SUPPLEMENT XV
Woody Allen to C. D. Wright

American Writers
A Collection of Literary Biographies

JAY PARINI
Editor in Chief

SUPPLEMENT XV
Woody Allen to C. D. Wright

CHARLES SCRIBNER'S SONS
An imprint of Thomson Gale, a part of The Thomson Corporation

THOMSON
™
GALE

Detroit • New York • San Francisco • San Diego • New Haven, Conn. • Waterville, Maine • London • Munich

THOMSON
★
GALE™

American Writers, Supplement XV
Jay Parini, Editor in Chief

Project Editor
Julie Mellors

Copyeditors
Gretchen Gordon, Robert E. Jones, Linda
Sanders

Proofreaders
Katy Balcer, Michelle Kazensky, Mary Ruby,
Maikue Vang

Permission Researchers
Margaret Abendroth, Timothy Sisler, Julie Van
Pelt

Indexer
Katharyn Dunham

Compositor
Gary Leach

Publisher
Frank Menchaca

LIBRARY OF CONGRESS CATALOGING-IN-PUBLICATION DATA

American writers : a collection of literary biographies / Leonard Unger,
    editor in chief.
        p. cm.
    The 4-vol. main set consists of 97 of the pamphlets originally published as the
University of Minnesota pamphlets on American writers; some have been rev. and
updated. The supplements cover writers not included in the original series.
    Supplement 2, has editor in chief, A. Walton Litz; Retrospective suppl. 1, c1998, was
edited by A. Walton Litz & Molly Weigel; Suppl. 5 has editor-in-chief, Jay Parini.
    Includes bibliographies and index.
    Contents: v. 1. Henry Adams to T.S. Eliot — v. 2. Ralph Waldo Emerson to Carson
McCullers — v. 3. Archibald MacLeish to George Santayana — v. 4. Isaac Bashevis Singer
to Richard Wright — Supplement[s]: 1, pt. 1. Jane Addams to Sidney Lanier. 1, pt. 2.
Vachel Lindsay to Elinor Wylie. 2, pt. 1. W.H. Auden to O. Henry. 2, pt. 2. Robinson
Jeffers to Yvor Winters. — 4, pt. 1. Maya Angelou to Linda Hogan. 4, pt. 2. Susan Howe
to Gore Vidal — Suppl. 5. Russell Banks to Charles Wright
.   ISBN 0-684-19785-5 (set) — ISBN 0-684-13662-7
    1. American literature—History and criticism. 2. American
literature—Bio-bibliography. 3. Authors, American—Biography. I. Unger, Leonard. II.
Litz, A. Walton. III. Weigel, Molly. IV. Parini, Jay. V. University of Minnesota pamphlets
on American writers.

PS129 .A55
810'.9
[B]   73-001759

ISBN: 0-684-31306-5

Acknowledgments

Acknowledgment is gratefully made to those publishers and individuals who have permitted the use of the following material in copyright. Every effort has been made to secure permission to reprint copyrighted material.

WOODY ALLEN Excerpts from *Without Feathers*. Random House, 1975. Copyright © 1972, 1973, 1974, 1975 by Woody Allen. From *Side Effects*. Random House, 1980. Copyright © 1975, 1976, 1977, 1979, 1980 by Woody Allen.

FRANK BIDART Excerpts from *Ploughshares*, v. 9, 1983 for "Frank Bidart—An Interview (with Mark Halliday)" by Frank Bidart and Mark Halliday. Copyright © 1983 by Ploughshares, Inc. Reproduced by permission of the authors. From *In the Western Night: Collected Poems 1965–90*. Farrar, Straus and Giroux, 1990. Copyright © 1990 by Frank Bidart. Reprinted by permission of the author's agent. From Desire. Farrar, Straus and Giroux, 1997. Copyright © 1997 by Frank Bidart. Reprinted by permission of the author's agent. From *Music Like Dirt*. Sarabande, 2002. Reproduced by permission.

WITTER BYNNER Excerpts from *Saturday Review of Literature*, August 18, 1951. Copyright © 1951 by Saturday Review. Wilbur, Richard. From "Critical Introduction," in *Selected Poems*. Edited by Richard Wilbur. Farrar, Straus, Giroux, 1978. Copyright © 1977, 1978 by The Witter Bynner Foundation. Reprinted by permission of Farrar, Straus and Giroux, LLC. From "A City of Change," in *Prose Pieces*. Edited and with an Introduction by James Kraft. Farrar, Straus, Giroux, 1979. Copyright © 1979 by The Witter Bynner Foundation for Poetry Inc. Reprinted by permission of Farrar, Straus and Giroux, LLC. From "Ave Atque Vale," in *Prose Pieces*. Edited and with an Introduction by James Kraft. Farrar, Straus, Giroux, 1979. Copyright © 1979 by The Witter Bynner Foundation for Poetry Inc. Reprinted by permission of Farrar, Straus and Giroux, LLC. From *The Way of Life According to Laotzu*. The John Day Company, 1944. Copyright 1944 by Witter Bynner. Renewed 1972 by Dorothy Chauvenet & Paul Horgan. Reprinted by permission of Harper-Collins Publishers. From *The American Academy of Arts and Letters*, for Witter Bynner BIO: Witter Bynner, (1881–1968) by Paul Horgan. Reproduced by permission. From "Lorenzo," in *The Selected Witter Bynner: Poems, Plays, Translations, Prose, and Letters*. Edited by James Kraft. University of New Mexico Press, 1995. Copyright © 1995 by the University of New Mexico Press. Reproduced by permission of the Witter Bynner Foundation for Poetry, Inc. From *The Chinese Translations*. Farrar, Straus, Giroux, 1978. Copyright © 1978 by The Witter Bynner Foundation. Reprinted by permission of Farrar, Straus and Giroux, LLC. From "Ezra Pound," in *Prose Pieces*. Edited

and with an Introduction by James Kraft. Farrar, Straus, Giroux, 1979. Copyright © 1979 by The Witter Bynner Foundation for Poetry Inc. Reprinted by permission of Farrar, Straus and Giroux, LLC. From "Autobiography in the Shape of a Book Review," in *Prose Pieces*. Edited and with an Introduction by James Kraft. Farrar, Straus, Giroux, 1979. Copyright © 1979 by The Witter Bynner Foundation for Poetry Inc. Reprinted by permission of Farrar, Straus and Giroux, LLC. From "On Teaching the Young Laurel to Shoot," in *Prose Pieces*. Edited and with an Introduction by James Kraft. Farrar, Straus, Giroux, 1979. Copyright © 1979 by The Witter Bynner Foundation for Poetry Inc. Reprinted by permission of Farrar, Straus and Giroux, LLC. From "The Persistence of Poetry," in *Prose Pieces*. Edited and with an Introduction by James Kraft. Farrar, Straus, Giroux, 1979. Copyright © 1979 by The Witter Bynner Foundation for Poetry Inc. Reprinted by permission of Farrar, Straus and Giroux, LLC. Kraft, James. From *Who is Witter Bynner? a biography*. 1st Edition. University of New Mexico Press, 1995. Copyright © 1995.

MICHAEL CUNNINGHAM Excerpts from *Poets & Writers Magazine*, v. 27, July, 1999. Reproduced by permission. From *The Gay & Lesbian Review*, v. 10, March–April, 2003. Copyright © 2003 by The Gay & Lesbian Review, Inc. All rights reserved. Reproduced by permission. From *Christian Science Monitor*, May 4, 1984 for "Giving New Twists and Fresh Style to Timeless Coming-of–Age Theme (review of Golden States)" by Ruth Doan MacDougall. Copyright © Ruth Doan MacDougall. Reproduced by permission of the author. From Shoup, Barbara and Campanello, Kimberly, in "Interview: Michael Cunningham," *Other Voices web site*, fall–winter, 2002.

PETER EVERWINE Excerpts from *Snake Nation Review*, n. 19, 2005 for "An Interview with Peter Everwine" by Jon Veinberg, Christopher Buckley, and Peter Everwine. Reproduced by permission of the authors. From *From the Meadow: Selected and New Poems*. University of Pittsburgh Press, 2004. Copyright © 2004, Peter Everwine. All rights reserved. Reproduced by permission. From "Lullaby," in *Speaking of Accidents*. Sutton Hoo Press, 2003. Reproduced by permission of the author. Anonymous, From "To Tlaloc of Rain," in *In the House of Light*. Translated by Peter Everwine. Stone Wall Press, 1970. Copyright © 1969. Reproduced by permission. From *Collecting the Animals*. Atheneum, 1972. Copyright © 1969, 1970, 1971, 1972 by Peter Everwine. Reprinted with the permission of Scribner, an imprint of Simon & Schuster Adult Publishing Group. Sach, Nathan. From *Keeping the Night*. Atheneum, 1977. Translated by Peter Everwine. Copyright © 1973, 1974, 1975, 1976, 1977 by Peter Everwine. Reprinted with the permission of Scribner, an

Nebraska Press, Bison Book, 1960. Copyright 1975, by the University of Nebraska Press, © renewed 2003 by the University of Nebraska Press. Reproduced by permission of the University of Nebraska Press. From "1926," in *The Collected Poems of Weldon Kees*. Edited by Donald Justice. University of Nebraska Press, Bison Book, 1960. Copyright 1975, by the University of Nebraska Press, © renewed 2003 by the University of Nebraska Press. Reproduced by permission of the University of Nebraska Press. From "Travels in North America," in *The Collected Poems of Weldon Kees*. Edited by Donald Justice. University of Nebraska Press, Bison Book, 1960. Copyright 1975, by the University of Nebraska Press, © renewed 2003 by the University of Nebraska Press. Reproduced by permission of the University of Nebraska Press. From "The Locusts, the Plaza, the Room," in *The Collected Poems of Weldon Kees*. Edited by Donald Justice. University of Nebraska Press, Bison Book, 1960. Copyright 1975, by the University of Nebraska Press, © renewed 2003 by the University of Nebraska Press. Reproduced by permission of the University of Nebraska Press. From "Aspects of Robinson," in *The Collected Poems of Weldon Kees*. Edited by Donald Justice. University of Nebraska Press, Bison Book, 1960. Copyright 1975, by the University of Nebraska Press, © renewed 2003 by the University of Nebraska Press. Reproduced by permission of the University of Nebraska Press. From "Farrago," in *The Collected Poems of Weldon Kees*. Edited by Donald Justice. University of Nebraska Press, Bison Book, 1960. Copyright 1975, by the University of Nebraska Press, © renewed 2003 by the University of Nebraska Press. Reproduced by permission of the University of Nebraska Press. From "For My Daughter," in *The Collected Poems of Weldon Kees*. Edited by Donald Justice. University of Nebraska Press, 1975. Copyright 1975, by the University of Nebraska Press. © renewed 2003 by the University of Nebraska press. Reproduced by permission of the publisher and the literary estate of the author. From "Letter to Maurice Johnson," in *Weldon Kees and the Midcentury Generation: Letters, 1935–1955*. Edited by Robert E. Knoll. University of Nebraska Press, 1986. Copyright © 1986 by University of Nebraska Press. Reproduced by permission. From "Letter to Sarah Kees," in *Weldon Kees and the Midcentury Generation: Letters, 1935–1955*. Edited by Kobert E. Knoll. University of Nebraska Press, 1986. Copyright © 1986 by the University of Nebraska Press. Reproduced by permission. Hoffman, Paul. From *New York Public Library Special Collections*. 1941. Kazin, Alfred. From Yaddo Foundation. Crane, Milton. From *New York Times Book Review*. 1948. Aiken, Conrad. From *Huntington Library Special Collections*.

X. J. KENNEDY Excerpts from *Breaking and Entering*. Oxford University Press, 1971. Copyright © 1971 by X. J. Kennedy. Reprinted by permission of Curtis Brown, Ltd. From *Nude Descending a Staircase*. Doubleday & Company, Inc., 1961. Copyright © 1961 by X. J. Kennedy. Reprinted by permission of Curtis Brown, Ltd. From *Three Tenors, One Vehicle: A Book of Songs*. Open Places, 1975. Copyright © 1975. Reproduced by permission of the author. From *Growing into Love*. Doubleday & Company, Inc., 1969. Reproduced by permission of the author. From *Emily Dickinson in Southern California*. Godine, 1974. Copyright © 1973. Reproduced by permission of the author. From *Hangover Mass*. Bits Press, 1984. Reproduced by permission of the author. From *Cross Ties: Selected Poems*. University of Georgia Press, 1985. Copyright © 1985 by X. J.

Kennedy. Reproduced by permission of the author. From *Dark Horses*. Johns Hopkins University Press, 1992. Copyright © 1992 X. J. Kennedy. All rights reserved. Reprinted with permission of The Johns Hopkins University Press. From *The Lords of Misrule*. Johns Hopkins University Press, 2002. Copyright © 2002 X. J. Kennedy. All rights reserved. Reprinted with permission of the Johns Hopkins University Press. From *Brats*. Atheneum, 1986. Text Copyright © 1986 by X. J. Kennedy. Reproduced by permission of the author. Kennedy, Dorothy M. From *Exploding Gravy: Poems to Make You Laugh*. Little, Brown and Company, 2002. Copyright © 2002 by X. J. Kennedy. By permission of Little, Brown and Co., Inc. From "X. J. Kennedy (journal entries)," in *The Poet's Notebook: Excerpts from the Notebooks of Contemporary American Poets*. Edited by Stephen Kuusisto, Deborah Tall, David Weiss. W. W. Norton and Company, 1995. Copyright © 1995 by Stephen Kuusisto. Reproduced by permission of the author.

KENNETH KOCH Excerpts from *The Art of Poetry: Poems, Parodies, Interviews, Essays, and Other Work*. University of Michigan Press, 1996. Copyright © 1996 by the University of Michigan. All rights reserved. Reproduced by permission. From *Thank You and Other Poems*. Grove Press, Inc., 1962. Copyright © 1962, renewed 1990 by Kenneth Koch. Reproduced by permission. From *The Art of Love*. Random House, 1975. Copyright © 1972, 1974, 1975 by Kenneth Koch. Reproduced by permission of the literary estate of the author. From *The Burning Mystery of Anna in 1951*. Random House, 1979. Copyright © 1977, 1978, 1979 by Kenneth Koch. Reproduced by permission of the literary estate of the author. From *Seasons on Earth*. Elisabeth Sifton Books, Viking Penguin, 1987. Copyright © 1959, 1975, 1976, 1977, 1987. Copyright renewed Kenneth Koch, 1987. All rights reserved. Reproduced by permission of the literary estate of the author. From *Ko, or A Season on Earth*. Grove Press, Inc., 1959. Copyright © 1959, renewed 1968 by Kenneth Koch. Reproduced by permission of the literary estate of the author. From *Days and Nights*. Random House, 1982. Copyright © 1982 by Kenneth Koch. Reproduced by permission of the literary estate of the author. From *New Addresses: Poems*. Alfred A. Knopf, 2000. Copyright © 2000 by Kenneth Koch. Reproduced by permission of Kenneth Koch Literary Estate.

ED LACY Excerpts from *New York Times Book Review*, October 3, 1948; November 15, 1992; October 29, 2000. Copyright © 1948, renewed 1976 by The New York Times Company. All reproduced by permission.

LI-YOUNG LEE Excerpts from *The City in Which I Love You*. Boa Editions, Ltd., 1990. Copyright © 1990 by Li-Young Lee. Reproduced by permission of BOA Editions, Ltd., www.BOAEditions.org. From *Book of My Nights*. Boa Editions, Ltd., 2001. Copyright © 2001 by Li-Young Lee. Reproduced by permission of BOA Editions, Ltd., www.BOAEditions.org. Hsu, Ruth Y. From "Li-Young Lee," in *Dictionary of Literary Biography, American Poets Since World War II, Fourth Series*. Edited by Joseph Conte. Gale Research, Inc., 1996. Copyright © 1996 by Gale Research. From *Prairie Schooner*, v. 63, no. 3, fall, 1989. Copyright © 1989 by University of Nebraska Press. Reproduced from Prairie Schooner by permission of the University of Nebraska Press. Li-Young Lee with Michael

List of Subjects

Introduction

Real writers aim high. The great American novelist, William Faulkner, spoke of this aim in his Nobel address, on December 19, 1950, in Stockholm, where he said it was the writer's "privilege to help man endure by lifting his heart, by reminding him of the courage and honor and hope and pride and compassion and sacrifice which have been the glory of his past. The poet's voice need not merely be the record of man, it can be one of the props, the pillars to help him endure and prevail." Of course, by "poets" Faulkner meant all writers with a creative vision, whether they be novelist, poets, playwrights, critics, or memoirists.

In this fifteenth volume of *American Writers,* we offer eighteen articles on American writers of fiction, drama (including film), and poetry; they are all accomplished writers who have displayed many of the virtues that Faulkner notes above, yet none of them has yet been featured in this series. These articles should prove helpful to readers who wish to dig more thoroughly into the work of these writers, so that they can see how each—in his or her own way—has added something of great value to American culture.

This series had its origin in a remarkable series of critical and biographical monographs that appeared between 1959 and 1972. *The Minnesota Pamphlets on American Writers* were incisively written and informative, treating ninety–seven American writers in a format and style that attracted a devoted following of readers. The series proved invaluable to a generation of students and teachers, who could depend on these reliable and interesting critiques of major figures. The idea of reprinting these essays oc-

curred to Charles Scribner, Jr. (1921–1995). The series appeared in four volumes entitled *American Writers: A Collection of Literary Biographies* (1974).

Since then, fourteen supplements have appeared, treating well over two hundred American writers: poets, novelists, playwrights, essayists and autobiographers. The idea has been consistent with the original series: to provide clear, informative essays aimed at the general reader and intelligent student. These essays often rise to a high level of craft and critical vision, but they are meant to introduce a writer of some importance in the history of American literature, and to provide a sense of the scope and nature of the career under review. A certain amount of biographical and historical context is also offered, giving a context for the work itself.

The authors of these critical articles are mostly teachers, scholars, and writers. Most have published books and articles in their field, and several are well-known writers of poetry or fiction as well as critics. As anyone glancing through this volume will see, they are held to the highest standards of good writing and sound scholarship. The essays each conclude with a select bibliography intended to direct the reading of those who want to pursue the subject further.

Volume Fifteen treats a wide range of authors from the past and present. Among them are two interesting novelists from the late eighteenth and nineteenth centuries, Susannah Rowson and Elizabeth Stoddard, both of whom were extremely popular in their time. The novels of Rowson and Stoddard have only recently attracted the attention of scholars, and these essays go a considerable distance toward making their careers accessible to students and general readers, who might wish to explore their books.

The main focus of this volume is poetry, and twelve poets considered in this collection: Frank Bidart, Witter Bynner, Peter Everwine, Carol Frost, Dana Gioia, Weldon Kees, X. J. Kennedy, Kenneth Koch, Li-Young Lee, Gjertrud Schnackenberg, Louis Untermeyer, and C. D. Wright. Most of these are contemporary, although Bynner, Kees, and Untermeyer belong to the first half of the twentieth century. I believe readers will find a rich feast in these essays, and an invitation to read some of the finest poets of the past century, most of whom are still at work, creating American culture with each new volume.

Two essays focus on novelists Michael Cunningham and Ed lacy. Cunningham recently won the Pulitzer Prize for his novel *The Hours,* which was made into an award–winning film. He is a writer of astonishing emotional depths and linguistic skills, still in midcareer. Ed Lacy (a pseudonym for Leonard S. Zinberg) wrote innovative and compelling detective novels in the 1950s and 1960s, and was best known for creating the first highly credible black detective, Toussaint Moore. He won an Edgar Award in 1957.

Two writers of plays and screenplays treated in Supplement Fifteen are Woody Allen and Wendy Wasserstein, two of our most vibrant creators of work for the stage and screen. Both have had long and rich careers, and have been extremely influential in American drama and film. These essays look at their origins and track their development to the present, offering broad assessments of their work, and the impact of this work on American culture.

The critics who contributed to this collection represent a catholic range of backgrounds and critical approaches, although the baseline for inclusion was that each essay should be accessible to the non–specialist reader or beginning student. The creation of culture involves the continuous reassessment of major texts produced by its writers, and my belief is that this supplement performs a useful service here, providing substantial introductions to American writers who matter, and it will assist readers in the difficult but rewarding work of eager reading.

—*JAY PARINI*

Contributors

Bert Almon. Professor of English and Film Studies at the University of Alberta. He is the author of *William Humphrey: Destroyer of Myths* (North Texas State University Press, 1998), *This Stubborn Self: Texas Autobiographies* (TCU Press, 2001) and eight collections of poetry. He has published essays on English, American, Canadian, and Australian poets. LI-YOUNG LEE, C. D. WRIGHT

Charles R. Baker. Poet, essayist and short story writer. A long time contributor to *American Writers, British Writers,* and *American Writers Classics,* Mr. Baker also wrote seven entries for the *Oxford Encyclopedia of American Literature.* He is the curator of " Mark Twain: Father of Modern American Literature" at Southern Methodist University. MICHAEL CUNNINGHAM

Jonathan N. Barron. Associate Professor of English at the University of Southern Mississippi. He is coeditor of the following books: *Jewish American Poetry: Poems, Commentary, and Reflections, Roads Not Taken: Rereading Robert Frost,* and *New Formalist Poets.* He is also Editor in Chief of *The Robert Frost Review.* LOUIS UNTERMEYER

Kim Bridgford. Directs the writing program at Fairfield University, where she is a professor of English and editor of *Dogwood.* She has received fellowships from the National Endowment for the Arts and the Connecticut Commission on the Arts. Her books of poetry include *Undone* (David Robert Books, 2003), which was nominated for the Pulitzer Prize, and *Instead of Maps* (David Robert Books, 2005). DANA GIOIA

Christopher Buckley. He has published thirteen books of poetry, most recently, *Sky* (2004), and

Closer to Home (2003). For his poetry he has received four Pushcart Prizes, two awards from the Poetry Society of America, a Fulbright Award in Creative Writing to the former Yugoslavia, and is the recipient of NEA grants in poetry for 2001 and 1984. PETER EVERWINE

Nancy L. Bunge. A professor at Michigan State University. She is the author of *Nathaniel Hawthorne: A Study of the Short Fiction,* the editor of *Conversations with Clarence Major,* and the interviewer and editor of *Finding the Words: Conversations with Writers Who Teach* and *Master Class: Lessons from Leading Writers.* She has been a senior Fulbright lecturer at the University of Vienna, the Free University of Brussels and at Ghent University. WENDY WASSERSTEIN

Gerry Cambridge. Scots-Irish poet and editor. His books of verse include *The Shell House* (Scottish Cultural Press, 1995), *Nothing but Heather!: Scottish Nature in Poems, Photographs and Prose* (Luath Press, 1999), illustrated with his own natural history photographs, and *Madame Fi's Farewell and Other Poems* (Luath Press, 2003). He edits the Scottish-American poetry magazine *The Dark Horse* and was the 1997-1999 Brownsbank Writing Fellow, based at Hugh McDiarmid's former house, Brownsbank Cottage, near Biggar in Scotland. His website is at: www.gerry-cambridge.com. X. J. KENNEDY

Susan Carol Hauser. Her books include *Outside after Dark: New and Selected Poems; You Can Write a Memoir; Wild Rice Cooking: History, Natural History, Harvesting & Lore* (which one a 2001 Minnesota Book Award); *Sugaring: A Maple Syrup Memoir with Instructions; Outwitting Poison Ivy; Outwitting Poison Oak;* and *Meant to Be Read Out Loud* (which won a 1989

Minnesota Book Award). She has a Master of Fine Arts degree in poetry from Bowling Green State University and is a Professor of English at Bemidji State University. WITTER BYNNER

Ernest Hilbert. His poetry has appeared in *The New Republic, The Boston Review, Mc-Sweeney's, The New Formalist, The American Scholar, Verse, Fence, Volt,* and in the anthology *And Gentlemen: Younger American Male Poets.* He is the editor of NC, an annual journal of new writing, and is a contributing editor at the *Contemporary Poetry Review.* He is a regular reviewer for the *New York Sun* and *American Poet.* Hilbert received his doctorate in English Literature from Oxford University, where he earlier completed a Master's Degree and founded the *Oxford Quarterly.* He is an agent at Bauman Rare Books. GJERTRUD SCHNACKENBERG

Denise Larrabee. Writer and historian specializing in American women's history and literature. She is the author of *Anne Hampton Brewster: 19th-century Author and "Social Outlaw"* (1992) and editor of *Meridian Bound: Fiction, Essays, Poetry, and More* (2000). Her work has appeared in numerous reference books, anthologies, and publications. SUSANNA ROWSON

Robert Niemi. Teaches film, literature, and critical theory in the English Department and American Studies Program at St. Michael's College, Colchester, VT. Niemi has published books on Weldon Kees and Russell Banks and numerous articles on American literature and cultural history topics. He has just completed *History in the Media: A Reference Guide* for ABC-CLIO. ED LACY

James Reidel. Author of *Vanished Act: The Life and Art of Weldon Kees* (Lincoln: University of Nebraska Press, 2003). His poetry and translations appear in *New Yorker, Paris Review, Tri-Quarterly, Ironwood, New Criterion, Verse, Poets Lore, Ploughshares, Conjunctions, Härter* and in such online journals as *Cortland Review, Pierian Springs, WebConjunctions, Adirondack*

Review, and *Slope.* An independent scholar, he is researching and writing about the photography of Weldon Kees and the novelist Robert Lowry. An extensive biographical and critical essay on Lowry appears in *Review of Contemporary Fiction* (Summer 2005). WELDON KEES

Lacy Schutz. Poet and writer living in Brooklyn, New York. Her poetry has appeared in *Fence, Denver Quarterly, Black Warrior Review, New Orleans Review,* and many other journals. Her critical work has been published in *The Oxford Encyclopedia of American Literature, Post Road,* and elsewhere. She earned her MFA in poetry from Bennington College and is currently pursuing a master's degree in Information and Library Science at the Pratt Institute. KENNETH KOCH

Lisa Sewell. Author of two books of poetry, *The Way Out* and *Name Withheld.* She has published essays and articles on Brenda Hillman, Ted Hughes, Louise Gluck and Sylvia Plath and is co-editing a collection of essays on contemporary American poetics for Wesleyan University Press. She is an assistant professor of English at Villanova University. FRANK BIDART

Corinne Wohlford Taff. Affiliate assistant professor of English at Fontbonne University. She was a finalist in 1999 for the Grolier Poetry Prize, and her poetry has been published in *Harvard Review, Pleiades, Plainsongs, Margie,* and other journals. She is a graduate of the MFA program in poetry at Washington University in St. Louis, where Carol Frost was among her mentors. She and her husband, Jason Taff, live in St. Louis and are awaiting the adoption of their first child. CAROL FROST

Daniel Vilmure. A twice published novelist (*Life in the Land of the Living,* Knopf, Faber & Faber, 1987) and *Toby's Lie* (Simon & Schuster, Bloomsbury, 1995.) He is a graduate of Harvard and Stanford Universities, a former Fulbright Lecturer at the University of Jordan in Amman, Jordan, and Director of the Villanova University Literary Festival, which has included such guests as Jonathan Franzen, Michael Cunningham, and Robert Creeley. He is currently Assistant Professor of English and Creative Writing at Villanova University. WOODY ALLEN

Ellen M. Weinauer. Associate professor in the Department of English at the University of Southern Mississippi. She is the co-editor, along with Robert McClure Smith, of *American Culture, Canons, and the Case of Elizabeth Stoddard* (University of Alabama Press, 2003) and the author of articles on Hawthorne, Melville, Elizabeth Stoddard, and others. ELIZABETH STODDARD

SUPPLEMENT XV
Woody Allen to C. D. Wright

Woody Allen

1935–

*L*IKE SO MANY of the legendary humorists who preceded him—Mark Twain, Oscar Wilde, Charlie Chaplin, and Lenny Bruce—Woody Allen has spent a lifetime playfully deconstructing himself and his audience through the inestimable power of laughter. Early writing for notable television shows, successful Broadway and off-Broadway plays, best-selling books of satirical prose, and three dozen original film scripts comprise a career of a scope and a variety unmatched by any American humorist of the later twentieth century.

Armed only with his self-deprecating wit and an endearingly fumbling charm, Allen's central persona is that of the neurotic everyman trying to get by in a world of nonstop angst. His popularization of psychoanalysis, endlessly quotable one-liners, densely comic exploration of Judaic tradition, and trademark spectacles through which he quizzically examines his out-of-focus world have all combined to make Allen one of the most cherished and recognizable humorists on the planet.

But, as with the careers of Twain and Chaplin, Allen's career has developed well beyond the boundaries of mere popular comedy. Works such as *Interiors* inhabit the dark existential spaces of films like Ingmar Bergman's *Persona; Stardust Memories* exudes the self-referential angst of Federico Fellini's *8 1/2; The Purple Rose of Cairo* plays Pirandellian games to melancholy effect; and *Crimes and Misdemeanors,* with its tortured central protagonist, plumbs Dostoevskian depths that are a far cry from the easy farce of Allen's Swinging Sixties debut, *What's New, Pussycat?* After five decades as a gag writer, stand-up comic, essayist, playwright, actor, screenwriter, director, clarinetist, and kvetching philosopher, Allen is more than the sum of his punch lines. He is a central American literary figure.

EARLY YEARS

Born Allan Stewart Konigsberg in Brooklyn, New York, on December 1, 1935, Woody Allen was raised by Orthodox Jewish parents. His mother, Nettie Cherry Konigsberg, kept the books for a flower shop while his father, Martin, shifted from job to job. Over a decade the Konigsbergs moved a dozen times before Martin, reportedly toting a gun, settled into a position at a Bowery saloon. At the impressionable age of three Allen was taken by Nettie to see Walt Disney's *Snow White and the Seven Dwarfs.* "Even as a kid I always went for the wrong women," Allen would joke years later in *Annie Hall.* "Everyone fell in love with Snow White. I immediately fell for the Wicked Queen." However doubtful Allen's early taste in women, his first trip to the movies was love at first reel.

"In my neighborhood in Brooklyn in those days," Allen told the film critic Richard Schickel, "there were fifty movie theaters virtually within walking distance of [my] house." Proximity to the cinema nurtured a passion that would grow throughout his childhood and blossom into a career. After seeing a Tyrone Power pirate movie called *The Black Swan,* Allen began to fantasize about one day making movies. In time his early interest in Disney femme fatales would develop into a taste for more sophisticated fare—*Double Indemnity, Casa-*

blanca, and *Shane* were early favorites. By the 1950s and 1960s the teenage cineast had graduated to the imported art house offerings of Bergman and Fellini—directors who would later prove influential to Allen's own formidable mise-en-scène.

Despite a high IQ and placement in an accelerated academic program, Allen was a lazy and unimpressive student. Nicknamed "Red" because of his ruddy hair, Allen thrived outside of the classroom. Adept at basketball, football, baseball, even boxing, a figure now famous for his bumbling insecurities cut a dazzling swath across the playgrounds of Flatbush. Allen was also fascinated by magic, a fascination that would materialize years later in several of his films as well as in a Broadway play, *The Floating Light Bulb.* At age fifteen Allen took up the clarinet—an instrument he insists on playing at New York venues like Michael's Pub even when his films are competing for Academy Awards, which they do frequently. But the clarinet is not the only thing Allen took up during this pivotal period. In 1952, writing jokes incognito for newspaper columnists, Allan Stewart Konigsberg took up a new name: Woody Allen. A young man attracted to movie houses, baseball diamonds, magic tricks, and clarinets had now undertaken the trickier business of inventing himself as an artist.

In 1953 Allen attended New York University but soon dropped out to join the NBC Writers' Program. Recruited at twenty by *The Colgate Variety Hour,* Allen was eventually hired to write for *Your Show of Shows,* the *Gary Moore Show,* the *Tonight Show,* and *Candid Camera.* Allen married Harlene Rosen in 1956; the two divorced in 1962. By then Allen had begun to write original plays and short comic pieces. Even more importantly, he had become a fixture of the New York City stand-up circuit, where his intellectual, anxious, lovable persona riffed on God, sex, death, and everything in between.

Allen's first film script was *What's New, Pussycat?* (1965), a wacky farce about Michael James (Peter O'Toole), a sex addict who consults Dr. Fritz Fassbender (Peter Sellers), a gonzo psychiatrist who is even more of a sexual loose cannon than Michael. In the opening scene Fassbender is berated by his wife, who repeatedly calls him a "lascivious adulterer." "Don't you dare call me that again until I've looked it up!" he fires back. As the colorfully named Victor Skakapopulis, Allen made his acting debut in a movie that is probably remembered more for its bouncy Burt Bacharach title song than for any intrinsic merit as an early Allen comedy. There are some phenomenal moments—a dead-on Fellini parody in which O'Toole, à la Marcello Mastroianni, repels a bevy of beauties with a whip—but the farce as a whole feels forced and frantic. Instead of being thrilled to realize the dream of finally seeing his work and himself on the same big screens that had weaned him in Brooklyn, the twenty-nine-year-old Allen was altogether horrified: "I couldn't bear the picture when it came out.... I vowed that I would never write another film script unless I could direct it." After thirty-one films as writer and director, Allen has more than made good on that promise.

Discounting *What's New, Pussycat?* and the 1972 Herbert Ross film adaptation of Allen's Broadway hit *Play It Again, Sam,* Allen's oeuvre may be divided into three parts: the early comedies (1966–1975), beginning with the uproarious *What's Up, Tiger Lily?* and concluding with the giddy Tolstoy satire *Love and Death;* the master films (1977–1989), beginning with his breakthrough *Annie Hall* and concluding with the moral drama *Crimes and Misdemeanors;* and the later films (1990–2003), beginning with the Mia Farrow fantasy *Alice* and concluding with the romantic comedy *Anything Else.*

Because of the sheer mass of Allen's enormous screenwriting corpus, this overview of his career will examine only select works. Of his several Broadway and off-Broadway plays— *From A to Z* (1960), *Don't Drink the Water* (1966), *Play It Again, Sam* (1969), *Death* (1975), *God* (1975), *The Floating Light Bulb* (1982), and *Three One Act Plays* (*Riverside Drive, Old Saybrook,* and *Central Park West,* 1995)—two will be considered. Of his three best-selling collections of comic prose—*Getting Even* (1971), *Without Feathers* (1975), and *Side Effects* (1980)—highlights from each will be examined, followed by a brief consideration of new directions in which the perennially prolific writer may be headed.

EARLY COMEDIES (1966–1975)

"I'm chatting with Woody Allen, the author of this film," an interviewer says at the beginning of *What's Up, Tiger Lily?* (1966), Allen's frisky reworking of a Japanese gangster flick in which the entire soundtrack is overdubbed to hilarious effect. "Is the word 'author' quite the correct word to use?" Considering the loaded meaning the word "auteur" took on in the postwar film community of the 1950s and 1960s, the monumentally silly *What's Up, Tiger Lily?* would seem a wobbly peg on which to hang Allen's early bid for auteur status. But slight as it is, this frolicsome forerunner of *Airplane!* and *Mystery Science Theater 3000* shows all the markings of the work of a filmmaker with cinematic fingerprints entirely his own.

Liberated from the heavy farcical mechanics of *What's New, Pussycat?, What's Up, Tiger Lily?* permits Allen's comic sensibility to run rampant as his Japanese tough-guy hero (improbably named Phil Moscowitz) joins forces with Teri and Suki Yaki to beat the rival gangsters Shepherd Wong and Wing Fat in their search for a "secret recipe for egg salad.... A salad so delicious you could plotz!" When Fat is accused of being Wong, the confusion over Wongs leads Moscowitz to crack, "Two Wongs

don't make a wight." Groovy musical interludes by the Lovin' Spoonful date a movie whose comic exchanges feel precociously timeless. "I can't break the door down because of my bursitis!" Moscowitz complains. "Get the dynamite!" a desperate Suki replies. "And could you also bring me a regular coffee?" Brilliant formal moments—silhouetted lovers in a projection room stop the film cold to discuss their liaison—suggest how the older Allen (*Zelig, The Purple Rose of Cairo*) will challenge the very limits of cinema as a medium. And Allen gives Wong—"that poor unfortunate egg salad junkie"—one of the great in-extremis lines in cinematic history: "I'm dying! Call my rabbi!"

Documenting the life of Virgil Starkwell, a schlemiel career criminal who spends most of his hapless life behind bars, *Take the Money and Run* (1969) is the first Allen script that put him both behind and in front of the camera. At once a true-crime spoof and a parody of prison films, Allen's freshman writer-director-actor effort ups the wisecrack quotient of *What's New, Pussycat?* "The prison psychiatrist asked me did I think sex is dirty," Starkwell recounts, adding: "It is if you do it right." *Take the Money and Run* also showcases Allen's flair for physical comedy in an extended chain gang sequence that would work marvelously in a silent film. Cowritten, like *Bananas,* with his childhood friend Mickey Rose, Allen's script is more rhetorically sophisticated than his first, displaying a fondness for loopy tautologies ("The prison has not been built that can hold me," Virgil boasts, "and I'll get out of this place if it means spending my entire life here") and sideswiping hyperboles ("Sentenced to eight hundred years in federal prison ... [Starkwell] tells his lawyer confidently that with good behavior he can cut the sentence in half").

Allen's second outing is most noteworthy for its use of the same fake documentary elements—mock interviews, inserted newsreel footage, sanctimonious music, voice-over narration—that will be deployed to even sharper effect in more mature works like *Annie Hall* and *Zelig*. In particular, Jackson Beck's deadpan narration casts a *Dragnet*-like shadow over the proceedings. The film's portentous tone makes vignettes like the one in which Allen gives a bank teller a poorly scribbled note ("ACT NATURAL I AM POINTING A GUB AT YOU") even more sidesplitting. When the fans in *Stardust Memories* lament that Allen's alter ego Sandy Bates no longer makes movies like his "early funny ones," it's a dearth of movies like *Take the Money and Run* that is really being lamented. But with four slapstick masterpieces right around the corner, for Allen and his fans the fun was just beginning.

If Graham Greene had spent his formative years on the borscht belt, *Bananas* (1971) might have been the result. After a bittersweet opening in which the romantic loser Fielding Mellish (Allen) strikes out with his political activist girlfriend Nancy (Louise Lasser, Allen's second wife, whom he married in 1966 and divorced in 1969), Fielding travels to the politically unstable republic of San Marcos. To impress Nancy, Fielding's goal is to research the country, the chief export of which "is dysentery." Immediately the subject of an assassination plot ("Blood! That should be on the inside!"), Fielding is recruited by guerrillas to overthrow the dictator, a man to whom citizens of San Marcos must annually pay "their weight in horse manure." Assisted by the United Jewish Appeal—in lieu of the CIA—Fielding winds up default *presidente* and returns to America to raise money for San Marcos wearing a beard and mustache Fidel Castro wouldn't be caught dead in. Described by one politico as "a New York Jewish intellectual Communist crackpot ... but I don't wanna cast no aspersions," Fielding is arrested by the FBI and subjected to a ticklishly Kafkaesque trial from which he emerges unscathed before winning the hand of a now-enamored Nancy.

Allen's gift for physical comedy in *Bananas* remains impressive: gags with machine guns, TV dinners, machetes, subway thugs, surgical instruments, and kidnap victims drugged with sodium pentothal offer a field day to the Keaton-inspired comic. But even more impressive are the throwaway sight gags, most of which are Buñuelian in the suggestiveness of their absurdity. In a dream sequence Fielding is carried crucified through the streets of New York City by robed acolytes only to find his followers battling *another* crucified man's followers for a parking space. At Fielding's trial a juror drinks with a straw from a fish bowl while a bound and gagged Fielding mumblingly cross-examines a witness who exclaims, "Don't put words in my mouth!" In the guerrilla camp, Fielding's first attempt at camouflage ends in disaster when a comrade casually urinates on him. And as the dictator's palace is stormed, a runaway baby carriage bounces down the steps in homage to *Battleship Potemkin*. Highbrow slapstick, *Bananas'* Marxism is equal parts Karl and Groucho.

From the body politic to the body erotic, *Everything You Always Wanted to Know about Sex* (1972) rivals *Gulliver's Travels* in its microscopic, macroscopic assault on the fleshly battleground that is the human body: pre-ejaculation sperm outfitted with parachutes banter nervously as a man approaches orgasm; a giant, milk-squirting, B-movie breast pursues a cross-wielding Woody through a bucolic pasture; foolproof chastity belts prove the downfall of a randy court jester; and in the film's most notorious episode the deliriously poker-faced Dr. Doug Ross (winsomely underplayed by Gene Wilder) makes love to a nonplussed sheep named Daisy—perhaps the only character to maintain her dignity in Allen's cornucopia of kink. *Everything* aggressively courts bad taste in a scene from *What's My Perversion?* in which a tied-up rabbi is gleefully whipped by a fashion model while the man's frowning wife, "whom we've flown in from Indiana, will sit at the rabbi's feet and eat pork!" But the remainder of the movie—more intellectually risky than Allen's previous comedies—offers crackerjack dialogue that is more outrageous in the end than outraging. At the murder scene in which a victim of the colossal, mutant, marauding breast lies in a puddle of sticky lactose, Allen's young scientist observes: "The cream slowed him up and the milk killed him. We're up against a very clever tit. It shoots half and half!"

The 1973 science fiction spoof *Sleeper*—co-scripted by Marshall Brickman, who would later cowrite *Annie Hall, Manhattan,* and *Manhattan Murder Mystery*—is the first Allen film to feature the nondescript white-on-black opening credit sequence (typically accompanied by percolating jazz) that would become a staple of the director's work for the next three decades. Cool futuristic production design and set decoration by Dale Hennesy and Gary Moreno, respectively, as well as sheeny photography by David M. Walsh give *Sleeper* an added dash of visual panache: it's the first Woody Allen film to look as clever as it sounds.

Miles Monroe (Allen), a Greenwich Village health food store owner, wakes up drooling from cryogenic deep freeze two hundred years after a botched ulcer operation and can't stop bellyaching about the brave new world that has been thrust upon him. "I can't believe this," Miles gripes. "My doc said I'd be up and on my feet in five days! He was off by 199 years!" Miles hasn't had sex for 200 years: "204 if you count my last marriage." Enlisted by revolutionaries to overthrow a corrupt leader, Miles goes undercover as a robotic domestic servant and falls in love with the salivarily named Luna Schlosser (Diane Keaton), an aspiring poetess influenced by Rod McKuen who spends most of her time doing recreational drugs (in the form of an "orb") and having recreational sex (in the form of an "Orgasmatron"). Allen is making the

same points here about the blissed-out future that he makes in *Annie Hall* about blissed-out California: "If [you] get too mellow, [you] ripen and [you] rot." However content, Luna and her arty friends are as emotionally and intellectually alive as the giant produce Miles clubs someone with ("Oh, my God! I beat a man insensible with a strawberry!") when he and Luna go on the lam from the authorities. By the end of the film—after parodic salutes to *A Streetcar Named Desire, Modern Times,* and the Miss Universe Pageant—Miles and Luna have left behind their brave new world and, as they will in three more films to come, turned to each other.

Again teaming Allen and Keaton, *Love and Death* (1975) is dress rehearsal for the more mature themes of *Annie Hall,* while the billowy white clouds and rousing Prokofiev score anticipate the celebrated Gershwin-meets-Big-Apple opening of *Manhattan.* Both "militant coward" and fabulous lover ("I practice a lot when I'm alone"), Boris Grushenko would rather bat eyelashes at the beautiful Sonja (Keaton) than leave with his brothers for the Napoleonic wars. "You've always been our favorite nephew, even though you're an incredible coward," Boris's uncle tells him. Butterfly collection under his arm, Boris is soon off to fight the French. But confronted on the battlefield by a bloody heap of bodies, Boris replies to his comrade's remark that "God is testing us" with the skeptically glib rejoinder "If he's gonna test us why doesn't he give us a written?" To escape battle Boris crawls into a cannon, which discharges him like a human missile, killing several enemy generals. Boris returns home a hero, but marital bliss with Sonja does not prevent the onset of a very deep, very Russian existential despair. Looking directly at the camera, Boris says: "Nothing. Nonexistence. Black emptiness." "What are you saying?" Sonja asks. "I'm just planning my future."

Circular babble about ontology, epistemology, and moral imperatives interrupts *Love and*

Death's most crucial moments. Boris can't flirt with Sonja without engaging her in abstract debates, and a critical opportunity to assassinate Napoleon slips away when the lovers bicker about God ("The worst thing you can say about him is he's an underachiever"). Throughout the movie Boris begs for a sign of God's existence, but when his angel indeed materializes to assure Boris (falsely) that he won't be executed, all Boris can do is misquote the Bible. The misquotation is significant: "Though I run, though I *run* through the Valley of the Shadow of Death...." Death appears to Boris at the beginning of the film, and at the end of the movie, in a nod to *The Seventh Seal,* the two hold hands as they gambol toward the horizon. *Love and Death* is more than just a send-up of Tolstoy: it is Allen's first gesture to the darker side of comedy and a worthy forerunner of the masterful period that would characterize his next decade and a half as an artist.

MASTER FILMS (1977–1989)

Annie Hall's (1977) reputation as Allen's first masterpiece is understandable if only for the way in which it explodes all of the themes that had been fizzing through Allen's work up to that point: the attraction/repulsion of Jewish and WASP cultures, the sexual smorgasbord of postwar America, the alienation of the intellectual in a pseudo-intellectual world, the absence of God, the hassle of childhood, and the high-wire act of finding love and maintaining it. But *Annie Hall* pushes out in an even bolder, fresher direction: it's funny, very funny, but it's not *simply* funny. Allen told the interviewer Stig Bjorkman that he wanted to "make some deeper film and not be as funny in the same way [as his previous work]." *Annie Hall* entailed not merely a radical departure from the frantic farce of his first effort but signaled a shift from the broader parodic agendas that had put Allen on the map of classic Hollywood comedy. *Annie Hall*'s greatest asset may in fact be its earnestness; its best moments come when the laughter stops coming. Alvy Singer, Allen's neurotic alter ego par excellence, is forever making light of himself, to be sure. But the aim he takes at love is as true as it is serious.

The plot is pleasantly thin: successful stand-up comedian Alvy (Allen) falls for struggling nightclub performer Annie Hall (Keaton)—an androgynously dressed, carefree spirit whose trademark "la-de-da" betrays insecurities about life and love that are as appealingly real as Alvy's. But Alvy's possessiveness, Annie's restlessness, and a history of romantic casualties on both sides dooms them from the start. "A relationship ... is like a shark," Alvy tells Annie after a revealing detour to Los Angeles. "It has to constantly move forward or it dies. And what we got on our hands here ... is a dead shark." Using split screens, animated footage, subtitles, man-on-the-street interviews, and fourth-wall-breaking direct addresses to the camera that enlist the audience as partners in heartbreak, *Annie Hall* chronicles the slow, painful death of Alvy and Annie's sick-shark relationship with all the formal inventiveness of *Take the Money and Run* or *Zelig.* Potshots at academia (a pompous professor is told off by Marshall McLuhan), at TV (Alvy has an anxiety attack when he discovers the dubious uses of a laugh track), at family (Alvy's boisterous Jewish clan shares the screen with Annie's uptight Protestant brood), and at drugs (Alvy sneezes Chaplin-like into a box of expensive cocaine) keep the laughs coming until a showstopping performance by Keaton of "Seems Like Old Times." But long before then it has become apparent that far more is at stake here than in previous Allen comedies. In the film's final moment, highlights of Alvy and Annie's love affair—accompanied by a tender reprise of "Seems Like Old Times"—flash across the screen, communicating the message behind Alvy's closing joke: "This guy goes to a psychiatrist and says, 'Doc, uh, my brother's crazy. He thinks he's a chicken.' And, uh, the doctor says, 'Well, why don't you turn him in?' 'I would but I need the eggs.'" A certifiable madness, love is also a sustaining one. The closing shot shows Alvy and Annie saying goodbye as traffic rushes by on Sixty-third Street.

"Certifiable" may be used in a more clinical sense to describe the suicidal heroine of Allen's *Interiors* (1978). In a wrenching performance, Geraldine Page plays Eve, the damaged interior decorator whose attorney husband Arthur (E. G. Marshall) abandons her for the vivacious "vulgarian" Pearl (Maureen Stapleton). Of their three adult daughters, Renata (Diane Keaton) is a tormented poet, Joey (Mary Beth Hurt) a floundering photographer, and Flyn (Kristin Griffith) a marginally successful television actress. To varying degrees of success the daughters try to keep Eve together mentally as the prospect of reconciliation with Arthur becomes more and more remote. Eve is so in denial that when Arthur ironically announces in a church his intentions to finalize their divorce, she replies, "I know it's perhaps a little too soon to talk about a reconciliation, but I don't see why we have to finalize a divorce." Moments later Eve flees the sanctuary after overturning an altar of votive candles.

In the two films following *Love and Death,* the accent in *Annie Hall* was on love, but the accent in *Interiors* is on death. All dramatic action—devoid of even the slightest comic relief—inclines toward Eve's self-destruction. When Renata's ineffectual husband remarks of a Broadway play that "it was pessimistic to the point of futility," his evaluation seems to apply to the larger project that is *Interiors.* Gordon Willis' exquisitely etiolated photography complements a project whose main concern is turning inside-out the psychology of an emotionally repressed family whose spiritually damaged matriarch is "really too perfect … to live in the world," as her daughter Joey says of her: "All

[your] beautifully furnished rooms, carefully designed interiors … everything so controlled. There wasn't any room for … any real feelings." Bergman's influence is sizable here, but the courage of Allen's project, and its relentlessness, are his own. When at the end of the film Pearl gives a half-drowned Joey the kiss of life, she awakens only to shield her eyes. Death's shadow looms across the figures of *Interiors,* but unlike Boris at the end of *Love and Death,* no one seems particularly inclined to want to dance with it.

As if to shake off the terrible solemnity of *Interiors, Manhattan* opens with a bang: pyrotechnics erupt to the soaring strains of Gershwin as Allen, in a Damon Runyonesque monologue, salutes the city he adores. Allen is having fun goosing his myth as the single most famous New Yorker on Earth, but the real star again is Gordon Willis' photography, which in this razzle-dazzling sequence and throughout *Manhattan* is as outsized, affirming, and unabashedly romantic as his work in *Interiors* was muted, stark, and inward. Widely recognized as Allen's masterpiece, *Manhattan* is in fact *Annie Hall*'s perfect bookend: the two lean together as tragicomic salutes to love—and to the city that is *there* to be loved—even when funny valentines, as they always do, elude you.

Isaac Davis (Allen) is a disgruntled television writer conducting an affair with seventeen-year-old Tracy (Mariel Hemingway), whom Isaac describes poetically as "God's answer to Job." A mere teen whose insights into love are invariably more substantive than Isaac's, Tracy is constantly being told by Isaac, "Hey, don't be so precocious, Okay?" At the same time, Isaac's academic friend Yale (Michael Murphy) is cheating on his dutiful wife Emily (Anne Byrne) with the high-strung, volatile editor Mary Wilkie (Diane Keaton), an opinionated woman given to spouting non sequiturs like: "I'm just from Philadelphia … we believe in God." Yale's desire to call it quits with Mary coincides with

Isaac's growing attraction to her. Soon Isaac has left Tracy for Mary, only to be abandoned in the end by Mary for Yale, who finally leaves his wife. In the film's final sequence a miserable Isaac lies alone on a couch speaking into a tape recorder reasons for living: "*Sentimental Education* ... Marlon Brando, Frank Sinatra ... the crabs at Sam Wo's ... Tracy's face." Isaac's epiphany is followed by shots of him hurtling through the streets toward Tracy's apartment, only to find her late for a plane to London. In a moment that plays like a conflation of the finales of *La Dolce Vita* and *Casablanca,* Isaac begs Tracy to stay. She refuses, saying she will be back in six months; Isaac claims that by then she will be a changed person. "Not everybody gets corrupted," the wise-beyond-her-years Tracy replies. "You have to have a little faith in people." On the word "faith" Isaac hooks his eyes at the sky, but the grudging smile Tracy wrings out of him suggests that it is Isaac who will change, and for the better. What makes *Manhattan* itself a reason for living is its status as the first Allen film in which "faith" does not come off sounding like a dirty word.

But faith has abandoned Allen at the outset of *Stardust Memories* (1980). "I don't wanna make funny movies anymore," Woody whines while framed against a blown-up backdrop of the My Lai massacre. "They can't force me to." At once Allen's *ars regretica* and a protracted homage to Fellini's *8 1/2, Stardust Memories* offers a tour of a comic imagination punch-drunk from punch lines and the claustrophobia of celebrity. Sandy Bates (Allen), a barely disguised portrait of the artist, is invited to a festival honoring his work. There Sandy juggles memories of a disastrous love affair with Dorrie (Charlotte Rampling), a mentally-ill actress; current flirtations with Daisy (Jessica Harper), an introverted violinist; and his ongoing relationship with Isobel (Marie-Christine Barrault), an adoring mother of two. All the while Sandy is beset by legions of fans who never give him a moment's peace. "Have you ever had intercourse with any type of animal?" an academic inquires. "Would you sign my left breast?" one woman asks. "Can I have your autograph?" a fan says suddenly, adding apropos of nothing: "I was a Caesarean."

"For a guy who makes a lot of funny movies," Daisy tells Sandy during a ramble along the beachfront, "you're kind of a depressive." Like the Fellini classic from which it takes its cues, *Stardust Memories*—whose alternate title as Allen's eleventh film might as well have been *10 1/2*—is the work of a filmmaker weary of filmmaking and wondering where his art fits into the Big Picture. "I look around the world," Sandy explains, "all I see is human suffering." A visit from space aliens in one of the film's more inspired moments provides Sandy with the answer he might not be looking for. "You want to do mankind a real service?" one fuzzy-voiced alien barks at the bewildered auteur. "Tell funnier jokes." After an imagined assassination by a deranged fan and a commitment from Isobel that seems like a romantic deus ex machina, Sandy Bates, more ill at ease than ever, spends the final frames of *Stardust Memories* staring blankly at an even blanker movie screen. Allen's greatest love, the cinema, has become a cross to bear. The faith in people posited by *Manhattan* has only led Allen to a radical doubt in the very medium—cinema—intended to convey that faith.

This doubt may explain the middling reception of *A Midsummer Night's Sex Comedy* (1982), a slight homage to Bergman's *Smiles of a Summer Night.* More notably, it was Allen's first of eleven collaborations with Mia Farrow—whom he would famously never marry but with whom he would more infamously part after establishing relations with her adopted daughter Soon-Yi Previn (whom he *would* marry in 1997).

Allen and Farrow's second collaboration—1983's *Zelig*—captures their love affair at its height and Allen back at the top of his game. Clocking in at seventy-nine minutes, Allen's fleetest comedy chronicles the life of Leonard Zelig (Allen), a Jazz Age "human chameleon" who takes on the physical, racial, ethnic, and personality traits of anyone with whom he is in close proximity. Traumatized years before by a group of bright students among whom he was ashamed to admit that he had never read *Moby Dick,* the hypnotized Zelig tells Dr. Eudora Fletcher (Farrow) that "It's safe...." "What do you mean safe?" "To be like the others." Dispensing with the deliberately lead-footed approach of *Take the Money and Run, Zelig's* more fluid documentary style seamlessly interweaves an astonishing array of technical devices: sham interviews (Saul Bellow and Irving Howe); doctored newsreel footage (Pope Pius XI swatting Zelig with a sacred decree); cheesy clips from nonexistent movies ("Somewhere behind that vacuous face ... is a real human being!"— *"The Changing Man,* Warner Bros., 1935"); phony billboards ("Leonard Zelig says ... *We* smoke Camels"); fake Socialist placards ("ZELIG UNFAIR TO WORKERS HOLDS FIVE JOBS"); vintage footage of bad Yiddish theater (an Orthodox version of *A Midsummer Night's Dream* featuring Zelig's father in prayer curls and tights); fabricated dance fads ("Do the Chameleon!"); mock paraphernalia (board games, dolls with interchangeable heads); and concocted songs saluting Leonard's cute mutability, including "You May Be Six People but I Love You" and the dreamy "Reptile Eyes":

You have such reptile eyes!
Eyes like a lizard
That weave their spell!

"Chameleon" might be a Freudian slip for "comedian"; the same anxiety to satisfy his audience that tormented Sandy Bates in *Stardust Memories* is at the core of Zelig's more crushing desire to please absolutely everybody. "One could really think of him as the ultimate conformist," Dr. Bruno Bettelheim says in one

mock interview. As Zelig and Eudora's sessions become more revealing, and as the two gradually fall in love, this profoundly funny film becomes a profoundly serious meditation on self. To discover love with Eudora, Zelig must first discover himself. It's somewhere in there, and using mesmerism Eudora at last roots out the real Leonard: "Your pancakes ... I dump them in the garbage when you're not looking.... I love you.... You're the worst cook.... I wanna take care of you.... No more pancakes!" By *Zelig's* conclusion a rehabilitated Leonard proclaims to his adoring masses that "It shows exactly what you can do if you're a total psychotic!" The closing shot is of Zelig and Eudora stumbling bashfully off as jazz music fondly plays.

The affectionate tone of *Zelig* carried over to 1984's endearing *Broadway Danny Rose* and 1987's nostalgic *Radio Days,* Allen's generous, heartfelt tributes to Vaudeville and his childhood years, respectively. But it was the intervening back-to-back critical and commercial successes of The *Purple Rose of Cairo* (1985) and *Hannah and Her Sisters* (1986) that reestablished Allen's reputation as a screen author of the first rank.

The Purple Rose of Cairo extends *Stardust Memories'* suspect examination of the sustaining power of film in the face of grim reality. Cecilia (Mia Farrow) is a Depression-era waitress whose wastrel husband Monk (Danny Aiello) philanders, beats her, and spends her money. Addicted to the movies, Cecilia is alarmed when on her fifth viewing of *The Purple Rose of Cairo* its archaeologist hero Tom Baxter (Jeff Daniels) spots her in the audience, declares "I've got to speak to you," and steps off the screen to woo her. Anarchy ensues. The picture's producers worry that other Toms on other screens will also go AWOL; stranded members of Tom's cast await his return, petrified that the projector will be switched off at any moment ("Don't! ... It gets black and we disappear!"); and the audience is understandably miffed. Meanwhile the actor who portrays Tom, Gil Shepherd (also Daniels), is sent to find Baxter and salvage his career. Both Tom and Gil make a play for Cecilia. But Cecilia, more attracted to Tom, is worried about her prospects for more practical reasons: "You're not real." Tom kisses her and says, "Was that real enough for you?"

Line for line *The Purple Rose of Cairo* is as zippy as any of Allen's "early funny movies," but the laughs exude a creeping existential dread. The bored Countess (Zoe Caldwell) in the movie-within-the-movie glares out at the audience and says contemptuously, "They don't look like they're having too much fun to me." And when her panicky costar Henry (Edward Herrmann) exclaims, *"We're* reality; *they're* a dream!" the Countess replies: "You've been up on the screen *flickering* too long." In one of the movie's incredible moments Tom drags Cecilia up into his picture for a glamorous night on the two-dimensional town. Sipping champagne, Cecilia remarks, "These bottles are filled with ginger ale!" "Welcome to the movies, kid," Tom's smart-alecky costar Rita (Deborah Rush) snaps back. In the end Cecilia must choose between Tom ("I'm honest, dependable, courageous, romantic, and a great kisser") and Gil ("I'm real"). She chooses Gil and breaks Tom's celluloid heart, only to be abandoned by Gil when she finally finds the courage to leave Monk. At the end of the picture, in a coda full of pathos, Cecilia sits in the theater with her suitcases beside her while Fred Astaire and Ginger Rogers float on ether to the heavenly strains of "Cheek to Cheek."

Mia Farrow is the title character and once again the emotional center of the leisurely paced, expansive *Hannah and Her Sisters.* In the fashion of *Interiors,* but with incandescent light, the film explores the relationships among three sisters—Lee (Barbara Hershey), an unemployed student living with a bitter painter (Max von Sydow); Holly (Dianne Wiest), a caterer and cocaine addict who falls first for a dashing architect (Sam Waterston) then for Hannah's ex-husband Mickey (Woody Allen); and the stage actress Hannah, whose financier husband, Elliot (Michael Caine), is conducting an affair with Lee. The film also offers intricate portraits of the sisters' parents—the alcoholic Norma (Maureen O'Sullivan) and her long-suffering husband, Evan (Lloyd Nolan), whose troubled relationship stands as a template for all of the other relationships in the film. Though Farrow's nurturing, oblivious character remains the soul of *Hannah and Her Sisters,* this is the first Allen film in which family may be said to be the central character—which may account, in fact, for its resounding popularity.

Though Allen's canvas in *Hannah and Her Sisters* is large, it never feels crowded or busy. Quiet moments of desperation like Hannah's unheard plea to Elliot that she has "enormous needs" clearly communicate the way in which individuals get lost or taken for granted in the family shuffle, and when Holly tells Mickey at the climax that she is pregnant, Allen's happy ending seems earned, not forced. Happier still is a woozy subplot involving Mickey's hypochondria. "I wonder how he'd handle it if there was ever something really wrong with him," Hannah jokes prophetically at the beginning of the film. As comic relief, Mickey's increasingly panicky visits to a series of physicians about a possible brain tumor amusingly undercut the intensity of the increasingly dangerous relationship between Lee and Elliot, which threatens the larger harmony of the family as a whole. At the film's conclusion Elliot has returned to Hannah, Lee is engaged to marry her Columbia professor, and even the incurable worrier Mickey finds himself a father to be; his earlier, on-the-brink-of-suicide revelation that life is something to "enjoy ... while it lasts" seems dramatically and philosophically valid. "The heart," as Holly observes at *Hannah and Her Sisters'* luminous conclusion, "is a resilient muscle."

The heart of *Crimes and Misdemeanors* (1989) beats strongly as well, but darkly. On the heels of the less convincing Mia Farrow vehicle *September* (1987) and the Gena Rowlands tour de force *Another Woman* (1988), this last great work of Allen's middle period chronicles the descent of Dr. Judah Rosenthal, a philanthropic ophthalmologist trying to disengage himself from his desperate mistress Dolores Paley (Anjelica Huston), who is determined to reveal their relationship to Judah's wife, Miriam (Claire Bloom). Judah contracts his hit man brother Jack (Jerry Orbach), all the while obsessed by the words of Rabbi Ben (Sam Waterston), a friend who has been seeing Judah for a degenerative eye disease: "I couldn't go on living if I didn't feel with all my heart a moral structure with real meaning and forgiveness and some kind of higher power; otherwise, there's no basis to know how to live." After the hit goes down, Judah finds himself existentially at sea: "God have mercy on us," he says pointedly. Never have the philosophical issues of an Allen film been freighted with such weighty consequences. Where *Love and Death* lampooned the grand pronouncements of Tolstoy's *War and Peace*, *Crimes and Misdemeanors* with inexorable gravity captures the psychological vertigo of Dostoevsky's *Crime and Punishment*.

Disintegrating emotionally, Judah returns to his childhood home, where in an *Annie Hall*-like flashback he overhears his family at seder debating the "nonsense" and "mumbo-jumbo" of Judaism. "[God] punishes the wicked," Judah's father affirms in a moment unique in Allen's work for the manner in which it affirms ethical imperatives inherent in belief. For the symbolically named Judah, an ophthalmologist who has been taught by his father to remember that "the eyes of God are always on us," the moment proves devastating. Caught between irreversible action and inescapable guilt, this "man of science … [who has] always been a

skeptic" must now learn to navigate blindly a world where the awful possibility of God has suddenly become more palpable than ever. A diverting subplot in which the independent filmmaker Cliff (Allen) makes a documentary about a showbiz blowhard named Lester (Alan Alda) while both compete for the hand of the film's producer, Halley (Farrow), offers a surprising turn when Halley, selling out morally like Judah, abandons Cliff for the phony but successful Lester. By the end of the film no moral center remains. Judah, who has said that "without God the world is a cesspool," gets away with "the perfect murder." But the implication, rare for an Allen film, is that the real moral bill will be presented to Judah with considerable interest in the next world—if there is one.

After setting the bar so high for himself in the half-dozen masterful films that comprised Allen's phenomenal stretch from 1977 to 1989, the more immediate question became, "Would there be life after *Crimes and Misdemeanors*?"

LATER FILMS (1990–2003)

The wistful Mia Farrow comedy *Alice* (1990) and the expressionistic dead end *Shadows and Fog* (1992) answered this question equivocally, kicking off as they did a decade and a half that by critical consensus has not measured up to Allen's early and middle periods. Works such as *Celebrity* (1998), *Small Time Crooks* (2000), *The Curse of the Jade Scorpion* (2001), *Hollywood Ending* (2002), and *Anything Else* (2003)—were unevenly received. But before them minor gems like the freewheeling Marshall Brickman–Diane Keaton reunion *Manhattan Murder Mystery* (1993), the effervescent Mira Sorvino comedy *Mighty Aphrodite* (1995), the affectionate, ersatz musical *Everyone Says I Love You* (1996), and the hard-nosed *La Strada* homage *Sweet and Lowdown* (1999) showcased Allen's strengths, not the least of which continues to be his prodigious cinematic output. Of the fourteen films made during this period, three in particular stand out: the marital exposé *Husbands and Wives* (1992), the boisterous Douglas McGrath collaboration *Bullets over Broadway* (1994), and what is arguably the strongest film of Allen's later period, the excoriating *Deconstructing Harry* (1997).

Bergman's *Scenes from a Marriage* would seem to be the model for *Husbands and Wives,* but handheld camerawork and an unhurried pace contribute to a more casual if no less searing analysis of marital strife. When Jack and Sally (Sydney Pollack and Judy Davis) announce to their best friends Gabe and Judy (Allen and Farrow) that they are splitting up, Gabe and Judy seem more upset than Jack and Sally. Judy takes it especially hard and asks Gabe, "You think we'd ever break up?" Gabe's reluctance to have a child by Judy ("You would never tell me you were putting your diaphragm on and then not do it, right?"), his flirtations with his talented writing student Rain (Juliette Lewis), and Judy's infatuation with her handsome coworker Michael (Liam Neeson) give Judy's question increasing heft as the film unfolds. Gabe and Judy's breakup is not a question of "if" but "when." Meanwhile Sally pursues an unsatisfying relationship with Michael while Jack falls for an aerobics instructor who refers to King Lear as "King Leo." After a climactic electrical storm in which Gabe kisses Rain but goes no further, Jack and Sally are back together, Judy leaves Gabe for Michael, and the only person Gabe has left to talk to is his analyst, whom he asks pointedly in the last shot: "Can I go now?"

The paucity of shtick and the rawness of emotions in *Husbands and Wives* suggest that Allen has no easy answers for the seemingly random ways in which couples unite, split, reunite, and split again. The chaos of coupling is enigmatic and maddening: "It's the second law of thermodynamics.... Sooner or later everything turns to shit." Even the twenty-year-old Rain seems like a battle-weary veteran of love: "Aren't our choices between chronic dissatisfaction and suburban drudgery?" There is a fleeting moment during the electrical storm in which Rain's mother tells her husband, "it'll be our twenty-fifth anniversary in June" before kissing him. Then the lights go out. "Maybe in the end the idea was not to expect too much out of life," Gabe concludes earlier, before strolling home alone—without Rain—in the rain.

Allen remains firmly behind the camera for the rambunctious *Bullets over Broadway,* but the question of "authorship" is really divided between the aspiring playwright David Shayne (John Cusack) and the mafia thug Cheech (Chazz Palminteri) who "cowrite" a play featuring the mob moll Olive Neal (Jennifer Tilly), for whom Cheech is a bodyguard and whose gangster boyfriend has financed David's play as Olive's star vehicle. When David's mediocre script is brought to dramatic life by Cheech's increasingly savvy suggestions, and when it becomes ever more apparent to the artistically sociopathic Cheech that Olive's horrible performance "is gonna ruin my play," Cheech takes matters into his own hands. "I think you should know this," Cheech states before shooting Olive point-blank, "you're a horrible actress."

Bullets over Broadway asks the same moral question posed by *Crimes and Misdemeanors.* Although "an artist creates his own universe," is murder ever justified? At the same time, the farce flips the ontological equation of *The Purple Rose of Cairo:* instead of characters breaking the fourth wall with a vengeance, *writers* ravage reality, murdering with abandon in the higher name of art. "She kills my words! ... She makes my stuff not work!" Cheech rages. "That's no reason to kill her!" David responds, adding: "I'm an artist! But first I'm a human being!" Featuring an Academy Award-winning performance by Dianne Wiest as a diva named Helen Sinclair, who preempts David's declarations of love with the basso profundo pronouncement "Dooon't speak!," *Bullets over Broadway* scores huge laughs but scores even deeper points about the potentially lethal collision of art and reality. "To an ideal world with no compromises," Helen toasts David as she watches his star rise, unaware that his muse is a conscienceless mob goon. After attending the dying Cheech in a grisly backstage hit, David renounces art and is reunited with his girlfriend. Closing credits are accompanied by "Let's Misbehave," which also accompanied the opening credits of *Everything You Always Wanted to Know about Sex.* There its use was comic, here seriocomic: artists, however brilliant, may create their universes, but just like the rest of us they must *behave* in them too.

Deconstructing Harry seems determined to misbehave. The pyrotechnics that opened *Manhattan* with a burst of joie de vivre are replaced here by fusillades of off-color language that suggest we are in for a misanthropic show: "You schmuck! … I'd like to cut your fucking head off!" Lucy (Judy Davis) rails at her ex-lover, the novelist Harry Block (Allen), after learning their affair has been revealed in his book. "I'm not gonna stand up here on this roof with a world-class meshugganer cunt and beg for my life!" Harry shouts back when Lucy fires a gun at him. Harry, a writer suffering from his last name, would rather be shot than go back to work. After a lifetime of exposing wives and girlfriends ("Kill the black magician so he can't spin any more gold out of human misery!" Lucy screams), Harry has run out of people to exploit and turns on himself with terrible avidity. "I'm spiritually bankrupt," he tells his sister, who agrees with him: "Your whole life—it's nihilism, it's cynicism, it's sarcasm and orgasm!" "You know in France," Harry replies, "I could run on that slogan and win."

In *Stardust Memories,* Sandy Bates's hostility, represented by a rampaging gorilla, roamed the countryside pursued by the police. Harry makes that gorilla look like a softie. Unapologetic

about fooling around ("Does the president of the United States want to fuck every woman he sees? *Bad* example!") and denied visitation rights with his son by his embittered ex-wife ("He's *not* gonna spend the afternoon with his pill-popping, alcoholic, beaver-banging excuse for a father!"), Harry kidnaps his son and drives to a college ceremony in his honor accompanied by a prostitute named Cookie (Hazelle Goodman) and a friend (Bob Balaban), who dies of a heart attack en route. Pursuing him too are his literary characters, who upbraid him for his past, much to Harry's irritation: "I'm not gonna stand here and get lectured by my own creation[s]!" Arrested for kidnapping, Harry is bailed out by his ex-lover Fay (Elisabeth Shue) and ex-best friend Larry (Billy Crystal) but not before indulging in an infernal fantasy in which he goes to Hades ("Floor seven, the media—sorry, that floor is full") and confronts the devil ("For two years I ran a Hollywood studio, but you can't trust those people"). Having finally hit bottom in the hell of his own conscience, and supported only by his characters, who give him a Felliniesque round of applause, an unblocked Harry Block bangs away at his typewriter at *Deconstructing Harry*'s upbeat conclusion. As brave as it is profane and as hilarious as it is bracing, *Deconstructing Harry* locates salvation in "writing, which in more ways than one had saved [Harry's *and* Allen's] life."

PLAYS AND PROSE

"I [would have been] very content to have a life in the theater," Allen has said, "and was looking forward to being a playwright…. You could really do something substantial in theater." *From A to Z,* Allen's 1960 musical review for Hermione Gingold, the autobiographical *Floating Light Bulb,* and one acts like *Central Park West* are accomplished, but Allen stands far more of a chance of being remembered for his work for the screen than for the stage. Nonetheless, two of his Broadway smashes—*Don't Drink the Water* and *Play It Again, Sam*—should be remembered with the same high regard as his early film comedies.

In Allen's cold war caper *Don't Drink the Water,* the inept Axel Magee ("You started on top and you worked your way to the mail room") is put in charge of the American embassy of an unnamed Communist country by his departing ambassador father. An international incident ensues when the Hollander family from New Jersey seeks asylum for snapping sensitive photos ("What did you think it was—a place that sold guards and dogs and barbed wire?"). Magee negotiates a swap: the Hollanders for a captured spy. But when the spy hangs himself ("What do you expect from a Gray Fox. Is that a name for a grown-up person?"), Axel disguises the Hollanders in the clothes of the drunken sultan of Bashir and smuggles them out, only to have Mr. Hollander shoot Axel's own returning father in the foot. By then Axel has become engaged to the Hollanders' daughter, Mr. and Mrs. Hollander are Jersey-bound in the most absurd manner imaginable ("While we're aboard the submarine, you wire us your silverware pattern"), and the Catholic-priest magician ensconced in the embassy for political reasons who has acted throughout as delirious chorus informs us in an epilogue that Axel's father "has sent him five thousand miles away to Bolivia, where for the first time in two hundred years that country had a plague of locusts." A breezy, delightful romp, *Don't Drink the Water* has more farcical confidence than *What's New, Pussycat?,* which was penned at around the same time. Its continuing popularity—a 1969 film starring Jackie Gleason and Allen's own 1994 TV adaptation featuring Michael J. Fox—is understandable.

Not as funny but more substantial, *Play It Again, Sam* anticipates the illusion-versus-reality clash of movies like *The Purple Rose of Cairo* in the manner in which Humphrey Bogart steps out of *The Maltese Falcon* to help the recently divorced Allan Felix succeed again with women. The play also has the loosely structured feel of Allen's best comedies; it isn't just about Bogey's too-cool attempt to coach Allan romantically, it's also about the slowly burgeoning romance between Allan and his friend Linda (played on stage and in the screen adaptation, significantly, by Diane Keaton). Linda's husband, Dick, neglects her, and through cinematic scene shifts and fantasy fades (a boat-row through Central Park improvised in a hammock, trips to New York nightspots and the Museum of Modern Art) the two nearly come together in a way that points upward and outward to Allen's later, more mature film work. When Allan buys her a stuffed pet skunk from FAO Schwartz and Linda replies, "I'm so touched … I don't know what to say," we all but expect her to add: "La-de-da." Bogart's help seems peripheral; *Play It Again, Sam* is a dry run for *Annie Hall.* And even though Linda returns to her husband in the end, Allan comes close to winning her before bidding her adieu in an unavoidable tip of the hat to *Casablanca:*

ALLAN: If that plane leaves the ground and you're not with him, you'll regret it. Maybe not today, maybe not tomorrow, but soon and for the rest of your life.

LINDA: That's beautiful.

ALLAN: It's from "Casablanca." I waited my whole life just to say it.

If Woody Allen had never written plays like *Play It Again, Sam* or screenplays like *Annie Hall,* his prose pieces would be enough to establish his reputation as a significant humorist in the American canon. Published over three decades in magazines like the *New Yorker,* the collected sketches in *Getting Even, Without Feathers,* and *Side Effects*—and many currently uncollected—showcase the same comic gifts apparent in his works for stage and screen. Some of these—"The Kugelmass Episode," which won the O. Henry Award, just to name one—are classics in their own right. A selected overview can only hint at their pleasures and of more pleasures to come.

As if getting even with the colleges Allen fled, *Getting Even* lampoons academic rhetoric. In "The Metterling Lists" scholars scrutinize a famous writer's laundry lists down to the last odd sock; "My Philosophy," a spoof of crackpot philosophical discourse, dissects the "Critique of Pure Dread," "Eschatological Dialectics as a Means of Coping with Shingles," and "The Cosmos on Five Dollars a Day"; the mock course catalog "Spring Bulletin" offers "Yeats and Hygiene"; and in "Conversations with Helmholtz," a colleague of Sigmund Freud and Otto Rank defends his radical theories: "I did not particularly care for Rank since he had recently referred to my paper on 'Euphoria in Snails' as 'the zenith of mongoloid reasoning.'" But the freshest pieces in *Getting Even,* as with Allen's early films, are parodic. "Mr. Big" captures the zero-affect delivery of detective fiction as a smart Vassar coed is accused by a private dick of murdering God: "When the Supreme Being gets knocked off, *somebody's* got to take the rap." "Viva Vargas!" anticipates *Bananas'* send-up of guerrilla manifestos: "[The] CIA has reconsidered our chances of bringing off the revolution and as a result threw Arroyo and his cabinet a conciliatory brunch at Wolfie's in Miami." And Bram Stoker is skewered to bloody perfection in "Count Dracula," a gothic farce in which the Count arrives at the home of two victims only to be asked: "Did you come by to watch the eclipse with us? ... A few moments of darkness from noon until two minutes after." To which the Count replies: "I'm in big trouble."

The title of Allen's second collection stands Emily Dickinson ("Hope is the thing with feathers") on her head. *Without Feathers* also

upsy-daisies the occult ("it was actually my body that left my spirit, although all it did was get a rubdown"); ballet ("A melodic prelude recounts man's relation to the earth and why he always seems to wind up buried in it"); the Old Testament ("[And] Job calleth out: 'Why doth thou slay my kine? Kine are hard to come by. Now I am short on kine and I'm not even sure what kine are"); circus romances ("[his mother] was a trapeze artist ... his father ... was the human cannonball. The two met in midair and were married before touching the ground"); and, perhaps most surprisingly, the author himself ("Following are excerpts from the hitherto secret private journal of Woody Allen, which will be published posthumously or after his death, which ever comes first"). The strongest piece here is "The Whore of Mensa," in which a call-girl network of sexy pseudo-intellectuals gets big bucks to talk deep: "For three bills, you got the works: A thin Jewish brunette would pretend to pick you up at the Museum of Modern Art, let you read her master's, get you involved in a screaming quarrel at Elaine's over Freud's conception of women, and then fake a suicide of your choosing—the perfect evening, for some guys. Nice racket. Great town, New York."

Side Effects rounds up the usual suspects and some unusual ones too: moral angst ("It seemed the world was divided into good and bad people. The good ones slept better ... while the bad ones seemed to enjoy the waking hours much more"); UFOs ("Experts do agree that any glowing cigar-shaped aircraft capable of rising straight up at twelve thousand miles per second would require the kind of maintenance and sparkplugs available only on Pluto"); Kafka ("One day, for no apparent reason, F. broke his diet"); the Heimlich maneuver ("He hugged sharply, causing a side order of bean curd to rocket out of the victim's trachea and carom off the hat rack"); haute cuisine fettuccine ("Pasta as an expression of Neo-Realistic starch"); and burglary

("Where I grew up, you had to steal to eat. Then you had to steal to tip").

But the high point of *Side Effects* is "The Kugelmass Episode," where, in another foretaste of *The Purple of Rose of Cairo,* the unhappily wedded Kugelmass ("bald and as hairy as a bear, but he had soul") ditches his psychoanalyst in favor of a magician who pops him into a box with a copy of *Madame Bovary* and transports him to Yonville, where a fictional tryst with Emma lies in wait. But when Emma is whisked to New York with Kugelmass and can't get back to Yonville, this postmodern fairy tale (whose influence can be noted in screenwriter Charlie Kaufman's *Being John Malkovich*) begins to show telltale signs of a moral: "It's over," says Kugelmass, "I learned my lesson. I'll never cheat again, I swear it." Nonetheless Kugelmass is back three weeks later with a copy of Philip Roth's *Portnoy's Complaint.* When the magician inserts the book his fantastic box explodes, and Kugelmass is last pictured in *"Remedial Spanish* ... running for his life over a barren, rocky terrain as the word *tener* ('to have')—a large and hairy irregular verb—raced after him on its spindly legs."

From the sublimely ridiculous to the ridiculously sublime, Allen one-ups "The Kugelmass Episode" with "My Speech to the Graduates," a rummage sale of clichés concealing the odd ironic treasure: "More than any other time in history, mankind faces a crossroads. One path leads to despair and utter hopelessness. The other, to total extinction. Let us pray we have the wisdom to choose correctly."

As he enters his seventh decade as an artist, Woody Allen's creative fountain of youth would appear to flow eternal. Allen is reportedly in negotiation to write a multimillion-dollar memoir, he continues to publish regularly in the *New Yorker,* he still plays his clarinet religiously at Michael's Pub, and his thirty-seventh film— *Melinda and Melinda*—has been released. With three dozen award-winning original film scripts,

three best-selling books of humorous prose, legendary stints in television and stand-up comedy, a pair of Broadway hits, and international status as a bona fide pop cultural icon, Allan Stewart Konigsberg of Brooklyn, New York has come a long way from the playgrounds of Flatbush. Alvy may have fallen out of love with Annie Hall, but the world's affair with Woody Allen would appear to be a shark that will never stop moving.

Selected Bibliography

WORKS OF WOODY ALLEN

FILMS
What's New, Pussycat? Famous Artists, 1965.
What's Up, Tiger Lily? American International Pictures, 1966.
Don't Drink the Water. Avco Embassy, 1969.
Take the Money and Run. Palomar Pictures, 1969.
Bananas. United Artists, 1971.
Everything You Always Wanted to Know about Sex* (*But Were Afraid to Ask). United Artists, 1972.
Play It Again, Sam. Paramount Pictures, 1972.
Sleeper. United Artists, 1973.
Love and Death. United Artists, 1975.
Annie Hall. United Artists, 1977.
Interiors. United Artists, 1978.
Manhattan. United Artists, 1979.
Stardust Memories. United Artists, 1980.
A Midsummer Night's Sex Comedy. Orion Pictures, 1982.
Zelig. Orion Pictures, 1983.
Broadway Danny Rose. Orion Pictures, 1984.
The Purple Rose of Cairo. Orion Pictures, 1985.
Hannah and Her Sisters. Orion Pictures, 1986.
Radio Days. Orion Pictures, 1987.
September. Orion Pictures, 1987.
Another Woman. Orion Pictures, 1988.

Crimes and Misdemeanors. Orion Pictures, 1989.

New York Stories ("Oedipus Wrecks"). Touchstone Pictures, 1989.

Alice. Orion Pictures, 1990.

Husbands and Wives. Columbia-TriStar, 1992.

Shadows and Fog. Orion Pictures, 1992.

Manhattan Murder Mystery. Columbia-TriStar, 1993.

Bullets over Broadway. Sweetland/Miramax, 1994.

Mighty Aphrodite. Sweetland/Miramax, 1995.

Everyone Says I Love You. Sweetland/Miramax, 1996.

Deconstructing Harry. Sweetland/Fine Line, 1997.

Celebrity. Sweetland/Miramax, 1998.

Sweet and Lowdown. Columbia-TriStar, 1999.

Small Time Crooks. DreamWorks, 2000.

The Curse of the Jade Scorpion. DreamWorks, 2001.

Sounds from a Town I Love. TV short, 2001.

Hollywood Ending. DreamWorks, 2002.

Anything Else. DreamWorks, 2003.

Melinda and Melinda. Fox Searchlight Pictures, 2004.

Match Point. DreamWorks, 2005.

PLAYS

From A to Z. Unpublished. April 20, 1960. Plymouth Theater, New York.

Don't Drink the Water. New York: Random House, 1967.

Play It Again, Sam. New York: Random House, 1969.

The Floating Light Bulb. New York: Random House, 1982.

Three One Act Plays. New York: Random House, 2003. (Includes *Riverside Drive, Old Saybrook,* and *Central Park West.*)

PROSE

Getting Even. New York: Random House, 1971.

Without Feathers. New York: Random House, 1975.

Side Effects. New York: Random House, 1980.

The Complete Prose of Woody Allen. New York: Wings Books (Random House), 1991.

PUBLISHED SCREENPLAYS

Woody Allen's Play It Again, Sam. New York: Grosset & Dunlap, 1972.

Four Films of Woody Allen. New York: Random House, 1982. (Includes *Annie Hall, Interiors, Manhattan,* and *Stardust Memories.*)

Hannah and Her Sisters. New York: Random House, 1987.

Three Films of Woody Allen. New York: Vintage Books, 1987. (Includes *Zelig, Broadway Danny Rose,* and *The Purple Rose of Cairo.*)

CRITICAL AND BIOGRAPHICAL STUDIES

Allen, Woody. *Woody Allen on Woody Allen.* Edited by Stig Bjorkman. New York: Grove, 1985.

Bailey, Peter J. *The Reluctant Film Art of Woody Allen.* Lexington: University Press of Kentucky, 2001.

Benayoun, Robert. *The Films of Woody Allen.* New York: Harmony, 1986.

Blake, Richard A. *Woody Allen: Profane and Sacred.* London: Scarecrow Press, 1995.

Canby, Vincent. "Woody Allen Continues to Refine His Cinematic Art." *New York Times,* July 17, 1973, p. 15.

"Deconstructing Woody: A Critical Symposium on Woody Allen's *Deconstructing Harry." Cineaste,* summer 1998, p. 35.

Didion, Joan. "Review of *Annie Hall, Interiors,* and *Manhattan." New York Review of Books,* August 1979, p. 18.

Fox, Julian. *Woody: Movies from Manhattan.* Woodstock, N.Y.: Overlook Press, 1996.

Gittelson, Natalie. "The Maturing of Woody Allen." *New York Times Magazine,* April 22, 1979, pp. SM1, 4.

Hirsch, Foster. *Love, Sex, Death, and the Meaning of Life.* New York: McGraw-Hill, 1981.

Hirschberg, Lynn. "Woody Allen, Martin Scorsese." *New York Times Magazine,* November 16, 1997, p. 91.

Jacobs, Diane. *But We Need the Eggs: The Magic of Woody Allen.* New York: St. Martin's Press, 1982.

Kael, Pauline. *Reeling.* Boston: Little, Brown, 1976.

Kael, Pauline. "The Frog Who Turned into a Prince / The Prince Who Turned into a Frog." *New Yorker,* October 27, 1980, pp. 183–190.

Kakutani, Michiko. "How Woody Allen's *Zelig* Was Born in Anxiety and Grew into Comedy." *New*

York Times, July 18, 1983, p. 13.

Lax, Eric. *Woody Allen: A Biography.* New York: Knopf, 1991.

Meade, Marion. *The Unruly Life of Woody Allen.* New York: Scribners, 2000.

Rich, Frank. "An Interview with Woody." *Time,* April 30, 1979, pp. 68–69.

Sarris, Andrew. " 'S Wonderful." *Village Voice,* April 30, 1979, p. 51.

Schickel, Richard. *Woody Allen: A Life in Film.* Chicago: Ivan R. Dee, 2003.

Siskel, Gene. "Woody Allen on Love, Life, and Ronald Reagan." *Chicago Tribune,* June 11, 1982, p. 5.

Turan, Kenneth. "The Comic Genius of Woody Allen." *Progressive,* March 1973, pp. 44–46.

Wernblad, Annette. *Brooklyn Is Not Expanding: Woody Allen's Comic Universe.* Rutherford, N.J.: Farleigh Dickinson University Press, 1992.

Yacowar, Maurice. *Loser Take All: The Comic Art of Woody Allen.* New York: Frederick Ungar, 1979.

—*DANIEL VILMURE*

Frank Bidart

1939–

FRANK BIDART IS one of the leading poets of his generation. His books have consistently been nominated for many of America's major prizes for poetry, including the Pulitzer Prize, the National Book Award, and the National Book Critics Circle Award, and he has received honors from all the significant organizations concerned with the arts—the Wallace Stevens Award from the Academy of American Poets, the Shelley Award from the Poetry Society of America, the Morton Dauwen Zabel Award from the American Academy of Arts and Letters, the Rebekka Bobbitt Prize from the Library of Congress, the Lannan Literary Award, and the Lila Wallace–Reader's Digest Foundation Award. Eschewing many of the conventions of contemporary poetry, his work looks and sounds singular and unique. At a time when irony is de rigueur, Bidart is not afraid to grapple with questions that have long been central to Western metaphysics, venturing grand statements about life and death, body and spirit, guilt and meaning. At the same time, his work is grounded in the quotidian, mixing eloquence with bathos and portraying a deeply American vision. The approbation of one's peers is probably the greatest tribute a poet can receive, and in awarding Bidart the Wallace Stevens Award, the jury honored him with high praise indeed. In her citation, the chair of the jury, U.S. poet laureate Louise Glück, wrote, "Frank Bidart has patiently amassed as profound and original a body of work as any now being written in this country.... He is, in the feeling of our jury, one of the great poets of our time."

SURPRISING ORIGINS

Because he has lived in Cambridge, Massachusetts, since the early 1970s, Bidart perhaps seems to be the consummate New Englander. In fact, however, he was born into a family of farmers and grew up in the farm and ranchlands of southern California. The family business, Bidart Brothers, is one of the largest diversified farming operations in Kern County. Bidart's father, Frank, ran a thriving potato farm, but he was an alcoholic and a womanizer, and his personal life was relatively disastrous. Bidart's mother, Martha Yarnos, who considered herself a great, undiscovered beauty, eventually suffered a "nervous collapse." His parents' marriage ended when Bidart was only five, and he was raised primarily by his mother, who eventually remarried.

Bidart, who was born on May 27, 1939, grew up among the bleak, uncultured farm and ranchlands of Bishop and Bakersfield, California, but he never expected to join the family business. He did not have much exposure to the performing arts, but from an early age he was drawn to the glamour and mystery of the cinema—the only real "art form" he had access to. At first, he was determined to be an actor, but by the time he began his undergraduate education at the University of California at Riverside, he had fixed on the idea of becoming a serious film director. He seems to have invested art with a significance and possibility that is surprising in such a young man. As he told Mark Halliday in an interview for the literary journal *Ploughshares* (reprinted at the end of his 1990 volume of collected poems, *In the Western Night*): "I wanted films to be as ambitious and complex as the greatest works of art—as Milton, Eliot, Joyce." Once he had begun his studies, his interests shifted toward literature and philosophy, but the cinema continued to be an intense interest and influence in his work. As Helen Vendler and other critics have acknowledged, his best known dramatic work splices together sundry materials to create a movement that is distinctly cinematic. Likewise, a sense of drama and an awareness of the performative aspects of identity are always present in the work.

THE EDUCATION OF A POET

As an undergraduate at Riverside, Bidart was exposed to thinkers and writers whose teachings made a lasting impression on him. He studied philosophy with Philip Wheelwright, whose interests included myth, symbolism, imagination, ethics, Aristotle, Heraclitus, and Aeschylus. Wheelwright also introduced Bidart to opera, which became a significant interest and influence. Another important mentor was Thomas Edwards, an eighteenth-century scholar who had been a student of Reuben Brower and was famous for tutoring his students in the art of careful, attentive reading, emphasizing "voice" and "tone of voice." These concepts became central to Bidart's aesthetic and to his aims for his poetry. At Riverside, Bidart also discovered the work of modernist writers like T. S. Eliot and Ezra Pound; Eliot became a favorite, but reading Pound had a profound effect on his ideas about how to make a poem. He found the possibility of bringing together "many different kinds of thing" in a poem, as Pound had in *The Cantos,* to be enormously liberating: "if you can create a structure that is large enough or strong enough, *anything* can retain its own identity and find its place there" (*Western Night*). He also encountered the critical writings of Lionel Trilling and Francis Fergusson, and as he explained to Halliday, he was

equally influenced by their ideas. In particular, Trilling's notion that a work of art can conclude without bringing the various elements to conclusion allowed Bidart to write poems that revolve around irresolvable tensions. Fergerson's theory of "unity of action" in theater influenced Bidart's belief that a poem, like a drama, must both imitate an act and be an action.

In 1962 Bidart began graduate studies at Harvard University—a move that initiated his transformation into an East Coast intellectual. Though he has characterized his graduate studies as unfocused and he never completed his doctorate, his time at Harvard put him into contact with poets, teachers, and intellectuals who would be influential in his life, as well as his work and career. Certainly working as a teaching assistant in Brower's humanities course at Harvard reinforced the ideas about "voice" and careful reading that he had first gleaned from Thomas Edwards. Working with Brower no doubt helped inspire Bidart in his attempts to find a notation that could "fasten" the "voice in [his] head" to the page. While at Harvard, he also studied with Robert Lowell, a poet who was to be the subject of his doctoral thesis. This encounter would have a lasting effect on Bidart's life and work, for the two men became good friends. Indeed, Bidart became Lowell's confidant, editor, and amanuensis. He has said he felt "incredibly lucky" to have met Lowell when he did; being able to be "useful, both as a reader of his poems and a friend to someone [he] so revered, was a profound event in [his] life" (*Western Night*). Lowell came to depend on Bidart's candid responses to his poems, relying on his assistance in the editing of his last four books of poetry. Bidart's relationship to Lowell has continued to be important throughout his career. He is executor of Lowell's literary estate and a coeditor of his *Collected Poems,* which appeared in 2003. Lowell introduced Bidart to Elizabeth Bishop, another important poet from the generation that precedes his own. Bidart and Bishop also became good friends and had a lasting relationship; Bidart is the coexecutor of Bishop's literary estate.

Bidart joined the faculty of Wellesley College in 1972 and has continued to teach courses in literature and poetry writing there. He has also taught at other colleges and universities, including Brandeis University and the University of California at Berkeley. His adopted home is still Cambridge, Massachusetts, and he has said that he feels quite lucky to have gotten a job in the Boston area where he has found a real poetry community, which includes writers like Jay Cantor, Seamus Heaney, Lucie Brock-Broido, Tom Sleigh, Louise Glück, and the former U.S. poet laureate Robert Pinsky.

A VOICE-CENTERED PROSODY

Bidart's poems are noticeably unpoetic—devoid of many of the elements traditionally associated with poetry: imagery, figurative language, and the music of assonance, alliteration, and rhyme. From the start of his career, Bidart's readers and critics have commented on his singular style and vision: in a review for the *Atlantic Monthly,* Donald Hall wrote that the poems in *The Book of the Body* (1977) made him feel that he was "in the presence of something new," likening Bidart's innovations to Eliot's *The Waste Land* (1922) and William Wordsworth's *Lyrical Ballads* (1798). Following in the footsteps of these and other of his literary heroes, Bidart has seemingly attempted to reinvent poetry, or at least redefine what is "permissible" as poetic language.

The most radical aspect of this inventiveness can be found in his prosody, which is based in his interest in the capacity of poetic language to "fasten" a voice to the page. Of course, Bidart is not the first to explore this idea. Robert Frost is well known for his dedication to capturing the "speaking tone of voice" in his work and for his belief that poems are only dramatic when

that voice is "somehow entangled in the words and fastened to the page for the ear of the imagination" (quoted in *Western Night*). Powerfully influenced by Frost, Bidart is equally invested in this idea, although for him, this "fastening" and "entanglement" cannot be realized in regular iambic pentameter. He instills his poems with the pacing of speech but resists pervading assumptions about measure and music. In addition, unlike Frost who hoped to revivify spoken language in his poems, Bidart presents the internalized voice of the educated mind, analyzing, questioning, and deliberating. He has said that in addition to getting the materials of the world into his poems, he wants to portray the action of the mind confronting, ordering, and resisting those materials.

In order to "deploy" these internal voices, and register shifts in tone and intensity, Bidart makes idiosyncratic use of what he calls "expressive punctuation." As he explained to Halliday, "punctuation allows me to 'lay out' the *bones* of a sentence visually, spatially, so that the reader can see the pauses, emphases, urgencies and languors in the voice" (*Western Night*). This includes using italics, quotations marks, capitals, semicolons, dashes, and white space. Consequently, even with his first book, *Golden State* (1973), Bidart's poetry had a unique shape. Instead of fairly even lines of verse organized more or less into neat stanzas, or single columns of text, Bidart's poems stagger and bound across the page. Lines of greatly varying length and spacing may end abruptly, giving way to unlineated prose that creates a stark visual and tonal contrast to the lines of verse. By his third book, he was making use of the full range of expression allowed by this prosody: a line might begin flush with the left margin or in the middle of a page; phrases and single words, even whole lines might appear in all capital letters, or in italics, or in italicized capitals; a dash might follow a comma or precede a semicolon. This passage from "The

War of Vaslav Nijinsky," from his third book, *The Sacrifice* (1983), illustrates the variation in Bidart's prosody:

—Now, for months and months,
I have found

ANOTHER MAN in me—;
                    HE is *NOT* me—; *I*
am afraid of him ...

He hates my wife and child,—
and hates Diaghilev;

because he thinks GOODNESS and BEING
are incompatible,—

... HE WANTS TO DESTROY THE WORLD

This unusual use of punctuation is one of the hallmarks of Bidart's work. For many critics, the dashes, semicolons, italics, and capitals succeed in creating a lyric voice that paradoxically has its origins in prose. Others find the elaborate use of typography distracting, and even irritating, wondering whether differences in voice or tone can only be conveyed in this manner. Another complaint is that because he uses this prosody to represent shifts in tone in many poems, all of the speakers come to sound the same. But as Bidart has suggested, he is not as interested in creating character as he is in representing the voice of the imagination: specifically the internal voice of the mind in crisis attempting to sort through existential dread.

POST-CONFESSIONAL POETRY

Partly because of his relationship with Robert Lowell, but also because he has written candidly about his family, Bidart is often considered to be an inheritor of the "confessional" tradition of poetry—a tradition associated with other mid-century poets like John Berryman, Sylvia Plath, and Anne Sexton. But he distinguishes himself from these writers in important ways. While a cursory glance at the work of these poets confirms that "confessional" is a misleading term, implying that they sacrifice art and craft in favor of unfiltered emotional outburst, the work of these writers does produce the sense that the poet is speaking directly and earnestly of his or her life. Bidart's poetry explores the impulse toward self-disclosure and self-examination, but also questions that impulse, explicitly calling attention to the artful and constructed aspects of private personal expression.

Bidart's best known poems are highly dramatic, engaging speakers who are suffering some form of existential crisis. But all his poems also involve personal self-disclosure. Traditional dramatic monologues, such as Robert Browning's "My Last Duchess," exclude the experiences and emotions of the poet, but Bidart uses the consciousness of others to explore personal history, often drawing on material that arises out of his own life. Bidart's dramatic personae—whether the speaker is a child molester, a patient in a mental institution, or a version of Bidart himself—are neither simply disguised representations of the poet nor dramatic fictions that are wholly separable from him. They are something in between, infusing the calculated artifice of the dramatic monologue with a confessional stance. At the same time, he broadens the scope of the dramatic monologue form by incorporating materials from the "real" world: reported speech, medical evaluations, instructions, letters, and other written documents that provide a counterweight to the point of view of the central persona. Even when the speaker in the poem is not an assumed persona and is closer to Bidart himself, the poem may recount incidents that did not happen to him. Bidart creates a poem that opens the exclusive, closed circle of the confessional speaker to the world and also humanizes the depersonalized stance of the dramatic persona. In this way, he reveals the intersection between autobiographical self-revelation and imaginative self-invention, between the immediacy of personal experience and abstract philosophical idea.

GOLDEN STATE

Bidart's first book, *Golden State* (1973), was published as part of the Braziller poetry series, edited by the poet Richard Howard. In many ways *Golden State* introduces the structures and themes that Bidart will continue to explore in his later work. The book includes two dramatic poems, several more or less confessional pieces, and announces Bidart's investment in classical literature by including a translation of the opening lines of Vergil's *Aeneid* and a version of a poem by Catullus. *Golden State* also instigates Bidart's exploration of some of the fundamental questions and conundrums that inform existence: what does it mean to have a body, what does it mean to make art or poetry, what is the meaning of the specific path a life takes. Throughout his oeuvre, Bidart presents speakers who are in the midst of crisis, unable to accept the emotional, social, physical givens of their lives. They struggle against themselves, their inner desires, their bodies and fates. In this first book, Bidart approaches these questions primarily by focusing on the past, articulating, as he puts it, "his argument with the past." Speaking with Mark Halliday about his initial impulse as a poet, Bidart explained that he knew that his subject matter had to be his relationship to his family history:

> I was someone who had grown up obsessed with his parents. The drama of their lives dominated what, at the deepest level, *I* thought about. Contending with them (and with the worlds of

Bakersfield and Bishop, California, where I had grown up) was how I had learned ... to "think my life." (*Western Night*).

Bidart explores the drama of his past most pointedly in the three poems that compose the second section of the *Golden State:* "California Plush," "Book of Life," and the title poem. These poems clearly make up the heart of the collection, presenting the reader with a grim family history: an irresponsible, alcoholic, delusional father; an indifferent, racist stepfather; and a mentally unstable, ineffectual mother who "has had her / bout with insanity" ("California Plush" *Western Night*). Desolation and emotional impoverishment are the parents' legacy to the child, reflected and embodied by the physical structures and landscape of the place. The California of *Golden State* is not a rediscovered Eden but a place of fool's gold and self-delusion: Its memory is of poverty,

> not merely poverty of means,
> but poverty of history, of awareness of
> the ways men have found to live.

Visiting with his father in a coffee shop in Bishop, California, Bidart's speaker in "California Plush" recounts the tasteless random décor:

> plastic doilies, papier-mâché bas-relief wall ballerinas,
> German memorial plates "bought on a trip to Europe,"
> . . . .
> frilly shades, cowhide
> booths—

and mentally contrasts it with "the lovely congruent elegance / of Revolutionary architecture" of Cambridge (*Western Night*). His sense of alienation is clear, but he also feels guilty for harboring such feelings. For Bidart California is a place "without memories, or / need for a past," and these poems suggest that his flight to the East was motivated in part by the need to remake himself in a place with a history, a place with traditions (*Western Night*).

These poems are the starting point for Bidart's ongoing struggle with the irresolvable paradoxes of existence, focusing in particular on his relationship with his father. The ten short poems that form the title sequence, "Golden State," are addressed to Bidart's father and chart the son's failed attempts to come to terms with their relationship. The father is presented as an embittered, miserly, self-deluded man who dreamed of being "a movie star / cowboy, empire builder," but also as a god-like man who wore a "nimbus of / furies" around his "awesome, graying head" (*Western Night*). The poem also details a mutual ambivalence between the two men: the father is both proud and disappointed with his effete, intellectual son and the son desires and disdains the father's approval. In the final section, the son accepts his failure to come to terms with the contradictions that characterize both his father and their relationship, recognizing that

> no such knowledge is possible;—
> as I touch your photographs, they stare back at
> me
> with the dazzling, impenetrable, glitter of mere
> life ...

The poems that make up the middle section of *Golden State* are by far Bidart's most directly "confessional" work. But even in this first book, he juxtaposes his personas' observations and internal monologues with reported speech and written letters. The sixth section of "Golden State" incorporates a letter written by the father, "Shank," which provides a striking contrast to the voice of the son. The reader gets a clear sense of their strained relationship, the father's failures to take care of himself, and his general inability to express himself. The letter begins, "Sorry I haven't wrote to you sooner but glad to hear that you are well and enjoying *Paris*" (*Western Night*). By including the letter in the poem, Bidart shifts the register of the language and provides a slightly different perspective on the relationship between father and son.

Golden State also introduces Bidart's reimagination of the dramatic monologue. The book opens boldly with the poem "Herbert White," which is spoken by a psychopathic child murderer and necrophiliac. The opening lines are unforgettable:

> "When I hit her on the head, it was good,
>
> and then I did it to her a couple of times,—
> but it was funny,—afterwards,
> it was as if somebody else did it ..."

The reader is immediately brought into contact with the alien and alienating mind of a psychopath, a person whose behavior and way of speaking and thinking suggests total self-absorption and disregard for others but also a radical alienation from the self:

> "...like I said, she didn't move: and I
> saw,
> under me, a little girl was just lying there in the
> mud:
>
> and I knew I couldn't have done that,—"

The only way White is able to live with the knowledge of his transgressions is by convincing himself that the crime was committed by someone else—another person who was and was not him. The poem ends with the breakdown of this pretense. White cannot maintain the split between his two selves—he can no longer believe that "somebody else did it." The poem closes with the chilling lines

> "—Hell came when I saw
>   MYSELF ...
>   and couldn't stand
> what I see ..."

In exploring the mental processes of a monster, Bidart locates the human in the monstrous and the monstrous in the human. As Richard Howard suggests in his introductory note to *Golden State,* what becomes truly disturbing and harrowing about White's monologue is his similarity to the "Frank Bidart" presented in the clearly autobiographical poems. Like the speaker in "Golden State," White is angry at a father who abandoned him and then late in life remarried and inherited a new family. When White declares, "To think that what he wouldn't give me, / He *wanted* to give them ... ," he sounds uncannily like the speaker in "Golden State." Clearly, Bidart wants the reader to recognize that these similar histories carry very different resonances but also represent alternate versions of each other. Indeed, Bidart told Halliday that White represents a kind of "anti-self" for him, someone "whose way of 'solving problems' was the *opposite* of that of the son in the middle of the book" (*Western Night*). He also underscores the idea that White's way of splitting himself off from his own behavior can be a coping mechanism for other, presumably "normal" people.

In addition to presenting subject matter that will continue to obsess and possess Bidart, the poems in *Golden State* make a strong aesthetic statement. Throughout, Bidart's language is decidedly spare and unadorned. In "Golden State," the speaker pleads with his dead father: "Oh Shank, don't turn into the lies / of mere neat poetry." (*Western Night*). These lines point to Bidart's concern that poetry often aestheticizes and idealizes in ways that may betray its subject. Bidart counters this tendency throughout *Golden State,* using punctuation and spacing to re-create the cadences of speech, or at least the internalized speech of the educated mind. Several poems juxtapose prose paragraphs with verse that moves erratically across the page, and shifts in tone and intensity are indicated by italics or capitalization; in his later books he continues to work hard to keep the expression of ideas from being "mere," and his poetry from becoming "neat."

THE BOOK OF THE BODY

The Book of the Body was published by Farrar, Straus and Giroux in 1977. In this second book,

Bidart continues to stage his "argument with the past," but as the title suggests, the unacceptable givens of physical, corporeal existence become a central concern. The poem "Elegy" is the most similar to those in *Golden State* as it deals directly and explicitly with family history, providing insight into Bidart's intense and vexed relationship with his mother. The poem is divided into sections that allow the reader to consider the relationship between the death of the mother's dog, her own death from cancer, and her mother's death. Throughout, Bidart reproduces his mother's voice, conveying her simultaneously possessive and cruel love for her son, as well as her guilt about her own mother's death and her need to induce a similar kind of guilt in her child:

"I know I made a lot of
mistakes with you, but I couldn't count on
anyone—

I had to be both father *and* mother ..."

The sequence suggests that inadequate ways of expressing love are passed along from generation to generation, but also that in the end such failures are all we have and will be missed, even longed for. The final poem in the sequence is a harrowing villanelle that expresses the speaker's rage and guilt over the loss of his mother: "Mother, I didn't forgive you. Conceal / unreal forgiving. Show me your face in fury—; not dead." (*The Book of the Body*). As James Atlas suggests, the "Envoi" of this poem brilliantly examines "the grotesque menace of a past that resists resolution and yet insists on its primacy."

It is the mother's body that finally betrays her, and betrays her son too. The body as a source of conflict and disappointment is a central theme in the other poems in *The Book of the Body* as well. "The Arc" concerns an amputee's musings about the "reality" of the body as he fluctuates between trying to believe that he has lost his arm, and not wanting to believe it. A car accident leaves him with "a space" where his arm one was and this event transforms the world into a place where there is either no meaning, or too much. While the accident was a seemingly arbitrary event, it changes everything in his life and this change is intolerable. The paradox presented in the first few lines of the poem sums up the narrator's dilemma:

> When I wake up,
> 　　　　　I try to convince myself that my
> arm
> isn't there—
> 　　　　to retain my sanity.
> Then I try to convince myself it is.

Inspired by a three-legged dog he sees running that seems "without consciousness / of what he lacked," he tries to tell himself he has always had one arm. But he comes to understand that in telling himself this, he effectively wipes out his entire past. The world becomes flat, a "cardboard" place that has lost all "dimension, resonance, and grace" ("The Arc" *The Book of the Body*). The narrator's simultaneously complete and incomplete body provides Bidart with a physical metaphor for an intolerable reality. In a very different way from poems like "Elegy" or "Golden State," which focus on the need to accept family history, "The Arc" suggests that no matter how painful the past may be, it is what gives meaning and nuance to the present.

The struggle between the mind and the body suggested by "The Arc" comes even more acutely into focus in "Ellen West," one of Bidart's best-known dramatic poems. Based on the case study of an anorexic patient that was recorded by the existential psychiatrist Ludwig Binswanger, "Ellen West" explores the woman's struggle with her disorder. Bidart uses this material to address larger, existential and metaphysical questions. The speaker in "Ellen West" is dissatisfied with the "givens" of her existence, caught up in a struggle against "nature." Bidart shows that while this struggle appears to be in the realm of the merely physical, it has a crucial metaphysical dimension. Ellen says that while she loves sweets, and for her, "heaven / would be dying on a bed of vanilla ice cream," her ideal self is

> … thin, all profile
>
> 　　　　　… the sort of blond
> elegant girl whose
> 　　　　　body is the image of her soul.

Her belief that her physical body somehow masks and distorts her "true self" suggests a Cartesian understanding of the relationship between the mind and the body, and her "ideal of being thin" conceals the much more profound question of how the body seems to be both the container the self or soul inhabits, and inseparable from that self. As she attempts to work out this relationship, Ellen concludes:

> without a body, who can
> *know* himself at all?
> 　　　　　Only by
> acting; choosing; rejecting; have I
> made myself—
> 　　　　　discovered who and what *Ellen*
> can be …
> —But then again I think *NO*. This *I* is anterior
> to name; gender; action;
> fashion;
> 　　　　MATTER ITSELF,—

In this poem, and in many others, Bidart explores the difficulty of distinguishing between body and soul, the impossibility of finally locating a true and essential self that is known and knowable. As Steven Cramer has suggested, in Bidart's poems, "the self peers into its soul and finds its true identity: a stranger".

In addition to introducing increased psychological and philosophical complexity to the questions that preoccupy Bidart in his poetry,

"The Arc" and "Ellen West" further extend Bidart's experiments with the dramatic monologue. In "Ellen West," Bidart includes prose passages from Binswanger's case history, quoting from them almost verbatim. By juxtaposing the psychiatrist's comments with Ellen's discourse about her internal conflict, Bidart conveys the clinical detachment that is part of scientific investigation, but also provides an alternative to Ellen's self-presentation. These passages make the reader aware of the brutal realities of her physical condition, providing a shocking contrast to her intellectualized spiritual struggle: "Every evening she takes sixty to seventy tablets of a laxative, with the result that she suffers tortured vomiting at night and violent diarrhea by day, often accompanied by a weakness of the heart. She has thinned down to a skeleton, and weighs only 92 pounds." (*The Book of the Body*).

Shifting between interior argument and the clinical prose of doctors, the reader comes to see that while Ellen is clearly thoughtful and intelligent, she is also quite insane. Through this process, Bidart forces the reader to recognize that even more than Herbert White, her behavior is on a continuum with "normal behavior." Thus Bidart asks us to reconsider the categories of "sane" and "insane."

"Ellen West" and "The Arc" also provide examples of Bidart's innovative use of autobiographical detail in the dramatic monologue form. In "Herbert White" the use of personal and autobiographical material revealed something of Bidart's past, but in "Ellen West" and "The Arc" he incorporates autobiography in order to consider questions about art and meaning, and to comment on his own project as a poet. This is particularly clear in "Ellen West" when Ellen explores her admiration for the great opera diva Maria Callas, who is well known for having lost a tremendous amount of weight at the height of her career. There is no evidence that the patient called "Ellen West" in Binswanger's case study knew of Maria Callas. On the other hand, in the interview with Mark Halliday, Bidart mentions Callas and it is clear that she is an artist who matters to him a great deal. Jeffrey Gray suggests that this passage of the poem can be considered a kind of *ars poetica* for Bidart, for in it Ellen meditates on the pathos of the deterioration of Callas's voice due to weight loss as an expression of a truer kind of art—an art that moves beyond virtuosity, custom, and fashion to achieve "the true voice of feeling." Clearly this is what Bidart strives to accomplish in his own poetry: authentic expression that is fashioned out of diverse materials. Ellen says that watching Callas perform, she felt she was "watching / autobiography—," and this is precisely how the reader feels reading Bidart's dramatic monologues. Ellen West is a compelling and believable character, and yet part of Bidart's genius is that his artist's hand is never completely out of view. In his later books, he further melds dramatic artifice with personal revelation, blurring the boundary between the two with even more subtlety and finesse.

THE SACRIFICE

While Bidart's first two books earned him a small but loyal following, with the publication of *The Sacrifice* (1983) he began to receive widespread recognition as a major voice in American letters. His interest in classical literature resurfaces with a translation of Catullus' epigram "Odi et Amo" (I hate and love)—a brief poem that encapsulates the conflict that informs much of Bidart's poetry. Many critics considered the long poem "The War of Vaslav Nijinsky" to be a tour de force. Elaborating and extending the project begun in "Ellen West," this poem also explores the distinction between sanity and insanity. But instead of adopting a relatively obscure persona, Bidart turns to the legendary Russian dancer, who in his day was considered a "god of the air." Nijinsky's career was tragically cut short by mental illness; at the age of twenty-eight he was diagnosed with schizophrenia and spent the remainder of his life in and out of institutions. Basing his portrait on the diary Nijinsky kept prior to his first period of institutionalization, Bidart creates another character in an extreme state of existential crisis. Like Ellen West, the speaker in "The Arc," and even Herbert White, Nijinsky is at war with himself, trapped by the unresolvable paradoxes of his existence. Bidart presents him as a highly intelligent, intensely introspective artist driven to represent his internal struggles in his art.

To create contrast in this poem, Bidart juxtaposes Nijinsky's verse monologues with prose passages from biographies, including one written by his wife, Romola de Pulszky. The reader learns of Nijinsky's introduction to the dance world, his vexed romantic and professional relationship with Sergey Diaghilev, the director of the Ballets Russes, and his increasingly erratic, violent behavior toward his wife and child. Bidart's most radical invention, Nijinsky is by turn rational, hysterical, elegiac, grief stricken, enraged, and supremely restrained. At the core of his struggle lies an implacable sense of guilt: a communal guilt about the First World War, "when the whole world painted its face // with blood," and a private guilt for the suffering he has brought to those he loves ("The War of Vaslav Nijinsky" *The Sacrifice*). The central action of the poem is Nijinsky's final performance in which he attempts to expiate his guilt. Unable to kill himself, tormented by his guilt over having tried to hurt his wife and child, he arrives at a solution:

My BODY spoke to me:

There is no answer to your life.
You are insane; or evil.

There is only one thing that you can do:—

You must join YOUR GUILT
                    to the WORLD'S GUILT.

In order to do this, he creates a dance in which he figuratively sacrifices himself. A prose passage describes the performance. After staring at the audience for half an hour, Nijinsky says:

"Now, I will dance you the War, which you did not prevent and for which you are responsible." His dance reflected battle, horror, catastrophe, apocalypse. An observer wrote: "At the end, we were too much overwhelmed to applaud. We were looking at a corpse, and our silence was the silence that enfolds the dead."

There is something utterly irrational about Nijinsky's belief in such expiation, and yet, through art, through the dance he creates, he is able to enact the impossible—to convincingly embody the horrors of war. Through this conundrum, Bidart asks the reader to consider how difficult it is to differentiate between "sane" and "insane," particularly in light of a catastrophe like the First World War. While in the end, Nijinsky comes to see himself as mad—when Diaghilev comes to visit him in the hospital and tells him he must "dance again for the Russian Ballet and for me," Nijinsky responds, "I cannot because I am mad"—Bidart suggests that his insanity may have been chosen, preferable to living with the intolerable givens of a reality that includes the insanity of war ("The War of Vaslav Nijinsky" *The Sacrifice*). Our understanding of "sane" and "insane" are held up for interrogation. The prose passages should provide an objective view of Nijinsky, and yet somehow do not fully resolve the question. Bidart makes it clear that Nijinsky's behavior toward Diaghilev and toward his family is anathema, and yet he also makes it impossible not to empathize with the dancer in his existential struggles.

Nijinsky is also an important figure within Bidart's canon because he was a genius and an innovator; his ballets *Afternoon of a Faun* (1912) and *The Rite of Spring* (1913) were well ahead of their time. In addition to exploring questions of identity, through this persona, Bidart is able to consider questions of invention and authenticity that are germane to his own art. Speaking of his ballet *The Rite of Spring*, Nijinsky explains that he wanted the ballet to reflect his experience of life. He says that while his training in ballet emphasized "*Effortless-ness, / Ease, Smoothness, Equilibrium*," these were not the qualities that he found in his own life ("The War of Vaslav Nijinsky" *The Sacri-fice*). The ballet Nijinsky makes is heavy, effort-ful, uneasy, and jagged, and without equilib-rium—much like Bidart's prosody. His irregular, uneven lines, erratic spacing, multiple forms of punctuation, and mixture of typographies may attempt to "fasten" the voice of the mind to the page, but they also convey the effort involved in this project. Bidart's poetry is not sonorous or incantatory; it does not conjure up beautiful imagery and apt metaphors. Instead, it conveys the intense difficulties involved in human exist-ence by recording the anxious, straining of a mind at work.

Guilt is the focus of many of the poems in *The Sacrifice*. Two short poems, "For Mary Ann Youngren" and the title poem, convey the tragic deaths of women plagued by guilt. In another long poem, "Confessional," Bidart explores this terrain, returning to the subject of his relation-ship with his mother. Bidart has said that he returned to this theme because "Elegy," which was written close to the time of his mother's death, no longer represented the way he felt about their relationship. (*Western Night*.) In "Confessional" the speaker presents his conflict-ing feelings about his relationship with his mother to a silent interlocutor who comes to represent both a father confessor and a psycho-analyst. Through a series of conversations, he explores his distress about his unresolved feel-ings about his mother, revealing the terrible yet gratifying enmeshment that characterized their relationship:

> we seemed to be engaged in an ENTERPRISE together,—
>> the enterprise of "figuring out the
> world,"

figuring out her life, my life,—

THE MAKING OF HER SOUL,

>> which somehow, in our
> "enterprise"
> together, was the making of my soul,—

The speaker recalls this "enterprise" with sentimental longing but then goes on to explain that as a young adult he felt suffocated and could no longer tolerate the terms of such enmeshment:

> what he found so deeply INSIDE HIM,
>
> had its hands around his neck,
>> strangling him,—

He concludes that in order to survive, he "HAD TO TO KILL HER INSIDE ME." But of course, in order to kill the part of her that he had absorbed he would have to kill himself. As with Ellen West's struggle, the battle takes place within the self and again Bidart underscores the fundamental conundrum of the divided self.

Demonstrating the increasing sophistication and complexity of Bidart's poetry, "Confes-sional" also brings philosophical and theologi-cal systems to bear on the relationship between mother and son. A large part of the second sec-tion of the poem is devoted to a comparison of their relationship to that of the early Christian philosopher Saint Augustine and his mother, Monica. According to *The Confessions*, once Augustine converts to Christianity, he and Monica succeed in resolving their bitter differ-ences and are able to attain an ideal relation. Over several pages, Bidart describes the idyll between Augustine and his mother in sentences and clauses that powerfully convey the rapture of their spiritual flight. Bidart contrasts this with the reality of his mother's life, which came to nothing:

> She was afraid to die
> *not* because she feared an afterlife,
>
> but because she didn't know what her life had
> been.

The comparison only makes the speaker more envious and dissatisfied with his lot, and also underscores that at heart this is a poem of metaphysical crisis. Like Bidart's other personae, the speaker wants his life, and his mother's life, to be meaningful, but as his interlocutor insists at the end of the poem, *"Man needs a metaphysics; / he cannot have one"* ("Confessional" *The Sacrifice*). This irredeemable truth is the paradox that Bidart explores in one way or another in much of his work. But the long lyric flight that he creates for Monica and Augustine in this poem also argues that release from this paradox can take place—but only in the momentary consolations that are afforded by art. This reprieve from the angst of never finding meaning or resolution also informs the final poem in the volume. *The Sacrifice* ends with an inventive translation of the first section of the biblical book of Genesis. Moving closer to coming to peace with the terrible conflicts that inform his poetry, Bidart closes the book with a sense of optimism and revelry.

IN THE WESTERN NIGHT

Bidart's fourth book of poems, *In the Western Night: Collected Poems 1965–90* (1990), brings together his three previous books, two sections of new poems, and also includes the interview with Mark Halliday. Some reviewers remarked that it seemed early for Bidart to be publishing a volume of his collected poems, but given the scope and ambition of his work, most critics concurred that it seemed appropriate. The organization of the book begins with the title collection, *In the Western Night,* which presents previously unpublished work: five brief elegiac lyrics, including a free translation of St. John of the Cross's "Dark Night." This section is followed by his three previously published volumes, but they are presented in reverse chronological order. In other words, *The Sacrifice* follows the first section, then *The Book of the Body* and then *Golden State.* This order creates the sense that Bidart's work transcends the temporal and biographical. It also highlights the fact that his concerns have remained fairly constant: the legacy of the dead to the living, the need for a metaphysics that will make the harsh realities of life tolerable, the possibility that art can somehow reveal what is hidden by the surfaces of ordinary life. At the same time, Bidart shows that as his career has moved forward, he has been able to invent vehicles that allow him to explore his obsessions with more subtlety and complexity. After reading "The War of Vaslav Nijinsky," "Confessional" and even "Ellen West," the poems in *Golden State* seem almost naïve in their simplicity and directness.

The closing section, "The First Hour of the Night," presents new work, including several shorter poems and the long, ambitious title poem—which, at over forty pages, is Bidart's longest poem. It is the first installment in a projected series of twelve poems, one for each of the twelve hours of the night through which the sun must pass before rising, according to the ancient Egyptian funerary text "The Book of Gates." In this poem, Bidart further stretches the limits of the dramatic monologue. Whereas the speakers in his earlier poems suffer from afflictions that come to symbolize metaphysical and existential crises, in this challenging poem, Bidart presents a speaker whose crisis is over the failures of metaphysics and philosophy as systems of belief. The poem is more abstract and philosophical than Bidart's earlier work, related by a speaker who has an even more ambiguous and fluid identity than Bidart's previous personae. The first line, *"This happened about twelve years before I died,"* tells us that he is speaking from beyond the grave ("First Hour" *Western Night*). All we know about him is contained in the narrative of the events of the night the poem focuses on—and most of what happens takes place in a dream. It is by far

Bidart's most complex poem, circular and convoluted both in content and in structure, interweaving accounts of several deaths and dreams within a narrative frame that is never returned to.

The narrator recounts a visit he pays to the son of his best friend, who had died several years earlier. Here, Bidart focuses on the problems of familial inheritance, but this time through the account of a third party. The son admits that he feels trapped by his inheritance of his father's "GREAT HOUSE" and wealth, and he recounts a recurring dream in which his father returns. Like the narrator in "Confessional," the son is plagued by the fact that

> " ...everything ever unresolved
> clearly FOREVER
>   is unresolvable between us—; "

Nonetheless, in the dream he is aware that he does not wish that his father were alive again; when he wakes up, he is overcome with shame that what he wants is for his father to remain dead. The speaker responds to this account, by telling a rather sentimental story about the pony he loved as a child, but eventually outgrew. The pony dies and he experiences this death as a reproach; later, he is plagued by dreams in which the pony comes back and wants the speaker to ride and play with him again. But the speaker finds that the pony "was now / *TOO SMALL* to ride—" ("First Hour" *Western Night*). He believes his friend's son's dreams express a similar mixture of guilt and regret and concludes that the son's feeling of shame does not stem from having to confront his own pettiness or greed, but from the recognition that there is something structural and therefore impersonal in human relations. In despair at coming up against this truth once more, the speaker retires, hoping to escape this grim reality through sleep.

Bidart then gestures toward the tradition of the "dream-vision" poem, as the speaker dreams himself into Joannes Volpato's etching of Raphael's fresco *School of Athens,* which hangs above his bed. The fresco represents the whole of Western philosophy up to the Renaissance; at its center are Plato and Aristotle. Over the course of the dream, which recounts the various fine points of Western thought, the harmony suggested by the groupings in the frieze completely breaks down into cacophony and chaos. As more figures crowd in, the scene degenerates into spitefully warring factions. Bidart's speaker expresses personal anguish at witnessing

>   "PHILOSOPHY itself
>
> divided, torn,
>   into three, or even *more* direc-
>   tions—;"

The nightmare gets worse as Bidart infuses the dream with the postmodern belief that "truth" depends upon historical and social conditions; for it eventually becomes clear that within each group of philosophers the search for truth is actually an attempt to gain social power.

> The speaker wakes,
>   "...infected with the desolation of
>   HISTORY's
>   leprosy,—*LEPROSY* of SPIRIT,—"

and is again suffused with despair. ("First Hour" *Western Night*). After waking from this highly abstract dream of order that turns into a nightmare about the collapse of Western metaphysics, the speaker has another dream about his pony, which allows him to come to terms with his feelings of guilt. He is able to ride the pony, finding that he is

>   "—now
>
> somehow *NEITHER*
> *NOT* THE SAME SIZE, NOR THE SAME
> SIZE,—"

The perfect harmony they once had is not achieved, but some sense of balance is found.

In contrast to the engulfing despair of the earlier dream, the speaker wakes with a sense of

"beneficence:—

an emotion which, though it did *not*
erase, TRANSFORMED
                                    what earlier had
    overwhelmed"

This notion of transformation allows the speaker to live with a past that had seemed unbearable. He makes no attempt to reflect on the relationship between the two dreams, but the connection between human experience and philosophical idea is embodied and enacted in the poem. This tentatively hopeful ending strikes a new note in Bidart's oeuvre, pointing toward a capacity to experience joy despite the insurmountable paradoxes his poems painstakingly illuminate.

DESIRE

In many ways, Bidart's fourth book, *Desire* (1997), continues the project that he has involved himself in from the beginning of his writing career. But it also marks out new territory both formally and thematically. As the title suggests, the unifying theme is Eros. While forbidden erotic love is the specific focus of the long poem that closes the volume, Bidart exposes the compulsive, unbidden component that is present in all forms of desire. The fourteen poems that make up the book are varied, including hybrids that mix original and existing materials, a prose poem, a retelling of classical history, a "found" poem, and several translations, in addition to the long final poem, "The Second Hour of the Night." The formal variation of the work highlights Bidart's genius for taking existing materials and combining and rearranging them to create a unified and coherent vision. Thematically he continues to convey the agony created by the existential, erotic, and familial contradictions that have been at the heart of his work—he includes a second version of his translation of Catullus' "Odi et Amo,"

this time titled "*Catullus: Excrucior*" and emphasizing the self-punishing erotics of the body that "hammering a nail nails / itself" (*Desire*). But in general the poems suggest that he is more at peace with what cannot be changed. The reader finds more of the cautious optimism suggested by the closing lines of "The First Hour of the Night."

Throughout the book, desire is presented as a repetitive, universal, and almost impersonal force that takes many forms; Bidart connects it to physical compulsion, religious hunger, the core of identity, and the drive for power. "Overheard through the Walls of the Invisible City" points to unappeasable, carnal desires, describing a subject who is

… telling those who swarm around him his
    desire
is that an appendage of each of them
fill, invade each of his orifices,—

At the end of this poem, Bidart writes "(we are the wheel to which we are bound)," suggesting that the craving that inhabits the soul creates the self and inevitably gets repeated again and again, but also that these inner struggles define and humanize us (*Desire*). "Adolescence," a poem that Bidart shaped from "anonymously published prose," reshapes a scene of what appears to be coerced fellatio in order to explore a sadomasochistic dynamic in which the victimized speaker admits that being abused created a desire both for the abuse and to be the one wielding the power (*Desire*). In "The Return," the second longest poem in the volume, desire is explored as it manifests itself in the drive for power and revenge. Here, Bidart explicitly addresses the horrific repetitions and compulsions of war. As he explains in a note at the end of the book, the poem "steals from Michael Grant's translation of *The Annals of the Tacitus*" (*Desire*). Bidart retells the history of the engagement of the Romans with the German Bructeri in 15 C.E., and includes a flashback to a battle fought on the same site six years earlier. In that battle, the Bructeri annihilate the Roman legions commanded by Varus. The "Teutoburgian Wood" becomes the site of two irrational, bloody battles that resulted in the deaths of tens of thousands.

Several of the shorter poems are elegiac, mourning the passing of friends and lovers, including the artist and poet Joe Brainard, who died from AIDS in 1994. While these poems express the insuperable experience of loss, they also express a sense of peace and resolution. The speaker in "In Memory of Joe Brainard" never succeeds in breaking the "code" of the beloved, who had somehow been able to "erase" "not only / meanness, but anger" in himself, despite having succumbed to "the plague that full swift runs by" (*Desire*). But the poem suggests that his "*purity and / sweetness*" remains with the speaker, for the AIDS epidemic, "*in the end, could not / take you, did not break you—*" (*Desire*). "The Yoke," confirms this idea of the everlasting presence of the deceased beloved, as the speaker implores:

> turn your face again
> toward me
>
> when I hear your voice there is now
> no direction in which to turn

In both poems, the sense of anguish fused to acceptance is conveyed by the careful repetition of particular lines and phrases.

The long poem that constitutes the entire second half of the collection, "The Second Hour of the Night," fuses this theme of mourning with compulsive, insurmountable, and ultimately destructive desires. In this poem, Bidart joins materials that are much less obviously related than those that form the basis for his earlier long poems; he also shifts away from the dramatic monologue form, abandoning the artifice of a central persona. The poem is framed by a meditation on the dead that is based on the Roman philosopher Plotinus's discussions of reincarnation, according to which, the soul after

death seeks the body of a congenial former being in which to return to the physical world. The other sources for the poem include the memoirs of the great French composer Hector Berlioz and the tale of Myrrha and Cinyras from Ovid's *Metamorphosis*. The sections from the memoirs, which focus on Berlioz's feelings about his wife Henriette-Constance Berlioz-Smithson, are juxtaposed with Bidart's memories of mourning his mother's death. Berlioz is tortured by guilt about his wife's life and death; he regrets his treatment of her, and is overwhelmed by "*a sense of pity*" that he finds unbearable. Berlioz's emotions echo Bidart's feelings about his mother, and by framing these mixed emotions within a marriage, this section of the poem prepares us for the second part, with its focuses on taboo, forbidden love.

The tale of Myrrha and Cinyras is one of the "tales of love" sung by Orpheus in Ovid's *Metamorphoses*. By emphasizing this, Bidart adds another layer to his poem, for Orpheus is a figure for the poet and famous for his beautiful, maddening singing. In addition, like Berlioz, Orpheus tragically disappoints his wife Eurydice, condemning her to spend eternity in Hades because he cannot keep himself from turning to look back at her as he leads her back up to the world. But this song is a tale of explicitly forbidden love—of incest between Myrrha and her father, Cinyras: a coupling made inevitable by Myrrha's unquenchable desire for him, and more crucially by Cinyras's vanity. Their union leads to the conception of the god-like Adonis, who as a young man torments the goddess Venus with his indifference to her love. Through their story, Bidart further elucidates the inescapability of one's desires. He shows that Myrrha realizes that her desire for her father is destructive and wrong—she tries unsuccessfully to commit suicide—but she cannot help herself. Myrrha's desire provides Bidart with a type that has implications for all love, sanctioned and unsanctioned. Her desire is an inescapable given, and as Bidart told Andrew Rathmann in an interview, "There's no solution to Myrrha's life". The idea of being in thrall to and constituted by one's desires is central to Bidart's concerns here. In the poem, he writes that Myrrha is "not free not to desire" and "not free not to choose" ("Second Hour" *Desire*). But he makes this paradox even more fraught and complex. When Myrrah succeeds in tricking her father into sleeping with her, she discovers that her resistance and abhorrence of her desire are important, necessary parts of it:

> *... the resistance you have*
> *marshalled against it*
>
> *failing utterly leaves*
> *open, resistless, naked before it*
>
> *what if you do NOT resist it CANNOT be*
> *reached:—*

Of course Myrrha and Cinyras do not escape punishment for their act. When he discovers his daughter in his bed, Cinyras tries to kill Myrrha, but she escapes. He murders Myrrha's nurse, who has set up the encounter in order to have revenge on Cinyras, and ultimately kills himself. Myrrha flees to the island of Sheba, where she lives through the gestation of her child. Before she is able to give birth, Myrrha asks the gods *Make me nothing / human: not alive, not dead,"* and her request is granted: she is turned into a myrrh tree, "her tears new drops glistening everywhere on its surface:—" ("Second Hour" *Desire*). Amazingly, Bidart manages to convert this tragedy of taboo, forbidden love into an affirmation of human emotion. He notes that the resin of the Myrrh tree is considered to be an aphrodisiac, an anodyne, a "gift fit for the birth and death of // prophets," presenting the residue of Myrrha's sorrow as complex and valuable ("Second Hour" *Desire*). To those whose desires are "lawful" and "common" he suggests: *"before the mirror / anoint your body with myrrh // precious bitter resin"* ("Second Hour" *Desire*). While some reviewers found Bidart's suggestion that taboo, incestuous love is a type for all unbidden desire to be too extreme, most critics found the poem to be profoundly honest and moving.

"The Second Hour of the Night" is also concerned with inheritance and the ways children's lives are shaped and informed by those of their parents. While he is in the womb, Myrrha's child Adonis absorbs her tale of woe and then grows up to avenge his mother's suffering by punishing Venus. Of Adonis's destiny Bidart writes *"We fill pre-existing forms, and when / we fill them, change them and are changed: —"* ("Second Hour" *Desire*). This statement also appears in "Borges and I," a poem that explores Bidart's ideas about the nature of artistic creation. A kind of *ars poetica*, in this prose poem, Bidart responds to the well-known essay in which Jorge Luis Borges differentiates between his writing self and the self that lives out his ordinary life, and suggests that his writing self is somehow false and artificial. As Bidart notes, Borges "asserts a disparity between [his] essential self and [his] worldly second self" ("Borges and I" *Desire*). Bidart feels that this is a false distinction because he believes that any act or action, any role or form we try to fill, must change us and be changed by our interaction with it. For Bidart, writing, creating a poem, is inseparable from his life, for once he has written about that life, his understanding of it is inevitably changed. For the "Frank" in the poem, and presumably for the poet, this is a cruel and terrifying truth, but one that he must come to terms with: "he had written about his mother and father until the poems saw as much as he saw and saw more and he only saw what he saw in the act of making them" ("Borges and I" *Desire*). Once he has written something about the past—an example might be the poems in *Golden State* about his father—the writing becomes the charged container for that past.

MUSIC LIKE DIRT

Published as part of the Quarternote Chapbook Series by Sarabande Books, *Music Like Dirt* (2002) is something of a departure for Bidart. The chapbook presents fourteen relatively short poems—although as with his other work, the collection is unified by a central theme. Taking up the ideas suggested by "Borges and I," *Music Like Dirt* is a sequence of fourteen poems that consider various forms of making, from having children to making love, from creating jazz music to the establishment of a career. In a note on the back, Bidart explains that he "wanted to make a sequence in which the human need to make is seen as not only central but inescapable" (*Music Like Dirt*). The poems in the collection suggest that humans are all essentially makers of art, but also that the things we create can be horrific as well as sublime, and can have both positive and negative consequences.

In the opening poem, "For the Twentieth Century," Bidart praises the technology that allows him to appreciate and relive the artistry of "...*Callas, Laurel & Hardy, Szigeti*," but also mourns the fact that so many great performances and their makers

> are lost, a mountain of

> newspaper clippings, become words
> not their own words.

Even those who were legends in their own time are obliterated by the march of time, the short memory of the public. "For Bill Nestrick (1940-96)" memorializes a literary critic who wrote a seminal essay on George Herbert but died without ever finishing and publishing his book. "Advice to Players" addresses the theme of the collection directly. In it, Bidart suggests that each person's life is something made and created, and we make our lives through living: "*being* is making: not only large things, a family, a book, a business: but the shape we give this afternoon, a conversation between two friends,

a meal." (*Music Like Dirt*). In Bidart's view we cannot know ourselves unless we shape our lives, but the poems also suggest that suffering and cruelty stem from not bothering to truly make oneself or one's life, from borrowing one's image from ready-made sources. For Bidart, this kind of making entails denying one's desires in a kind of self-betrayal.

Some of the poems explore this self-betrayal through human interactions. "Luggage" critiques the cold disinterestedness of a lover who believes that "Wisdom of the spirit // ... lies in condescension and poise" (*Music Like Dirt*). The poem ends with a curse:

> In your stray moments, as now in
> mine, may what *was not*

> rise like grief before you.

The title poem, "Music Like Dirt" portrays the mutual but unfulfilled love between two lovers and closes "I will not I will not I said but as my body turned in the solitary / bed it said But he loves me which broke my will" (*Music Like Dirt*).

In this collection, Bidart once again makes reference (if obliquely) to the Catullus epigram "Odi et Amo": it seems to be a poem that articulates an essential aspect of human nature for him. In *The Sacrifice* he translated the epigram as "I hate *and* love. Ignorant fish, who even / wants the fly while writhing," (*The Sacrifice*) and in *Desire,* under the title "*Catullus: Excrucior,*" as "I hate and—love. The sleepless body hammering a nail nails / itself, hanging crucified" (*Desire*). In an interview he has said that the poem is not translatable, and his repeated published attempts may suggest just how apt the epigram is for Bidart. Catullus makes a veiled appearance in *Music Like Dirt,* in the short poem "Hammer": "The stone arm raising a stone hammer / dreams it can descend upon itself" (*Music Like Dirt*). Here the impossible frustration is focused in the problem of distinguishing the maker from his work, or as

William Butler Yeats put it, "the dancer from the dance." This ghostly presence of Catullus throughout Bidart's books points to the remarkable unity of his work and its variety as well. The fundamentally contradictory nature of human experience is present for Bidart in all of life's struggles; it can be returned to and explored again and again, yet always remade and recreated into something entirely new.

Selected Bibliography

WORKS OF FRANK BIDART

POETRY

Golden State. New York: Braziller, 1973.

The Book of the Body. New York: Farrar, Straus and Giroux, 1977.

The Sacrifice. New York: Vintage, 1983.

In the Western Night: Collected Poems 1965–90. New York: Farrar, Straus and Giroux, 1990.

Desire. New York: Farrar, Straus and Giroux, 1997.

Music Like Dirt. Louisville, Ky.: Sarabande, 2002.

Star Dust. New York: Farrar, Straus and Giroux, 2005.

ARTICLES, CRITICISM, AND BOOKS EDITED

"On Elizabeth Bishop." In *Elizabeth Bishop and Her Art.* Edited by Lloyd Schwartz and Sybil Estess. Ann Arbor: University of Michigan Press, 1983. Pp. 214–215.

"Like Hardy." *Harvard Review* 10:115 (spring 1996).

"On Robert Lowell." In *The Critical Response to Robert Lowell.* Edited by Steven Gould Axelrod. Westport, Conn.: Greenwood, 1999. Pp. 54–55.

"What's American about American Form?" Presentation for What's American about American Poetry Festival, November 12–14, 1999. Sponsored by New School Writing Department and Poetry Society of America. Available at http://www.poetrysociety.org/wabidart.html.

"Panel: Lowell on the Page." With Wyatt Prunty and Richard Tillinghast. *Kenyon Review* 22, no. 1:234–48 (winter 2000).

"You Didn't Write, You Rewrote." *Kenyon Review* 22, no. 1:205–15 (winter 2000).

"Pre-existing Forms: We Fill Them and When We Fill Them We Change Them and Are Changed." *Salmagundi* 128–129: 109–122 (fall 2000–winter 2001).

Collected Poems/Robert Lowell. Coedited with David Gewanter. New York: Farrar, Straus and Giroux, 2003.

CRITICAL AND BIOGRAPHICAL STUDIES

Atlas, James. "The Poetry of Mere Prose." *Nation* 224, no. 24:763–766 (June 18, 1977).

Bedient, Cal. "Frank Bidart, Tragedian." *Salmagundi* 118–119:328–29 (spring-summer 1998).

Bowditch, Lowell. "Classical Tragedy as Lyric Dialectic: The Ideological Struggle of God and Nietzsche in Frank Bidart's 'The War of Vaslav Nijinsky.' " *Classical and Modern Literature* 17, no. 4: 319–340 (summer 1997).

Burt, Stephen. "Desire." *New Leader* 180, no. 16:16–17 (October 6, 1997).

Chiasson, Dan. "Presence: Frank Bidart." *Raritan* 20, no. 4:117–138 (spring 2001).

Cramer, Steven. "Four True Voices of Feeling." *Poetry* 157, no. 2:96–114 (November 1990). (Review of *In the Western Night.*)

Crenshaw, Brad. "The Sin of the Body: Frank Bidart's Human Bondage." *Chicago Review* 33, no. 4:57–70 (winter 1983).

Donoghue, Denis. "The Visible and the Invisible." *New Republic* 202, no. 20:40–44 (May 14, 1990). (Review of *In the Western Night.*)

Dyer, Joyce. "Frank Bidart's *The Sacrifice.*" *Notes on Contemporary Literature* 11, no. 3:8–10 (May 1981).

Glück, Louise. "The Forbidden." In her *Proofs and Theories: Essays on Poetry.* Hopewell, N.J.: Ecco Press, 1994.

Gray, Jeffrey. "'Necessary Thought': Frank Bidart and the Postconfessional." *Contemporary Literature* 34, no. 4:714–739 (winter 1993).

Hall, Donald. "Other Voices, Other Tores." The Atlantic Monthly 240, no. 4:100-104 (October

1977). (Review of The Book of the Body.)

Hammer, Langdon."Frank Bidart and the Tone of Contemporary Poetry." *Southwest Review* 87, no. 1:75–91 (winter 2002).

Heaney, Seamus. "Frank Bidart: A Salute." *Agni* 36:270–71 (1992).

Hoey, Allen. *"In the Western Night: Collected Poems, 1965–90." Southern Humanities Review* 26, no. 1:90–93 (winter 1992).

Howard, Richard. "A Note on Frank Bidart." In *Golden State,* by Frank Bidart. New York: Braziller, 1973. Pp. vii–ix.

Keniston, Ann. "'The Fluidity of Damaged Form': Apostrophe and Desire in Nineties Lyric." *Contemporary Literature* 42, no. 2:294–324 (summer 2001).

Kirsch, Adam. *"Desire." New Republic,* October 27, 1997, pp. 38–41.

Lehman, David. *"The Sacrifice." Newsweek,* January 30, 1984, p. 71.

Nadel, Alan. "Wellesley Poets: The Works of Robert Pinsky and Frank Bidart." *New England Review and Bread Loaf Quarterly* 4, no. 2:311–325 (winter 1981).

Peseroff, Joyce. *"In the Western Night, Collected Poems 1965–90." Ploughshares* 16, no. 4:281–82 (winter 1990–1991).

Pinsky, Robert. *The Situation of Poetry: Contemporary Poetry and Its Traditions.* Princeton, N.J.: Princeton University Press, 1976.

Quinn, Justin. "Frank Bidart and the Fate of the Lyric." *P.N. Review* 27, no. 6:40–42 (July-August 2001).

Rathmann, Andrew. *"Music Like Dirt." Chicago Review* 49:109–115 (spring 2003).

Spiegelman, Willard. "The Poem as Quest." *Parnassus* 17, no. 2:423–441 (fall 1992). (Review of *In the Western Night.*)

Stitt, Peter. "A Variegation of Styles: Inductive, Deductive and Linguistic." *Georgia Review* 37, no. 4: 894–905 (winter 1983). (Review of *The Sacrifice.*)

Vendler, Helen. *The Music of What Happens: Poems, Poets, Critics.* Cambridge, Mass.: Harvard University Press, 1988.

Williamson, Alan. *Introspection and Contemporary Poetry.* Cambridge, Mass.: Harvard University Press, 1984.

Yenser, Stephen. "Poetry in Review: *Desire." Yale Review* 86, no. 2:153–168 (April 1998).

Young, David. "Out beyond Rhetoric: Four Poets and One Critic." *Field* 30:83–102 (spring 1984). (Review of *The Sacrifice.*)

INTERVIEWS

Halliday, Mark. "Frank Bidart: An Interview." *Ploughshares* 9, no. 1:11–33 (spring 1983).

Liu, Timothy. "Punishing Love: Tim Liu Interviews Frank Bidart." *Lambda Book Report* 6, no. 9:1–2 (April 1998).

Rathmann, Andrew, and Danielle Allen. "An Interview with Frank Bidart." *Chicago Review* 47, no. 3:21ff. (fall 2001).

—LISA SEWELL

Witter Bynner

1881–1968

Harold Witter Bynner (BIN-ur) was born on August 10, 1881, in Brooklyn, New York. His parents, Thomas Edgarton Bynner (1853–1891) and Annie Louise Brewer (ca 1858–1937), had married on December 11, 1880, in Massachusetts. Members of both families exhibited qualities that carried into Bynner's life. His father wrote poetry. A paternal uncle, Edwin Lassetter Bynner (1842–1893), published several novels and graduated from Harvard Law School. His paternal grandfather, Edwin Bynner, a newspaper editor and writer, was known as a storyteller and a man of character and was in demand at social functions because of his ready wit and skillful repartee. On his mother's side Bynner was descended from clergy, educators, and successful businessmen who were generally driven by propriety moderated by a sense of individuality, a fact that is evidenced by Bynner's mother's request that the word "obey" not be included in her wedding vows.

Both sides of the family contributed less desirable attributes as well, including a penchant for alcohol—Bynner's father was called Dive after his unrepentant patronage of drinking establishments—and vulnerability to depression. The latter was occasionally a factor in Bynner's life. In 1888, Bynner's mother left Dive and took Bynner and his younger brother Edwin Tyler (1885–1959), called Tim, to live with relatives in Connecticut. Dive commented on the separation with his characteristic acceptance of his failings: "The breach is made—it is wide enough and there should be an end of talk."

In 1891, Bynner's father died at the age of thirty-eight from a combination of alcoholism,

depression, and tuberculosis. In 1892 the family moved to Brookline, Massachusetts, to live with Dive's sisters, who helped raise their nephews and supplemented the support provided by their mother, who played piano and taught school for a living. In high school Bynner strained against the demands of the aunts, who, along with his mother, called upon him to behave with decorum and thus redeem the family reputation. About the same time he discovered, as editor of the Brookline High School literary magazine, an interest in writing and publishing that eventually informed his life.

In 1898 at the age of seventeen Bynner graduated from high school and entered Harvard with the aid of a scholarship. Away from the pressures of a family dedicated to the social norm, he nurtured an approach to life that became a pattern: he studied eclectically, allowing himself to be drawn along by his interests and without much concern for end results, trusting instead the inclinations of his will. Much later he would find this choice articulated in the work of the Chinese philosopher Laotzu.

Bynner's course work at Harvard focused on the humanities and the arts, feeding his growing hunger for literature. It included the study of Greek, Latin, French, German, philosophy, and drama, though with varying success. His approach to extracurricular activities was similarly focused. He was invited by his classmate Wallace Stevens (1879–1955) to join the staff of the Harvard *Advocate*. He attended operas and plays, started a book club to read George Meredith novels, and taught French (to one person) in an extension class. He was also known, among friends and to the dean responsible for discipline, for boisterous, often disruptive, partying. Still he won the Boylston Prize for Elocution and the Bowdoin contest for best literary essay in 1902 and graduated summa cum laude in English. Also at Harvard, Bynner took up the nickname Hal, by which he was known to friends for the rest of his life. Assuming a new name fittingly symbolized the new man. Among his other activities, he became involved in the suffrage movement, the beginning of a lifelong history of social concern. And he made a lifelong friend, Arthur Davison Ficke (1883–1945), a fellow writer.

Bynner's mother and aunts held onto modest hope for his success. In his biography *Who Is Witter Bynner?* (1995), James Kraft reports that when Bynner made a prosuffrage speech back in his home community of Brookline in 1901, "a woman said to Bynner's mother, 'You must be very proud of your son,' to which she replied with frankness and pleasure, 'You don't know him.'" And Kraft says that upon Bynner's graduation from Harvard, one of his aunts in a letter "accepted his interest in literature, provided what he wrote was proper and correct."

In 1901 Bynner's mother married Walter L. Wellington, a wealthy businessman. He died in 1914, and when his daughter, Ruth, died five years later, Annie inherited substantial wealth, with smaller inheritances going to Bynner and his brother. Through successful management and investment of his share, and with the addition of an inheritance from his mother on her death in 1937, Bynner was self-sustaining by the 1940s. Bynner and his mother remained in touch throughout her life, though she never fully approved of his move away from home. He also remained in contact with his brother, Tim.

LITERARY TIMES

In October 1902, after graduation from college and a grand tour of Europe that was a gift from his stepfather, Bynner moved to New York City where he took a position at *McClure's Magazine,* a successful periodical dedicated to exposing corruption in politics and society and to the publication of literature. He was only twenty-one and started work as a glorified office boy. However his sharp literary eye was soon detected by Mr. S. S. McClure (1857–1949) himself, and Bynner became embroiled in the literary affairs of the magazine. When he recommended a story, "The Sculptor's Funeral," by an unknown writer named Willa Cather, McClure insisted that it be cut by several hundred words. Bynner accepted the task, unaware that Cather knew nothing of the editorial imposition. When she discovered it, she was furious, and McClure laid the blame on Bynner, who accepted it.

But McClure's whimsy also worked in Bynner's favor. Bynner recommended for publication a story, "Tobin's Palm," by another unknown writer, O. Henry. Following office protocol, he forwarded his recommendation to a second editor, who would normally have responded to Bynner. When she did not, Bynner discovered that she had sent the story back to O. Henry with a rejection letter. Bynner immediately went to McClure, who accepted Bynner's judgment and gave him permission to go directly to O. Henry with the word. In "Autobiography in the Shape of a Book Review" (1963), Bynner recounts his visit to O. Henry:

> I bounded across to the Lion d'Or restaurant and, in a bleak room overhead, found O. Henry—like a Western Buddha—occupying an unpadded rocker and on a trunk nearby I saw a sealed envelope. "Tobin's Palm?" I asked. "Yes," he said. "Accepted," said I, grandly and with young pride.

McClure's continued to publish O. Henry's stories, along with those of Cather. Bynner considered one of his major accomplishments to be the publication of poems from A. E.

Housman's *A Shropshire Lad* (1896). Bynner recalls that

> McClure let me not only republish poems already contained in a published volume, but to pay for them at a higher rate than most verse in those days received. Incidentally, Mr. Housman returned the first check and received none further because of his statement to me that he never took payment for his verse.

Immersed in an editorial career, Bynner continued to lead a vigorous literary life with Harvard classmates Wallace Stevens and the muralist Barry Faulkner, as well as a wide circle of newfound friends, including Mark Twain, Booth Tarkington, the artist Rockwell Kent, John Dewey, and Henry James. He also knew the Yeatses—father John, and sons William Butler and Jack—who visited him when they traveled to New York from Ireland.

After four years at *McClure's* Bynner decided it was time to devote himself to his own writing. He had suffered some ill health, which he attributed in part to his inability to govern his own willful pleasures, and he wanted further distance from his mother, who now also lived in New York. He was concerned about the wisdom of his decision, but was encouraged in a letter from his "friend and counselor" Mark Twain:

> Dear Poet: You have certainly done right—for several good reasons; at least, of them, I can name two: 1. With your reputation you can have your freedom and yet earn your living. 2. If you fall short of succeeding to your wish your reputation will provide you another job. And so, in high approval I suppress the scolding and give you the saintly and fatherly pat instead.

Bynner left *McClure's* in October 1906; he accomplished the distance from New York and acquired the solitude and the space for his writing by moving in 1907 to Cornish, New Hampshire, to room with his good friends the sculptor Homer Saint-Gaudens and his wife Carlota.

He remained there for ten years.

Throughout his tenure at *McClure's,* Bynner had continued to write poetry, and after he moved to New Hampshire, *An Ode to Harvard and Other Poems* was published by Small, Maynard & Co. in Boston. The first of more than twenty books of poetry that saw print in his lifetime, it was, as indicated by the title, in part a paean to his college years. It was republished in 1925 by Knopf as *Young Harvard: First Poems of Witter Bynner*. His second book of poems, *The New World* (1915), not published until eight years after the first, was republished by Knopf in 1922. For Bynner the poems in both books represented a departure from the romantic and idealistic poetry of the time and followed instead the trail blazed by Walt Whitman (1819–1892). As James Kraft reports, "Bynner himself said of the *Ode*":

> Apart from my other verse, I take a defiant sort of pride in the *Ode,* feeling it to be of the poetry of today concerned with real things. I am hoping that you will find in it not mere pleasantry, but a sincere expression of worthier material than is to be found in the more conventionally poetical pieces preferred by some of the critics.

In *The New World,* Bynner not only continued to write about "real things" but also began to show a sense of the democratic self and democratic life. He used the term in the general sense of social equality, a sense that had been simmering within him for a long time, as indicated by his participation in the suffrage movement and his appreciation of Whitman. In a prose pamphlet published in 1871, Whitman addressed his concern about materialism in America and proposed that a new generation of artists could bring about a nation that was not dependent on its heritage from abroad, for "the work of the New World is not ended, but only fairly begun."

Bynner issues a call to arms for this new world at the beginning of "In Temporary Pain":

> In temporary pain
> The age is bearing a new breed

Of men and women, patriots of the world
And one another. Boundaries in vain,
Birthrights and countries, would constrain
The old diversity of seed
To be diversity of soul.
      O mighty patriots, maintain
Your loyalty!—till flags unfurled
For battle shall arraign
      The traitors who unfurled them, shall
 remain
And shine over an army with no slain
And men from every nation shall enroll
And women—in the hardihood of peace!

The poem shows his vision and his faith that such democracy was possible.

This awareness of the possibilities for life in America had been stirred further by Bynner's earlier tour of Europe. Many of his contemporaries—T. S. Eliot, Ernest Hemingway, Ezra Pound, and Gertrude Stein among them—sought their muses and their raison d'être in faraway places across the Atlantic Ocean. Bynner however was not taken with what he saw there in 1902 and did not return for fifty years. Like the poet William Carlos Williams, he was taken with the beauty of the American experience rather than with the European foundations from which so much of it sprang.

Although Bynner's home base during this period was in New Hampshire with the Saint-Gaudens, he was not homebound. From 1907 to 1922 he lectured around the country on poetry, literature, and suffrage, contributing to a national *renascence,* a so-described movement around 1910 exemplified by a burgeoning awareness of the possibilities of the American spirit and embodied in poetic schools that embraced free verse, which took its cadence from meaning rather than from form. Bynner fed on the energy of this rebirth, contributed to it, and celebrated it in *The New World.*

Even while he lectured, he continued to write and to expand his literary circles. His plays *Tiger* (1913) and *The Little King* (1914) were published by Mitchell Kennerley in New York.

Through that association he arranged for Ezra Pound's first American book publication. He wrote a play, *The Mechanic,* with Cecil B. DeMille, though it was not produced, and translated Euripedes' play *Iphigenia in Tauris* (1915) for the dancer Isadora Duncan. He and his friend Arthur Ficke were enamored of Edna St. Vincent Millay's poem "Renascence," published to great acclaim in *The Lyric Year* in 1912, and they wrote to her, beginning a lifelong friendship among the three of them. In fact Millay (1892–1950) is said to have fallen in love with Ficke, who was married, and it is known that Bynner proposed to her, though perhaps half in jest. She accepted, but they later agreed not to marry for fear of disrupting the threesome.

Bynner was by then well aware of his interest in men, an orientation that was not easily acknowledged at the time. In 1917 he began his first deeply affecting love relationship, with the Swiss artist Paul Thévenaz, who died in 1921 of a ruptured appendix. After moving permanently to Santa Fe in 1922, Bynner had a serious relationship with Willard "Spud" Johnson, and then in 1926 he met Robert Hunt, twenty-five years his junior, with whom he lived, as in a marriage, from 1930 until Hunt's death in 1964. Although Bynner was not an activist in what has come to be called gay rights, he did not conceal or deny these partnerships, living, as he had long tried to do, with quiet integrity. His book of poems *Eden Tree* (1931), published the year after Hunt came to live with him, is dedicated to Hunt and declares their relationship to the world. This was unusual and, as Kraft says, "not ... even minimally accepted" at the time. It probably cost Bynner friendships and professional opportunities. Bynner was well aware of the statement he was making in *Eden Tree:* "I am relieved that its honesty has been understood. I am sick of literary glazing over the truth. Most writers do it. Poets, at any rate, shouldn't. So much the Chinese have taught me."

THE SPECTRA HOAX

The lecture tour years before he settled in Santa Fe spawned another change in Bynner's life and writing. He and Ficke were disgruntled with the schools of poetry that rose to the top of the free verse movement, such as imagism and vorticism. The two were especially scornful of imagism. This school, defined by Ezra Pound, T. E. Hulme, Amy Lowell, Hilda Doolittle, and others, took free verse to extremes, insisting on pure, unfettered image and observation. Although imagism marked an important break from the constraints of traditional poetry, as did Bynner's poems, and brought Asian verse into the mix, Bynner and Ficke found it to be pretentious. Ever playful they decided to skewer schools such as imagism by creating one of their own, one which proclaimed meaning but was in fact spurious.

Thus was born spectrism, which sought, as Kraft says, "to see the spectre in our life and capture the varied light of the spectrum." Using the pseudonyms Emanuel Morgan (Bynner) and Anne Knish (Ficke), they published spectric poems that were reviewed widely—by themselves using their real names, as well as by others—in the literary journals of the time. They published a volume, *Spectra: A Book of Poetic Experiments,* with Mitchell Kennerley in 1916. Spectrism was generally proclaimed a success and had a coterie of followers and practitioners.

The Spectra Hoax, as it was known after the culprits confessed their deed around 1918, had two unexpected consequences. Readers and critics who had applauded the movement felt betrayed, and some never again trusted Bynner. Ficke was spared this judgment for the most part, because he was not—and did not seek to be—widely published. The other consequence was to Bynner's poetry. Bynner was tall and handsome with—for all his insistence on the American idiom—the genteel bearing and ease of an old-world gentleman. His poetry before Emanuel Morgan tended also toward a nicety of bearing and phrase. Emanuel had no such restraint, and through that door the playful Bynner—the wit, the prankster, and the protest marcher—stepped into the writing. When the hoax was revealed and Emanuel's name disappeared, his voice did not.

Bynner was aware of this transformation in his writing and of the trouble it caused him. He wrote to Harriet Monroe, the editor of *Poetry* magazine, on April 30, 1918:

But—Emanuel Morgan wishes to continue as the person he has become—a person quite distinct from WB and a person enjoying himself in a manner not altogether foreseen by WB. In other words he has got away from me and refuses to be called back. He is doing his own work and has every intention of going on with it—and, to my confusion, it isn't my work any longer. I've certainly split myself in two and found that the two parts wriggle separately and away from each other. Dual personality? Something of the sort—which accounts for my continued insistence on him as Emanuel, even against the testimony of

Yours as ever.

This declaration notwithstanding, the voice of Emanuel Morgan was imbedded in Bynner's earlier poetic voice, and it was with the newly amalgamated persona that Bynner traveled with Arthur Ficke and his wife to Asia in 1917. They stayed four months, visiting Japan and China, and Bynner discovered a new worldview that accommodated, complemented, and expanded the Bynner/Morgan vision. Prior to the visit Bynner had not imagined that there could be more to life and writing than to affirm the democratic.

Bynner found in China that there could be more, including timeless answers to timeless questions. Bynner's poems subsequent to the China trip exhibit a clarity and sweetness unobstructed by romantic diction, as can be seen in "Lightning" from *The Beloved Stranger* (1919):

> There is a solitude in seeing you,
> Followed by your presence when you are gone.
> You are like heaven's veins of lightning.
> I cannot see till afterward
> How beautiful you are.
> There is a blindness in seeing you,
> Followed by the sight of you when you are gone.

Although the clean and natural new voice is distinct, its origins are easily discernable in some of the poems in *Ode to Harvard,* for example, such as "The New Life" with its investigation of what is seen and heard:

> Perhaps they laughed at Dante in his youth,
> Told him that truth
> Had unappealably been said
> In the great masterpieces of the dead:—
> Perhaps he listened and but bowed his head
> In acquiescent honour, while his heart
> Held natal tidings,—that a new life is the part
> Of every man that's born,
> A new life never lived before,
> And a new expectant art.
> It is the variations of the morn
> That are forever, more and more,
> The single dawning of the single truth.
> So answers Dante to the heart of youth.

These qualities of observation were present earlier as well in *The Grenstone Poems,* not published until 1917 but written before the *Spectra* poems and the introduction of Emanuel Morgan's voice in 1916 and before the trip to China. "At the Last" is exemplary:

> There is no denying
> That it matters little,
> When through a narrow door
> We enter a room together,
> Which goes after, which before.
>
> Perhaps you are not dying:
> Perhaps—there is no knowing—

> I shall slip by and turn and laugh with you
> Because it mattered so little,
> The order of our going.

Not only the larger passages in Bynner's life were reflected in his poems; smaller moments and specific events found a place there. "The Dead Loon," also published in *Grenstone* and one of the few poems of his that has been anthologized, is an example of such a moment and shows how Bynner's poetic voice was ingrained in his everyday life. The poem finds its origins in a letter written on June 15, 1908, from a cabin in Maine:

> I'm very tired, and anxious besides to be in bed for the reason that I am alone in the cabin this gusty night, De Mille having taken his pack for a three-day tramp in the woods. There's a dead loon in camp, shot by a clever fool, and down the lake a live loon, calling. Big drops of rain sound like footsteps and the creak of the wind now and then like the lifting of the latch. Shadows glue their faces to the windows;—and yet a revolver is to me a fearsome bedfellow. Something's whimpering on the lakes—and there again, and nearer, comes that hollow scream of the loon. I wish I were in bed, in spite of the bedfellow; and I wish I were awake and it were morning.

The narrative of the letter becomes the basis for the poem, illustrating Bynner's ability to fuse experience into art:

> There is a dead loon in the camp tonight, killed
>   by a clever fool,
> And down the lake a live loon calling.
> The wind comes stealing, tall, muscular and cool,
> From his plunge where stars are falling—
> The wind comes creeping, stalking,
> On its night-hidden trail,
> Up to the cabin where we sit playing cards and
>   talking.
> And only I, of them all, listen and grow pale.
> He glues his face to the window, addressing only
>   me,
> Talks to me of death and bids me hark
> To the hollow scream of a loon, and bids me see
> The face of a clever fool reflected in the dark.

That dead loon is farther on the way than we are.
It has no voice, where it hangs nailed to the gate.
But it is with me now and with the evening star.
Its voice is my voice and its fate my fate.

THE MIDDLE YEARS

Bynner's trip to Asia came in the midst of World
War I (1914–1918), and his travel was in part a
rejection of the war, which he vigorously opposed. In 1918, however, he volunteered for
"military service" as a professor of oral English
for the Students' Army Training Corps at the
University of California at Berkeley. Although
his assignment lasted only a month, ending with
the war, he stayed on at Berkeley to teach in
the English department. While there, inspired
by his recent trip to China, he immersed himself
in the study of Chinese literature and culture
and started working with the distinguished
Chinese scholar and political refugee Kiang
Kang-hu (1883–1954), who would guide Bynner through the translation of two major works:
an anthology of three hundred T'ang Dynasty
poems and the *Tao Teh Ching*. Bynner did not
speak or read Chinese, and his poetic translations were made from Kiang Kang-hu's literal
translations into English.

Bynner felt comfortable in Berkeley and
intended to make it his home. However in 1919
his outspoken support for releasing conscientious objectors became a public issue, as did his
practice of entertaining students in his apartment. Called home to the deathbed of his
stepsister, Ruth Wellington, he did not return to
Berkeley. For the next several years, 1919–
1922, with his home base still at the Saint-
Gaudens' in New Hampshire, Bynner continued
his work on the public speaking circuit, now
including lectures on China. In 1920 he returned
to China, this time staying for ten months, and
began work on the Laotzu translation, steeping
himself deeper in the culture that would influence his life and art. In 1922, tired of his fifteen-
year peripatetic life as a lecturer, he visited

Santa Fe, New Mexico, and fell in love with the
city and with its people, its art, and its cultural
ways. Until then it had been as though he were
traveling from place to place in search of a
home. In Santa Fe he rented a house that he
later bought, and he lived there for the remaining forty-six years of his life.

In his essay "A City of Change" (1924), Bynner describes the effects of the city on him:

Soon I had found my own adobe, one of the oldest, with a broad-beamed roof to shed homely dirt
on me in windy weather and primitive rain in wet.
I was above the troubled world. I was washed
clean of the war, I was given communion each
night when sunset would elevate the host on the
Sangre de Cristo mountains. I was writing to
friends who lived on another planet.

He also found sympathy and comfort in Santa
Fe's eclectic population that included American
Indian and Hispanic peoples. In their art,
architecture, and lives he found a parallel to
what attracted him in Chinese people and
culture: a sense of democratic, unpretentious
living. He was well known in Santa Fe and well
loved, and he easily entered the community by
participating in events and projects, even running for the state legislature on the Democratic
ticket in 1926, a bid he lost. As is stated on the
website of the Witter Bynner Foundation for
Poetry, "He presided throughout five decades,
by common consent, over the cultural and
convivial life" of his chosen city.

Bynner was forty-one years old when he
settled in Santa Fe. He gave up, for the most
part, the lecture circuit; he settled into the community; and he became friends with D. H.
Lawrence and his wife Frieda. He continued to
write and publish his own work—he had more
than a dozen books, including poetry, criticism,
and drama—and he played an important role in
the publishing world, helping acquire manuscripts for literary presses such as Small, Maynard and Mitchell Kennerley. He had strong,

enduring friendships with Arthur Davison Ficke, Edna St. Vincent Millay, the teacher and writer Haniel Long, and others.

Over the years, Bynner expanded his modest adobe house and fitted it with a grand mix of artifacts from his travels in China and the art and accoutrements of his adopted home place. He continued to develop friendships with artists and writers and to work on Chinese translations. Among his acquaintances was Mabel Dodge Luhan, a wealthy patron of the arts who had moved to Taos, New Mexico, in 1917 to escape East Coast life. She shared with Bynner a sense of renewal in the Southwest landscape and peoples, but otherwise their relationship was strained, as Luhan often vied for the friendships that came easily to Bynner.

In the fall of 1922, less than a year after Bynner settled in Santa Fe, Luhan contacted him and asked if D. H. and Frieda Lawrence could stay with him on their way to Taos. The visit resulted in the Lawrences, Bynner, and Willard Johnson traveling together to Mexico in 1923, an extended journey that had several important consequences. Lawrence and Bynner collided over their opposite appreciations of Mexican life. While Bynner embraced friendship with the people, Lawrence, though sometimes professing sympathy, generally denigrated them. Yet Bynner and Lawrence were deeply attracted to each other as writers. The attraction and disagreement were borne out in writings by both of them. While they were in Mexico, Lawrence was writing a novel, *The Plumed Serpent,* published in 1926, and he based an unappealing minor character, Owen Rhys, on Bynner. In 1925, Bynner published three poems—"D. H. Lawrence," "Lorenzo," and "A Foreigner"— critical of Lawrence's nature.

Twenty-one years after Lawrence's death, Bynner published a biographical memoir about their travels, *Journey with Genius: Recollections and Reflections Concerning the D. H. Lawrences* (1951). In it he describes the majestic turmoil of Lawrence's emotional life, and the book was both praised and decried for its forthrightness. In a review published in the August 18, 1951, issue of the *Saturday Review of Literature,* Paul Horgan said,

> It is a moving experience given to us here to progress through the disorderly and fear-ridden life of such a man [as Lawrence], from what on first acquaintance seem like irredeemable absurdity and malice, to deeper knowledge of him that yields in the end another true glimpse into the complex nature of man.

A happier outcome, perhaps happier than the trip itself, was Bynner's discovery that, as with Santa Fe, the landscape and people of Mexico were highly compatible with his lifestyle and vision. He eventually purchased a home in Chapala and returned there frequently until the last few years of his life. A book of poems, *Indian Earth* (1929), based mostly on his visits to Mexico and considered by many to be Bynner's best volume, reveals an awareness and appreciation of non-European cultures that was unusual for his time, though today we might think it commonplace. Bynner's travels with the Lawrences also resulted in a deep affection and permanent friendship between Bynner and Frieda, and she eventually settled in New Mexico after her husband's death.

THE CHINESE TRANSLATIONS

Bynner's visits to China in 1917 and 1920 led to his translating two major works of Chinese literature, *Three Hundred Poems of the T'ang* and the *Tao Teh Ching,* a religious text attributed to Laotzu, who lived in the sixth century B.C. Work on the translations covered nearly three decades, from Bynner's first visit to China to the publication of *The Way of Life According to Laotzu* in 1944, and it deeply influenced Bynner's own poetry at the same time it affirmed his life vision, summarized perhaps in his epigraph to the *Tao Teh Ching* translation: "The way to do is to be."

Three Hundred Poems of the T'ang is an anthology of work from the latter years of the T'ang Dynasty, which ruled from A.D. 618 to 907, a period sometimes called the Golden Age of Chinese civilization. The arts, literature, and science were encouraged and flourished, as did Taoism, a religious system well over a thousand years old by the time of the T'ang Dynasty. The T'ang poets include Li Po, Tu Fu, and Wang Wei. Bynner's translation of *Three Hundred Poems* is titled *The Jade Mountain: A Chinese Anthology, Being Three Hundred Poems of the T'ang Dynasty 618-906* (1929) and was the first complete book of Chinese poetry to be translated by an American. The poetry in *The Jade Mountain* is generally written in the complex prosody of the *shih* form, which combines Chinese monosyllabic hieroglyphic characters, each of which has a fixed tone, with rules of syntax, number of characters per line, lines per poem, and similar restrictions on form. The poems are usually based in nature, but speak to human experience. According to Burton Watson's introduction in *The Chinese Translations* (1978), the successful *shih* poem sheds ego, and rather than saying "Look what is happening to me!" as much modern poetry does, it says, "Look what happens to man." In spite of its complex structure, the *shih* poem is simple and direct in its presentation, as for instance in Li Po's "In the Quiet Night":

So bright a gleam on the foot of my bed—
Could there have been a frost already?
Lifting myself to look, I found that it was
   moonlight.
Sinking back again, I thought suddenly of home.

The translation of any text from one language to another is fraught with choices that must be made between the literal and the figurative. This problem is exacerbated in the translation of poetry, in which so much of the meaning is in the figure of the poem. Bynner was not spared

this conundrum, and it would be a mistake to think that he only converted Kiang's English translations, from which he worked, into a close approximation of the literal poems. Rather he undertook extensive study of the content and form of the poetry and, through a process of synthesis with his own sensibilities, working back and forth with Kiang, he wrote poems that remain most faithful to the spirit of the originals.

He was criticized for this by some but more often was applauded. In the February 1930 issue of *Poetry* magazine, Eunice Tietjens says,

The Jade Mountain is at once magical and scholarly, sensitive and practical, human and trustworthy. It is this by the very nature of the collaboration which went to its making, that of an admirable Chinese scholar of the old school, and a western poet distinguished in his own right, who is by temperament peculiarly fitted to understand this ancient poetry of the Chinese. What one of the collaborators may have lacked is amply supplied by the other; and the whole has been supplemented by a patience and loving care common to both, but all too rare.

The translation of the poems was followed by the translation of the sacred text of Laotzu, the *Tao Teh Ching,* again in collaboration with Kiang. Taoism, a philosophy and religion, arose in China around 600 B.C., about 1,200 years before the T'ang Dynasty. Confucianism arose at about the same time, and the two presented nearly opposite life paths. Both refer to tao, which simply means "the way," though the way of Laotzu is referred to as Taoism. Taoism embraces a transcendent reality that accommodates being, nonbeing, and change and encourages yielding to harmony with the ineffable tao of the universe. Confucianism is more rule oriented, calling for adherence to social order and duty. The *I-ching,* or *Book of Changes,* is a text in the Confucian canon.

Bynner found in the *Tao Teh Ching* an articulation of his personal approach to life, in which even the mundane is worthy of meditation, and judgment is suspended in favor of harmony. The forty-ninth poem, or chapter as the sections are sometimes called, extols harmony among human hearts:

> A sound man's heart is not shut within itself
> But is open to other people's hearts:
> I find good people good,
> And I find bad people good
> If I am good enough;
> I trust men of their word,
> And I trust liars
> If I am true enough;
> I feel the heart-beat of others
> Above my own
> If I am enough of a father,
> Enough of a son.

The origins of the *Tao Teh Ching* are obscured in history and myth. It is said to be the oral teachings of Laotzu that were written down by a gatekeeper who begged that they not be lost. Whatever their actual beginning, the eighty-one brief sections have survived for more than 2,500 years and are still of interest to readers. It is perhaps the single most important book to come out of China. Bynner titled his work *The Way of Life According to Laotzu: An American Version;* it was first published in 1944 and has been reprinted several times since then. He recognized in it the accommodation of contradiction. In his introduction Bynner says that Laotzu's choice not to "leave a set record of his own spoken belief"

> was not, as has been widely assumed, vacant inaction or passive contemplation. It was creative quietism. Though he realized the fact that action can be emptier than inaction, he was no more than Walt Whitman a believer in abstention from deed. He knew that man can be a doer without being an actor and by no means banned being of use when he said that "the way to do is to be." Twenty-five centuries before Whitman, he knew the value of loafing and inviting one's soul.

As with *The Jade Mountain,* Bynner concentrated his translation on the truth of such spirit of the matter. Reviewing *The Way of Life,* Arthur Ficke said in *Poetry* in April 1945 that Bynner

> has produced a clear, sparkling, vigorous flow of speech that seems as if it must carry some of Laotzu's own eager honesty and directness … the road of spontaneity and humanness of speech [has been chosen], and has [been] written as if the lines had been put down by a living man out of the deep springs of his personal awareness.

In Kiang's response to the final manuscript of *The Way of Life,* which Bynner quotes in the book's dedication, Kiang also approves of Bynner's approach: "It is impossible to translate it without an interpretation. Most of the [earlier] translations were based on the interpretations of commentators, but you chiefly took its interpretation from your own insight. It was your 'fore-nature' understanding—or in Chinese, hsien-t'ien—that rendered it so simple and yet so profound." Kiang's words came to Bynner in a note from a prison cell in Shanghai. Kiang had returned there in 1932 "to suffer with my people. I want to dispossess everything in the World so I can be what I am again." He was arrested in 1945 after a change in government and remained in prison until his death in 1954 despite Bynner's many attempts to secure his release. He was allowed some correspondence, and Bynner sent him *The Way of Life* in 1948. Kiang's response was not received until the year of his death.

The *Tao Teh Ching* is said to be the second most translated book in the world after the Bible. However, many if not most of the translations of the time suffered from the failures of literal reading of the text. In his preface to *The Way of Life,* Bynner expresses his desire to overcome such failures: "Above all I have been prompted by hope to acquaint Western readers with the heart of a Chinese poet whose head has been too much studied."

LETTERS AND PROSE

Bynner was a habitual letter writer, as were many people in the first third of the twentieth century. He never gave up the habit. From early in his life he kept copies of his correspondence, and more than seven thousand of his letters exist, written to more than thirteen hundred recipients. Many are written to his longtime friends Arthur Davison Ficke and Paul Horgan, Haniel Long, and to Robert Hunt. But the list also shines with the names of some of the twentieth century's finest women and men of arts and letters, including Ansel Adams, Robert Frost, R. Buckminster Fuller, Christopher Isherwood, Henry James, Amy Lowell, Edna St. Vincent Millay, Harriet Monroe, Ezra Pound, Carl Sandburg, Margaret Sanger, Louis Untermeyer, and William Carlos Williams.

While the letters afford a gossipy look at Bynner's life, the prose pieces provide another link. They have the conversational voice of the letters, and cover as broad a range of topics, but with more specific purpose. Perhaps most like the letters are the character sketches. *"Ave Atque Vale,"* an elegy for Ficke first published in *Poetry* in April 1946, describes the first writing of the Spectra poems:

> There was satire too, a keen sense of it, as who should know better than I, particularly from our experience in putting *Spectra* together. Our pitch was such, in writing those poems, that we would not sleep nor eat and were at last banished by his rightly exasperated wife from the house in Davenport, finishing them at a hotel across the river in Moline. In this book for once we wholly liked each other's verse.

Bynner was equally frank with his descriptions of other writers, as in "Ezra Pound" (1956), in which he recounts his first meeting with the poet, who came to Bynner as the poetry editor of *McClure's* to ask his blessing: "Would I look at these poems and see if I thought they warranted his being sent abroad for stimulus and study." Bynner rendered the desired affirmation and fifty years later recalled the visit:

> My memory of Pound ... is the eager face, voice and insistent spirit behind them and then a sense of his being an even more happily cuckoo troubadour than the young Vachel Lindsay. But never have I seen Lindsay attired for it as Pound was. I should say that his jacket, trousers and vest had each a brave color, with a main effect of purple and yellow, that one shoe was tan, the other blue and that on a shiny straw hat the ribbon was white with red polka dots.

But the prose pieces are perhaps most valuable for their statement of Bynner's aesthetic beliefs. He begins his long essay "The Persistence of Poetry" (1929) with an attempted definition of poetry:

> Perhaps its very brevity will leave it vague enough to cover or suggest the reaches of poetry.... Here is it then. Two words. *Passionate patience.*
>
> Of all of the arts, music and poetry are those nearest to the heart, and most immediately echo the heart. Any definition of the elements of poetry must define also the elements of life nearest to the heart. No one would question passion as the prime element in live things; nor would anyone, I think, considering the cosmic silence which meets man's passionate and thwarted demands, question the element of patience as necessarily inhering in the life we have to live and try to understand.

After an extensive discussion of the culture, craft, impulse, and history of poetry, he closes the essay with the import of the matter:

> It is not necessary that culture bring about the death of poetry, as it did in the Rome of Virgil. The cynics are wrong who see in our future no place for an art which belongs, they say, to the childhood of the race. The head of a man and the heart of a child working together as in the Chinese have made possible with one race and may make possible with any race, even in the thick of the most intricate culture, the persistence of the purest poetry.

Both passages readily reflect values that can be inferred from his own work and that he applies to his criticism of the work of others and to his philosophy of teaching.

Opening his essay "On Teaching the Young Laurel to Shoot," published in the *New Republic* on December 5, 1923, Bynner asks the question, "Can the writing of poetry be taught?" To which he answers, "To poets, yes; to others, no." He believed that poetry should be taught as it is written: with passion and freedom, and with as much disregard for propriety as can be mustered.

> Knock the nonsense out of them—the affectations, the self-deceptions, the guesses toward what will seem poetry to others, the catches at vogue. Release them from the dead hand of English literature.... Encourage them to write in the open: to give terms of themselves to the sky.... Let them say or write anything which genuinely impels them, discovering among one another that honesty is the best poetry.

He concluded with a repetition of his statement that poetry can be taught to poets and added, "There are more poets born than insurance agents."

The prose also indicates that as Bynner matured, many of his long held beliefs about how best to be human stayed with him. A treatise on religion, "Credo," published in 1958, included this note: "This Credo, phrased mostly as here, was set down in my twenties. In my seventies I find little reason to change it." The "Credo" itself professes the faith of acceptance and inclusion that Bynner cultivated throughout his adult life, and includes these lines: "who shall be my enemy / When he is I and I am he?"

"A LONG-PURSUED CRAFT"

Bynner's talent for translation was not limited to his interpretation of Chinese classics. In 1915 he published *Iphigenia in Tauris,* a revision of English translations from the Greek of Euripides, for performance by Isadora Duncan. It was subsequently revised and published in the University of Chicago Press's *The Complete Greek Tragedies: Euripides II* in 1956. In 1923 Bynner published *A Book of Love,* translated from the French of Charles Vildrac. The *Iphigenia* translation followed naturally from his interest in the stage. As a student at Harvard and thereafter, he frequently attended the theater and over his lifetime wrote a number of plays, including *Tiger, The Little King,* and *The Mechanic.* In 1926 he published the verse play *Cake,* which is generally based on the life of Mabel Dodge Luhan. It plays off Bynner's ongoing spar with her and was highly acclaimed.

Although other writing was consistently in the background, it was poetry that continually stood up front for Bynner. His first book of poems after the Spectra Hoax and the 1917 trip to China, *The Beloved Stranger* (1919), embodies the energetic mixture of the two new strains in Bynner's work, that of Emanuel Morgan and of the T'ang Dynasty poets.

The new note released in *The Beloved Stranger,* an acknowledgement of a more difficult and sometimes dark current, continued in later work, and in *Caravan* (1925) edged over into the cynical.

But "Lorenzo," another poem in *Caravan,* eases the charge:

> But I had not known that there could be
> Men like Lorenzo and like me
> Both in the world and both so right
> That the world is dark and the world is light.

Some critics wondered which poet was the real one—"the celebrant ... in a gospel of beauty" or "a man who loathed humanity when it was nearest him." This concern was perhaps exacerbated by the Spectra Hoax, but the disparities were consistent with the overall development of the poet. From youthful idealism he graduated to acknowledgement of the human vicissitudes.

From here forward the poetry integrated the eternal questions, solitude against loneliness, ego against unity, love against desire. The books, as they always had, continued to tumble out: *Eden Tree* (1931); *Guest Book* (1935); *Selected Poems* (1936); *Against the Cold* (1940); *Take Away the Darkness* (1947); *Book of Lyrics* (1955); and *New Poems 1960,* published when Bynner was seventy-nine. Each volume received generally good reviews, sometimes outright praise, sometimes complaints about the uneven qualities of the poems. But as Bynner aged, the question that continually formed was not so much about the poetry but about his status as a poet. Many of his contemporaries, who were also friends or acquaintances, had been clearly stamped with the mark of success, success often gained with Bynner's help: Willa Cather, T. S. Eliot, Robert Frost, Edna St. Vincent Millay, Ezra Pound, and others. Bynner wrote, published, and was extraordinarily successful with the Chinese translations, yet by the end of his life his name was barely known outside literary circles. Richard Wilbur says in his critical introduction to *Selected Poems* (1977):

How to explain the forgottenness of a poet who was so valued, in his day, by other poets whom we still read and esteem? A simple answer might be that writers are often seen, in retrospect, to have overvalued their contemporaries, out of proximity and a natural gratitude to all who are helping their moment to find its voice. I think it no injustice to say that Bynner had not the final stature of some who praised him. Yet he was and is a true and valuable poet.

Bynner may also have fallen by the wayside because of a trend toward anthologizing, especially for classroom texts, which repeatedly selects many of the same major poets over and over and leaves no room for poets of the margins. Some have suggested that Bynner wrote too much, or published without discretion, or experimented too much, or that his writing changed too much throughout his career. The reviews, even those that were begrudging, acknowledged the longevity of the work. Winfield Townley Scott says in his assessment of *New Poems 1960* that "Bynner may be scarcely more than a name from the remote past," but Scott understands why Bynner "has not yet been defined or placed: he has been, as it were, too various.... None the less it is evident that [his] subconscious shaped [his poems] out of a long-pursued craft."

Others considered Bynner's subject matter problematic. He wrote about minority cultures and societies before his own society was interested. He placed himself squarely in the United States and within its cultural diversity, while other important writers took their stand in Europe. Even William Carlos Williams, who championed the American voice, held fast to the East Coast, while Bynner migrated to the west. He fought early for rights of others—conscientious objectors, women in their struggle to vote—and he lived his life openly as a gay man at a time when that was rarely done. Still his poetry leaped over those obstacles and championed both the tao of the universe and the difficulties of the human experience.

THE LEGACY

Bynner did not seem to rail against the injustice of his lapse into obscurity, perhaps because early in his life he decided that the "way to do is to be." He lived with personal integrity, was encircled by faithful friends and companions, and lived in a home amidst the art and mementos of his well-traveled life. In 1950, when Bynner was sixty-nine, he and Hunt took a six-month trip to Europe and North Africa. Bynner had not been there for nearly fifty years. They visited numerous friends, including James Baldwin, George Santayana, Alice B. Toklas, and

Thornton Wilder. Back in Santa Fe, on the night before his seventieth birthday he reflected on his age with his usual frankness and optimism:

When a man has reached seventy, he has lived his natural life and ought to be able to begin to use it. At least he can look around him and without fear or favor face the truth.... Once more I say in my heart: You have lived your life, now use it; you have spent it, now earn it. And I feel a clutch at the throat of what breath is left me, realizing that my breath still blows away like the down of a dandelion or the airy spokes of any day's sun. But there is sudden exhilaration too. I am free. I have lived and not died and the space between life and death feels like an eternal space in which not only to continue but to begin as with new youth; small lungs full of all breath, small fingers probing all touch, small eyes focusing infinity, but with the reach of human living behind me as well as ahead of me, made into a new youth and a stronger honesty, with a fuller warmth of everlasting responsibility. At first responsive, now responsible. Though there be gaps in the plumes, there is a sweet preening of old wings. I can still fly. And how often do you find a dead bird?

Although few people today recognize his name, Bynner's literary legacy is secured through two sets of publications. *The Works of Witter Bynner* are collected in five volumes edited by James Kraft, with biographical and probing critical introductions written by others: *Selected Poems* (1977), *Light Verse and Satires* (1978), *The Chinese Translations* (1978), *Prose Pieces* (1979), and *Selected Letters* (1981). Kraft is also the author of a biography, *Who Is Witter Bynner?* (1995), and an accompanying compilation of works from the series, *The Selected Witter Bynner* (1995). His letters, papers, and photographs are held in numerous archives.

He left another legacy as well, in the form of the Witter Bynner Foundation for Poetry, based in Santa Fe. In 1997 the foundation awarded the Library of Congress an annual Witter Bynner Fellowship to be selected by the poet laureate of the United States. It also offers various grants and awards for translation, for the development of audiences for poetry, and for uses of poetry; and it honors Bynner's life. In a brief biography of Bynner posted on the foundation's website, Paul Horgan says:

Anyone who spent an intimate evening in his fine library, at Santa Fe, with a handful of like-minded men and women of wide culture and high wits, will keenly remember his presence, his gusty humor, his generous sensibility in honor of any honest human manifestation, his range of civilized and often hilarious reference, and above all his feeling for the common cause of human life itself, with all his hopes, wonders, and satisfactions, which he saw as deserving of tolerance and respect even at its most pathetic or misguided. Beyond all this, his generous and time-giving encouragement of younger poets was legendary.

Robert Hunt died on January 18, 1964, in Santa Fe. Two days short of a year later, on January 16, 1965, in Santa Fe, Bynner suffered a disabling stroke. After three and a half years of isolation within his body, he died at home at the age of eighty-seven, on June 1, 1968. His last words, suddenly articulated despite his paralyzed state, were said to be, "Other people die, why can't I?"

A Stream

Cool, moving, fruitful and alive I go,
In my small run reflecting all the sky.
I see through trees, I see through melting snow,
I see through riffles which the wind and I
Have made, and through the shadow of a man,
Nor know where I arrive, where I began.

Selected Bibliography

WORKS OF WITTER BYNNER

POETRY

An Ode to Harvard and Other Poems. Boston: Small, Maynard, 1907. Republished as *Young Harvard:*

First Poems of Witter Bynner. New York: Knopf, 1925.

The New World. New York: Mitchell Kennerley, 1915. New York: Knopf, 1922.

Spectra: A Book of Poetic Experiments. New York: Mitchell Kennerley, 1916. (Cowritten with Arthur Davison Ficke and published under the pseudonyms Emanuel Morgan and Anne Knish. Reprinted with additions in William Jay Smith's *The Spectra Hoax.*)

The Grenstone Poems. New York: Frederick A. Stokes, 1917. New York: Knopf, 1926.

A Canticle of Praise. San Francisco: John Henry Nash, 1918. (First delivered in the Greek Theatre at the University of California, Berkeley, on December 1, 1918.)

The Beloved Stranger: Two Books of Song and a Divertissement for the Unknown Lover. New York: Knopf, 1919.

A Canticle of Pan and Other Poems. New York: Knopf, 1920.

Pins for Wings. New York: Sunwise Turn, 1920. (Published under the pseudonym Emanuel Morgan.)

Caravan. New York: Knopf, 1925.

Witter Bynner. Edited by Hughes Mearns. New York: Simon and Schuster, 1927.

Indian Earth. New York: Knopf, 1929.

The Jade Mountain: A Chinese Anthology, Being Three Hundred Poems of the T'ang Dynasty 618–906. New York: Knopf, 1929. (From the texts of Kiang Kang-hu.)

Eden Tree. New York: Knopf, 1931.

Against the Cold. New York: Knopf, 1933. (A sonnet sequence printed as a chapbook.)

Guest Book. New York: Knopf, 1935.

Against the Cold. New York: Knopf, 1940. (A full length collection of poems that includes the sonnet sequence first published as a chapbook by the same title in 1933.)

The Way of Life According to Laotzu: An American Version. New York: John Day, 1944. (A verse translation of the *Tao Teh Ching* from the texts of Kiang Kang-hu.)

Take Away the Darkness. New York: Knopf, 1947.

Book of Lyrics. New York: Knopf, 1955.

New Poems 1960. New York: Knopf, 1960.

PLAYS

Tiger. New York: Mitchell Kennerley, 1913. Great Neck, N.Y.: Core Collection Books, 1977.

The Little King. New York: Mitchell Kennerley, 1914.

Iphigenia in Tauris. New York. Mitchell Kennerly, 1915. Reprinted in *The Complete Greek Tragedies: Euripides II,* edited by David Grene, et al. Chicago: University of Chicago Press, 1956.

Snickerty Nick. New York: Moffat, Yard, 1919. (Cowritten with Julia Ellsworth Ford.)

A Book of Plays. New York: Knopf, 1922. (Contains *The Little King, A Night Wind, Tiger, Cycle,* and *Iphigenia in Tauris.*)

Cake: An Indulgence. New York: Knopf, 1926.

OTHER WORKS

The Persistence of Poetry. San Francisco: Book Club of California, 1929. (An essay, part of which first appeared as Bynner's introduction to *The Jade Mountain.*)

Journey with Genius: Recollections and Reflections Concerning the D. H. Lawrences. New York: John Day, 1951. New York: Octagon, 1974. (A memoir.)

COLLECTED WORKS

The Works of Witter Bynner. 5 vols. Edited by James Kraft. New York: Farrar, Straus, 1977–1981. (Volume I: *Selected Poems.* Edited with a biographical introduction by Kraft and a critical introduction by Richard Wilbur; Volume II: *Light Verse and Satires.* Edited with an introduction by William Jay Smith; Volume III: *The Chinese Translations.* With introductions by Burton Watson and David Lattimore; Volume IV: *Prose Pieces;* Volume V: *Selected Letters.*)

The Selected Witter Bynner: Poems, Plays, Translations, Prose, and Letters. Edited by James Kraft. Albuquerque: University of New Mexico Press, 1995.

MANUSCRIPTS AND PAPERS

Houghton Library, Harvard University. (Has more than seventeen thousand letters written by and to Bynner, as well as numerous other holdings.)

Bancroft Library, University of California, Berkeley.

University of New Hampshire Library.

D. H. Lawrence Collection, Witter Bynner Collection of Photographs, University of Nottingham, England.

Harry Ransom Humanities Research Center, University of Texas, Austin.

Haniel Long Papers, Department of Special Collections, Research Library, University of California, Los Angeles.

Beinecke Rare Book and Manuscript Library, Yale University.

CRITICAL AND BIOGRAPHICAL STUDIES

Benet, William Rose. "The Phoenix Nest: Contemporary Poetry." *Saturday Review of Literature,* December 5, 1936, p. 40. (Review of *Selected Poems,* 1936.)

Blackmur, R. P. "Versions of Solitude." *Poetry* 39:217–221 (January 1932). (Review of *Eden Tree.*)

Ficke, Arthur Davison. "The Luminous Chinese Sage." *Poetry* 66:40–42 (April 1945). (Review of *The Way of Life According to Laotzu.*)

Fitts, Dudley. "Poetry and Tradition." *Saturday Review of Literature,* October 26, 1940, p. 16. (Review of *Against the Cold,* 1940.)

Horgan, Paul. "Details on Greatness." *Saturday Review of Literature,* August 18, 1951, pp. 9–10. (Review of *Journey with Genius.*)

———. "Witter Bynner (1881–1968)." The Witter Bynner Foundation for Poetry (*http://www.bynnerfoundation.org/witterbynner/index.htm*). (A brief biographical article posted on the foundation's website.)

Kraft, James. *Who Is Witter Bynner?: A Biography.* Albuquerque: University of New Mexico Press, 1995.

Lindsay, Robert O. *Witter Bynner: A Bibliography.* Albuquerque: University of New Mexico Press,.

Long, Haniel. "Mr. Bynner's Philosophy of Love." *Poetry* 15:281–282 (February 1920). (Review of *The Beloved Stranger.*)

Scott, Winfield Townley. "Nothing Is Static." *The Nation,* November 5, 1960, pp. 352–353. (Review of *New Poems 1960.*)

Smith, William Jay. *The Spectra Hoax.* Middletown, Conn.: Wesleyan University Press, 1961. (Contains an account of Bynner and Ficke's hoax, the poems first published in *Spectra,* and additional poems written by Bynner and Ficke under their pseudonyms.)

Tietjens, Eunice. "From the Chinese." *Poetry* 35:289–292 (February 1930). (Review of *The Jade Mountain.*)

"Witter Bynner (1881–1968)." *Gay Bears: The Hidden History of the Berkeley Campus.* (*http://sunsite3.berkeley.edu/gaybears/bynner/*). (Part of the University of California at Berkeley's website.)

—SUSAN CAROL HAUSER

Michael Cunningham

1952–

THE QUESTION OF how ought we to live our lives has puzzled and intrigued humankind from the moment we became capable of formulating such an inquiry. Philosophers, theologians, academicians, poets, and countless others have presented their answers over the centuries, but the question arises anew as each generation seeks to find the good and worthwhile life in its own time. In his novels Michael Cunningham looks for his answer by unflinchingly examining contemporary American family life, revealing its flaws and suggesting alternatives.

Michael Cunningham was born to Don and Dorothy Cunningham on November 6, 1952 in Cincinnati, Ohio. Cunningham's early years were a time of unsettled residence; his father's career in advertising took the family as far away as Germany. By the time Cunningham was ten years old, however, a degree of permanence was established in Pasadena, California. In high school Cunningham shared the prevailing ambition of many teenage boys who were experiencing the wild social and artistic dynamics of the late 1960s: he wanted to be a rock star. Once after he had expounded upon the poetic merits of Leonard Cohen and Bob Dylan, Cunningham was asked by an older classmate, "Have you ever thought about being less stupid?" The questioner, a girl whom Cunningham remembers being "tall and mean and beautiful and smart," added, "Why don't you read some books? Why don't you read Eliot and Virginia Woolf?" The school library did not have any works by T. S. Eliot but Cunningham found the one Woolf novel it owned, *Mrs. Dalloway* (1925). The intricate complexities of the novel were beyond the teenager's understanding, and he returned the book before finishing it. But he appreciated the similarity between what Virginia Woolf (1882–1941) did with language and what Jimi Hendrix did with an electric guitar. Admitting his lack of musical talent, Cunningham thought perhaps he could express himself through literature.

After graduating with a bachelor's degree in English from Stanford University in 1975, Cunningham spent the next two years working at a bar in Laguna Beach and trying to write. His friends were mostly nonreaders, and he found that life in the beach community was not conducive to literary pursuits. Cunningham immersed himself in his chosen art by entering the University of Iowa Writers' Workshop. There he found a sanctuary filled with like-minded men and women who respected one another and took their calling seriously. The budding writer was fortunate to have the novelist Hilma Wolitzer as an instructor. With her guidance and encouragement Cunningham began to submit stories to magazines. His work was published in the *Paris Review, Redbook,* and the *Atlantic Monthly.* Cunningham left Iowa in 1980 with a master of fine arts degree in writing and accepted a one-year residency at the Provincetown Fine Arts Work Center. In 1984, Crown published Cunningham's first novel, *Golden States.* In a 2002 interview conducted by Barbara Shoup for *Other Voices* magazine Cunningham had this to say about the novel's creation:

> I wrote it very, very quickly. I was about to turn thirty, and I realized what I had for my years of writing thus far was seventeen abandoned beginnings.... I was working in a bar and I suddenly had

this vivid image of myself at sixty, still in the bar, still talking about the novel I was going to write someday. So I said to myself, "Sit down now and finish something. It doesn't matter what. Just start it in the beginning, write through the middle and reach the end and then stop."

GOLDEN STATES

The story begins with a brief description of weather conditions that have caused problems ranging from the merely annoying to the catastrophic for the citizens of Los Angeles. Drought has forced coyotes down from the hills into residential neighborhoods in search of water. The coyotes slake their thirst at swimming pools and make meals of docile house cats and what they can reach in garbage cans and fast-food dumpsters. The months-long drought ends with a sudden fury of torrential rain. Homes are lifted from their foundations and sent gracefully down muddy hillsides to their ultimate destruction in canyon bottoms. The coyotes are driven back to their natural habitat by the deluge, but their eerie nightly howling reminds everyone that they linger nearby. This feeling of impending menace permeates all that follows.

Cunningham's protagonist is twelve-year-old David Stark, and David's story is told in third person. David lives in Rosemead, a comfortable, secure middle-class city twelve miles east of Los Angeles, with his mother, Beverly, and his ten-year-old sister, Lizzie. Beverly is a forty-eight-year-old assistant administrator in the Rosemead school system. Cunningham hints several times throughout the novel that Beverly is in poor health. When Beverly returns from a doctor's appointment, she reassures her worried son that she is fine but immediately increases David's sense that all is not well by asking him to help take care of his sister, Lizzie. Not knowing whether to be flattered or terrified, David reminds his mother that he is only twelve. She responds that she knows, but he is the one who guards the house.

The children's father, Beverly's second husband, Frank Stark, exists in the past and future tense in the novel, his threatening presence lingering on the outskirts of the story like the coyotes at the edges of town. The reader does not learn what Frank does for a living or what act caused Beverly to divorce him, but it is clear that he is a brutal man. Years earlier Frank had bolted out of his bedroom after a shouting match with Beverly and bumped into David, sending the young boy hurtling down the stairs. In answer to David's question about the event, his mother tries to assure him that his father would never have hurt him on purpose. David is not convinced and Cunningham cites enough examples of Frank's past brutality to convince the reader that the children's fear of going to Spokane for their annual three-week, court ordered visitation is well founded. Nevertheless David waivers between his fear and an idealized vision of his father gained when the two were at a shooting range.

David's best friend since second grade is Billy. Like most boys their age, the two enjoy role-playing adventures. On the day the story opens they greet each other at the appointed place as British detectives, complete with affected accents. But soon the mood changes. Billy is angry and wants nothing more than to "punch somebody." The boys enter the town drugstore together, but David separates himself from his friend when Billy asks him to shoplift. David instead focuses his attention on a young woman who is buying rat poison. In his sleuthing mode David imagines she is bent upon suicide and stealthily follows her through the store and out to her car in hopes of rescuing her. Left at the curb, David turns his attention to a commotion in front of the drugstore. A crowd has gathered around Billy, who has been caught in the act. As two men go through Billy's pockets extracting stolen items, David watches his friend's public humiliation from the sidelines. When Billy, who has passively submitted to the search, sees David, he hoists an imaginary rifle and fires a shot at the bewildered boy. The imaginary shootings continue whenever the two boys meet, and David grows desperate to repair the fractured friendship.

Cunningham presents in a gentle manner the troubling sexual ambiguity of preteen boys like David. Cunningham only implies Billy's own confusion regarding his friend, but he makes it clear that whereas David is curious about his feelings, Billy is filled with aggressive anger toward David. During lunch at school David is granted an epiphany. Billy is still not speaking to David but he sits near him in the schoolyard while they eat their lunches. He looks at David "with avid eyes that were not like Billy's at all." "He loves me, said the voice inside David's head." Billy's violence escalates however. From high in a tree he hurls a pinecone at David and counts off the seconds as if it were a live grenade. Days later he leaps from the same tree, throws David to the ground, and savagely beats him, then stands over him with his hand cocked to simulate a pistol and fires.

David's sexual confusion is aggravated by the arrival of his twenty-three-year-old half sister, Janet. Fourteen years earlier Janet's father, Beverly's first husband, Ray, had been hit and killed as he was crossing a street. As if that were not enough for Janet to endure, she was also a victim of her stepfather's brutality, with implied sexual abuse as well. An example of this is shown on one occasion when Janet was preparing to go out with a friend. Shortly after this incident Janet decided she wanted to become a doctor. Beverly encouraged her to apply to Berkeley instead of UCLA because it would put more distance between Janet and her stepfather.

Janet was not at Berkeley long before she met Rob Schmidt, a law student who wore overalls and Birkenstocks and impressed Janet with his determination to help the poor. But

during the three years Janet lived with Rob his countercultural zeal dissolved into middle-class conformity. When Janet didn't get into medical school, the couple turned their thoughts to marriage; but something in Janet suddenly changed. She fled Rob and returned to her mother's home to sort things out. David is strongly attracted to Janet. He spies on her when she swims nude in the backyard pool and agonizes over how to get close to her. When she tells him that she does not love Rob, he decides to be more careful and to become a man that deserves to be loved.

Rob, his constant phone calls not producing the desired effect of winning Janet back, arrives at the Stark home. This throws the family into a state of confusion. Beverly is cordial to Rob and supportive of Janet, but she is incapable of offering more than motherly advice. Lizzie adores Rob and craves his attention, and Janet's initial desire to be rid of him weakens. But it is David who exhibits the most curious behavior. Cunningham neatly presents a portrait of preadolescent angst as David at one moment wants his imagined rival to leave and at another wants him to stay in order to learn how to be a man Janet could love. David is also somewhat attracted to Rob. Cunningham adds another element to David's confused state of mind.

Janet's indecision drags on for a few days, but she finally chooses to return to San Francisco with Rob. Unwilling to face her family, she leaves a note on the breakfast table and departs. David is awakened at three in the morning by a sense of something wrong. He reads Janet's note and develops a plan to bring her back home. David is no longer role-playing as he did when he sought to rescue the woman in the drugstore; now he is determined to fulfill his fantasy of being the family protector. Thus David enters the coming-of-age ranks found throughout literature.

For a boy who we have been told is afraid to be outside by himself at night, David suddenly displays remarkable courage and determination.

He pockets what money he can find—$15.77—steals the handgun from his mother's nightstand, wraps it in a towel and stuffs it in his backpack, and sets off in the predawn. His first idea, recruiting Billy, is negated when Billy's mother discovers David trying to awaken her son by tossing pebbles at his window. Undeterred, David makes his way alone to the bus station. He buys a ticket that will take him as far as he can get without exhausting his funds. When he arrives in Santa Barbara, he relies on what he considers "his certain power to make cars stop for him" and is picked up by a black man who drives him to Buellton, treats him to breakfast, and buys him a ticket to San Francisco. All the man asks of David is that he call home when he arrives at his destination and let his mother know he is all right. David is reluctant to take the man's charity and promises to repay, but his benefactor leaves without giving his name or address. Cunningham does not let this act of altruism go without inserting a threat that feeds David's life experience that men are to be feared and women protected and rescued: shortly after picking up David and learning his age the man announces that he's taking David to the sheriff. But the man accepts David's story that he is trying to get to his girlfriend.

Back on the bus David drifts off to sleep and wakes to see most of the passengers getting off at a large station. He goes into the station to ask for directions and discovers that he is in Oakland; his bus has left; and he once again must use his hitchhiking talents. This time he is picked up by Warren, who misreads David. He offers to share a joint, and David, who has smoked marijuana with Janet and gotten drunk on Irish whiskey with Rob, readily accepts. Although the drug clouds his mind, David manages to avoid answering Warren's questions truthfully. The misunderstanding leads David to agree to stop at Warren's apartment where the stoned twelve-year-old is unbelievably unaware of the man's intentions. It is only when Warren

kisses him that David snaps out of his stupor. Fortunately for the vulnerable boy, Warren is embarrassed and apologetic. He gives David a Japanese parasol to protect him and sends him on his way in the rain. As he waits at a bus stop, David realizes that he had wanted Warren to touch him.

Two officers in a patrol car spot David and, based on a police bulletin, realize they have found a runaway. David is released to Janet and Rob after being questioned about the gun in his backpack. David claims he has no idea why he took the gun; it just seemed like something he should carry with him. Rob is not so sure and remains sullen as he and Janet take David to the airport to catch a flight back home. But in his imagination anything is possible, so as he is boarding the plane David "raised his right arm, thumb and index finger erect, and fired three shots. He made the sounds. 'Pshiew.' 'Pshiew.' 'Pshiew.' He shot Rob straight in the head."

David's mother and sister pick him up at the airport, and his fifteen-hour odyssey comes to an end. Like Odysseus, David has traveled far from home and encountered the strange and exotic and has returned to protect what is his. Additionally he has discovered who he is just as surely as Truman Capote's character Joel Knox realizes his true nature in *Other Voices, Other Rooms*: "Someday he would go back to San Francisco. Warren would still be there."

Golden States was well received by critics. The novelist Ruth Doan MacDougall in a review for the *Christian Science Monitor* of May 4, 1984, wrote,

Cunningham has a magical way with figures of speech—coffee steams "with a black adult life of its own," a purse droops "like a sack of jelly"—and he eases them into a 12-year-old's viewpoint with stunning skill. However much one might object to the theme of the protection of women, one cannot help savoring every moment of this novel. Funny, tender, it is a joy to read.

Anne F. Wittels in the *Los Angeles Times Book Review* and Elizabeth Royte in the *Village Voice* found the book appealing and well written, although Wittels was disappointed by how it ends.

Given this favorable attention to a first novel by an unknown writer, it is surprising that the book did not sell well. That proved to be a source of embarrassment for Cunningham, and *Golden States* is rarely included in his list of works. Cunningham explained to Barbara Shoup:

> Not listing it, frankly—though I didn't fight this— was a sort of marketing ploy, when my second book came out. It's much, much easier to sell a first novel. [Golden States] had sold about seventeen copies and nobody knew about it. The irony, of course, is now they sell for several hundred dollars on the Internet.

Cunningham felt that his first attempt was a modest success that achieved modest aims, and he turned down an offer from his publisher to release a paperback edition. He told Shoup, "I never felt good about that book, because I wrote it too fast. Because I knew it wasn't the best book I could write."

Cunningham went to work as an annual report and press release writer for the Carnegie Corporation in New York City in 1986. Two years later he met the man who became his life companion, the psychologist Ken Corbett. In the four years that followed the publication of *Golden States,* Cunningham became convinced that the literary world had lost what little interest it had shown him. To prove his theory to Corbett, Cunningham submitted a chapter from a novel in progress to the *New Yorker* feeling certain that it would be rejected. The magazine confounded his pessimism by accepting the chapter and publishing it as the short story "White Angel" in its July 25, 1988 issue. It subsequently was chosen for *Best American Short Stories, 1989.* The story of Bobby, Carl-

ton, and their counterculture parents captured the imagination of readers, critics, and publishers. Impressed by the writing, Roger Straus of Farrar, Straus and Giroux informed Cunningham that his firm would like to publish the novel from which this segment had come.

A HOME AT THE END OF THE WORLD

Cunningham's ambition to write a book that would not merely sit and gather dust in bookstores was better served by his next novel, *A Home at the End of the World* (1990). In it he abandons the third-person narrative technique he used in *Golden States* and divides his story into three parts; each part is further divided into chapters that are designated by the name of the character whose first-person viewpoint is being presented. Part one is told by Bobby Morrow, Jonathan Glover, and Alice Glover and covers a period of nearly fifteen years, from when the boys are preschool age through their high-school graduation. Bobby's parents, Burt and Isobel, are teachers; Burt teaches music at Roosevelt High and Isobel works with exceptional children. Bobby has a brother, Carlton, seven years his senior, and the two are inseparable; Carlton shares his drug and alcohol experiments with Bobby, and the younger boy is able to boast, "I was, thanks to Carlton, the most criminally advanced nine-year-old in my fourth-grade class." The two endure the more mundane aspects of their lives by dreaming of escape to an imaginary Woodstock Nation where they will be free to stay perpetually stoned on LSD.

Tragedy strikes when Carlton accidentally runs through a sliding glass door during a party thrown by his parents. "Carlton reaches up curiously to take out the shard of glass that is stuck in his neck, and that is when the blood starts. It shoots out of him." Despite his parents' frantic efforts to stop the flow, Carlton bleeds to death before the ambulance arrives. The family is as shattered as the door, and the survivors retreat into their separate lives of pain and loss.

The tragedy that affects Jonathan and his parents, Ned and Alice, occurs when Jonathan is five. Ned owns and operates a small movie theater and is away from home most of the day. Alice stays home and raises Jonathan, "When my father was away at work my mother and I were alone together. She invented indoor games for us to play, or enlisted my help in baking cookies." Cunningham captures Jonathan's early crisis of sexual identity in a scene wherein the young boy adorns himself with his mother's makeup and then lathers his face with his father's shaving cream. Jonathan studies the results in the bathroom mirror. His eyes, blackened by mascara, "glittered like spiders above the lush white froth. I was not ladylike, nor was I manly. I was something else altogether. There were many different ways to be a beauty."

Alice is pregnant with a child she does not want, and arguments rage between her and Ned, arguments that are barely audibly to young Jonathan who has found comfort in caring for a pink vinyl baby doll. The baby dies during childbirth, and, "after an awkward period we would resume our normal family life, find our cheerfulness again. My mother and father would invent a cordial, joking relationship that involved neither kisses nor fights." Alice thrives and becomes an accomplished cook, but Ned's life begins to shrink: "His wife shunned him, his business was not a success, and his only son—there would be no others—loved dolls and quiet indoor games."

Jonathan and Bobby meet when their separate elementary school classes are combined in junior high. Bobby is living alone with his father, his mother having killed herself shortly after Carlton's death. In obvious ways Bobby has become Carlton, perpetually smoking dope and wearing his dead brother's clothes. Jonathan finds him exotic, and soon the two spend much of their free time in Jonathan's room getting high and listening to music. Alice is drawn to Bobby; Ned is tolerant of the boy's constant presence. Bobby is equally curious about Alice and is fascinated by her cooking skills. Over Jonathan's objections Bobby invites Alice to join them in their favorite pastime. Soon Alice is enjoying their music, dancing with Bobby, and sharing their marijuana. She comes to think of herself as Wendy in *Peter Pan,* a young woman taking care of lost boys. Her idyllic time with them comes to a halt when she discovers the boys engaged in sex. Following a brief period of embarrassment realignment occurs: Jonathan spends most of his time alone in his room while Alice teaches Bobby the art of mastering recipes. By the end of part one, Jonathan leaves for college in New York, and Bobby enrolls in a culinary institute, eventually opening his own restaurant, "Alice." A freak accident claims the life of Bobby's father; the restaurant is unsuccessful; and Bobby finds himself bankrupt, living back in Jonathan's old room and working at a bakery.

In part two Jonathan, now twenty-five, is sharing an apartment in New York with a thirty-six-year-old jewelry designer, Clare Rollins. After graduating from New York University, Jonathan was hired by a weekly newspaper and has worked his way up from typist and occasional reporter to food columnist and restaurant critic. His relationship with Clare is sexless but loving: "Clare and I told our worst secrets and admitted to our most foolish fears. We ate dinner and went shopping together, assessed the qualities of men who passed on the streets." Clare has become jaded and bitter after an abortion, a divorce, and a succession of disappointing relationships with men. Jonathan has had several sexual yet loveless encounters with a variety of men; the latest, Erich, looked promising but in the end Jonathan admits to himself that "we shared an intimacy devoid of knowledge or affection." He and Clare have resumed their habit, born of depression, of imagining a future that includes such things as opening a breakfast-in-bed catering service, moving to the coast of Spain, and their most persistent fantasy of having a baby. It is after Jonathan's breakup with Erich that Bobby calls.

For eight years Bobby has lived contentedly with Ned and Alice, cooking their meals, cleaning their house, and earning a living at the bakery. It all ends when Ned's doctor recommends that the couple move to Arizona for the sake of Ned's ailing lungs. Bobby expects to go with them, but Alice decides it is time for him to leave the nest. Disturbed by the prospect of life alone in Cleveland, Bobby seeks out the only other person with whom he shares a familial bond, Jonathan. After some hesitation Jonathan agrees to let Bobby stay with him while looking for a job and an apartment. Jonathan tells him, "I'll see what I can do to keep you safe here."

Cunningham reveals Bobby's painful sense of otherness immediately upon the young man's arrival in New York. He feels his clothes are not right, his luggage is an embarrassment, and his attempts to talk to Jonathan are awkward. In contrast the streetwise Jonathan is full of irony. At the apartment Bobby realizes that "over the years we'd lost our inevitability together; now we were like the relatives of two old friends who had died." He attempts to reclaim the past relationship by pulling out some record albums he has brought,

"Oh, hey, have you got this Van Morrison?"

"No. I don't think I've listened to Van since I was in Cleveland, to tell you the truth."

"Oh, this record'll kill you," I said. "He's still, like, one of the best. I'm going to put it on, okay?"

"We don't have a turntable," he said. "Just a cassette player. Sorry."

"Oh. Well," I said.

But Jonathan is sensitive to his friend's feelings and treats him to a shopping trip for cassette tapes. "This is your welcome-to-New-York present.... Buy me something when you've got a job." At dinner Clare takes Bobby under her wing when he says that he hopes to find a job as a baker: "Now, sweetheart, listen to your aunt. One of the great features of New York is, you can do anything here." Bobby begins to feel comfortable with the exciting twosome: "Clare and Jonathan were both good talkers. I rode their talk as if it was a hammock stretched between them." Later, however, when the two young men are alone, the subject of their past sexual acts comes up. Bobby knows that he had participated only because he loved Jonathan. "This was a hard subject. I had realized by then that I didn't feel what others called 'desire.' Something was missing in me."

Unsure and inarticulate, Bobby finds comfort in safe activities, the sort he enjoyed with Ned and Alice in Cleveland: housecleaning, grocery shopping, meal preparation, and spending evenings with television, popcorn, and Diet Coke. But Clare decides it is time for Bobby to have a makeover; she cuts his hair short, adds vintage clothing to his wardrobe, introduces him to new music, gets his ear pierced, and makes an earring for him. The new Bobby is more attracted to life outside the apartment, and Clare finds herself more attracted to Bobby. When he learns that she had been at Woodstock, he is in awe of her experience of his own long held escape fantasy. Clare's seduction of Bobby is easy, and he cries himself to sleep in her arms afterward, astonished that he had the ability to have sex with a woman.

Bobby finds work as a prep chef at a small restaurant, and a sense of normalcy arises. The three pretend among themselves to be a family named Henderson. Clare is Mom, Bobby is Junior, and Jonathan is Uncle Jonny. Three events disturb this arrangement and cause Jonathan to disappear and try to form a separate life: he learns that a friend has been hospitalized and the fact of sexually transmitted disease and his own possible infection becomes an issue; a visit to his parents in Arizona unsettles his concept of family; and his confusion over his love for both Bobby and Clare pushes him farther away from the new family he had hoped to create. After more than a year the three are reunited in Arizona for Ned's funeral, then they return together to New York by automobile, visiting tourist attractions and spending a few moments in Bobby and Jonathan's hometown. As they near New York, still unsure of what form their relationship will take, Bobby suggests that they find a place in the country, a home where they can rebuild the family they once were. This is too much for Clare who has not revealed that she is pregnant, and she bolts from the car—a terrified, pregnant, forty-year-old woman in love with two men. At this point in the story Clare cannot foresee any alternative to her situation.

In parts one and two Cunningham shows the destructive power of the conventional family. Bobby, Jonathan, and Clare have emerged from their upbringings as undefined, directionless adult children who yearn for a tenable alternative structure. Part three documents their attempt. With Clare's inheritance they purchase a two-story house outside of Woodstock and open a nine-table restaurant they name Home Café. Bobby cooks, and Jonathan waits tables, and Clare stays home with the baby, Rebecca. Cunningham could have ended his novel here with an idyllic happy ending, but he is painfully aware that in an age when sex can kill, happy endings are rare.

Death enters the story in the form of Erich, Jonathan's former lover, who is in an advanced stage of AIDS. Jonathan has suspected for some time that he himself is infected and is curious to see how the disease has affected his partner. As Erich's visits to Woodstock increase and lengthen, it is clear that he will soon need professional care. Rather than abandon him to the impersonal health care available to the uninsured, Jonathan and Bobby take Erich in for the duration of his illness. Clare cannot bear to raise her daughter in this morbid atmosphere and flees for the West Coast, leaving behind the two men she loves to care for their dying friend. Cunningham seems resigned to the idea that no union of individuals is healthy or nondestructive. The only hope for people may lie in abiding friendships. Bobby says late in the story:

> Here is what's unsayable about us: Jonathan and I are members of a team so old nobody else could join even if we wanted them to. We adore Clare but she's not quite on the team. Not really. What binds us is stronger than sex. It is stronger than love. We're related. Each of us is the other born into different flesh. We may love Clare but she is not us. Only we can be ourselves and one another at the same time.

A Home at the End of the World was written during the early years of the AIDS epidemic, a time of fear, ignorance, and denial. Cunningham says in his interview with Shoup that presidents Ronald Reagan and George Bush never used the word AIDS in public, although many Americans were dying from the disease. Cunningham wanted to write a novel with characters and circumstances that reflected what was happening to his friends. The critical reaction was favorable. Richard Eder wrote in the *Los Angeles Times* of November 18, 1990, "We come to feel that we know Jonathan, Bobby and Clare as if we lived with them; yet each one retains the mystery that in people is called soul, and in fiction is called art." Joyce Reiser Kornblatt in the *New York Times Book Review* on November 11, 1990, likened Cunningham's work to that of Charles Dickens and E. M. Forster and stated, "Although [this novel] pretends to be a novel of voices, it is in fact the author's voice that informs every page, reaching at times that lyrical beauty in which even the grimmest events suggest their potential for grace."

FLESH AND BLOOD

Elements of Cunningham's first two novels are found in his third, *Flesh and Blood* (1995). The family structure in *Golden States* is mirrored in the Stassos family: an angry and clueless father, Constantine; a passive-aggressive mother, Mary; oldest daughter, Susan; middle child, Billy; and youngest daughter, Zoe. All bear characteristics similar to their counterparts in the Stark family. Even the refrigerator magnets that adorned the refrigerator in the Stark kitchen have found their way to the Stassos home: "On the refrigerator, old drawings of Billy's and Zoe's were held with magnets shaped like fruits. A plastic apple, an orange, a banana." Each member of the Stassos family, like the main characters in *A Home at the End of the World,* is seeking a means of coping with what they see as unfulfilling and stultifying lives.

Like its predecessor this novel is divided into three parts, but in this case chapters within the parts are identified by the year in which the action takes place, spanning a hundred years. Part one, "Car Ballet," covers the thirty-five-year period from 1935 to 1970. During that time Constantine Stassos, a Greek immigrant and construction worker, marries Mary Cuccio, an Italian immigrant, and the two eke out a precarious life of quiet desperation as they raise three children on Constantine's meager salary in a poor neighborhood of Newark, New Jersey. Constantine's dissatisfaction with his life often explodes in violent physical and verbal abuse. Even when his fortunes improve after partnering with an unscrupulous builder, and he moves his family to a better home in an upscale neighborhood on Long Island, Constantine remains a man at war with himself, swinging from hateful outbursts to pitiful apologies. He finds solace in alcohol and sexual play with his older daughter. For her part Susan, who wants and does not want her father's attentions, justifies her father's acts by telling herself, "He wasn't to blame, not really. She had started it

and now it existed, a secret they shared. Saying no would have given it a name."

Susan escapes by accepting a marriage proposal from her handsome and popular high-school sweetheart, Todd Emory. Billy's escape takes the form of long hair, outlandish clothes, alcohol, and joyriding with disreputable friends. The almost feral Zoe escapes into physical unattractiveness and animality: "Billy knew Zoe thought of herself as an animal. She snatched food off her plate and ate in small, eager bites. She slept curled up in a nest she made out of blankets and sheets." And Mary, who suspects something is going on between her husband and daughter, finds she can cope with the aid of "pale yellow pills" and an occasional shoplifting spree.

Part two, "Criminal Wisdom," relates events from 1971 through 1982. Billy, who by his academic brilliance and Constantine's newfound money gains admittance to Harvard, experiences his homosexual nature through the ministrations of an older man. Susan and Todd live on campus at Yale where Todd is an undergraduate prelaw major and Susan, who is trying to separate her life from her parents' by becoming pregnant, works as a secretary in one of the university's offices. Zoe migrates to New York, shares an apartment with two friends, works in a secondhand clothing shop, and spends much of her time stoned on various drugs. She is attracted to and "adopted" by Cassandra, a striking transvestite who instructs her "daughter" in the finer points of choosing men. Constantine, neglectful of and neglected by Mary, takes pleasure in having lunchtime sex with his partner's secretary, Magda.

Cunningham directs his characters to continue making the worst choices possible so that by the end of part two the reader finds Susan pregnant but unsure whether the father is Todd or Joel, an arborist with whom she has experienced erotic satisfactions beyond the imagination or inclination of her husband; Constantine thrown out of his home by Mary, who can no longer pretend she knows nothing of Magda; Zoe four months pregnant and hospitalized by a drug overdose. There seems to be some hope for Billy, who goes by the name Will now. He has used his Harvard degree to become a fifth-grade teacher on Beacon Hill in Boston and, after suffering a humiliating experience with a man who wanted to experience "fag stuff" before marrying, is determined to rebuild himself, at least physically. Mary seems to be the most vulnerable at this point, standing in her daughter's hospital room trying to absorb difficult facts: that Zoe is dangerously careless with drugs, that she has not been told of her advanced pregnancy, and that the woman who appears to offer her daughter the most care and protection and acts as her second mother is in fact a man. Mary has yet to learn that the father of Zoe's child is black.

Part three, "Inside the Music," presents the next thirteen years, 1983 to 1995, plus a vision of 2035. A poignancy pervades this section as Cunningham brings a close to the lives of his characters. Constantine marries Magda, becomes a millionaire building and selling substandard housing, erects a Gatsby-like mansion on Long Island, settles into the role of adoring and adored grandfather, and finally dies after a series of strokes. Will (Billy) meets his soul mate, Harry, and the two live happily into old age. Mary lives alone in her large house, works in sales at Anne Klein, meets Cassandra for lunch in Greenwich Village occasionally, and takes pleasure in watching Constantine's beloved garden wither and die.

Two children are added to the Stassos family: Susan's son Ben, and Zoe's son Jamal. Both boys are troubled. Jamal is frightened by the fact that his mother has begun the long process of death by AIDS, and Ben is tormented by shame and guilt as he desperately tries to exorcise his own homosexual nature. In his unnatural battle Ben silently expresses his hatred

of his Uncle Will and Harry, refusing even to sit where either of them has sat. He does, however, indulge in sexual play with Jamal until Jamal puts a stop to it by declaring he has a girlfriend. In addition to this humiliation, Ben discovers that his grandfather has been nearby as he pleaded with Jamal to let him perform oral sex. "His grandfather could see the remnants of what had happened. Ben felt certain of it." Leaving Jamal behind, the two go for a short trip in Ben's sailboat.

The horror that grips Ben is palpable; he cannot accept who he is and thinks for a moment he will blame Jamal for what Constantine may have seen and heard. Constantine's image of Ben is precisely what Ben wants to be: "This perfect boy, this kid who could do anything, who had nothing to hold him back. Nothing. He was handsome and strong and smart and rich." But he is also gay, a condition that he knows his beloved grandfather will abhor. Reckless in his agony, the fourteen-year-old capsizes the boat and swims out to sea. "He swam hard, to exhaust himself, to drain off the wrongness of his being." Cunningham lingers over the boy's last moments, filling six and a half pages with his death by drowning. Intermingled with Ben's struggles is Zoe's peaceful, poetic death sitting in the sunshine on her father's terrace with Jamal at her side holding her hand. At Ben's funeral Susan settles an old score with her father. In front of the gathered mourners she takes the shaken man's chin in her hand and,

> still holding his jaw, she put her mouth on his. She kept her eyes open. Soon he tried to pull away but she kept her mouth on his. She held her mouth in place and she continued looking into his eyes until she saw that the knowledge had entered him. Then she held her mouth over his a little longer, until she felt sure he knew he was not forgiven.

In this long novel's penultimate chapter, Cunningham forecasts the fates of most, but not all, of his remaining characters. Curiously the reader is not informed of the details of Mary or

Cassandra's ultimate ends. We are told, however, that two years later, after her father's death, Susan will leave Todd, marry the owner of a printing company, and give birth to a daughter she will name Zoe. Finally, in 2035, the story comes to an end as Jamal, who lives in California with his adored second wife and two children, prepares to take a box containing the cremated remains of Will and Harry to the bay. Cunningham's compassion for all his characters in this novel is evident. No one is beyond hope, but it is those who face themselves and the world honestly who finally enjoy some sort of peace.

Reviews were favorable. Meg Wolitzer, daughter of Cunningham's former writing instructor at Iowa, praises Cunningham's courage in the *New York Times Book Review* of April 16, 1995: "As Mr. Cunningham well knows, there's a great deal hidden inside those identical suburban houses. In this novel, he throws all their doors wide open." And in the January 15, 1995, issue of *Booklist*, Donna Seaman writes, "Cunningham, in a remarkable performance, inhabits the psyche of each of his striking characters as they find themselves in one surprising situation after another." She calls Cunningham "a tenacious and word-perfect writer with acute insight into the eccentricity of personalities and the chemistry of intimate relationships." And Cunningham himself said this about *Flesh and Blood* in an interview with Michael Coffey printed in the November 2, 1998, issue of *Publishers Weekly:* "I wanted *Flesh and Blood* to have some of the easier virtues of a pulpier kind of book. There were things I would do differently now, but I was pleased with the real range of responses it got." *Flesh and Blood* was adapted for the stage by the writer and actor Peter Gaitens. The three-and-one-half-hour play originated in the New York Theatre Workshop in 2000 and was performed several times before receiving a two-month run in the summer of 2003, following

the critical acclaim given to the motion picture adaptation of Cunningham's next novel, *The Hours* (1998).

THE HOURS

On May 14, 1925, Leonard Woolf, co-owner and operator of the Hogarth Press in London, published his wife Virginia's fourth novel, *Mrs. Dalloway.* The novel tells the story of one day in the life of Clarissa Dalloway, a character who had appeared in Woolf's first novel, *The Voyage Out* (1915), and several of her short stories. Mrs. Dalloway, still attractive in her fifties and married to a member of parliament, begins her day by deciding she will go out and buy flowers for the party she is hosting that night, leaving the rest of the preparations to her servants. She emerges into the bright, promising June day and is filled with what Robert Frost would have recognized as "sheer morning gladness at the brim." Her joy diminishes gradually throughout the day as she remembers events in her past. Particularly disturbing to her is the remembrance of a rejected suitor who will attend her party. Mrs. Dalloway doubts her husband's fidelity and is disappointed in her daughter, but she deliberately maintains her poise, successfully suppressing the rage within her.

Less successful in controlling demons is Septimus Warren Smith, a man "aged about thirty" and a budding poet whose mind has been destroyed by the horrors he recently endured on the battlefield. Smith descends deeper and deeper into madness and ultimately in a frenzy of fear he throws himself from a window and dies horribly. Later that evening a guest arriving late at Mrs. Dalloway's party apologizes and explains that he was detained by a young man's suicide. Mrs. Dalloway is aghast that something so sordid would intrude on her well-planned festivity, and she retreats to a private room. There she enjoys an epiphany: one can choose to throw life away, choose death over life. For that moment Mrs. Dalloway chooses life and returns to her party, her life.

It would serve a reader of *The Hours* well to read *Mrs. Dalloway* first. In addition to the enjoyment of reading one of the seminal novels of modern literature, the reader will gain a greater appreciation of Cunningham's accomplishment. In *Poets and Writers Magazine*, Cunningham told interviewer David Bahr,

> I've always had this thing with *Mrs. Dalloway* since I was very young, and it has always felt like a part of me. I don't exactly know why. I don't know if it was the greatest book ever written. I don't know if it's the greatest book Virginia Woolf ever wrote. But I read it when I was pretty young and it just stuck with me like nothing else has, to the point that it felt as much like something for me to write about as my childhood, my first love affair, or all the more traditional material.

Bahr wrote that it was Cunningham's original intention simply to rewrite *Mrs. Dalloway* "as a social commentary on gay life, with its protagonist a 52-year old gay man living in Manhattan." But after three years of research and many false starts Cunningham "ended up with three female protagonists and a story that, among other things, is a paean to the palliative effects of reading and writing during times of psychic pain."

The novel's prologue relates the final hours of Virginia Woolf's life. Haunted for decades by bouts of mental instability and feelings of artistic and personal failure, Woolf suffered a profound and overwhelming attack of despair on March 28, 1941. On the morning of that day, at the age of fifty-nine, wearing a coat that she weighted down by placing a large stone in one of its pockets, she walked into the river Ouse near her home in Sussex and drowned. Her body, wedged against a bridge support, was discovered by children playing near the river on April 18. The final four sentences in her farewell letter to her husband read; "If anybody could have saved me it would have been you. Every-

thing has gone from me but the certainty of your goodness. I cant [*sic*] go on spoiling your life any longer. I dont think two people could have been happier than we have been."

As in his previous two novels, Cunningham eschews the traditional form of chapter divisions. Each section of *The Hours* is identified by the name of that section's protagonist, Mrs. Dalloway, Mrs. Woolf, and Mrs. Brown. Mrs. Dalloway is Clarissa Vaughan, nicknamed "Mrs. Dalloway" in college by her friend and former lover, Richard, a poet and novelist. It is on Richard's behalf that the prosperous and beautiful fifty-two-year-old Clarissa goes out on an errand in Manhattan on a June morning in the late 1990s. She intends to throw a party to honor Richard's winning the prestigious Carrouthers Prize. As her fictitious namesake had done, Clarissa starts her day by going to a florist. The parallels between Mrs. Dalloway's morning and Clarissa's are numerous: both days are bright and sunny; both women love the life of their respective cities; they both run into friends to whom they issue invitations; and both witness the crowd-gathering presence of celebrities— Mrs. Dalloway sees a car carrying perhaps members of the royal family or the prime minister, and Clarissa sees a member of modern day America's nobility, a movie star she recognizes as either Meryl Streep or Vanessa Redgrave. (Cunningham is playing with his readers here; he had no way of knowing that Streep would be cast as Clarissa Vaughan in the 2000 motion picture of his novel, but he perhaps trusts that his readers will know that Redgrave starred in Marleen Gorris's 1998 motion picture adaptation of *Mrs. Dalloway*.)

The Mrs. Woolf sections of the novel take place on a day in 1923. Virginia Woolf is struggling with the opening line of a novel in progress whose working title is *The Hours* but is published two years later as *Mrs. Dalloway*. Cunningham convincingly presents Woolf's possible state of mind as she creates, rejects, accepts, and seeks the necessary balance, always careful to not let her work (or herself) "wander into a realm of incoherence from which it might never return." Like Clarissa, Virginia is planning a party too, a tea for her sister Vanessa and Vanessa's children.

Laura Brown is the third protagonist. Laura's day begins in Los Angeles in 1949, and like Clarissa and Virginia, Laura is planning a party: a birthday party for her husband, Dan. While Laura has characteristics of all of Cunningham's struggling mothers, she is most similar to Alice Glover: both women are married to dull but well-meaning men, endure unwanted pregnancies, spend their days in the house entertaining and being entertained by their young sons, and find some release from their frustrations through baking. Laura is enthralled by Virginia Woolf and is reading all of her work, "fascinated by the idea of a woman like that, a woman of such brilliance, such strangeness, such immeasurable sorrow; a woman who had genius but still filled her pocket with a stone and waded out into a river." Laura imagines that she too has "a touch of brilliance" and desires some time away from Dan, her three-year-old son, Richie, and a bothersome neighbor to explore her capabilities, even just two hours alone to read *Mrs. Dalloway* would be greatly appreciated.

Cunningham intricately weaves the activities and the innermost thoughts of his three protagonists—Virginia the writer, Laura the reader, and Clarissa the character—and transports his reader back and forth through time. Clarissa stops at Richard's apartment to check on his condition and to remind him of the party. Richard is in the advanced stages of AIDS, and it is unlikely that he will be strong enough to attend either the presentation of his prize or Clarissa's party; but Clarissa, who loves him, publishes his work, and has taken care of him as his illness made it more and more difficult for him to take care of himself, reassures him that all will be well and she will return to pick him up that afternoon.

Virginia struggles with her novel, her servants, and her husband, Leonard. Leonard has moved Virginia to their home in the countryside hoping that some time away from London might be good for her. Her unhappiness is reflected in her intention of having Mrs. Dalloway commit suicide. The visit from her sister and the children, however, increases her desire to return to the life she loves in the city. Leonard acquiesces to Virginia's wish. The day comes to an end with Virginia deciding on Mrs. Dalloway's fate: "Clarissa, sane Clarissa—exultant, ordinary Clarissa—will go on, loving London, loving her life of ordinary pleasures, and someone else, a deranged poet, a visionary, will be the one to die."

Laura makes a decision too. Her morning has been a time of disappointment, desire, and desperation. The birthday cake is imperfect; a visit from her neighbor Kitty awakens a latent lesbianism in her; and nothing she does escapes the ever watching eyes of Richie. When Kitty leaves, Laura tips the birthday cake into the garbage, bakes another and decorates it to perfection, takes Richie to a sitter, and drives to an expensive hotel, the Normandy. Safely settled in a room Laura allows herself the luxury of considering the possibility that she is on the brink of a nervous breakdown or even the madness that drove Woolf to suicide. She opens her copy of *Mrs. Dalloway,* and for the next two and one half hours, "it seems, somehow, that she has left her own world and entered the realm of the book." And like Mrs. Dalloway, Laura discovers the peaceful contentment that results from the realization that life can be ended, that suicide is a readily available option. "It would be as simple, she thinks, as checking into a hotel." But she has not reached that stage yet. "She loves life, loves it hopelessly, at least at certain moments." She returns to her family, those "certain moments" strengthened by the knowledge that she is free to choose an alternative.

Clarissa arrives at Richard's apartment in the afternoon to prepare him for the evening's festivities. She finds him "perched on the sill of the open window, straddling it, with one emaciated leg still in the apartment and the other, invisible to her, dangling out over five stories." To the terrified Clarissa, Richard looks "insane and exalted." He tells her, "I don't know if I can face this. You know. The party and the ceremony, and then the hour after that, and the hour after that." Clarissa tries desperately to assure him that he does not have to do anything he does not want to do and that better days lie ahead for him. Unconvinced, Richard tells her he loves her, and speaking the final words Woolf wrote to her husband—"I don't think two people could have been happier than we've been,"—he slides off the windowsill and falls to his death.

Late that night Clarissa and her long time companion and lover, Sally, arrive home with an elderly woman. All the party preparations except for the flowers have been put away by Julia, Clarissa's daughter conceived through artificial insemination. They make the old woman comfortable and put together a late night buffet. The old woman, whom Clarissa and Sally have brought from Toronto, is a retired librarian, a woman who left her husband, son, and daughter decades earlier and began a new life for herself in Canada. Her husband died of cancer; her daughter was killed by a drunk driver; and her son committed suicide that afternoon. She is Laura Brown, mother of Richie/Richard. It was her abandonment of him that haunted Richard's life and made his work soar. As the four women gather to eat, Clarissa thinks,

> We throw our parties; we abandon our families to live alone in Canada; we struggle to write books that do not change the world, despite our gifts and our unstinting efforts, our most extravagant hopes. We live our lives, do whatever we do, and then we sleep—it's as simple and ordinary as that.... There's just this for consolation: an hour here or

there when our lives seem, against all odds and expectations, to burst open and give us everything we've ever imagined, though everyone but children (and perhaps even they) knows these hours will inevitably be followed by others, far darker and more difficult. Still, we cherish the city, the morning; we hope, more than anything, for more.

This is perhaps Cunningham's answer to the question of how ought we to live: we should live honestly, hopefully, and lovingly, remaining open to life's offerings.

The novel was a critical and commercial success. Robert Plunket, a contributor to the *Advocate,* confessed that although he has "a very low tolerance for arty writers who publish stories in the *New Yorker* and then write novels that turn out to be homages to Virginia Woolf," reading Cunningham's book he was "overwhelmed by the possibilities of art." Of all the accolades, however, the one that may best summarize Cunningham's accomplishment can be found in an unsigned *Publishers Weekly* review of August 31, 1998, which says that *The Hours* "makes a reader believe in the possibility and depth of a communality based on great literature, literature that has shown people how to live and what to ask of life."

A RESPITE IN PROVINCETOWN

The Hours won the Pulitzer Prize for fiction and the PEN/Faulkner Award in 1999. Cunningham had previously been awarded a Guggenheim fellowship (1993), a Whiting Writers' Award (1995), a National Endowment for the Arts fellowship (1998), and an O. Henry Award (1999) for his short story "Mister Brother." Cunningham took a break from writing fiction in 1999 and accepted an offer from Crown Publishers to contribute a volume to their series of literary travel books. For his subject Cunningham chose a place that had been a refuge for him since 1981—Provincetown, Massachusetts. The book is not only an account of the history of

Provincetown since its incorporation in 1720 but also an exhaustive guided tour led by Cunningham through the small town, which is "three miles long and … two blocks wide." Chapters on Provincetown's homes, commercial buildings, weather, year-round citizens, and summer tourists are interspersed with prose and poetry by those who have experienced the town's peculiar charms: Norman Mailer, Stanley Kunitz, Mark Doty, and others.

In his *New York Times* column "At Home With" for October 24, 2002, John Leland reported that writing *Land's End: A Walk through Provincetown* was a way for Cunningham to shelter himself "from the emotional whirlwind" that followed the success of *The Hours.* Leland quotes Cunningham as saying, "I was bouncing off the walls. I was trying to start a novel, and I couldn't even think about it, let alone write it." He described this work in progress (scheduled for publication under the title *Specimen Days* by Farrar, Straus and Giroux in 2005) to Tony Peregrin in an interview for the March–April 2003 issue of the *Gay & Lesbian Review Worldwide:*

> I can't reveal the project's title just yet but I will tell you that it features three linked novellas: the first is a gothic horror story set in the past, the second is a thriller set in the present day, and the third is a science fiction story that takes place in the future. Each novella contains the same set of characters, including an appearance by Walt Whitman!

Ernest Hemingway admonished budding authors to write what they know. Cunningham knows what it is to be a gay man in America, and he is acutely aware of the societal changes that have given a new look to the American family photo album, but he cannot be pigeonholed as a genre writer, because he so skillfully presents a character's sexuality as only one aspect of the whole person. However, he is concerned that some who would benefit from his work may avoid or overlook it if it is retailed as mainstream fiction. Cunningham told Barbara Shoup:

> That's the kind of funny doubleness. On the one hand, I want them to be on the shelf with all the other books, not in a special section. On the other hand, if it could be of some help to a sixteen-year old gay kid, yeah. And if that kid's more likely to find it in a gay and lesbian section—this is where it gets complicated. I get criticized—I have arguments with other gay and lesbian writers—about the relative absence of politics in my books, which is intentional…. Part of what's fascinating and difficult about human life is that everybody is the hero of their own story, everybody thinks they're doing the right thing. It seems to me that novels are uniquely equipped to help us understand that.

Selected Bibliography

WORKS OF MICHAEL CUNNINGHAM

NOVELS
Golden States. New York: Crown, 1984.
A Home at the End of the World. New York: Farrar, Straus and Giroux, 1990.
Flesh and Blood. New York: Farrar, Straus and Giroux, 1995.
The Hours. New York: Farrar, Straus and Giroux, 1998.
Specimen Days. New York: Farrar, Straus and Giroux, 2005.

NONFICTION
I Am Not This Body: Photographs by Barbara Ess. New York: Aperture, 2001. (Cunningham contributes brief personal essays about science and Ess's photographic art.)
Land's End: A Walk through Provincetown. New York: Crown, 2002.

UNCOLLECTED SHORT STORIES
"Cleaving." *Atlantic Monthly,* January 1981, 60–66.
"Bedrock." *Redbook,* April 1981, 92–93, 146–155.
"Pearls." *Paris Review* 24, no. 86:202–209 (winter 1982).

"White Angel." *New Yorker,* July 25, 1988, 25–33.

"Ghost Night." *New Yorker,* July 24, 1989, 30–40.

"Clean Dreams." *WigWag,* August 1990, 53–58.

"Grave." *Blind Spot* 10:52–53 (spring/summer 1997).

"Mister Brother." *DoubleTake* no. 14:92–94 (fall 1998).

"A Room at the Normandy." *New Yorker,* September 21, 1998, 120–131.

CRITICAL AND BIOGRAPHICAL STUDIES

Allen, Brooke. "A Feeling of Disjunction." *New Criterion* 17, no. 10:81–84 (June 1999). (Review of *The Hours.*)

Eagan, Joseph M. "Michael Cunningham." In *Gay & Lesbian Literature,* Vol. 2. Edited by Tom Pendergast and Sara Pendergast. Detroit: St. James, 1998. Pp. 101–103.

Eder, Richard. "Squaring a Triangle." *Los Angeles Times Book Review,* November 18, 1990, pp. 3, 12. (Review of *A Home at the End of the World.*)

———. "The Greater the Risk." *Los Angeles Times Book Review,* April 9, 1995, pp. 3, 7. (Review of *Flesh and Blood.*)

Hattersley, Michael. "Is Provincetown Doomed?" *Gay & Lesbian Review* 9, no. 5:39–41 (September–October 2002).

Jones, Paul Christian. "Michael Cunningham." In *Dictionary of Literary Biography,* Volume 292, *Twenty-First-Century American Novelists.* Edited by Lisa Abney and Suzanne Disheroon-Green. Detroit: Gale, 2004. Pp. 55–61.

Kornblatt, Joyce Reiser. "Such Good Friends." *New York Times Book Review,* November 11, 1990, pp. 12–13. (Review of *A Home at the End of the World.*)

Leland, John. "This Is the House the Book Bought." *New York Times,* October 24, 2002, sec. F, pp. 1, 8. (An article concerning *Land's End* in Leland's "At Home With" column.)

MacDougall, Ruth Doan. "Giving New Twists and Fresh Style to Timeless Coming-of-Age Theme." *Christian Science Monitor,* May 4, 1984, p. 20. (Review of *Golden States.*)

"Michael Cunningham." In *Contemporary Authors New Revisions, Vol. 96.* Gale, 2003. Pp. 81-83.

"Michael Cunningham." In *Contemporary Literary Criticism,* Vol. 34. Edited by Sharon K. Hall. Detroit: Gale, 1985. Pp. 40–42.

Plunket, Robert. "Imagining Woolf." *Advocate,* December 8, 1998, p. 87. (Review of *The Hours.*)

Publishers Weekly. Review of *The Hours.* 245, no. 35 (August 31, 1998), p. 46.

Royte, Elizabeth. "Family Affair." Review of *Golden States. Village Voice,* September 4, 1984, p. 52.

Seaman, Donna. "Flesh and Blood." *Booklist* 91, no. 10:868–869 (January 15, 1995).

———. "Where the Artists and Writers Are." *Booklist* 98, no. 21:1818–1819 (July 1, 2002).

Wittels, Alice F. Review of *Golden States. Los Angeles Times Book Review,* April 22, 1984, p. 6.

Wolitzer, Meg. "Suburban Sprawl." *New York Times Book Review,* April 16, 1995, p. 13. (Review of *Flesh and Blood.*)

INTERVIEWS

Bahr, David. "The Difference a Day Makes: After Hours with Michael Cunningham." *Poets & Writers Magazine* 27:18–23 (July–August 1999).

Coffey, Michael. "Michael Cunningham: New Family Outings," *Publishers Weekly* 245, no. 44:53–54 (November 2, 1998).

Coleman, Chris. "Novel to Stage: A Family's 2nd Act." *American Theatre* 18, no. 8:50 (October 2001). (A brief talk with Cunningham about the stage adaptation of *Flesh and Blood.*)

Gambone, Philip. "Michael Cunningham." In his *Something Inside: Conversations with Gay Fiction Writers.* Madison: University of Wisconsin Press, 1999. Pp. 142–154.

Peregrin, Tony. "Michael Cunningham after Hours." *Gay & Lesbian Review* 10, no. 2:30–33 (March–April 2003).

Shoup, Barbara (with Kimberly Campanello). "Interview: Michael Cunningham." *Other Voices* 37:175–184 (fall–winter 2002).

FILMS BASED ON NOVELS OF MICHAEL CUNNINGHAM

The Hours. Screenplay by David Hare. Directed by Stephan Daldry. Paramount Pictures and Miramax Films, 2002. (In 2003 it won a Golden Globe

Award for best picture, and Nicole Kidman, who plays Virginia, won best actress; Kidman also won an Academy Award for best actress that year.)

A Home at the End of the World. Screenplay by Keith Bunin. Directed by Michael Mayer. Warner Independent Movies, 2004.

—*CHARLES R. BAKER*

Peter Everwine

1930–

FROM 1962 THROUGH 1991, the poet Peter Everwine taught at the California State University, Fresno. Along with Philip Levine, and later C. G. Hanzlicek, he was responsible for establishing there one of the most productive and renowned creative writing programs in America (sometimes referred to as "the Fresno School," though in fact there was no "school" aspect to it, given the wide range of styles and voices among the poets). Forty or more well-known and nationally published poets today owe their careers and writing lives in large part to the influence of Peter Everwine, his poetry, and his teaching. The poets Larry Levis, David St. John, Roberta Spear, Gary Soto, Dixie Salazar, Ernesto Trejo, Kathy Fagan, Greg Pape, and Luis Omar Salinas are but a few whose skills and poetic sensibilities were influenced and shaped by the poetry and poetic sensibilities of Peter Everwine.

During his time at Fresno, Everwine was known not only for his poetry writing workshops but also for courses in which he taught poetry in translation. He presented eastern European, Aztec, Swedish, and Israeli poetry among many others. Everwine published translations of the Nauhuatl/Aztec (*In the House of Light,* 1970) and later of the Israeli poet Natan Zach (*The Static Element: Selected Poems of Natan Zach,* 1982). These voices and strategies had a profound effect on the poetry Everwine began to write in the 1960s and afterward and contributed greatly to the original voice he would develop in his own work.

Prior to the 1960s Everwine had attended the Iowa Writers Workshop and was writing and publishing poems in traditional forms, largely in the starched manner and voice of the early 1950s. The new modes of expression he began to explore in the 1960s and early 1970s, however, led in 1973 to the volume *Collecting the Animals,* which won the Lamont Poetry Prize from the Academy of American Poets and established his reputation as a poet of unique voice and vision in America. Since then he has published five more poetry collections and seen his poems published in the *New Yorker, Antaeus, Field, Iowa Review, Ohio Review, Crazyhorse,* and *Kayak,* among many other prominent literary journals, and his poems have been widely anthologized.

Everwine's is a singular voice in American poetry. The influences of other cultures and their poetry have been distilled in his poems so that there is little occasional information offered, unlike much American poetry over the last thirty years. In addition to the subtle influences from the Aztec and Israeli poetry, Everwine discovered some different possibilities for his poems from reading many eastern European poets. His poems speak in a more universal voice than we see in much contemporary American poetry, a voice that is elemental, uncircumscribed in its imagery and symbols. The themes and occasions of his poetry often take up emotion or build a vision that stretches across the centuries, that is not limited by a strict time and setting. Yet he is one of the most accessible of poets. Although he rarely points to the facts and details of his own, autobiographical life, the humanity at the emotional center of each of his poems is unmistakable. He values the myth and the fable, the cross-cultural and almost Jungian images that connect all readers.

LIFE AND CAREER

Everwine's parents, Peter Borello and Lena Castelnuovo, were married in 1928 and lived in Leechburg, Pennsylvania. His mother was pregnant with Peter when his father was killed in an auto accident. She went to live with her half-brother, Joseph Grosso, and his wife, Nota, in Detroit where Peter was born on February 14, 1930. Not long after his birth, Everwine and his mother returned to Leechburg to live with his maternal grandmother, who had returned to the United States from a stay in Italy. His grandfather Paolo remained in Italy, and Everwine did not meet him until he was about nine years old. Leechburg, about forty miles north of Pittsburgh, had many coal mines and a steel mill, and all of Everwine's uncles worked in one or the other.

His mother worked, so his grandmother, Pinota (a nickname for Josepina) and her friends looked after him as a child. Pinota came from Perosa Canavese, a village in Piemonte (the Piedmont region in northern Italy), and the first language in the house was a dialect of Piemontais. All his uncles and his mother spoke the dialect, and it was really his first language, before English. He saw his paternal grandparents only once or twice in his life due to some long-standing quarrel.

While he was still a child, Peter's mother married a local doctor, Merle Everwine, who was a widower. He adopted Peter, provided a good education for him, and Peter always thought of him as his father. In 1947 Everwine enrolled at Northwestern University for premed and discovered English, studying with Jean Hagstrum, Richard Ellmann, and Frank O'Connor among others. W. H. Auden and Dylan Thomas came to campus, and Everwine heard them read.

In 1951 Everwine married Katharine Lammers, and he attended the Bread Loaf Writers Conference, trying to write fiction. He was drafted into the army and served in Germany from 1952 to 1954. Sid Corman was publishing a magazine called *Origin* then, and Everwine found a copy, began to try his hand at poetry, and sent in submissions. Corman returned the poems but each time wrote encouraging and patient notes advising him which poets to read. Everwine was discharged from the army in 1954 and went to Iowa for graduate school. There he met and befriended many poets in the writers workshop: Donald Justice, Philip Levine, Robert Mezey, Michael Harper, Don Petersen, Mark Strand, Henri Coulette, Constance Urdang, and others. Robert Bly was at Iowa teaching for a while, but Everwine missed the years of Robert Lowell and John Berryman.

In 1956 Everwine and his wife had a son, Christopher Borello. Everwine was awarded a Jones Fellowship (now called the Stegner Fellowship) from Stanford, and in 1958 he moved his family west to Palo Alto, California. He had long admired the poetry and criticism of Yvor Winters, who taught there. Everwine's poetry at this time was formal, and he had begun to publish in the *Paris Review, Poetry, Western Review,* and *Perspective,* among other literary journals. The Hillside Press of Mt. Vernon, Iowa, published a collection of his formal poems in 1958 in a book titled *The Broken Frieze.* After the year at Stanford, Peter and his family moved back to Iowa, where he taught in the English department and completed his Ph.D. thesis, *Winter Stop-Over.* Not long after that the writing froze up for him, and his marriage to Katharine ended in divorce.

In 1962 Everwine married Sandra Shearer, and with help and encouragement from Philip Levine he moved to Fresno to teach at California State University, Fresno (then Fresno State College). His son, David Dominic, was born to them in Fresno in 1963. Everwine took a sabbatical in 1968 and went to Jocotepec, Mexico, a small fishing village near Guadalajara. The writing had been stalled for some time now, but in Jocotepec, Everwine came across some Spanish translations of Aztec poems; working the Spanish versions into English had Everwine working again, and this would lead to the breakthrough for his own new work. The Aztec translations were published as *In the House of Light,* in a striking limited edition by Kim Merker's Stone Wall Press in 1970, and some were included with the new free-verse poems Everwine wrote between 1969 and 1971 in *Collecting the Animals,* his first trade book, published by Atheneum in 1973. In addition to winning the Lamont Award for that year, *Collecting the Animals* was also a finalist for the National Book Award.

In 1975 Everwine traveled to Italy. He had received a National Endowment for the Arts grant in poetry for 1975 and also was awarded a Guggenheim Fellowship for 1976. In Italy he visited Perosa Canavese, his grandparents' hometown, where he still had relatives; he also had family in Ivrea, close by, both towns not far from Turin in the Piedmont region. This trip led to the section of Italian poems in *Keeping the Night,* published by Atheneum in 1977. About this time his marriage to Sandra Shearer ended and he met an Israeli, Shulamith Starkman, whom he would marry in 1990. She introduced Everwine to a good deal of Israeli-Jewish culture, and he became familiar with and very fond of Tel Aviv. With Shulamith he began to translate Israeli poetry, especially the work of Natan Zach, who was largely unknown then in the United States. Everwine introduced himself to Zach and showed him his translations as well as his own work. This led to the book of translations of selected poems by Zach, *The Static Element,* which Atheneum brought out in 1982, a year in which Everwine also received a Fulbright to Israel. A year later, in 1983, Everwine was invited by the State Department/United States Information Agency to represent the United States at the Struga International Festival in Macedonia. There he met and read with the eminent Spanish poet Rafael Alberti.

Everwine retired from teaching at California State University in Fresno in 1991, and his marriage to Starkman ended in divorce in 1992. In 2003 Sutton Hoo Press published a selection of new poems, *Speaking of Accidents,* in a limited edition. With William Kelly of Brighton Press, Everwine collaborated on an artist's book, a limited-edition handmade volume titled *Figures Made Visible in the Sadness of Time* (2003), which combines new poems by Everwine with original etchings by Kelly. In 2004 the University of Pittsburgh Press brought out *From The Meadow: Selected and New Poems,* and in 2005 Sutton Hoo Press will publish a book of new translations from the Aztec, *From the Flower Courtyard.*

EARLY WORK

The Broken Frieze, the collection of Everwine's early formal poems published in 1958 by the Hillside Press as No. 26 in the Cornell College Chapbook Series, contains fifteen poems, most of them one-page lyrics cast in the strict, formal structures of the 1950s—quatrains, iambic pentameter, rhyme schemes often in an *abab* pattern. Some of the poems had appeared in notable journals—*Poetry, Western Review,* and *Perspective.* The one longer poem, "The Voyager," had appeared in the anthology *Homage To Baudelaire,* published in 1957 by the redoubtable Harry Duncan's Cummington Press. "The Voyager," a blank-verse poem in two eighteen-line sections, is a meditation taking off from Baudelaire's poetic quest and can be viewed as an ars poetica or a kind of secular metaphysics. It is cast largely in a formal voice and diction, and yet as the poet Henri Coulette asserts in the preface to the book, a contemporary idiom and concrete aspect of vision is at work here. The following passage from the middle of the first section is much more limber and accessible than the phrasing in much formal poetry from those times:

Might follow with his mind the sail's goodbye
To what the mind enclosed, for images
Released the infinite expanse of things—
Horizons, archipelagoes that burned
Past Martinique, past China and the dreams …

In "The Glass Tent" a reader comes across a quality and specificity of imagination that is fresh and unusual in such forms:

…. Luminous fish that looked
like uncles; a whiskered face puckered
in an old aunt's kiss; tall, lacy kelp
waving in a tin-type parlor.

Indeed, this elegy for his father is the most direct and emotionally complete poem in the book as well as the least formal. It is a poem of dark puns and highly inventive imagery and diction, yet a poem rendered close to the bone, without any unearned embellishment.

Most of the poems are cast in *abab* quatrains or are sonnets or variations on the sonnet form; they struggle in their forms and attendant dictions, which are often holdovers from earlier decades and centuries. Here is part of the first stanza of "Angel and Unicorn and Butterfly," a poem of five six-line stanzas rhymed *abbcac:*

That I would have portend your birth,
And from the fabled woods wherein they lie
Come hence to bless your worth.

Nevertheless, despite the poems' muscle-bound restrictions of inherited form and end rhyme, and their penchant for proclaiming generalities, a reader can often find in these early poems the original and clear phrasemaking that adumbrates and announces Everwine's specific talent and poems to come. The sestet from the Petrarchan sonnet "Designs on a Point of View" offers a considerably more natural and contemporary idiom:

Design means supper to the bird, not flight,
Not simply the release, although that, too,

Is part of it. And the tree that shapes the night
Will also aim the bird, give contour to
A local habitation where the eye
Is rooted, where the bird defines the sky.

A number of the poems that came after this book, and which were contained in Everwine's 1959 thesis, *Winter Stop-Over,* are masterfully handled, employing a diction and phrasing appropriate to a specific subject and vision. As such they are some of the best—if least celebrated—formal work of the time. (The thesis is available in the stacks of the University of Iowa library.) Especially compelling are "Small Voice from the Wings," "Winter Stop-Over," and "To My Father's Ghost," whose third and last stanza runs:

Old mole,
Oh dear, unsponsored ghost, lie still!
The mind, unravelled, would be whole.
I am my own, my own increase.
Yet from your savage hill
The dead still walk where definitions cease.

IN THE HOUSE OF LIGHT

Following his return to the University of Iowa in 1959 Everwine's writing hit a stasis; he became disenchanted with formal poetry and did not write for several years. In "An Interview with Peter Everwine" with Jon Veinberg and Christopher Buckley in *Snake Nation Review,* Everwine explained that during his sabbatical year in Mexico he discovered the need for writing again and that the discovery of the Spanish translations of the Nahuatl/Aztec poems helped restore his poetic energy and vision.

I got hold of some Spanish translations, and was struck by how extraordinarily simple and beautiful and clear and resonant those poems were, and I started to work with those and feed back and forth my own work into that. They were influential, I think, somehow they fit, if not my style or my voice of whatever it is one talks about in poetry, they filled some sense of need you have to be in touch with what you think of as legitimate poetry. That was in important source; it fed something and while not by direct imitation, it fed a sense of what is important in language, what is important to do with words.

Everwine had intended to spend his sabbatical time in Guadalajara, but he happened to meet some Americans there who were returning to the States and who needed to rent their house in the fishing village of Jocopetec. This change was fortuitous, for it enabled Everwine to meet Jesus Urzua, an agronomist in the area who showed him the Spanish versions of Aztec poetry by Angel M. Garibay in the second and third volumes of *Poesía náhuatl* (Mexico City, 1965, 1968) as well as Miguel León-Portilla's *Trece poetas del mundo azteca* (Mexico City, 1967).

Returning to Fresno, Everwine found a letter from Kim Merker, a poet he had met in Iowa City and a printer of limited-edition books who had gained a substantial reputation in the poetry world from printing volumes of Ezra Pound as well as first books by such young poets as Mark Strand and Philip Levine. Kim asked if Everwine had a book he might consider for publication. Everwine had thirty translations/adaptations of the Spanish derived from the Nahuatl that he thought were worthy, and the result was *In The House of Light,* published by Merker's Stone Wall Press in 1970. In the preface to the book Everwine addresses the question of rendering versions of poems at two languages removed:

the Spanish itself is likely to be far removed from the original systems of the Nahuatl.

And yet, the poems seemed worth doing. In Mexico the continuity of Indian life is inescapable and real. The Aztec poets speak from four and five centuries in the past. Yet I lived in a village that rose form the dust of Nahuatl-speaking tribes and still bore its Nahuatl name. My neighbor, to the north, spent an afternoon pointing out to me the flowers in his garden, naming them in that strange tongue. The poems, beautiful in themselves, still carried this presence.

Everwine continues in his preface to advise the reader of the nature of the Aztec poetry, that it was/is a public poetry, a ceremonial and oral poetry, and the many repetitions were evidence of a "quality of mind" committed to a religious order. To praise the gods and the beauty of the world that derives from them in the natural elements is one of the main themes of these Nahuatl poets. A representative poem for its themes, its rich imagery, and its simple and direct address is "To Tlaoc of the Rain"; here are the second, third, and last stanzas:

God of water and rain
Is there anything
Is there anything great as you are
How many flowers you have
How many songs
Giving delight in the time of rain

Everything I have you have given me
My fan my fine green plumes and tobaccos
My curved staff my ensigns of flowers
Here in the house of moss
In the house of light

How many flowers you have
How many songs
Giving delight in the time of rain
To you I give this song
This single flower
Which is my heart

While Everwine's own poems do not take up the same voice and images of the Aztec, there is a concision, a directness of statement linking the two. Like all good poets, the Aztec poets were as much concerned with the human condition as with the beautiful elements of the natural world, the simple pleasures of song. There is an introspective quality in much of this work, a sophistication of thought that belies the simplicity of the rhetoric. "Moquihuitzin's Answer" is a short poem that contains all of these qualities:

I have been considering everything
And what I think
Is this—
I was born to suffer on this earth
I, Moquihuitzin.

Each time I feel satisfied
Or happy
I say to myself—
Perhaps it will end.
Then I go wandering everywhere
Everywhere, shouting about things.

Wherever flowers are opening
Or the dancers whirl, there
My heart lives.
Perhaps it will end.

Herbert Leibowitz, in reviewing *Collecting the Animals* (which contains thirteen of the poems from *In The House of Light*) for the *New York Times Book Review* (April 12, 1973) commented particularly on what he felt was the favorable influence of the Aztec translations upon Everwine's new poems: "His reverence for the earth, for 'the god of living things' and 'the place of the dead,' his ability to look at things clearly, seem to have been strengthened by his contact with Aztec poetry." As recently as June 22, 2003, the poet Edward Hirsch, in the "Poet's Choice" column of the *Washington Post,* was praising the power and gravity of the songs and meditations of ancient Aztec poetry, a poetry he discovered thirty years previously in the translations of Peter Everwine.

COLLECTING THE ANIMALS

In 1972, when *Collecting the Animals* was the Lamont Poetry Selection, there were many fewer poetry prizes than there are presently, and the Lamont Award—then for a first book—was one of the most notable and coveted. In many ways this was Everwine's most important book, as it announced a new talent and important poetic voice on the American scene. At the same time, this collection gave us a poet who had gone his own way, who was not aligned with any of the contemporary schools or styles. In addition to the selected Aztec poems comprising the second section of the book, *Collecting the Animals* opens with a translation of the Israeli poet T. Karmi, "The Condition." The poem has striking connections with both Everwine's own voice in his new free-verse poems and to the Aztec adaptations. In the first few stanzas of the translation we can see an economy, a simplicity, and an introspection that is at once human, accessible, and complex:

First, I'll sing. Later, perhaps, I'll speak.
I'll repeat the words

Like someone memorizing his face at morning.
I'll return to my silences

The way the moon wanes …

The poems here may also echo some reading of the eastern European poets, for they are not occasional, not ego-centered. The voice is often objective, almost disembodied, and yet it speaks without elevation or self-importance. Among many eastern European poets Everwine has read, taught, and admired is the German poet Johannes Bobrowski. In the interview quoted earlier, Everwine commented on him:

I guess I get more and more interested in the kind of poem that doesn't need all that information coming into it, is very close to the sense of—it's almost a physical sense, a kind of suspended sense where everything is just about ready to break into meaning.… And especially Bobrowski; he has that lyrical voice, but he's in touch always with kind of imminence, and he's the poet among all those others I've mentioned who I really feel is a spirit of poetry, or what is a spirit of poetry for me. I'm not trying now to talk about direct imitation of a technique or a voice, just the sense of where does the poem sit, for your spirit.

There is a credible humility in these poems, a tenderness for the least detail in the world, which his attention and care make luminous. Bone, leaf, panorama, or part of speech, Everwine works to identify in any particular how our lives—at least in the attention of the moment—might claim transcendence. In Miguel de Unamuno's story "Saint Emmanuel the Good, Martyr" the protagonist, although failing in his orthodox beliefs, posits that there is another, more luminous world, but it is shining within this one. The poems of *Collecting the Animals* call us time and again to what we can find shining in this world, and with his first poem in the book, he shows us "How It Is."

> This is how it is—
>   One turns away
>   and walks out into the evening.
>   There is a white horse on the prairie, or a river
>   that slips away among dark rocks.
>
>   One speaks, or is about to speak,
>   not that it matters.
>
>   What matters is this—
>
>   It is evening.
>   I have been away a long time.
>   Something is singing in the grass.

The essential eloquence of this poem of homecoming is compelling. Where we usually push for specifics, identifiable, occasional details, Everwine has given us imagery that is archetypal, almost Jungian in its place. And yet the place the poet sees is a place every one of us knows almost by heart. This is the clearest of visions, of voices, beyond any poetic pretension. This, like so many other poems in the book, is something singing.

The Pure Clear Word is almost a cliché of contemporary poetry. But Everwine, as surely as James Wright, valued it, found it in these poems. Imagine a child growing up, speaking

Italian first, finding the magical names for birds in English, the first simple and generic word multiplying into the exotic syllables and naming the varieties of birds—then years later writing the poem that would be faithful to that moment, to the direct and mellifluous images, the small bell-like ringing, the flight of the sounds. Here is "Learning to Speak."

> As a child running loose,
> I said it this way: *Bird.*
> *Bird,* a startled sound at field's edge.
> The sound my mouth makes, pushing away the cold.
> So, at the end of this quiet afternoon,
> wanting to write the love poems I've never written,
> I turn from the shadow in the cottonwood
> and say blackbird, as if to you.
> *There is the blackbird. Black bird,* until its darkness
> is the darkness of a woman's hair falling
> across my upturned face.
> And I go on speaking into the night.
> *The oriole, the flicker,*
> *the gold finch....*

Everwine's transitions and moves here are seamless and amazing. After the child's first word and the wonderful image of the mouth pushing away the cold, he turns to the end of a *quiet* afternoon, an afternoon just waiting for the sounds of the poem. He is writing a love poem—an ars poetica perhaps, a poem about the pure love of language and sound, and at the same time a poem of romance to a "you" who is the object of the line "Wanting to write the love poems I've never written." Everwine joins two joys here, two loves, and finds that full way around the cliché of the heart to find the fresh language and trust it, and to go on speaking into the night.

Many poets have written "double" poems, and object or riddle poems are an old strategy; however, few, if any, have combined the two and written a poem that so subtly takes on the enigma of mortality, a poem that allows the conceit of the poem to rise out of its subject, as effortlessly as Everwine's "The Coat."

> After so many years,
> standing with me in the same mirror,
> it is almost transparent.
> In the morning I rise up and enter it—
> this skin frayed at the wristbones; this suitcase
> of old weathers, slick with shine, sagging
> with the weight of inner pockets.
>
> At night I slide it off, and the darkness
> slides into it, slips its fingers inside
> and touches what the day has left—
> old bills, dry webs of hair, salt,
> a leaf thin and sharp as a birds' thigh.
> What do I care what the dark does,
> rifling my coat like an old wife?
>
> Throw it on a stool to beg,
> dance with it the long nights,
> fold it after the funeral—what do I care?
> When I lie down naked to sleep
> it wears my own slouch.
> I breathe in. Breathe out.
> in a dark corner, it fills.

The coat, having been with the poet so long, is almost a second skin, and how wonderfully apt and resonant that it sags "with the weight of inner pockets," implying of course all that is carried and kept hidden, inward in oneself, and at the same time coming quite accurately and naturally from the regular construction of coats. And what a precise imagination we are presented with here as the darkness fingers what is left in the coat's pockets—the "dry webs of hair" and that closely, so impeccably observed "leaf thin and sharp as a bird's thigh." Now, at night, without him it starts to breathe, to take on a life of its own. It is rare to find a poem with so much fidelity to the natural object and equally with so much resonant imagination.

"The Heavy Angel" makes a similar connection. Hunting, perhaps hiking, crossing a salt slough the poet feels the weight of the "other" among the natural elements, sees his spirit/ psyche, a vague image of himself, of us all before we were weighted down with a society of concerns and were, perhaps like Adam, fresh from the waters. Here is the end of the poem:

> I seek you down the acrid street of dead fathers
> or in the dark lakes of the child I was,
> sensing your presence then, the shadow
> you make behind my closed lid.
> But it is here I know you best,
> surprise you in the solitary places—
> my boots sinking in the dark muck
> and the snipe leaping from the grass,
> crying its shrill *scape, scape.*
> and I bend to meet you,
> my likeness, my heavy angel,
> seeing as if for the first time
> your face wild and shining,
> still wet with the sea.

Collecting the Animals is filled with poems that speak this clearly, with such a charged imagination anchored in the luminous world. But also Everwine establishes a unique voice and rhetoric in many of these poems, especially in the elegies, wherein he combines a tightly made, deep imagism with a direct and almost angry address to the fates and losses in life, and yet he cherishes, fiercely, the affection he can remember and reclaim. "Drinking Cold Water" is an elegy for his grandmother and for his lost childhood. There is, in the clipped and fresh phrasing, a laconic realization, an original voice. Following are the last two stanzas of one of the most memorable poems in the book:

> Tonight I brought my bundle of years
> to an empty house.
> When I opened it, a boy walked out—
> drinking cold water, watching the
> moon rise slim and shining over your house.
> whatever it was I wanted
> must have come and gone.
>
> Twenty years, grandmother.
> Here I stand
> In the poverty of my feet,
> And I know what you'd do:
> you'd enter your black shawl,

step back into the shadows of you hair.
And that's no help tonight.
All I can think of is your house—
the pump at the sink
spilling a trough of clear
cold water from the well—
and you, old love,
sleeping in your dark dress
like a hard, white root.

Almost all of the poems have a mystical and inner shining and create a vision of the earth that is almost preternatural. The last poem in the book, "Gray Poem," is the longest and adumbrates the concerns of the volume to follow, which takes up the lives of many of Everwine's relatives. "Gray Poem" begins in the months of San Joaquin Valley fog, an atmosphere so thick and dim that it is easily otherworldly. In this kind of limbo, the poet's grandmother and father return, the world is usual and strange. Here are two of the four sections:

1

Another gray morning
in this month of valley fog.
Everything seems old, little threads and roots
sucking a cold sea.

When I look into it, the mirror
cups my face in its silver hands.
I hear my grandmother whispering
beneath her shawl—

Cloth of forgetfulness
Skull of the one night
Shag of wisdom
White grass of misery

In the yards, our children
are turning into clouds.

4

The window darkens.
A man bends over me
and kisses my cheek.

When the sun rose, he says,
I turned up my hands to the light.
Every road was on fire.

I call him father.
He is gray
and his shoes are gray.

Everwine has a superb ear for speech and imagery, for capturing the spells, the poetry of the past—he knows a sure economy whether he is writing the poem of images or the poem that relies on turns of rhetoric, and most all of the poems give us a brilliant combination of both.

In *Collecting the Animals* a reader does not come across any religious terms or orthodox beliefs or justifiable arguments with God about our precipitous place on earth facing the unknown. Yet Everwine holds out a world to us in a language both rich and spare and works at everyday phenomena to understand and appreciate a life and a world that in parts, and with the right eyes and attention, is elementally sacred.

KEEPING THE NIGHT

In 1977 Everwine published his second book with Atheneum, *Keeping the Night.* Just prior to the release of this trade edition, a letterpress edition was issued by Penumbra Press of Lisbon, Iowa, in a signed and numbered edition of 230, bound in boards covered with a midnight-blue cloth. In its imagery and economy of phrasing, *Keeping the Night* presents a vision even more distilled than that of *Collecting the Animals.* A darker book, *Keeping the Night* is a book of elegies, really, elegies for his Italian relatives but elegies truly for us all, for the poems take up themes of mortality in the more subtle aspects of life as well as in the more dramatic or obvious. The cover of the Atheneum edition displays an etching by Samuel Palmer, "The Homeward Star." It is a night scene, and in its two-tone blue and black sets the atmosphere for the book—the peasants are at their rustic table amid the orchard and their flocks, celebrating a meal despite the dark surrounding them, and a crescent moon and one star glimmer beyond the distance of the mountains.

This book too opens with a translation of an Israeli poet. Before section 1, Everwine offers a translation of Natan Zach, which works as a kind of invocation.

> Be careful. Open your life
> only to the wind that has touched distance.
> Suffer the absent. Speak up
> only in the nights of solitude. Know the day
> the fixed season, the moment,
> and don't beg. Pay attention to what is still.
> Learn to bless
> the shadow just beneath the skin. Don't
> hide in words. Sit with the counsel of worms,
> the wisdom of the maggot. Don't wait.

These are wise, if dark, admonitions—for the writer, for us all. In the face of mortality, take risks, pay attention, praise the spirit, live with dignity, don't waste time being clever, "hiding in words"—live. And in the first poem of the book, "Memory," Everwine show us how it is to carry that weight of mortality in your unconscious as well as your conscious mind, how it is we all give ourselves false comfort about the end of our lives. He wakes from sleep, remembering speaking a different language, being somewhere else, but there he is in his own room, realizing he was speaking with the dead and that what is important is that there is a story, a continuance. Yet he realizes he is comforting himself with this affirmation: "*Yes,* I say *Yes* / putting on my clothes, my shoes, / lying as one does to the old."

In some ways "Routes" is a more obvious poem as the speaker, recalling his boyhood house, tells us, "My window faces the funeral home. / When the exhaust fan / starts to hum /something is flying, something / is leaving at the level of the trees." But the poem moves much more subtly than one might expect past the plain facts of death. This too is a poem of memory, and the imagery, which is somewhat derived from fable, suggests a grander and more common metaphysical experience. The second section of this short poem concludes:

> I enter a street
> where the sun is falling.
> I look over my shoulder
> and follow a thread that was my coat.
> And its end is a vacant room
> and a little bench of sleep.
>
> I sit down quietly.
> A few others arrive,
> their eyelashes shining like crystals.
> One coughs in a cloud of incense.
> One closes his silver telescope.
>
> A lost town circles overhead in the dark.
> The houses hang out their lanterns.
> On a blue bike
> I race the shadows of the trees.

The imagery here is resonant, dreamlike, and fablelike with its "thread," and it concludes with a boy remembering, trying to hold onto all of the "shadows" from his town, racing them, racing mortality on his bike.

"The Fish / Lago Chapala" is a poem that also makes use of myth/fable. There is a connection here, on one level, back to Everwine's earlier book *In the House of Light,* for it is set in the village along Lake Chapala in Mexico, where he learned of the Aztecs and the rituals of their descendents still living there in Jocotepec. The poem is in two sections. The first describes the burial of a child in the village, and how everything in that village depends upon the fish and the fishing on the lake. What makes the poem—what keeps the first section from becoming a simple and spare witnessing—is the second section, which connects the past to the present. Along Lago Chapala many tear pots or vials have been found. The Aztecs who first lived there placed drops of blood and/or tears into the vials and threw them into the lake to propitiate the gods of sun or water, the ranking gods. The ritual, the memory of the past, continues to sustain life, and the italicized lines in the short second section of the poem indicate the connection to an ancient voice and my story.

the land was mesquite
prickly pear
rock
he saw his face in the water
into a tiny bowl shaped like a black nut
he let fall one tear
one drop of blood
and cast it into the lake

this happened so long ago
the tear became a fish
the drop of blood became a fish
we eat the harvest

The voice here, the style and diction, are even more concentrated, more noun-centered than the first, more narrative section of the poem. This is a style closer to the Aztec poetry, closer to chant, in which myth and magical transformation were part of a religious life and worldview and were seen as necessary to preserve that world.

The second section of *Keeping the Night* is a sequence of poems titled "Perosa Canavese," the town in the Piedmont region of northern Italy from which Everwine's family emigrated. While these are family poems, narrative poems that relate what happened to whom and when, they are also larger poems of witness, poems that by extension deal with the common experiences of immigrant families. For the most part the poems locate the incident or the most resonant image that will release the quality of that life. Typically the Everwine poem avoids discursiveness, the freighting of too much information. In the poem titled "The Wedding," Everwine selects a single moment, the event that, without a long narrative or dramatic development, best reveals the character of his grandmother and the quality of her life. She has arrived on a train in Pennsylvania with nothing more than a letter to tell her of a new land and her new husband, whom she meets for the first time as she steps off the train. The last half of the poem shows us her life and what it will come to.

They enter the grocery store of Tony Maridon,
paisano who has come before them.
There, in the dress she has worn for days,
with no blessings and no flowers,

she marries him. She marries the garlic, the wine,
the bags of salt, the dead rabbits hanging,
like bloody sleeves, the star of oil
the moon of bread …

Pinota Castelnuovo.

She never learns English.
She attends many funerals.
She herself dies, her house
is razed, her garden paved with cement.

Only then does she enter America.

No romanticizing—only the hard, spare facts make up this tribute to his Italian grandmother, whose unadorned life was emblematic of that of so many immigrants. Appropriate to her life, the poet's gesture of affection is the one line with her name.

Everwine offers a similar poem dedicated to his grandfather's life in America, "Paolo Castelnuovo." Leaving the poverty of Italy in the late 1920s, many Italian immigrants came to America and, though they found work, they were not able to escape poverty. Despite the lack of reward for hard work, the injustice of companies and bosses, Everwine looks for value in the lives of his relatives. From his grandparents he learned a sense of work and a sense of love, and from his grandfather especially, a sense of dignity in the face of the failed promise of justice and a better life. The epigraph for this poem tells a reader that each time his grandfather got mad at the bosses, he would leave and return to Italy, but he always turned back to his home in the States and to work. "The mayor struts in a green sash," and Paolo Castelnuovo curses him and leaves. But he is worn down, and when he returns from Italy for the last time, he "stands in the doorway like a man emptying / his pockets." Still, in the end, the poet sees his grandfather defying all those who oppressed him and people like him. Here is the end of the poem.

> Let the wind scatter his elements.
> I write down here
> the will he didn't leave:
> *I, Paolo, give my stone to the priests.*
> *Tell them to make it bread.*
>
> *Water I give to those loving how money sweats.*
>
> *Fire I leave to my children.*
>
> *As for air,*
> *give it to the buzzard who is the first*
> *and last of kings.*

Upon his death, all he has are the basic elements of the earth—dirt-poor, as the cliché has it. And there is irony and defiance for a hard life lived. The ability to burn it all down, to consume it, he leaves to his children. The buzzard, who lives off of the dead, survives us.

"Perosa Canavese," the title poem of the section, speaks to the poet's desires and the project of this group of poems. Everwine traveled to Italy in 1975 to see his ancestral village, looking, perhaps, to reaffirm some continuity; as the poems demonstrate, he was searching out some personal witnessing, and at the same time he did not let his observations, his poems, become overburdened with anecdotal or biographical information. He was taking the larger view of an entire community of people and wrote an elegy despite going there no doubt to discover

some personal relationship. This is the poem in its entirety.

> What I came for
> —all those miles—
> was to see the face of the village
> my people spoke of
> in the hour before sleep,
>
> and which I was given for my own
> like an empty locket,
> like a mirror in a locked room.
>
> I thought there would be a lamp
> Set among the vineyards,
> Burning a thousand years.
>
> There was, in fact, a white cemetery
> —stone after stone
> saying the alphabet of his childhood,
>
> and faces floating on the polished surfaces
> like small brown clouds that promised
> neither light nor water
> but what my shoes had brought.

There is a simple and stark elegance to these lines. The poet arrives expecting the romance of the past, of his family history, only to find in the cemetery all the same names; the entire village's descendants had moved to America. The final image of his shoes shows us a speaker who discovers nothing, nothing more than he brought with him—the weight of dust and flesh and bone, the weight of mortality. Such witnessing, such cherishing as these eleven poems provide in the elegiac mode is almost necessarily melancholy. Yet Everwine is never sentimental, and the poems are never inflated. His distilled phrasing coupled with the economy of his images and detail preserves and honors his subjects. These simple lives he holds up to the harsh light shine for us all.

The third section of *Keeping the Night* contains a sequence of love poems, "Night Letters," which in imagery and subject are entirely unpredictable. This section also offers translations of four poems from the Hebrew of Natan Zach and two of Everwine's best imagistic lyric poems, "Distance" and "Late Hour." It is, however, the penultimate poem, "Desire," that is a signature poem for this book and most of Everwine's poetry. In the space of twenty short lines, Everwine is able to suggest the scope and simple panoply of the individual human struggle. The poem works in terse images and statement, and we see and feel the speaker standing, perhaps, outside at night, ruminating about the past as the present rushes by in the dark. Then the dead arrive in memory, followed by the realization of what we truly desire.

> Like the wind
> that abandons everything.
>
> Like the drift of stars
> across the window.
>
> Something loose in my life,
> in this night that lies slack
> and heavy in my hands.
>
> A moment ago,
> I thought of the dead in their rags,
>
> One foot in the grave,
> The other—the slow one—
> Turning like an ox
> In its circle.
>
> Now another night arrives
> From years ago:
>
> Winter. The new snow banked high
> In the back yard, lit by the moon.
> A boy almost asleep,
> A low rumbling
> Deep inside the house.

What gnaws at the heart, the soul, the poet suggests, is the ongoing loss, the condition of our mortality in the face of all that we desire, which is the world, the ability to stay alive, to thrive in peace and cherish it all. How subtly yet exactly that desire is conveyed in Everwine's view, a view as simple and luminous as the images of the new snow banked high at night, that feeling of basic contentment in childhood upon which death has yet to press in, with the child drifting off to sleep, warm in winter, the furnace rumbling in the basement of the house.

Keeping the Night is less openly celebratory than *Collecting the Animals,* due probably to the poet's aging. Here joy is replaced by the small lamp of memory, the discovery of human values and affection among the litanies of loss. When Everwine writes the poem of childhood or uses imagery from the past, that poem does not move or function on simple recollection or particular autobiographical detail. Rather, as in "Desire," the image from the past is called up and tempers the darker cast of the poem. The extraordinary feature of these elegiac poems is contained in Everwine's ability to move seamlessly in and out of time, presenting the reader with the complete scope of a life; the events, tied together and informing one another, maintain a sense of immediacy in these poems. While the book does not offer joy, the poet rescues what muted light and understanding are available from the conditions and outcomes of these lives.

THE STATIC ELEMENT

In 1982 Everwine published *The Static Element: Selected Poems of Natan Zach.* His then wife, Shulamit Starkman, an Israeli, had introduced him to Zach's poetry. She would render a literal gloss of a poem and Everwine would work from that, discussing and researching the allusions and complexities of language. Zach was born in Berlin in 1930 and immigrated with his family to Israel in 1935. He is one of Israel's most important writers and was virtually unknown and untranslated in America. *The Static Element*

For me the hour will be familiar. Come now,
I'll tell myself, it isn't the first time,
you've seen them come and go.
The sun, of course, will be indifferent to my
  words.
Blood red, it will go down behind the far
  mountains
as if I were bereft in the world. There is no other
  sun.…

It is a stoic vision, a realistic one; there is no other sun. The speaker is "on to himself," aware of his own habit and self-indulgent feelings. Yet he acknowledges a creator, and angels, so it would seem he is not totally bereft—alone in the world perhaps, but he has some belief of life beyond the world. At the same time, it is the feeling that comes regardless of what he knows or believes that keeps him from joy, from contentment. The glory of the world passes again as always, no matter how well he understands his own condition, his own mortality. He must do his job, alone, facing the landscape. Here are the last four lines.

The creator puts aside his handiwork,
The angels' verdict is in the locked book.

The gate must be closed, logic tells me. At night
The dark is darkest.

Whether this scene is set one hundred or a thousand years in the past, the emotion and understanding of the speaker is the same. He knows the situation he—and by extension mankind—finds himself in regardless of logic or belief. He is facing the dark. Aside from the universal and self-contained weight of the imagery, Everwine selects and admires this poem for its timelessness, its unending immediacy.

In addition to their archetypal imagery and situations, Zach's poems also display great wit and irony, a sly, defiant humor as we find in "When God First Said": "When God first said Let there be light / He meant it would not be dark for him." God is admiring his creation and not paying attention to people multiplying on the earth, involving themselves in various strategies of pain. Zach concludes the poem with an almost existential view of the human condition: "When God first thought of night / He didn't think about sleep. / So be it, God said, I will be happy. / But they were multitudes." In Zach's view, we are clearly abandoned to our own devices.

Zach's later poetry continues to employ biblical references and a view that does not find great consolation in the sources of belief. Here is the book's last poem, "The Countries We Live In."

These flickering lights
are also typical lights—
landscapes, elements,
their end: to go on. Their end: to go out.
The sun also rises and the sun goes down
following its path to the sea
through the narrow corridor set aside for it.
From east to the uttermost end of the west
there is no new shadow
and the order of things is good—
also, there is no other order.

Here the irony and despair are conveyed more in a tone of enervation, in lines cast closer to the rhetoric of speech, lines not as embellished or embedded with images. Yet again Zach manages to give us a speaker capable of credible observations, a legitimate, suffering "I" to speak the poem, who is at once not specific or historical and yet who is not pretentious. The Old Testament phrase about "the sun also rising" is easily recognized, but almost immediately Zach undercuts its traditional resonance and power by pointing out that we have no choice in any of this. In choosing to translate such a generous selection of Zach's poems, Everwine offers readers a poetry whose strategies are unlike those of most American poetry. These translations present poems that, while not occasional and specific with autobiographical detail, nevertheless are accessible in voice and offer a consistent thematic gravity.

FROM THE MEADOW: SELECTED AND NEW POEMS

In recent years Everwine has collected his new poems in limited edition books. *Speaking of Accidents,* a group of eleven new poems, with woodcuts by Gary Young, was published in 2003 in an edition of 200 copies in boards by Sutton Hoo Press in Winona, Wisconsin. Also in 2003 Everwine collaborated with William Kelly of Brighton Press in San Diego to publish *Figures Made Visible in the Sadness of Time,* a book of new poems by Everwine and etchings by Kelly. All of these new poems are collected in the *From the Meadow: Selected and New Poems* (2004), most of them in the last two sections of the book. Everwine's interest in translation is evident in the arrangement of the poems in this book. Unlike most selected poem books, the sections here do not proceed forward or backward, book by book chronologically. While the earlier work is generally presented first, leading to the new work, the six sections are organized to display affinities of theme, subject, and voice. As well, translations are mixed in to dramatically support or contrast the dynamics inside of each section. Everwine includes some uncollected translations of the Jewish poet David Vogel, a poet largely unknown to American audiences, who was killed in a concentration camp in World War II. Selections of Aztec poems, Zach, and the T. Karmi translation from *Collecting the Animals* are also included. In the interview previously quoted, Everwine says the following about the inclusion of translations and the ordering of his *Selected and New Poems:*

> I like what takes place when poems—often from a different time and culture—are juxtaposed. We all sit down to write our poems in rooms that are crowded with ghosts—poet ghosts among them.

Why not openly invite this community of poets into our work, as if we talked together and found a common ground? It's a way of talking across borders, and I think it makes for a richer book.

Also in that interview, Everwine addresses the fact that some of his later work has a more narrative edge to it. "In general, I think I have less capacity—less interest?—these days in inventing images, and this may lead to a different perception of narrative elements. It may have something to do with aging. I don't want to lose that economy and concentration I desire." New poems—such as "Speaking of Accidents" and "In the Last Days," both of which appeared in the *New Yorker*—demonstrate this extension of method or style. In the first lines of "Speaking of Accidents" we encounter, for Everwine, a more discursive voice that admits dialogue, a little more irony, and wordplay:

> Given the general murkiness of fate
> you might, in my mother's words, "Thank
> your lucky stars," a phrase she'd drop
> into the lull between calamities
> like a rubbed stone, then nod wisely
> while it sank home, pure poetry,
> meaning she loved the sound of it
> more than its truth.
> But precisely here one needs discrimination.

Everwine maintains his economy, and images amplify the ideas, but the syntax is more embedded and complex. This more attenuated structure allows him to play off words, clichés, to work in more wit as the poem goes on to tell us of the town drunk who is run over at night by a train, transfixed by its headlight. From the wit and wordplay, Everwine concludes on a considerably more serious note, speaking eloquently about our collective desire:

> The trick is to risk collision,
> then step back at the last moment:
> that ringing in your ears
> might be construed as the rush of stars.
> We all want stars, those constellations

with the lovely names we've given them blossoming
in the icy windblown fields of the dark.
Desire is always fuming into radiance,
though even a drunk can't hope to ignore
some fixity underfoot, some vivid point
closer to home where all the lines converge—
scars, I mean,
not stars.

"In The Last Days," a poem about the death of his father long ago, is very different from the poem on the same subject in his first book, *The Broken Frieze*. The earlier poem developed image upon image, and while engaging, lacks the directness, the exact voice and profound suggestion that this new poem offers. The poem centers on the final days of his father's illness, when he sits up from a coma-like state and slaps his hands together at something invisible in the room before he goes off to sleep again. Here are the last two stanzas of the short four-stanza poem.

I don't know what my father saw then, wandering
in some mazy episode of time.
That was forty years ago. Forty years, like
yesterday.
Almost his own age now, I can see
his face before me: his wry smile of wonder,
as if something had leapt up underfoot
in the dark and sped away
as he watched.

Of course we surmise that what went speeding away—at least on one metaphorical level—was his life. So it happens to the poet speaking forty years later "like yesterday." Everwine's concision here, the exact and emblematic phrase, direct and for the most part unadorned, gives us lines of great and understated poignancy. To reach a point in poetry writing at which direct and simple expression can be rendered so seemingly effortlessly requires, it would seem, great talent and a good deal of time.

Among the new poems there is a prose poem, "Story"; a very compelling longer sequence of images and vignettes for the poet's mother, "Elegiac Fragments"; and a poem of village curses from Italy that contains a great deal of wry folk humor, "Poem for Two Voices." In the new sections of *From the Meadow* a reader will encounter poems of great range in voice, poems that explore a variety of styles and subjects. Yet at the heart of the new work, as well as the old, is the hallmark Everwine lyric in which an honest and human voice speaks in a direct music, having turned over the problems of mortality for awhile. The achievement of these poems lies not only in luminous imagery and precise statement but in their ability to come to some common and compassionate understanding about the human condition despite the dark that awaits us all. Here is the last half of "Lullaby":

No, this isn't another metaphor
meant to adorn a romantic tale.
like you, I'd kill a mosquito in a moment.
But it does make one stop and think
how driven we are—even the least—to hear
the world's incessant undersong—
even if it was never meant for us
or never anything but clamor we wanted to *be*
song—
and how much we love it, and with what sadness,
knowing we have to turn away
and enter the dark.

Selected Bibliography

WORKS OF PETER EVERWINE
The Broken Frieze. Mt. Vernon, Iowa: Hillside Press, 1958.
In the House of Light. Iowa City, Iowa: Stone Wall Press, 1970.
Collecting the Animals. New York: Atheneum, 1973. Pittsburgh: Carnegie Mellon University Press, 2000.
Keeping the Night. New York: Atheneum, 1977. Lisbon, Iowa: Penumbra Press, 1977.

The Static Element: Selected Poems of Natan Zach. New York: Atheneum, 1982.

Speaking of Accidents. Winona, Wis.: Sutton Hoo Press, 2003.

Figures Made Visible in the Sadness of Time. San Diego: Brighton Press, 2003.

From the Meadow: Selected and New Poems. Pittsburgh: University of Pittsburgh Press, 2004.

BIOGRAPHICAL AND CRITICAL STUDIES

Book World. Review of *Collecting the Animals.* Vol. 7, November 1973, p. 15.

Buckley, Christopher, and Jon Veinberg. Snake Nation Review. No. 19, 2005. "Interview with Peter Everwine."

Buckley, Christopher. "Where We Are." *American Poetry Review,* May-June 2000, p. 46.

Choice. Review of *Collecting the Animals.* Vol. 10, October 1973, p. 1191.

Choice. Review of *Keeping the Night.* Vol. 15, April 1978, p. 228.

Cooley, Peter. "Self-Reflections." *North American Review.* Vol. 11, no. 3, fall 1974, pp. 70–71.

Cotter, James Finn. "Poetry Reading." *Hudson Review* 31:207–220 (spring 1978).

Dollard, Peter. Review of *Collecting the Animals.* *Library Journal,* June 15, 1973, p. 1923.

Ewart, Gavin. "Events in the Mind." *Times Literary Supplement,* January 13, 1978, p. 38.

Georgia Review. Review of *Keeping the Night.* Vol. 32, spring 1978, p. 242.

Jacob, John. Review of *Keeping the Night. Booklist,* December 15, 1977, p. 659.

Hirsch, Edward. "Poet's Choice." *Washington Post,* June 22, 2003, p. T12.

Leibowitz, Herbert. "Poetry with and without People." *New York Times Book Review,* August 12, 1973, p. 5.

Logan, William. Review of *Keeping the Night. Library Journal,* December 1, 1977, p. 2435.

O'Neil, Catherine. Review of *Keeping the Night. New Republic,* October 22, 1978, p. 38.

Ramsey, Paul. "One Style—and Some Others: American Poetry in 1977." *Sewanee Review* 86:454 (July 1978).

—CHRISTOPHER BUCKLEY

Carol Frost

1948–

CAROL FROST, NÉE Carol Perrins, and her identical twin, Suzanne, were born in Lowell, Massachusetts, on February 28, 1948, to Renee Fellner Perrins and William Arthur Perrins. Frost barely knew her biological father, but she deeply admires her mother, a native of Vienna who arrived in America only a year before the twins' birth. At three years old, Frost moved with her mother and sister to her grandparents' apartment in Vienna. A Viennese dialect of German was her first language, but her mother forbade it in their home after she returned with her daughters to the United States for their grammar school education.

In America, Frost's childhood was turbulent. Fellner divorced Perrins shortly after their return and worked as a model, waitress, and secretary to support her children. She married Douglas Angus Kydd Jr. about four years later, when the girls were eight; the children adopted their stepfather's surname. The marriage produced a sister, Nancy, and a brother, Douglas, nine and eleven years younger than the twins, respectively. The twins dressed identically until they reached sixth grade, but Frost's memories of childhood revolve more around her mother than her siblings. Although she seldom explicitly writes of them, in her essay "A Secret Gladness" Frost credits both her twin and her mother for endowing her with "the qualities I needed to be a poet, practicing imagination's magic and invisible power." She points out, "The word *twin* is double, but their natures are single. A mother cannot solve this: the paradox is the solution. So it is in poetry."

Another formative influence was nature. The family moved often, and Frost had difficulty making friends. She found solace in nature, which consoled and freed her from what she perceived as the hypocritical adult world. In a March 6, 2003 interview for the present essay, Frost said, "I had my inclinations to be alone. I liked the great silence.... As I watched wind flicker sedges or waves break over a sandbar or as I ran from clearing to clearing in the woods, my mind settled." Her connection to the natural world—evidenced in her many poems treating nature, natural history, and its moral landscape—has never wavered and has provided her not only subject matter but also a frame for understanding herself and the world.

However Frost has never confused the natural with the divine. She attended an Episcopal church as a child and derived her early notions of morality from religious values. She sang in the church choir, memorized much of the Book of Common Prayer, and enjoyed Bible stories, but by the age of fifteen she began to feel that a religious framework was too simple. She left the church when she was seventeen and came to consider herself agnostic, but her early experiences with the church remained important. Singing in the choir engendered a lifelong interest in music and composers; the rhythms of the Book of Common Prayer exposed her to one sort of poetry; and the biblical stories offered a moral lens on the world.

A swimmer, Frost worked her way through the State University of New York College at Oneonta with money earned as a lifeguard and swimming teacher. This income also funded her study at the Sorbonne in Paris during her sophomore year. Traveling alone to Europe at nineteen resembled in ways Frost's earlier explorations into nature—frightening, exhilarating, private, and freeing. Lured by art museums, she hitchhiked around Luxembourg, Germany, Spain, and Austria, where she was reunited with her grandmother after fifteen years. Frost lingered for hours at each museum seeking out religious art and the lush architecture of churches in particular, which provided a formal understanding that would shape her poems for years. She admired the idea that a building—a thing that had been crafted—could be so beautiful and could house such powerful emotions. In her essay "Petrarch, Shakespeare, and the Blues," published in the summer 1997 issue of the *New England Review,* Frost argued a similar point: that a "poem's words and sentences" work the way "a well-structured jazz solo or house makes its material—the notes or the stone lintels—expressive."

After returning to America, Frost married the poet Richard Frost (born 1929) on August, 23, 1969, a semester before her graduation in 1970 with a bachelor's degree. Her husband had been one of her undergraduate teachers and had been among the first to encourage her writing. Although both Richard Frost and Donald Petersen, another undergraduate teacher, were active in the contemporary poetry scene (Petersen had been in John Berryman's famous University of Iowa workshop), Frost knew few of her peers and ignored much of contemporary poetry, concerned that her voice might become derivative. Through literature courses she focused instead on Robert Browning, John Donne, George Herbert, John Keats, Percy Shelley, and Wallace Stevens, and she admired William Faulkner's fiction and Shakespeare's plays. The works of these writers, she sensed, were complete; she knew that the poems she and her classmates would submit to writing workshops were not. Thus the older literature could provide better models for her work.

After her sons Daniel and Joel were born in 1970 and 1971, respectively, the family moved to the village of Breuberg-Wald-Amorbach in Germany for a year in 1972–1973, during her husband's sabbatical. Frost wrote while her sons napped and at other free moments. She estimates having written about a hundred poems that year, many of them "awful," from assignments she gave herself. Her efforts yielded her earliest publications—in the *North American Review* and the *Seneca Review*. After Frost submitted poems to the journal *12 Poems,* the editor, Scott Walker, requested a manuscript. She did not yet have one, but it was in the works. *The Salt Lesson,* a chapbook, was published by the Graywolf Press in 1976 while she was a graduate student in literature and creative writing at Syracuse University.

At Syracuse, Philip Booth and W. D. Snodgrass were influential teachers "in part because they hardly ever agreed," says Frost in an interview for the present essay. "Booth attended to the poem's details while Snodgrass was interested in the poem's energy. Both could spot felicitous phrasing and were generous in praising that." George P. Elliot became an important mentor, securing her a fellowship to the Bread Loaf Writers' Conference in 1976 and recommending her for three Yaddo fellowships—in 1978, 1980, and 1982. Yaddo was pivotal. She wrote prolifically, met other poets, and developed what she calls a "fierce ... but private" ambition to become a part of the "historical literary continuum."

If Frost's ambition was growing fiercely, she still maintained her humility. Even as she garnered critical praise for her poems she treated her writing as an apprenticeship. She reads voraciously and writes not only to explore her own mind but also to imitate and absorb the methods of poets she admires. As a result her style has evolved slowly and carefully. Although themes remain similar throughout the four decades in which she has published poetry, we see a movement toward the higher lyric style that she prefers today—but only after an entire book, *Day of the Body* (1986), was dedicated to narrative poems. Frost wanted to prove to herself that she could write narrative poems. During her thirties Frost realized that abstraction is at times necessary in poetry, despite Ezra Pound's exhortation to "go in fear of abstractions." The abstract poems in *Pure* (1994) and *Venus and Don Juan* (1996) are no doubt the result of her brooding over the question of how to make abstractions.

Frost's essay "Self Pity," published in the spring 1998 issue of *Prairie Schooner,* offers insight into her writing process by exploring the use of pronouns in poetry. She begins by describing a dream that might make the material of a poem. She goes on to explain, however, the difficulties of using the first-person pronoun to ask in a poem the questions that the dream elicited. From there she looks to other poets: John Berryman, Donald Justice, and Walt Whitman for examples of the first-person pronoun used well, with praise also for Randall Jarrell, Robert Lowell, Frank O'Hara, and William Wordsworth; James Wright to discern what, in her view, makes his use of the pronoun unsuccessful. The essay ends with two poems, "Waking" and "Thaw," preceded by the sentence "I have sat at my desk and written two poems in the first person as a beginning." The poems, then, are explorations that work out the problems she has outlined. She is teaching herself, and the end of the essay is only the beginning of the process. It is clear that even at this advanced point in her career Frost remains in her own mind an apprentice, but she insists that all students of poetry ought to maintain the belief that "it's possible to be great," even if that means a lifelong pursuit that yields only a handful of truly great poems. Although Frost does not consider herself to have attained greatness, Donald Justice names her "one of the three or four best poets of her generation."

Frost's first full-length book—*Liar's Dice,* written mostly during her Yaddo fellowship in 1978—was awarded second place for the University of Cincinnati's Elliston Prize that same year. Frost began teaching composition at Hartwick College in Oneonta, New York, in 1981. The first of two National Endowment for the Arts fellowships also came that year, and a second chapbook, *Cold Frame,* was published the following year by the Owl Creek Press. Since then she has published seven more full-length collections of poetry and has won three Pushcart Prizes as well as other awards. With her gradual but continuous publication success Frost has remained at Hartwick in various positions, including writer-in-residence and founder and director of the Catskill Poetry Workshop, a summer program for which she has coordinated courses and readings with many noted American poets. She has also taught in the master of fine arts program at Warren Wilson College and as a writer-in-residence at Wichita State University and Washington University in Saint Louis.

Teaching has provided more than financial support for her writing. It has encouraged helpful aesthetic debates with other poet-teachers, and Frost has called teaching "an opportunity to come to understand, which is to say to articulate, my own aesthetics." She judges the success of her teaching by "how unnecessary I become" and claims that young writers need only to learn to read like writers to sharpen their aesthetic judgments and decisions. Frost's discussion of the teaching and learning process recalls Rainer Maria Rilke's famous exhortation in *Letters to a Young Poet* to "live the question" so that "perhaps you will gradually, without even noticing it, find yourself experiencing the answer, some distant day."

Although Frost has traveled extensively in the United States and in Australia, New Zealand, Europe, Mexico, and elsewhere, her home base has remained her 143-acre farm in Otego, New York, where she and her husband have lived their entire married lives. Here Frost has hunted, fished, gardened, landscaped, skied, snowshoed, and tracked weather and animals. In 1999 she began spending her winters in Cedar Key, Florida. She has said that "travel, family, and writing have been fairly well integrated" throughout her thirty-five years on the farm, but she does not write every day, especially when she is teaching. However, she claims that her mind is constantly making notes and that the pent-up feeling she gets after not writing for several days is a pleasurable excitement. Despite open-heart surgery in 1991, a breast cancer diagnosis in 1996, and a broken back resulting from an automobile collision in Cambridge, Massachusetts, in 2001, she remains physically active through kayaking, swimming, hunting, and walking.

THE LIMITS OF BIOGRAPHY

In her poem "Liar's Dice," Frost writes, "One way of ownership / is not to tell how much you have." And in "Icarus in Winter," she writes, "who knows who feels what and how much?" These passages suggest the difficulty in reading Frost's poems with her biography in mind. Asked in a PoetryNet interview whether her work is autobiographical, Frost is equivocal: "Do the experiences and the emotions in my poems refer to me? Yes and no. My son nearly *did* fall off a mountain in Venezuela, like the boy in my poem 'Nothing.' But as far as I remember at the time, I thought nothing. I was too stunned." Frost considers all poetry autobiographical in the sense that it records the movement of a mind. A poem "can tell us as much about the writer as a chair ... tells us about the woodworker," she continues but suggests that we might enjoy the chair as a chair rather than as a reflection of its maker. Frost claims that the "authenticity" of a poem trumps in importance any autobiographical context and that poems that depend too much upon their topical context often seem voiced inappropriately to their mood or argument. Thus, she contends, readers

distrust the poem itself.

One might turn to "Mozart," a poem that appears in her collection *Chimera* (1990), to understand the irrelevance Frost assigns to the artist's life in relation to his art:

The books say genius, prodigy.
This means so little. Or that he loved his canary perched on a wire swing.

These descriptors do not matter, nor do "his trouble with women, his difficult love / for his father, his debts." What matters rather are "his bits of song making architecture." Frost admires the way the structure that Mozart, her favorite composer, builds through music—and, one might argue, that a poet builds through poems—is imbued with spirit, with something greater than himself: "a gust of melody / no one has known." This building of music, of course, recalls similar ideas about the building of the religious architecture that Frost admired in Europe.

Like a Mozart composition, poems ought to be, as she says in "Self Pity," "universal and memorable" for the reader; the "particular experience that a poem is" is more important than the experience of any particular person— namely the poet. For some writers subject matter is at least partly a choice that reflects what is "appropriate" for poetry. Frost leaves that decision to readers. "The audience ... will end up deciding what is essentially adequate as truth or beauty or expression," she writes in her essay "The Poet's Tact, and a Necessary Tactlessness," published in the *New England Review* for summer 1999. She continues, "What one hopes for ... that for whatever sort of poetry it was, sensations and emotions, abstractions and concretions were presented with freshness and some sense of proportion, an excitement ensuing." Although she is not particularly interested in everyday objects in her poems, Frost indicates that this tendency reflects her personality and interests more than any judgment on poetry itself. Asked if she finds poetry about the things of daily life inappropriate, Frost says no: "I am interested, only for myself, in our origins—moral and emotional." She acknowledges that this refusal to address contemporary culture in her poems may be considered old-fashioned and unpopular, and it may exile her from the contemporary literary scene, but that does not worry her.

DOMINANT THEMES

Despite Frost's frequent return to themes of the natural world, she claims that her thematic interest is not exactly nature. "Were anyone to criticize me for being a nature poet, I'd say that my poems were about mind and emotion … and helplessly entangled with what I call moral dreaming." The term "moral dreaming" is one to which Frost often turns in discussing her work; thus it behooves any student of her poetry to understand it. One might call moral dreaming an exploration of the natural history of feeling. Where do our emotions originate? What are our living relationships with death and nature? How are instinct and imagination intertwined? How do image, myth, and metaphor access the unconscious? What is animal in humans and vice versa? How do the mind and body shape and reshape their worlds? How do beauty and structure express these ideas?

These kinds of questions are well described in "Seagulls and Children," a poem from *Chimera:*

> I do not know how it is possible to walk through
>   the landscape
> at the time without asking questions: not the
>   riddle
> of egg and hen …
> . . . .
> but just thinking out loud that life here in the
>   sunflat between inlet
> and ocean seemed impossible.

Questions that attempt to unravel the world and

discern how it could become possible yield only speculative answers; thus they are a kind of dreaming. Although they are often explorations of morality, they never moralize. Although they ask questions, they answer usually with only more questions. Nonetheless an examination of Frost's themes across her career offers a surprisingly coherent worldview.

For Frost the human is another animal in a landscape in which all bodies are parts of a primordially true nature: amoral and without language. We see this clearly in "Komodo," one of the new poems in *Love and Scorn: New and Selected Poems* (2000). In it a man, Baron von Biberegg, is eaten by a Komodo dragon, and the poet can find "neither heart nor devil nor god figure; no perfidy in the reptile's ambush; no metaphor; / only viscera, anatomy." She writes of the lizards:

> … if they completely inhabit themselves, there
>   are no morals
> or excuses. None for the disemboweled,
>   disembodied: goats, pigs, horses,
> the blazing cockatoo, the pink, lightless, inner
>   tissues of the Baron.

The Baron's body is no more than another of the animals, and no lesson—nor even metaphor—is offered upon his death.

Sex, illness, and dying—common themes in her work—are rendered as connections, even if fleeting, with this deep nature that resides in all bodies. As she writes in "Songs for Two Seasons," also a new poem in *Love and Scorn,* "The body … doesn't exist to be changed; / it itself changes." Not human sentiment, imagination, nor language can alter the course of nature. Frost marvels, nonetheless, at the uniquely human endowments of love, imagination, and language. These gifts of expression and feeling are rich and contradictory, sometimes at odds with the realities of the natural world. Thus Frost wonders how such feelings take root and also how and why they disintegrate, leaving humans back at that primordial origin. In "Lying in the Pollen and Water," a poem in *I Will Say Beauty* (2003), for example, Frost writes:

> and I feel
> my mind swerve, spring's malignity whispering
> and singing what
> it knows and I've always known,—that I will be
> covered
> over by snow, or stone, or light, or moldering
> dark, the body the grave,
> its lineaments and fibers great and less, the
> details of a sort
> of fermentation at the bottom of all sweetness....

As these passages illustrate, the ultimate intimacy in Frost's poems is between the mind and our natural origins (its substance: "lineaments and fibers"), because what is conventionally moving, beautiful, or sweet falls away. Another poem in *I Will Say Beauty,* "Given," says of death, "Faith and love into atoms without form and limb."

Even in beauty exists, as that earlier Frost, Robert (no relation, but a poet Carol Frost much admires), knew so well, an awesome darkness. It is full of potential rather than fixed truths, except for the truth of the grave, as in "Lying in the Pollen and Water." Art gives structure to this potential and thus affords us the closest measure of truth we can access through language, even if, as *Love and Scorn*'s "Sin" argues, "We'll never know the all of it."

These themes appear in some incarnation in most of Frost's books. Indeed she often reprints earlier poems in later collections, thus carrying forward her themes. A single poem may reappear in as many as five of her collections. "The Winter without Snow," for example, first appears in *Cold Frame* and then reappears in *Liar's Dice* and several later books. While thematic content remains somewhat constant, the gradual evolution of Frost's style over the years distinguishes her books from one another.

EARLY COLLECTIONS

Frost's first four books are two chapbooks, *The Salt Lesson* (1976) and *Cold Frame* (1982), and two full-length collections, *Liar's Dice* (1978) and *The Fearful Child* (1983). Her subjects and landscapes in these early collections are more various and commonplace than those that characterize her later work: a cafeteria scene, sorting a mother's belongings, a child's haircut, a washed-up circus performer. Nonetheless her rendering of these subjects, as well as those more typical of her later work, establishes premises both thematic and stylistic for future work. Many of the poems overlap among these collections.

In the title poem of *The Fearful Child* the speaker reflects upon a sad adolescence in which she "wept salt onto my knuckles" in the "bleak bed before sleep" while her parents quarreled in another room. At dawn redemption arrives:

> In the serene light of sun-up, before sparrows
> tumbled up from the earth, whispering and singing,
> and the exquisite sea and sky mobilized
> their heavy, blue currents, I was consoled.

Here we see Frost's sense of nature as a comfort and a place of redemptive beauty. Whereas elsewhere in the poem her syntax is direct and prosaic, here the simple thought "I was consoled," expressed in a three-word independent clause, is postponed until the end of what is one of the two longest sentences in the poem.

Compare this lingering syntax with these lines from the first stanza:

> I was fearful of people as well as things,
> and my faithful toy shepherd with his painted
> face
> sat by me on the bed in the gloom.
> I was disdainful of dolls as weak people.

It is not the length nor quality of image but rather the directness of these sentences—the ordinary syntax and diction, the unsurprising line breaks—that differentiates their subjects from the subjects of beauty, which of ten come from the natural world. Beauty merits a syntactical excitement that the world of things and human behavior does not, for, as her essay "Passing Beauty" indicates, she finds "complexity beautiful." In that essay she also says, "The more like prose [that poetic language] seems, the more transparent." "Packing Mother's Things" illustrates the transparency of everyday things through relatively prosaic sentences:

> I call the Goodwill and say
> that they can have everything else.
> . . . . . .
> They are incredulous that I would leave
> her shag rug red as cabbage, an aviary,
> a homemade bookcase.

In contrast, "Unfinished Song," a few poems later in *The Fearful Child,* foreshadows the syntactic variety that figures more prominently in later work and requires more of the reader to unpack:

> All day long, before the sun sings a requiem,
> I walk through the thicket-rich hills
> along deer paths where the finely cleft hooves
> make wells in the mud, and the peace of mind
> of water under grasses is sung quietly.

If, to quote "Passing Beauty" again, "poetic imagination forms patterns and effects out of a range of sounds," the syntactical structure of these lines helps the reader experience the lingering pleasure of Frost's daylong journey.

A typical structure emerges in many of these early poems: an introductory scene-setting and then, often late in the poem, a comment upon or recoloring of the scene, almost as the last six lines of a sonnet react to the eight that precede them. For example, the first three stanzas of "The Embroidery" say:

> Grandmother embroiders the summer day.
> She sits amid the bodies and light of childhood,
> lilac-scented, perspiring,

> sewing life-like flora in cloth the color of cream.
> Pollen is strewn in the air;
> some spices her hair.

> The design on the porch sofa isn't far off
> from the green and golden scene,
> a water-garden, she inextricably sews into new
>   cloth.

After this seemingly innocuous description the second half of the poem moves toward a more serious tone: "To look at her face, you would not see birth or death." The last line ominously reports that "mildew casts its net around." What at first seems like a sweet grandmotherly scene becomes pregnant with death. In "Eating with My Fingers," the introductory stanza describes the speaker's substandard housekeeping tendencies. The last stanza, however, replies glibly about how much the housekeeping really matters; the speaker decides, "My shepherd's pie is done when I am ready."

This two-part structure is the form taken by the lyric impulse that Frost considers natural to her writing. It begins with observation and then expands to a moment of reflection and wonder, toward a more meaning laden vision. Of her early writing days the poet has said, "I remember very strongly coming to the conclusion that you always needed to take a left-hand turn somewhere in the poem or you couldn't end it." We see these "left turns" throughout Frost's early work. Her later work moves toward a higher lyric style in which this two-part structure is less apparent and her writing becomes more headstrong. However the themes explored in these early poems are articulated in ways much as in her later work. A fine example of what Frost calls "moral dreaming" is the poem "Aubade of an Early Homo Sapiens." The speaker asks:

> Was it in your eyes, where my elongated face
>   shone,
> I saw for the first time
> . . . .

a hunger that was not wholly animal?

Here the speaker's "strange blood rises," as she ponders her own vision in a lover's eyes and feels "a hunger" that must be love. Is this how love first stirred in humans? The poem concludes with the images of "Wild, beautiful petals all around. / A beast's face. And something, something else." As love takes its place in natural history, the image intertwines beauty, eeriness, and awe.

AN EXPERIMENT IN NARRATIVE

Published in 1986, *Day of the Body* reprints several poems from earlier collections alongside new ones. Although by this time Frost had published in numerous prestigious literary magazines, in the summer 1987 issue of the *Georgia Review,* Peter Stitt calls her work "a well-kept secret, known to the sort of people who give out Poetry Fellowships for the National Endowment for the Arts, but hardly to anyone else." He says that Frost's poems in this collection are "realistic to an astonishing degree, thanks to a dense physicality of image and a palpable texture of sound."

Many of her subjects in *Day of the Body* are fittingly corporeal, although the body in question is not always human and is perhaps less often living. "Mallard," for instance, describes cleaning up a dead bird in the garden; "Death in Winter," a dying lamb; "The New Dog: Variations on a Text by Jules Laforgue," the burial of a family dog. The preoccupation in this book with dead or dying bodies seems not so much a morbid fascination with death as an engaging search for the human soul, a term rarely used in Frost's later poems. These poems represent another kind of moral dreaming: is there a soul, and if so what is it? How is the soul tethered to or separate from the body? What imbues the body, made as it is of the things of nature, with a soul? With imagination? With the ability to make art? The answers are not simple.

In "The Undressing" aging lovers with "calluses" and "round tough moons on their extremities, / shadows under their eyes," and "a sour smell" eventually "woke up" and "were dead." The poem closes:

> They opened their mouths
> and crawled out, pitifully soft and small,
> not yet souls.

The last line suggests that the soul exists separately from the body, as does a line in the next poem in the book, "Girl on a Scaffold," in which a woman is hanged, and, as she is dying,

> Within her now
> a feeling rises like the soft clashing of wings
> to be free of red clay and the world twisted.

The last part of the five-part title poem opens, "The looser his skin gets, / the more he gets used to his soul," as if the soul emerges as the body wanes.

But what is the soul? The closest answer may lie in "Prayer for my Son," which does not involve death but offers a helpful discussion of how Frost imagines the physical body. Addressing the baby resting in her hands, the speaker states,

> So little of what
> I see is what you are. Fingernails,
> cartilage, cell deaths, layers of skin,
> the garden in your head:
> wild pig, the air's dragons,
>
> a humming thick as honey just below sense,
> and the picked castles of bone
> which held essences once, and still do.

This passage marvels at the human endowments of imagination and dreaming (the "wild pig, the air's dragons") that make the human more than the sum of its body parts. The "soul" of the other poems in this collection seems very similar to the "garden in your head" that is "below sense" in this one. Death seems to reduce us to those "essences" to which the body merely gives shape.

At death, however, the soul—or "essences" or imagination—is not headed for any particular heavenly destination. As Peter Stitt points out, the poem "Redbirds" describes what he calls "the harrowing landscape beyond death" as continuous with this world but only, as Frost writes, "a farther field / waning west." "Who shall say," the poem asks bravely, whether this vision is right or wrong? In "The Salt Lesson," Frost offers, "The mind is a sullen scavenger / with the belly and bowels of a god." Stitt reads this line as a statement of the role of the poet and also uses it to explain the role of death in Frost's work. He writes, "The poet's task is to accept the real world's grossest ore and refine it into precious metal. For Carol Frost, the world's grossest ore is often the fact of death, its most precious metal always poetry."

In many ways this collection is her least characteristic, despite characteristic themes. Frost has said that she had to prove to herself that she could write narrative poems before she went on to writing in a higher lyric style. Some titles, such as "The Gardener Delivers a Fawn" and "Country Marriage," more obviously connote a narrative structure; however, although many of these poems are more narrative than most of Frost's other poems, it is difficult to imagine that a reader would consider them purely narrative. "Mallard" is an example of a narrative poem infused with the lyric tendency for which Frost is better known. It begins, "I raked up a mallard in the garden, / its body rolled in dirt." Frost adopts a simple chronological structure to narrate the poem:

> A horsefly landed on my leg
> and a stink filled my nostrils.
> Then the whole garden, dirt and air,
> gave way to the death.

Although the structure is narrative, the expansive moment characteristic of the lyric poem shines prominently. Immediately after "gave way to death," Frost wraps the moment in a simile—

> as a birdflock,
> thick at the center and jagged at the edges,
> with a slight but irresistible movement,
> veers south above a stubble field
> or the sun enters the world

—that spans five lines and diverts the reader from the narrative by conjuring new images out of the imagination. Moreover the poem's final six lines recolor the scene with a terrifying comparison of the mallard's breast to

> the breaths of the just-born
> or the sweet howling of the dog
> that buried it.

This closing feels very much like the "response" in the two-part structure typical of Frost's early poems—the structure that she has called a basis for the lyric poem.

Other poems in this collection might not be considered narrative at all. "Lines Written in Manassas," for example, is one of the poems in this collection most like her later work. Abandoning now the two-part structure, Frost opens without explanation or any obvious link to the poem's title:

> What is Art? Not
>
> a battlefield
> where the high cold star is now
>
> as years
>
> before in place?

With its clipped stanzas and surprising line breaks, the poem is striking on the page, if for nothing else than its obvious visual difference from the densely written lines of some of her earlier poems, many of which reappear in this collection. The rhythms surprise as they jostle the syntax of the sentence against the syntax of the line. For example, we might read the first line as the question "What is art not?"

We can read "Lines Written in Manassas" as a kind of *ars poetica*. Answering her question "What is Art?" and thinking about the dead at Bull Run, Frost writes,

> There must be ecstasy: The soldiers
> must get to the top of the hill.
>
> And protocol: They crumple
> and fall from the grapeshot
>
> like leaves out of season. Over and over
> in art.

She concludes,

> Art is the habit of this place.
> In it the wounded tree
> is wise,
>
> and the ground is wise.
> In it only the dead sleep.

These lines are useful in understanding why poetry matters to Frost. Art must have feeling ("ecstasy") and structure ("protocol"), just like the churches she visited in Europe. Art preserves and livens our senses to constant wonder ("only the dead sleep"). Her argument recalls Keats's "Ode on a Grecian Urn," but it goes further. Art does not, in Frost's rendering, preserve that eternally sweet moment that Keats described but rather enacts the moment, sweet or not, "over and over."

A TRANSITION

Examined in the context of overall movements in Frost's career, *Chimera* (1990) might be considered a transitional book. Its syntax is more ornate and lyric, but its subject matter remains more concrete than in her later works. It is the book that at once shares most in common with her earliest and her latest books; indeed about a quarter of the poems appear again ten years later in *Love and Scorn*.

In "Sunfish," Frost reacts to Elizabeth Bishop's famous poem "The Fish" while recapitulating some of her own characteristic themes. In both poems the narrators catch fish, and in both color figures prominently. After catching her "battered and venerable / and homely" fish, Bishop exclaims,

> oil had spread a rainbow
> . . . . .
> until everything
> was rainbow, rainbow, rainbow!

Frost addresses her fish this way:

> I have held you—spinous, slimy,
>
> and fragrant as dead leaves—in my bare hands
> to admire your aegis of blue-greens
> and yellows shading into one another
>
> as if formed by sunbeams through a shower.

Bishop's "rainbow" line suggests a celebratory excitement, and she, respecting the fish's venerability, throws it back. Frost, on the other hand, "can't make of the life history of fish / a lesson," and she kills the fish. "So naturally was death wrought," Frost writes,

> I felt no evil, and so glorious the colors
> lying on the surface of the water
> robbed of moral.

In her essay "The World as We Know It" in the winter 1996 *Gettysburg Review*, Dorothy Barresi calls this moment "a triumph of amorality."

Amorality is characteristic of Frost's world. Despite the allusion to another poem and the halfhearted attempt to compare the fish to the world of myth—

Vertebrate, kin to the fully armed form
sprung upon the earth like Athena
from the head of Zeus

—Frost cannot find any greater meaning in her catch. Whereas Bishop privileges her fish's experience and beauty, Frost writes:

How is it no love

or scruples are stirred as you flap
at the end of my line, foul-hooked
glistening?

Frost's use of the passive voice in this question is particularly noteworthy because the creature who feels neither love nor scruples is not specified. Is the poet marveling at the fish's lack of feeling or at her own? The poet and the fish are in the same moral realm. Just as in the fish "there are no inhibitions, moments of hesitation, / no book of pain borne in your mind," neither are such feelings aroused in the narrator as she kills the fish.

This amoral stance toward the violence of nature reappears elsewhere in the book. For example, in "A Field Full of Black Cats"

There is no
reaching into the heart
of violence

when the cat paw sweeps
suddenly toward
the mole.

In "Eating the Whole" a cat kills and eats a mouse without "a guilty murmur." In both poems the cats' actions cannot be read as anything but a reflection of hunger and instinct; it is not a moral situation. It is likewise for the human in "Red Deer":

I stand in violence, in death,
and I am happy—with the chill of fear.
The light withdraws; chills me; alters
nothing. At the root of humanness
a cup of blood
nature spills. And this is part
of everything I see or make or am.

TOWARD ABSTRACTION

Triquarterly Books of Northwestern University published *Pure* in 1994. The book is comprised of three sections, the middle and longest of which contains poems with one- and two-word abstract nouns for titles—for example, "Truth," "Art," "Mind," "Her Beauty," "Obedience." All of these poems have eleven lines, with the exception of "Crying Wolf" and "Alto." The form recalls the Petrarchan sonnet; often around the seventh or eighth line one finds the slight change of focus common between the octave and sestet of a sonnet and in Frost's early poems. "Harm" is a fine example, hinging on the sentence "So it seemed," where the poem moves away from a hospital patient's passive response to physical pain and toward a seemingly angry power. Frost uses her invented form, which usually adopts a third-person voice, as a "room" in which she can experiment with the design and work out "the dramatic process," as she explains in her PoetryNet interview. In "Self Pity" she expresses interest in these poems, "plastic qualities" [and has] "made small rhythmic phrases and placed them against others, tried new ways … of making metaphors, and, ultimately, worked in each poem at defining an abstraction."

The poems in this book show Frost's movement toward a higher lyric sensibility but not the looser ties to narrative that figure more prominently in later poems. The title poem, for example, narrates a story in which a hunter accidentally kills his son rather than the deer he thought he was shooting. While the poem recounts an event, its eerie closing lingers over a single moment in syntactically complex form:

> He only had left to him his pure hunter's sense,
>   still clean under his skin,
> a gun, the example of wounds, a shell's ease in
>   the chamber, as he loaded,
> the speed of the night chill, while his mind like a
>   saint's tried to bear
> that which God took from His own mind when
>   he could not, not for another moment....

Dorothy Barresi's discussion of *Pure* comments on "the violence reflected in our innermost selves" in poems such as this one. "Beneath their surfaces," she writes, "lie all sorts of unconscious dangers."

Frost's book suggests that the living body—albeit in different forms—is the common thread between animal and human. Although the poet chooses not to anthropomorphize her "Sunfish" (the poem is reprinted here), in "To Kill a Deer," the speaker animalizes herself. Running after a deer she had just shot, she "felt myself a part of the woods, / a woman with a doe's ears"; and after she leaves the deer dead in the forest, she "heard riot in the emptied head." Killing the deer has intertwined the animal and the human; she imagines she can hear what happens in the deer's body.

"Apple Rind" describes the speaker, "perfectly drugged" and "swallowing oxygen / from a tube," after an unspecified surgery. The deer imagery reappears, and the speaker muses as the poem closes:

> How to explain directions a mind takes
> or why I told no one how much I wanted
> to come back to this beautiful, stupid world.

Here the human is nearly as vulnerable—and as speechless—as the dead doe in "To Kill a Deer." Moreover, the world is complex, beautiful and stupid (in the senses both of idiocy and of numbness). Importantly, however, Frost eschews any sentimentality about this vulnerable moment. The poem "Refusal," later in the collection, suggests that such sentimentality would be less comfort than the refusal to be moved: "Isn't there a human stillness in shapes labored / over," she asks, "and comfort to be taken from feeling nature's refusal to be much moved?"

Nature may be unmoved, but humans are moved—and sentimental. We respond to beauty and experience as Bishop does in "The Fish." We respond to a host of other associations that, Frost suggests, nature does not obey. In "Small" she addresses a boa constrictor and mocks her own species: "Beware. When it comes to people, you'll have to think of religion, Eden, ethics committees, / all that fuss." In "Self Pity" she writes, "Fatigue, illness, the swelling chords of violins—these and many other circumstances can make our emotions too facile. Farewells, reunions, landscapes of a certain quality, sunsets, the rich smell of lilacs—we could blush for our inappropriate responses."

Critics have often noted Frost's refusal to sentimentalize her topics. In its review on April 25, 1994, of *Pure, Publishers Weekly* wrote, "Fate and the natural world intersect in the book as a whole, producing exacting poems with a serious tone and a clarity of vision that, to Frost's credit, is not romanticized." By refusing sentimentality, Frost challenges the reader to avoid facile interpretations of experience, for all experience undoubtedly holds something more mysterious, awesome, terrifying, and usually contradictory than our minds easily can interpret. "How to describe the beauties of this / violence and this fatigue, even to herself?" she asks in "Refusal."

LOVE'S DISINTEGRATION

Frost continues her "abstraction" poems in *Venus and Don Juan,* published in 1996 by Tri-Quarterly Books. The poems—with their one-word titles and eleven-line form—in this book draws from all of Zach's major collections published between 1955 and 1979.

In the aforementioned interview with Veinberg and Buckley, Everwine was asked why he chose to translate Zach and if that translating had any effect upon his own work. In part, Everwine replied:

> He's my age—What is an Israeli poet my age doing at this point? He also doesn't write very much like me. I feel closer an affinity to say the Aztec stuff if I were talking about relationships of technique and so on, than I do to Zach, because Zach is in many ways a very intellectual poet.... He is often a man who works in intellectual structures, ironic structures, and I found that immensely attractive, partly because I didn't know how to do it, because to a degree it's almost foreign to my own sense of writing.... his use of language is very complicated and dependent on a whole network of playing-off these Biblical allusions....

Everwine's own poetry shows more of an affinity for the earlier work of Zach, which is more concentrated, image-centered, and direct when compared with his later, more discursive poems. "Be Careful," which Everwine translated and used as a proem, or invocation, for *Keeping the Night* (and quoted earlier in this essay) is also the first poem in *The Static Element*. "Failure" is also very representative of Zach's early work; while it employs biblical allusiveness, it also proceeds with straightforward statement before turning on the unexpected lyric image of the heart at its end.

> Seven times the wolf said to the lamb,
> Beware! On the eighth, he devoured it.
>
> What brought me to want
> whatever it is the heart wants?
>
> Or led me to believe I might divide
> water from water
>
> that cannot be divided
> and only in the sky

> is altered to air?
> Meanwhile
>
> only the heart is still there, wishful
> as ever,
>
> and whatever was not fished up
> on its hook.

Like "Failure," "When the Last Riders" is a poem translated from Zach's *Various Poems* (1960). The sensibility of the poet here, the viewpoint of the speaker, is not very far removed from that of Everwine; most readers may well find a similarity of approach and texture between this poem and Everwine's "How It Is." Although the poem is written/spoken in the first person, there are really no autobiographical or historical details. Rather, the speaker is—certainly by the thrust of the more universal imagery—more of an everyman than a particular individual in a specific time and place. From the poem, we know only that he is a gatekeeper, perhaps at some frontier—certainly an occupation of times past. The poem may contain a biblical allusion given Zach's style, but it is not at all overt—not like the lamb and wolf and use of the number seven are in "Failure." If there is any biblical connotation, it may be recognizable only to those fluent in Hebrew and steeped in Old Testament lore. The focus is more directly on fate, a common desire, and/or realistic expectations of the human condition. The speaker "knows the score"—the riders come and go, the sun goes down, and he has his job. The tone and imagery suggest that the speaker understands the larger significance of these daily and seemingly insignificant actions and therefore understands himself as a singular and mostly unnoticed part of the world turning, the day giving way to darkness.

> When the last riders disappear over the horizon
> and even the dust of their horses no longer rises
> I'll know it is time to lock the gate.
> The spent day will look at its hands and be
>   content.

look not unlike those in *Pure;* however, here the titles reflect abstract human emotions and psychology: "Obsession," "Conscience," "Hypocrisy," "Joy," "Failure," and so on. Likely because of this shift in subject, the *Publishers Weekly* review of October 28, 1996, admired the development of "a sense of personal connection, especially in the latter of this volume's seven sections, that was absent from Frost's earlier work," whereas the *Library Journal* of September 15, 1996, praised Frost's "uncanny ability to dissociate from and observe emotion" through objectifying "her analyses by transforming her observations into shimmering and haunting images."

As the title suggests, this book's dominant theme is erotic love. Sexual union is often portrayed as the means to—not the result of—love. "Compatibility" is a fine example. "Never after was life so filled with meeting," the poem opens (one nearly hears "meeting" as "meaning"), "as then, when bed-hot, filled with surges, / the man and woman began to know each other." The couple's sexual relationship is used to bring them toward love, as they

> opened entirely, bending to two wills,
> striking down vanities, feeling what lay deep
> inside—the darker compatibilities—
> until love seemed causal, not just related.

The poem's final line is most intriguing. Rather than speaking the word "love," the couple performs it: "Their sinuous tongues used the word, over and over, without speaking." Physical, natural lust has transformed into love through the exploration of each other's bodies, through reaching, as much as one can, inside another human—into the primordial realm.

"Untitled" explores a similar question. "When, // when, and whenever lust became love was the question." Speaking to a lover and remembering an early sexual encounter, the speaker states,

> I tasted our sweat as it washed

over us and felt us moving toward our earliest
 natures—
what the bone frame (ribs and hips) is made for.

As in "Compatibility," here love is consummated rather than spoken: "We were alone and there were no appropriate words." The body is a primordial, prelingual realm.

Ultimately Frost's vision of love is unconsoling; it does not hold. "Apology" puts it plainly:

> What induces
> then weakens the greater and lesser passions is
> what she'd like to know
> . . . .
> she is someone who *had* loved.

Almost all the poems in the wrenching final two sections of the collection explore the issues of love's creation and ultimate dissolution: another kind of moral dreaming. The final poem, "Venus and Don Juan," finds these two legendary lovers in the same bed, where "they lovingly went forth and lost themselves." But immediately their love disintegrates, and the speaker is left resigned to love's loss: "But hadn't they rehearsed, / the pale moon slipping out of the sky each morning, doors shutting, the bedclothes smoothed dry?" It is a lonely conclusion.

A STUDY IN CONTRADICTION

Love and Scorn, a collection of both new and selected poems, documents what Jeffrey Shotts calls in an online review Frost's "remarkable development," although he laments the choice to arrange the older poems alphabetically rather than chronologically, as it obscures the arc of her development. Nonetheless Shotts rates the book "one of the finest collections likely to be published" in 2000.

The three-part collection opens with twenty new poems, followed by a grouping of thirty-five "Abstractions" from *Pure* and *Venus and Don Juan,* and finally forty-six other poems selected from earlier work. In her PoetryNet interview Frost calls the new poems in this collection "a departure from my eleven line poems," and goes on to say, "What I was trying to write began to feel a little too familiar. I could still play with the shape, ... but I knew a little too well how to work through the various tensions set up in the eleven lines." Another shift in these poems is toward a higher lyric sensibility. Shotts deems her "surprising formal and syntactical shifts" as representative of her "most stylistically developed" work to date. *Publishers Weekly,* however, gives qualified praise, admiring the imagery and energy of Frost's "headlong free verse" but accusing the poems of "not much formal or intellective control."

Indeed these poems are among Frost's most challenging. The poems are syntactically complex, and they often lack narrative. Many of the poems are less expository and speak in fragments, thus at times dislocating the reader from a phrase's referent. The syntax makes the grammar difficult as well. An interesting example is the first three lines of "Thaw." The first two words are "Clouds brown," but whether "brown" is an adjective or verb never becomes completely clear. The clause reads,

Clouds brown in a puddle
                              like the skies Job learned
to find beautiful,

but is the simile here a modification of how the clouds brown or of "a puddle"? The image is double, reflective, and perhaps richer—but certainly not easier—for it.

After this clause the sentence continues:

        the fields
                              chaste, yes, but far away
violet and blue-green trees
                              on dawn's cold sleeve;
manger-rich, ah, sweet, the dirt;

                              the music of melting
gathering head
                              where blind fishes wait, cold
and unable to tell mercy
                              from fathomless grace
in this presence, this absence,
                              this cold presence.

Throughout this passage and indeed throughout many of these new poems, the reader finds traditional structure slipping: does "far away," for example, modify "fields" or "violet and blue-green trees"? The answers are not obvious.

Then again, the answers to the questions of these new poems are not obvious, and their structures often reflect their subjects. In "Thaw" the speaker states later in the poem, "I am no longer / what I thought myself to be." What could be a more jarring sentiment? Thus the poem's shifts and uncertainty seem appropriate as well. Many of these poems, written around the time of Frost's breast cancer diagnosis and treatment, explore frightening realities about illness and death. Writing about recovering from her mastectomy and chemotherapy in an expanded version of "Self Pity" published in Kate Sontag and David Graham's *After Confession: Poetry as Autobiography* (2001), Frost says,

> Was I healing or uncured? No one could say for certain, and I would look in the mirror and see hairlessness and strain. Who was I then? I, who had always had a physical relationship with the world and built my trust on that bedrock, felt the ground shifting.... [M]y thoughts wore a groove: *and if I die, and if I die.*

It follows that these poems are highly lyric: brooding, meditative, sometimes reticent, enlivened by dark epiphanies. "What is structure?" asks Frost in "Petrarch, Shakespeare, and the Blues." And she answers, "... the element in art that exposes art to the contradictions and complexities of immediate experience."

The book's title, *Love and Scorn,* itself suggests these "contradictions and complexities" through embracement of opposites. Tara Neelakantappa writes in the *Boston Review* that the poems are "sensitive to complexity and contradiction." She points out that in "Matins," the opening poem, "guilt and ecstasy" are treated "as if they were two halves of the same emotion." Likewise "Scorn" closes, "they gave up themselves a little so that they might both love and scorn / each other, and they ate from each other's hands." Here the allowance of the conflicted emotions makes for the fullest experience. Perhaps nowhere else is this more poignant than in "Thaw." The poem is in part a realization that "I may have to leave this place / sooner than I want," but the poem studies both "overwhelming regret" and "joy." "Pear Tree" finds in a deer's carcass "ruin and beauty." This attention to contradiction fits perfectly with Frost's claim in "Petrarch, Shakespeare, and the Blues" that "the unfamiliar no less than the familiar needs our full attention to be properly appreciated."

"HAVE I LIED TO MYSELF ABOUT ART?"

I Will Say Beauty, published by TriQuarterly in 2003, is divided into ten small sections of two to four poems each, most of which describe scenes in Cedar Key, Florida. Despite the book's mostly favorable reviews, critics complain about the overall structure of the book. Writing for the *Library Journal,* Rochelle Ratner calls the use of many "short sections … nothing more than padding," and in its April 21, 2003, issue *Publishers Weekly* complains that "Frost's speakers often introduce the natural world in precious, childlike terms" and that "cuteness is a distraction throughout the book," citing the speakers' occasional direct speeches to nature as "particularly perilous." Also controversial is Frost's choice to right-justify all but the first poem of the thirty-eight-poem collection. Ratner claims that this choice "interferes with reading the poems for themselves," and *Publishers Weekly* calls it "a seemingly arbitrary choice."

In personal communication with the author, Frost's editor Reginald Gibbons, however, praises the decision to align the poems against the right margin, which he says is done "to invert the reader's print-culture expectations concerning the visual emphasis given to line-initial and line-final words and effects." He admires the effect of "two different instances of enjambment, moving in opposite directions, since the line-initial words now construct a ragged-left vertical margin," which creates "twice as many phantom utterances formed mentally by the reader on the basis of words vertically contiguous rather than syntactically related." Gibbons adds,

> [The] flush-right margin has yet another effect, subtler but equally startling, when line-initial words, now much more apparent, cause the eye to leap from line-beginning to line-end, pairing first and last words to create with this device, in a way I have never before registered, yet another phantom utterance that adds even further to the complex layering of the poem.

The book's title itself might be considered another instance of what Gibbons calls "a phantom utterance." Although the title comes from "The Part of the Bee's Body Embedded in the Flesh," in which the word "will" is italicized for emphasis, Frost omits the italics from the book's title. Thus it can be pronounced one of four ways, depending on which word the speaker emphasizes. The title then has four possible connotations: the willful, assertive "*I* will say beauty"; the affirmative—as if after hesitation—"I *will* say beauty"; the deceptive "I will *say* beauty"; and the unintimidated, annunciatory "I will say *beauty*." None of these four readings cancels out the other; all renderings of the title are shades of meaning the book engages. However, in *Publishers Weekly* criticizes this range, arguing that "the title affirmation ends up overwhelming the book's subject."

Prefacing the first section are two poems, one of which—"Winter without Snow"—appeared originally as "The Winter without Snow" in *The Fearful Child,* published twenty years earlier, and reappeared in *Day of the Body, Pure,* and as the final poem in *Love and Scorn.* Whereas all the other poems in this collection are right-justified, "Winter without Snow" keeps the left margin of the original. Interestingly nothing else notes the difference of this poem from the others in the collection; even its slightly more prosaic qualities seem reflected in the rest of the collection as Frost shifts toward a slightly simpler diction after the more ornate poems of *Love and Scorn.* The poem's central frustration is expressed as the speaker watches a man carrying

> bucket after bucket of plaster dust
> up the earthen ramp of the barn that caught fire
> . . . .
> with all the coldness I had,
> yet it would not snow.

As if the speaker's will might be enough to bring snow, the poem continues,

> Nothing could make it snow.
> Not the burst water pipes, the leggings,
> the sleds, or the white horses.
> Not the smoky fountains, the clouds.

Again here we see Frost's acknowledgment that neither things of the world nor her own will can control the whims of nature, however fervent her "wish for a white field / like a fresh beginning." She reminds us that, try as we might, we cannot make meaning in the face of things greater than us, and this realization undermines any metaphor Frost constructs by its very attempt to remake one thing into another.

The intractability—even through imagination and art—of reality pervades this book. In "Hydrangeas," for example, "Desire came and went, / explaining nothing." Here no metaphoric connection is even attempted in the discussion of desire; it passes without consequence.

Nonetheless metaphor—what we *say* (to use one enunciation of the book's title)—can comfort, as in "Apiary IX," in which Frost writes,

> there's beauty in small lies.
> I say bees lick nectar after dark
> and bring it to the bough of the honey tree.
> Royal jelly keeps the larvae from falling
> from the cells. *Broodcomb, honeycomb, bee bread—*
> this is a harmless thought.

This passage recollects the "I will say *beauty*" pronunciation of the title. Frost suggests that the language we use to understand the world and to console ourselves can be beautiful and harmless. "I think with very great care with words one can have some truth and/or beauty," she says in the interview for the present essay.

While the themes of imagination, reality, and the role of art endure throughout her work, in *I Will Say Beauty,* Frost stops to question this mode of understanding. "Driftwood" reports:

> I consider my own similes—gardens, trees,
> an orchard still rooted, light marine
> in the blown air, fruit drunken on the swirl,
> like everything that leads up to a legend
> of leaving.

This impressive line break suggests a double entendre in the phrase "legend / of leaving." First it offers the sense that the images are themselves "legend" rather than reality; the enjambment leading to "of leaving" then adds the sense of departing, of leaving the real. We see this even in the progression of images: "gardens, trees, / an orchard" are all "still rooted" in the real, the concrete. "Light marine / in the blown air, fruit drunken on the swirl" begins to move into a high lyric style that no longer suggests obvious images; they depart from the rootedness.

Except in the poem's actually discussing the role of simile and metaphor, the refusal to make simple metaphors is nothing new to Frost. She has often used metaphoric association without explicitly rendering the metaphor itself. For example, bees easily symbolize sweetness; Frost lets that association stand, but seldom acknowledges it. In "The Part of the Bee's Body Embedded in the Flesh" she asks instead, "Why not say it hurts?" Early poems, such as "Liar's Dice," also use metaphor in subtle ways. In that poem Frost uses the dice metaphor about lying—but suggests that metaphor itself is a kind of lying. We don't know what is *not* being said, and the metaphor helps to obscure rather than to reveal.

More surprising are questions like the one that opens "Driftwood": "Have I lied to myself about art?" "Everything can't be art," it suggests. "Bird not bird / but driftwood roughed up by the sea." This image strikingly recollects the image in "Ellipsis," a poem published in Frost's first chapbook:

> your vision clears.
> The man's head in the road
> is no more than a dead hedgehog—

In both this very early poem and in Frost's latest work, we see imagination preceding reality, imagination's assumptions being jostled back to reality. At the close of "Driftwood," Frost laments, "Poor driftwood, poor / bird, with your premise of wings." Imagination, metaphors, art, even love as *Venus and Don Juan* suggests—none of these can transform the driftwood or the bird permanently. For Frost, for whom art has given whatever shape truth can have and thus has acted like religion might for many others, this question—"have I lied to myself about art?"—is a wrenching one.

Typically, however, she remains cool. "A Woman Like Yourself" describes a chance encounter with

> a woman like yourself,
> but older,
> only she isn't,

which compels "as strong a desire not to die / as anything you've felt before." This urgent but quiet realization continues to acknowledge the futility of the inconsequential *things* of a life:

> her friends, the bric-a-brac
> in her dressing room, blouses, even a gesture
> as her daughter turns her head
> will outlast her presence here.

The sentiment is frustrating and sad, but rather than rail against it, Frost resigns herself:

> you resume
> the day, lured by something,
> but as if nothing at all
> happened.

FROST'S ART

Carol Frost may be among the most respected writers living today about whom the least has been written. Her work is seldom easy; it prides itself on complexity and embraces a darkness many find difficult to confront. From that darkness, however, Frost conjures imagination, love, and beauty and holds them to the light, marveling at them. Ultimately, however, it is her art that matters most. The poems themselves house that marvel. Frost's gift is the inextricability of her keen insights from her structural mastery of her poems. In this she surpasses her own standards for excellence and distinguishes herself as a singular talent in American poetry today.

Selected Bibliography

WORKS OF CAROL FROST

POETRY
The Salt Lesson. Port Townsend, Wash.: Graywolf, 1976.

Liar's Dice. Ithaca, N.Y.: Ithaca House, 1978.

Cold Frame. Missoula, Mont.: Owl Creek, 1982.

The Fearful Child. Ithaca, N.Y.: Ithaca House, 1983.

Day of the Body. Memphis: Ion Books, 1986.

Chimera. Salt Lake City: Gibbs Smith, 1990.

Pure. Evanston, Ill.: TriQuarterly, 1994.

Venus and Don Juan. Evanston, Ill.: TriQuarterly, 1996.

Love and Scorn: New and Selected Poems. Evanston, Ill.: TriQuarterly, 2000.

I Will Say Beauty. Evanston, Ill.: TriQuarterly, 2003.

UNCOLLECTED ESSAYS

"Petrarch, Shakespeare, and the Blues." *New England Review* 18, no. 3:118–131 (summer 1997).

"A Secret Gladness." In *From Daughters to Mothers: I've Always Meant to Tell You.* Edited by Constance Warloe. New York: Pocket Books, 1997.

"Self Pity." *Prairie Schooner* 72, no. 1:9–18 (spring 1998). Reprinted in an expanded form in *After Confession: Poetry as Autobiography.* Edited by Kate Sontag and David Graham. St. Paul: Graywolf, 2001.

"A Poet's Tact, and a Necessary Tactlessness." *New England Review* 20, no. 3:196–204 (summer 1999).

"Hunting Journals '98–'00, Excerpts." *New England Review* 22, no. 1:60–67 (winter 2001).

"Frost's Way of Speaking." *New England Review* 23, no. 1:119–133 (winter 2002). (Carol Frost's essay about Robert Frost; they are not related.)

"Passing Beauty." *New England Review* 24, no. 1:91–103 (winter 2003). Online at http://www.poems.com/essafros.htm.

REVIEWS OF FROST'S WORK

Barresi, Dorothy. "The World as We Know It." *Gettysburg Review* 9, no. 1:55–72, pgs. 162-175, (winter 1996).

"Carol Frost." On *PoetryNet.* Edited by John Canaday. Online at http://www.members.aol.com/poetrynet/month/archive/frost/intro.html. (A brief article built around an interview with Frost.)

Daly, Catherine. "Miltons: Susan Mitchell's *Erotikon* and Carol Frost's *Love and Scorn: New and Selected Poems.*" *Valparaiso Poetry Review* 4: no. 1 (fall–winter 2002–2003). Online at http://www.valpo.edu/english/vpr/dalyreviewmiltons.html.

Disch, Thomas M. "Poetry Roundup." *Hudson Review* 50, no. 3:501–507 (autumn 1997). (Includes a brief negative review of *Venus and Don Juan.*)

Drayton, Fiona Russell. Review of *Venus and Don Juan. Blue Moon Review* 4 (1998–1999). Online at http://www.thebluemoon.com/4/russell1.html.

Greenwall, Garth. Review of *I Will Say Beauty. Pleiades Book Review* 24, no. 2:150–154. Online at http://www.cmsu.edu/englphil/Frost.html.

Killough, Ann. "Navigating Poetic Traditions." *Women's Review of Books* 21, no. 4:17–18 (January 2004). (Review of *I Will Say Beauty.*)

Lynch, Doris. Review of *Love and Scorn. Library Journal* 125, no. 7:96 (April 15, 2000).

Neelakantappa, Tara. Review of *Love and Scorn. Boston Review* 25, no. 6:58 (December 2000–January 2001). Online at http://www.bostonreview.net/BR25.6/micropoetry.html.

Publishers Weekly. Review of *Pure.* 241, no. 17:64 (April 25, 1994).

Publishers Weekly. Review of *Venus and Don Juan.* 243, no. 44:77 (October 28, 1996).

Publishers Weekly. Review of *Love and Scorn.* 247, no. 8:84 (February 21, 2000).

Publishers Weekly. Review of *I Will Say Beauty.* 250, no. 16:57 (April 21, 2003).

Ratner, Rochelle. Review of *I Will Say Beauty. Library Journal* 128, no. 10:126 (June 1, 2003).

Satterfield, Jane. Review of *I Will Say Beauty. Antioch Review* 62, no. 2:370–371 (spring 2004).

Seaman, Donna. Review of *I Will Say Beauty. Booklist* 99, no. 15:1366 (April 1, 2003).

Shotts, Jeffrey. Review of *Love and Scorn. Rain Taxi Review of Books, Online Edition* (summer 2000). Online at http://www.raintaxi.com/online/2000summer/frost.shtml.

Stenstrom, Christine. Review of *Venus and Don Juan. Library Journal* 121, no. 15:72 (September 15, 1996).

Stitt, Peter. "Realism, Death, and Philosophy." *Georgia Review* 49, no. 2:397–408 (summer 1987). (Review of *Day of the Body.*)

Travisano, Thomas. Review of *Chimera. Prairie Schooner* 65, no.3:140–143 (fall 1991).

Wunderlich, Mark. Review of *Venus and Don Juan*. *Boston Review* 22, no. 2 (April–May 1997) Online at http://www.bostonreview.net/BR22.2/poetrymicro.html.

—CORINNE WOHLFORD TAFF

Dana Gioia

1950–

Dana Gioia (pronounced "Joy-a") is the best-known figure of the New Formalist movement, which, in the late 1970s and early 1980s, argued for a return to traditional forms in poetry. Believing that academic poetry alienated readers and that free verse lacked memorability, the New Formalists argued for accessible, even popular, subjects and a return to rhyme. The group distinguished itself from the formalists of the 1950s, including Donald Justice, Richard Wilbur, and Anthony Hecht, among others, who did not see themselves as writing primarily for the general public. While their free-verse detractors said that poetic forms were dead, the New Formalists felt that traditional forms were a way to revitalize poetry. Gioia himself prefers the term "expansive" over "New Formalist," in order to embrace the best of both the formal and free-verse traditions. His own work is written roughly half in each.

CENTRAL THEMES AND SUBJECTS

Central to Gioia's work is the notion of loss. Some of Gioia's best work (particularly the poem "Planting a Sequoia," written in free verse) is about his grief following the loss of his son, Michael Jasper Gioia, who died of sudden infant death syndrome (SIDS) at the age of four months. Yet human loss in general pervades his work; he is aware of the inability to sustain transcendent moments in the midst of the commonplace. He uses the motif of the journey in particular to explore this theme, one that often brings the traveler back to the same place. In addition, he writes about the landscape of California as well as the landscape of New York,

tracing his own literal journey from the West Coast to the East, and back again. Ultimately, he questions the efficacy of words to capture experience, but realizes they are necessary to create both personal and public memory.

BIOGRAPHY

Michael Dana Gioia was born to working-class parents in the Los Angeles suburb of Hawthorne, California, on December 24, 1950. His father, Michael Gioia, drove a cab, and his mother, Dorothy Ortiz Gioia, was a telephone operator for AT&T. His family nurtured his love for the arts, as April Lindner notes, "driving him on their days off to galleries where he could look at paintings and literary manuscripts." Moreover, when his uncle Theodore Ortiz died in a plane crash, he left an impressive collection of recordings and scores that played an important role in Gioia's development; his first choice of careers was music.

Gioia was educated in Catholic schools, which were significant in his development as an artist, particularly in his use of religious iconography. He was valedictorian of Junipero Serra High School, although his conduct was less exemplary than his scholastic achievement: he was suspended three times. In 1969, he entered Stanford University, the first in his family to attend college.

At Stanford, he majored in English with a minor in German. Although he loved music, he felt like an outsider because his teachers did not encourage his interest in tonal music. He was the naysayer in his English classes, too. "Coming to maturity as a writer in the California of

Haight-Ashbury, one was engulfed in waves of fashion," he has said. "I found myself resisting. My literary sensibility tends to be contrarian. Had I grown up in a period when people write sonnets and villanelles, I would probably have gone off to Black Mountain College" (as quoted in Lindner). He was active on campus, becoming the editor of the literary magazine *Sequoia* and writing reviews for the *Stanford Daily*. After graduating Phi Beta Kappa and summa cum laude in 1973, he went to Harvard University to study comparative literature.

Although he was influenced by his teachers Elizabeth Bishop and Robert Fitzgerald, and he ultimately completed all of his coursework for the doctorate, he decided to leave Harvard before taking his degree in order to pursue an M.B.A. (completed in 1977) at Stanford. His reasons were partly financial: his siblings Ted (born in 1957), Gregory (1970), and Cara (1971) were considerably younger, and he could help to support his family. But his reasons were also literary. Gioia has explained,

> I entered business because I needed to make a living and wanted some control over my life. The other reason I left academics was to become a poet. That sounds paradoxical, but I felt that I was becoming a worse writer with each passing year in academia. My poetry was becoming too studied and self-conscious. (as quoted in Lindner).

At Stanford he met his future wife, Mary Hiecke, in 1975. The two married in 1980 and had three sons. The death of the couple's first son of SIDS in 1987 was one of the most devastating experiences of Gioia's life. He said at the service remembering his son, "Our son was bright, healthy, and happy till the last night we put him into bed. We had no inkling of the death which was so suddenly to take him from us. So we were utterly unprepared for this grief" ("A Remembrance"). The Gioias went on to have another child, Theodore Jasper Gioia, shortly after (in 1988), and five years later (in 1993) Michael Frederick Gioia was born.

Gioia became a successful businessman, rising through the ranks at General Foods in White Plains, New York, and eventually becoming a vice president. His Kool-Aid account was one of the company's most profitable. Yet he kept his poetry a secret; he has joked that he bought up copies of his poetry when they appeared in the company store. After he was selected one of *Esquire*'s most influential leaders under forty, however, the secret was out. Since most poets have academic jobs, his unusual journey to poetic fame earned him the tag "businessman poet."

Gioia began by publishing his poetry through fine arts presses, maintaining the longest relationship with Aralia Press; many of his finest poems, such as "Planting a Sequoia," appeared first in chapbooks published by Aralia. By the time he was in his mid-fifties he had published three books of poetry: *Daily Horoscope* (1986); *The Gods of Winter* (1991), chosen for the British Poetry Book Society; and *Interrogations at Noon* (2001), winner of the American Book Award, all published with Graywolf Press. He had also become a noted critic; his books of criticism include *Can Poetry Matter?: Essays on Poetry and American Culture* (1992), *Barrier of a Common Language: An American Looks at Contemporary British Poetry* (2003), and *Disappearing Ink: Poetry at the End of Print Culture* (2004). His essay "Fallen Western Star: The Decline of San Francisco as a Literary Region," first published in the winter 1999–2000 issue of the *Hungry Mind Review,* set off a regional debate that culminated in the collection of essays titled *The "Fallen Western Star" Wars: A Debate about Literary California* (2001), edited by Jack Foley.

Among other projects, Gioia was also the translator of poems by the Italian Nobel Prize winner Eugenio Montale, in a volume titled *Mottetti: Poems of Love: The Motets of Eugenio Montale* (1990); the author of *Nosferatu: An Opera Libretto* (2001); and a prominent textbook editor, of which an *An Introduction to Poetry* (2005), coedited with X. J Kennedy, is the best known. In 1995, with Michael Peich of Aralia Press, he founded the West Chester Poetry Conference in West Chester, Pennsylvania, the only conference devoted to formal poetry in the United States, and in 2001 he founded Teaching Poetry, a conference based in Santa Rosa, for high school teachers. He is also a frequent commentator for the British Broadcasting Corporation. Because of Gioia's versatility, Matthew Brennan has called him "the Auden of our time" (Brennan, "The Poet as Public Intellectual").

Perhaps it was this versatility—in addition to his background in business—that made Gioia the Bush administration's choice to head the National Endowment for the Arts in 2003, an appointment that made him simultaneously the first Italian chairman and the first Hispanic chairman (his father was Sicilian, his mother Mexican) after he was approved unanimously—in Senate confirmation hearings in which his business background was almost exclusively the focus. Because the religious right had criticized the way in which NEA grants had funded controversial exhibits, such as those of Robert Mappelthorpe, as well as individual performance artists, such as Annie Sprinkle, Gioia moved quickly to diffuse controversy by creating a national tour of Shakespeare plays. He told Geoff Edgers of the *Boston Globe,*

The average American wants art in … communities and in … schools. It's not a program of the left or the right. It's mainstream American opinion. One of the major needs is to build a public consensus for the support of art and arts education, and we're going to do that by building a kind of inclusive coalition, by refusing to polarize.

"CAN POETRY MATTER?"

Although Gioia is arguably the best poet of the New Formalist movement, he is at the same time its most ardent spokesman. His essay "Can Poetry Matter?," originally published in the *Atlantic Monthly* in 1991, was one of the most controversial pieces in that magazine's long history and perhaps one of the best literary essays in the past fifty years. This essay, collected in a 1992 volume titled *Can Poetry Matter?* that also included Gioia essays such as "Notes on the New Formalism" and "Business and Poetry," support Matthew Brennan's claim that Gioia has the "uncanny ability to finger the pulse of poetry in our culture" (Brennan, "The Poet as Public Intellectual"). In addition, Gioia makes the case for poets like Robinson Jeffers, Weldon Kees, and Ted Kooser, who have been largely forgotten by mainstream literary critics. Ultimately, however, Gioia believes (as he told Gloria Brame), "The culture will take the discussion where it need[s] to go."

The conservative critic Hilton Kramer underscores, on the one hand, why many poets and critics find Gioia's book significant:

From time to time there appears a volume of criticism that, in the course of its attention to particular works of art, illuminates a good many more questions about our artistic and cultural affairs…. To these questions Mr. Gioia brings the gift and experience of a first-rate literary artist, the intellectual rigor of a tough-minded critic, and an outlook on the world that is the reverse of everything we associate with the word 'academic.' He also brings a generosity of spirit that lives on easy terms with the obligation to make distinctions, including distinctions of quality.

Stephen Yenser, in "Some Poets' Criticism and the Age," on the other hand, sums up why many other critics find Gioia infuriating. Yenser argues that

Gioia is a classic conservative in certain respects: he is nostalgic for less "complex" apprehensions of the world; he thinks that American literary history has been all downhill for the last century or so; and he prefers the viewpoint of the (purportedly) independent businessman or entrepreneur to that of the (supposedly) beholden academician.... in view of his acumen and his knowledge of craft [the book] ... is anything but a carefully thought-out undertaking."

Yenser takes issue with what Gioia sees as a paucity of good literary criticism and a lack of good contemporary poetry. Yet he does applaud Gioia's work on Weldon Kees and Robinson Jeffers, bringing these forgotten poets to the eyes of the public.

H. L. Hix underscores the appeal of Gioia, no matter what side of the poetic—or political—fence the reader is on: "His judgments, whether one agrees with them or disagrees, never fail to interest and instruct: Gioia writes a criticism that counts."

The purpose of the essay "Can Poetry Matter?" was threefold: to demonstrate that poetry is irrelevant in American culture, to postulate why this situation has occurred, and to offer some solutions. "American poetry now belongs to a subculture," Gioia says. "No longer part of the mainstream of artistic and intellectual life, it has become the specialized occupation of a relatively small and isolated group." The irony of the situation, argues Gioia, is that there are more writing programs than ever before, more books of poetry being published, and more poets giving readings. While such facts would indicate a "golden age of American poetry," the reality is just the opposite. Members of the general public are simply not interested in poetry. Since major daily newspapers rarely review poetry—and then not in a timely manner—Gioia concludes that newpapers, which are in the business of selling their product, do not see poetry as being of interest to their readership.

At the same time, he sees poets as writing for their own "subculture," reviewing the work of friends and thus not pointing out the true quality of the work, and being based, almost entirely, in universities, so that there is no diversity of occupation (and presumably experience) with poets. As a result, poetry has become banal. He suggests that poets should write to appeal to the general cultured reader, be more honest in their criticism, participate in the larger culture outside academia, and be less self-absorbed with regard to their own work. In short, poets should make poetry more relevant to others. Further, poets at their readings should include work by poets they admire; intermingle other arts, such as dance, in the performance of poetry; and work harder to appeal to a younger audience. He implies that the joy of the art of poetry has been lost as poets become more concerned with tenure and promotion than with the cultural importance of poetry. Gioia argues, instead, that poets should become less concerned with their own self-promotion and more cognizant of their role as poetic ambassadors to the larger culture. In short, if people do not have positive experiences with good poetry, they will continue to feel that all poetry is irrelevant. Gioia's implication is that New Formalist poetry—accessible, traditional, memorable—will help to make poetry relevant again.

In "Notes on the New Formalism," Gioia sketches out the relationship between free verse and metrical poetry in the American literary scene and posits his theory regarding the phenomenon of New Formalism. Gioia, who writes both free verse and metrical poetry, makes clear that "formal verse, like free verse, is neither intrinsically bad nor good." Gioia makes this claim in the context of a larger argument; as H. L. Hix has pointed out, many American poets see metrical poetry as "elitist" and no longer poetically viable. Nothing could be further from the truth, argues Gioia, who traces metrical poetry to its origins in oral tradition. He points out that free verse had taken over the literary scene by 1980; he finds it troubling that many younger poets "could not write with minimal competence in traditional meters;" and he gives examples of what he calls the "pseudo-formal poem," written by talented poets without any real understanding of meter. The New Formalists, in Gioia's view, through their understanding of meter and tradition, attempt to bridge the gap between the academic and general audience. Because he prefers the term "expansive," he is suggesting that New Formalism is not a substitute for free verse but has its own role to play.

In keeping with his theory that poetry should not be a property exclusively of the university, he goes on to sketch a different life for poets in "Business and Poetry," in a way turning the notion of artist as outsider on its head, because most poets are part of the academic establishment. Along with Wallace Stevens, the famous insuranceman-poet, Gioia points to the poets A. R. Ammons and James Dickey, in addition to lesser-known poets, such as Edmund Clarence Stedman and William Bronk, to illustrate poets who have had careers outside academia. He notes that "business provided these men with the same security and satisfaction that many of their contemporaries found in teaching." Gioia argues that because they have been outside the academy these businessmen-poets have sometimes developed more idiosyncratic voices. He maintains that "working in nonliterary careers taught them a lesson too few American writers learn—that poetry is only one part of life, that there are some things more important than writing poetry." Because their livelihoods do not depend on poetry, they may have more perspective. Ultimately, the essay argues that academic poets should value what businessmen-poets offer.

Lastly, in this volume Gioia brings lesser-known poets to the eyes of the public, and in so doing carries out his poetic ambassador mission. Three of his favorites are Robinson Jeffers, Weldon Kees, and Ted Kooser. These are strikingly different poets—Jeffers a Californian with an emphasis on thorny, long lines and environmental issues; Kees a Nebraskan with a penchant for Eliotic pronouncements and moroseness; and Kooser a plain-speaking Iowan with a preoccupation with regional landscapes.

Yet Gioia's criterion is simply quality. While many take issue with this and other essays in the book, most critics applaud his foregrounding of such poets.

THE "FALLEN WESTERN STAR" WARS

Not only has Gioia participated in national poetic controversies, he has participated in regional ones. His essay "Fallen Western Star: The Decline of San Francisco as a Literary Region," argues that California is not an important center of literary activity. The essay produced a range of responses: from incredulous anger at its claims to sympathetic relief at their finally being articulated. So spirited was the debate, and so wide-ranging the participants, that a collection featuring Gioia's essay and a range of responses was published in 2001 by the California-based Scarlet Tanager Press.

Gioia argues that "in 1899 San Francisco was a major literary center—a city where influential new trends emerged and young writers achieved national reputations." Jack London, Bret Harte, and Frank Norris called it home. Not only was the city's literature important but also its newspapers. He tells the story, for example, of Edwin Markham's poem "The Man with the Hoe," which after its appearance in the *San Francisco Examiner* quickly became the most popular poem in America.

Yet Gioia points out that California's literary influence has disappeared. He says that there are few California literary magazines, and most of them are financial failures. In fact, he claims that "there is not a single major literary quarterly currently published in California." Because there is no place for young writers to flourish, Gioia says that most of them escape to the academy or publish elsewhere.

Why has this happened? For Gioia, the answer partially lies in geography. California is a highway culture, as opposed to New York, which has more of a social center. He makes the point that in the East, "cultural life tends to be public and social," while in the West, "literary life ... tends to be private and individualistic." What to do about this situation? His essay calls for a movement that transcends local "boosterism" to establish a serious literary culture. After all, Gioia writes, "Local culture matters because human existence is local."

The response to his essay started with outrage, with Howard Junker leading the pack. In "Thus Do I Refute Gioia," collected in *The "Fallen Western Star" Wars,* Junker says that "Dana Gioia is so estranged, so painfully oblivious, that if he weren't also so pompous and inaccurate, it would be cruel to take him to task." The gist of Junker's refutation is that Gioia should open his eyes to California's literary riches, its universities, its magazines, its writers, its billionaires, and its actors. How can California be seen as lacking, Junker argues, when it is home to everyone from Alice Walker, to Sandra McPherson, to Gary Soto, to Sharon Stone, to Danny Glover? Jonah Raskin agrees with Junker, finding Gioia's take "odd." He argues that there is much "richness and diversity" in California, but that regionalism has been made over into a new internationalism. Richard Silberg sees Gioia's essay as logically flawed; he points out that the Bay Area is rich in poetry, although he does agree with Gioia that fiction is not California's strong suit (he says that economics determine this and that fiction is marketed nationally, not locally). Like Junker he ends his piece with a list, although his contains only poets.

By contrast, others see Gioia's piece as an articulation of a serious problem. David Mason, a Colorado writer, detects defensiveness on the part of many of the respondents, saying, "I think we in the West had better ask ourselves why so much of our cultural energy is spent in or sustained by the East." He sees the points in Gioia's essay as "challenges," calling people to consider Gioia's claims seriously. Jack Foley does the same, saying that "for Ruskin, Junker, and Silberg, the fact that Dana doesn't agree with them means that he must be missing something. If he weren't missing something, he would agree with them! That is an indication of their tolerance for genuine disagreement: he's just an outsider, don't listen to him, he's been in New York for twenty years." He says that "Gioia's essay *asserts* that there are many, many fine writers in the Bay Area" but "that they don't *talk* to one another." Gioia's provocative article did, however, seem to get people talking. And his 2003 anthology *The Misread City: New Literary Los Angeles,* edited with Scott Timberg, may be a continuation of that discussion. This book, which contains essays as well as poetry and prose by and about California's writers, attempts to cover a broad swath of perspectives. Here Gioia positions himself as a California writer, perhaps to answer any questions people may have had about his calling himself one.

BARRIER OF A COMMON LANGUAGE

Dana Gioia is a skilled translator, particularly of Romance languages, and so it is almost paradoxical to encounter a critical volume in which the language he is translating for the public is English—British English, that is. The 2003 volume *Barrier of a Common Language: An American Looks at Contemporary British Poetry* collects Gioia's articles and book reviews on British poetry over the past twenty years. In the preface, he claims that "American literati no longer read new British poetry" and bemoans the fact that a situation that he noticed thirty years ago has not yet been rectified.

The title essay outlines why there is such a disjunction between contemporary British and contemporary American poetry. While American poets were shaped by modernism, British poets saw it as only one influence; and while Americans took the international stage in the second half of the century, they exhibited an arrogance that the British resented as much in their poetry as their politics. During this time, British poets became more regional and inward.

Some of the names in modern British poetry are well-known, even to Americans—Philip Larkin, Wendy Cope, Ted Hughes, and Kingsley Amis—yet there are some surprises in Gioia's observations even there: he shows us Wendy Cope as a serious love poet and Philip Larkin as a smutty letter writer. What is perhaps most useful about the collection is the discussion of poets less known: James Fenton and Charles Causley, to name only two. Gioia points out the range of Fenton's work and praises his war poems in particular; in Causley's case, he uses the argument for New Formalism to bring him to attention. Causley is a popular poet, who was both Ted Hughes's and Philip Larkin's choice for poet laureate of England. As Gioia writes, *"Best loved. Most needed. Man of the people.* These are not phrases one is accustomed to hear concerning a contemporary poet. Surely some readers find them embarrassing." While these may not be popular ways to gain cynical American interest, he is unabashed about what draws him to Causley. That is the strength of the book: the way Gioia illustrates why these internationally unappreciated poets should be brought to the attention of the American public.

LETTERPRESS PUBLICATIONS

While employed at General Foods and living in Bronxville, New York, Gioia met Michael Peich, who would go on to found Aralia Press, one of the best fine presses in the country. Although Gioia would publish with other fine presses—Bowery Press and Windhover Press are two examples—it is Gioia's long-term publishing relationship with Aralia that epitomizes his attitude about the importance of letterpress printing. Gioia's two-poem chapbook *Summer* (1983) was Aralia's first publication. In

the essay "Dana Gioia and Fine Press Printing," Michael Peich writes that he was "attracted … by the clarity and perfection of Dana's writing," adding, "Gioia's crafting of a poem is similar to the construction of a finely printed book of poetry." Gioia went on to become Aralia's editor.

Of Gioia's publications at Aralia, it is perhaps the 1991 chapbook *Planting a Sequoia* that is best known, dedicated to his infant son who died of SIDS. The poems "Prayer," "All Souls'," "The Song," "The Gods of Winter," and "Planting a Sequoia" explore the inconsolable nature of grief. Two poems, "Night Watch" and "Veterans' Cemetery, " address the death of Gioia's uncle Ted, who was such a musical influence on him. These poems, which interrupt those about Gioia's son, serve both as buffer and intensifier: a buffer in that the beautiful poems about a dead child are easier to bear, an intensifier in that the poems in the book deal with the deaths of two of the most important people in Gioia's life.

No stranger to grief, Gioia was the perfect choice to write the introduction to Aralia's reissue as a chapbook of W. H. Auden's poem "September 1, 1939," following the terrorist attacks on New York and Washington, D.C., of September 11, 2001. Gioia writes,

Like virtually everyone else in America the terrorist attacks of September 11 left me stunned, anguished, and confused. Watching the gruesome televised images, repeated almost hypnotically, of the World Trade Center burning and collapsing, I can't imagine that anything I felt was not replicated in a hundred million other viewers—all united by our common shock and grief…. Poetry is a vast and flexible art that should be able to express all of human experience—public and private. The horrors of September 11 remind us that the art should be able to articulate our common sorrows as well as our private ones. Sometimes great poetry is not conspicuously individual, original, or complex, but communal, familiar, and direct. What matters most is not its stylistic novelty, but its expressive power. (Introduction, "All I Have Is a Voice").

This philosophy concerning the importance of poetry to answer both personal and public concerns dominates Gioia's work.

DAILY HOROSCOPE

Responses to the collection *Daily Horoscope* (1986) fell along predictable lines, with New Formalists praising the book and detractors criticizing its neoconservatism. At the heart of the division is the question of what is more important: risk taking or tradition preserving? Greg Kuzma sums up the negative camp: "*Daily Horoscope* is a rather dull thing. If it does indeed exemplify where our poetry is going in the next twenty years, we should all of us give up reading. Gioia seems oblivious to the poetry of commitment and risk-taking" ("Dana Gioia and the Poetry of Money"). Radcliffe Squires turns the risk argument on its head by saying, "the very quiet of his poetry constitutes a species of revolution by insisting that life belongs to life rather than to ideology and that we see it not as a transient loyalty but as the unmoving dapple of light on the stream that is always moving." Or as Robert E. Knoll puts it, "These are patterned poems addressed to the general reader about recognizable human experience." One's poetic philosophy determines whether these are admirable criteria or not.

Gioia begins *Daily Horoscope* with "The Burning Ladder," which deals with one of Gioia's major concerns: transcendence. Jacob misses his own opportunity for transcendence, and, as Gioia argues elsewhere, we all do—or, more precisely, we lack the ability to sustain our realizations (a premise that both James Joyce and Virginia Woolf have also argued, but in prose). As Gioia writes in "Flying over Clouds," we might glimpse but cannot "breathe" perfection:

O paradise beyond the glass,
beyond our touch, cast and recast,
shifting in wind. Delicate world
or air too thin to breathe, of cold
beyond endurance.

Gioia is, among other things, a poet of longing for the "platonic script," the world of the ideal, like his poetic forebear, Donald Justice.

While loss and missed opportunity frame the book, critics are often drawn to Gioia's poems about California, and possibly because he is a different type of California poet—businessman rather than bohemian—he has been criticized for these poems, which strike some as wooden. Such a poem is "Cruising with the Beach Boys," with its resounding iambs and end-stopped lines:

Some nights I drove down to the beach to park
And walk along the railings of the pier.
The water down below was cold and dark,
The waves monotonous against the shore.
The darkness and the mist, the midnight sea,
The flickering lights reflected from the city—
A perfect setting for a boy like me,
The Cecil B. DeMille of my self-pity.

Kuzma, for one, sees this passage as "verse" rather than "poetry." Yet Lewis Turco defends the passage—and poem—noting, "there are many rhythmic variations Gioia has worked into the poem.... they do not 'jingle'... The meter imitates the motion of the waves" (Turco *American Poets Since WWII* 86). However, the critic Kevin Walzer, who in general is an advocate of Gioia, admits, "Gioia's most distinctive work is much better than 'Cruising with the Beach Boys'."

While in "Cruising with the Beach Boys" the meter is the poem's foremost concern, the issue in "California Hills in August" is the landscape:

I can imagine someone who found
these fields unbearable, ...

. . . .
An Easterner especially

The poet favors the "gentle" offering over the garish display, a connoisseur's savoring of the not-so-obvious. Or, as Lindner sums up, "The poet values these dry California hills precisely because they can only be appreciated by the initiated." This savoring of landscape is also clear in Gioia's homage to Raymond Chandler, "In Chandler Country." The poem captures the hot, gritty atmosphere of a Chandler novel, furthering Lindner's claim that in Gioia "atmosphere and content are inseparable from one another." She unequivocally sees Gioia as a Western writer.

Yet this vice president of General Foods, and longtime resident of New York, covers not only the natural landscape of California but the suburban landscape of John Cheever. Gioia's poems on East Coast suburban life are often misread—some do not hear the longing for escape in the poems, taking them at face value—but they do articulate Gioia's intimate knowledge of another part of the country. As Robert McPhillips notes, "Both Cheever and Gioia share the experience of creating their own fragile domestic paradises, their own careers and marriages, their own 'homes,' as adults" (McPhillips *The New Formalism*). "In Cheever Country" illustrates the "glimpse" so characteristic of Gioia's vision:

If there is an afterlife, let it be a small town
gentle as this spot at just this instant.
But the doors close.

Gioia is preoccupied with the alienated person, and nowhere is this clearer than in the title poem. "Daily Horoscope," with its use of second person, invites the reader into the experience, one whose terror lies in its ordinariness. "Today will be like any other day," the first poem in the series indicates, and it is that awareness that is most frightening of all, that life is an exercise in learning how to accept "less," as the second poem in the series admits. Although many comment on Gioia's poetic kinship with Donald Justice, it is also important to remember that Gioia's teacher was Elizabeth Bishop, and his work often deals with the theme that "the art of losing isn't hard to master." The series ends with a mysterious phone call at night:

Soft and familar,
it mentions names you haven't heard for years,
names of another place, another time,
that street by street restore
the lost geography of childhood.

After the call, the disoriented "you" is left with only himself, which feels impossible to bear—an idea that is one of Gioia's central subjects.

In addition to longing and loss, and East and West Coast landscapes, Gioia's themes include music, women, and journeys, all of which hold out the possibility of transcendence and escape. Most notable of the poems on music are "Bix Beiderbecke (1903–1931)," "The Memory," and "Song from a Courtyard Window." Not surprisingly, the most effective poems on music also involve loss. As "Song from a Courtyard Window" points out,

This was the only music we had hoped for:
something to make us close our eyes and lose
the courtyard full of people, silence all
the conversations at the other tables
and stop us from believing that we heard
the sunlight burning in the open sky.

But the transcendent moment "never lasts."

For the romantic Gioia, women, too, offer possible transcendence. In "Photograph of My Mother as a Young Girl," the speaker looks at a picture of his mother from years ago. The speaker is captivated by the picture, but the moment has been lost, and the speaker is powerless to change time or experience from his vantagepoint in the future. Also of note are "His

Three Women" and "The Country Wife," which might serve as mirrors of each other. While "His Three Women" emphasizes a man's relationship with women, "The Country Wife" illustrates the unsustainability of relationships. Both poems concern longing; yet in the latter, the romantic longing evident in Gioia's work is transferred to death. Presumably ordinary life is too much for the country wife, and the implication is that she has committed suicide.

Journeys also play an important role in the poems, but sadly they often take one back to the same place. In "An Emigre in Autumn," the "you," who is miles from home—his greatest journey has taken place before the poem begins—is told to

Count the steps you take each day—
Miles that span no distances,
Journeys in sunlight toward the dark.

While there is a sense of brief escape in the sunlight and "glistening" autumn leaves, Gioia reminds us that

But even here the subtle breeze
Plots with underlying shadows.
One gust of wind and suddenly
The sun is falling from the trees.

In "Instructions for the Afternoon" the "you"—presumably a tourist—is told to "Leave the museums, the comfortable rooms, / the same distractions of the masterpiece." Instead the journey of the self must come through "the dark churches / in back towns that history has forgotten." The tourist must blend into the place, "wait like a mirror," "wait like the stone / face of a statue waits." Once again the epiphany may be that this is all there is. At the end of the poem Gioia sums up the paradox of such a journey:

Not a vision to pursue, and yet
these insufficiencies make up the world.
Strange how all journeys come to this: the sun

bright on the unfamiliar hills, new vistas
dazzling the eye, the stubborn heart unchanged.

"The Journey, the Arrival and the Dream" follows a similar path; the "you" has made an arduous journey to a place far from modern life, and Gioia writes,

did it cross your mind that this same village
lost in the dry mountains was all
there ever would be?

The use of the second person, as in other poems, implicates the reader—although there are physical details in the poem that indicate that the character is a woman—and also creates the effect of a hyperawareness of the character, the way a voiceover in a movie does. This woman, who has journeyed so far only to be disoriented from her own self, is told to "Close your eyes. Accept / that some things must remain invisible." Ironically, the swallows at the end of the poem—which recall the pigeons at the end of Wallace Stevens' "Sunday Morning"—have the capacity to "glid[e] downward in the valley / as if the light would last forever." But human beings' self-awareness makes it impossible to dive into a moment in just that way. Or as Gioia sums up in "The Letter," one of the last poems in the book,

And in the end, all that is really left
Is a feeling—strong and unavoidable—
That somehow we deserved something better.

One poem that glimpses this "something better" is "The Room Upstairs," a dramatic monologue uncharacteristic of the style of the rest of the book. Ironically, though, in this case, the person who is transformed is the reader, not the speaker, as is the case in dramatic monologues. Robert Richman notes that "*Daily Horoscope* would be a lesser book were it not for the inclusion of the poem," arguing that it highlights "the main peril of Gioia's own undertaking, namely, permitting dream and reality to intermingle." At the same time, the poem may be exploring the irony that, even if we are transformed, we may not know it when we see it, or, particularly in terms of repressed sexuality, what we have closed off to the world we may have closed off to ourselves.

The speaker of the poem is a landlord, an older man who is showing someone a room (the situation is remarkably similar to that in Robert Browning's "My Last Duchess"); he unwittingly reveals his love for David, a student who used to rent a room from him and was killed in a tragic mountain-climbing accident. The speaker foreshadows this lack of self-knowledge by admitting,

> I never look in mirrors anymore,
> Or if I do I just stare at the tie
> I'm knotting, and it's easy to pretend
> I haven't changed.

This freeze-frame of time makes it possible for him to bemoan the fact that he has never had a child (particularly a son), without registering in his own psyche the depth of his loss. At the same time, when he talks about David, he reveals to the reader the ways in which his dreams to be a writer and his longing for a son merge in his sexual longing for David. While living at the rooming house, David becomes hurt while saving a fellow climber, and afterward, cleaning up his wounds, David invites the speaker to see them:

> I watched him standing in the steamy
>   bathroom—
> His naked body shining from the water.
> . . . .
> Wounds deep enough to hide your fingers in.
> I felt like holding him but couldn't bear it.

Later, after David's death, the speaker dreams of him, and David offers himself up as a Christ figure: "'I've come back to you,' he said. 'Look at me. / Let me show you what I've done for

you.'" In the dream, the speaker gets to do what he couldn't do in real life: hold David in his arms. Yet, as in so many of Gioia's poems, loss overtakes the joyous transformation of the moment. The speaker admits, "he grew lighter, slipping silently away / Like snow between my fingers, and was gone."

THE GODS OF WINTER

The Gods of Winter, published in 1991, and arguably Gioia's best collection, was virtually ignored in the United States, although it was well received in Britain. Richard Francis of *PN Review* says that *"The Gods of Winter* can be poignant and directly expressive," but also exhibits "a determination to get the moral hammered out with the same assiduity as the structure." Joyce Walter writes,

> all I could do by the end of the book was fall in love. In love with his firm control, and lack of it. In love with the masterly way he crafts his lines— like someone who has lived for 200 years and learned his skill all along the way.

Anne Stevenson, in a long review, says,

> Seeking a precise adjective to describe Dana Gioia's poetry, I came up with beautiful.... *The Gods of Winter* is an important book, if only because it exemplifies Gioia's courageously aesthetic approach to poetry—to its language and rhythms.

The book is framed by a quote by Ben Jonson on the death of his son, "Farewell, thou child of my right hand, and joy," and is thoroughly permeated in grief. Its most important poem, "Planting a Sequoia," is about what we do to commemorate the living and the dead. The speaker, whose son has died, cannot follow the usual Sicilian custom of honoring the *life* of his first son with the planting of a fruit-bearing tree, but instead he turns the custom on its heels, by honoring the *death* of his son with a tree: in

California, the speaker can plant a giant redwood, with the hair and birth cord of his son, and through this tree, known for its longevity, the dead son can live longer than the rest of this family. Because this tree can do for the child what the father and other family members cannot—make him live—the speaker addresses the tree with both sadness and reverence:

> And when our family is no more, all of his
>   unborn brothers dead,
> Every niece and nephew scattered, the house torn
>   down,
> His mother's beauty ashes in the air,
> I want you to stand among strangers, all young
>   and ephemeral to you,
> Silently keeping the secret of your birth.

While "Planting a Sequoia" honors loss and nature, "Counting the Children" explores the horror of loss. Mr. Choi, an accountant, is called to the home of a dead woman, who has inexplicably left behind a collection of maimed and broken dolls. This eerie collection emblemizes both lost children and lost childhood, for Mr. Choi asks, "Where were the children who promised them love? … Was this where all lost childhoods go?" It is loss expressed by multitude, by this broken anonymity, that bothers Mr Choi, or, as Gioia writes, "Dust has a million lives, the heart has one."

The speaker in "Planting a Sequoia" is clearly haunted by his grief; however, he has found a way to channel it. Mr. Choi has no such channel. He is haunted by the dolls, dreaming first of frenzied numbers that he cannot add up, then of family members drifting off in his ancestral tree. Finally, in the dream, he must add things up, or his daughter will die. When he fails, Mr. Choi says, "I saw the dolls then—screaming in the flames."

In waking up, he thinks of his daughter and how he used to check, each night, to see if she was breathing. At that time he thought,

> How delicate this vessel in our care,
> This gentle soul we summoned to the world,

> A life we treasured but could not protect.
> This was the terror I could not confess—
> Not even to my wife.

Seven years have passed since then. Yet, in the wake of the dream, he is driven to check her again:

> She was asleep—the blankets softly rising
> And falling with each breath, the faint light trac-
>   ing
> The sleek unfoldings of her long black hair.
> Then suddenly I felt myself go numb.

What he sees is the multitude of children that his daughter represents, a blessed innocence lost first through adulthood and then through death. In a flash he realizes that our hopefulness is based in our beginnings, and, while we yearn for immortality, what binds us together is the gathered force of our communal loss. In viewing his daughter, he notices her own dolls, and they haunt him as symbols of childhood that cannot last. They seem to have the knowledge that he has just acquired:

> Their sharp glass eyes surveyed me with
>   contempt.
> They recognized me only as a rival,
> The one whose world would keep no place for
>   them.
> I felt like holding them tight in my arms,
> Promising I would never let them go,
> But they would trust no promises of mine.
> I feared that if I touched one, it would scream.

The magnitude of human loss strikes him with revulsion, and he is left in horror. Yet what the reader tastes in the imaginary situation of Mr. Choi is the ash-in-the-mouth taste of Dana Gioia's own grief (in fact the poem directly follows "Planting a Sequoia"). In the loss of his own son, held forever like a doll in childhood, is the loss of every child and the loss of every person. Once one has gained that knowledge of the universality of loss, there is no going back.

Gioia breaks the mood of this somber book through humor and distance of material. While *The Gods of Winter,* as a whole, intensifies Gioia's recurrent theme of loss, and many poems, like "Rough Country," "Places to Return," and "Guide to the Other Gallery" return to the daily loss of human life, in this book Gioia makes a clear choice to diversify. What may be appropriately intense in a chapbook may feel relentless in a full-length collection. While "My Confessional Sestina" pokes fun at the proliferation of mediocre sestinas, "The Homecoming" is about a escaped convict who returns home to kill his foster mother. Both poems deal with an illusion of power—one over poetic form, the other over life and morality; on another level, these poems may further a theme of helplessness in the book. In both, it is the speaker who points out the paradox.

"My Confessional Sestina" is a good example of Gioia's attitude toward form. He wittily writes another sestina while already bemoaning that there are too many in the world already. The poem begins with the speaker's gripe:

> Let me confess. I'm sick of these sestinas
> written by youngsters in poetry workshops
> for the delectation of their fellow students,
> and then published in little magazines
> that no one reads, not even the contributors
> who at least in this omission show some taste.

With the word *youngsters,* the speaker emphasizes the absurdity of this form being the form of choice in many workshops, a form for which there are only a handful of good examples in all of literature. Also, by framing the poem as a confession, he pokes fun at confessional poets such as Anne Sexton and Sylvia Plath, who discuss everything from menstruation to mental illness to suicide in their poems. As a New Formalist poet, Gioia makes his confession about form rather than content, and he makes the point that some critics make about his own poems: that form without content is dull, perhaps even meaningless. (Paradoxically, his "confessional" poems about his son are among his most powerful, though Gioia never calls them confessional.) Finally, Gioia's poem is formally looser than traditional sestinas—many of which are written in iambic pentameter or syllabics—yet still with an underlying iambic beat that is lacking in many contemporary sestinas (which may preserve the blocky look and end-words of the sestina, but little else). In this sense, Gioia is willing to go only so far in abandoning the form, although at times he does "soften" his end-words by using slight variations of them.

The speaker realizes that readers may find a formalist more persnickety about form than others. Not so in this case, argues the speaker:

> Is this merely a matter of personal taste?
> I don't think so. Most sestinas
> are such dull affairs. Just ask the contributors
> the last time they finished one outside of a
> workshop.

He goes on to argue, "Let's be honest. It has become a form for students." He points out, tongue in cheek, that even his barber, enrolled "in a rigorous correspondence school workshop," has published his own sestina in a national magazine for barbers. Gioia bemoans the fact that there seems no end to this proliferation, and he uses his own characteristic "glimpse" to view sestina heaven:

> Perhaps there is an afterlife where all contributors
> have two workshops, a tasteful little magazine,
> and sexy students
> who worshipfully memorize their every sestina.

Of course, even when the glimpse is good in Gioia, it does not last. Here there is a sense that, instead, we are trapped in sestina hell on earth.

"The Homecoming," a dramatic monologue written in blank verse, is reminiscent of "The Room Upstairs" from *Daily Horoscope*. In the poem, the speaker confesses to the reader and to the police why he has killed his foster mother. Gioia could not have included a poem more dissimilar to "Planting a Sequoia," in that this poem involves a child killing a parent figure and finds the bonds that unite family largely illusory.

The poem is written in eight sections, the first of which sets the scene by welcoming the police officers. The second explains that his family gave him up when he was small, although he does not know why. The third section involves the speaker's realization that "God didn't care" about him. Because he feels abandoned by everyone, he, like Satan in Milton's *Paradise Lost*, prefers to "rule in Hell." Through the visitation of a crow, section 4 shows the speaker's realization of his own power: that others are afraid of him. He admits, "That's when I started getting into trouble;" he goes on in section 5 to explore the relationship between the weak and the strong:

> power was the only thing that mattered.
> The weak made up the rules to penalize
> the strong, but if the strong were smart enough,
> they always found another way to win.

To test his own power, he starts killing animals, then committing petty thefts. The speaker is caught and goes to prison in section 6. While there, he plays sadistic games with spiders and flies, realizing that "spiders always win," and this game spins into the only thing that can keep him going in prison: a plot to kill his foster mother.

The speaker proceeds home to face his foster mother in section 7, after killing a guard and escaping prison, then killing a woman who has picked him up hitchhiking. These deaths are mere encumbrances to him, obstacles that prevent him from reaching his destination. Yet when he comes face to face with his foster mother, he comes face to face with himself, the same smile:

> It was the smile I greeted in the mirror.
> I never knew till then where I had learned it.
> How strange the people we are closest to
> become almost invisible to us
> until we leave them. Then, on our return,
> we recognize the faces in our dreams.

He cannot regain his childhood, nor separate her from it.

What propels him to kill the woman is the repetition of the cycle of his life: there is now another foster child living in the house. By saving him, the speaker feels that he can save himself. The speaker approaches the foster mother as she washes dishes and kills her. At first the speaker "felt a sudden tremor of delight" but then realizes he will remain trapped. It is not only the living who haunt us, the dead do, too.

And it is this realization, although in a more tender, palatable form, that ends the book. These bonds with the living and the dead are part of the webwork of life. In "Speaking of Love," the issue is looking for the words that need to be said, presumably in the face of loss. As the speaker and his partner speak platitudes to each other, the speaker asks,

> Was it then that words became unstuck?
> That star no longer seemed enough for star?
> Our borrowed speech demanded love so pure
> And so beyond our power that we saw
> How words were only forms of our regret.

The speaker says that he and his partner are both

> Surrendering ... voices to the past,
> Which has betrayed us. Each of us alone,
> Obsessed by memory, befriended by desire

> With no words left to summon back our love.

While the ending is haunting, the next poem illustrates that they do summon love back: in "Equations of the Light" the speaker and his companion stumble upon a street of dark houses that they cannot enter. It becomes a figurative street of death. Yet this moment outside time is interrupted by traffic. Life goes on, and, as the speaker points out,

> Our shadows moved across the street's long wall,
> and at the end what else could we have done
> but turn the corner back into our lives?

INTERROGATIONS AT NOON

The ten-year gap between *The Gods of Winter* and *Interrogations at Noon* created a sense of anticipation about the book. Here Gioia returns to some of his central subjects—loss, journeys, and his connection to California—but from the perspective of middle age. While Gioia continues to explore the transcendent glimpse, there is a new emphasis on language and its role in defining human existence. The British critic William Oxley, though perhaps more effusive than most, captures the tenor of the reviews of the book by calling Gioia "the most exquisite poet writing in English" (Oxley "The First Shall Be the Last").

The collection begins with "Words," a subtle rendering of the biblical Adam's naming in the Garden of Eden. The argument of the poem is that, even though the world does not need us to name it, *we* need to name *it,* and, through a series of steps concerning the relationship between language and experience, the poem brings us to that realization.

First, Gioia writes that "the world does not need words," and he gives a list of things that get along fine without them: "sunlight, leaves, and shadows," for instance, or "stones on the path," or a kiss. That is true, of course. Moreover, any word changes an experience through its connotations: "*illicit, chaste, perfunctory,*

conjugal, covert." Yet, while unmediated experience is admirable, such experience is "less real" to human beings without language. The only way we can make sense of things is to name them: "To name is to know and remember."

Along with the necessity of naming, however, Gioia also explores the necessity of confronting loss, the aftertaste of experience. Three poems, "The Voyeur," "Failure," and "The Litany," all take on Gioia's recurrent theme. In "The Voyeur" a husband is in his bedroom, watching his wife get ready to bathe. Matthew Brennan calls it "one of the best marriage poems we have" (Brennan, "MidLife Regret"), and Leslie Monsour comments on "a paradoxically strained but fluid self-consciousness" that she sees in this and other poems in the collection (Monsour, "O Dark, Dark, Dark"). There is an ethereal quality to the poem, as the speaker feels like an outsider in the presence of the mysterious woman who is his wife, a feeling exacerbated by the fact that the poem is written in the third person. In addition to underscoring loss—the man is not participating in the moment but is an outsider watching—the poem epitomizes Gioia's characteristic glimpse: the wife is seen as otherly beautiful, like moonlight. But there is a price for the distance of this glimpse:

> what he watches here is his own life.
> He is the missing man, the loyal husband,
> sitting in the room he craves to enter,
> surrounded by the flesh and furniture of home.

By watching the moment, he cannot participate in it.

Gioia's poem "Failure" does what Anne Bradstreet's "The Author to Her Book" does: it suggests that one's accomplishments can be viewed as one's children, and the comparison accepts both their strengths and failures. Yet while Bradstreet's poem is specifically about writing, Gioia's is more general. Moreover, Bradstreet's poem is more playful; Gioia's takes a world-weary, yet almost perverse pleasure, in embracing failure:

As with any child, you find your own more
  beautiful—
eager to nurse it along, watch over it,
and taking special pride as each day
it grows more gorgeously like you.

He argues that failure is its own accomplishment: "Satisfaction comes from recognizing what you do best." The ending of the poem turns Emily Dickinson's "Success Is Counted Sweetest" on its head: "You only fail at what you really aim for."

The development of the poem "Litany" is similar to that of Elizabeth Bishop's "One Art" in that there is a cumulative effect to loss. The poem is a "liturgy of rain," "a prayer to unbelief," "a litany to earth and ashes." Like Bishop's poem, this one becomes more personal at the end: "This is a prayer, inchoate and unfinished, / for you, my love, my loss, my lesion." Finally at the end of the poem, the reader is implicated as well: "it is our litany, *mon vieux*, / my reader, my voyeur." Here Gioia's view of the beauty and loss of life is crystallized. In pointing out the beauty of "mist / steaming from the gorge, this pure paradox," he illustrates the "luminous" vanishing moment that is both our litany and our life.

Gioia returns to the subject of California in "A California Requiem." Rather than revisiting the brittle California hills, he visits a cemetery and confronts what lies beneath the landscape:

My blessed California, you are so wise.
You render death abstract, efficient, clean.
Your afterlife is only real estate,
And in his kingdom Death must stay unseen.

In turning to leave the cemetery, he is visited by the voices of the dead, who ask to be forgiven for their lack of understanding of the landscape and their pillaging of it. The dead ask Gioia to be a spokesperson for them, in a grandiose way, as befitting California:

Forget your stylish verses, little poet—
So sadly beautiful, precise, and tame.

We are your people, though you would deny it.
Admit the primal justice of our claim.

Although Gioia pokes fun at himself as a New Formalist, he is of course at the same time the poet of loss: "Become the voice of our forgotten places. / Teach us the names of what we have destroyed." He is offered his own subject matter.

Gioia revisits the theme of the journey in "The End of the World," a poem that is a hyperbolic rendering of his journey motif in *Daily Horoscope,* at the same time as it is playful: " 'We're going,' they said, 'to the end of the world.'" The speaker's guides, presumably, take him there, and finally the speaker says, "I stood alone, / As the current streaked over smooth flat stone." And what awaits him? No clear answer, as always:

I stood at the edge where the mist ascended,
My journey done where the world ended.
I looked downstream. There was nothing but sky,
The sound of water, and the water's reply.

There is a new irony in this collection, particularly in "Song for the End of Time" and "The Archbishop." "Song for the End of Time" is similar to Auden's "As I Walked Out One Evening" in a variety of ways. The poems have a somewhat similar rhythm; they illustrate the world gone wrong; and they employ the same tone:

The hanged man laughs by the garden wall,
And the hands of the clock have stopped at the
  hour.
The cathedral angels are starting to fall,
And the bells ring themselves in the gothic tower.

Auden's poem is a hyperbolic vision that leads us back to the ordinary horror of human life; Gioia's poem, while using the same poetic strategies, is more literal: he's writing about the apocalypse. Auden hopes for some self-awareness in his poem; Gioia points out the uselessness of such a wish: "But the moon is burning under the sun, / And nothing you do will stop what appears." This poem, then, is an extension of his usual thesis on loss, with the ultimate horrifying conclusion.

"The Archbishop" takes an ironic look at a pompous archbishop and, in the process, underscores some of the criticisms of inaccessible poetry (some would make the same argument about New Formalism); it makes a nod to Robert Browning's "The Bishop Orders His Tomb at St. Praxed's Church," which also deals with a bishop more interested in acquiring worldly accoutrements than saving souls. Since Gioia was brought up Catholic and educated in Catholic schools, this poem points out his belief in substance over style, especially since elsewhere in his work religious symbols are valued.

The archbishop does not want to have anything to do with his people, finding "Their notions of God unrefined." Because he does not believe in what the Bible tells him about the poor—"The first shall be last"—he "has that troublesome passage revised." More preoccupied with his personal appearance than with his flock, he refuses to wear his glasses, and this literal choice becomes symbolic: he does not see. Meanwhile, beggars, orphans, and choirboys need sustenance that is not offered them. The poem is a damning portrayal of a church removed from its people.

In addition, it is a damning portrayal of a poetry removed from its people. Since the poem is dedicated to "a famous critic," the piece suggests that poetry must be relevant and connect to people. The use of the ballad stanza, a staple of the oral tradition, underscores this claim.

"Summer Storm" also uses the ballad stanza and, perhaps more than any of Gioia's poems, most encapsulates the New Formalist philosophy. The poem—which is Gioia's most popular—is about a man who, many years later, looks back on a wedding, where he met a woman he never saw again. The two had an intimate moment together, removed from the rest of the wedding party:

To my surprise, you took my arm—
A gesture you didn't explain—
And we spoke in whispers, as if we two
Might imitate the rain.

After the storm passed, the two separated, and only said "goodnight" to each other; the moment recalls Robert Frost's "The Road Not Taken" but with a twist; Gioia's poem emphasizes that we can never take every road:

There are so many *might-have-beens,*
What-ifs that won't stay buried,
Other cities, other jobs,
Strangers we might have married.

And memory insists on pining
For places it never went, As if life would be happier
Just by being different.

MOTTETTI: POEMS OF LOVE: THE MOTETS OF EUGENIO MONTALE

It seems fitting that Gioia would translate *Mottetti: Poems of Love: The Motets of Eugenio Montale* (1990), because the central concern of Montale's poetry is the same sense of loss and longing that pervades Gioia's own work. In his introduction to the volume, Gioia expressed his hope that the edition would make available to an American audience "one of the great lyric works in modern European poetry."

This twenty-poem sequence by Italy's Nobel Prize–winning poet is about the longing caused both by separation and by love. Because the poems have often mistakenly been read as separate poems and contain cryptic imagery, Gioia's introduction, after underscoring the importance of the sequence, addresses the issue of their approachability: "The *Motets* tell a story that no one has trouble understanding: a tale of impossible love. The poet is irrevocably separated from the woman he loves. From the beginning of the sequence he knows that he has lost her forever, yet he cannot stop himself from needing her. She was the center of his world, and that world is now painfully empty."

The first motet begins, "You know this: I must lose you again and cannot," underscoring the pervasive quality of loss. Curiously, there is some comfort in that the universe seems to speak signs that enable the speaker to communicate with his beloved, but the signs are obscure images that unfold, over the course of the twenty poems, to reveal a longing that cannot be quenched. Gioia's introduction describes Montale's motets as being "among the loneliest poems ever written."

NOSFERATU: AN OPERA LIBRETTO

Nosferatu: An Opera Libretto (2001), based on F. W. Murnau's film version of the Dracula story, combines Gioia's literary and musical interests. In fact, Gioia writes, "*Nosferatu* offered a librettist the positive virtues of a compelling plot, strong characters, and vivid, indeed often unforgettable, images." The storyline of *Nosferatu* is thus: Eric Hutter is asked by his employer, Henrich Sculler, to sell a piece of real estate to Count Orlock, Nosferatu. The place is "a ruin." Although Eric's wife, Ellen, pleads with him not to go, he does so and ultimately succumbs to Dracula. But Dracula's real goal is Ellen. While Eric goes insane, Ellen hears the Count calling, and eventually she succumbs also.

Gioia included sections from *Nosferatu* in *Interrogations at Noon:* "Ellen's Dream" (during which she glimpses Eric's future), "Nosferatu's Serenade," and "Mad Song." While there is a strong emotional resonance in the poems, it is Gioia's use of repetition and hypnotic urgency that is powerful:

I am the image that darkens your glass,
The shadow that falls wherever you pass.
I am the dream you cannot forget,
The face you remember without having met.

Not only does Gioia return to his first love, music, in this project, but he brings the tenets of new formalism to a new arena.

Loss is Gioia's milieu, and *Nosferatu* is about loss. Gioia writes,

working on the libretto touched ... childhood memories of religion, family, and poverty. Memories of my beautiful Aunt Felice dying of cancer, the "Salve Regina" being recited at the end of our parochial school's daily morning mass, and the constant family worries about money intermingled naturally with my first sighting of Max Shreck's shadow climbing up the stairway toward his shuddering victim.... the new form invited new subjects, and I could disguise my life as part of someone else's story since the underlying myth was big enough to hold it all.

Gioia's entire project is about this "disguise" and finding the arguments, the forms, and subjects to "hold it all." The recurrent theme of his project is the paradox—that is, both the difficulty and beauty—of doing so.

CONCLUSION

Gioia plays many roles in the arts—poet, critic editor, translator, librettist, poetic ambassador—but among his disparate achievements, one of his most significant roles has been to define the state of poetry and invite others to do so. He has found it important to value tradition, particularly in terms of poetic forms, and to see himself as a part of that tradition. For Gioia, the businessman-poet, this is no small matter: "The role of a civilization is to decide what things you cannot put a price on," he told Hillel Italie. For him, this concept has both private and public significance. Out of the inconsolable grief following the death of his son, and again out of the grief of September 11, 2001, he explored the significance of poetry to address both private and public moments. As Gioia said at the service for his son Michael Jasper, "Our dear Michael Jasper, our sweet B. D., will never grow old.... or lose one atom of his innocence. We will try to bear the crushing grief of his loss without bitterness or despair. We will remember the wisdom he gave us—to appreciate life's joy and wonder, to open ourselves to love. To do any less would betray his memory" ("A Remembrance"). His poem "Unsaid," the last in the collection *Interrogations at Noon,* implies the need to articulate the private:

> So much of what we live goes on inside—
> The diaries of grief, the tongue-tied aches
> Of unacknowledged love are no less real
> For having passed unsaid. What we conceal
> Is always more than what we dare confide.
> Think of the letters that we write our dead.

Gioia's work is about human loss, and moving on, with love, in spite of it.

Selected Bibliography

WORKS OF DANA GIOIA

POETRY COLLECTIONS
Daily Horoscope. St. Paul, Minn.: Graywolf, 1986.
The Gods of Winter. St. Paul, Minn.: Graywolf, 1991.
Interrogations at Noon. St. Paul, Minn.: Graywolf, 2001.

POETRY CHAPBOOKS
Daily Horoscope. Iowa City, Iowa: Windhover, 1982.
Two Poems. Bowery Press, 1982. (Contains "An Elegy for Vladimir de Pachmann" and "Lives of the Composers.")

Summer. West Chester, Pa.: Aralia, 1983. (Contains "Summer" and "The Summoning.")
Journeys in Sunlight. Cottondale, Ala.: Ex Ophidia, 1986.
Two Poems/Due poesie. Bilingual edition. Italian translations by Massimo Bacigalupo. Verona, Italy: Stamperia Ampersand, 1987. (Contains "Equations of the Light" and "Maze without a Minotaur.")
Words for Music. Tuscaloosa: University of Alabama, Parallel Editions, 1987.
Planting a Sequoia. West Chester, Pa.: Aralia, 1991.

MISCELLANEOUS LETTERPRESS PUBLICATIONS
"A Remembrance: Michael Jasper Gioia." West Chester, Pa.: Aralia, 1988.
"The Gods of Winter." West Chester, Pa.: Aralia, 1989.
"All Souls'." West Chester, Pa.: Aralia, 1990.
"Two Small Prayers." West Chester, Pa.: Aralia, 1990. (Contains "Prayer" and "Planting a Sequoia.")
"Curriculum Vitae." West Chester, Pa.: Aralia, 1996.

CRITICISM
Can Poetry Matter?: Essays on Poetry and American Culture. St. Paul, Minn.: Graywolf, 1992.
Barrier of a Common Language: An American Looks at Contemporary British Poetry. Ann Arbor: University of Michigan Press, 2003.
Disappearing Ink: Poetry at the End of Print Culture. St. Paul, Minn.: Graywolf, 2004.

ESSAYS
"Longfellow in the Aftermath of Modernism." In *The Columbia History of American Poetry.* Edited by Jay Parini and Brett C. Miller. New York: Columbia University Press, 1993. Pp. 64–96.
"What Is Italian American Poetry?" In *Beyond "The Godfather": Italian American Writers on the Real Italian American Experience.* Edited by A. Kenneth Ciongoli and Jay Parini. Hanover, N.H.: University Press of New England, 1997. Pp. 167–174.
"Discovering a Lost Poem." In *Contributor's Note,* by Weldon Kees. West Chester, Pa.: Aralia, 1999.
"Fallen Western Star: The Decline of San Francisco as a Literary Region." In *The "Fallen Western Star" Wars: A Debate about Literary California.*

Edited by Jack Foley. Oakland, Calif.: Scarlet Tanager, 2001.

"Sotto Voce: Notes on the Libretto as a Literary Form." In his *Nosferatu: An Opera Libretto.* St. Paul, Minn.: Graywolf, 2001. Pp. 67–85.

"All I Have Is a Voice." Foreword to *September 1, 1939,* by W. H. Auden. West Chester, Pa.: Aralia, 2002.

VOLUMES EDITED

The Ceremony and Other Stories, by Weldon Kees. Port Townsend, Wash.: Graywolf, 1984. (Includes an introduction by Gioia.)

Poems from Italy. Translations, coedited with William Jay Smith. St. Paul, Minn.: New Rivers, 1985.

New Italian Poets. Translations, coedited with Michael Palma. Brownsville, Ore.: Story Line, 1991.

Certain Solitudes: On the Poetry of Donald Justice. Coedited with William Logan. Fayetteville: University of Arkansas Press, 1997.

Selected Short Stories of Weldon Kees. Lincoln: University of Nebraska Press, 2002.(Includes an introduction by Gioia.)

The Misread City: New Literary Los Angeles. Coedited with Scott Timberg. Los Angeles: Red Hen, 2003.

ANTHOLOGIES

The Longman Anthology of Short Fiction: Stories and Authors in Context. Coedited with R. S. Gwynn. Compact ed. New York: Longman, 2001.

Twentieth-Century American Poetics: Poets on the Art of Poetry. Coedited with David Mason and Meg Schoerke. Boston: McGraw Hill, 2004.

Twentieth-Century American Poetry. Coedited with David Mason and Meg Schoerke. Boston: McGraw Hill, 2004.

An Introduction to Fiction. Coedited with. X. J. Kennedy. 9th ed. New York: Pearson Longman, 2005.

An Introduction to Poetry. Coedited with. X. J. Kennedy. 11th ed. New York: Pearson Longman, 2005.

Literature: An Introduction to Fiction, Poetry, and Drama. Coedited with. X. J. Kennedy. 9th ed. New York: Pearson Longman, 2005; 4th compact ed. New York: Longman, 2005.

OTHER WORKS

Mottetti: Poems of Love: The Motets of Eugenio Montale. Translations. St. Paul, Minn.: Graywolf, 1990. (Includes an introduction by Gioia.)

Juno Plots Her Revenge. Translation of act 1 of *Hercules Furens* by Seneca. West Chester, Pa.: Aralia, 1992.

The Madness of Hercules. Translation of *Hercules Furens.* In *Seneca: The Tragedies,* vol. 2. Edited by David Slavitt. Baltimore, Md.: Johns Hopkins University Press, 1995. Pp. 49–104.

Nosferatu: An Opera Libretto. St. Paul, Minn.: Graywolf, 2001.

CRITICAL AND BIOGRAPHICAL STUDIES

Brame, Gloria G. "Paradigms Lost: Part One." *ELF: Eclectic Literary Forum,* spring 1995. Available at http://gloria-brame.com/glory/gioia.htm. (Interview with Dana Gioia.)

Brennan, Matthew. "Dana Gioia: The Poet as Public Intellectual." *South Carolina Review* 35, no. 2:167–176 (2003).

———. "Midlife Regret." *American Book Review* 23, no. 3:17 (March-April 2002). (Review of *Interrogations at Noon.*)

Edgers, Geoff. "He Wants NEA To Bring Art to All Americans." *Boston Globe,* April 3, 2003.

Foley, Jack. "The Black Hole of Criticism: Richard Silberg on Dana Gioia's 'Fallen Western Star.' "In his *The "Fallen Western Star" Wars: A Debate about Literary California.* Oakland, Calif.: Scarlet Tanager, 2001. Pp. 49–60.

———, ed. *The "Fallen Western Star" Wars: A Debate about Literary California.* Oakland, Calif.: Scarlet Tanager, 2001.

Francis, Richard. "Bread and Circuses." *PN Review* 82 (18.2): 60. (Review of *The Gods of Winter.*)

Hagstrom, Jack W. C., and Bill Morgan. *Dana Gioia: A Descriptive Bibliography with Critical Essays.* Jackson, Miss.: Parrish House, 2002.

Hix, H. L. "Dana Gioia's Criticism." In *Dana Gioia: A Descriptive Bibliography with Critical Essays.* Edited by Jack W. C. Hagstrom and Bill Morgan.

Jackson, Miss.: Parrish House, 2002. Pp. 283–296.

Junker, Howard. "Thus Do I Refute Gioia." In *The "Fallen Western Star" Wars: A Debate about Literary California.* Edited by Jack Foley. Oakland, Calif.: Scarlet Tanager, 2001. Pp. 29–31.

Italie, Hillel. "New NEA Chair Hopes to Restore Agency." *Washington Post,* April 1, 2003.

Knoll, Robert E. *Prairie Schooner* 60, no. 3: 122–125 (1986). (Review of *Daily Horoscope.*)

Kramer, Hilton. "Poetry and the Silencing of Art." *New Criterion* 11, no. 6: 4–9 (1993). (Review of *Can Poetry Matter?: Essays on Poetry and American Culture.*)

Kuzma, Greg. "Dana Gioia and the Poetry of Money." *Northwest Review* 26, no. 3:111–121 (1988). (Review of *Daily Horoscope.*)

Lindner, April. *Dana Gioia.* Western Writers Series, no. 143. 2nd ed. Boise, Idaho: Boise State University, 2003.

———. "Michael Dana Gioia: A Chronology." In *Dana Gioia: A Descriptive Bibliography with Critical Essays.* Edited by Jack W. C. Hagstrom and Bill Morgan. Jackson, Miss.: Parrish House, 2002. Pp. ix–xiii.

Mason, David. "Letter to *Poetry Flash.*" In *The "Fallen Western Star" Wars: A Debate about Literary California.* Edited by Jack Foley. Oakland, Calif.: Scarlet Tanager, 2001. Pp. 47–48.

McDowell, Robert. "New Schools and Late Discoveries." *Hudson Review* 39, no. 4:673–675 (1987). (Review of *Daily Horoscope.*)

McPhillips, Robert. "Dana Gioia and the Visionary Realism." In his *The New Formalism: A Critical Introduction.* Charlotte, N.C.: Volcanic Ash, 2003. Pp. 33–58.

Monsour, Leslie. "O Dark, Dark, Dark amid the Blaze of Noon: The Poetry of Dana Gioia." At http://www.ablemuse.com/current/l-monsour_gioia-review.htm. Winter 2002. (Review of *Interrogations at Noon.*)

Oxley, William. "The First Shall Be the Last." *Acumen* 41 (September 2001). Available at www.danagioia.net/about/oxley.htm. (Review of *Interrogations at Noon.*)

Peich, Michael. *Aralia Press: Poetry and Fine Printing.* West Chester, Pa.: Aralia, 2000.

———. "Dana Gioia and Fine Press Printing." In *Dana Gioia: A Descriptive Bibliography with Critical Essays.* Edited by Jack W. C. Hagstrom and Bill Morgan. Jackson, Miss.: Parrish House, 2002. Pp. 255–258.

Raskin, Jonah. "Local Literary Scene Is Worth Celebrating." In *The "Fallen Western Star" Wars: A Debate about Literary California.* Edited by Jack Foley. Oakland, Calif.: Scarlet Tanager, 2001. Pp. 32–34.

Richman, Robert. "Impatient Faith." *New Criterion* 5, no. 6: 71–74 (1987). (Review of *Daily Horoscope.*)

Silberg, Richard. "On 'Fallen Western Star': Dana Gioia Stirs It Up in the *Hungry Mind Review.*" In *The "Fallen Western Star" Wars: A Debate about Literary California.* Edited by Jack Foley. Oakland: Scarlet Tanager, 2001. Pp. 35–46.

Squires, Radcliffe. *Southern Humanities Review* 22, no. 1:92–94 (1988). (Review of *Daily Horoscope.*)

Stevenson, Anne. "The Poetry of Dana Gioia: Review of *The Gods of Winter.*" In her *Between the Iceberg and the Ship: Selected Essays.* Ann Arbor: University of Michigan Press, 1998. Pp. 156–158.

Turco, Lewis. "Dana Gioia." *American Poets since World War II: Third Series.* Edited by R. S. Gwynn. Detroit: Gale, 1992. Pp. 84–90.

Walter, Joyce. "Ambushed by Typescript." *Poetry Review* 81, no. 1:56 (1991). (Review of *The Gods of Winter.*)

Walzer, Kevin. *The Ghost of Tradition: Expansive Poetry and Postmodernism.* Ashland, Ore.: Story Line, 1998.

Yenser, Stephen. "Some Poets' Criticism and the Age." *A Boundless Field: American Poetry at Large.* Ann Arbor: University of Michigan Press, 2002. Pp. 9–16.

—*KIM BRIDGFORD*

Weldon Kees

1914–1955?

ON THE FIRST weekend after Weldon Kees's car had been found abandoned in a parking lot near the Golden Gate Bridge, his radio program *Behind the Scenes* aired for the last time across the Bay Area. His cohost Michael Grieg and a friend from his Yaddo days, the writer Nathan Asch, did the show without the usual repartee on Hollywood and the latest films. Instead they improvised an elegy for a poet whose status as missing person or suicide was as uncertain as his reputation or how to define it. Grieg played a demo tape that he had found in Kees's empty apartment—empty save for the aptly, ironically named cat of a cultured, busy man who was rarely home, "Lonesome." On the tape the nightclub vocalist of the legendary Purple Onion nightclub performed Kees's "Daybreak Blues" to his accompaniment on piano. Now the torch song had taken on a new meaning as the young woman—better known as Ketty Lester—sang, "Got the bad news."

At the song's end, there was hesitancy in Grieg's voice as to what to say next. This was grief, naturally, and the very doubt surrounding Kees's death. However, just where to place Kees was a problem in itself, as though the theme of existential mystery that appears throughout his poetry had really come to life in him. Up until the day he disappeared, on July 18, 1955, he had been involved in making experimental and documentary films. He had taken hundreds of photographs for a book on nonverbal communication. During the first half of the year he had produced a literary burlesque show, the Poets' Follies, that featured not only poets reading but Oakland's most celebrated stripper. He had been composing and recording with a number of Bay Area jazz musicians. He had turned an old auditorium into a theater and concert hall, which had unfortunately been closed by the San Francisco Fire Department just days before his new play for three women, *The Waiting Room,* was to open. Though his hiatus from abstract expressionism had not come to end, he was again reviewing art, this time for *Art News,* as well as writing book reviews for the *New Republic.* Certainly his friend's range of interests and accomplishments held Grieg back before he turned to Kees's core art. The songwriter, Grieg said, was really "one of the most distinguished poets writing in this country, though not as recognized as he, I think, should be." And the uncertainty here, as though Kees wanted it this way, also had other dimensions that Nathan Asch apprehended. To him Kees was a "strange figure for a poet," one who did not look the part,

> if that means anything to anybody who tries to imagine what a poet looks like. I always thought he looked more like a Broadway character. He was always very well dressed, right in a Brooks Brothers' style. And he always had a slightly confidential look about him … as if he was about to buttonhole you and impart to you something of extreme importance.

Grieg read Kees's last poem to be published in the *New Yorker,* "Colloquy," and one of his longer poems, "Travels in North America," a concatenation of driving and listening to Patti Page on the car radio, seeing a "Navajo in levis" reading a Pocket Book edition of Sartre, Los Alamos—"the Capital of the Atomic Age," the screaming girl who "threw a cocktail shaker at a man in tweeds," and "Joe's Lunch [that] appears again, town after town." It is a favorite method of Kees, a kind of Buddhist prayer of his fragmented American experience. Though he is miles from Allen Ginsberg and Jack Kerouac, it shows him to be the missing, eliotic bridge to their generation. And with such a method, he achieves this "serenity of a saint" that the editor of his *Collected Poems,* Donald Justice, saw above Kees's "ultimate expression" of bitterness—the other intense flavor note of Kees's oeuvre, as in "Travels in North America":

> Here, sodden, fading, green ink blending into
> blue,
> Is Brooklyn Heights, and I am walking toward
> the subway
> In a January snow again, at night, ten years ago.
> Here is Milpitas,
> California, filling stations and a Ford
> Assembly plant. Here are the washboard roads
> Of Wellfleet, on the Cape, and summer light and
> dust.
> And here, now textured like a blotter, like the
> going years
> And difficult to see, is where you are, and where
> I am,
> And where the oceans cover us.

After hearing the poem close with these lines, Nathan Asch spoke in a halting voice, with a Central European accent and described Kees's work as though he were one Beat's, calling it "a beautiful evocation of America, Under the Road of America" "I would hate, absolutely hate to think," Asch continued, "that this particular giftedness for bringing back America to us poignantly, be lost. I am hoping that it isn't." But this would be the case, and it would take decades before Kees's poetry made Harold Bloom's American canon and another European, the late Nobel Prize–winner Joseph Brodsky, could say, indeed, that on that July day in 1955, "America lost a very tough poet."

EARLY YEARS

Harry Weldon Kees was born on February 24, 1914, in a midwestern town that would not have seemed out of place in a Booth Tarkington novel or a Wallace Stevens poem: Beatrice, Nebraska, pronounced with a strong, long syllable on the letter "a," the way it was said by the conductors of the three railroads that ran along the nearby Blue River. His father, John Kees, was a hardware manufacturer and the son of German immigrants. His mother, Sarah Green Kees, was a former schoolteacher and an amateur genealogist whose efforts brought her memberships in the Sons and Daughters of Pilgrims, the Americans of Royal Descent, and the Daughters of the American Revolution. An only child, Kees, to use his own description of the time, grew up in the "civilized, elegant, and lush world of the Wilson-Harding-Coolidge years," of the "shock-absorbing twenties." Much of this comfort zone came from his parents, who saw to it that their preternaturally gifted son had everything to stimulate his imagination. Weldon, as he was called, seemed more like a small adult than a child. He preferred to call his parents by their first names and paid special attention to his appearance, a fastidiousness that lasted throughout his life. (The wife of one friend could not believe that he could have jumped off the Golden Gate simply because the water would soil and ruin his clothes.) This even found its way into "Aspects of Robinson," Kees's *New Yorker* everyman and alter ego:

> Robinson in Glen plaid jacket, Scotch-grain
> shoes,
> Black four-in-hand and oxford button-down,
> The jeweled and silent watch that winds itself,
> the brief-
> Case, covert topcoat, clothes for spring, all cover-
> ing
> His sad and usual heart, dry as a winter leaf.

Despite his world of indoor games—puppet shows, his homemade Hollywood movie magazines typed on his father's office typewriter, listening to jazz records, and play dates with Beatrice's other "mama's boy," Spangler Arlington Brugh, better known as the actor Robert Taylor—Weldon liked camping with his Boy Scout troop, telling mystery stories on the neighbor girl's porch, and gliding across frozen farm ponds on iron skates made by his father's firm and sold in Chicago's department stores. He especially enjoyed going to the town's two motion picture theaters, the memory of which—along with the rest of his Nebraska childhood—informs the estranged, negated nostalgia of the poem "1926":

> The porchlight coming on again,
> Early November, the dead leaves
> Raked in piles, the wicker swing
> Creaking. Across the lots
> A phonograph is playing *Ja-Da*.
>
> An Orange moon. I see the lives
> Of neighbors, mapped and marred
> Like all the wars ahead, and R.
> Insane, B. with his throat cut,
> Fifteen years from now, in Omaha.
>
> I did not know them then.
> My airedale scratches at the door.
> And I am back from seeing Milton Sills
> And Doris Kenyon. Twelve years old.
> The porchlight coming on again.

A family pew in the Presbyterian church (the source of that "fierce Calvinist spirit" that Brodsky praised) and being the son of one of the town's few Democrats and freethinkers early on imprinted Kees with both a sense of place and a disassociation from it. The Great Depression and the lingering effect of a bad investment on his family's fortunes intensified this alienation and Kees's incredulity with the surface calm of things. Nevertheless, he was not considered an overly serious or even intellectual young man. In high school he liked to sing in the glee club, act in the school plays, and perform in little jazz bands. On graduating in 1931 he saw

himself working as a "drummer" for the F. D. Kees Company, selling his father's ever-expanding line, including the Kees Frost Kleerer, a suction cup windshield defroster, and the Kees Krawler, the original lawn sprinkler tractor. (That genius for assembling objects and trivia into poems and abstract collages may owe to the father's factory, its lathes and metal bits and pieces.) But this would come after dutifully attending Doane College, a small, Congregationalist liberal arts school in nearby Crete, Nebraska, where Kees continued the same pattern he had in high school and where it seemed if he did anything adventurous it might be to follow Robert Taylor, another Doane student, out to Hollywood. However, at Doane, Kees, like other young people of his day, settled on a vocation picked from that heroic American triumvirate of the 1920s and early 1930s: screen actor, aviator, and novelist. He started to read Ernest Hemingway, William Faulkner, F. Scott Fitzgerald, John Dos Passos—and collect entire runs of the little Depression-era literary magazines that published new work.

Kees had already written plays for his drama club and, for an English assignment, an amusing send-up of a Hollywood comedian with a name that parodied Clark Gable's—Percy Poggle, who, on the verge of fame with his first film, refuses success and escapes to Australia to live under an assumed—and distinguished-sounding—name. In this student work, Kees, who as a child was already porous to the film industry's influence, reveals what would become both a life theme and a theme for his work: to be a part of the movies but on his own terms, as a kind of private existential *showing*.

Doane, like many schools before World War II, lacked creative-writing classes, and Kees soon realized that he needed more than just the encouragement of his friends and a few supportive teachers. In the fall of 1933 he transferred to the University of Missouri in Columbia, where the Department of Journalism offered an elective in short-story writing. Once there, however, he found the course hardly what he had imagined and began instead showing up at the home of Mary Paxton Keeley, an English teacher at nearby Christian College (and a childhood friend of Harry Truman), who held quaint "literary evenings" for students.

Kees proved different from the others who came to her apartment for tea, coffee, and conversation. They might write something to enter in newspaper contests or what had been assigned to them in class. Kees brought his new mentor one story after another—and he did not just talk about writing the Great American Novel. He actually brought over chapters for her to read. Like other young writers, however, Kees relied too much on his imagination and did not have enough experience with real events and people to go on. This would soon change for him in a rather traumatic way. His good looks soon attracted the attention of more than one man. One of his professors even exposed himself to Kees. And they had reason to think that he might be receptive to their passes (or simply uninitiated). He was not seen dating girls, and as one of his male admirers told Keeley, it was his eyes, which had this "sadness and longing" in them.

What happened at Missouri only half-contributed to Kees's decision to transfer to the University of Nebraska in Lincoln in 1934. There Lowry Wimberly, the editor and founder of *Prairie Schooner,* had helped Kees through the mail over the spring and summer to revise and lengthen his first published short story, "Saturday Rain," which appeared in the literary review's fall issue. Though Kees did not have a girlfriend like the one his protagonist loses, he had used leaving the town of Beatrice, which the girl personifies. He also used the Hemingway he had been reading in his first finely polished jewel of estrangement. He gave Wimberly's magazine—and his new classmates—a small-town Orpheus and Eurydice.

Only Kees's protagonist takes the steps off a porch rather than up from the underworld, and he does not turn back to look at Arlene but only stops to make sure she is dead to him:

> The streets were shining, and the grass suddenly seemed greener than it had ever been. I stopped in the middle of the sidewalk for a long time, looking about me, listening to the stillness. Then when I began to hear cars going by and the sound of water dripping from the trees, I picked up my bag and walked on.

FROM FICTION TO POETRY

Kees did find love at the University of Nebraska if not back home. In the fall semester he began dating Ann Swan, who had also just transferred, from Pomona College. Quiet and reserved, with pale skin and brown hair much like his, the couple struck other students as both ideally matched and more like brother and sister. Ann took an immediate interest in Kees's writing and his desire to be a published novelist. Kees also began to cultivate a small circle of friends among the other students in the English Department, notably Maurice Johnson and another aspiring novelist, Dale Smith. It was another student, Norris Getty, whose attraction to Kees provided this description of the new standout who had already been published in *Prairie Schooner:*

> Kees has all accomplishments, has had all experiences, and has money. At first sight of him, as he came into the first meeting of Wimberly's class, I thought "pale fish" and "my God, if I have to look at that face all semester." An anthropoid slouch under Englishy tweeds, as if he were trying to touch his shoulders together in front.... But I've come to like his appearance—his unearthly cleanliness, dark eyes, neatness of lashes and hair.... His obsessions are the Communist Party and the stupidities of middle-class America. He is so discouragingly well read, knows and has done so much that I must feel that my lack of interest in the Cause is a serious deficiency. I have been

reading the Communist poems of K. Fearing, and have tackled O'Hara, Hermann, and Dos Passos in a wistful attempt to attain some sort of even standing with him.... He is so much more clever than I, a better satirist.

Though Kees dutifully attended such courses as "The Continental Novel" and "Eighteenth-Century Prose" taught by Wimberly and the renowned Louise Pound (the companion of Willa Cather), he preferred discussing Faulkner and James Joyce and groaning about the over-rated writers of the moment. "William Saroyan in the Yale Review ... again ... again," Maurice Johnson complained in a letter to Kees from the voluminous correspondence that followed their graduation, whereas Kees parodied *Ulysses* and the installments of *Finnegans Wake* in his letters, making up words like "rainsound," "gluesmell," and similar neologisms. On the serious side, he had committed himself to writing a novel for publication, which was why he had to take a class in the summer of 1935 to graduate before setting out to his parents' campsite on the Big Thompson River in Colorado, where he finished *Slow Parade*.

Kees felt that he had crafted a socially conscientious story even if it did not reflect the robust social realism of *New Masses*. *Slow Parade* seemed good "propaganda," despite its grimness. Writing to Johnson while admiring the rushing river nearby, Kees even seemed to be moving away from the very current that would run through his poetry:

Isn't Faulkner trying to "sell" us on the futility of futility? Isn't Wolfe trying to put across his "lostness"? T. S. Eliot is the poet who sings the song of Oswald Spengler.... It seems to me that anyone can be a futilitarian right now: it's the easiest, simplest thing in the world—because it is *negative*..... But surely we should have more admiration for those writers with some guts, those who are trying to find a rational solution and are willing to fight a little, than for those pale and hopeless young men who have little more to say than Booth Tarkington and Kathleen Norris.

Though no manuscript of *Slow Parade* survives, Kees's letters tell that he employed a technique similar to Dos Passos', yet inverted. Where Dos Passos (whom Kees linked to Charles Dickens and found procrustean) would take isolated characters and bring them slowly closer and closer to each other, Kees tried to take the members of one family and show them growing farther and farther away from each other. The method and content, however, intrigued some editors—and violated the sensibilities of others. Harold Strauss of Covici wrote Kees that *Slow Parade* was "unrelievedly grim." Donald Elder of Doubleday, Doran felt "almost unqualifiedly enthusiastic" about the book. His only reservation, however, was not so much the book itself but getting Kees to revise it so that it could pass the "prudish standards" of his house. "Cynthia's sexual aberration" was one thing, the editor told Kees, and there was all the "dialogue which doesn't meet the purity standards."

With Lowry Wimberly's encouragement Kees had applied to and was admitted into University of Chicago's graduate program in English literature beginning in the fall of 1935. Wimberly wanted to make sure that his most interesting student writer had a career to fall back on, as a high school teacher or English professor, in case the fiction Kees was now publishing regularly in the little magazines did not provide an income. To Wimberly, Kees also needed another kind of grounding: he feared Kees as a new type, a person whose mind was fixed in the present and future, who saw the past as something to be discredited and discarded. But Kees only lasted a few weeks at Chicago when it became clear to him that the reading and work required for his advanced degree would get in the way of his next novel and all the latest books and magazines he wanted to read instead. With the new two-volume set of Alfred Döblin's *Berlin Alexanderplatz* in English translation, Kees took the train back to Nebraska, where he stayed until January 1936, having decided to find work in Hollywood that would not interfere with becoming a published novelist.

With bipolar-like fascination and disgust, Kees reacted to his new setting in this "mad and terrifying region." The stories he had heard about Los Angeles overflowing with "oil, orangejuice," and "the sperm of moviestars" seemed true. "Augment them," he advised Maurice Johnson in one of his first letters back to Nebraska, "with recollections of all the satires written about it, and that is the actual and genuine Hollywood. Ben Hecht's remark, to the effect that out here they're all 'either drunk or crazy' is fairly accurate."

Finding steady work as a writer, musician, actor, extra, or anything proved nearly impossible. There was already a Beatrice contingent in Hollywood, as well as young people from all over the country, seeking what few jobs the film industry had left. Kees, for his part, had the advantage of his connection to Robert Taylor. But a canceled meeting with the leading man (perhaps proving his patriotic bona fides well before he testified before the House Subcommittee on Un-American Activities) quickly led to their estrangement. "My erstwhile friend Arlington Brugh," Kees wrote back to Dale Smith, "now Robert Taylor of the silver screen, would not even see me, and you may instruct the local Bolsheviki that they are more than welcome to boycott his pictures without any denunciatory mutterings from me."

Kees, waiting for the phone to ring in his rented room in a bungalow on South Kingsley Drive, thought about "chucking it all and coming back to the Cornhusker State." Instead he worked prodigiously on his fiction—and, perhaps unselfconsciously—the quality of his own letter writing. Much of Kees's talent, when it had no where else to go, found its way into his correspondence, and his entertaining and piquant observations of American society and culture practically mark the end of what is now a lost

art. He also assuaged his frustrations seeing the latest films in Hollywood's famous movie palaces as well as seeing Ann Swan, who discreetly lived in her own apartment.

What few good jobs Kees found "blew up with a crash." Then, in the spring of 1936, he lost several manuscripts and his typewriter when fire gutted his house on South Kingsley, forcing him to return to Lincoln in June. With the help of Dr. Wimberly, Kees was hired for one of the good-paying editorial jobs compiling the state guide of Nebraska, part of a nationwide series sponsored by the Federal Writers' Project, a New Deal relief program under the Works Progress Administration. This reunited Kees with his former classmate Norris Getty, who now sat across from him in a facing desk. It did not take long for Kees to find much in common with his new friend, whose interest in poetry Kees himself took up with the intensity of someone wanting to change his life. Philip Horton's biography of Hart Crane's troubled life also fed into Kees's new passion. He talked about the book for days and was moved by Crane's jump from the S.S. Orizaba and how—apocryphally—he had swum away from the ship, back to Mexico, leaving his poems behind. This came out one hot summer afternoon while Getty and Kees were on assignment, visiting a graveyard in Lincoln. As soon as they entered the cemetery, Kees sat in the shade of the nearest evergreen tree. He said he would vouch for anything Getty wanted to write as he observed the names and dates on the headstones. "More and more," Getty heard Kees say, "I think Hart Crane had the right idea."

By the fall of 1936 Kees was showing his own poems to Getty, who would eventually give up his own verse to be Kees's critical reader and editor. The early efforts show the influence and politics of Kenneth Fearing—but without Fearing's bad ear and social realistic noise. Kees in a matter of months had hit a high note of the mature poet he would become in a few years' time. One of these poems from late 1936, "Subtitle," the first to be published (in John Malcolm Brinnin's magazine *Signatures*), shows Kees had not found his Hollywood experience to be a waste but something to appropriate in giving his poems an edgy contemporary power that they still would have today even without The Movie Channel:

We present for you this evening
a movie of death: observe
these scenes chipped celluloid
reveals unsponsored and tax-free.
We request these things only:
all gum must be placed beneath the seats
or swallowed quickly, all popcorn sacks
must be left in the foyer. The doors
will remain closed throughout
the performance.
. . . .
Look for no dialogue, or for the
sound of any human voice: we have seen fit
to synchronize this play with
squealings of pigs, slow sound of guns,
the sharp dead click of empty chocolatebar
  machines.
We say again: there are
no exits here, no guards to bribe,
no washroom windows.
NO FINIS to the film unless
the ending is your own.
Turn off the lights, remind
the operator of his union card:
sit forward, let the screen reveal
your heritage, the logic of your destiny.

That restlessness with placenames and people that became something of a modus operandi began to work on Kees while he worked on the state guide. Around the office, a warehouse overlooking the Union Pacific yards, he, Getty, and Dale Smith were known for their irreverence for their boss, barely literate contributors, and the onus of having to live in the hell of churchgoing Lincoln. They were called the "Unholy Trio"—and Kees, the reddest of the three, had even volunteered to do union organizing, more to bother the "bourgeois" elements as

he called them than out of any real commitment. This and his need for a personal politics of experiential volition even makes for a proto-confessionalist moment in another of Kees's early efforts, "Statement with Rhymes," in which he showed, as much from listening to jazz as reading his Eliot, a precocious gift for form that was as natural as conversation but had all the "good numbers" of an Elizabethan poet's meter and rhyme. The authority of W. H. Auden, by way of Nebraska, is present too, especially where themes preternaturally surface as if from nowhere given Kees's youth—and for a body of work that he considered still a sideshow to his latest novel-in-progress:

propelled by zeros, zinc, and zephyrs, always I'm
pursued
by thoughts of what I am, authority,
remembrance, food,
the letter on the mezzanine, the unemployed,
dogs' lonely faces, pianos and decay.

Plurality is all. I sympathize, but cannot grieve
too long for those who wear their dialectics on
their sleeves.
The pattern's one I sometimes rather like; there's
really nothing wrong
with it for some. But I should add: It doesn't
wear for long,
before I push the elevator bell and quickly leave.

Toward the end of the summer of 1937, Kees, the model for the ironic Futurist figure in this poem, found himself trying to land a staid job behind a reference desk. It was a move that was decidedly middle class and to placate Sarah Kees, whose influence over her son was exercised with a worried face that practically rose from the longhand of her letters. He enrolled in the graduate library program at the University of Denver, which included working in the city library, and he married Ann Swan that October. She had already been living and working in Denver—and keeping her often one-sided relationship from flagging with frequent train trips to Lincoln.

The new couple increased the handful of cultured people who provided prewar Denver with its own Bloomsbury set. Their first "arty" cocktail party, given for the benefit of the Spanish Loyalists, became a starting point for the small circle that Kees formed around himself in his new city. The host, Michael Stuart, had once served as Joyce's confidante and aide in Paris, a connection testified to by an autographed picture of "J. J."—as Kees remarked in one of his letters—prominently displayed. The writer and translator of Federico García Lorca, Gilbert Neiman, and his wife Margaret, a painter—who later became fixtures in entourage of Henry Miller—entertained him with their plans to live in Mexico among the dissolute expatriate Americans already there.

The relationship that Kees cultivated with James Laughlin, the young publisher of New Directions, grew out of their correspondence and personal contacts, for Laughlin was a passionate skier who made special trips to the Colorado slopes. His New Directions annuals of advanced writing had impressed Kees, who had written a favorable review of the 1937 anthology, and it did not take long for Laughlin to "discover" the talented Denver librarian for his series. Disturbing, provocative short stories appeared in *New Directions 1939* and *New Directions 1940,* including "I Should Worry," a distillation of what Kees's novels must have read like, with a deaf young woman pimped by her brother for drinking money; and the subversively pacifist and surreal "The Evening of the Fourth of July." Kees's fiction had also been noticed by the editor of the *Best Short Stories* volumes, Edward O'Brien, who listed Kees short stories in the back pages of his anthologies, where he acknowledged the work he had no room to reprint. O'Brien would eventually include Kees's "The Life of the Mind" in his *Best Short Stories 1941* and dedicate the volume to Kees—O'Brien's custom of acknowledging rising young fiction writers.

During the late 1930s Kees developed something of a national reputation by the frequent appearances of his short stories, poetry, and book reviews. He also moved from the reference desk of the Denver Public Library to become head of the Rocky Mountain Bibliographic Center for Research, a pioneering effort to create a union catalogue for a number of western states that also provided Kees with a small staff and even more privacy to work on his own writing. (Unlike friends such as Theodore Roethke, who turned to creative-writing and English instructorships, especially after the war when the GI Bill filled postwar campuses, Kees found employments that would be "symbiotic" for his work, and he rarely had to resort to being clandestine while typing poems and stories at his desk.)

He even felt settled in Denver despite it being, to him, a cultural backwater. Ever the cineaste, Kees enjoyed going to the Hiawatha Theatre, which had been converted into an art house that showed foreign-language, English, and good Hollywood pictures. He also contributed to the local scene by appearing on the Denver radio station KOA, where he talked about new books and authors such as Nathanael West, Robert Cantwell, Katherine Anne Porter—and William Carlos Williams, whose work could not be found in the Denver Public Library until Kees came on the staff. He made it part of his routine to drop in on the library's order department to see what new books had arrived—and to convince the department's head that more collections of experimental writing and literary magazines should not be passed up "in the anxiety to stock eighty copies of *Gone with the Wind.*"

With his luminous correspondence and long trips to San Francisco and New York, Kees's milieu went far beyond Denver to include Kenneth Rexroth and the "*Partisan Review* boys," as Ann Kees called Philip Rahv, Dwight Macdonald, and Lionel Trilling—whom Kees met during the 1940 English Institute Conference at Columbia University—along with Alan Tate, James T. Farrell, and the art critic Clement Greenberg. Kees also circulated among literary agents and editors and, with the help of Mari Sandoz, he signed a contract with Knopf in early 1941 to produce an academic comedy set in the Midwest, *Fall Quarter* (1990).

What should have come as a milestone for Kees, however, was really to him only the teaser to getting Knopf to publish his first book of poems. Despite all the attention his fiction had received, Kees was beginning to walk away from it in yet another permutation of his career's restlessness. He had created something of stir with an antiwar poem, "June 1940," in *Partisan Review* the year before—and indeed much of his new poetry was fired by his growing antipathy toward an America being prepared by the Roosevelt administration for entering the war in Europe and the Pacific. The most striking of these poems is considered one of Kees's signature works, "For My Daughter," which appeared in the spring 1940 issue of *Kenyon Review:*

Looking into my daughter's eyes I read
Beneath the innocence of morning flesh
Concealed, hintings of death she does not heed.
Coldest of winds have blown this hair, and mesh
Of seaweed snarled these miniatures of hands;
The night's slow poison, tolerant and bland
Has moved her blood. Parched years that I have
  seen
That may be hers appear: foul, lingering
Death in certain war, the slim legs green.
Or, fed on hate, she relishes the sting
Of others' agony; perhaps the cruel
Bride of a syphilitic or a fool,
These speculations sour in the sun.
I have no daughter. I desire none.

As war loomed throughout 1941, Kees occupied himself with the bibliographical center, his novel, and his current Selective Service classification. His 3A status was intended for men with dependents but not engaged in activities essential to the war effort—suggesting that he

had not been honest with the local draft board about Ann's job as a legal secretary and their lack of children. And if it came down to being drafted, Kees did not see himself becoming a conscientious objector like his friend Kenneth Rexroth, for that would mean some kind of alternative service or even imprisonment that would compromise his work and his jealously guarded freedom to push the existential elevator button and leave. Though he always alluded to the pacifism of Randolph Bourne during World War I, the hunchbacked essayist of the old *New Republic* was not Kees's model. Nor was Kees afraid of death. What he did fear was the next wave of the incipient fascism that would come with the reorganization of American society for war—Kees wanted to find a third way through it as a matter of pragmatism as much as a quiet protest. The military-industrial complex and the imperial America of Gore Vidal's nightmares were already presciently being apprehended by Kees as he and Ann listened to the droning from nearby Logan Airfield. In "The Locusts, the Plaza, the Room,"

You woke me when they turned the streetlights
  off.
Then new lights raced across the wall from
  windows to the door.
We made love while the bombers roared on by,
Gone seaward. The room rocked and the world
  closed in your eyes.

Pearl Harbor had the dual effect of forcing the United States into the war and making Kees's novel, the now finished *Fall Quarter,* an anachronism overnight. In his reader's report of December 8, 1941, the Knopf editor Paul Hoffman wrote, "It may be that last night and this morning were not precisely the best of times to read a light novel about campus life in the Middle West.... At first I thought things I objected to were merely lapses in discrimination and began to make notes as cuts and revisions but as I got into the new text, I gave up. Every one without exception behaved more and more like a screwball and presently even the properties, so to speak, of the piece began to take on a look of incongruity." Indeed, Kees had written an experimental fusion of the Hollywood screwball comedy and surrealism. ("If you read my story," he wrote the editor Ray West, " 'The Evening of the 4th of July' … you'll have an idea of the sort of thing that got them down; although such effects are much more sparingly employed in the novel.") However, his Dust Bowl answer to Evelyn Waugh's *Decline and Fall* flew in the face the war-themed productions that the publishing industry now needed on its lists. "Can you help me to discover what type of mind is operating here?" he asked Norris Getty, who had read and praised Kees's manuscript. "I just feel as though I'd told my favorite joke and nobody even smiled."

Though his new agent, Henry Volkening, was willing to take the novel to other publishers, Kees wrote and published only a handful of short stories and directed most of his energy to new poems. He could also console himself with what he already knew: that his first book would be a book of poems, *The Last Man,* which William Roth, the Matson Shipping Lines heir, had accepted in the fall of 1941 for the printer Janet Grabhorn's new Colt Press in San Francisco. While a guest at Yaddo during the spring and summer of 1942, Kees hardly looked like the defeated novelist to another guest, the young Alfred Kazin, but rather one of the most "up-to-the-minute writers":

> At Yaddo in 1942 he was a brash young librarian from Beatrice, Nebraska…. He was unbelievably well informed on the smallest details of modernist literature, eagerly presented himself as a walking encyclopedia on every little magazine ever published between Reykjavik and Pinsk. He was a poet who desperately wanted to be "up there," as he used to say, with Eliot, Pound and other stars in our firmament.

NEW YORKER POET AND PAINTER

Kees's experience with Yaddo, where he had met many of his contemporaries for the first time (he sent his friends "McCullersgrams" to keep them informed of the drinking and sexual doings of period's most interesting young writer) made it hard for him to return to his life in Denver and to his waiting wife. Over the summer his marriage had been stressed by Ann's increased drinking and paranoia, which could be traced back to his being involved in Rexroth's scheme to hide Japanese-Americans to keep them from being interned. Kees also faced the increased likelihood of being drafted, and he had a number of projects he wanted to close before that happened, including an anthology of "light" verse—the first of many side projects and vocations with which Kees intentionally tried to dilute the intensity—perhaps even the emotional price—of his own poetry writing.

In February 1943 he left for New York, where he assumed he would enjoy a few more months of freedom and where the Selective Service had "real" psychiatrists who he hoped might classify him as unfit. For several weeks Kees was the guest of Edmund Wilson and his wife Mary McCarthy, John Cheever, and others, including Malcolm Cowley, who had been Kees's "press agent" among the country's literati since 1941, when he wrote that Kees was the poet to publish for his take on the "critical state of this country and the world" and his "sense of incongruity." One string that Cowley pulled for Kees when Kees's savings were running out was to recommend him to his old friend T. S. Matthews, the managing editor at *Time.*

The cachet of writing book—and later film and music—reviews for *Time* was not lost on the "lean, gangling Weldon Kees"—as he described his new job to friends and family, mocking the magazine's hard-boiled prose style (that would be deconstructed by his contemporary Marshall McLuhan in his essay "The Psychopathology of Time & Life"). There was also the camaraderie of working with other poets on the payroll, among them Howard Moss and James Agee. Though his *Time* pieces lacked bylines—which at least ameliorated the onus of working for Henry Luce—Kees made sure his parents received copies of the pieces he was especially proud of. One of these included "How Tom is Doin'," a celebration of a man who could "put the phonebook to music," "Fats" Waller, written only weeks before the jazz composer's death.

The workload as a movie critic eventually wore on Kees. At least the movie studio projection rooms in New York "have very comfortable leather chairs," he wrote Norris Getty, "if only the pictures were up to the chairs." Kees's lack of enthusiasm frequently and piquantly showed up in his copy, such as his review of the remake of *The Phantom of the Opera,* which

> contains more opera than phantom, more trills than thrills.... The 1943 Phantom is bantam-sized Claude Rains, who attempts to terrify by sheer force of character, scar tissue, and Technicolor. Scuttling about in a robin's-egg blue mask, Cinemactor Rains scares nobody but his fellow cinemactors.

Kees's career at *Time* was cut short by his new boss, Whittaker Chambers, better known now as the Soviet agent turned patriot who accused a young State Department employee named Alger Hiss of espionage in 1948. "Our readers," Chambers said on letting him go in early September, "don't want to hear you groan."

Getting fired was hardly a setback for Kees. He received a generous severance, and his self-esteem was assuaged by at last receiving finished copies of his first book of poems, *The Last Man* (Colt Press, 1943), which in turn received respectable reviews. (Horace Gregory acknowledged the Kees's "unfaked" world-view—but also observed that the gloom in his poetry might stand "in the way of its receiving greater notice.") The Selective Service had rejected him on psychiatric grounds, and since the early summer he had been reunited with Ann, who had joined him New York. The couple had subleased a furnished apartment on East Tenth Street near St. Mark's Church, and with her job as an associate editor at *Antiques* magazine and his new position as a writer and editor for Paramount Newsreel Service, they now were relatively comfortable financially.

Having the art critic Harold Rosenberg for an upstairs neighbor and Clement Greenberg for a frequent guest contributed to Kees's taking up painting abstractions in the spring of 1944, a vocation that he initially kept private and performed without the cold-water loft and the anxiety of authenticity so well documented by Tom Wolfe in his 1975 book *The Painted Word* (a book that Kees's art writing to come might have influenced). What more interested Kees was the person he was becoming in New York, that "*sympathique,* very tense, but charming" man Saul Bellow knew to the generous one noted in the diary of Joe Gould, the Village's most famous panhandler, and the man standing apart, even missing from this man. Poetry was the medium used for a self-portrait in which selfhood is a dubious construct. The result was "Robinson":

> The dog stops barking after Robinson has gone.
> His act is over. The world is a gray world,
> Not without violence, and he kicks under the
>   grand piano,
> The nightmare chase well under way.
>
> The mirror from Mexico, stuck to the wall,
> Reflects nothing at all. The glass is black.
> Robinson alone provides the image Robinsonian.
>
> Which is all of the room—walls, curtains,
> Shelves, bed, the tinted photograph of Robinson's
>   first wife,
> Rugs, vases, panatelas in a humidor.
> They would fill the room if Robinson came in.
>
> The pages in the books are blank,
> The books that Robinson has read. That is his
>   favorite chair,
> Or where the chair would be if Robinson were
>   here.

All day the phone rings. It could be Robinson
Calling. It never rings when he is here.

Outside, white buildings yellow in the sun.
Outside, the birds circle continuously
Where trees are actual and take no holiday.

The first readers to encounter Kees's alter ego—
who would "appear" and "disappear" in three
other Robinson poems—certainly recognized
the connection to Robinson Crusoe and his now
urban displacement. Less obvious is Kees's
synthesis of French existentialism imported in
translation by *Partisan Review*. Though Kees
did not win when he entered it in Houghton
Mifflin's poetry contest in the summer of 1945,
he achieved more with its publication in the
New Yorker in October—for there the poem had
the effect of counterpointing the very imago of
the magazine's readership. (Interestingly,
though, one of the contest judges did write Kees
anonymously and make the connection between
Robinson and Kees's easel: "This is intellectual
art with a strange emotional impact characteristic of some contemporary painting. I find in it
brutality and violence and salt.")

The appearance of Kees's second book of
poems, *The Fall of the Magicians* (Reynal &
Hitchcock, 1947) placed him in the first rank of
a new generation of postwar poets. In their
reviews critics listed him with Robert Lowell,
Elizabeth Bishop, and other younger poets who
had recently published books. Milton Crane, the
historian of the New Deal era, saw that Kees
had managed to freshen up the Waste Land
motif in time for the new Republican congress.
Writing in the *New York Times Book Review*, he
saw Kees's work as forming "a chapter in the
history of the disintegration of our world, written by an intelligent, witty, and detached mind.
[Kees]—like many a contemporary and ancestor—[takes] refuge from chaos in irony. But the
refuge is only temporary at best, and the
destruction that will at the last be universal
begins, as the poet well knows, in the drawing
room." Ambrose Gordon's review in *Furioso*

praised Kees's fresh use of formalism, his use
of such difficult forms as the villanelle and sestina to convey entrapment. Elder poets like Conrad Aiken also noticed Kees and gave him
advice—more in reaction to the last part of the
Magicians, which included more derivative efforts from *The Last Man*—on who not to sound
like in his next book:

You're embarrassingly and rewardingly skillful
and use the light touch sometimes quite murder-
ously, and if I have any complaint (meaning of
course that I have) it's of the pale red current of
vin audenaire that now and then stains your own
aqua pura—or if not the vin audenaire, the professional dye that came to be made of it, if you know
what I mean.

Though he took this advice about sounding
like Auden, Kees also poured more of himself
into his critical and cultural writing for the
Partisan Review and his painting. The latter fed
off his summers in Provincetown and his friendships with gallery owners such as Samuel Kootz
and artists such as Hans Hofmann, William Ba-
ziotes, Adolph Gottlieb, Mark Rothko, and Ro-
mare Beardon, who was surprised to learn,
while visiting the Keeses' new apartment in
Brooklyn Heights, that the abstraction over the
sofa was Weldon's. With the same precocious-
ness that marked Kees's debut as a poet, he had
his first one-man show at the Peridot Gallery in
November 1948. The only disappointment—
perhaps more than the few sales—was that his
friend Clem Greenberg had not reviewed the
show in his influential art column in the *Nation*.
Greenberg, however, only sent Kees a private
note, in which he wrote that Kees's work was
"some of the most respectable contemporary
painting there is to be seen anywhere." But he
urged Kees to paint "a lot" and to have a second
show. What he was presenting to Kees was the
issue of commitment, which ran counter to what
Kees did not want to do, to specialize in one
thing or the other, to be either a poet or painter.
This "pigeonholing," as Kees called it, would

become something that he wanted to cheat more than death. And it came at a price when he learned that his next book of poems had been rejected for being too thin, even with the addition of the two new Robinson poems that had appeared in the *New Yorker.*

Kees's "entanglements" increased throughout 1949. On the one hand, he seemed to heed a warning he had long ago planted in the poem that closes *The Last Man,* "The Smile of the Bathers": "No death for you. /You are involved." And on the other, the culture required an almost superhuman intercession on his part after the Cultural and Scientific Conference for World Peace, held at the Waldorf-Astoria in March. Seeing it as a Stalinist front for appropriating the culture, Kees organized a more depoliticized symposium for assessing art, literature, the dance, and even the popular culture of jazz music and films: Forum 49, which ran throughout the summer in Provincetown. Even Greenberg, who had warned Kees about being distracted by "public affairs" (much the way he cautioned his real project, Jackson Pollock, whose drip painting *No. 17* hung next to one of Kees's in the Forum 49 exhibition) was impressed with the people and topics Kees covered as well as the gallery converted from a Provincetown garage. "What you have scheduled," the critic wrote, "looks like the most exciting thing in art ever to run outside of New York in the summer—or in the winter too."

Forum 49 and Kees's increasing presence in New York's art scene during the rise of abstract expressionism resulted in his replacing Greenberg as the art reviewer for the *Nation* during the art gallery season of 1949–1950. He and Ann also moved to a loft on Stanton Street, where he continued to paint for his next one-man show. Only a very few of his close friends, such as Norris Getty, knew that he was still a poet at the core. Getty had reservations about his friend's paintings and collages—but he did not realize that Kees had already hinted at why

he went in this direction and that it might have contributed to his surviving as long as he did and to write the rest of his poems. On the eve of his first one-man show he had told the *Brooklyn Eagle* that his painting and poetry complemented one another: "I don't get into the periods of absolute sterility that are often experienced by writers who just write, or painters who just paint…. In my own case I find the change from writing to painting a joyous, spontaneous experience." Nevertheless, in late 1950 and early 1951 he felt his poems and paintings were moving in the "direction of a mess." He did have "happier efforts," however. "Farrago" was added to the manuscript Kees had expanded and retitled *A Breaking and a Death.* It sends up Auden without being so *vin audenaire* or being (or overdoing) Robinson:

> —I sit in a bar
> On Tenth Street, writing down these lies
> In the worst winter of my life. A damp snow
> Falls against the pane. When everything dies,
>
> The days all end alike, the sound
> Of breaking goes on faintly all around,
> Outside and inside. Where I go,
>
> The housings fall so low they graze the ground
> And hide our human legs. False legs fall down
> Outside. Dance in a horse's hide. Dance in the
>   snow.

Kees may have seen his life as a death performance of madness and falseness, but he was not going to count himself with Ted Roethke, whose recent mental breakdown had caused Kees to observe that "poets are unstable fellows." Instead he slipped into his new profession as a documentary filmmaker and, as the *Nation's* art critic, lent himself to Robert Motherwell's artists' roundtable and their boycott of the Metropolitan Museum's juried exhibition of new American art. The resulting contretemps, during which Kees featured the boycotters' manifesto in his art column, led to an Abstract Expressionist coup in the art world and the famous group portrait titled "The Irascibles," which appeared in *Life* in January 1951. But Kees was not among them. After becoming bored and disenchanted with what he saw as selling out during his last summer in Provincetown, he had left New York for San Francisco, where he hoped to find a fresher avant-garde scene that was not giving itself over to careerism and the hurried, mercenary competitiveness that he identified with the intellectual life in New York. Writing in the *New York Times* at the end of 1950, in the one piece he submitted as its roving West Coast art reporter, he felt that the cultural life in San Francisco should "set New York's avant-garde seismographs aquiver."

POET'S FOLLIES OR FULFILLMENT?

"San Francisco must have seemed like rebirth to Weldon," one friend observed, "it looked so civilized and easy and full of possibility." To him it was "one of the few beautiful cities left in the world. Unlike either contemporary New York or Paris, San Francisco and environs offer the possibility of at least a measure of serenity." During the first months of 1951 he began turning out his best and most ambitious poems (as well as colorful and even colorless, dark paintings). He gave readings at Kenneth Rexroth's Potrero Hill home and had now worked alongside the anthropologist Gregory Bateson at the Langley Porter Clinic making documentary films. Nevertheless, a rejection letter from Robert Giroux—the editor who was then putting the most poets on the American Parnassus—took its toll on Kees. In a letter drafted for his mother, he defended his painting and writing and leaving New York—and he defended himself from expectations as old as his childhood:

> I have written 150 poems—all of which have been published and alone would be considered a lifetime's work for most individuals. My new book of poems will eventually find a publisher. I believe in my work, and I even believe in the eventual success and acceptance of my work in painting.

The real satisfaction that Kees derived from his work was in outflanking what came to be called manic depression (though he would have disdained this interpretation of his motivations despite close working relationships with psychiatrists and the behavioral research in which he was involved). He found comfort in being the polymath, in having so many vocations to spread what was pain to him—to which he added filmmaker and jazz composer after his collaboration on James Broughton's new experimental film, *Adventures of Jimmy* (1951). The vocations left him open as well to picking up different and elusive trails of the 1920s avant-garde for which he had been born too late. He liked hearing what Truman Capote once said in comparing him to ambitious poets such as Robert Lowell ("I can tell from the way you act you don't want to be a success"). But Kees was hardly finished with writing poems.

A few days after Christmas 1951, Norris Getty received a new batch and a new direction—especially in "The Testimony of James Apthorp." "A natural further step in a certain line of development," he wrote Kees, "so natural that you seem not to have broken your stride at all, in spite of your long verseless interlude." But the new poem also disturbed Getty. Kees had always alluded to murders and the like to invoke the violent century. But now Kees spoke in a blur of murderer and self-murderer, with scene splicing that shows his cinematic influences in a pre-Peckinpah verbal slow motion that is almost religiously serene even where there is no cure, no comfort taken in the act, for the cosmic joke being played out in one more of Kees's variations:

> I could not mean to kill
> A druggist at a store. But seeds,
> Black and predictable, fall from the peonies
> And tick along the hardwood floor, like beads.
> Sparse grass

Grows through the cracks. That isn't Rheims.
  Rheims cracks apart.
Why don't they all give up and give it to you
  straight
And say they can't heal anything? Those shrines
Where cripples dump their trusses and their
  canes—
Throw me there, too, against the crutches;
Let me die. Not silica, not cinnabar,
Not parsley out of Macedonia. I did not mean to
  kill
The druggist at the store. I felt the ice
That cracked as Rheims went down. A wall.
A chair. A chiffonier.—I broke his head in
With a jar of facial blemish cream. He kept on
  grinning,
Going down. So many hairnets, all those salves....

Throughout 1952 and 1953 Kees produced some of the last and most important poems—including "A Distance from the Sea," a poem about a raft rigged by the apostles for Christ to perform the miracle of walking on water; and "The Hourglass," Kees's meditation on time. He also gave up his basement studio in his new apartment on Dana Street in Berkeley soon after finishing his last major consignment for Peridot—a series of collages in which the association between Kees's poetry and visual art come closest—to play piano and compose music with the jazz clarinetist Bob Helm. Kees also took hundreds of photographs to illustrate *Nonverbal Communication: Notes on the Visual Perception of Human Relations* (1956), which he coauthored with the psychiatrist Jurgen Ruesch of the Langley Porter Clinic. Though the images were considered scientific data, they can stand apart as art photography, with a vernacular that has a remarkable affinity with the social commentary of Kees's sardonic poems.

The crisis that took place inside his marriage during the summer of 1954 dramatically changed Kees's life. Ann Kees, whom he described as a "mild, controlled alcoholic," became obsessed with the televised Army-McCarthy hearings in June and developed symptoms of extreme paranoia over tapped phone lines, her husband's government-funded research at Langley Porter even a child rival for her husband's attention, as though the girl from "For My Daughter" had come to life. After committing her, Kees moved out of their Berkeley home to San Francisco and began seeking a divorce. Though callous in hindsight, Kees himself was desperate. His job was uncertain and underfunded. His musical ventures had failed to find a music publisher as popular music began to evolve in the direction of Elvis Presley. Poetry tastes had changed too, and though Kees had had significant appearances in the international journal *Botteghe Oscure* and the *New Yorker,* he was, even from his place in San Francisco's poetry scene, not interested in prefiguring or crossing over to the Beats as his rival Rexroth had. At last he allowed the printer Adrian Wilson to publish what was now simply to be titled *Poems, 1947–1954* (1954) in a limited, subscription edition, with some copies featuring original ink drawing frontispieces by Kees.

The book had the intended effect of resuscitating Kees's spirits and even a little of his former reputation as a poet. However, as though he were almost disassociating himself from it, Kees intensified his other alignments and interests. He jammed and recorded with the bluesman Jesse "Lonecat" Fuller and another African American musician, the Purple Onion nightclub's singer, Ketty Lester. He scripted ideas for feature films with fellow poet Vincent McHugh and the critic Hugh Kenner—and he tried to make Hollywood come to him by forming San Francisco Films, a partnership with local filmmakers and television people, and hosting *Behind the Movie Camera* on KPFA, whose panel of guests included Pauline Kael before she became the *New Yorker*'s film critic.

Kees recycled his jazz music and other entertainments into a variety show for a troupe of San Francisco actors that eventually became the Poets' Follies of 1955, a literary burlesque that featured a favorite Oakland stripper reading, of course, Sarah Teasdale. Its local success and national press coverage put Kees into a manic-depressive high that resulted in yet another venture to add to the ones that came after his divorce. He leased an old auditorium and rechristened it the Showplace. After weeks of rehabbing its interior, Kees at least enjoyed seeing it used for a housewarming and fund-raiser dance during the rehearsals of his play *The Waiting Room.* However, the financial burden that came following its closure took its toll on Kees—as did his attempts to find someone to replace Ann. His affair with a local art museum director and his infatuation with one of his actresses had ended badly—as did his affair with his latest companion, a clinical psychologist he met at Langley Porter. He began to talk about killing himself in a way that was hard to take seriously. He talked of jumping from the carillon on the Berkeley campus and about going away too. On different evenings he met with friends for dinner, including Pauline Kael, to discuss his future or futureless plans. He had, he said, been influenced by Rilke's poem "Archaic Torso of Apollo," which ends with the dictum: "You must change your life." And yet he had not followed the script in his own poems—something he, an exacting reader and editor of his own work, would know. Their *thanatos* and detective story clueisms (of which there are enough to add murder to the unknown fates he left behind) required a resolution that begged the question: "Who could be alive after writing all this?" There is now new scholarship that proposes that Sylvia Plath gave her life to the "doctrine" of the *Ariel* poems, so as to make them credulous and real—and it may be that Kees preceded her with as much conscious design. Nevertheless, even in his last days, he was collecting materials for a book with the working title of *Famous Suicides* as though he would be around to finish it as well as be judgmental on the dead celebrities he wanted to profile.

On the last of what turned out to be his "farewell" evenings, Sunday, July 17, Kees met the last friend to see him alive, Michael Grieg. After talking about an unsuccessful attempt to jump to his death and about maybe going to Mexico instead, the two friends drank half a bottle of Jack Daniel's and then had dinner at the Italian Village. Kees then returned to his apartment. There he made some telephone calls the next day and, presumably, when the fog rolled in later in the day, drove to the Golden Gate Bridge. He has not been seen since—or for very long if the apocryphal, glance-like sightings are true—and his name and dates, as long as there are library catalogs, will forever bear a question mark.

Selected Bibliography

WORKS OF WELDON KEES

POETRY
The Last Man: Poems. San Francisco: Colt Press, 1943.
The Fall of the Magicians: Poems. New York: Reynal & Hitchcock, 1947.
Poems, 1947–1954. San Francisco: Adrian Wilson, 1954.
The Collected Poems of Weldon Kees. 1960. 3d ed., edited with prefaces by Donald Justice and David Wojahn. Lincoln: University of Nebraska Press, 2003.

FICTION
Fall Quarter: A Novel. Edited with an introduction by James Reidel. Port Townsend, Ore.: Story Line Press, 1990.
Selected Short Stories. Edited with an introduction by Dana Gioia. Lincoln: University of Nebraska Press, 2002.

CORRESPONDENCE
Weldon Kees and the Midcentury Generation: Letters, 1935–1955. Edited and with commentary by

Robert E. Knoll. Lincoln: University of Nebraska Press, 1986.

OTHER WORKS

Nonverbal Communication: Notes on the Visual Perception of Human Relations. With Jurgen Ruesch. Berkeley: University of California Press, 1956. (Contains many photographs by Kees.)

Reviews and Essays, 1936–1955. Ann Arbor: University of Michigan Press, 1988.

MANUSCRIPT PAPERS

Papers. City Libraries of Lincoln, Nebraska, Bennett Martin Special Collections Room. This collection also contains films, recordings, and artwork by Kees.

Papers and paintings. Gertrude Stein Gallery, New York. Private archive.

CRITICAL AND BIOGRAPHICAL STUDIES

Brodsky, Joseph. "Weldon Kees." *Wilson Quarterly* 17, no. 2:92–93 (spring 1993).

Elledge, Jim. *Weldon Kees: A Critical Introduction.* Metuchen, N.J.: Scarecrow Press, 1986.

Gioia, Dana. "The Afterlife of Weldon Kees." *Boulevard* 4:37–43 (fall 1989).

Gioia, Dana. "The Loneliness of Weldon Kees." In his *Can Poetry Matter?: Essays on Poetry and American Culture.* St. Paul, Minn.: Graywolf Press, 1992. Pp. 61–91.

Niemi, Robert, and Gillane, Daniel. *The Bibliography of Weldon Kees.* Baton Rouge, La.: Parish House, 1997.

Reidel, James. *Vanished Act: The Life and Art of Weldon Kees.* Lincoln: University of Nebraska Press, 2003.

Reidel, James, ed. "Where's That Happy Ending?" Special feature on Weldon Kees. *Verse* 14, no. 3:63–127 (1998).

Ross, William T. *Weldon Kees.* New York: Twayne, 1985.

Siedell, Daniel A., ed. *Weldon Kees and the Arts at Midcentury.* Lincoln: University of Nebraska Press, 2003.

—JAMES REIDEL

X. J. Kennedy

1929–

X. J. KENNEDY—JOE to his friends (the "X" being a typically spirited invention)—was in the 1990s co-opted as a tutelary poetic spirit by a new generation of American poets, commonly known as the New Formalists, freshly interested in the aesthetic possibilities of meter and rhyme in poetry. Kennedy, however, is an old—though far from staid—Formalist, with a no-nonsense view of his art. He quotes with approval lines from the Duke Ellington–Irving Mills song "It Don't Mean a Thing (If It Ain't Got That Swing)" and, in a long artistic life stretching back over fifty years, has stayed true to his own aesthetic preferences. As a poet he is serious, but not solemn; his poems often crack jokes, or make satirical asides; he can be a caustic writer of epigrams; and, while a good deal of New Formalist writing can appear characterized by aesthetic caution, its content formal as well as its technique, Kennedy's work has, at times, a devil-may-care heedlessness, reflected in his work's regular preoccupations with sexual peccadillos and a wide range of unusual characters—many of them outsiders. While he has been a formal master of verse since his thirties, the distinction of his work comes from the tension set up between his forms' rigor and their offbeat, risqué, or otherwise unusual subject matter—what he has referred to, with a glance at his Cornish, Irish, and German ancestry, as his "Celticly wild, teutonically fussy" stance.

LIFE

Joseph Kennedy—his middle name, Charles, he did not take until his confirmation in 1939—was born in the fourteen-thousand-strong town of Dover, New Jersey, on August 21, 1929, the only child of Joseph Francis Kennedy, a time-keeper and paymaster for the local Dover Boiler Works, and Agnes Rauter, who had worked as a registered nurse until her marriage. Kennedy's background was Cornish and Irish on his father's side, and German and Irish on his mother's.

Both parents are affectionately remembered by the poet. From his father, a gentle man whom his wife christened "St. Francis" from his habit of feeding the birds every morning, and his memorized anthology of verse, the child may have taken an early liking for poetry; his mother ensured that, in illness, he received the best of care: having given birth to her only child with complications when past the age of forty, she could have no further children. While the poet's paternal grandfather, Mike Kennedy, had died before his grandchild was born, his widow, the poet's Cornish grandmother, Caroline, was a constant presence, remembered for her baking skills and saws based upon the King James Bible.

Kennedy was a child of the economic depression of the 1930s, and his father's wage had consequently been "trimmed" to twenty-five dollars a week. The family escaped the worst poverty partly helped by the poet's Aunt Effie, who redirected occasional bags of loose change from her husband's haulage business. Fortuitously, shortly before the Wall Street crash of 1929, Kennedy's father had cashed in his stocks to have a house built. Kennedy's childhood home, 84 Baker Avenue, was a modest but comfortable dwelling.

As the son of a mixed marriage—Kennedy's father was Catholic, his mother Methodist—the Catholic side of Kennedy's upbringing would later influence a good deal of his sensibility and, arguably, his poetry; attending St Mary's church in nearby Wharton, he underwent such doctrinal rituals as First Holy Communion, though a terror of the nuns who oversaw the local Catholic school made him beg to attend public rather than parochial school.

It was in the third grade of Northside Elementary School, under his teacher Miss Smith's instruction, that he first tried poetry, writing a piece of pastiche considered accomplished enough to be published in the local newspaper. As the poet later whimsically recalled, his classmates' hoots of derision—"Hey, Longfellow!"—kept him from committing no more poetry than school dictated for at least a few years.

Like many intense adolescent males influenced by Catholicism, Kennedy seems to have sublimated, for interest in girls, with an obsession while a junior at Dover High School—in his case, with science fiction in which he read widely and tried to write, with little success, though he became, by age fourteen, "a widely-published letter hack." The poet-to-be published mimeographed science-fiction magazines such as *Terrifying Test Tube Tales* and *Vampire*. His mixing with skeptical sci-fi fans may have encouraged his drift away from the Catholicism of his youth.

By September 1946, his interest in science fiction beginning to wane, Kennedy had enrolled at the Catholic Seton Hall College in South Orange, New Jersey, then an unusual establishment full of former GIs who would play card games at the back during classes. In 1950 Kennedy graduated from the college with a B.Sc. degree in English. That same year, he began practice teaching at Dover High School.

Upon realizing he was unlikely to make a living as a science-fiction writer, he began, too, a year's study at Columbia University, where his teachers included notable critics such as Lionel Trilling and Mark Van Doren. By the time he graduated in 1951 with an M.A. in English with a concentration in American literature, realizing the difficulty of finding a teaching position, Kennedy had decided to join the navy. He signed up for four years, failing entry into officers' training school on account of poor eyesight—a circumstance that led to his placement instead at the Naval Journalist School at Great Lakes, Illinois, and four years of what the poet later described as "better than receiving four Guggenheim Fellowships in a Row." (*Contemporary Authors,* Vol. 9.) Not only was he sent on cruises, visiting countries in the Caribbean, the North Sea, and the Mediterranean, but his workload was so light that, after photographing sailors for their home newspapers, he could indulge his interest in publishing by mimeographing daily single-page news sheets for an eager crew. He also wrote verse, some of it influenced by W. B. Yeats' *Collected Poems,* bought in the famous Gotham Book Mart in New York while Kennedy was a student at Columbia. Two poems from this period, submitted in 1955, were accepted for publication by the legendary Howard Moss at the *New Yorker,* at which point Kennedy, dismayed by the associations of his given name, permanently adopted the "X" for his byline. One of the pieces was "On a Child Who Lived One Minute," among Kennedy's finest earlier poems.

By summer 1955, his stint in the navy finished, Kennedy was in Paris, having enrolled at the Sorbonne for a year on the GI Bill. His year at the University of Paris was notable not only for the improvement in his French—he received a *certificat littéraire* from the Sorbonne, and a *certificat* from the Institut de Phonetique—but for exposure to the local life of the city, including encounters with the American expatriate litterateur Cid Corman, a poet and little magazine editor. Corman was the first totally committed poet Kennedy recalled meeting.

Kennedy was missing America, however. He was also anxious about his future. He decided to take a Ph.D. and to teach. Corman suggested applying to the University of Michigan at Ann Arbor, which promptly hired him as a teaching fellow. There for six years, not only did he earn $2,400 in prizes from the Avery Hopwood writing contests, but he learned how to face students in class, as well as meeting poets such as the erudite Englishman John Heath-Stubbs and American contemporaries such as Donald Hall, W. D. Snodgrass, and Keith Waldrop. With Waldrop he indulged in a variety of high-spirited japes, including a 1959 hoax evening of beatnik poetry billed as "fresh from San Francisco"—a precursor perhaps of his interest in the "sociology" of the poetry world, later to be whimsically and acerbically featured in aspects of his verse.

More fundamentally, the years at Ann Arbor produced two further big developments for Kennedy: the publication of his first book of verse, *Nude Descending a Staircase,* in 1961—which won a Lamont Award from the Academy of American Poets—and his marriage, in January 1962, to Dorothy Mintzlaff. They remain married; Dorothy, a considerable literary presence in her own right, would later collaborate with the poet on many publishing projects.

In spring 1962, determined to survive as a writer, Kennedy dropped out of the Ph.D. program at Michigan (though he had completed all formal requirements bar the dissertation). He failed to be awarded any of the grants or awards he had applied for, however and, with Dorothy newly pregnant, was bailed out by the offer of a job "teaching basic courses" at the Women's College of the University of North Carolina, in Greensboro. There, the couple spent a busy year, with Kennedy marking student papers, editing poetry for the *Paris Review*—he had recently

succeeded Donald Hall as editor—and meeting, among others, that acute poet-critic Randall Jarrell. Jarrell deeply impressed Kennedy, if more for the "mastiff wit" of his criticism than for his "muzzled" poetry, as the younger poet would later shrewdly observe in an epigram.

By mid-1963, not only was Kennedy father to a first child, Kathleen, but he had been offered a teaching position at Tufts University in Massachusetts, an institution at which Kennedy would remain, after being appointed a full professor in 1973, until 1977. That year, he resigned to concentrate full time on his own writing and on his second career as a textbook writer. (His books for teaching literature include *An Introduction to Poetry,* first published in 1966, and *Literature,* first published in 1976, volumes which had gone into ninth and eleventh editions respectively by 2005, and been used by some one and a half million students.) The intervening fourteen years had been busy ones: he and Dorothy had added four sons—David, Matthew, Daniel, and Joshua—to the family, and the poet had published his second collection, *Growing into Love* (1969), and then *Breaking and Entering* (1971), a third collection for a mainly British audience which reprinted work from the first two books. In 1972, depressed by the low standing of rhyme and meter—the Beats were then in full sway in American poetry—Kennedy and his wife had also begun *Counter/Measures,* a journal hospitable to formal poetry; although it reached only three issues, and had to be closed down in 1974 when Kennedy's aged parents required nursing care, it proved that the tradition of formal poetry still had life in it.

Soon after the closure of *Counter/Measures,* a letter from the children's poet and anthologist Myra Cohn Livingston, started the poet off on a considerable third career as a children's author. Livingston enquired if Kennedy had written any more children's verse like the two examples he had printed in *Nude Descending a Staircase;*

the result in 1975 was *One Winter Night in August*. Kennedy discovered that qualities such as meter and rhyme, which at the time seemed drawbacks in an American poetry scene dominated by free verse, had never gone out of fashion with children. Since 1977, the year he retired from teaching, Kennedy has developed three strands of his activity: editing teaching textbooks, writing for children, and consolidating his reputation as a gifted formal poet. Describing himself as "an earnest, dependable ham" who, as a poetry reader, shows up "more or less sober," he has also established a name as an engaging performer of his own verse, often singing classics such as "In a Prominent Bar in Secaucus One Day." With numerous books for children to his credit, several adult collections, and a number of chapbooks, Kennedy has continued to produce new work. In 2002 he published a collection of verse for adults titled *The Lords of Misrule*. Increasingly honored with awards and recognitions such as honorary degrees bestowed by Lawrence University (1988), Adelphi University (1998), Westfield State College (2002), and having received the Award For Excellence in Children's Poetry from the National Council of Teachers of English in 2000, he is widely respected and admired as one of contemporary America's finest verse craftsmen, a poet with an offbeat sense of humor and a light touch.

NUDE DESCENDING A STAIRCASE

Kennedy was thirty-one when his first book of poems appeared, revealing the poet as already a mature voice. Among its forty poems were numerous future anthology pieces. Although Kennedy has thrown scorn on the idea that the arrangement of a volume's poems was important, his first book showed evidence of an awareness of audience that would later serve the poet well as performer. Subtitled "Poems | Songs | A Ballad," the book was divided into three sections with an additional, drolly titled, "Intermission with Peanuts" consisting of two children's poems, epigrams, and what seems to have been considered, rather arbitrarily, as light verse. The epigrams included his celebrated "Ars Poetica," Kennedy's downbeat take on the danger of self-consciousness when composing poetry.

The volume began, however, with "First Confession," a memory of the poet's Catholic upbringing, which would mark a whole seam of verse about Catholicism throughout his career. Neatly written in rhyming quatrains, with slant rhymes in many of the odd-numbered lines which, as the Kennedy specialist Bernard E. Morris has pointed out, set up a disjunction between the authority figure of the priest and the uncertain child, the poem expertly captures the young narrator's mix of intimidation, cooperation, and reluctance in the face of his first confession before the priest, "the robed repositor of truth," in the confessional. If one reads the poem biographically, Kennedy seems to have been an unusually truthful and trusting confessor, even telling the priest how he'd "bribed" his "girl to pee" so that he could "spy her instruments." "Doled"—given—by the priest, "as one feeds birds," seven Our Fathers and a Hail Mary as penance, he says them twice to "double-scrub" his soul. "Doled" implies a haughty superiority on behalf of the giver, and a neediness on behalf of the recipient. Thus absolved, the child is fit to take Communion the following Sunday when, kneeling at the altar rail, he tells us, he stuck his "tongue out at the priest: / A fresh roost for the Holy Ghost." At the time the poem records, the Catholic communicant was not permitted, as now, to take the Communion wafer into his or her hands, but had to have it directly placed on the tongue by the priest. Kennedy wittily subverts this action of humble cooperation to one of covert rebellion. The young confessor's attitude is deeply ambiguous. His tongue, organ of speech, is both an instrument of subversion and only a "roost," that is, a sleeping place, for the Holy Ghost, here symbolized as a bird, though there is a rustling gorgeousness in the phrase "fresh roost."

Two poems interrelated, "On a Child Who Lived One Minute" and "Little Elegy," are elegies for a baby and a young girl respectively. Both deal with understated images of great violence: in the former, the world is one "where children shriek like suns / Sundered from other suns on their arrival." A baby is made a cosmic force here; it is compared to a sun, a giver of light, and the violence of the image is accentuated by the verb "shriek" and the alliteration with and elevated gravity of the verb "sundered"; after describing how, with an ironic daintiness, "a blackness tiptoed in her / and snuffed the only candle in her castle," the poem ends:

> O let us do away with elegiac
> Drivel! Who can restore a thing so brittle,
> So new in any jingle? Still I marvel
> That, making light of mountainloads of logic,
> So much could stay a moment in so little.

While the poem's narrator refuses "elegiac / Drivel," even referring to such an elegiac poem—and, implicitly, his own—as "any jingle," this has the paradoxical effect of increasing the poem's poignancy, an effect increased by the pun on "making light" in the poem's penultimate line. "Mountainloads of logic" are made light of not only in the sense of counting for little but by being returned, as light, to the poem's and the infant's source. The repetition of the alliteration on the "m" and the "l" in that line help reinforce the action described.

"Little Elegy" is an eight-line "mouthful of melody" as Ezra Pound would have called it, with no biographical context but, as we know from Kennedy himself, produced entirely as a result of his liking for the delicate lyrics of the seventeenth-century English poet Robert Herrick. Subtitled "For a Child Who Skipped Rope," its very title indicates a desire to avoid, as in "On a Child Who lived One Minute," "elegiac drivel," though it also implies that the child is dead, a conclusion the poem's eight lines leave ambiguous. The first quatrain reads:

> Here lies resting, out of breath,
> Out of turns, Elizabeth
> Whose quicksilver toes not quite
> Cleared the whirring edge of night.

Here, night is, terrifyingly, like the blade on some massive circular saw; Elizabeth has been caught by it. Lines one, two, and four are tetrameters which each begin with a strong stress; they set up the regular rhythm of the little girl skipping, accentuated by the comma breaks in lines one and two. In line three, however, the cramming together of stressed syllables unsettle the soothing rhythm and imitate sonally the little girl's frantic attempt to clear "the whirring edge." The poem's closing stanza ends with the poet's invocation that the earth "Shelter now Elizabeth / And for her sake trip up Death." This implies that she has been injured but is not yet dead; an implication denied by the valedictory "Elegy" of the poem's title. Kennedy may well be, however, invoking Death as a death of the spirit even beyond the death of the body. One also notes the skillfulness of Kennedy's rhymes: the girl's name is rhymed with "breath," symbol of life, in stanza one, and wholly negated by the closing rhyme in stanza two.

Kennedy's first book included numerous poems whose subjects and themes would remain preoccupations throughout his career. Section 2, "Songs and a Ballad," opened with his classic "In a Prominent Bar in Secaucus One Day"— spoken by an old lady down on her luck who, in her glamorous younger days, had been the delight of men infatuated by her beauty and sexual allure, who would scrabble for her sexual favors. While nothing in the poem indicates she was a prostitute, it is plain that she used her sexual power to help her live the high life. Now, she tells us, "I'm saddled each night for my butter and eggs / And the broken threads race down the backs of my legs." The poem's literary antecedents include "The Old Woman of Beare," an Irish Gaelic poem whose speaker (though she has not turned to prostitution) similarly laments her old age. The poem begins Kennedy's fascination in his verse with outsiders and misfits. It comprises ten quatrains rhymed as closed couplets, with a predominantly anapestic/dactylic beat which gives an energetic, ironic bounce to the poem's grievous subject matter. In performance, Kennedy sings it to the tune of "The Old Orange Flute," a melody which, poised between gaiety and sadness, seems entirely fitting for the poem's tone of jaunty grief. While "the lady in skunk" offers advice which social changes have made seem outdated—she recommends that women get themselves married off young—"or be left—an old barrel with many a bung," her difference from modern women, not least in this attitude toward marriage, simply serves to increase her isolation and therefore the central poignancy and point of the poem.

Kennedy's interest in and partial empathy with social misfits continued here in poems such as "The Aged Wino's Counsel to a Young Man on the Brink of Marriage" and "B Negative." In the first, the old wino who has married the bottle instead of a woman contrasts it favorably with a range of possible nightmare wives—self-obsessed, acid-tongued, thriving on gossip—and exhorts the young man in what seems half a challenge, half a threat, to "wed half as well" as he has to his "two quart virgin" of alcohol. The poem exemplifies men's sexual reliance on women: the old wino is full of bitterness, which he has handled as best he can, transforming it via alcohol into a barren triumphalism. Variations on the theme of marriage—its difficulties, and the results of separation—and bachelor or

spinsterhood will remain a constant throughout Kennedy's oeuvre.

The speaker in "B Negative" is known to us only by his blood group, which as the poem's title also acts as a faint pun, and by his poem's subtitle: "M/60/5ft 4/W PROT," as if to emphasize the anonymity of contemporary American urban society. This sixty-year-old, white, Protestant, fairly diminutive man appears to be working as a litter attendant in Central Park—unless he is a vagrant on the hunt for leftovers. He sees the world from an unusual angle: April he recognizes, he tells us, because there are fewer "coughdrop boxes" dropped. He prefers the honest barrenness of snow to the painful awakenings of spring: "The snow, at least, keeps tracks of people's feet." Spring and its energies, the implication is, unsettle everything, including human relationships—for in stanzas five and six of this sixteen-stanza poem, in quatrains whose rhyme scheme is that of the *Rubáiyát of Omar Khayyam* in Edward Fitzgerald's translation, the speaker gives us a clue as to his "story":

It used to be that when I laid my head
And body with it down by you in bed
    You did not turn from me nor fall to sleep
But turn to fall between my arms instead

And now I lay bifocals down. My feet
Forget the twist that brought me to your street.
    I can't make out your face for steamed-up glass
Nor quite call back your outline on the sheet.

The bifocals are an indication of his increasing incapacity. The rest of that stanza is characterized by its negatives—of forgetting and of inability. Out of a failed relationship, the poem's narrator lives in despair, on the edge; he sleeps on the subway because it is cheaper than a room; at the poem's close he tells us

I know how, lurking under trees by dark,
Poor loony strangers out to make their mark
    Reach forth shy hands to touch a woman's
    hair—
I pick up after them in Central Park.

The speaker has compassion for those messed-up men, too shy or inadequate for relationships with women, and not necessarily potential rapists and molesters, who, it could be implied, masturbate under the trees: that "know" implies more than just intellectual knowledge. They are "poor" in every sense, and the "loony" gives them a certain pathetic acceptability. Here, men separate from women are seen to be imbalanced, likely to go off the rails. The deep melancholy and bleakness in the speaker's voice is emphasized by what he notices, and the gloominess is set ironically against the energy and fluency of the rhyming quatrains: the speaker barely pauses for breath. There is a manic urgency to his own utterance.

Another outstanding related poem, "Solitary Confinement," is a sixteen-line narrative meditation about a woman lying in bed who has remained too long in a marriage she cannot now escape. The poem comprises two eight-line stanzas. In the first, she considers the possibility that she could still escape. In the second, resignation has taken over:

> She put the notion back
> And turned her look up where the clock,
> Green ghost, swept round its tethered hand
> That had made off with many nights
> But no more could break from its shelf
> Than she could quit this bed where breath
> By breath these years he'd nailed her fast
> Between two thieves, him and herself.

The "green ghost" may refer to the luminosity of the clock in the dark: stored with captured light—an image in this context with a rich resonance—its "tethered hand" can only sweep around ineffectually; time is a jailer, and she is as imprisoned by it as the clock's hand. By the poem's closure the woman is compared, ironically, to the crucified Christ between the two thieves at the Crucifixion. The Christ, in this context, seems to be her better self, the one with aspirations. She, however, by her inability to break out of the marriage by sheer force, is considered as much a thief of her own freedom and its potential as her husband. The repetition

of the word "breath" across the line break leads to a halt in the voice as one reads the lines, serving to mimic the jolt of realization the reader experiences.

Nude Descending a Staircase closed with Kennedy's celebrated twelve-line vignette, the book's title poem, followed by a likeable Yeatsian dialogue, "One A.M. with Voices," in which a wife admonishes her rhymester husband for trying to make verses while she lies cold in bed, awaiting him. The book's title piece is loosely associated with Marcel Duchamp's painting of the same title, first exhibited in New York in 1913, where it caused a stir with its somewhat mechanistic attempt to convey movement via a still image. Kennedy's poem is considerably more gorgeous than Duchamp's representation and depicts the nude "sifting" "in sunlight down the stairs / With nothing on. Nor on her mind." It is a poem appropriate to a writer raised in a Catholic tradition in which praise of the Madonna is central. The last stanza is:

> One-woman waterfall, she wears
> Her slow descent like a long cape
> And pausing, on the final stair
> Collects her motions into shape.

In the final line, her stillness coalesces; she becomes "a shape" once more rather than the movements she has been throughout the poem—"a snowing flesh," "a one-woman waterfall." While some commentators have made considerable claims for this poem written in jaunty tetrameters, it seems, finally, a celebration of pure being; the woman has "nothing on," and nothing "on her mind": claiming too great a complexity for it seems to negate the very state it delicately celebrates.

Nude Descending a Staircase marked a powerful debut for the young poet; his next major collection, *Growing into Love*, which appeared eight years later, helped consolidate that early achievement.

GROWING INTO LOVE

Kennedy's new book of fifty-four poems was divided into three sections, respectively titled "Experiences," "Countrymen," and "Growing into Love." The volume began with the poem "Cross Ties"—later to be the title poem of his volume of selected poems that appeared in 1985: a brief, complex piece rich with symbolism. The poem's title puns on the narrator's binding connection still to the symbolic cross of his early Catholicism. The piece's narrator is walking on cross ties out on a disused railway track, symbolic, for the speaker, of his outmoded Catholicism; he can "take stock" in a "something," "Hell-bent" approaching from behind his back—"a thing to sidestep or go down before." The possibility of damnation is symbolized as a train approaching from behind, which the narrator can either take seriously or sidestep by opting for purely pragmatic realities. He concludes:

> Out of reach
> Or else beneath desiring, I go safe,
> Walk on, tensed for a leap, unreconciled
> To a dark void all kindness.
> When I spill
> The salt I throw the Devil some and, still,
> I let them sprinkle water on my child.

Death is "a dark void all kindness"; the narrator is, however, "unreconciled" to it and still remains superstitious enough to throw the Devil some accidentally spilled salt and to "let them"—a phrase which marks his separation from his former faith—baptize his child with holy water. The poem elucidates the narrator's unresolved dilemma in regard to Catholicism. Highly ambiguous, it flirts with Pascal's Wager that it is better to believe and avoid damnation, as one will have lost nothing by doing so, than to not believe and risk eternal perdition.

Other outstanding poems in the first section included "Poets," a portrayal of poets when schoolboys which was apparently prompted by a negative comment by D. H. Lawrence, writing from Dover, New Jersey, Kennedy's hometown, in August 1923. The comment functions as the poem's epigraph: "The people here are … quenched. I mean the natives." Kennedy added to the epigraph the first line (which is also the title) in its original French of a Stéphane Mallarmé sonnet, "Le vierge, le vivace, et le bel aujourd'hui." ("The virginal, lively, and lovely here-and-now," in Kennedy's version.) The sonnet depicts a swan with feet frozen in ice, wings buffeting the sky.

Kennedy's poem begins by speculating what poets were like in childhood, suggesting a range of unflattering possibilities. It then becomes directly autobiographical, with the poet recalling how, in his hometown, swans on the local pond would let the ice "glaze about their feet," so that

> A fireman with a blowtorch had to come
>
> Thaw the dopes loose. Sun-silvered, plumes aflap,
> Weren't they grand, though? Not that you'd
>   notice it,
> Crawling along a ladder, getting bit,
> Numb to the bone, enduring all their crap.

In one reading this can be Kennedy's apologia for being a poet himself. In another, however, this is Kennedy standing up for his own people enduring all "the crap" of poets such as a cynical D. H. Lawrence who feels justified in making judgments of communities he is not part of, though Kennedy acknowledges, too, the concomitant "grandness" of the poet. One of the strengths of Kennedy's verse is his instinctive distrust of the fake and the inflated; here, he grants both the pragmatic world and the world of art their respective says. The poem is stronger as a consequence.

In Kennedy's fine variation on a Petrarchan sonnet, "Nothing In Heaven Functions as It Ought," a chaotic dailiness, originally thought negative, proves to be a source of hope. In the octet, heaven is rather disorganized; rather than turning "with a hush of gold as Milton had thought," St. Peter's gates "lurch with the cackle of a cock"; it is "sleek Hell," in the sonnet's sestet, which "hath no freewheeling part": everything functions there with mathematical precision. Here, organization is terrifying; randomness, being human, is closer to genuine heaven. The piece seems shadowed by knowledge of the attempted efficiency of the death camps of the Holocaust.

The book's middle section, "Countrymen," assembles an impressive cast of characters, again confirming Kennedy's fascination with outsiders: in "O'Riley's Late-Bloomed Little Son," the death of a child of parents too mature to have another is conveyed in a scene reminiscent of the bereaved couple in Frost's "Home Burial"; "The Self-Exposed" is the monologue of a sexual flasher; there is a portrait of a barren maiden lady, of a disgruntled scholar's wife deserted by her husband for his studies, and a weird portrait of an "Absent-Minded Bartender" who accidentally killed a woman in bed and has been on the run ever since. Among the section's outstanding pieces, "Loose Woman" depicts a Mary Magdalene—by contrast to the Madonna elsewhere found in Kennedy's oeuvre—in a trim pair of rhyming octets the shapeliness of which is in ironic contrast to the poem's content. In the first stanza, two boys coming from fishing discover the woman with her throat cut, "her chin," which she would toss haughtily at taunts from local "firehouse oglers" as she passed, "flung up higher than she'd want / Just held fast by a little hinge of skin." Here is the closing octet:

> Her next-best talent—setting tongues to buzz—
> Lasts longer than her best. It still occurs
> To wonder had she been our fault or hers
> And had she loved him. Who the bastard was,
> Though long they asked and notebooked round
>   about
> And turned up not a few who would have known

> That white inch where her neck met shoulder-
>   bone,
> Was one thing more we never did find out.

Here, the community's tongues are transformed into wasps that "buzz"; the narrator has enough insight and humanity to speculate on whether this "loose woman" was a symbol for the repressed desires of, at least, the male segment of the community: her taunters in stanza one "ogle" her at the same time as they mock her. There is a grudging respect in the narrator's recognition of her haughtiness. She becomes a mystery, and the three closing sentences of the poem, which increase in length until the final beautifully modulated speculation is sealed by the flat declaration of the last line, help enact that sense. While she is considered, for her willful promiscuity, a "fault," irrespective, one senses the narrator's sympathy with the character.

Despite Kennedy's avowal that the ordering of a collection is of little importance, section 3 of this book, "Growing into Love," shows evidence of careful ordering; the poems notate something of the growth that the section's title suggests. The section begins with the sonorous "Transparency," in which the narrator informs us in his opening stanza:

> Love was the woman I loved,
> A grave, inhuman woman.
> At night in our room alone,
> I, self-sufficient Adam,
> Laid hand on my cold bone.

The narrator is in love with an ideal, not the particular; he masturbates, fantasizing about this abstract, which can take various women's faces like a mask. Most noticeable here is the skillfulness of Kennedy's rhymes. "Loved," has no rhyme, emphasizing the speaker's isolation; "woman" and "Adam" are half-rhymes, and "woman" is the general rather than the particular represented by "Adam," emphasizing the narrator's inability to meet his match. "Alone" and "bone," meanwhile, are full rhymes which echo like a vault being closed. The poem is a depiction of the barrenness of its narrator; masturbation, in fairly judicial terms, becomes a form of death. By the poem's end its speaker, having obtained physical release, "even through gorged eyes" is able to "see through" his fantasy object's "skull."

The theme of the overscrupulous male, sexually self-contained, separated from nature and authentic femaleness, continues in the following poem, "Artificer," in which the character, in love with perfection, attempts to construct his own perfect universe: "His thrushes tried tin whistles in their bills; / His oaks bore pewter acorns that unscrewed." The natural, organic world, however, which contains birth and therefore death, will not be denied: "All night, the world that lolled outside / Kept slipping newborn rats under his door."

Immediately after this was the ironically titled "Ode," a paean of acceptance to a sort of id, or the earthly slapstick part of the self, without which, the narrator asks: "How could the stuck-up spirit in me bear / Coming back down to earth?"

The narrator is well down to earth with two poems near the end of the sequence, "Daughter in the House" and "Giving in to You." Both are addressed to the narrator's wife; the first is about their daughter, whom the poet regards with rapt fascination, and the second is a sort of hymn to giving in to the feminine principle, though Kennedy has rewritten the poem since, mainly by deleting the middle sections. The book closes with "The Shorter View," a profound poem contrasting the poet's attitude to that of his wife, who has been reading a book about astronomy and humanity's inexorable fate of cosmic extinction. Grasping the relativity not just of a single human life, but of humankind itself for the first time, she

... lets her book fall with stricken face.
She'd thought tomorrow set and rooted here,
And people. That some morning will occur
Without a sunrise hadn't dawned on her.
Kathleen some great pink shell held to her ear,
And, wistful, staring through me to an earth
Littered with ashes, too dried-up to bear—
Though I say, *What the Hell, we won't be there*—
She doesn't see much point in giving birth...

The poem contrasts the wife's grief at the prospect of our species' extinction with the narrator's temporal pragmatism. There is a deep irony in the poem's colloquialism of the day without a sunrise not having "dawned on" the poet's wife. She stares through her husband "to an earth / Littered with ashes, too dried-up to bear" both metaphysically and biologically. With "littered" Kennedy puns, again ironically, on the word's other meaning, to give birth to a litter. The husband's response to his wife is "What the hell, we won't be there." On the contrary, he would "recklessly make love." The poem concludes with his wife, however, who, her arms tight shut, "for this night will not give / One inch of ground for any shorter view." Pragmatism and idealism are powerfully contrasted. The man's sensibility in "The Shorter View" is temporal; his wife's, absolute. The latter, in absorbing the lesson of cosmology, in keeping her arms shut and not giving ground for "any shorter view," for this single night ironically comes to exemplify the barrenness which that lesson teaches. There is a pun, too, in the phrase about "giving ground," with its allusion to the possibility of fertility. The irony is that "The Shorter View" is the one that produces life.

BREAKING AND ENTERING

Kennedy's next book took the form of an unofficial "selected works" for the British reader: it established something of a British reputation for him. The London Poetry Book Society made it their recommendation for that year. The new volume collected fifteen poems and twenty-two poems respectively from Kennedy's first and second books; it added "Bulsh," a sequence of two-line rhyming epigrams on the eponymous Bulsh, an unpleasant, lecherous, and wholly cynical Catholic priest, which Kennedy reprinted from a chapbook published the previous year, and it also included six new poems plus a sequence of "Japanese Beetles," epigrams which demonstrated Kennedy's mastery of the form.

The "Bulsh" sequence continues that strand of poems in which Kennedy explores his relationship to Catholicism, though there is nothing exploratory about his investigation of Bulsh, who appears as nastiness incarnate. Kennedy's take on him is breathtakingly one-sided: Bulsh is almost pure id. (He is a creation who became only more convincing in the wake of twenty-first-century scandal and lawsuits over sexual abuse by Catholic clergy.) He is the priest as sex addict, a cynical showman for the cameras, and he embodies some of the paradoxes and contradictions Kennedy senses about the faith he was raised in. While sexuality is at the root of Bulsh's perversion, he also exemplifies the paradox of forgiveness of sins: "When Bulsh found out he hadn't long to live / He fell to giving God more to forgive." The possibility of redemption irrespective of the sin committed seems to be the doctrine that Kennedy is satirizing here. Bulsh's indulgence in sin accrues to the greater glory of a God who seems the more generous the more his pleasurably sinning disciple gives him to absolve. Both parties gain dubiously from this "spiritual" transaction.

The other group of epigrams, "Japanese Beetles," show a wide range for a form especially suited to the expression of pithy, often satirical, asides. Many, as in "Teutonic Scholar," cram a biography into two lines; others comment wittily on the sociopolitics of contemporary poetry, that world which has little to do with genuine creativity but which a modern poet arguably has to understand and manage sensibly

if he or she is to organize a career which helps advance the most important thing, the work itself. The form also allows Kennedy to file his acerbic wit to a razor edge. Here, in "To a Now-Type Poet," Kennedy both criticizes a vogue for shapeless confessionalism in contemporary poetry and implies by his epigram's form an alternative aesthetic: "Your stoned head's least whim jotted down white-hot? / Enough confusion of my own, I've got." As Ezra Pound would have said of this, Kennedy has a meaning in each of his terms: it is hard to see what could be removed without altering the sense. All but "Your" and the second syllable of "jotted" in the first line carry primary stresses, which, crowded together, ironically mimic the "intensity" of the "now-type" poet; the second line, placing the speaker in direct opposition, is a more balanced iambic pentameter, with a weak third stress (on the "of").

In the final "Japanese Beetle," the six-line "To a Young Poet" (which Kennedy would later reduce to its final rhyming couplet), Kennedy advises the aspirant to "Be heavy, man, as this grave day commands." He comments acerbically on the tendency in the poetry world to favor grand schemes, solemnity and the appearance of seriousness above wit, vivacity, and gaiety. The verse concludes: "On solemn asses fall plush sinecures, / So keep a straight face and sit tight on yours."

To Kennedy's credit, such solemnity is something he never managed especially well; he distinguishes between solemnity and its more attractive cousin, seriousness, even if, having thus "blown his cover," as it were, it could be at his own expense in the often humorless poetry scene.

Among the strong new poems added to *Breaking and Entering* were "Consumer's Report," a validation of the American proverb which serves as epigraph, "They don't make things like they used to." It shows Kennedy returning, as often, to the Dover of his childhood, peopled with eccentrics and memorable characters such as this poem's John Dowd, a maker of powerful horseradish from "cream and home-ground roots," the fumes of which, it was said, "get to your brain." In decline, Dowd is stoically aware of his coming death, an awareness compared favorably with the ignorance of "those other guys," those "who use white turnip filler," whose death, the narrator believes, will take them by surprise. Kennedy's poem harks back nostalgically, yet not necessarily unjustifiably, to an older world presumed more authentic.

"Last Child," dedicated, ironically, to Kennedy's second-to-last son, Daniel, is a thirteen-line expression of a father's decidedly ambiguous feelings toward a late-born son. An extraordinarily honest poem, it opens: "Small vampire, gorger at your mother's teat, / Dubious claim I didn't know I'd staked." Even in this harsh poem, one notes Kennedy's characteristic wordplay: the pun on "staked," as well as having its primary meaning of "officializing," or "establishing the boundaries to," sets up a reverberation implying that, as the father is partly responsible for his son's birth, so he will be as a corollary, too, for his eventual death; he has "staked," in the sense of "stabbed," this "small vampire" by fathering him. The narrator here is the child's "stop-and-fetch-it-pimp," and the child itself is, in the father's eyes, the wholly self-seeking life principle which proceeds without concern for its environmental effect: the child's fingers are "anemones / A decent ocean ought to starve." The father makes "tries at a caress," and the poem closes: "You should not be. I cannot wish you dead." The child's innocent life urge is contrasted with the father's culpable awareness of the environmental damage another human on earth will cause merely by existing, and the poem ends with two opposing statements, set like weights on either end of a balance; the closing sentence, which has one stress more than the penultimate one, is a small, grudging affirmation. "Last Child" may seem to some readers an unpleasant poem. A lesser poet may well have omitted it from a collection. Kennedy, on the other hand, has reprinted it since in a slightly rewritten version which increases the bleak honesty.

After *Breaking and Entering,* it would be fourteen more years before another of Kennedy's books of poetry for adults would be brought out by a sizeable trade publisher. A journal entry by the poet from the 1970s explains that he had been

> born just a little too late for the crest of formal poetry that rose in the 1950s, so that my stuff didn't begin to appear till the great stampede out of traditional form was on. So I came to the poetry scene like some guest who shows up just when the party is ending, the punchbowl drained, the streamers all tromped to the floor.

Despite this gloomy diagnosis, Kennedy persisted in writing in meter and rhyme and in producing unfashionable satire about contemporary poetry for a common reader, an activity primarily likely to alienate him in the somewhat ingrown and nepotistic poetry world. He published only chapbooks for more than the ensuing decade, ten years in which he began a substantial career as a children's poet and novelist.

BOOKS FOR CHILDREN

When the children's anthologist Myra Cohn Livingston showed her publisher, Margaret K. McElderry at Atheneum, examples of Kennedy's work for children, the result was, in 1975, Kennedy's first book of children's verse, *One Winter Night in August.* Since that year have followed numerous otherbooks of verse for children, the editing of several anthologies, and two children's novels, *The Owlstone Crown* (1983) and *The Eagle as Wide as the World* (1997).

In the verse for children Kennedy was able to use aspects of his adult work to good advantage—his offbeat humor, exaggerated and married to his command of form, interest in word games, and sheer pleasure in verbal malarkey proved advantages where they had seemed to be drawbacks in the 1970s adult poetry scene. The children's verse has an anarchic voltage; it features crazy relatives, eccentric characters, bizarre food, a whole cast of witches, dragons, dinosaurs, giants, and the astonishments of the natural world.

Frequently, the books of verse have a thematic cohesion. In one of Kennedy's more popular series, which began with *Brats* (1986), later to be followed by *Fresh Brats* (1990) and *Drat These Brats!* (1993), a general motif is that of the overly curious or mischievous child who does something he or she shouldn't, often with consequences so dire and overblown that the result is humorous. In such poems, Kennedy makes the most of children's liking for unusual names and wacky incidents; the series' pieces are full of action, and seldom longer than ten lines, most being considerably shorter:

Noticing an open-doored
Spacecraft, Nora sneaked aboard.
Now where is she?
            Moved, poor dear,
Several million miles from here.

Conversely, *The Beasts of Bethlehem* (1992) is a gentler book which utilizes the old belief that on Christmas Eve the animals attending Jesus' birth in the manger in Bethlehem can speak. A range of creatures, from the lowliest such as beetle and worm, to the highest, such as the eagle, speak briefly. The sequence has an appropriately venerating tone, though one feels that Kennedy is more at home with the zanier happenings in many of his other children's poems. They form part of a world in which a volcano appears and erupts in someone's backyard, or a great grandmother is implored not to sleep in her treehouse tonight, or in which "The Cat Who Aspired to Higher Things" prefers chasing rhinoceroses to chasing mice. (The mice thrive; but rhinoceroses are, naturally, nonexistent.) It is a world of exploding gravy and "choosy" wolves who turn their noses up at eating children, preferring natural food that "nothing has been done to." Some of the poems are simply delineations of ordinary—if not ordinarily written about—situations, likely to be recognized by child and adult alike, such as "Alarm," in which a slightly sanctimonious older sister once again calls her mother to see the extraordinary mess made by her younger brother, or "In the Motel," a depiction of a family holiday in which everything goes dramatically and flamboyantly wrong. Others, such as "Making Light of Auntie," begin with ordinary phenomena such as a child making static electricity by rubbing socks on the carpet and end with an aunt for a lightbulb. Still others, such as "Living on a Giant," are surreally daft to begin with; the poem plays out the daftness. Yet others, such as "The Whales off Wales," have great fun with word sounds: "With walloping tails, the whales off Wales / Whack waves to wicked whitecaps." Kennedy never loses his sense of significant language in the verse for children. In the twelve-line, three-stanza "Woolly Mammoth," for instance (from the 2002 collection *Exploding Gravy*), which describes this prehistoric giant, Kennedy closes by recounting how

By someone in Siberia
A bunch of these vast geezers
Were once discovered big as life
And fresh as fish in freezers.

The use of colloquialisms such as "bunch" and "geezers" helps convey a friendliness to the animals without diminishing their power to awe, and the closing line's alliteration has a wonderful lip-smacking relish which powerfully conveys the shivering cold; comparing the vision of this bunch of "vast geezers" to something much closer to the children's experience, refrigerated fish, both increases and makes more realizable the astonishment of this discovery.

The children's poems are notations of the world's absurdity and paradox when it is looked at too literally; the often rollicking wordplay counterpoints what could seem risky subject matter; chaotic and anarchic happenings are safely bounded within rigorous metrical patterns and sing-song jauntiness.

Kennedy's two novels for children, *The Owlstone Crown* and its sequel, *The Eagle as Wide as the World,* have many of the linguistic virtues of the poetry. *The Owlstone Crown* is an adventure story cum ecological fable with offbeat characters including a talking detective ladybug and a prophetic snail. Twins, Timmy and Verity Tibb, the book's central characters, believing themselves to be orphans, are working in misery for Maw and Paw Grimble until, told by the detective ladybug that their grandparents are still alive, they escape in search of them. They find, by accident, Other Earth, which has been taken over by Raoul Owlstone and his sidekick, Baroness Ratischa Von Bad Radisch; having corrupted a good scientist's labor-saving invention to their own ends, they rule over Other Earth with an army of stone owls and have placed a large glass dome over the Moonflower, which is a sort of symbol for creativity, harmony, and ecological balance. The story is the action-filled account of the liberation of the moonflower and the restoration of ecological and psychic harmony to Other Earth. Among its virtues are the wonderful touches of quirky humor and description. The book enjoyed the distinction of being reissued in a mass-market paperback.

Fifteen thousand words cut from the original draft of *The Owlstone Crown* formed the basis for the sequel, published some fourteen years later. All the original characters reappear, though the pace seems gentler, and some of the invention seems incidental to the central plot. Meadea, a giant queen bee, has plotted, with her sidekick, Professor Drone, to take over rights to the Moonflower, so that only the giant bees can have access to its nectar, a ruse which would mean the death of all other life on Other Earth. They kidnap Timothy and Verity's half-brother, Mustard, as hostage to get the twins' grandfather, also chief elder, to agree to this dastardly scheme. Notwithstanding the kidnapping, the twins go off at the insistence of their grandfather to school, the School of Sweetness and Light, an institution newly taken over in secret by giant bees, where the only lessons taught are on bee lore and husbandry, with the eventual aim of turning the students into bees, paragons of industry and efficiency. The youngsters, accompanied by the ladybug and the giant bear, Fardels, escape in search of their half-brother, having learned he is probably on April Fool Isle, where all the animals grow to giant size and where the Eagle as Wide as the World, which also happens to be invisible, lives. After many adventures, they rescue their half-brother, expose the plot of the giant bees, and the story ends in harmony with the bees still being permitted to visit the moonflower, which has enough nectar for everyone.

THE CHAPBOOK DECADE, 1974–1984

While beginning to establish himself as a children's author, Kennedy had by no means given up on his poetry for adults, publishing numerous chapbooks, some of them handsome. Of these, the first, *Emily Dickinson in Southern California,* appeared in 1974. It was named after the title poem, which had nine sections and, in a manner reminiscent of Emily Dickinson, imagines her in that state. The poem has its comic moments—as here, where Dickinson records how

I walked a pace - I tripped across
Browned couples - in cahoots -

No more than tides need shells to fill
Did they need - bathing suits -

The piece can seem to fall uncomfortably between parody and serious imitation, however, in comparison to Kennedy's "own" work. The reader feels uncertain as to the point of the exercise.

Perhaps to extend his potential audience for this chapbook, Kennedy also reprinted "Last Child," some of the "Japanese Beetles" and other epigrams from *Breaking and Entering*, and added several new poems. These included "Onan's Soliloquy," which continued Kennedy's exploration of aspects of sexuality, in particular masturbation as opposed to sex within relationship, which for him seems to have psychic and spiritual consequences. The "Onan" of his poem's title, who seems to refer only generically to the biblical character, infuriated by being rebuffed by a woman, "possesses" her by fantasizing about her while masturbating. The poem comprises four taut rhyming couplets and ends with the speaker unpleasantly fumbling "the dim unconscionable tits" of his fantasy object. His victory, however, the poet implies, is empty: the poem's last line reads: "Darkness all mine for lover. And I its." Masturbation is futureless; the poet associates it with the implied negative of "darkness"; and the crudity of "tits" rhyming with "its" helps to hammer home the bitterness: the narrow vowels of the rhyming words hammer the poem closed like nails into the coffin of the speaker's isolation.

Emily Dickinson in Southern California would be followed the same year by *Celebrations after the Death of John Brennan,* a limited edition printing Kennedy's fine affirming elegy in ten sections for a gifted student who died of suicide, later reprinted in his selected poems, *Cross Ties* (1985). The following year, 1975, he featured in another chapbook, *Three Tenors, One Vehicle: A Book of Songs,* along with the poets James Camp and Keith Waldrop, highlighting eleven poems by Kennedy, including

the wittily playful "Flagellant's Song," a paean to sadomasochism as aphrodisiac, delivered in a comic sing-song stanza:

So whip away!
Flail, flog, and flay!
    Hooray! the birchbark's thwacking!
That whistling wood
Incites my mood,
    And soon I'm hot attacking.

The gaiety of tone, and the poem's strict formality contrasted with the transgressive contents, are richly comic.

It was 1983 before Kennedy's next publication, *Missing Link,* a retrospective self-published chapbook "offered as a freeby to a patient listener, in thankfulness"; the circumstances of its production show how far the poet's stock had fallen: all his books of adult poetry were out of print. It was published the same year as *French Leave,* a dozen translations of eight French poets including Charles-Pierre Baudelaire, Pierre de Ronsard, and Jules Laforgue. In 1984 Kennedy followed this with a large-format chapbook, *Hangover Mass,* a limited edition of 333 copies, containing fourteen poems, many of them excellent. It opened with the title poem, a childhood memory again utilizing Kennedy's Catholic background, focusing on the sexually damaged and concomitantly lonely old bachelors encountered in his boyhood. "Dirty English Potatoes," meanwhile, is an almost hangdog admission, despite Kennedy's admiration for the characters and authenticity of his childhood, of his American sanitized sensibility. Living for a year in Yorkshire, England, the poem's narrator compares the "steam-cleaned," "same-sized," Idaho and Maine potatoes with their "British Kindred," the muck still clinging to them. "The New World's impatient taint" sticks to the narrator's bones; he wants "unreal meals risen from sheer mist." There is an ironic religious connotation in the verb "risen"; the narrator longs for the easy miracle of the American counterpart.

"At the Last Rites for Two Hot Rodders," meanwhile, contrasts the two of the title who, as the result of a successful dare to "meet head on" are being buried together, "inseparable," having "steered / towards absolute success." The failures who, by dint of being so, survived, bury them; the poem has an ironic logic.

"Aunt Rectita's Good Friday" continues this ironic note. Washing dishes and preparing food at a sink, the frail aunt asks with rhetorical ruefulness how birth and death can continue while Christ is being crucified, traditionally at 3 P.M. on Good Friday. The noise of a beer truck as it passes "desecrates" Christ's passion: a symbol of human enjoyment, forgetfulness, and license, temporal and ordinary, it has a cheerful ignorance of the grimness of the moment. Preparing the ham for dinner, "brooding on sorrowful mysteries," the aunt righteously concludes, "He died for those who do not give a damn," while she shoves into the ham's "clean white forehead fat," a "thorn crown of cloves." She fails to see that, even in preparing food, she is also implicated in the whole business of daily living which she castigates. The dead flesh she will eat is part of a crucifixion, too. The poem is a small gem of irony and ambiguity in a dozen lines.

Other notable poems include "Old Men Pitching Horseshoes," a beautifully constructed descriptive poem in rhyming pentameter couplets, and a love sonnet to Kennedy's wife, "To Dorothy on Her Exclusion from The Guinness Book of Records." The octet deftly wrong-foots the reader by describing the poet's wife by apparent negatives: three of its lines begin with the word "Not" before going on to describe perpetrators of the bizarre and marvelous (but, ultimately, trivial) feats detailed in the famous annual volume. The close of the sestet then describes, by contrast, his wife's effect on the poet:

> yet you win
> The world with just a peerless laugh. I stand

Stricken amazed: you merely settle chin
Into a casual fixture of your hand
And a uniqueness is, that hasn't been.

There is, as one might expect with Kennedy, the ghost of a sexual pun in that "stand" poised at the line's end, and his response to his wife still has all the helpless ardor of genuine smittenness. The occurrence of the transformation brought about by his wife is deftly emphasized by the comma in the closing line, which splits his wife's transformed and transforming state from what preceded it. The line would be far less effective without its separating comma.

CROSS TIES: SELECTED POEMS

When *Cross Ties* appeared in 1985, it marked Kennedy's return to mainstream publication for adults. Its 168 pages gathered together much of the work he valued from previous books. Ever a rewriter and rearranger of his poems, however, not only did he not reprint the poems in the order in which they had first appeared in book form, but he divided the new book into nine sections, four of which were "Intermissions"—of "Songs," "Light Verse," "Epigraphs and Epigrams," and "Poetry for Children," respectively. The volume won the Los Angeles Times Book Award for poetry and also helped consolidate Kennedy's reputation, gathering as it did almost a quarter of a century's fruit of writing verse. Of its 122 poems, 28 had been previously uncollected or were new, primarily some of the epigrams and a number of poems in the book's closing section, which was dated 1978–1984. Among the strongest of these were "Flitting Flies," "Epiphany," and an exquisite four-line love poem, "You Touch Me," the title of which also serves as its first line. It concludes:

One by one
In each cell of my body
A hearth comes on.

Not a "fire," but a "hearth." The use of the more homely term, so evocative of an untwee domesticity, mark this as a domestic love poem. The gradually increasing radiance of all those hearths coming on is wonderfully achieved. The touch of the beloved grants the narrator, trapped in the prison of his flesh, "each cell" of his body, a warming succor.

"Flitting Flies," on the other hand, sees Kennedy returning to theme of sexual, specifically Catholic, guilt. The "flies" of the poem's title are *muscae volitantes,* the dead cells which are caught in the fluid at the back of the eyes of most of us; looked at suddenly against a pale background, they can be seen sliding across our vision like tiny amoebas, or with the same motion as eggs sliding in oil in a frying pan; occasionally indicative of eye disease, most commonly they are harmless, but noticed by individuals in hypersensitive states. Kennedy observes:

> When in the heat of puberty
> These vague May flies first rose in me,
> I thought my hangdog soul abhorred
> In the fierce eyeball of the Lord—
>
> Took them for Limbo's brats let loose
> To strike me blind for self-abuse...

The narrator, suffering Catholic guilt over masturbation as an adolescent, and with typical adolescent hypochondria, believed the "flies" indicated a punitive god's retribution would be to make him blind; his own "hangdog soul" is characterized as just such a speck in God's "fierce eyeball"; at the poem's closure, however, the narrator has realized that a selective blindness to this eye quirk and all the issues it implies is, paradoxically, his "best hope of seeing clear." He is:

> No longer certain there can be
> Ideal fish of porphyry
> Nor indiscriminately fond
> Of lurkers deep in my own pond.

The poet is no longer certain of the perfection, in this or any other realm, which his narrator formerly foregrounded as obsessiveness with its opposite, bodily decay; he has moved on from the self-absorption which once made him so focused on this presumed physical manifestation of guilt. He no longer thinks himself important enough to be worth such egoistic self-concern.

Instead, in "Epiphany," the poet, "flat on his belly," is sorting through junk mail, "bills, begs, and bull," on the kitchen floor, when a sudden glare of sunlight, highlighting the "legs and rungs of chairs" and "how they joined," astonishes him "to take mere things in." The narrator can scarcely get any lower but, remarkably, his epiphany comes from such a lowly position. Increasingly, Kennedy has moved from turgid theology to a Zen-like valuing of the present moment, awareness of which is that self-forgetfulness he indicates as a release of sorts at the closure of "Flitting Flies."

The new poem "One-Night Homecoming" also showed Kennedy's openness to writing on realist themes associated with middle age. The poem depicts a middle-aged narrator, a father, visiting his own aged parents in the house of his childhood. He sleeps in "childhood's bed"; it is his turn "to read the writing crayoned on the wall"—that is, the bleak knowledge that our children supplant us.

DARK HORSES

Cross Ties had helped reestablish Kennedy's presence in contemporary American verse. His next collection, *Dark Horses* (1992), was not only brought out by the prestigious John Hopkins Press, but showed the poet, now in his early sixties, writing at the height of his powers.

In the interim between *Cross Ties* and the new collection, Kennedy had printed the chapbook *Winter Thunder* in 1990. The poet reprinted some two thirds of *Winter Thunder's* fifteen pieces in *Dark Horses*. The volume gathered forty-three poems into three sections of twenty, seven, and sixteen pieces respectively. The volume exemplified what had seemed Kennedy's aesthetic strategy all along: to write self-sufficient poem after poem, each seldom longer than two pages, most substantially shorter, and all characterized by a hammered clarity of diction. The volume opened with an attractive sixteen-line poem, "Woman in Rain," a portrait reminiscent of the "Nude Descending a Staircase" of Kennedy's first book. It is a praise poem, addressing its subject at its close as

>   ...still unaware
> That she as we behold her there
> Might grace a page or fill a frame.
> But then, what planet knows its name?

The poem notates through its four stanzas the woman's progress through rainy streets until, in the last stanza, the narrator has the reader and himself "beholding" the woman, elevatedly; by the last line she is a "planet," a piece of affectionate hyperbole effective because of the commonplaces of the rainy streets described in the previous three stanzas. What the narrator perceives as her lack of self-consciousness is part of the woman's attraction. As often when writing about women, Kennedy here adopts a gentler, somewhat venerating tone—a legacy of his Catholic background, though this can also lead him into objectifying in a way some women readers may find unappealing. In "Overnight Pass," for instance, a prostitute or a promiscuous woman is compared in wartime to a "front" where "regiments came scatheless through / The barbed wire of her hair." The woman here is an objectified cipher for the satisfaction of the men. Kennedy seems on stronger ground where he gives voice to his female characters, as in "Speculating Woman," in which the woman character, disappointed in love and jilted, opts to "bed down with a dollar

bill"; she marries financial speculation instead of the depreciating value of a "mortal husband." More commonly, however, woman is regarded as a spiritual and bodily center in the poems. In "Veterinarian," the capable woman doctor has "hands as sure as planets in their course." She is one who "murmurs words to soothe the languageless," is "a carpenter of flesh," and, at the poem's close, she

> Leaves like a plowman order in her wake.
> Home for a hot tub and a single feast
> Of last night's pizza, watching cold dawn break,
> Knowing that some will live—a few, at least—
> Though foam-jawed, wild-eyed, the eternal beast
> Annihilation with perpetual neigh
> Takes worlds like ours with water twice a day.

Here, as in a poem such as "The Shorter View," and in "Overnight Pass," for all that poem's objectification, Woman is seen as nurturer and healer, the mortal representative of the iconic Madonna and child of Kennedy's own childhood. "Veterinarian" achieves a substantial metaphoric leap in its closing three lines; the ironic image of the destructive beast compared to the suffering beasts earlier depicted is both impressive and unexpected. Ever fond of a pun, Kennedy uses one as the last word of line six in the stanza quoted, to beautiful effect: death is a form of "nay-saying" it is implied, and as habitual as the regular meal-taking of a beast, perhaps a stallion. Lines five and six in the stanza quoted, with their elevated register, are all the more impressive for their juxtaposition with homelier language. "Annihilation," in particular, with its Latinate gravitas and emphatic position at the beginning of a line, seems fresh and unexpected.

Dark Horses also showed that Kennedy's technical mastery was undimmed. He was plainly adept at a variety of forms—couplets, epigrams, sonnets, rhyming quatrains, and his own invented varieties. While, occasionally, he seemed still to invert word order to get rhymes—he can refer, in an elegy, to his fellow

American poet J. V. Cunningham's "lore immense," to get a rhyme with "sense" for instance—in general his syntax is seldom other than that of heightened ordinary speech. In poems such as his comic "Song: Enlightenment," about an elephant "selected to carry what is believed to be the tooth of Buddha in an annual festival," his command of word music and metric can be breathtaking: "Hear the bong of the gong and the sigh as the throng of worshipers whooshes aside / Like a bowing grain-row that that tooth may go and its grandiose pachyderm stride." Not only does the poet end-rhyme in couplets this rollicking twelve-line piece, but he handles the predominantly anapestic meter deftly, and just for fun he adds internal rhymes to the first, second, and fourth strong stresses of a number of the poem's heptameter, or seven-beat, lines. These add to the knockabout carnival air which reinforce Kennedy's conclusion: "It can strike like the jolt of a billion-volt bolt and leave one a bit the wiser, / Knowing any old tooth as immense in truth as that elephant-borne incisor." Kennedy subverts the culture's veneration of the Buddha's Tooth in an ironically Buddhist fashion, scotching the notion that any tooth, even the Buddha's, is any more important than any other.

Dark Horses ranks as one of Kennedy's most outstanding individual collections. Its title implies not only that the contents may be unlikely successes but, as Bernard E. Morris has suggested, may be imbued with graver undertones too. "The Arm," for instance, is a horror poem based on a childhood memory of finding a doll's arm (and is reminiscent of the scene in Emily Brontë's gothic novel *Wuthering Heights* in which the phantom child, Catherine Linton, tries to enter by the window of the room where Mr Lockwood is to sleep). In "The Animals You Eat" a four-year-old newly struck by the horror of eating meat questions a weary-cynic adult. "Family Reunion" is a parched portrayal of a family Christmas in eight lines, at

the close of which the family "fork white meat in through the family face." Meanwhile, in "Finis" the progress of life is compared to a child's party at which, at the end,

Like a tired child impatient parents drag
Out to the car you're strong-armed, all your winnings
Clutched in a little star-decked paper bag.
It's cold, it's growing dark. You go off screaming.

"Bullets" and "winnings" are the only two non-rhyming end words of this two-stanza poem of ten lines; twinned, the non-rhymes make an ironic point. The "little star-decked paper bag" is the one decorative note struck by the poem; it is simultaneously charming, paltry and poignant, and Kennedy chooses the phrase's qualifiers with understated care. "Star-decked," the bag is precious, yet, being "paper," subject to decay, though in a writerly context this adjective could imply something more lasting.

Kennedy also continues his verse of relationships and their psychology with "Winter Thunder," six terse off-rhymed lines, in which, at least in one reading, a married couple "at odds in numb December / Hear overhead the widening crack of thunder." If this implies, in the poem's context, the danger of adverse external circumstances, far from driving the couple farther apart, this reminder of their individual vulnerability is a "friendly dynamite"; it reunites them from the "separate cells" in which their dispute or differences had imprisoned them.

Dark Horses was a substantial collection by a master craftsman; it would be nine years before his next collection for adults. In the interim, Kennedy published modestly: an edition of the journal the *Epigrammatist* in August 1994 gave over a complete issue to a new gathering of Kennedy epigrams, and in 1996 the same publisher, Robert C. Barth, published a limited edition of one hundred copies of *The Minimus Poems,* a set comprising thirteen postcards with an epigram printed on each. The title was an ironic response to, and doubtless an implicit criticism of, the wordy free verse of Charles Olson's *The Maximus Poems*.

THE LORDS OF MISRULE

Kennedy's 2002 book takes its title from the English medieval Christian spirits charged with keeping the Christmas revelers under control during medieval festivities, a role which in Kennedy's book is to be carried out by the verse's formal rigor. The trope brings together the Celtic wildness and Teutonic fussiness Kennedy identifies as part of his aesthetic. The volume showcases the work of an old poet with an achieved style to whom authenticity, it appears (to paraphrase W. H. Auden), is more important than originality. In "A Snapshot Rediscovered," for instance, the second poem in *The Lords of Misrule*, Kennedy simply reworks the trope of elegizing a relative in an old photograph: he does it, however, in four immaculately crafted stanzas exemplifying Thomas Hardy's statement that in poetry only emotion, contentwise, is likely to be lasting. Appropriately enough—Kennedy was seventy-three when this book appeared—the poet at times looks back in these poems, as in "Jimmy Harlow," a touching elegy for a schoolfriend, or in "Naomi Trimmer," a memory of another colorful eccentric from the poet's Dover, New Jersey, childhood. Yet, too, the book is full of contemporary America, of pizza parlors, cafés, airport bars, and police courts. A narrator in "Heard through the Walls of the Racetrack Glen Motel" overhears a fraught conversation between an older woman terrified of being deserted and a younger man who wants to go out ostensibly for a drink. The "Street Moths" of the poem of that title are sexually frustrated young men able only to watch the passing haughty and uninterested young women: again, women are portrayed as the sexual center, the source of sexual power. In "Police Court Saturday Morning," the participants in domestic disputes face the magistrate's "hard glare"; the poem ends flatly: "Love's short / And when it's gone what else is left." What should have been an interrogative is a flat statement, emphasizing despair. Such bleakness is seen, too, in "Pie," a poem about the strained aftermath of a couple's dispute; the narrator is reminded by the cherry pie left over by the previous customer in a café, with its red seepage, of "a thing not yet altogether dead," like the couple's simmering argument. In "Shriveled Meditation," a terse twelve-line paean to decay and the endless winding down of everything to nothing, the narrator "and everyone alive / Go right on growing deader." There is a sort of willed bleakness in this last example, however, which verges on a comic note which other poems explicitly celebrate.

"Fat Cats in Egypt," for instance, a three-part sequence about being well-off American tourists amid the poverty of the third world, closes with "Mustafa Ferrari," a genial portrait in expert blank verse of a young surrey driver, who takes the poet and his wife as part of a convoy to the shrine of Horus:

> Tousled black hair, BULLS t-shirt. Merriment
> Glints from his eyes. Deftly he swings aboard
> And cracks his buggy whip. Away we lurch
> Like a greased storm cloud down the mud-rut
>   street.
> "Come on, you sit up front!" Mustafa shouts—
> I'll play his game. I climb up by his side—
> "Is better to take picture." So I snap
> A portrait of our horse's steaming ass.

Among the artificiality and moneyed privilege, the teenager is a piece of irrepressible gaiety, admired as such by a narrator slightly repressed by age and circumstances who, while Ferrari is being bawled at by the guide for risking an American tourist's life, sits, "chastened, in the safe back seat." The poet closes with the valediction, "Farewell, Mustafa Ferrari. You have style." One meaning hovering below the literal one of his closing line could be that style cannot survive in the pragmatic world. The poet acknowledges this, yet the stylist in himself cannot help admiring it, too, in the boy. The poem illustrates one of Kennedy's most refreshing qualities as poet: his interest in others and the world. He has a novelist's eye for detail.

Other pieces which contrasted with the volume's bleaker notes included the caustically funny "A Curse on a Thief," invoked upon the purloiner of a box of fishing tackle lovingly gathered over many years; "Décor," in which the past in the form of relatives on the walls of a pizza parlor can only stare down "at blue-jeaned lovers making assignation"; and the almost surreal "A Beard of Bees," subtitled "At the Farmer's Market," which depicts a bee-keeper with, literally, a "beard" of swarming bees. The very situation here is bizarre enough to be astonishing when described. The poem closes: "A whir—his mustache flies / Away in search of nectar."

The Lords of Misrule closed with a twelve-line poem, "September Twelfth, 2001," about the morning after the greatest tragedy on American soil in recent times. It is a modest poem which, in three four-line stanzas, undergoes three deft transformations. In stanza one, the poet is having a nightmare about leaping out of one of the twin towers holding hands with his wife; in stanza two, waking with a start, he realizes that the couple in the nightmare "aren't us," himself and Dorothy; relieved, he is astonished at being alive, faced with "the incredible joy of coffee / and the morning light." The final stanza leaps from the particular and personal to the general:

> Alive, we open eyelids
> on our pitiful share of time,
> we bubbles rising and bursting
> in a boiling pot.

The poem's understatement and quietness both valorize ordinary existence and emphasize the inability of art to console in the face of such catastrophe. Kennedy sounds no bass notes; the poem is a threnody in a minor key. It exemplifies the irony of happiness existing alongside such disaster, of being happiness more acute, indeed, precisely because of such disaster and its horrific outcome. In a long and distinguished career, X. J. Kennedy has rewardingly sought out in his poems such clarifying, and not always comfortable, truths as these.

Selected Bibliography

WORKS OF X. J. KENNEDY

POETRY FOR ADULTS

Nude Descending a Staircase. Garden City, N.Y.: Doubleday, 1961. 2nd ed. Pittsburgh, Pa.: Carnegie Mellon University Press, 1995.

Growing into Love. Garden City, N.Y.: Doubleday, 1969.

Bulsh. Providence, R.I.: Burning Deck, 1970.

Breaking and Entering. New York: Oxford University Press, 1971.

Celebrations after the Death of John Brennan. Lincoln, Mass.: Penmaen Press, 1974.

Emily Dickinson in Southern California. Boston: Godine, 1974.

Three Tenors, One Vehicle: A Books of Songs. With James E. Camp and Keith Waldrop. Columbia, Mo.: Open Places, 1975.

Missing Link. Bedford, Mass.: Scheidt Head, 1983.

Hangover Mass. Cleveland: Bits Press, 1984.

Cross Ties: Selected Poems. Athens: University of Georgia Press, 1985.

Winter Thunder. Florence, Ky.: Robert L. Barth, 1990.

Dark Horses: New Poems. Baltimore: Johns Hopkins University Press, 1992.

Epigrammatist 5, no. 2 (August 1994). A quarterly magazine, this issue being given over entirely to X. J. Kennedy's work.

The Minimus Poems. Edgewood, Ky.: Robert L. Barth, 1996.

The Lords of Misrule: Poems 1992–2001. Baltimore: Johns Hopkins University Press, 2002.

The Purpose of Time. West Chester, Pa.: Aralia Press, 2002.

POETRY FOR CHILDREN AND YOUNG ADULTS

One Winter Night in August and Other Nonsense Jingles. New York: Atheneum, 1975.

The Phantom Ice Cream Man: More Nonsense Verse. New York: Atheneum, 1979.

Did Adam Name the Vinegarroon? Boston: Godine, 1982.

The Forgetful Wishing Well: Poems for Young People. New York: Atheneum, 1985.

Brats. New York: Atheneum, 1986.

Ghastlies, Goops, and Pincushions: Nonsense Verse. New York: McElderry Books, 1989.

Fresh Brats. New York: Atheneum, 1990.

The Kite That Braved Old Orchard Beach: Year-Round Poems for Young People. New York: McElderry Books, 1991.

The Beasts of Bethlehem. New York: McElderry Books, 1992.

Drat These Brats! New York: McElderry Books, 1993.

Uncle Switch: Loony Limericks. New York: McElderry Books, 1997.

Elympics. New York: Philomel, 1999.

Elefantina's Dream. New York: Philomel, 2002.

Exploding Gravy: Poems to Make You Laugh. Boston: Little, Brown, 2002.

NOVELS FOR CHILDREN AND YOUNG ADULTS

The Owlstone Crown. New York: Atheneum, 1983.

The Eagle as Wide as the World. New York: McElderry Books, 1997.

EDITED WORKS

Mark Twain's Frontier: A Textbook of Primary Source Materials for Student Research and Writing. With James E. Camp. New York: Holt, Rinehart and Winston, 1963.

An Introduction to Poetry. Boston: Little, Brown, 1966. 11th edition, with Dana Gioia as coeditor.

New York: Pearson Longman, 2005.

Pegasus Descending: A Book of the Best Bad Verse. Compiled with James E. Camp and Keith Waldrop. New York: Macmillan, 1971.

An Introduction to Fiction. Boston: Little, Brown, 1976. 9th edition, with Dana Gioia as coeditor. New York: Pearson Longman, 2005.

Literature: An Introduction to Fiction, Poetry and Drama. Boston: Little, Brown, 1976. 9th edition, with Dana Gioia as coeditor. New York: Pearson Longman, 2005.

Tygers of Wrath: Poems of Hate, Anger, and Invective. Athens: University of Georgia Press, 1981.

Knock at a Star: A Child's Introduction to Poetry, with Dorothy M. Kennedy. Boston: Little, Brown, 1982; rev. ed., 1999.

The Bedford Guide for College Writers. With Dorothy M. Kennedy as coeditor. New York: St. Martins, 1987. 7th edition, with Dorothy M. Kennedy and Sylvia A. Holiday as coeditors. Boston: Bedford, 2004.

Talking Like the Rain: A Read-to-me Book of Poems, with Dorothy M. Kennedy. Boston: Little, Brown, 1992.

The Bedford Reader. 8th edition, with Dorothy M. Kennedy and Jane E. Aaron as coeditors. Boston: Bedford, 2003.

MISCELLANEOUS PROSE

"Making a Name in Poetry." In *The Writer's Handbook.* Edited by Sylvia K. Burack. Boston: The Writer, 1988. P. 364–370.

Autobiographical essay. In *Contemporary Authors: Autobiography Series.* Vol. 9. Edited by Mark Zadrozny. Detroit: Gale, 1989. Pp. 73–88.

"The Present State of American Poetry." *New York Quarterly* 20 (1993): 93–99.

"Roads in a Wood: The Choices Writers Make." *Gettysburg Review* 7, no. 2:289–303 (spring 1994).

"A Selection of Notebook Entries by X. J. Kennedy." In *The Poet's Notebook.* Edited by Stephen Kuusisto, Deborah Tall, and David Weiss. New York: Norton, 1995. Pp. 121–133.

"The Loneliness of the Writer." In *Facing the Lion.* Edited by Kurt Brown. Boston: Beacon, 1996. Pp. 104–113

Autobiographical essay. In *Something about the Author.* Vol. 22. Edited by Gerard J. Senick. Detroit: Gale, 1996. Pp. 105–24.

"About 'B Negative.' " In *Introspections: American Poets on One of Their Own Poems.* Edited by Robert Pack and Jay Parini. Hanover, N.H.: University Press of New England, 1997. Pp. 138–144.

"Robert Frost Overheard." *Michigan Quarterly Review* 36, no. 1:129–138. (winter 1997).

CRITICAL AND BIOGRAPHICAL STUDIES

Morris, Bernard E. *Taking Measure: The Poetry and Prose of X. J. Kennedy.* Selinsgrove, Pa.: Susquehanna University Press, 2003.

Bennani, Ben, ed. "The World of X. J. Kennedy." In *Paintbrush: A Journal of Poetry and Translation* 25 (autumn 1998). Special issue on Kennedy, in celebration of his sixty-fifth birthday.

INTERVIEWS

Mancini, Foster. "X. J. Kennedy: An Interview." *Paintbrush* 25:12–22 (autumn 1998).

Rice, William. "A Conversation with X. J. Kennedy." *Dark Horse,* no. 1 29–34 (spring 1995).

Baer, William. "An Interview with X. J. Kennedy," *The Formalist,* vol. II, no. 2, 19-34 (2000).

—GERRY CAMBRIDGE

Kenneth Koch

1925–2002

WHETHER GREAT, SMALL, serious, pleasureable, or even indifferent, he still has the life, ease, and beauty of the operations of the daily planet. Even where he seems dull and commonplace, his brightness and originality at other times make it look like a good-natured condescension to our own common habits of thought and discourse; as though he did it but on purpose to leave nothing unsaid that could bring him within the category of ourselves. His charming manner intimates that, instead of taking thought, he chooses to take pleasure with us, and compare old notes; and we are delighted that he does us so much honour.

These words of Leigh Hunt, from his essay "Ariosto: Critical Notice of His Life and Genius" published in 1846 in volume two of his *Stories from the Italian Poets,* could as easily be applied to Kenneth Koch as to the fifteenth-century Italian poet. Ludovico Ariosto (1474–1533) was a particular favorite of Koch's, and like Koch he was overlooked during his lifetime, because critics perceived his work as merely comic. Speaking of Ariosto's epic poem *Orlando Furioso* (1516), on which Koch based his own long poem *Ko; or, A Season on Earth* (1959), Hunt says, "Instead of being mere comic writing, such incidents are in the highest epic taste of the meeting of extremes,—of the impartial eye with which Nature regards high and low." Koch was one of the most unusual and inventive poets of the twentieth century. His dedication to pleasure and wit caused many readers and critics to overlook his more serious underlying themes, such as egalitarianism, the universality of the human experience, and the importance of happiness. Koch was immensely energetic and prolific. He produced many volumes of poetry, drama, and fiction, and he revolutionized the way poetry is taught to children. He was also a founder of the New York School of poets.

BIOGRAPHY

When Jay Kenneth Koch (pronounced *coke*) was fifteen, his maternal uncle Leo Loth took him to the family furniture store and opened up a big safe. He confessed to the young Koch that he'd written poems when he was a teenager. They were all sonnets, and all of them were about an unrequited love of his youth. He had no illusions about their quality, but he wanted to show them to his nephew anyway and also to give the boy a volume of the complete poems of Percy Bysshe Shelley. Both his uncle's poems and the complete Shelley were revelations to Koch, who had been writing poetry since he was five years old. His uncle's sonnets gave him the notion that anyone could write poems, even a teenager, and Shelley opened up to him the actual world of poetry. Koch immediately began writing his own sonnets, which he confirmed later were exaggerated and pretentious. In his lecture "Educating the Imagination," delivered in 1994 at a conference celebrating his educational endeavors and published in *The Art of Poetry* (1996), he says, "I wrote … one, not exactly based on my experience, which began 'And as a growing eaglet.' You can imagine I'd seen a lot of eaglets!"

Kenneth Koch was born in Cincinnati, Ohio, on February 17, 1925, to Stuart J. Koch and Lillian Loth Koch. Stuart Koch was an executive in the family's store, and the Kochs epitomized a typical upper-middle-class family in a Midwestern American town. In "Educating the Imagination" Koch recalls, "My parents were very nice. The first time I wrote a poem, my mother gave me a big kiss and said, 'I love you.'" He had conflicting feelings of wanting to escape from that environment but also of taking pride in his family's stability. The Kochs were members of a country club, and the boy was inducted into a world of affluence with its tennis, swimming, and snootiness:

> The whole idea of writing poetry had a lot to do with escaping, escaping from the bourgeois society of Cincinnati, Ohio, escaping from any society … anywhere. The first thing I had to find out to be a poet at all was that there was a bigger world, a bigger world than that of my school and my parents and their friends.

When Koch was a junior in high school, he was fortunate to have an English teacher who supported and encouraged his writing. When he first shared his poems with Katherine Lappa, he was nervous and a little thrilled imagining how she would react to what he considered risqué work, full of sensuality and aggression. Lappa earned his lifelong affection when she took the poems in stride, admired them, and encouraged him to write more. Koch's first book on teaching poetry to children, *Wishes, Lies, and Dreams: Teaching Children to Write Poetry* (1970), is dedicated to her.

Koch was the kind of student who easily earned A's and occasionally took down his lecture notes in unrhymed iambic pentameter. He earned a perfect score on the verbal portion of the Scholastic Aptitude Test and spent the second half of his senior year of high school at the University of Cincinnati, where he trained as a meteorologist. The United States was engaged in World War II when Koch graduated in 1943, and he was promptly drafted into the army. His eyesight wasn't good enough for him to be a meteorologist, so after basic training at Fort Hood in Texas the military sent him to study engineering in the Army Specialized Training Program (ASTP), which was for academically talented enlisted men and was generally reserved for privileged upper- and middle-class recruits like Koch. The training took place at the Illinois Institute of Technology, where the famed linguist S. I. Hayakawa was teaching. Koch showed his poems to the linguist and received his first professorial encouragement from him. The ASTP was dissolved in 1944 while Koch was still in training, so he was sent to train with the Ninety-sixth Infantry Division in California. He was deployed as a rifleman to the Philippines and discharged at the rank of corporal in 1946.

Koch immediately enrolled at Harvard on the GI Bill and earned his bachelor's degree in 1948. At Harvard he met John Ashbery (born 1927) and Frank O'Hara (1926–1966), who would join him as founding members of the influential New York School of poets and artists. At the time, Harvard was rich with students who would become some of America's leading poets, including Robert Bly, Donald Hall, and Adrienne Rich. Ashbery and Koch were editors at the *Harvard Advocate,* the college's literary magazine, and thus wielded much power over the literary climate. When Koch was in his early twenties, he went to France on a Fulbright scholarship. He returned to the United States in 1951 and worked briefly as a teaching assistant at the University of California at Berkeley. There he met Mary Janice Elwood, whom he married on June 12, 1954. They returned to New York for a few years, where Koch wrote his master's thesis on the physician in literature at Columbia University. He and his wife then moved to Italy, where their daughter, Katherine, was born in 1956. His doctoral dissertation was about the influence of American poetry in France in the first half of the twentieth century. He earned a Ph.D. in 1959 and immediately joined the tenured faculty at Columbia. He also taught at the New School from 1958 till 1966. Koch and his first wife separated in the 1970s and she died in 1981. On December 29, 1994, Koch married Karen Culler. They'd met years earlier when Karen's educational consultancy firm hired Koch to instruct teachers in Pennsylvania.

In the decades between his first high school poems and his death from leukemia in 2002, Koch distinguished himself as a poet, a playwright, an educator, a novelist, and a friend. He received numerous prizes, including the Bollingen Prize from Yale University in 1995 for his books *One Train* and *On the Great Atlantic Rainway: Selected Poems, 1950–1988,* both of which were published in 1994; the Rebekah Johnson Bobbitt National Prize for Poetry from the Library of Congress in 1996, also for *One Train;* and the Phi Beta Kappa Poetry Award in 2001 for *New Addresses* (2000), which was also a finalist for the National Book Award in the year of its publication. In 2000 Koch received the Chevalier des Arts et des Lettres, or Insignia of the Order of Arts and Letters, from France in recognition of his promotion of French writers and literature. He was also awarded honors from the American Academy of Arts and Letters and from the Fulbright, Guggenheim, and Ingram-Merrill foundations.

THE NEW YORK SCHOOL OF POETS

The milieu in which Koch and his literary cohorts were living and working was one rich with camaraderie, collaboration, and friendly rivalry. Three of the four principles in the New York School—Ashbery, Koch, and O'Hara—had met at Harvard. They became friends with James Schuyler (1923–1991) after moving to New York City. There they also became affiliated with the abstract expressionist painters Willem de Kooning, Jackson Pollock, and Larry Rivers, with whom they collaboratred on various projects.

Several distinguishable schools of poetry were born in the years following World War II. The United States struggled to cope with the notion of the atomic bomb, the economic impact of the war and of the soldiers returning from it, and the inevitable changes in the structure of society. The Black Mountain school led by Charles Olson, and the Beats with Allen Ginsberg at the helm, shared the changing cultural landscape with Koch and his colleagues. Although their styles differed markedly, they were all in rebellion against middle-class life and values, established literary conventions, and T. S. Eliot's influence in particular. In "Educating the Imagination," Koch says, "I grew up in a time when T. S. Eliot was, as Delmore Schwartz said, the literary dictator of the West, and not only were you supposed to be serious, you were supposed to be a little depressed." Having created a model of impersonality and metaphysics around which the cult of New Criticism arose, Eliot recoiled from vulgar revelations about the individual self and from popular culture. The New Critics rejected the notion that a reader should consider anything except the actual text. They felt that there should be no context beyond the words on the page, and readers should not take into account the poet or the poet's historical or social setting, all of which were elements embraced by the New York School.

Differentiating the New York School from contemporaneous movements was the poets' admiration for the French avant-garde tradition. They adopted its styles and modes, including absurdist attitudes and collaborations with visual artists. As an undergraduate, Ashbery read the work of the notorious French playwright Alfred

Jarry (1873–1907) and informed Koch that they must strive to be crazier. Jarry shocked Paris in 1896 with his play *Ubu Roi,* which opened with the French word *merde,* a vulgar expression on the level of "shit" or "turd." Jarry was part of a group of French artists, writers, and composers, including Henri Rousseau, Guillaume Apollinaire, and Erik Satie, dedicated to breaking open traditional forms. From this milieu arose cubism, surrealism, fauvism, dadaism—among the most significant literary and artistic movements of the twentieth century. Ashbery and Koch were galvanized by Jarry's artistic derring-do; his example gave them license to introduce jokes and silliness into their writing. Like many of their French predecessors, they were fixated on the *blague,* a farce or practical joke.

Ashbery and Koch both lived in France during their young adulthood. They picked up not only the recent history of the avant-garde, but became familiar with their contemporaries, such as Michel Deguy, Max Jacob, Saint-John Perse, and Pierre Reverdy. They carried this knowledge and these proclivities back home and mixed them with the philosophies of Jackson Pollock and Willem de Kooning and particularly with those of the second generation of New York School painters, Jane Freilicher, Red Grooms, Fairfield Porter, and Larry Rivers. It was an era rich in collaboration. Together the poets and artists created comic strips and collages. The painters constructed sets for the writers' plays. The poets together produced a short-lived literary journal called *Locus Solus.* Ashbery and Schuyler cowrote a novel called *A Nest of Ninnies* (1969).

Ashbery, Koch, O'Hara, and Schuyler were not only friends and colleagues but were editors and cheerleaders to one another. Their work was linked by aesthetics of pleasure, irony, intellect, and wit. In an interview with Jordan Davis, which is included in *The Art of Poetry,* Koch said, "We inspired each other, we envied each other, we emulated each other, we were very critical of each other, we admired each other,

we were almost entirely dependent on each other for support. Each had to be better than the others but if one flopped we all did." There were many constants among the four: Koch, O'Hara, and Schuyler all fought in World War II; Ashbery, O'Hara, and Schuyler were homosexual; Ashbery, Koch, and O'Hara shared a Harvard education; O'Hara and Schuyler both worked at the Museum of Modern Art organizing exhibits, and Ashbery and Schuyler were both critics for *Art News.*

Each poet's work, however, differs significantly from that of the others. Ashbery, who outlived the rest, has had the most profound effect on poetics, and the work of many contemporary poets can be traced to his influence. Although widely published, James Schuyler was the least prolific and the last to gain recognition. He was hampered by years of mental instability. His poems were less urban and more pastoral than the others'. When he won the Pulitzer Prize in 1981, however, readers across the nation discovered the talent his friends had known for years. O'Hara was the dynamo behind the entire group and had a coalescing effect on both the writers and painters. He was a curator at the Museum of Modern Art and possessed an immense charisma. He died at the age of forty, struck down by a dune buggy on a Fire Island beach on July 25, 1966. The poet and critic David Lehman neatly sums up their differences and similarities in *The Last Avant-Garde: The Making of the New York School of Poets* (1998):

As good as Schuyler is at capturing a moment of warmth and comfort, or O'Hara one of buoyancy and glee, or Koch one of orgasmic delight, or Ashbery one of spiritual exaltation, there is an air of profound sadness in Schuyler, of melancholy in O'Hara, of incurable nostalgia in Koch, and of wry resignation in Ashbery. What they were seeking was not an artificial paradise but a new mode of writing to chart out the progression of their hearts, and the movement of their minds, without the sentimentality that customarily imperils such efforts.

EARLY POEMS

Koch's first publication was a pamphlet of radically inventive poems put out by the Tibor de Nagy Gallery. The gallery was an early supporter of work by the New York School, and it encouraged, fostered, and provided a forum for collaborations between writers and artists. Koch's *Poems,* with prints by Nell Blaine, was published in 1953. Aside from this rare limited edition, the poems Koch wrote during the early stage of his development were not collected until nearly fifty years later, when they were published posthumously in *Sun Out: Selected Poems, 1952–1954* (2002).

When Koch first went to France as a young man, he understood French imperfectly and enjoyed the experience of being between languages. "Words would have several meanings for me at once," he says in the introduction that he wrote for *Sun Out* shortly before he died. "*Blanc* (white) was also *blank* and, in the feminine, *Blanche,* the name of a woman. The pleasure—and the sense of new meanings—I got from this happy confusion was something I wanted to re-create in English." Koch dared to be carried forward on the strength of sound alone and in fact commented several decades later on that rush of sound in this stanza from the poem "Days and Nights":

Sweet are the uses of adversity
Became Sweetheart cabooses of diversity
And Sweet art cow papooses at the university
And Sea bar Calpurnia flower havens' re-noosed
  knees.

"When the Sun Tries to Go On," the crowning poem of *Sun Out,* was written in 1953 but not published in book form until 1969. "When the Sun Tries to Go On" consists of a hundred stanzas, each twenty-four lines long. There is

no narrative, no characters, and little sense in the lines. The poet Charles Simic compares reading the poem to walking through a library, taking books off the shelves at random, and reading a phrase or two in each. A reader's enjoyment of these poems lies exactly in not being able to understand them. Paul Hoover, also a poet and critic, calls it "mouth joy" in his essay "Fables of Representation: Poetry of the New York School." The idea is to turn loose of conventions and inhibitions, to get caught up in the cumulative silliness of absurd images, and to enjoy the music of the language without worrying what it means—much as Koch did as he sat in the cafes of Paris listening to conversations only half comprehended.

In a sharply negative review of Koch's first book, the poet Harry Roskolenko says in the July 1954 issue of the staid literary journal *Poetry* that Koch "has a rare combination of words rattling about in his skull, but it is difficult to call any of his word combinations ... even *lazy verse.*" Roskolenko says that Koch is "precious and puerile when he is not merely futile." Eight months later in its March 1955 issue, *Poetry* published Frank O'Hara's defense of his friend's poetry. O'Hara says that "there is another way of reading the work." Koch, who "embraces the vulgar and inanimate objects of everyday life," has "the other poetic gift: vivacity and go, originality of perception and intoxication with life. Most important of all, he is not *dull.*"

O'Hara's vindication exemplifies the close bond of the New York School poets and the efforts they made to support and promote one another. In the introduction of *Sun Out,* Koch writes about the heady environment in which he created those early poems: "We poets and painters hung around a lot together, showed each other our works, and were made by this camaraderie very (or more than otherwise) ambitious, envious, emulous, and, I think lucky. Everyone had an immediately available audience that had no reason not to be critical or enthusiastic."

Koch's poetry was closest in character to O'Hara's. Both wrote litanies and celebrations of products and of pop culture icons. In "Days and Nights" he quips, "Athena gave Popeye a Butterfinger filled with stars / Is the kind of poetry Z and I used to stuff in jars." Koch and his fellow poets were some of the first practitioners of postmodernism, and they dressed up modernism's disjunction in postmodernism's surrealism. They discovered that the creative process was as important as the product. David Lehman writes,

> They learned that it was okay for a poem to chronicle the history of its own making—that the mind of the poet, rather than the world, could be the true subject of the poem—and that it was possible for a poem to be (or to perform) a statement without making a statement.

One of the signature features of postmodernism is that any subject is fair game. Koch made liberal use of this notion, tossing into his poetry everything from Mickey Mouse to the Dodgers to Japanese Noh plays. As David Chinitz points out in his essay "'Arm the Paper Arm': Kenneth Koch's Postmodern Comedy," Koch's is a poetics of inclusion. In "When the Sun Tries to Go On," excrement appears next to Timon of Athens. In "The Pleasures of Peace" Koch talks about himself and the process of writing the poem and incorporates imagined responses to the poem: "'A wonder!' 'A rout!' 'No need now for any further poems!'"

POETICS OF INCLUSION

Ko; or, A Season on Earth, written in the first years of his marriage and published in 1959, is a mock epic composed by a young and happy Koch, newly married and living in Florence. The poem is written in ottava rima, a form that originated in Italy and was commonly used for heroic poems, including Ariosto's *Orlando Furioso* and Lord Byron's *Don Juan.* Koch read the latter while he was working on *Ko.* He observed that it contained almost no reflection whatsoever and was entirely concerned with action. He imitated both the form and the content. An ottava rima stanza consists of eight iambic pentameter lines, in an *abababcc* rhyme scheme. Though he takes liberties with the form, it serves Koch well with its constant bouncing rhythm, creating a giddy feeling of motion. Koch played fast and loose, breaking up words across lines, often using eleven syllables in a line instead of ten, giving his characters nonsense names:

> Meanwhile, in London, Huddel and his family
> Were going to a big display entitled
> The Dog in Britain, they and their dog Ammily,
> A small and pleasant not at all a bite-all d-
> Og, not big enough to halfway dam a lee,
> And very like a spaniel, Sir, despite all d-
> Ifferences which we, if we were purists,
> Would have to take into account; but, tourists....

Koch wanted to write a poem that included all the things he liked: baseball, love, high jinks, and adventure. The poem begins with Ko, a young Japanese man, traveling to America on a quest to play ball with the Dodgers. He joins the team, and the poem evolves into a series of absurd plots, subplots, and sub-subplots involving a Cockney fellow named Huddel, who is not happy at home; the Dog Boss who wants to control all the world's dogs; a group of girls in Kansas who take off their clothes in order to protest dullness; and other ridiculous characters navigating surreal scenarios.

"The Departure from Hydra," published in 1962's *Thank You and Other Poems,* further examines the importance of pleasure. The narrator of the poem, walking home in Greece, experiences a general sense of pleasure, which is interrupted momentarily by his awareness of bodily pains. He overcomes the disruption by resolving to write about the initial pleasure

KENNETH KOCH / 181

when he gets home, thereby solidifying it and preserving it. The narrator goes on to reflect on pleasure as necessary to a full life:

> Vitality, however, usually
> Appeals to an answering vital force in others
> And brings about making love or great events,
> Or it at least gives pleasure—I can't judge
> Vitality in any way but the way
> It gives me pleasure, for if I do not get
> Pleasure from life, of which vitality
> Is just the liquid form, then what am I
> And who cares what I say? I for one don't.

INFLUENCES

"Fresh Air," written in 1956 and published in *Thank You,* partners with Frank O'Hara's essay "Personism" to form a statement of the New York School's poetics. "Fresh Air" became one of Koch's best-known poems. In it Koch assaults academic poetry and the poets who write it. The poem begins with a meeting of the Poem Society. A man stands up in the midst of the meeting to denounce poets who have "restraint and mature talent"; another laments the "baleful influence" of the likes of T. S. Eliot and W. H. Auden. Koch goes on to say,

> Where are young poets in America, they are
>   trembling in publishing houses and universities,
> Above all they are trembling in universities, they
>   are bathing the library steps with their spit,
> They are gargling out innocuous (to whom?)
>   poems about maple trees and their children,
> Sometimes they brave a subject like the Villa
>   d'Este or a lighthouse in Rhode Island,
> Oh what worms they are! They wish to perfect
>   their form.

Koch conjures the Strangler, whose mission is to annihilate bad poets.

> The Strangler's ear is alert for the names of Or-
>   pheus,
> Cuchulain, Gawain, and Odysseus,

> And for poems addressed to Jane Austen, F. Scott
>   Fitzgerald,
> To Ezra Pound, and to personages no longer liv-
>   ing
> Even in anyone's thoughts—O Strangler the
>   Strangler!

Yet for all his protestation Koch freely admitted his debt to the "baleful influence" of Ezra Pound, William Butler Yeats, Walt Whitman, and many of the forebears he excoriates in "Fresh Air." He credited Pound for leading him to Chinese and Provençal poetry, to Japanese Noh plays, Ovid, and George Saintsbury's *History of English Prosody,* published early in the twentieth century. Saintsbury's book gave Koch the grounding he needed to concoct wild subversions of forms like the sestina and the alexandrine and ottava rima. Such influences are more transparent in Koch's work than in those of his peers. In his epic poems *Ko; or, A Season on Earth* and *The Duplications* (1977), predecessors such as Edmund Spenser's *The Faerie Queene* and John Milton's *Paradise Lost* are visible in long narratives tricked out with multiple story lines.

Koch, like the Beat and Black Mountain poets, rebelled against the influence of Eliot. Yet in his interview with Jordan Davis in the summer of 1995 Koch was able to look back on his experience of first reading Eliot's *The Waste Land* and recognize the poem's profundity: "It seemed more than a mere work. With its vagueness, its clarity, and its dissociations, it was like a big spacious mystery voyage." Despite his protestations against academic poetry, Koch dearly loved and continually referenced many favorites among his poetic ancestors. His gripe was with poets who exercised their knowledge of literature rather than simply reveled in the breadth and beauty of their forebears. These poets, he felt, held up their knowledge as a sort of shield between themselves and the vital pleasures of living in the world. Worse, they wielded that knowledge to deny to those they considered less educated the enjoyment poetry could offer. In "Some General Instructions," published in *The Art of Love* in 1975, are lines that sum up Koch's aesthetic:

> Do not be defeated by the
> Feeling that there is too much for you to know.
>   That
> Is a myth of the oppressor.

If Koch is at all a political poet, it is in this notion—that one ought not to feel oppressed, whether by the morbid influence of Yeats or by an early teacher who made you feel you must have some specialized knowledge in order to understand poetry.

French poetry provided another set of influences for Koch. In addition to the work of Alfred Jarry, the poetry of Raymond Roussel (a particular favorite), Guillaume Apollinaire, Max Jacob, Pierre Reverdy, and many others acclimated Koch to surrealism and radical juxtapositions. He compared reading French authors to discovering an entirely new kind of art, and he described his love of them, their mystery and elegance, as the kind of puppy love one feels as a teenager. Koch also looked to William Carlos Williams, in particular to the older poet's ability to blur the lines between fantasy and reality, interior and exterior. His early exposure to Shelley was of course pivotal as was his introduction to John dos Passos.

MIDDLE YEARS

Koch reveled in the pleasures of sexuality and put forward the possibility of experiencing the world through gleeful lust and erotic frolic. *The Art of Love* contains some of his most burlesque poetry. In a *New York Times* review on September 28, 1975, the poet and novelist Aram Saroyan calls the volume "the best of [Koch's] books to date," and says that "beneath the lighthearted nonsense … you feel the poet exploring the real nature of sex and romance, and love

itself, with unexpected seriousness." Indeed the seven long poems that make up the book display a broader range of interest along with an emotional maturity and complexity largely absent from the earlier work.

Koch was not an antiformalist like the Beat poets. He revived outdated forms and fledged them with new feathers. In addition to his use of obscure rhyme schemes such as ottava rima, Koch introduced a kind of moral proclamation long defunct in poetry. With poems entitled "Some General Instructions," "The Art of Poetry," and "The Art of Love," the book is rife with directives for everything from what kinds of questions to ask yourself as you write poetry to what to do with a woman once you've got her into your bed. Though Koch undoubtedly adored women and does not seem to have been actually sadistic or misogynistic, some of his instructions in "The Art of Love" do not hold up well. The poem is clearly meant to be funny, not malicious, but readers may fail to see the humor in lines like these about tying up one's lover:

> Of course with the girl tied this way
> You can hit her up and down if you like to do
>   that
> And she will never be able to get up and walk
>   away
> Since she can't walk without her feet, and they
>   are tied to the bed.

The Burning Mystery of Anna in 1951, published in 1979, introduced the first notes of melancholy and nostalgia into Koch's oeuvre. Koch, by then in his fifties, was no longer simply a poet of humor and pleasure. Frank O'Hara had long been dead; Koch's marriage had dissolved; and the poets who remained of the original New York School were not the same enthusiastic, driven young men. Their work had continued to mature, but they no longer stayed up all night drinking and going to parties with painters and other New York City luminaries.

Koch begins in this volume to look back on his life and to reflect on friendships and other relationships that have come and gone. In "Fate" the poet relates the tale of an afternoon in 1951, when he was in a New York City apartment with O'Hara and Ashbery and the painters Larry Rivers and Jane Freilicher. He's telling them excitedly about his first trip to Europe, and they're listening politely but are clearly more interested in gossiping. They are drinking Irish whiskey, and Koch remembers it both ecstatically and sadly.

> I don't know what and why do I think
> That my being so happy is so urgent
> And important? it seems some kind
> Of evidence of the truth as if
> I could go back and take it? or do
> I just want to hold what
> There is of it now?"

In his essay "Kenneth Koch's 'Serious Moment,'" the literary critic David Spurr compares Koch, especially the Koch of these volumes published in the 1970s, to Walt Whitman with a sense of humor. Koch matches Whitman's passion for life and his commitment to experiencing the pleasures (and the pains too) that come with being human. At this point in his career Koch has drawn a bead on his primary thesis: that life is simple and we're all here in it and there's no point being anxious about what we know or don't know. In "The Problem of Anxiety" he wrote, "This / I cannot answer, but surely life is better off the floor. / To take a walk with you, how good it is! and / To talk about recoveries from anxieties! to pick / This blossom, it's a purple one, I shall name it / *L'Innocence retrouvée* what does that mean? It's / French." Koch indicates that worrying what the French words mean is no more useful than worrying about any of life's other concerns, and it's far better to enjoy a walk in the park and pick flowers.

LATE POETRY

Koch's epic poem of the 1950s, *Ko,* was followed in 1977 by the sequel, *The Duplications.* In 1987 both were published together in one volume, *Seasons on Earth.* When the combined edition was published, Koch struggled to write an introduction, and in the end he wrote it in ottava rima to match the poems. In contrast to the frolics packed into the two epics, the introduction raises issues of pain and regret. Continuing the themes of *The Burning Mystery of Anna in 1951,* Koch looks back on happiness through a veil of loss: the loss of his wife, the loss of his youth. Koch is uncertain for what feels like the first time.

> What is, I want to know, the truth if there is
> Truth in the view of things I had, and what is
> The source, if it's mistaken, of its errors?
> Do we come into life with minds and bodies
> Ready to live in some ecstatic Paris
> Or is the limit of our lives more modest?
> Is there seed in us? are we the pod? Is
> The blossom pleasure, and the fruit the goddess?
> Did you too ever feel it, like a promise,
> That there could be a perfect lifetime, Janice?

Koch provides a sort of backstory for things that were taking place thirty years earlier while he worked on *Ko.* He talks about how his wife miscarried in the sixth month of pregnancy and almost died. He calls it "the saddest thing that ever happened to us," and the reader gets the sense that it was the saddest of many sad things, masked by the joyful wit of the poem. He asks more questions in the introduction than he answers, as he ponders what it means to have witnessed so much of the pleasures and tragedies of life already.

> I don't know. Don't know any of this. My
>   decades
> Six now, with the beginning of a seventh,
> Counsel me, sure, to dance to slower records,
> But I'm still trumped and bumped by
>   glimpsed-up heavens

And think they may be true—but just for
  seconds.
Two words, one word, it used to be a sentence.
Nothing has come of this except my wonder
What it's about, before I'm shoveled under.

Though they separated much earlier, Janice died several years before *Seasons on Earth* was published, and it is to her memory that Koch dedicates the book.

Koch published two volumes of new work in the 1990s: *One Train* in 1994 and *Straits: Poems* in 1998. Both contain accomplished, inventive poems. *New Addresses,* however, published in 2000, continues most intently along the path of melancholy laid out in the poetry of the late 1970s. The volume carries the apostrophe to new heights. Apostrophe, another dated rhetorical device, is an address to an absent or deceased person or to an inanimate object or idea. While the poetry is still witty, the reader gets the feeling that Koch is tying up loose ends, saying things he has long meant to say and addressing subjects he has long sidestepped, including his Jewish heritage and World War II. Koch gave the poems such titles as "To Psychoanalysis," "To Knowledge, My Skeleton, and an Aesthetic Concept," and "To Jewishness, Paris, Ambition, Trees, My Heart, and Destiny." In the poem "To World War Two," Koch talks for the first time about his experiences as a rifleman in the Philippines and the way poetry sustained him through the war.

"I can't be killed—because of my poetry. I have
  to live on in order to write it."
I thought—even crazier thought, or just as
  crazy—
"If I'm killed while thinking of lines, it will be
  too corny
When it's reported" (I imagined it would be
  reported!)
So I kept thinking of lines of poetry. One that
  came to me on the beach on Leyte
Was "The surf comes in like masochistic lions."
I loved this terrible line. It was keeping me alive.

A Possible World, published posthumously in 2002, maintains the theme of aging and looking back, and it is more than anything a book of farewells. Koch writes with rueful wonder, amazed gratitude, and candid humor about things like his friendship with Delmore Schwartz, who died in 1966, traveling through Asia, and teaching poetry to elementary school students in Haiti. The final poem in this final book of poetry is called "A Memoir," and it goes on for twenty-one pages. Calling it "A Memoir" instead of just "Memoir" communicates that this is one of many possible memoirs. Koch's poetry was almost always autobiographical, less emotionally confessional than that of some of his contemporaries, such as Robert Lowell and Sylvia Plath, but still it was culled from the events and observations of his own life. "A Memoir" bumps through a haphazard conglomeration of episodes. All the usual players—John Ashbery and Frank O'Hara and Larry Rivers—make appearances, as do Koch's grandson, the writer Grace Paley, the artist Jim Dine, and the playwright Lionel Abel. Koch remembers such minutiae as makes up, in the end, the sum of a life: reading the poetry of Poliziano with Janice; an Italian girl he met in London; getting a haircut in Kansas City. Within the poem Koch comments on the writing of it:

I could have made a memoir that was all loss
Lost Marina lost marriage lost Paris lost inspira-
  tion
I would live in this Memoir for days
But a birthday was obvious
Became all too clear
I hadn't wasted my life because it wasn't wasted.

CRITICAL LEGACY

Koch's humor has been the primary impediment to critical attention and respect. He is excluded from many anthologies of twentieth-century poetry, including ones edited by the influential critic Helen Vendler and the new formalist poet

J. D. McClatchy. David Perkins, author of the two-volume *History of Modern Poetry* (1976, 1987), uses a bit of *When the Sun Tries to Go On* as an example of what he calls "the weaker side of the New York School." Perkins says that Koch "offers strings of puns, homophones, and other types of irrational connection" and that "the more effort we spend, the less we feel rewarded." These editors perform a disservice to their readers. As David Chinitz says in "Arm the Paper Arm," "In a world where almost anything one might wish to express has already been reduced to a cliché, comedy is often deployed to capture and reproduce the force of serious feeling." Despite the privilege of his upbringing and the sophisticated company he kept at home in New York City and abroad, Koch was a populist. He didn't take himself too seriously, and though he was serious about poetry, he didn't bring to it the kind of grim weightiness people like Vendler so admire. Academia and the "serious" poets never forgave him, it seems, for suggesting in "Fresh Air" that they should all be strangled.

With his death, however, and the publication of his late work, readers have begun to recognize the versatility of style and the complexity of emotion Koch achieved. Charles Simic wrote in "The Water Hose Is on Fire," a critical appreciation of Koch's last volumes, "Comedy, one realizes, reading him, casts its net much wider than tragedy and melodrama, which tend to be claustrophobic. It's a rich, multifaceted world.... Koch carries out here a comic examination of seriousness."

FICTION

Koch's first volume of fiction was short stories, with illustrations by the artist Alex Katz. *Interlocking Lives* (1970) contains five stories by Koch and twenty-one black-and-white line drawings by Katz, used in different contexts for each story. Katz, a pop artist who became

friends with the New York School poets in the fifties and who collaborated with them on many projects over the years, gave Koch the drawings, and Koch wrote five stories based on them in an attempt to address the philosophical issue of a picture's relationship to text.

In 1975 Koch published his novel, *The Red Robins,* which became a play a few years later. The sprawling story follows a group of young aviators, the Red Robins, as they travel from place to place in Asia and engage in high jinks, adventure, and romance. The young and attractive Red Robins are in the thrall of their leader, the international criminal Santa Claus. Santa Claus in turn is in love with Jill, one of the Red Robins. When Jill's parents come to Asia and plead with her to return home, she declares her love for Santa Claus and introduces him as her fiancé. There are dozens of supporting characters, including Mike the man-eating tiger and a gland named Pyotor. The brave and dashing aviators must overcome many obstacles such as engine failure, mysterious Slimy Green Things, and the continuous machinations of the Easter Bunny, who is intent on destroying them. One of the Red Robins, Jim, discovers halfway through the book that he is in fact a poet, which gives Koch the opportunity to scatter verse throughout the chapters.

The Red Robins has no plot to speak of, but near the end it is revealed that a clandestine meeting is being held among a lecherous senator, Jill's father (who still wants her to come home), the Easter Bunny (who has disguised himself as a count), and the president of the United States (who has developed a crush on one of the Red Robins and secretly wishes to be part of their organization). They discuss what is to be done about the problem of the Red Robins. The Queen of Nigeria shows up to testify to the goodness of the Red Robins, and she recognizes and exposes the Easter Bunny. She introduces a voice of reason into the proceedings, instructing Jill's father to accept that his daughter is an adult who can make her own choices. Jill's father reveals that he's not actually Jill's father; he is Bud, the boyfriend of the Red Robin with whom the president is infatuated. Chaos ensues, but everything is sorted out happily in the end: the Easter Bunny is chased off, and the president is convinced that he isn't suited to be a member of the Red Robins.

Koch's prose reads much like his poetry, especially the long narrative verse of *Ko* and *The Duplications*. It vaults forward on the sheer energy of its own nonsense and is occasionally punctuated by moments of tender emotion. Also much like his poetry, his fiction matured over the years, and when *Hotel Lambosa and Other Stories* was published in 1993, it toned down the surreal jabber of *The Red Robins* and focused as much on melancholy and memory as on foolishness and extravagant escapades. The more or less realistic stories in *Hotel Lambosa* are based on events that happened while Koch was in his twenties and thirties, traveling through France, Italy, China, Mexico, and elsewhere. Koch didn't consider these short stories (none are longer than four pages) to be prose poems. He particularly enjoyed writing them because he felt that as fiction they could go on indefinitely, which may be seen as ironic given the length of his epic poems. He was inspired by a volume called *Palm-of-the-Hand-Stories* by the Japanese writer Yasunari Kawabata. The stories of both writers share quietly transient narratives ending with barely articulated realizations. The tales close with a neat click of the jewel box, in Yeats's analogy of the well-composed poem.

PLAYS

Koch became interested in writing plays as a child and wrote satires caricaturing his extended family. In college he drew from the verse dramas of T. S. Eliot, William Butler Yeats, Federico Garcia Lorca, and W. H. Auden, among others. Alfred Jarry's *Ubu Roi* was a revelation. In his interview with Jordan Davis, Koch says, "When I finally wrote some plays I liked … , it was because 'dramatic' and even more so 'crazy' were added to or substituted for 'poetic'—I read *Ubu roi* and everything was turned upside down." Later, especially during the 1960s and 1970s, Koch published dozens of plays. New York City was particularly receptive to experimental theater during those decades and productions were thrown together in tiny venues with sets designed by some of the leading artists of the time, including Roy Lichtenstein and Larry Rivers.

Koch was commissioned by Rivers to write the play *George Washington Crossing the Delaware*. Rivers had exhibited his controversial painting *Washington Crossing the Delaware* in 1953, creating a stir on the New York art scene, and the Museum of Modern art had bought and hung the painting in 1955. After seeing it there Frank O'Hara had penned his poem "On Seeing Larry Rivers' *Washington Crossing the Delaware* at the Museum of Modern Art." The painting is generally regarded as a significant forerunner of the pop art movement. In requesting the play from Koch, Rivers intended it to be staged by his son's high school. However, the auditorium where it was to be produced collapsed, and instead of being performed by high school students it was put on by adults several years later in 1962 at the Maidman Playhouse in New York City, with sets by Katz. It has since become a classic of avant-garde theater. This charming short play reads much like an elementary school history lesson about the triumph of Washington over the British general Charles Cornwallis at Yorktown in October 1781. Washington describes his plan for overcoming the American troops' lack of food, ammunition, and clothes:

For stealing is licensed if for a good cause,
And in love and war, boys, you know there's no
  laws.

So pack up your shyness, your shame, and your
  fear,
And throw them away, and come meet me, all,
  here,
At twelve o'clock midnight, and off we shall go
To the camp of the English that lies down below!
And we shall return in their splendid attire,
And every man present shall have his desire.

Collaborating with artists and performers on these small off-Broadway and off-off-Broadway productions was one of Koch's favorite things to do. In an interview on February 28, 1994, quoted in David Lehman's *The Last Avant-Garde*, Koch said, "One of the most wonderful ways in the world to be with someone's sweetness and brilliance is to collaborate with that person." These plays were the prototypes for "happenings," which were the apex of avant-garde vogue.

Two months after *George Washington Crossing the Delaware*, Koch's next play, *The Construction of Boston*, was staged at the Maidman. The artists Niki de Saint-Phalle, Jean Tinguely, and Robert Rauschenberg made the sets. The play was directed by the famous avant-garde choreographer Merce Cunningham. David Lehman quotes an interview in which Frank O'Hara remembered the chaos surrounding opening night and how the spirit of the production truly was collaborative:

> They were all battling till the very moment the curtain went up about what direction it was going to take.... And I don't mean in an unpleasant way, but they were—you know, it really was a collaboration in the sense that nobody had, absolutely, made themselves the key figure in it.

The most famous production of one of Koch's plays was the adaptation he wrote of his novel, *The Red Robins*. It opened on January 17, 1978, at the Theater at St. Clement's. Many artists created sets: cardboard airplanes for the aviators, jungle trees, clusters of octopuses, and others. Koch was so delighted with the cutouts Red

Grooms fashioned to represent Shanghai that he wrote another scene so the set would remain on stage longer. The production was further distinguished by Taylor Mead's playing six characters, including Jill's father and Mike the Tiger. Mead had achieved fame as the star of several Andy Warhol films and had been a fixture both at the Factory and amidst the Beat poets. Not surprisingly *The Red Robins* received a negative review from Richard Eder, preeminent theater critic for the *New York Times*. In a review published the day after the play opened, Eder condemned the script as a "poor play, poor poetry and poor fantasy." Koch's play fell victim to the same misapprehension his poetry suffered. Critics refused or were unable to see or appreciate the seriousness under the humor.

In 1988 Koch published *One Thousand Avant-Garde Plays*, a collection of 112 very short plays. The Obie Award–winning director Barbara Vann staged seventy-two of them in one night. Other productions have done five or ten at a time. Koch got the idea for these tiny plays from flipping through television channels. He was amazed by how he could become emotionally involved in something in just thirty seconds and realized that everything was potentially dramatic.

CRITICISM

In 1981 Koch published *Sleeping on the Wing: An Anthology of Modern Poetry*. Written and compiled with the poet Kate Farrell, the book contains poetry stretching from Walt Whitman and Gerard Manley Hopkins to Gary Snyder and LeRoi Jones, as well as brief essays on the poets and on reading and writing poetry. It was intended to be as much a primer on writing as an anthology. Each poet's section is followed by a brief explanation of the work and a writing exercise based on one of the poems. After the section on Gertrude Stein, for instance, Koch gives instructions for writing a poem about a special friend. He tells the writer not to make sense but to use words in new ways.

Also with Kate Farrell, Koch published *Talking to the Sun: An Illustrated Anthology of Poems for Young People* in 1985. This anthology supplemented the books Koch had published in the 1970s on teaching children to write. In 1996 *The Art of Poetry* came out. Part of the University of Michigan Press's Poets on Poetry series, the volume is a compendium spanning Koch's career. It compiles reviews he wrote in the 1950s, the transcript of a long talk he gave at the Teachers and Writers Collaborative Center for Imaginative Writing, an essay on collaborating with painters, excerpts from his books on teaching, and a wide range of other work. It draws from every genre Koch tried, including comic strips. At the end of the book Koch is interviewed by his assistant Jordan Davis. In the interview Koch comments informally on his relationships to things like Italian poetry, narrative, and teaching.

Making Your Own Days: The Pleasures of Reading and Writing Poetry, published in 1998, is a more ambitious version of *Sleeping on the Wing.* The second half of the book is an anthology presenting a wider selection of poets than the previous anthology, starting with Homer and Sappho and working through antiquity to John Donne and William Blake and arriving finally at Koch's friends, John Ashbery, Frank O'Hara, and James Schuyler. The first half of the book describes how to get the most out of reading poetry. Koch presents simple explanations of prosody and of how to listen for poetry's particular music. He goes on to talk about inspiration and how writing one's own poetry can increase the pleasure of reading poetry. The writing is lucid, unpretentious, and conversational. In the preface Koch says:

> The aim of this book is to say some clear and interesting things about poetry. Poetry ... has often been written about in ways that make it seem more difficult, mysterious, more specialized, and more remote than it actually is—it is written about as a mystery, as a sort of intellectual/aesthetic code that has to be broken.

Koch proceeds to do his best to demystify poetry and to make a case for the unique pleasures of reading it. *Making Your Own Days* is a supremely egalitarian book in which Koch gathers and articulates in a definitive, authoritative manner his rubric that poetry can be accessible to anyone, regardless of age, social class, or education.

TEACHING

One of Alfred Jarry's motivating philosophies was to bring his life and his art as close together as possible—to live out his artistic theories of chaos and impudence. For Jarry this spelled a life lived in crushing poverty, closed by an early death. Among the many ideas Koch borrowed from Jarry, the idea of life and art existing in close connection was one of the most important. However, because Koch's poetics were centered on humor and equality, the result was very different. The philosophy of inclusion, which allowed Koch to write about subjects as diverse as Mickey Mouse and grand opera, extended to his pedagogy. He believed anyone could understand, appreciate, be enriched by, and even write poetry, from elementary school students to the elderly and infirm. In several books and essays he made a case for teaching the likes of William Blake and William Butler Yeats to very young children, arguing that they can respond to the emotional appeal of many poems that teachers would commonly classify as too complex and difficult. This is probably Koch's greatest legacy.

In the spring of 1968, under the sponsorship of the Academy of American Poets, Koch began an experiment at P.S. 61, a lower- and middle-income elementary school in New York City's East Village. As John Ashbery had said to Koch when they were in college, Koch said to the children he taught: be crazy. The children responded instantly to Koch, and they would clap and shout when he entered the classroom. He possessed a special talent for recognizing lyrical prospects in practically anyone and, even more astonishingly, being able to encourage and extract those possibilities.

Koch looked at the poetry being taught in elementary schools and found it lacked serious emotion and didn't present a complex viewpoint. The poems were simplified, dull, and meant to be reassuring; and they were not worthy of childhood's lively imagination and eagerness to process the surrounding world. In *Rose, Where Did You Get That Red?: Teaching Great Poetry to Children* (1973) he says,

> The usual criteria for choosing poems to teach children are mistaken, if one wants poetry to be more than a singsong sort of Muzak in the background of their elementary education. It can be so much more. These criteria are total understandability, which stunts children's poetic education by giving them nothing to understand they have not already understood; "childlikeness" of theme and treatment, which condescends to their feelings and to their intelligence; and "familiarity," which obliges them to go on reading the same inappropriate poems their parents and grandparents had to read.

Koch determined not to be deterred if a poem he wanted to teach contained unfamiliar words or syntax. He reasoned that children are, after all, constantly learning new concepts and vocabulary as they play games, watch television, and generally navigate the world around them.

Koch developed a strategy for teaching the reading and writing of poetry through the use of "poetry ideas." He would introduce a poem like William Shakespeare's "Come Unto These Yellow Sands" from *The Tempest* and then instruct the children to write a poem in which they invite someone to a mysterious place full of sound

and color. Reading the poem helped them to write their own poems, and conversely, writing their own poems helped them to understand the example poem. He also created a free and engaging classroom environment in which students were allowed to make noise, read one another's work, and misspell words.

He discovered that children are particularly receptive to poems that list things, ask questions, make strange comparisons, or use language in the kind of verbal games children like to play. A typical class started with everyone getting a copy of the day's poem. The children would be asked to read it on their own, then Koch would answer whatever questions they had. He would then explain the poetry idea and give them time to write their own poems. Koch was one of those rare adults who retained from his own childhood a thorough understanding of the sorts of things that enchant and excite children, such as talking to animals or receiving an invitation to something. He further gained their trust and admiration by not condescending to them and by having faith in their powers of comprehension and creativity.

Wishes, Lies, and Dreams: Teaching Children to Write Poetry, published in 1970, is a practical guide to the method Koch developed at P.S. 61. It was followed in 1973 by *Rose, Where Did You Get That Red?.* Like the PBS series *Sesame Street,* which also had its genesis in the early seventies, these books shaped parents' and teachers' attitudes about ways to teach children and engage their interest. To an entire segment of the population, Koch is barely known, if at all, as a famous poet who has a glamorous background collaborating with some of the best and most innovative artists and writers of the twentieth century, but primarily as a sensitive, enthusiastic teacher who used poetry to shape and inspire the creative minds of a generation of young people.

After his experiences in the New York City public school system, Koch became curious about teaching poetry to children in other countries. He went on to teach in Haiti, Paris, Shanghai, Rome, and elsewhere. His overseas teaching began in 1975 at the Lycée Toussaint L'Oueverture in Port-au-Prince, Haiti. He was horrified to discover that the schoolmaster stalked the classroom carrying a whip. School officials assured him it was never used, but it was indicative of what he found among the students: hesitation, fear, and bewilderment. Creole is the language spoken on the streets of Haiti, but in school students were required to speak French. When Koch found a Haitian assistant, he began instructing the students to write in what was, after all, their native tongue. Writing in Creole was immensely liberating for the young people, and they soon overcame their trepidation and were able to find and express the same kind of joy and complex emotion Koch elicited from his American students. From Haiti, Koch went to France, and then to Italy, China, and Africa. He expanded his teaching to include native poets from each country, such as Charles Baudelaire, Cavalcanti, and Li Bai.

In 1977 Koch published *I Never Told Anybody: Teaching Poetry Writing in a Nursing Home*. He and Kate Farrell taught at the American Nursing Home on Manhattan's Lower East Side. Their students were in their seventies, eighties, and nineties, and most were incapacitated by age and illness. They hailed from lives as cooks, domestic servants, dry cleaners, and other working-class occupations, and few, if any of them, had much education. Koch and Farrell used the same method of the "poetry idea" that Koch used with children. Koch's extraordinary ability to hone in on the particular world of young people also allowed him to understand and empathize with the pains, complaints, memory loss, and other limitations of the elderly. He did not, however, patronize them by expecting too little of them. He recounts in *I Never Told Anybody* the exceptional experience of giving the marginalized

people in the American Nursing Home a voice for their memories, shining a light on forgotten feelings and events, and thus relieving the monotony in the lives of individuals who otherwise thought they had nothing left to offer.

There were challenges in teaching the elderly that weren't present in a classroom of boisterous fourth graders. Most of the students had impairments that prevented them from reading or writing, so classes were conducted with a greater emphasis on the oral. Koch would read poems aloud, and both he and Farrell would transcribe the work of the students. He says,

> The people we taught weren't used to the kind of respectfully determined interest in their imaginings and perceptions that we had. It seems possible they weren't used to being listened to that much at all. So it was understandable that we had, at first, to talk, to convince, to reassure, to explain.

In addition to his pioneering work teaching poetry to the young and the old, Koch was a beloved professor at Columbia University, where he taught for more than forty years, from 1959 until the end of his life. His class on humor in contemporary literature became legendary. His students and colleagues remember him as immensely energetic, enthusiastic, entertaining, and inspiring. His teaching was marked by a deep respect for language, a vast knowledge of poetry, and a commitment to finding what was most pleasurable in any subject. Among his students were the poet Ron Padgett and the critic David Lehman, both of whom are teachers as well and have worked to pass on Koch's legacy by bringing his ingenuous assignments and dedication to humor into their own classrooms.

In 2001 Koch discovered he had leukemia, which claimed his life on July 6, 2002. He went to the Anderson Cancer Center in Houston, Texas, to receive radical and often painful treatment. He was confined for many weeks in an isolation chamber. Soon after he arrived, however, Koch discovered a program at the hospital for teaching poetry to children who had cancer, exactly the sort of program his books and teachings had inspired around the country over the foregoing quarter of a century. Koch met with the two Houston poets who were running the workshops and spoke to them from behind a glass partition. He also set out to find and contribute poems that would address the anger and fear of children undergoing treatment for cancer. His friends and family were amazed by the energy he put into the writing program at the hospital. Until the end of his life Kenneth Koch worked to bring poetry to individuals who didn't have any other outlet by which to express themselves.

Selected Bibliography

WORKS OF KENNETH KOCH

POETRY

Poems. Prints by Nell Blaine. New York: Tibor de Nagy Gallery, 1953. (Limited edition.)

Ko; or, A Season on Earth. New York: Grove Press, 1959.

Permanently. Prints by Alfred Leslie. New York: Tiber Press, 1960. (Limited edition.)

Thank You and Other Poems. New York: Grove Press, 1962.

Poems from 1952 and 1953. Los Angeles: Black Sparrow Press, 1968.

The Pleasures of Peace and Other Poems. New York: Grove Press, 1969.

Sleeping with Women. Los Angeles: Black Sparrow Press, 1969. (Limited edition.)

When the Sun Tries to Go On. Illustrations by Larry Rivers. Santa Barbara: Black Sparrow Press, 1969.

The Art of Love. New York: Random, 1975.

The Duplications. New York: Random, 1977.

The Burning Mystery of Anna in 1951. New York: Random, 1979.

Days and Nights. New York: Random, 1982.

Selected Poems, 1950–1982. New York: Random, 1985.

On the Edge: Poems. New York: Viking, 1986.

Seasons on Earth. New York: Penguin, 1987. (Includes *Ko; or, A Season on Earth* and *The Duplications.*)

Selected Poems. Manchester, England: Carcanet, 1991.

One Train: Poems. New York: Knopf, 1994.

On the Great Atlantic Rainway: Selected Poems, 1950–1988. New York: Knopf, 1994.

Straits: Poems. New York: Knopf, 1998.

New Addresses: Poems. New York: Knopf, 2000.

A Possible World: Poems. New York: Knopf, 2002.

Sun Out: Selected Poems, 1952–1954. New York: Knopf, 2002.

The Art of the Possible: Comics Mainly without Pictures. Brooklyn, N.Y.: Soft Skull Press, 2004.

FICTION

Interlocking Lives. Illustrations by Alex Katz. New York: Kulchur Press, 1970. (Short stories inspired by Katz's artwork.)

The Red Robins. New York: Vintage, 1975. (Novel.)

Hotel Lambosa and Other Stories. Minneapolis: Coffee House, 1993. (Short stories.)

PLAYS

Bertha and Other Plays. New York: Grove, 1966.

A Change of Hearts: Plays, Films, and Other Dramatic Works, 1951–1971. New York: Random, 1973.

One Thousand Avant-Garde Plays. New York: Knopf, 1988.

The Gold Standard: A Book of Plays. New York: Knopf, 1996.

NONFICTION

Wishes, Lies, and Dreams: Teaching Children to Write Poetry. New York: Chelsea House, 1970.

Rose, Where Did You Get That Red?: Teaching Great Poetry to Children. New York: Random, 1973.

I Never Told Anybody: Teaching Poetry Writing in a Nursing Home. New York: Random, 1977.

Sleeping on the Wing: An Anthology of Modern

Poetry with Essays on Reading and Writing. With Kate Farrell. New York: Random, 1981.

Talking to the Sun: An Illustrated Anthology of Poems for Young People. With Kate Farrell. New York: Metropolitan Museum of Art, 1985.

The Art of Poetry: Poems, Parodies, Interviews, Essays, and Other Work. Ann Arbor: University of Michigan Press, 1996.

Making Your Own Days: The Pleasures of Reading and Writing Poetry. New York: Scribners, 1998.

CRITICAL STUDIES

Auslander, Philip. *The New York School Poets as Playwrights: O'Hara, Ashbery, Koch, Schuyler, and the Visual Arts.* New York: P. Lang, 1989.

Diggory, Terrence and Miller, Stephen Paul. *The Scene of My Selves: New Work on New York School Poets.* University Press of New England, 2001.

Eder, Richard. "Theater: *The Red Robins.*" *New York Times,* January 18, 1978. (Review of the first performance of Koch's play.)

Ford, Mark, ed. *The New York Poets: An Anthology.* Manchester, England: Carcanet, 2004.

Hoover, Paul. "Fables of Representation: Poetry of the New York School." *American Poetry Review* 31, no. 4:20–30 (July–August 2002).

Lehman, David. *The Last Avant-Garde: The Making of the New York School of Poets.* New York: Doubleday, 1998.

O'Hara, Frank. "Another Word on Kenneth Koch." *Poetry* 85, no. 6:349–351 (March 1955). (Favorable review of Koch's first book of poetry.)

Perkins, David. *A History of Modern Poetry,* Volume 2, *Modernism and After.* Cambridge, Mass.: Harvard University Press, 1987.

Roskolenko, Harry. "Satire, Nonsense, and Worship." *Poetry* 84, no. 4:232–234 (July 1954). (Includes a brief negative review of Koch's first book of poetry.)

Saroyan, Aram. "Ten Things Never to Say to a Younger Woman." *New York Times,* September 28, 1975. (Review of *The Art of Love.*)

Simic, Charles. "The Water Hose Is on Fire." *New York Review of Books* 50, no. 1:13–14, 16 (January 16, 2003). (A retrospective of Koch's career in the context of a review of *Sun Out* and *A Possible World.*)

—LACY SCHUTZ

Ed Lacy

1911–1968

ED LACY EXISTED in name only, as the principle pseudonym of a New York writer named Leonard S. Zinberg. (He also used the pseudonyms Steve April and Russell Turner.) An obscure but fascinating figure in the annals of modern American literary history, Zinberg was, like many of his contemporaries, a Communist in the 1930s. Driven underground by the postwar Red Scare, Zinberg transformed himself into "Ed Lacy," a reasonably successful and seemingly apolitical pulp fiction writer of the 1950s and 1960s. Writing in a traditionally conservative—even reactionary—literary genre, Lacy deftly turned the form to his own ends, advancing progressive social messages under the guise of lowbrow entertainment. A story of adaptation and survival, Len Zinberg's literary career is also the story of a sea change in American literary and cultural politics after World War II.

Leonard Zinberg was born in New York City on August 15, 1911, to Max and Elizabeth Zinberg. The marriage soon dissolved. Some years later, Elizabeth (nicknamed variously Bea or Bes) married Maxwell ("Mac") Wyckoff, a Yale-educated banking lawyer who worked for the Manhattan firm of Livingston, Livingston & Harris. (Coincidentally Wyckoff also had a son named Leonard from a previous marriage.) The family home, at 450 West 153rd Street, was in the northern section of Manhattan's Harlem district, a neighborhood that Len Zinberg would live in for most of his life. Little is known about Len Zinberg's youth and school years during the period of the Harlem Renaissance, but later book dedications to his mother and stepfather indicate a loving and supportive household.

EARLY FICTION

Brought up in a white, well-educated, and affluent household in the midst of New York's teeming black ghetto, Zinberg was attracted to the unpretentious manners and mores of the working class, black and white. Manifestations of his proletarian outlook were an abiding class and race consciousness and his lifelong love of professional boxing. When he was twenty-six years old he published "The Fighters," his first story in print and the first of many boxing tales, in the November 1937 issue of *New Mexico Quarterly*. A satire of racism and bourgeois machismo, "The Fighters" features Charley and Ed, two flabby office workers in their forties who convene every Saturday afternoon at the corner bar and grill to get "pleasantly pie-eyed." As they proceed to get inebriated, Charley and Ed get more vociferous in touting white boxers like the retired Jack Dempsey against the reigning African American heavyweight, Joe Louis. The bartender disagrees, noting that with his youth and speed, Louis would "murder Jack," an observation that reminds Charley and Ed that their own virility is on the wane. As is their unspoken custom, the two drunks assuage their fragile male egos by harmlessly brawling on the subway heading home. In a similar vein is "The Champ" (*Coronet*, April 1938), another satire of male machismo that features John K. Cote, a pathetically deluded upstate farmer who quite seriously regards himself as the light-heavyweight boxing champion of the world because his boxing correspondence course declared him as such. The theme of white masculine vanity run amok would pervade Ed Lacy's work.

In the late 1930s, after publishing stories and articles in the *New Anvil, Esquire,* and the New York edition of the *Daily Worker* (the newspaper of the American Communist Party), Zinberg began writing a boxing novel. Published in 1940 as *Walk Hard–Talk Loud,* Zinberg's novel predates Budd Schulberg's more famous fight novel, *The Harder They Fall,* by seven years. The protagonist of *Walk Hard–Talk Loud* is Andy Whitman, a proud and volatile nineteen-year-old black shoe shine boy from Harlem whose fighting prowess is discovered by a boxing manager named Max Stringer. After two months of intensive training, Andy wins his first two bouts handily. He also meets Ruth Grath, a young Communist, and the two become romantically involved. Andy dreams of making a quick fortune in the ring and then using his winnings to move to another country, where racism is nonexistent. All seems to be going according to plan until Andy and Max travel to Scranton, Pennsylvania, for a six-round bout with a white fighter. The day of the fight Andy is denied a hotel room because of the color of his skin but is ultimately accommodated after he threatens a discrimination lawsuit. That night Whitman easily defeats the white boxer on points but the judges give the fight to his opponent, who is white and a local favorite. Still smarting from the day's disillusioning events, Andy attends a victory party for Larry Bachelo, another boxer managed by Max. At the party, Lou Ross, the racist gangster who is the money man behind Max Stringer, attempts to eject Andy from the party simply because he is black. Enraged, Andy pummels Ross—normally a fatal error but reporters are present. Instead of having Andy killed, Ross buys his contract from Max so that Andy will never be able to fight again. His dream of personal escape shattered, Andy is comforted by Ruth, who gently advises him that a separate peace with American racism was a deluded notion in the first place.

A number of features that would become staples of Ed Lacy's pulp fiction are manifest in *Walk Hard–Talk Loud.* First, there is the "tough guy" style that dominated American fiction in the 1930s, 1940s, and 1950s. In keeping with the dictums of the hard-boiled school, Zinberg's perennial subject is the struggle for survival in modernity's urban jungle. Accordingly his prose is the nonliterary and unselfconscious vernacular of the street: plainspoken, direct, ironic, and unsentimental. Another element that would show up frequently in Zinberg's work as Ed Lacy is a concern with class and race oppression and systemic institutional corruption. On a more personal and psychological level, Andy Whitman's escape fantasy was shared by Zinberg himself and is a constantly recurring motif in his Ed Lacy writings. Zinberg's Marxism, as espoused by the Ruth Grath character, is necessarily watered down in his later pulp fiction, but an essential critique of capitalism's dehumanizing effects pervades all his work. In a contemporary review, Ralph Ellison praised Zinberg for "indicat[ing] how far a writer, whose approach to Negro life is uncolored by condescension, stereotyped ideas, and other faults growing out of racial prejudice, is able to go with a Marxist understanding of the economic basis of Negro personality." The ideological power of Lacy's novel was reaffirmed during the 1946 season of Harlem's American Negro Theatre (founded 1940, disbanded c. 1950). Producer Gustav Blum and playwright Abram Hill (author of *On Striver's Row*) brought a racially integrated production of *Walk Hard* to the stage at the Chanin Theatre at West Forty-sixth Street and Seventh Avenue.

THE WAR YEARS AND AFTER

America's entry into World War II interrupted Len Zinberg's budding career as a novelist. Joining the Army Air Corps, Zinberg served overseas for twenty months between 1943 and

1945. For much of that time Zinberg was stationed near Bari, in southern Italy on the Adriatic Sea, where he did public relations work for the Air Force and wrote for *Yank* and the *New Yorker* in his spare time. The *New Yorker* pieces Zinberg published during the war provide vivid glimpses of rear-echelon life that point to larger ideological and social issues. In "Come On, Baby" (*New Yorker,* January 15, 1944), Zinberg satirizes the sort of "tough guy" machismo epitomized by Humphrey Bogart in the 1940s. A credulous KP pusher (a "kitchen police" broom pusher) admires the taciturn style of Paul, a "tough, silent" GI, who is winning at a crap game until he breaks his customary silence. Uttering a hopeful "Come on, baby," Paul throws the dice and loses forty dollars after a long winning streak. The KP pusher condemns the utterance as a loss of nerve: "Forty bucks and he upset the dice by going out of character. Bogart wouldn't have talked. Bogart would have had that forty bucks." "Caramels" (*New Yorker,* July 1, 1944) subtly pokes fun at American cultural insularity as it follows an off-duty conversation between a young Air Corps waist gunner and another American soldier in the square of a small Italian town. Soon to be repatriated after having completed fifty missions, the gunner vents his resentment of "Eye-ties" (Italians)—their parsimonious ways, their growing weariness of Americans, their constant begging for candy and cigarettes: "It's the people, I wanted to be friends, but they made me feel like a stranger, like an invader." Sardonically stating the obvious, the gunner's acquaintance asks "That's what we are, isn't it?" In "Feud" (*New Yorker,* August 4, 1945), Zinberg draws an implicit connection between racism, sexism, and general meanness with a satiric character study of a "tall, sharp featured" sergeant named Eddie. Admitted to a military hospital for malaria sufferers, the irascible Eddie quickly alienates a "Negro engineer," his white roommate (the story's narrator), and their

normally good-natured caregiver, Nurse Donovan. Eddie's tough-guy veneer belies a squeamish nature; he vomits on himself and faints after being subjected to a routine blood-taking by Nurse Donovan. Blaming Donovan for his own neurosis, Eddie exacts a twisted vengeance by peppering her with obscenities while pretending to be delirious with fever. After recovering from her embarrassment, Nurse Donovan has the last laugh by informing Eddie that his blood sample has been dropped and that he will need to give another the next morning—a ruse that brings great amusement to the narrator and his friend.

Continuing to publish slice-of-life fiction in the *New Yorker* after the war, Zinberg deftly chronicled Americans' disillusionment, perplexity, and growing sense of unease at the emerging shape of the postwar world. Appearing ten months before the release of William Wyler's hit film *The Best Years of Our Lives,* Zinberg's story "Ploesti Isn't Long Island" (*New Yorker,* March 2, 1946) deals with the same subject matter—ex-servicemen struggling to readjust to civilian life—but handles the topic in a more somber and realistic way. Charlie, ex-infantry, now sells weather stripping in Jackson Heights. Killing time before a sales appointment with a housewife, he stops in at a small Long Island airport and strikes up a conversation with an ex-bomber pilot who now makes his living taking tourists on sight-seeing plane rides over New York City. The pilot admits that he and some of his ex–Air Corps buddies make pretend bombing runs over Huntington to break up the monotony. Asked why he would want to revisit his war days, the pilot sums up the shortfalls of Pax Americana. In sum, no matter how efficient at delivering consumer goods for the masses, the atomized, competitive, venal, and lonely world of postwar capitalist America will never resurrect the tremendous sense of human solidarity and purpose that inhered during the war: a feeling that pointed toward a more ethically and spiritually meaningful world.

Another story, "Something's Going to Happen" (*New Yorker,* June 22, 1946), also featuring Charlie, expresses dark foreboding about the state of the world and the atomic age just dawning. Stopping in at a gin mill for his "before supper beer," Charlie runs into Eddie Conrad, an old army buddy. To Charlie's astonishment Eddie is in uniform, having reenlisted only weeks after returning home. Besotted and maudlin after hours of heavy drinking, Eddie explains that his decision to return to army life springs out of a deep and unremitting sense of doom that came over him during the war and has never left him. Eddie goes on to confess that his perpetual state of dread is both subjective and generalized. Irrevocably estranged from his wife after a four-year separation, rattled by runaway inflation, the housing shortage, labor unrest, police repression, and the bleak political outlook overall, Eddie is especially frightened that "this fooling with the atom bombs will bust the earth into pieces." After Eddie's abrupt departure from the bar, the eavesdropping bartender supposes the man's despair must be the result of his extreme intoxication. Awakened to the truth contained in Eddie's dark vision, Charlie replies sardonically, "Yeah. I hope he's drunk. I hope to hell and back he's drunk."

At least initially, Zinberg's own prospects were much brighter than those of his fictional characters. After the war, Zinberg won a literary fellowship from 20th Century–Fox studios to write a novel that might be turned into a film. Living in Los Angeles for a year (circa 1945–1946), Zinberg wrote *What D'Ya Know for Sure,* a Hollywood novel published by Doubleday in early 1947 that represents a clear departure from the gritty social realism of *Walk Hard—Talk Loud.* Zinberg's protagonist, Pete Rands, an assistant director at Popular-Bricker Pictures, is assigned to bring Terry (a.k.a. Cherry) Evans, an erratic young starlet, to the studio to start a picture. Apparently drunk, Evans is in no condi-

tion to go to work. Captivated by her extraordinary beauty, Rands brings her to his apartment and soon learns that Evans is dangerously unstable. He offers to let her stay at his place—no strings attached—until she feels well enough to resume her faltering career. Fired from his job at Bricker Pictures for failing to deliver Miss Evans to the studio, Rands subsists on a rapidly dwindling savings account while he tries to cure Terry of her neurosis (which manifests as "spells" of uncontrollable amorousness). Rands does not succeed in curing Terry until she discovers that he is working at a part-time dishwashing job so that he can be with her as much as possible. Finally convinced that Pete harbors no ulterior motives, Cherry is able rid herself of her pathological mistrust and inability to love. The two fall in love and marry and Cherry urges Pete to make a movie (starring her) which she will help to bankroll. When the movie, a conventional mystery, meets with success Pete worries that Cherry will abandon him as her career takes off again, but she puts his worries to rest by declaring that she is sick of show business and would prefer to settle down and just be a housewife.

The Cherry Evans character may have been based on the actress Frances Farmer (1914–1970). A blond Scandinavian beauty from the Pacific Northwest, Farmer was an anomaly among starlets: an intelligent, spirited nonconformist with leftist leanings. After the bitter end of an emotionally wrenching affair with the radical playwright Clifford Odets, Farmer struggled with manic depression and alcoholism and suffered a highly publicized breakdown after being arrested for drunk driving in 1943. By the time Zinberg wrote *What D'Ya Know for Sure,* Frances Farmer was having her rebelliousness crushed by forced shock treatments and ice water immersion "therapy" at a mental hospital in Washington State. Apt to identify with a fellow radical and underdog, Zinberg seems to have constructed a wish fulfillment fantasy that cast a man not unlike himself as the savior of a troubled star not unlike Frances Farmer. The caretaking relationship turned romance between Pete Rands and Cherry Evans recalls Fitzgerald's 1934 novel *Tender is the Night* and also bears some resemblance to Frank Capra's 1934 hit comedy *It Happened One Night*. At any rate, the inter-class romance plot was, by the 1940s, standard Hollywood fare.

His manuscript completed and submitted to his publisher by the summer of 1946, Zinberg returned to New York City. In September of that year two events occurred that would fundamentally change the direction of his life. The first of these involved public censure. The newly formed Duncan-Paris post of the American Legion—to which Zinberg belonged—had its charter revoked by the New York State Department of the Legion on the grounds that some of the post's members had belonged to the Communist Party. Though by no means a hard-core activist, Zinberg was named in a *New York Times* article, along with the writers Dewitt Gilpin, Saul Levitt, and James Dugan, as a former Communist. The second event, possibly triggered by the first, was more alarming. One September morning, after suffering chest pains, Zinberg was examined by his doctor and informed that he had a serious heart condition and would have to take blood-thinning medication, watch his diet, and restrict his physical activities (a regimen that Zinberg routinely violated by smoking cigars). Clearly there would be no returning to Hollywood; the strenuous, high-pressure life of a script hustler was out—a verdict further confirmed by reviews of *What D'Ya Know for Sure,* which were less than enthusiastic. A critic at the *New York Herald-Tribune* thought the novel "tough and tawdry" but "not too convincing an argument that love can triumph, no matter how cruelly it is kicked around." The *New York Times* reviewer found Zinberg's protagonist, Pete Rands, "more than a little naïve, earnest, and old-fashioned—like a

threadbare partisan who has wandered out of an 'agit-prop' play from the middle Thirties." Not surprisingly, 20th Century–Fox did not exercise its option to turn the book into a movie.

Critics' dismissal of *What D'Ya Know for Sure* as politically anachronistic did not faze Zinberg. His next novel, *Hold with the Hares* (1948), was even more explicit and emphatic in its affirmation of prewar American radicalism. The title comes from an old American proverb, "To run with the hounds and hold with the hares." As it relates to this novel, the hounds refer to the powerful capitalist ruling elite, and the hares refer to ordinary people struggling to survive. In terms of structure, Zinberg employs the then-popular noir flashback device. Italicized framing portions of the narrative, set in the present, are spaced at half-hour intervals between 5 and 10 A.M. on a cold day during the winter of 1945–1946 in a Brooklyn diner. These segments are narrated by the diner's owner and record his observations of a mysterious stranger who comes into the diner that morning. The flashback segments, told in the third person, comprise the bulk of the narrative. These segments are arranged chronologically by selected years—1932, 1935, 1937, 1939, 1941, 1943, 1944, 1945—and follow the life and career of Steve Anderson, son of a disabled union activist, who aspires to make it big as a newspaper journalist.

The central conflict, established early in the novel, is the conflict between Anderson's progressive political beliefs and his fierce personal ambition, with the latter force usually winning out—until the end. Attending a small, upstate New York college on a football scholarship, Anderson is expelled for participating in an anti-ROTC demonstration. In a futile attempt to avoid expulsion, Anderson repudiates his leftist ideals in an editorial: a craven act that gets him a job offer as a reporter by a conservative Buffalo paper. As Keith Booker puts it, "Anderson accepts the offer and thus embarks upon a path of selling out his ideals for personal gain, a path that leads to the breakup of his relationships first with his college sweetheart, Bess, a leftist, and then with Edith Stone, a union activist who is Jewish and therefore might impede his ambitions were he to marry her."

Reviews of *Hold with the Hares* were predictably similar to those tendered for *What D'Ya Know for Sure.* Critics politely noted Zinberg's proficiency as a storyteller but castigated him for dwelling on the seamier side of life. Virginia Kirkus observed that Zinberg's third novel was "competently handled" but recorded "basic instincts" with an "often unpleasant" plausibility. *Library Journal* voiced comparable sentiments: "[The] plot is interesting and well-handled. It is, however, extremely modern in language and tone, with much vulgarity, drinking, and immorality. It is unfortunate that the author, who has ability, should have besmirched an otherwise entertaining novel with so much that will be offensive to many readers." A more urbane and sophisticated reviewer writing for the *New York Times* was unruffled by Zinberg's gritty realism. He found fault instead with the author's political stance: "... a curiously archaic quality about the idealism.... the most enthusiastic reader may ... like to take the author by the arm and say, 'Look, by all means, you may be absolutely right. But it is much, much later than you think.' "

Len Zinberg did not need a *New York Times* book critic to remind him that his political views were increasingly out of step with the reactionary temper of the times. A year after the American Legion post flap, J. Parnell Thomas's House Un-American Activities Committee (HUAC) publicly accused nineteen people in the Hollywood film industry of left-wing sympathies. Ten of the nineteen (the "Hollywood Ten") who refused to cooperate with HUAC were convicted of contempt of Congress and sentenced to prison terms of up to a year. Scores of others were subsequently blacklisted. Not to be intimidated by right-wing zealots,

Zinberg remained secretly active in the Writers' and Publishers' Division of the Committee of the Arts, Sciences, and Professions, a New York–based Communist organization formed to support Henry A. Wallace's unsuccessful Progressive Party presidential bid in 1948. In February 1950 Senator Joseph R. McCarthy (R-Wisconsin) made the first of many hectoring speeches alleging Communist infiltration of federal government agencies. In May 1950 Vincent Harnett, a right-wing television producer, joined three former FBI agents to promulgate *Red Channels,* a pamphlet listing 151 Hollywood writers, directors, and performers who had heretofore escaped the blacklist. The outbreak of the Korean War (in June 1950) further enflamed anti-Communist hysteria. Over the next several years America was in the grip of a full-blown Red Scare: widespread political paranoia that would wreck countless careers, severely damage democratic institutions, and chill the nation's civil life.

Even in the ideologically favorable climate of the 1930s, radical novels sold poorly; the average American wanted escapism, not revolutionary propaganda. In the postwar years there was no way Zinberg could have been able to make a living as a writer of leftist fiction and steer clear of government harassment. To further complicate matters, Zinberg and his African American wife, Esther, desperately wanted to adopt a child—always a difficult endeavor for an interracial couple but made especially problematic by Zinberg's public reputation as a Communist. Consequently, at the height of the Red Scare in 1950, Len Zinberg ceased to be Len Zinberg and reinvented himself as Ed Lacy, paperback mystery writer.

PAPERBACK WRITER

In the early 1950s, before the cultural ascendancy of television, cheap paperback mystery novels and magazines exploded in popularity.

Though looked down upon by bourgeois taste-makers as unliterary rubbish and seldom reviewed, pulp novels could make their authors a decent living. Zinberg embraced the burgeoning genre as his meal ticket, knowing full well that he would be severely constrained by its established limits. As for remuneration, he made between $5,000 and $10,000 a year in the 1950s and 1960s—enough to live a life of what he termed "modest comfort." Advances, foreign sales, and book royalties were only periodical windfalls; He made ends meet week to week by selling dozens of short stories through his longtime literary agent, Howard Moorepark (1907–1983). Though his wife Esther also worked, Zinberg adhered to a disciplined and steady writing routine in order to survive as a professional writer.

He brought out his first pulp mystery as Ed Lacy, *The Woman Aroused,* in 1951. Lacy's protagonist, George Jackson, is a recently divorced New York City man who earns a good living editing a monthly magazine for the Sky Oil Company. Jackson's friend, Henry "Hank" Conley, asks Jackson to hold $7,000 for him, to keep it safe from his apparently volatile wife, Lee. George insists that Hank sign an IOU which he then hides behind a panel in his home. When Hank dies (by falling out of a window of his Twenty-ninth Street apartment), George—ambivalent about holding money that is not his—visits Lee, intending to give her the money that would rightfully be hers by inheritance. Lee turns out to be a six-foot-tall blonde Amazon with a strange, helpless affect. Sexually attracted, George initiates a relationship and is soon "keeping" Lee, as an escort and virtual sex slave, with her own money (he gives her $100 a week, which she hides away). On a night out in Harlem, Lee is recognized by a black ex-serviceman. She mysteriously panics and beats the man to a pulp. George traces the man the next day, questions him, and learns that Lee had been a slave laborer in a German concentration camp and had been worked half to death and gang raped by Axis *and* Allied soldiers; hence her dazed, slothful, apathetic manner. George makes attempts to find out Lee's real name and identity but fails. Despite his guilty pity for Lee, George tires of keeping her and tries to evict her from his home. When she refuses to leave, George tries to pressure her by telling her he suspects that she killed Hank. Turning the tables, Lee blackmails George into letting her stay by disclosing she has found the IOU note. The note and the fact that George has taken up with his friend's wife immediately after his friend's death amounts to considerable circumstantial evidence that George murdered Hank. George has no choice but to move out and continue to pay Lee the $100 a week as hush money. Trapped and downwardly mobile, George finally has the idea to search the house while Lee is out buying food. He finds the IOU note, destroys it, and is finally off the hook. Ironically, George's friend Joe moves in on Lee and begins the whole sordid process again.

Though certainly presenting the ultimate male fantasy of having a large, buxom woman at one's beck and call, *The Woman Aroused* ends with Lacy's own commentary on the sociopolitical and moral implications that contradict the fantasy:

This is the era of fear and the fast buck, and look what it did to me; money made me rook poor Lee, slip her to a good-natured dope like Joe, made me try to blackmail a sweet old man like Henderson. And the fast buck turned Walt from a shy schoolboy to a tin-horn racketeer. It seems to me that as long as the fast buck makes this a dog-eat-dog world—if you'll pardon the trite expression (and you will, won't you?)—we have to follow petty lives.... But you see what it all adds up to: we're not really living. We straightjacket our lives with misery and stupidity, then spend our free time looking for an escape. We think we're living yet in reality we're merely killing time.

Tempted by money and sex, George Jackson succumbs to both temptations but in the end gains insight into human venality and weakness. The novel ultimately condemns the cynical selfishness and opportunism that seem to characterize modern life under postwar capitalism. Stripped down to animalistic survival tendencies, Lee embodies the degraded spirit of modernity by becoming a monster of blind need and nothing else. Lacy also decries the wholesale corruption—malingering, waste, graft, sexual exploitation, black-marketeering—that constituted the dark underside of the Allied war effort.

With his next novel, *Sin in Their Blood* (1952), Lacy turned his attention to the contemporary milieu. His protagonist, Matt Ranzino, a burly ex-heavyweight boxer, World War II vet, ex-cop, and private detective, returns from the Korean War in fragile mental and physical health. After killing Korean civilians by mistake, Ranzino suffers a near-fatal bout with tuberculosis and continues to have nightmares. Returning to his hometown in California after months convalescing in a VA hospital, Ranzino is hired by William Saxton III to find the killer of Saxton's sister, Beatrice Wilson, and to find her husband, Henry, who has disappeared (and thus looks like a strong suspect in his wife's murder). Acting on a clue, Matt soon finds Henry Wilson, dead in a remote cabin, apparently having hanged himself. Matt's cop friend Max considers the case closed, but Matt suspects the murder-suicide was a cover-up engineered by Saxton. His suspicions grow when he soon learns that Henry Wilson was not white but actually a light-skinned black "passing" as white—a fact, if known to Saxton, that might be a motive for killing his sister and brother-in-law. Looking for a place to live by the beach, Ranzino meets Mady Moore, a quasi-alcoholic war widow who happens to be Saxton's mistress. The two become roommates and then lovers. A subplot involves Ranzino's ex–private

eye partner, Harry Loughlin, who is now a professional Red Scare blackmailer. Loughlin digs up information on anyone and everyone who has been "guilty" of leftist or unionist activities. He contacts them and threatens public exposure unless they pay him off. Mady's brother Joe, a postal worker, is being blackmailed by Loughlin for past union organizing. Matt persuades Joe to trap Loughlin in a simulated homosexual encounter with him, photograph it, and have something with which to blackmail Loughlin so that he'll stop blackmailing Joe. The scheme works a bit too well; Loughlin, fearing public embarrassment, commits suicide by diving out his office window. Matt concocts a scheme to entrap Saxton, but the scheme backfires. Saxton captures Matt, beats him and tortures him with cold showers so as to reactivate his tuberculosis and make his death appear to be natural. Luckily Mady calls Max after Matt vanishes. They go to Saxton's home, subdue him, and rescue Matt.

War, racism, and anti-leftist hysteria are Lacy's principle targets in *Sin in Their Blood*. Ranzino is damaged in body and soul by what he has seen and done in Korea. Saxton murders his sister and her husband, Henry, because he discovers Henry is black, "passing" as white. Ranzino's ex-partner, Loughlin, takes cynical advantage of the Red Scare to run a blackmail racket, thus illustrating how political paranoia breeds other evils. Both villains eventually get their just desserts. Lacy also explores the cult of macho individualism. Ranzino has always lived by the "tough guy" code until tuberculosis makes him confront his own fragile mortality. He also has to confront the fact that he cannot do it all alone. In the end Ranzino has to rely on Mady and Max to save him—a far cry from the super-masculine vigilante private eye Mike Hammer, Mickey Spillane's right-wing *übermensch* just then appearing in print.

More than most pulp fiction writers, "Ed Lacy" derived plots and themes from his own life experience. In about 1954 Zinberg and his wife finally succeeded in adopting a child, a three-year-old African American girl they called Carla. Nothing is known about the adoption process, but two of Lacy's mystery novels from this period express apprehensions about childbirth, adoption, and outside threats to the integrity of fledgling families. In *Enter without Desire* (1954), Lacy's protagonist, a sculptor named Marshal Jameson, becomes involved with Elma Morse, a pregnant woman recently estranged from her husband, Maxwell. Desperate to start a family with Elma, Jameson murders Maxwell Morse to prevent him from claiming custody of the child once it is born. (Elma, an illegal alien, is in no position to contest Maxwell's suit.) In the end Jameson's worst nightmare materializes when he is shot by a private detective looking into Morse's killing. It is not unreasonable to assume that the fear at the center of *Enter without Desire*—fear of forfeiting custody of a nonbiological daughter—came out of Zinberg's own anxieties.

Zinberg further explored his feelings about adoption and fatherhood from a radically different angle in *The Short Night* (1957), written under the one-time pseudonym Russell Turner. His protagonist, Lester "Red" Dolsan, is an ex-pro baseball player working as a scout for the Brooklyn Dodgers. Returning from a months-long scouting trip in Central America, Dolsan learns that Peggy Fulton, a woman with whom he had a one-night stand, tried to contact him while he was out of town. Finding out that Peggy left her job after becoming pregnant, he suspects the child might be his and sets out to locate her. Referred to a Robert and Ruth Hemingway on Staten Island by Peggy's former landlady, Dolsan visits Ruth Hemingway, who tells him she just married Robert six weeks before and that his first wife died giving birth to the blind daughter they are now caring for. Dolsan hires a private detective and continues his search for Peggy. Eventually he is shocked to

discover that the Hemingways made an illegal adoption deal with Peggy, who did not want to keep the child. She signed into the maternity ward as Mrs. Hemingway, then died in childbirth and was buried as Mrs. Hemingway. Ergo, the Hemingway's blind baby is actually Dolsan's daughter—which also explains the warning calls from Peggy. Afraid that their illegal adoption will be exposed, Bob and Ruth Hemingway have been trying to shake off Dolsan. In the end Dolsan embraces fatherhood by buying off Bob (a closeted gay man) and marrying Ruth. Together Dolsan, Ruth, and their daughter will form a real family even though its origins were mostly a matter of accident and chance.

In 1952 Zinberg and his wife made the first of a series of trips to France. While sitting in a Paris café he overheard a black American pugilist talking about his difficulties trying to make it in Europe as a boxer. The fighter became a character named Bud Stewart in Lacy's ninth novel, *Go for the Body* (1954), a reprise of *Walk Hard—Talk Loud* but also a nod to Budd Schulberg's *The Harder They Fall* (1947). Schulberg's novel had been loosely based on the sad career of the Italian heavyweight Primo Carnera (1906–1967), a former circus strongman who, as a boxer, fell under the influence of organized crime. In Lacy's novel the Carnera figure is called Milo Massimo, a slow, dim-witted Italian heavyweight being groomed as the new Mussolini by a fascist aristocrat—a scheme foiled by Lacy's protagonist, Ken Francine, Bud Stewart's white manager and friend. (In actuality Carnera fought with the anti-fascist resistance in World War II.) Lacy's Massimo plot is implausible, but his handling of the black boxer Bud Stewart in Europe fulfills Andy Whitman's dream of escape from American racism.

Besides supplying the basis for *Go for the Body,* Zinberg's Paris sojourn also inspired *The Best That Ever Did It* (1955), the first of five hardcover detective novels Lacy would publish with Harper over the next few years. *The Best That Ever Did It* was aptly titled; it is one of Lacy's best mystery novels: fluid, plausible, tightly focused and replete with vividly realized characters. In January 1956 Lacy sold the movie and television rights to *The Best That Ever Did It* to the actor Lloyd Bridges for his *Pursuit* TV show for $5,000, but Bridges never brought the story to the small screen.

Lacy's *The Men from the Boys* (1956) may have been prompted by a growing sense of mortality brought on by middle age and his bad heart. His tough-guy protagonist, Marty Bond, is a divorced and disgraced alcoholic ex-cop who works as a "house dick" (really a bouncer and pimp) at the Grover, a third-rate New York hotel where prostitutes ply their trade. After seeing a doctor for a gastrointestinal problem, Marty convinces himself that he has cancer and is going to die. To avoid a long and agonizing death he tries to commit suicide twice, by gun and barbiturate overdose, but both times loses his nerve. Meanwhile Marty's long-estranged (adopted) son, Lawrence, an auxiliary cop, stumbles on an odd occurrence. A local butcher claims he was robbed of $50,000 and later says he wasn't robbed. Lawrence seeks Marty's advice on the case, which eventually leads to Lawrence being severely beaten by an unknown assailant. From Lawrence's description Marty has a hunch the man is Bob "Hilly" Smith, a syndicate enforcer. Marty suspects that the incident at the meat store and Lawrence's beating tie in with the recent murder of the mobster "Cocky" Anderson and determines to go after Hilly Smith—not only to break the case but deliberately to get himself killed. He succeeds on both counts but, as he is dying from gunshot wounds, he is informed by his doctor that he did not have cancer after all. As its title suggests, *The Men from the Boys* is an ironic commentary on macho bravura and on Marty Bond's relationship to his son, Lawrence, and to Hilly

Smith. Indeed the three men stake out points on a moral continuum. Lawrence is young, naive, and idealistic and has no idea how compromised the job of city policeman actually is. Marty is jaded by all the corruption and brutality he has seen. The mob assassin Hilly Smith is evil incarnate. In Lacy's scheme of things, moving from boyhood to manhood does not seem to be a desirable transformation.

Though several of his novels feature black characters, Lacy's use of an African American protagonist for *Room to Swing* (1957) was his first such use since *Walk Hard—Talk Loud* seventeen years earlier. His renewed fore-grounding of race was likely inspired by the dramatic emergence of the civil rights movement. (In 1954 the Supreme Court banned segregation in public schools, and the Montgomery bus boycott, launched by Rosa Parks on December 1, 1955, ended successfully on December 21, 1956—only weeks before *Room to Swing* was published.) Alan Wald astutely notes that "Lacy named his detective Toussaint Marcus Moore—suggesting Toussaint L'Ouverture, the Haitian revolutionary; Marcus Garvey, the most successful Black nationalist of the African Diaspora; and Richard B. Moore, the West Indian Communist who lived in New York." Framed for a murder he did not commit, the New York City detective "Touie" Moore must venture to southern Ohio to solve the case: an instance of cultural and racial border crossing that makes for pointed political commentary. Moore's immersion in southern redneck culture predates John Ball's more famous novel, *In the Heat of the Night,* by eight years. Coming out at a triumphant moment in the civil rights struggle, Ball's novel was soon made into an Oscar-winning film starring Sidney Poitier (and later spawned a sequel and a long-running television show). Optioned for a screenplay that was never produced, Lacy's book sank into obscurity, despite the fact that it won the 1957 Edgar Award for best detective novel.

In the late 1950s Zinberg and his family started spending their summers at the seaside resort village of Sag Harbor, Long Island, an hour's train ride from their home in Manhattan. The Sag Harbor environs would serve as the locale for Lacy's next novel, *Breathe No More, My Lady* (1958), an allegorical meditation on his own career as a "hack" writer. In the book, Lacy figuratively divides himself between Matt Anthony (a best-selling mystery writer), Norm Connor (a publishing executive), and Henry Brown (a blacklisted leftist academic)—a tripartite schema that evokes Freud's classic model of the psyche comprised of the id (Matt), ego (Norm), and superego (Henry). The three principles also suggest the uneasy interrelationship between art, commerce, and politics. Though outwardly a big, blustering Hemingway figure of large appetites—despite a heart condition—Matt is a disciplined wordsmith (as was Lacy on all counts). Pragmatic and cynical about the writing business, Matt writes for fame, ego gratification, and money. The morally and politically principled Professor Hank Brown embodies Matt's troubled social conscience (and in a larger sense, the repressed political consciousness of 1930s radicalism). Remorseful over his easy accommodation to bourgeois values and imperatives, Matt publicly threatens to kill his wife, Francine, for snubbing Brown: a classic case of guilty projection. When she dies accidentally, he feels compelled to restage her death to make it look more convincingly accidental and, ironically, is indicted for murder. Even more ironically, the murder trial is made moot by Matt's death of a heart attack—a fate that Lacy probably anticipated for himself. Fascinating as psychological self-disclosure, *Breathe No More, My Lady* fails as a mystery, a result not lost on the *New York Times* mystery critic Anthony Boucher: "I suspect that this story of a mystery novelist on trial for wife-murder is intended to be something of A Serious Novel; but it is merely, in comparison with Lacy's less pretentious work, unduly long, terribly talky and clumsily constructed."

Boucher was much more impressed with *Shakedown for Murder* (1958), another mystery that uses Sag Harbor as its setting. Lacy found the resort friendly on the surface, but underneath he found long standing feelings of frustration and prejudice for all outsiders who had not been born there. Reprising the city-country clash that animates *Room to Swing*, Lacy fashioned a story featuring Matt Lund, an aging city jailhouse cop in "End Harbor" (i.e., Sag Harbor) to visit his son's family. The murder of Dr. Barnes, the village's esteemed physician, draws Lund into an investigation that pits him against the village police chief, actually based on Sag Harbor's police "chief" at that time: a man described by Lacy as "a well built, handsome young fellow [but] a bit on the arrogant side." With his instinctual regard for the underdog, Lacy imagined the old warhorse teaching the young turk a thing or two about police work as he solves the murder and uncovers the intricate insurance fraud scheme behind it.

Lacy's *Be Careful How You Live* (1958) is a morality tale modeled, in structure and theme, on his 1948 novel *Hold with the Hares*. The book, expanded from a short story, derives its title from Ephesians 5:15–16: "Be careful how you live. Not thoughtlessly but thoughtfully. Make the most of your opportunities for the times are evil." A first-person narrative told by Bucklin "Bucky" Penn, a crooked police detective in hiding with his equally crooked partner, "Doc," *Careful* uses a typical noir framing device: Bucky and Doc have expropriated one million dollars in ransom money and are in hiding until they can safely leave town. The rest of the story, told in flashbacks, chronicles Bucky's dubious background, his bad marriage, his willingness to cheat and steal in order to further his career as a cop, his alliance with Doc, a master of corruption—all leading up to their decision to steal the ransom money. Considerable suspense is built as the reader wonders if Bucky and Doc will escape their hideout or whether one will double-cross the other for the extra half-million dollars, but the heart of the novel is Lacy's detailed character study of Bucky Penn, an otherwise ordinary man who gradually slips into evil through a series of self-serving choices.

Being something of a Francophile, Zinberg took a keen interest in the Algerian war for independence from France (1954–1962). He was therefore more shocked than most Americans to hear the news from Algeria on May 28, 1957. On that day a terrorist gang of uncertain affiliation slaughtered some three hundred men and boys near the Algerian village of Melouza, an atrocity so gruesome that battle-hardened French troops were sickened. At the end of 1958 Lacy set himself the complex task of writing a political novel about the Melouza massacre that, for commercial reasons, had to be disguised as just another pulp mystery-thriller. Lacy's imaginative solution, presented in a paperback original crudely titled *Blonde Bait* (1959), was rather ingenious. Mickey, his Caribbean island–hopping narrator-protagonist, gets involved with Rose, a woman on the run from unknown pursuers. As she is in possession of $50,000 and a mysterious manuscript written in a foreign language, Mickey suspects that Rose is a gangster's moll running from the mob with stolen money. As it turns out, her pursuers are actually after the manuscript: an invaluable eyewitness account of the Melouza massacre by Joseph Fedor, a Hungarian mercenary with whom Rose had had a relationship. Forces on the Left and Right are anxious to obtain Fedor's account as it promises to settle the mystery of Melouza once and for all. Mickey and Rose could sell the manuscript for a great deal of money but ultimately opt to turn it over to the authorities so as not to sully themselves with

"blood money." As Lacy's novel self-reflexively demonstrates, the key issue is not lucre but repressed historical truth, not crime per se but *political* crime—its hidden causes, effects, and international implications as the world moved inexorably away from nineteenth-century European colonialism in the latter half of the twentieth century.

Thoroughly imbued with the cranky outlook of a 1930s socialist, Zinberg had little patience for the bohemian counterculture beginning to flourish in Europe in the 1950s. Though he described a two-month stay in Nice in the summer of 1959 with his family as "delightful," he was somewhat bemused by the younger generation. This sense of cultural and temporal dislocation resulted in *The Freeloaders* (1961), a caper novel "about a couple of Americans willing to do anything to remain abroad."

In the fall of 1959 Lacy wrote *The Big Fix* (1960), a reworking of *Go for the Body* (1954) that is in part another exposé of corruption in professional boxing but more centrally a character study of "Irish" Tommy Cork, an aging professional boxer who has seen better days but cannot relinquish his dream of making it big—despite the fact that he is often beaten, drunk, hungry, homeless, and forced to sell his blood to survive. Arno, a predatory fight promoter, plays upon Cork's dreams of glory to enlist him as an unwitting victim in an insurance fraud scheme that involves fight fixing and Tommy's death in the ring so that Arno, as his beneficiary, can collect a large settlement. Suspecting that Tommy is being set up, a fight announcer, Alvin Hammer, alerts the police detective (and ex-boxer) Walt Steiner. Genre conventions dictate that Steiner, the stalwart cop, will crack the case and rescue the forlorn Tommy Cork at the last moment, but Lacy deliberately confounds expectations by having Tommy entrap and defeat his enemies on his own. Fashioning a classic victory of the underdog, Lacy emphasizes the nobility and heroism of little people who are poor, beaten, and have no decent prospects but carry on—and sometimes triumph.

HARBINGER OF DEATH

In the fall of 1959, shortly after finishing *The Big Fix,* Zinberg was stricken with a severe heart attack, the event he had long anticipated and feared. He worried about it, but then eventually realized that it could become a source of story ideas. His novel *Bugged for Murder* (1961) came about as a result. The *New York Times* mystery critic Anthony Boucher deemed *Bugged for Murder* "one of [Lacy's] best paperback originals.... a good study of a man coming to terms with his invalid body."

Some years later Lacy would reprise the painful topic of his disability with *The Hotel Dwellers* (1966), his first attempt at a non-mystery novel since *Hold with the Hares* eighteen years earlier. Obviously a companion piece to *Bugged for Murder, The Hotel Dwellers* also bears considerable resemblance to *The Men from the Boys* (1956). Set in fourth-rate New York City hotels, both books feature protagonists struggling to come to terms with serious illness, either real or imagined. In the earlier novel, Lacy's protagonist, a house detective named Marty Bond, recklessly puts himself in mortal danger because he falsely believes that he is stricken with a fatal disease. Ironically, Bond's fear of death propels him headlong into the abyss. *The Hotel Dwellers* offers a parallel but distinctly different scenario in which Lacy's protagonist, Howie Fisher, a normally cautious hotel lobby stand proprietor, recklessly undertakes both a new business venture and an extramarital affair with Cleopatra Nasser, an Egyptian belly dancer who lives at the same hotel. Trapped in a perfunctory marriage—a common Lacy theme—Fisher reasons that he owes himself real libidinal fulfillment before he dies. The problem, ironically, is that Fisher does

not die in short order, as he had expected, but lives on and must deal with a life made impossibly complicated by having a wife, a mistress, and a new business. If Marty Bond wrongly thought of death as an enemy he must beat to the punch, Howie Fisher wrongly regarded it as a safe refuge from life's moral vagaries. In the end both men are confounded by realities that have little to so with their distorted perceptions and deluded expectations. For Lacy, death is neither nemesis nor savior; it tends to come when called but cannot be counted on to make a perfectly timed appearance. Lacy was proud of *The Hotel Dwellers*. In a marketing blurb requested by his publisher, Lacy compared "the atmosphere and mood of the book" with Arthur Miller's *Death of a Salesman* or Paddy Chayefsky's *Marty*. Reviews were strong across the board. The often caustic *Virginia Kirkus Bulletin* dubbed Lacy's novel "one of the minor unforgettables, the sort of thing that would become a classic on *Studio One*—if there was still a *Studio One*."

After sufficient recuperation from his heart attack, Lacy returned to writing with *A Deadly Affair* (1960), a novel that resembled *Room to Swing* but with a Puerto Rican first-person narrator-protagonist named José rather than a black man and a story that takes place entirely within New York City as opposed to the northern city/southern country locales of the earlier novel. In both novels the protagonist, suspected of murder, slugs a cop, escapes, and must find the real killer to exonerate himself and must do so in a matter of days or hours. *A Deadly Affair* is a good, taut suspense yarn that suffers from some implausible plot twists (for example, the accidental killing of a man on a rooftop handball court by a wayward building crane). Nonetheless Lacy manages to comment on the bigotry that Puerto Ricans faced in New York at a time of their mass immigration (after 1953 tens of thousands of Puerto Ricans poured into New

York City). Lacy also uses the suspense yarn device to expose and critique housing discrimination. In the end, though, Detective London puts the Puerto Rican's plight in historical context by rightly noting that every new wave of immigrants faced the same sort of treatment: "The Germans, the Irish, the Italians, the Jews. My grandfather died of TB working in a stinking East Side sweat shop. I'm not saying it's right, or has to be, Joey, but only that it takes time. There must be an adjustment on both sides. Unfortunately, due to air travel, the Puerto Rican influx has been faster and greater than the others." (Four years later Lacy's mystery novel *Sleep in Thunder* (1964) would present another José, this time a fourteen-year-old Puerto Rican protagonist who is inadvertently caught up in the murder of a gangster and must use his courage and wits to solve the crime and exonerate himself. In an introductory note Lacy expressed hope that "many real life Josés will read the book and think of themselves as the novel's hero.")

Besides Nice and Sag Harbor, Zinberg and his family also vacationed in the Caribbean. In an article Lacy noted that books "on the history and customs of the South Seas" fascinated him. He also admitted that he was "an escapist at heart." In the first few years after his heart attack, he interspersed his pulp mysteries with a number of novels featuring exotic settings that suggest authorial wish-fulfillment fantasies of flight to sunny resort paradises safe from the ravages of time, failing health, and the bitter winters of the Northeast. These lesser Lacy novels include *South Pacific Affair* (1961), *Two Hot to Handle* (also published as *Murder in Paradise* and *The Coin of Adventure,* 1963), and *The Sex Castle* (1963).

"BLACK POWER" FICTION BY A WHITE WRITER

In 1964 Zinberg was jolted out of his death reveries by the events swirling around him. That summer the civil rights struggle entered a new and violent phase as a number of states passed legislation nullifying the Civil Rights Act of 1964 passed by Congress. Mounting frustrations in the black ghetto finally boiled over into race riots in Harlem, Chicago, and Philadelphia that left more than one hundred dead, hundreds arrested, and property damage in the millions. In August 1965 six days of rioting in the South Central Los Angeles district of Watts left thirty-four dead, a thousand injured, and approximately $200 million in property damage. Racial turmoil reached a crescendo in the summer of 1967; thirty-four cities erupted, scores were killed, thousands arrested, and hundreds of buildings burned. During the mid-1960s it began to look like America's cities might explode into a full-scale race war that would tear the country apart.

Already decades ahead of most of his white contemporaries in understanding the plight of African Americans, Lacy once again put race at the center of his fiction with *Harlem Underground* (1965), *In Black & Whitey* (1967), and *Moment of Untruth* (1964). Both *Harlem Underground* and *In Black & Whitey* feature Lee Hayes, a young black New York City police detective, as their first-person narrator-protagonist. In *Harlem Underground* Hayes goes undercover to infiltrate a black youth gang on 128th Street in Harlem that is terrorizing the city. Hayes ultimately succeeds in solving a murder and arresting the gang's dangerous leader, "Purple Eyes." Though acclaimed a "hero," Lee Hayes emerges from the experience profoundly ambivalent. He has done his job as a police officer but has also come to understand—and empathize with—the extreme alienation of black urban youth. For his sequel, *In Black & Whitey,* Lacy teams Lee Hayes with Al Kahn, a white, Jewish cop. Both go undercover in the Paradise Alley section of Harlem, a powder keg about to explode into yet another bloody race riot. Hayes and Kahn manage to root out the leaders of WON (Wipe out Negroes), a white supremacist group fomenting unrest, and prevent catastrophe.

In *Moment of Untruth,* the sequel to his Edgar Award–winning *Room to Swing* (1957), Lacy sends his black detective-protagonist, Toussaint Marcus Moore, to Mexico to investigate a murder. In the course of his investigations Moore discovers that José Cuzo, a top Mexican toreador, hedges his bets by drugging the bulls he fights (hence the title, *Moment of Untruth*). As is common in Lacy's fiction, Hemingway-style machismo is exposed as a cowardly illusion. The foreign setting also allows Lacy the opportunity to explore race relations in an entirely different context. Moore's relatively benign treatment in Mexico underscores the virulence of racism in the United States. Jennifer Hynes also notes that Moore turns down "what might have been a fling with no consequences because he is in love with his pregnant wife [thereby undermining] the stereotype of African-American males lusting after white women."

On January 7, 1968, Len Zinberg collapsed and died of a massive heart attack in a laundromat a few doors away from his apartment building at 75 St. Nicholas Place, New York City. He was fifty-six years old. Under his own name and as Ed Lacy, Russell Turner, and Steve April, Zinberg wrote and published thirty-two novels (translated into twelve languages) and scores of short stories, sketches, and articles. His books, hastily written and admittedly uneven in quality, are reputed to have sold some 28 million copies worldwide. Beyond his impressive productivity and commercial staying power in a tough literary market, Len Zinberg managed to stay true to a humane vision of social justice and racial tolerance—impressive achievements for a pulp fiction writer.

Selected Bibliography

WORKS OF ED LACY

Walk Hard—Talk Loud. As Len Zinberg. Indianapolis: Bobbs-Merrill, 1940; New York: Lion Books, 1950.

What D'Ya Know for Sure? As Zinberg. New York: Doubleday, 1947; as *Strange Desires,* New York: Avon, 1948.

Hold with the Hares. As Zinberg. New York: Doubleday, 1948.

The Woman Aroused. New York: Avon, 1951; London: Hale, 1969.

Sin in Their Blood. New York: Eton Books, 1952; as *Chasse aux sorcières,* Paris: Gallimard, 1953; Buenos Aires, Argentina: Editorial Trebol, 1956; as *Death in Passing,* London: Boardman, 1959; Rome: Vaglieri Editorial, 1962.

Strip for Violence. New York: Eton Books, 1953; New York: McFadden-Bartell, 1965; London: Mayflower, 1969.

Route 13. As Steve April. New York: Funk & Wagnalls, 1954.

Enter without Desire. New York: Avon, 1954; MacFadden-Bartell, 1964.

Go for the Body. New York: Avon, 1954; as *L'après-midi d'un fauve,* Paris: Presses de la Cité no. 204, 1955; London: Boardman, 1959.

The Best That Ever Did It. New York: Harper, 1955; as *Ça c'est du billard,* Paris: Presses de la Cité no. 235, 1955; London: Hutchinson, 1957; as *Visa to Death,* New York: Permabooks, 1956.

The Men from the Boys. New York: Harper, 1956; as *Enquête privée,* Paris: Presses de la Cité no. 280, 1956; London: Boardman, 1960; MacFadden-Bartell, 1967.

Lead with Your Left. New York: Harper, 1957; London: Boardman, 1957.

Room to Swing. New York: Harper, 1957; New York: Pyramid, 1958; London: Boardman, 1958.

The Short Night. As Russell Turner. New York: Hillman, 1957.

Breathe No More, My Lady. New York: Avon, 1958.

Shakedown for Murder. New York: Avon, 1958; Rio De Janeiro, Brazil: Editorial Atlântida, 1958; as

Devil for the Witch, London: Boardman, 1958; also Italian and Danish editions.

Be Careful How You Live. London: Boardman, 1958; New York: Harper, 1959; as *Dead End,* New York: Pyramid, 1960; Lisbon: Empresa Nacional de Pulicande, 1964.

Blonde Bait. New York: Zenith, 1959.

The Big Fix. New York: Pyramid, 1960; London: Boardman, 1961.

A Deadly Affair. New York: Hillman, 1960.

Bugged for Murder. New York: Avon, 1961.

The Freeloaders. New York: Berkley, 1961; London: Boardman, 1962.

South Pacific Affair. New York: Belmont Books, 1961.

The Sex Castle. New York: Paperback Library, 1963; London: Brown, Watson, 1968; as *Shoot it Again,* New York: Paperback Library, 1969.

Two Hot to Handle (Murder in Paradise and *The Coin of Adventure).* New York: Paperback Library, 1963; London: Brown, Watson, 1966.

Double Trouble. New York: Harper & Row, 1964; London: Boardman, 1965.

Moment of Untruth. New York: Lancer, 1964; London: Boardman, 1965.

Pity the Honest. London: Boardman, 1964; New York: McFadden, 1965.

Sleep in Thunder. New York: Grosset & Dunlap, 1964.

Harlem Underground. New York: Pyramid, 1965.

The Hotel Dwellers. New York: Harper & Row, 1966; London: Hale, 1968.

In Black & Whitey. New York: Lancer, 1967.

The Napalm Bugle. New York: Pyramid, 1968.

The Big Bust. New York: Pyramid, 1969; London: New English Library, 1970.

SELECTED STORIES

"Five Minutes After I Left You ...." As Len Zinberg. In *The Best From Yank—the Army Weekly.* New York: Dutton, 1945. P. 209.

"Great Day." As Zinberg. In *The Best From Yank—the Army Weekly.* New York: Dutton, 1945. P. 95.

"Immigrant." As Zinberg. In *Cross Section 1945: A Collection of New American Writing.* 3 vols. Edited by Edwin Seaver. New York: Book Find Club, 1945. Pp. 351–354.

"Up Queer Street." As Zinberg. In *Esquire's 2nd Sports Reader.* Edited by Arnold Gingrich. New York: Barnes, 1946. Pp. 136–143. (Part of Chapter 11 of *Walk Hard—Talk Loud,* pp. 153–162.)

"The Right Thing." In *Best Short Stories by Afro-American Writers, 1925–1950.* Edited by Nick Aaron Ford and H. L. Faggett Boston: Meador, 1950. Pp. 184–188.

"Stickler for Details." In *A Pride of Felons: Twenty Stories by Members of the Mystery Writers of America.* Edited by Hugh Pentacost. New York: Holt, 1962.

"Death by the Numbers." In *With Malice Toward All: An Anthology of Mystery Stories by the Mystery Writers of America.* Edited by Robert L. Fish. New York: Putnam, 1968.

SELECTED UNCOLLECTED PERIODICAL PUBLICATIONS

"The Fighters." As Len Zinberg. *New Mexico Quarterly,* November 7, 1937, Pp. 257–260.

"A Peaceful Death." As Zinberg. *Esquire,* January 1938, Pp. 64, 131.

"The Champ." As Zinberg. *Coronet,* April 1938, Pp. 8–10.

"Subway to Harlem." As Zinberg, *New Anvil,* March 1, 1939, Pp. 21–22. (Excerpt from *Walk Hard—Talk Loud.)*

"Long Brown Letter." As Zinberg. *New Anvil,* June–July 1939, p. 19.

"The Flatfooted Angel." As Zinberg. *Esquire,* April 1940, Pp. 63, 141–142.

"The Crazy Torpedo." As Zinberg. *Esquire,* February 1941, Pp. 23, 123.

"The Quiet Life." As Zinberg. *Matrix,* winter 1942–1943, Pp. 18–21.

"Prodigal's Off Day." As Zinberg. *Decade of Short Stories* 4, Second Quarter 1943, Pp. 16–18.

"Home Is Where ... ?" As Zinberg. *New Republic,* October 25, 1943, Pp. 570–571.

"A Little Girl Like Home." As Zinberg. *Matrix,* fall 1943, Pp. 19–27.

"Come On, Baby." As Zinberg. *New Yorker,* January 15, 1944, Pp. 61–62.

"Caramels." As Zinberg. *New Yorker,* July 1, 1944, p. 53.

"The Critics." As Zinberg. *New Yorker,* August 19,

1944, p. 18.

"Count Basie and Soft Italian." As Zinberg. *New Yorker,* October 28, 1944, Pp. 64–67.

"162nd Street and Amsterdam." As Zinberg. *New Yorker,* December 16, 1944, Pp. 56–57.

"The Temptation of St. Lucky Strike." As Zinberg. *New Yorker,* February 3, 1945, Pp. 66–69.

"Embrace Me—at My Mother's Knee." As Zinberg. *New Yorker,* March 24, 1945, Pp. 66–68.

"Death and Dick Tracy." As Zinberg. *New Yorker,* July 7, 1945, Pp. 46–49.

"Feud." As Zinberg. *New Yorker,* August 4, 1945, Pp. 54–57.

"A Guy Just Has to Learn." As Zinberg, *New Yorker,* October 6, 1945, Pp. 52–54.

"Brushoff." As Zinberg. *New Yorker,* February 16, 1946, Pp. 62–63.

"Ploesti Isn't in Long Island." As Zinberg. *New Yorker,* March 2, 1946, Pp. 65.

"Something's Going to Happen." As Zinberg. *New Yorker,* 22 June 22, 1946, Pp. 81–83.

"What You Going For?" As Zinberg. *New Yorker,* 19 October 1946, Pp. 122–123.

"Slam the Door." As Zinberg. *New Yorker,* November 9, 1946, Pp. 108.

"On with the New." As Zinberg. *New Yorker,* December 28, 1946, Pp. 57–58.

"I'm a Little Man." As Zinberg. *Esquire,* January 1947, Pp. 141, 142, 144.

"Convert." As Zinberg. *New Yorker,* February 1, 1947, Pp. 46.

"Guy Can Always Learn Something." As Zinberg, *New Yorker,* March 15, 1947, Pp. 94.

"The Man Who Wouldn't Say Uncle." As Zinberg. *Esquire,* March 1949, Pp. 49.

"Curiosity Is Expensive." *Men to Men,* October 1950.

"The Real Sugar." *Esquire,* April 1951, p. 85.

"The Paradise Package." *Esquire,* June 1951, Pp. 60, 120, 123, 124.

"World of the Pug." As Zinberg. *American Mercury,* November 1951, Pp. 71–79.

"Over the Transom." *American Writer,* October 1953, p. 13.

"Blood Won't Wash Out." *Montreal Standard,* August 20, 1955.

"The Devil in Black Lace." *Mystery Digest,* July 1957, Pp. 63–70.

"Wet Bullets." *Mystery Digest,* July 1957.

"As Cockeyed As Truth." *Sleuth,* October 1958.

"Life Sentence." *Alfred Hitchcock's Mystery Magazine,* October 1958.

"What Malcolm Wanted." *Alfred Hitchcock's Mystery Magazine,* October 1958.

"We Are All Suspect." *Sleuth,* December 1958.

"Kill Nymph." *Mystery Tales,* August 1959, Pp. 1–22.

"Big Brains, Big Dough." *Off Beat,* September 1959.

"The Reality of Unreality." *Bestseller Mystery Magazine,* November 1959.

"Estimate of Rita." *Weekend Magazine,* June 21, 1961.

"Lucky Catch." *Alfred Hitchcock's Mystery Magazine,* May 1962.

"The Damn Fool." *Men's Magazine,* July 1962.

"I Did It for—Me." *The Saint,* September 1962, Pp. 101–104.

"The Smell of Roses." *Mike Shane Mystery Magazine,* 1962, Pp. 88–94.

"The Frozen Custard Caper." *Ellery Queen's Mystery Magazine,* January 1963.

"The Devil You Know." *The Saint,* April 1963.

"Murder Caribbean Style." *Argosy,* November 1963.

"The Cruise to Hell." *Manhunt,* July 1964.

"The Square Root of Death." *The Saint,* October 1964.

"Specialists." *Manhunt,* January 1965.

"Little Things." *Alfred Hitchcock's Mystery Magazine,* June 1965.

"The Juicy Mango Caper." *Ellery Queen's Mystery Magazine,* February 1966.

"Sic Transit …" *The Saint,* March 1966.

"The Listening Cone." *Alfred Hitchcock's Mystery Magazine,* April 1966.

"Break in the Routine." *Ellery Queen's Mystery Magazine,* June 1966.

"The Eunuch." *The Saint,* August 1966.

"Murder in Paradise." *Argosy,* July 1967, Pp. 1–128.

"More Than One Way to Skin a Cat." *Ellery Queen's Mystery Magazine,* July 1968.

CRITICAL AND BIOGRAPHICAL STUDIES

Barnes, Melvyn P. *Murder in Print: A Guide to Two Centuries of Crime Fiction.* London: Barn Owl Books, 1986.

Booker, M. Keith. *The Modern American Novel of the Left: A Research Guide.* Westport, Conn.: Greenwood Press, 1999.

Browne, Ray B. "Ed Lacy: Passage through Darkness." In his *Heroes and Humanities: Detective Fiction and Culture.* Bowling Green, Ohio: Bowling Green State University Popular Press, 1986. Pp. 47–54.

Fikes, Robert, Jr. "Adventures in Exoticism: The "Black Life" Novels of White Writers." *Western Journal of Black Studies* 26:6–15 (spring 2002).

Hynes, Jennifer. "Ed Lacy, August 15, 1911–January 7, 1968." In *Dictionary of Literary Biography.* Vol. 226, *American Hard-Boiled Crime Writers.* Edited by George Parker Anderson and Julie B. Anderson. New York: Gale, 2000. Pp. 226–232.

Lachman, Marvin. "Ed Lacy: Paperback Writer of the Left." In *Murder Off the Rack: Critical Studies of Ten Paperback Masters.* Edited by Jon. L. Breen and Martin Harry Greenberg. Metuchen, N.J.: Scarecrow Press, 1989. Pp. 15–34.

Reynolds, Paul. "The Dollars and Cents of Mystery Writing." In *The Mystery Writer's Handbook: A Handbook on the Writing of Detective, Suspense, Mystery and Crime Stories.* Edited by Herbert Brean. New York: Harper, 1956.

Schaub, Thomas Hill. *American Fiction in the Cold War.* Madison: University of Wisconsin Press, 1991.

Wald, Alan M. "Ed Lacy." in E*ncyclopedia of the American Left.* 2d ed. Edited by Mary Jo Buhle, Paul Buhle, and Dan Georgakas. London: Oxford University Press, 1998.

———. "The Urban Landscape of Marxist Noir." *Crime Time,* December 26, 2002.

———. *Writing from the Left: New Essays on Radical Culture and Politics.* Haymarket Series. London and New York: Verso, 1994.

—ROBERT NIEMI

Li-Young Lee

1957–

*F*ROM THE PUBLICATION of his first book, *Rose,* in 1986, Li-Young Lee took a prominent place in the crowded front row of younger American poets. His poem "Persimmons" appears in many anthologies and textbooks. Lee is also an immigrant, who came to America at the age of six with his family, and he is a part of the Chinese diaspora, as his brilliant poetic memoir, *The Winged Seed: A Remembrance* (1995), recounts.

This poet has a history of extraordinary richness. Li-Young Lee was born in Jakarta, Indonesia, on August 19, 1957, to Lee Kuo Yuan (also known as Richard K. Y. Lee) and Joice Yuan Jiaying. His mother's grandfather was Yuan Shikai, a warlord who eventually became the first president of China and, very briefly, self-proclaimed emperor. His father's grandfather was a gangster. According to Matt Miller's profile of Lee in the *Far Eastern Economic Review* (May 30, 1996), the poet's father fought on the Nationalist side in the Chinese civil war, but his commander switched sides. Lee Kuo Yuan then served as personal physician to Mao Tsetung for about nine months. But as a Christian and former Nationalist he was obviously uneasy in the position. He emigrated with his wife to Indonesia in 1950, where he taught at Gamaliel University, a Christian institution he helped to found. His courses included medicine, philosophy, and the King James Bible as literature. In 1958, he was arrested by order of President Sukarno and incarcerated for nineteen months. Then the family was placed on a ship to Macao, China. En route, one of the father's former students came alongside the vessel, took the family off, and brought them to Hong Kong. After sojourns in Hong Kong, Macao, and

Japan, the family emigrated to the United States in 1964, where Lee Kuo Yuan studied at the Pittsburgh Theological Seminary, eventually taking up the post of minister at a Presbyterian church in Vandergrift, Pennsylvania, a small town northeast of Pittsburgh. Li-Young says in *The Winged Seed* that parishioners referred to his father as their heathen minister. He has also said that racism in western Pennsylvania made it impossible to live there. He prefers the cosmopolitan atmosphere of Chicago, where he lives in one house with his wife and children, his brother Li Lin Lee (a distinguished painter), his brother's family, and his mother. His pleasure in having his relatives under one roof is clear in his poetry, which celebrates family intimacy in rich detail.

After attending Kiski Area High School, Li-Young Lee entered the University of Pittsburgh (1975–1979), where he studied biochemistry. He turned toward poetry only in his senior year. He came under the influence of the poet Gerald Stern, whose prophetic stance and poems influenced by Old Testament forms had a deep appeal. Li-Young's father was, if not a prophet, a man of enormous charisma, and he used the King James Bible to teach his son English. Neither Stern nor Lee is a poet whose work can easily be separated from his own identity as the author: little of Lee's slow unpacking of family memories through his volumes makes sense if the reader tries to ignore the autobiographical basis of the writing. Both poets are heirs of the Romantics, given to exalted utterance.

Lee started the MFA program at the University of Arizona in 1979. He told Amy Pence, who interviewed him for *Poets and Writers* (2001), that he "flunked out"; certainly he left the program. He studied at the State University of New York at Brockport in the 1980–1981 academic year, where he came under the influence of the poets William Heyen and, especially, Anthony Piccione, who became an important mentor and editor. He did not complete a degree at Brockport. He married Donna Bozzarelli in 1978, and they have two sons. In Chicago he has made a vocation as a full-time poet; for financial employment, he has worked in warehouses at tasks like moving books, taught karate, and taken part in a program to build parks in slums with the assistance of the local young people. He has taught occasionally at universities and is a popular reader of his work. The MFA dropout has won the Delmore Schwartz Memorial Poetry Award for his 1986 debut, *Rose;* the Academy of American Poets Lamont Poetry Selection for his second collection, *The City in Which I Love You* (published in 1990); a Mrs. Giles Whiting Foundation Writer's Award (1988); a Lannan Foundation Award (1994); and numerous grants and fellowships, including a Guggenheim Fellowship (1989).

ROSE

Li-Young Lee's first collection, *Rose,* appeared in 1986 with a cover by his brother, Li Lin Lee, and a foreword by Gerald Stern. One of Stern's interests in his preface is to trace influences in the poems, and he suggests Walt Whitman and Theodore Roethke among older writers, and James Wright, Galway Kinnell, and Philip Levine among more recent ones. He quite plausibly suggests that two devotional poets, George Herbert and Thomas Traherne, have also been influences. Lee himself has deep admiration for Robert Frost and Rainer Maria Rilke. Of course, the visionary poetry of Stern himself is a presence in Lee's work as well. Stern must have offered a path to the Romantic visionaries for Lee.

In a dismissive review of *Book of My Nights* (2001), William Logan suggests that Lee's lack of irony is a major weakness, laughable, in fact. However, irony is not a necessary element in visionary poetry. It could in fact be counterproductive.

The sensuous imagery of the biblical Song of Solomon and the spiritual struggles in the Psalms are major presences in Lee's work. Lee told Bill Moyers in an interview (collected in the 1995 volume *The Language of Life)* that he hated his poems because they were not the Song of Songs or Ecclesiastes. Exodus, he said, was his favorite book in the Bible: "the wandering of the children of Israel has profound resonance for me." As a member of the Chinese diaspora, Lee has a logical interest in the wanderings of the Israelites. His father's admiration for St. Paul (the senior Lee was, in his way, a wandering preacher like the first century apostle) has also left a mark on the work.

Ruth Y. Hsu deftly summarizes Lee's preoccupations:

> his sense of being part of a vast, global Chinese diaspora; his desire to understand and accept his father, whom he both loves and fears; and his identity's dimensions and textures, at least to the extent that those can be garnered from his relation to words, to the sensual, to love and passion.

She points out that "these themes often merge, informing each other." The three poems that open *Rose* fit her characterization. "Epistle" makes a fine prologue to all of Lee's work. As happens so often in his poems, he works with memory: here, the memory of his father's house at a moment when a young boy heard inexplicable weeping that began to sound like laughter. This scene foreshadows the effort in later poems to understand the past and to decode the ambiguous story of his father, whose career showed extraordinary ranges of behavior and attitude. The image of the child overhearing adult matters is so fundamental in human lives that it has almost archetypal status. The poem ends with the assertion that there was wisdom in the experience.

The book's second poem, "The Gift," juxtaposes two scenes: a father removes a metal splinter from his seven-year-old son's palm; the son, grown up, removes a splinter from under his wife's thumbnail. The poem ends with the narrator's memory of spontaneously kissing his father. The kiss is a frequent gesture in Lee's poems, with the depth and range probably suggested by the biblical readings so important in his parents' household. This mark of intimacy is crucial in the Song of Solomon (1:1, "My beloved kisses me with the kisses of his mouth"), the Gospels, and the Epistles of St. Paul (in which the admonition appears four times to "Greet one another with a holy kiss"). Kissing is also a motif in the poetry of Whitman, one of Lee's American influences. "The Gift" radiates tenderness and is precisely the kind of poem that has led critics to call Li-Young Lee sentimental. In his review of *Rose,* Roger Mitchell praises the poems but suggests that tenderness is not enough for poetry: "For one thing, tenderness is not an aesthetic matter. The poet determined to be tender will come to care less how a thing is said than that tenderness be displayed. For another, tenderness does not always mix well with truth." Lee's tone does at times include anger, as in the next poem in *Roses,* "Persimmons."

"Persimmons" deserves its fame as anthology piece. It dramatizes the situation—never an uncommon one in America—of the immigrant child who struggles to fit into a society that regards him or her as alien and receives mispronunciation of English words with ridicule. Lee describes being slapped by a teacher, Mrs. Walker, for being unable to distinguish "persimmon" from "precision." Further, he was made to stand in the corner, a visible exclusion from the schoolroom, a place that should have served as a means of acculturation rather than exclu-

sion. The experiences in the school are juxtaposed with scenes of family life, domestic scenes. In one, he lies in the yard naked with his wife, Donna, teaching her Chinese words, a scene of instruction very different from the sixth-grade classroom. He also recalls his mother saying that a persimmon has the sun inside. Mrs. Walker, he remembers, referred to the fruit as a "Chinese apple," an imprecise label, and she revealed her ignorance by feeding them to the class without realizing that they are unripe and bitter. The excluded Chinese immigrant has his symbolic revenge: he knows better and watches the faces of the others. The poem shifts its emotional register considerably at the end, recalling a moment when his blind father was given literal persimmons by his son—and symbolic ones. In the remembered scene, the son unwraps three paintings by his father, one of which depicts persimmons. The father recalls with emotion how he painted them in his blindness. The poem has revolved the image of the persimmon within the imagination, subjecting it to different emotional lighting, and ending with a scene full of pathos, a scene that affirms the value of art.

Lee's attitude toward the Chinese aspect of his identity is complex. He deplores any form of tokenism or ghettoizing of his work. In an interview with James Kyun-Jin Lee, the poet observed that the label "Asian American" is acceptable if it empowers writers but not if it makes them smaller than they are. He was steeped in study of the Bible and recognizes that the theme of exile is universal. "Diaspora" (Greek for "a scattering") was a term invented to describe the exiled condition of the Jews after their dispersal from Israel by the Romans in the first century, and it has been applied to a number of dispersed groups in modern times. In his interview with James Lee, the poet says: "I thought that trying to find an earthly home was a human condition. It's arrogant of the dominant culture to think it's not part of a diaspora."

Having been brought up by parents whose classical Chinese education enabled them to memorize and recite many T'ang Dynasty poems, Li-Young Lee naturally takes an interest in Chinese poetics, which emphasize the image. His father taught him about Taoist alchemy, a discipline that, as Carl Jung demonstrated, has deep psychological symbolism. Explaining his religious vision to Eileen Tabios, he cites Buddhist concepts well-known in China, like "universe-mind." He also speaks of the shock of perception a reader experiences when a poem is good; in Chinese, the aesthetic term would translate as "raising the head." In the same discussion he uses the very colloquial American term, "WOW!" to describe the moment of lyric revelation. He also likes to refer to the impact of a poem as a "Zenist aha!" This kind of cultural syncretism seems to cause him no strain.

The poems of Li-Young Lee are remarkably sensuous. Images of food and of the human body abound. In a major article on Lee's work, "Inheritance and Invention in Li-Young Lee's Poetry," Zhou Xiaojing observes that he tends to build poems around a central image, like a rose or hair. In *Rose,* there are three poems about hair that rank among his best. "Dreaming of Hair" mingles erotic images of the beloved's hair with scenes of touching the hair of family members. He recalls sleeping beside his mother when he was a child, and waking with her hair in his mouth, and he also remembers stroking the hairline of his sleeping brother Li-En. Images of touch permeate the poem as a mark of family intimacy. Eventually he imagines his dead father's hair bursting out of the grave. He ends the poem with a vision of his wife's hair as a veritable universe, filled with objects: "apples, walnuts, ships sailing."

The next poem in the book, "Early in the Morning," is a compressed lyric narrative, a memory of his father watching the poet's mother as she combs and pins her hair, supposedly because he likes to see her make it "kempt." But the son believes that the father's pleasure is actually the anticipation of removing the pins later and watching the mother's hair fall. Near the end of *Rose,* a poem called "Braiding" unifies the collection, metaphorically braiding it together by echoing other poems. The narrator describes braiding his wife's hair in the same way that his father braided the mother's, mirroring the past-present juxtaposition in "Gift," the poem about removing splinters. And the act of grooming expresses the love of husband and wife as it does in "Early in the Morning."

The poems "Eating Alone" and "Eating Together" are placed so that "Eating Alone" comes at the end of the first section, and the companion poem appears at the start of the third. They help to tie the volume together by appearing in prominent positions. In the first poem, the speaker gathers young onions for a dish he is going to cook. He remembers looking at windfall pears with his father and recalls the way that his father turned the pear into a moral lesson by pointing to a hornet struggling drunkenly in the sweet juice of a wild pear. The poem ends with a veritable recipe for a Chinese dish. The solitary meal has a joy of its own. Savoring loneliness is a common feeling in the T'ang poets whose work he heard from his parents. The other poem, "Eating Together," describes cooking a trout, which is shared among the mother and siblings. The mother gets the sweetest meat, the trout's head, and she holds it as the recently deceased father did weeks before. The image triggered conveys grief and consolation: the father lay down "like a snow-covered road", one "without any travelers, and lonely for no one."

Flower images run all through the collection. The brief lyric, "My Indigo," one of Lee's best, celebrates a flower that lives "in two worlds / at once." In "Irises," the desire to find an affinity with the nonhuman is so powerful that the speaker wants to tear the flowers with his teeth and investigate their "hairy selves." They serve as a symbol of death, turning as they do from violet to blue as they wither. Lee constantly uses physical images to explore the metaphysical, as if to concur with the saying by Robert Frost in the famous 1931 essay "Education by Poetry," that "it is the height of poetry, the height of all thinking, the height of all poetic thinking, that attempt to say matter in terms of spirit and spirit in terms of matter." Li-Young Lee's poetry increasingly longs for the spiritual, which he refers to as the invisible, but he approaches it through the visible.

The long poem "Always a Rose" gives his first book its name, and uses the rose very ambitiously as a symbol in series of ten meditations. The inception of the poem is the rescue of a rose with "petals still supple" from a heap of discarded flowers. The tone of the poem evokes Allen Ginsberg's 1955 poem "Sunflower Sutra" and reaches back to one of Ginsberg's masters, the Walt Whitman of "When Lilacs Last in the Dooryard Bloom'd," another poem in leisurely, repetitive sections with a tone of immense tenderness. In the final section, Lee even uses one of Whitman's favorite words for a poem, "recitative," to describe his own work. The speaker returns to the rescued flower over and over, associating it with members of his family and their griefs. In his review of *Rose*, Roger Mitchell objects to the conventional uses Lee makes of the flower: "The title poem, unfortunately, does not discover the flower but uses it, ready-made, for a host of metaphoric ends which, while ambitious, strains credulity." However, as Judith Kitchen says in her review, "Speaking Passions," there is a line in which the speaker makes the rose "wholly his by naming it: 'Cup of Blood, Old Wrath, Heart O' Mine, Ancient of Days, Whorl, / World, Word.'" This line is indeed the heart of the poem: Lee is renaming the traditional flower, as this list of epithets conveys in turn sacrifice, anger, deep feeling, the eternal, geometric form, the uni-verse, and language. The ancient symbol has been renewed by such a list. The poem is overlong but still has to be seen as a major effort. Li-Young Lee's debut volume is an impressive one.

THE CITY IN WHICH I LOVE YOU

Lee's second book, *The City in Which I Love You,* won the Lamont Poetry Award. The collection was given thorough and perceptive reviews, including a fine article by Walter A. Hesford in 1996 that examines the unifying role of the intertextual references to the Song of Songs in the book. Although Lee includes some short poems, the volume is dominated by three major works: "Furious Versions," "The City in Which I Love You," and "The Cleaving." The poet has the same preoccupation with family as in *Rose*, but he has a new concern with personal identity and the immigrant experience. Although the book was published in 1990, it reveals a strong anxiety about the coming new era of the twenty-first century, generated in part by remembrance of the upheavals of the twentieth.

Lee's understanding of the instability of the contemporary world is based on personal experience, and he offers strong testimony in "Furious Versions," a seven-part poem about what he calls "the murderous century." The versions are versions of the self and versions of experiences that he and his family have undergone. Lee takes a postmodern view of the individual as fluid. His religious stance as he defines it later in *Book of My Nights* goes against the grain of much postmodern theory, especially Jacques Derrida's deconstructionism, as the discussion of that work will make clear. But in "Furious Versions" the self is shown to be fragmented in a way compatible with the contemporary theories that distrust the very term "self," with its assumptions of unity. Lee's poem takes a place alongside Frank O'Hara's remarkable poem "In Memory of My Feelings" as an exploration of the instability of the person. O'Hara goes through a whole repertory of alter egos to explode the very notion of a single self. His poem is witty, even fanciful. But Li-Young Lee experiences the fluidity of experience as one of the terrors of a world in which arbitrary arrest and exile come without justification or warning.

The poem opens with a section in which the speaker awakes every day in "the used light / of someone's' spent life," to discover that his various names have been stripped of meaning. He feels "dismantled" and wonders if he should arise and go into an American city, or into the wilderness sea—to the docks where he could bribe an officer to let him and his wife and children depart. The last alternative conflates memories of exile from Indonesia with his present life. At times he seems to be his father, as when he suggest that he should "answer / in an oceanic tongue" (suggesting the Indonesian archipelago) to the titles, *"Professor, Capitalist, Husband, Father."* This moment blurs into memories of dusting the pews in his father's snowbound church, a memory followed by one of coming to America. He next imagines that he is his own father in an Indonesian jail. No wonder he then says, "Memory revises me." The final scene in the opening poem is the scene of composition,

On a page a poem begun, something
about to be dispersed,
something about to come into being.

The poem is conceived of as an unstable entity, not as a Shakespearean composition outlasting "marble and the gilded monuments." At the end of the sequence, the narrator returns to the scene of writing, describing himself more objectively in the third person.

The third and fourth sections of the poem trace a moment in which the speaker goes out the back door and looks at three flowers. They serve as a focus for his meditations on his his-tory. He questions whether the luxury of writing about such beauty is appropriate in a convulsive world. He consciously puts the act of writing into the poems itself, speaking of the drafts he is creating as "furious versions / of the here and now." Of course, the moment of contemplating the flowers in the night is at a distance from writing poem about that moment. In what must be an echo of T. S. Eliot's *Four Quartets* (1943), a work permeated with images of the rose, Lee says at the end of the third poem in the sequence that

Here, now, one
should say nothing
of three flowers, only enter with them
in silence, fear, and hope,
into the next nervous one hundred human years.

In the first of his quartets, "Burnt Norton," Eliot wonders if there is any point in "disturbing the dust on a bowl of rose-leaves," and he ends the poem with an examination of a remembered moment of children laughing in a rose garden, a moment that is "Quick now, here now, always."

Lee's narrative cannot stay off the subject of roses, and the next poem, number 4, admits that they "seize / my mind." He uses the flowers more effectively in this poem than in "Always a Rose," for he transcends the conventional symbolism by talking about a very personal association. His family home in Pennsylvania had a climbing rose, a variety called "Paul's Scarlet." He calls it a "wandering rose," suggesting restlessness and exile. It would have appealed to his father because of the association with St. Paul, the much-traveled missionary who was an ideal for the senior Lee. St. Paul

promised the coming
of the perfect and the departing of the imperfect,
Else why stand we in jeopardy every hour?

The italicized scripture (1 Corinthians 15:30) is part of a discussion of eternal life. At the end of the fifth poem, he remembers his father's scarlet rose as something perishable, aphid-ridden and sickly but still crying out *I shall not die!*, making it as indomitable as the father it symbolizes.

The fifth poem in "Furious Versions" tells a poignant story that underlines the father's powerful identity: the son remembers a blind man in America who recognized his father by the sound of his footsteps on the sidewalk. The senior Lee had helped the man bury his dead wife in Nanjing as bombs fell around them. This story leads Li-Young Lee to imagine the legendary Chinese poets "of the wandering heart," Li Bay (usually known in the West as Li Po) and Du Fu (Tu. Fu) on the sidewalks of Chicago. Both poets wandered, but not, of course, as far as Chicago. He visualizes them sailing paper boats down the gutter, just as they sailed paper boats made of poems down streams in China. The poem asserts the poet's right to bring Chinese culture into America. When they note the narrator's surprise, they respond: *What did you expect? Where else should we be?* A quality of much diasporic writing is the maintenance of connections with the first culture: the melting pot is an obsolete metaphor.

The sixth poem uses a symbolism more complex and more personal to the poet than the scarlet rose that symbolized the father. He muses on the sound of wind in poplar trees and the way that it resembles the sound of the sea. Lee, who has lived landlocked in America, grew up on an island nation and lived in exile on other islands—Hong Kong, Japan—before coming to the United States. He compares himself to landlocked poplars: "Far / from water, I'm full of the sound of water." Beyond that sound he hears something else, a sound suggesting the continuity of the universe. But he does not wish to fly from the human to the cosmic in this poem: he will tarry to tell his human story. He is preparing to connect himself to his early history before immigration to the interior of America. When he tells his story, he does it in

the third person, as if to indicate the distance from his original self. He did not speak until he was three years old, and the first utterances came as the family sailed into exile. The language he spoke then was not Chinese but, rather, perfectly articulate Malaysian, learned from the servants: "a Malaysian so lovely it was true song." He did not speak again he says—speaking figuratively—for twenty years, by which he must refer to his decision to write poetry. By then he "wore a stranger's clothes" and "married a woman who tasted of iron and milk."

The final poem in the sequence returns to the scene of writing, using third-person narration to give himself objective reality as a writer. Lee has said that he does much of his writing in the middle of the night, and this is the situation in the poem, with a narrator who is unable to see in the one (literal) darkness and who "has shut his eyes / to see into another," a figurative darkness. What is that darkness? We are told that "Among the sleepers, he is one / who doesn't sleep" as he works on a poem

> birthing itself
> into the new
> and murderous century.

There was ample darkness in the twentieth century and Lee is apprehensive of more in the twentieth-first.

The second long poem in the book, "The City in Which I Love You" provided its title. The city is inspired by the dark urban setting of The Song of Songs. The poem has an epigraph quoted, with one omission, from that book, chapter 3, verse 2:

> I will arise now, and go
> about the city in the streets,
> and in the broad ways I will seek …
> whom my soul loveth.

Walter A. Hesford suggests that the word "him" after "seek" has been omitted so that the poem is appropriate for a male speaker, but Lee probably means to make the poem appropriate for a speaker of either gender. The object of the search, according to both Jewish and Christian traditions of interpretation, is God, cast symbolically as the lover of the soul (or the Church, in some Christian readings). The nature of the beloved in Lee's poem is not defined: he may refer to God, or an idealized "Other," who would complete the self—the possibilities are left open to interpretation. At one point the speaker addresses the sought-for person as "smooth other, rough sister," contradictions that insist on ambiguity.

Lee's city is a nightmare landscape. In the Song of Songs, a woman searching for her lover in the dark streets is victimized: "the watchmen that went about the city found me, they smote me, they wounded me; the keepers of the walls took away my veil from me" (Song of Solomon 5:7). Lee's speaker suggests that he may meet a similar fate:

Yet, how will you know me

among the captives, my hair grown long,
my blood motley, my ways trespassed upon?

Furthermore, the nightmare city in Lee's poem is a place of linguistic confusions "of accents and inflections" where the narrator's voice may not be understood. Hesford sees the city as possibly not an American city but perhaps instead a city in Asia, or even strictly a symbolic construction. T. S. Eliot's "Unreal City" in "The Waste Land" (and the comparison is surely valid) is London in a sense, but also a timeless metropolis of confusion and vice, as much Carthage as London.

Much of the poem is given over to a list of suffering people in the city, people whom the speaker does not chose to see. That is, he does not extend empathy to them. Hesford suggests an implied contrast with Walt Whitman, who always assures his reader that he achieves full

communion with those he observes in his journeys of the imagination in *Leaves of Grass* (1855), identifying with both sexes and all conditions of life. Lee is perhaps also implying the Christian teaching that those who do not serve the poor and the sick and the imprisoned (Matthew 25:41–46) have failed to serve God. The text is a favorite with preachers, and Lee would doubtless have heard it often in his father's church.

The quest for the other is not resolved in the poem. The seeker has come "Straight from my father's wrath / and long from my mother's womb." He creates a context for his life: "late in this century … // my birthplace vanished, my citizenship earned," which expresses Li-Young Lee's situation. The poem promises that the quest for the other in the city will continue: "And I never believed that the multitude / of dreams and many words were vain." That hopeful ending may appeal to the reader without seeming earned, at least not yet.

Lee's books are carefully organized, and the next poem, "The Waiting," has an interesting relationship to the title poem. "The City in Which I Love You" records a quest that seems as spiritual as it is erotic, while "The Waiting" records a complex sexual relationship between a man and a woman who are also father and mother to two children. With great candor, the poem takes the reader into the marriage bed in terms far more graphic than the Song of Songs, a poem that goes only so far as to say "he lies between my breasts all night." Lee's poem is not prurient for all its frankness.

The shorter poems in *City* are good, but none seems quite on the level of the lyrics in *Rose*, like "The Gift," "Eating Alone," "Eating Together," and "My Sleeping Loved Ones." The outstanding poems in the volume are the long ones: "Furious Versions," "The City in Which I Love You, and the final poem, "The Cleaving," a complex work exploring the poet's Chinese identity and a number of other themes through a moment in a butcher shop. In her long review of the book, "Auditory Imagination: The Sense of Sound," Judith Kitchen suggests that "The Cleaving" has "the feel of a major American poem." The scope and complexity of the poem encourages such a judgment. Furthermore, it confronts one of the key figures in American literature, Ralph Waldo Emerson, affirming the value of a multicultural society against Emerson's contempt for the Chinese. The poem has been discussed brilliantly by Jeffrey F. Partridge in an article, "The Politics of Ethnic Authorship: Li-Young Lee, Emerson, and Whitman at the Banquet Table."

The verb "to cleave" is one of those primal words that means its own opposite: a blade cleaves an object, a man cleaves to his wife. Sigmund Freud thought that such words were at the roots of language and thought. Divisions and unions run through this poem. The poet watches a skilled butcher cleave a duck, and yet he realizes that in eating food his extended family of thirteen becomes a "many-membered // body of love." Chopping up bodies for food makes the union of a family around the table possible. The poet seeks the soul but life is a process of bodies devouring bodies. "We are nothing eating nothing."

The butcher's skills involve blood and grease, but Lee admires their elegance, another paradox. The butcher himself becomes a means for Lee to identify himself with his Chinese origins: some features of the man suggesting the Northern Chinese, others the Southern. It is easy for outsiders to assume that the Chinese are homogeneous in appearance and culture, but in fact they are not. Lee has a quarrel with the New England poet and essayist Ralph Waldo Emerson, who has a crucial role in Lee's adopted culture. Emerson, we learn from Lee's poem, thought the Chinese had the ugliest features on earth and that they had preserved them intact for "three or four thousand years." The source of this slander is a journal entry of 1824, in

which Emerson applies the term "reverend dullness" to China and says that all it can say to the convocation of nations is "I made the tea." The New England writer's lofty talk about the soul somehow issued in racism, and Lee refers to Emerson's transcendentalist philosophy as "soporific." In defiance of Emerson's rather rarefied notion that the soul is transparent, Lee describes eating a carp's head.

The most uncompromising physical imagery in the poem comes when the poet contemplates the split-open skull of the duck being cleaved by the butcher. Its brain resembles a tiny man, a grey homunculus. The poet believes this is how he looked before he was born, "before I tore my mother open," the kind of cleaving that, in biblical terms, results because a man "cleaves" to his wife. They become one flesh and the woman's body is eventually "cleaved" in childbirth. Latent in this symbolic essence of the human being is the potential for all the crimes of the century. But, when offered the brain by the butcher, the speaker swallows it, the first of several sacramental acts of symbolic cannibalism in the poem. The human being is capable of crime, and also of communion.

Much of the text is devoted to describing various kinds of symbolic eating. The speaker wants figuratively to devour the butcher: his body and his motions. This is a moment of racial self-acceptance, a counter to the disgust aroused by Chinese features in Emerson. In this epiphany in the butcher shop, the speaker has learned that the soul is not ethereal. It must be cleaved so that it can be restored, the kind of paradox at the heart of many religious teachings. The world is violent, full of things eaten, things cleaved, and one word for violence is change. It is necessary, the poet says, to "cleave to what cleaves me." At the end of the poem, the speaker can perceive the butcher's physiognomy as a "Shang dynasty face," an African face. The butcher is also "my sister, this / beautiful Bedouin, this Shulamite" (like the dark woman in the Song of

Songs). His father's Christian instruction would have instilled in the author the mystical perception that all categories can be transcended. Lee would have learned the claim of St. Paul in Galatians 3:28 that in Christ there is neither bond nor free, male nor female, Greek nor Jew. Here he is using that kind of thinking without casting it in Christian terms. Human variety is celebrated as the poet acknowledges kinship with

... this Jew, this Asian, this one
with the Cambodian face, Vietnamese face, this
    Chinese
I daily face, this immigrant,
this man with my own face.

Otherness can be embraced because sameness is implicit within difference; cleaving is also "cleaving to." The movement in *The City in Which I Love You* has been from the exploration of a variety of selves in "Furious Versions" to a final epiphany in which the speaker's Chinese ancestry is defended at the same moment that he celebrates humanity in all its racial variety

THE WINGED SEED

Li-Young Lee's 1995 memoir, *The Winged Seed,* a winner of the American Book Award of the Before Columbus Foundation, is an autobiography in the form of an extended prose poem. It manages to be an immigrant autobiography about a family in the Chinese diaspora and at the same time explores that familiar terrain of memoirs in the 1990s, the dysfunctional family. The key figures are an immensely powerful personality, the poet's father, and his gifted poet son, the stone upon which the blade of the father broke, according to Li-Young Lee's mother. One of the ironies of the book is that the son's silence and forgetfulness were qualities that his father hated, but now that the father is silent in death, the son has become extraordinarily eloquent.

The only comparable works in recent American writing are Maxine Hong Kingston's *The Woman Warrior* (1976) and *China Men* (1980), which uses fantasy and a rich prose style to illuminate first-generation immigrant experience (her parents') and second generation (her own). Li-Young Lee arrived in America at the age of six, making his work first generation. He has much to say about the shock of arrival and the difficulties of acculturation in the racist environment of western Pennsylvania. He talks at length about a young woman he calls "Philadelphia Wong," Whom he met at a religious retreat, where she pretended ignorance of things Chinese, one kind of response to being an outsider in America. Particularly interesting are the comments on language: he is aware that non-European accents are grating on the ears of many Anglophones. Chinese is a pitch-based language, and the sounds are interpreted by the inexperienced ear as a repellent sing-song, as the young Li-Young discovered in school. He also learned in school that some people in East Vandergrift circulated disgusting rumors about his family, stories about grotesque diet and customs, and hints of incest.

As interesting as the book may be as an immigrant memoir, most of it is devoted to family dynamics. The source of the family's energy was the poet's father, a man with outsized abilities and a life that seems fictional. The book offers strong insights into a multicultural, multilingual family: Lee's exposure to the Javanese language and culture in childhood gets much attention. (English is actually his third rather than his second language.) Over the course of the memoir, Lee provides the history of his family in Indonesia, focusing on his father's imprisonment and the escape of the family in a daring rescue at sea. Lee's youth and his long ordeal caring for his dying father are covered in some detail.

The presentation of this history, however—and the experience, in general, of reading *The Winged Seed*—is profoundly nonlinear. The work is written in a lush prose heavily influenced by the Song of Songs, with sentences like "A man ringing, a man run with the twelve secret hips of honey, a signal odor of chrysanthemums, the recipe for snow, and the permanent address of the rose." The opening pages are built on a motif of night, and this passage is typical of the style of much of the book:

> Night is night as is, without hands. Night is night even if it's a basin of fire. Night is night though it's tentacle and maelstrom, night even a bloody custard, the body, dear trough, even if my hand a possible face ... night past the color of archipelago. O, how may I touch you across this chasm of flown things? What won't the night overthrow, the wind unwrite? Where is the road when the road is carried? What story do we need to hear, so late in childhood? This early in the future, roses exact all our windows, night the wound and way in, night my pink, rude thumb stopper and sink, mustard and ache, my club and good yam, the radish king in his red jacket and green embroidered slippers, writing his letter to the queen of the snails, saying *I crave your salty foot, give me a drink from your horn.*

The passage has several stylistic qualities that are typical of Lee's memoir: the use of metaphor, as in night is "a basin of fire"; the mysterious images, like "my club and good yam"; the rhetorical question; the bit of animistic mythmaking with creatures like the snail; the unabashed romantic tone, as in the apostrophe, "O, how may I touch you"; and the apparent double entendres in phrases like "pink, rude thumb stopper and sink" and "the radish king in his red jacket." The most vivid images in the text recall the Song of Songs, Lee's fundamental influence.

The narrative of *The Winged Seed* takes the form of an address to the poet's wife, Donna, and it moves from poetic meditations on poetically freighted subjects—like night or seeds—to anecdotes, often by what appears to be free association. Stories are embedded in other stories, so that the memory of a pastoral visit by Li-Young Lee and his father to see Mrs. Black contains an account of the father's evangelical work in Hong Kong and his days at the Pittsburgh theological seminary. The story of the family's life in Indonesia is interpolated into several episodes. The frequent use of highly symbolic dreams provides nonlinear narratives within episodes of the text.

The extraordinary organization of the work probably grew out of its unusual mode of composition. Lee wanted to capture his story in a text written in a single night, to make it somehow a single statement. That proved impossible. Instead, he repeatedly tried to write the story in three nights, fresh efforts made over a period of seven years, until he and his editor, Gary Lukeman, felt that he had a text worth publishing. He wanted to give "the feel of a moment's thought," he says on the first of his Lannan Foundation videos. As he tells Shawn Wong in an interview on that recording, the goal of autobiography is to uncover the self, and the self is different each time, so he created a succession of versions before he and his editor thought the work was right. This method is remarkably similar to Jack Kerouac's "spontaneous composition." Kerouac famously (or notoriously) wrote the published version of *On the Road* in twenty days on a long roll of paper, but that version was actually the third attempt to write the novel. Lee, like Kerouac, writes with words or phrases as leitmotifs: indeed, they happen to share the use of "night" as a recurring term.

The most important motif, as the title implies, is the symbol of the seed. Lee may be echoing the symbol of the "wingéd seeds" in Percy Bysshe Shelley's "Ode to the West Wind" (1819), which die but also serve as symbols of rebirth. He does in fact pronounce "winged" as two syllables in readings. The seeds in his poem do have a specific history: Lee's father carried a pocket full of morning glory seeds, which he told his son were for remembrance, which for a refugee is a poignant duty if a heritage is to be preserved. (The Hebrew term for "remember" appears over a hundred times in the Bible.) But that answer was not enough, and throughout the book Li-Young Lee ponders the meaning of the seed. It is a good symbol for the Chinese diaspora, for seeds wander and may, if conditions are right, take root. Winged seeds may wander very far. The seed, the son considers, can also be a symbol of "good news," the root meaning of "gospel." Christ's parable of the sower uses the metaphor of seed to suggest that the truth is spread like seed. He wonders too if a seed somehow embodies the Kingdom of Heaven, turning Christ's simile in Matthew 13:31, "the kingdom of heaven is like to a grain of mustard seed," into a metaphor. Lee recalls his father's "sermon on the seed," delivered in a church basement in Pennsylvania during a blizzard in 1975. The basic text for this memoir, the heart of its meaning, is surely John 12:24, which the King James Bible translates: "Verily, verily, I say unto you, Except a corn of wheat fall into the ground and die, it abideth alone: but if it die, it bringeth forth much fruit." One long episode in the book tells the story of a seed on a journey with the aspirations of "becoming a great rice." It encounters a knife who, in a familiar pattern from folklore and fairy tales, requires it to play a life-or-death riddling game. The riddles are really symbolic parables in a style evoking the poet W. S. Merwin, another product of small town Pennsylvania parsonage. No one would be likely to interpret the riddles if Li-Young Lee did not explain them. The seed wins the game but the angry knife kills it, which appears to make the riddle game futile. But of course the death of a seed is necessary for it to engender anything. The morning glory, which has only aesthetic rather than practical value, is one of those seeds that needs to be nicked with a knife or soaked overnight to generate. The parable prefigures the later image of the narrator as a stone against which the blade of his father's patience broke, a metaphor created by his mother near the end of *The Winged Seed*.

The seed is a symbol not only for a religious message but also a symbol of art, which can nourish like wheat or at least provide beauty like the morning glory. At one point, Lee reconstructs from memory a sermon his father gave at an Ambassadors for Christ retreat in Maryland. The sermon—which is clearly amplified by the poet-son—stresses that a seed is tiny but has an enormous house inside, a variation on the traditional microcosm-macrocosm symbolism. Lee likes to describe the great lyric poem as "manifold," and in his first Lannan Foundation videotape he reads Rainer Maria Rilke's *Sonnets to Orpheus,* 1:23, praising it highly for creating multiple modes of consciousness in a single fourteen-line sentence. Related to the seed as house symbolism is a model of Solomon's Temple that Lee says his father spent almost four years making. The description of the construction of the cardboard model comes immediately after Lee has suggested that a seed is a kind of house. The Temple, Lee reminds us, "lives only in the sentences of its description and only inside the reader of those sentences." Lee's father turned the sentences into a model. The reader of the sentences in *The Winged Seed* enters a temple of words which contains the lives and histories of the Lee family. Near the end of the memoir, Li-Young imagines a seed in his hand saying, *"It is not time to fly. Tell me a story."* So many stories have been packed into this house constructed of sentences: the life of Li-Young's mother as the child of aristocrats in China; the story of the ruthless paternal grandfather whose behavior was cruel and dishonest; the story of an early childhood spent in Jakarta with visits to the village of his nurse, whose world was shot through with superstitions; the story of persecutions and murders carried out against the ethnic Chinese by Sukarno's government.

The temple built by the father is one of the many things lost on the journeys of exile. Other things were deliberately destroyed: Li-Young Lee described the burning of most of his father's papers and painting after his death, without explaining the family's motives for doing so. But one son was burned by a spark from the fire, a visible sign of the indelible impression this charismatic father made on the psyches of his family.

Among other important symbols in the book, shoes as emblems are especially prevalent. Li-Young Lee opens his memoir with a dream in which his father returns from the grave and walks from Pennsylvania to Chicago to attend a family reunion: his shoes are naturally battered and worn. The shoe references work to suggest pilgrimage and also to suggest that the son cannot—as the saying goes—fill the shoes of his father. There is even a reference to his father's sermon on shoes.

The most exotic use of symbols comes in a discussion of Chinese characters. The pages on characters and their meaning is like a quick course in the pictographic nature of Chinese writing. For example, the character for the sun is explored in the text, and Lee proceeds to personify the sun and celebrate it as the capital letter R. (In Mandarin, the word for sun is pronounced, approximately, as "ri.") Lee makes the sun a companion, a seeker, an audience, and a new form of the East, a figure so powerful that "I put off my shoes to meet it," as Moses did when he saw the burning bush that represented God. Then, in a startling turn, the sun becomes a personification of his father's mortality, a being dwelling in the dying man's bones, something that mysteriously emerges on the day of the father's death out of a bouquet of roses carried by Donna Lee, the poet's wife.

Some of the strongest passages in *The Winged Seed* deal with the father's last days, when his eighteen-year-old son had to care for the helpless man. Lee moves from a long, tender description of bathing the father to a graphic description of donning rubber gloves to empty bowels that no longer move on their own. The range of this compact memoir is remarkable, taking in stark realism, magic realism (the description of mysterious hailstones on the family house in tropical Jakarta), dreams, animistic fables like the story of the rice and knife, and long passages of incantational prose poems built on refrains. These materials all illuminate the pilgrimage of a family that moved from the Far East to Pennsylvania, led by a Chinese patriarch of near-biblical stature. Throughout, love is the key emotion, though it is bound up with fear and antagonism when the father's mesmerizing role in the life of the family is described. Lee has said that his attitude to his father was awe rather than fear, but he must surely know that fear is one of the synonyms for awe. This demanding and harrowing book was not a best seller like the memoirs of Maxine Hong Kingston, Mary Karr, or Tobias Wolff, but its value cannot be measured by sales.

BOOK OF MY NIGHTS

Night is the most frequent setting in Li-Young Lee's work. His third book of poems, which won the William Carlos Williams Award from the Poetry Society of America, is essentially a set of nocturnes, poems of sleeplessness, of dreams, of death as a deeper form of sleep, of night as a setting for the spiritual to manifest itself. He told Amy Pence in *Poets & Writers* that "the writing of a poem is an uncovering of language to its sacred condition." The images of night and the stars, along with the melancholy tone in many of the poems, suggest Rilke, a poet whom Lee admires deeply. David Roderick's perceptive review of the book notes that the poems are all elegies. The language is more abstract than in the earlier volumes and the tone is less anguished, though it has touches of spiritual longing. The mood is restlessness, a desire to achieve the silence in which the divine can manifest itself. Like the great mystic St. John of the Cross, Lee assumes that illumination can come, paradoxically, in the dark night of the soul. Lee's interviews have increasingly emphasized his desire to go beyond the visible to invisible meanings. What his poems must avoid is that "transparent soul" that he found soporific in Emerson.

The opening poem, "Pillow," suggests that nocturnal restlessness contains everything: "Voices in the trees, the missing pages / of the sea," and "discarded wings, lost shoes, a broken alphabet." Under the pillow is "everything but sleep," a way of saying that the insomniac ponders everything. Two later poems, "The Sleepless" and "Our River Now," printed one after the other, suggest that sleeplessness points the way to richer experience. In "Our River Now," the sleepless child lies awake saying his given name over and over until he becomes aware that not only is he the self accounted for by this name, but also he is a "dumb throng," a multiple and illimitable panoply of potential selves. The poem ponders the possibility that we have a "beginningless past" that predates the limited self represented by the name bestowed by parents at birth.

Most of the poems are more abstract than Lee's previous work. They lack "the reek of the human," in William Wordsworth's phrase: there are no recipes for steaming a fish for a communal meal, no descriptions of braiding or loosening hair, no schoolroom scenes about persimmons. Lee has great metaphysical aspirations. In his first Lannan videotape, he suggests that the lyric poet aims at an ecstatic utterance, voice "free of gender, free of culture, free of time," and wonders if it would be possible to create a new interiority, as the surrealists did once. In an interview with Marie Jordan, he speaks of the world as saturated in what he calls "presence," and of poetry as a way of revealing a "transpersonal presence," saying that "to me, everything is saturated with luminosity and meaning." Lee told Tod Marshall in an interview that the poet is not simply a witness of the vis-

ible: "Our mission is witnessing the invisible and making it revealed in the visible so that everybody can line up and know what they are lining up with." Lee's work is a challenge, conscious or not, to the deconstructionist thought of the French philosopher Jacques Derrida, who believes that language can never deliver presence. Or more fundamentally, Derrida believes that it can never deliver the absolute, whether it is called God (Lee's term) or the transcendental signified (Derrida's term). Derrida's assumption that we are "logocentric," placing too much confidence in the word, is counter to Lee's belief, drawn from the opening verses of the Gospel of St. John, that the Word (*Logos* in the original) is with God and is God. Lee's poetry is increasingly a quest for God, though not in a narrow sectarian fashion. As he told Michael Silverblatt on a Lannan videotape:

There's a place in Hawaii where the island is being born and lava is pouring out, and several miles down it hardens into these patterns, and it seems to me formal religion is just the worship of those hardened patterns. Whereas the poet or the artist lives right at the mouth of that and suffers whatever ... has to happen. But one is constantly giving birth to new images, new symbols, new faces of God; you know, new symbols for God, for the Godhead.

Two of the best poems in *Book of My Nights* work particularly well because their images keep them anchored in the visible in spite of their concern with spiritual realities. Particularly fine is "Black Petal," a poem about his brother Tai, who died in Jakarta when he was very young, a victim of spinal meningitis. The dead brother is kept under the speaker's pillow through the imagination. Various evocative statements are attributed to the brother, who answers to metaphorical names like "Vacant Boat, / Burning Wing, My Black Petal" because he died too young to know his name. Lee's claim in "Our River" that human beings are more than the name given them by their parents is made more concrete here: the metaphors are potentially limitless, each conveying a strong emotion. The Word cannot be limited to an ordinary human name. In another poem, "Night Mirror," Lee suggests that we all enter into a state of being beyond the limits of mortal names:

> … Time is the salty wake
> of your stunned entrance upon
> no name.

One of the lessons Lee imagines learning from the dead brother in "Black Petal" is an acceptance of change:

> Does someone want to know the way to spring?
> He'll remind you
> the flower was never meant to survive
> the fruit's triumph.

The other outstanding poem in the collection is "My Father's House," one of Lee's most challenging. In it, he emulates Rilke by creating manifold meanings. His poem combines narrative and dream and is also a tissue of evocative metaphors. His work was written in response to his brother's series of sixteen paintings, *Corban Ephphata* that hang in the Art Institute of Chicago. Li-Young Lee's poem was published in Edward Hirsch's 1994 anthology of literary works responding to paintings in the Art Institute. In "Writing the Universe-Mind," Eileen Tabios, who benefited from conversations with the poet about his work and creative influences, discusses the genesis and successive drafts of the poem, some of which she reprints. Tabios writes that the poem was originally called "The Father's House," and one influence it reflects is that of the thirteenth-century German mystic, Meister Eckehart, whose writings (which Tabios effectively quotes) support Lee's interest in presence and sheer being. She also points perceptively to continuities between the poem and *The Winged Seed,* juxtaposing some passages from each. She asked Lee about the seed and night images that permeate the memoir, and he responded by suggesting that for him "seed" and "night" are one word: "One is so tiny and packed and the other is immense and without boundary. But because they're opposite, they're the same. I feel they are the same because the infinite can be so small—like (William) Blake's seeing the universe in a grain of sand."

The title of Li Lin Lee's *Corban Ephphatha* comes from a term Christ used in the Gospels when he healed people. "Corban" means a gift for God that remains for the time being in the possession of the giver, and "ephphatha" means "let it be opened." Lee told Eileen Tabios that the phrase seems to mean "that in healing the person Christ was offering 'a gift of God to be opened.' " It seems from the title that Li Lin's work is about healing or the desire to be healed. The series as a whole takes the form of a grid of symbols, some as simple as a cross or an hourglass, others suggesting stylized landscape features. The poet sees his brother's work as a depiction of the "universe-mind," which, he told Tabios, "connects us to who we really are." Such a connection would indeed be a form of healing, and Li-Young Lee's poem does deal with the desire to restore health after the trauma of a parent's death.

The poem focuses on the poet sweeping his father's house after that death. It affirms the continuity of life with the sentence, repeated with variations three times in the poem, "And someone has died, and someone is not yet born." The poem is written in couplets, most of them running over into the next couplet, providing slight pauses between the units without suppressing flow. The events are not straightforward realism: very quickly the speaker describes a letter his father never wrote to the family, one that uses the familiar image of the seed, suggesting that it must be tested by death and lightning before it can deliver a message. The letter itself describes a seed in characteristic terms, as house containing a thorn (a symbol of pain or grief) or

a wee man carving

a name on a stone, ...
the name of the one who has died, the name of
* the one*

not born unknown.

In the interval between the death and the coming birth, the speaker tells us that he occupies himself sweeping the three floors of his parents' house. Lee told Tabios that he considers such acts of housekeeping (including the folding of laundry later in the poem) a spiritual practice, and religions ranging from Catholicism and Zen Buddhism would concur. As he sweeps, he feels the presence and hears the voice of an unidentified female figure; he explained to Tabios that he himself finds the figure mysterious: perhaps she is a muse, or a Jungian anima—the archetype of the interpreter. As he continues with housekeeping chores by folding laundry, he hears women in a circle telling a story, the kind of activity common at any time but almost certain to take place after a death. He knows that he cannot capture the story but he obeys a command from the female voice to sleep, so he obeys, lying

down
on the clothes, the folded and unfolded, the life

and the death.

Ages go by and the elusive story has had an effect, creating a new reality: the firmament has become a domain, the domain a house (another example of the very large packed into the very small), and the boundaries of the story have enlarged to encompass the one dead and the one not born: the story seems to represent the poem in which it appears in a kind of self-reflective gesture. Some peace seems to have been achieved, for the speaker recalls two brothers, presumably the painter and the poet, reading a book to each other. So much of Lee's poetry has dealt with conflicts with the father. Now there is a new phase in the master narrative running through his work: a memory of perfect accord between the siblings, who read the story "Once in two voices, to each / other; once in unison." This event triggers a complex final epiphany, for the sun becomes an office that the brothers sit inside, and the birds "lend their church, sown / in air," created perhaps by the pattern of their movements. This imagined church is also a body "uttering / windows, growing rafters, couching seeds." Once again the microcosm and macrocosm have transformed into each other: the house is a body, the body a house. The poem is impossible to paraphrase because of its metaphoric richness, but it seems to end in a hopeful symbolic metamorphosis, a gift of healing. The final images are expansive. The poet's aspiration has been to find metaphorical terms to convey invisible realities and in this poem he has gone further than in any work in the collection.

Lee achieved a great deal in his first four books, the three poetry collections and the memoir. He pursues a more daring path in *Book of My Nights,* an effort to express the inexpressible. His lack of irony and his romantic diction make him vulnerable to critics like William Logan, who finds his poetry sentimental and obvious, but he has had many defenders and a considerable readership. On November 1, 2002, the website of *Poets & Writers* magazine noted that in the year since Li-Young Lee appeared on the cover of the magazine's November/December 2001 print issue, his collection *Book of My Nights* had sold more than ten thousand copies. For poetry in the early twenty-first century, this figure is very high. Li-Young Lee's work is a winged seed that has traveled very far and found earth in which to flourish.

Selected Bibliography

WORKS OF LI-YOUNG LEE

POETRY AND AUTOBIOGRAPHY

Rose. Brockport, N.Y.: BOA Editions, 1986.

The City in Which I Love You. Brockport, N.Y.: BOA Editions, 1990.

The Winged Seed: A Remembrance. New York: Simon and Schuster, 1995. Saint Paul, Minn.: Hungry Mind Press, 1999.

Book of My Nights. Rochester, N.Y.: BOA Editions, 2001.

CRITICAL AND BIOGRAPHICAL STUDIES

Baker, David. "Culture, Inclusion, Craft." *Poetry* 18, no. 3:158–175 (June 1991). Reprinted in his *Heresy and the Ideal: On Contemporary Poetry.* Fayetteville: University of Arkansas Press, 2000.

Engles, Tim. "Li-Young Lee's 'Persimmons.'" *Explicator* 54, no. 3:191–192 (spring 1996).

Hamill, Sam. "A Fool's Paradise." *American Poetry Review* 20, no. 2: 33–40 (March-April 1991).

Hesford, Walter A. "*The City in Which I Love You:* Li-Young Lee's Excellent Song." *Christianity and Literature* 46, no. 1:37–60 (autumn 1996).

Hess, David. "Letter to Kent Shaw, Revisited." *Jacket* 20 (December 2002). http://jacketmagazine.com/20/hess-shaw.html.

Hirsch, Edward, ed. *Transforming Vision: Writers on Art.* Boston: Little, Brown, 1994.

Hsu, Ruth Y. "Li-Young Lee." *Dictionary of Literary Biography.* Vol. 165, *American Poets since World War II.* Fourth Series. Edited by Joseph Conte. Detroit: Gale, 1996. Pp. 139–146.

Huang, Yibing. "*The Winged Seed: A Remembrance.*" *Amerasia Journal* 44, no. 2:189–191 (summer 1998). (Review.)

Kitchen, Judith. "Auditory Imagination: The Sense of Sound." *Georgia Review* 45, no. 1:154–169 (spring 1991).

———. "Speaking Passions" *Georgia Review* 42, no. 2:407–422 (summer 1988).

Knowlton, Jr., Edgar C. Review of *The City in Which I Love You. World Literature Today* 65, no. 4: 771–772 (autumn 1991).

Logan, William. "The Real Language of Men." *New Criterion* 21, no. 4:73–80 (December 2002).

Miller, Matt. "Darkness Visible: Li-Young Lee Lights up His Family's Muky Past with Poetry." *Far Eastern Economic Review,* May 30, 1996, Pp. 34–36.

Mitchell, Roger. "*Rose.*" *Prairie Schooner* 63, no. 3:129–137 (fall 1989).

Moeser, Daniel. "Lee's 'Eating Alone.'" *Explicator* 60, no. 2:117–119 (winter 1002).

Muske, Carol. "Sons, Lovers, Immigrant Souls." *New York Times Book Review,* January 27, 1991, Pp. 7, 20–21.

Neff, David. "Remembering the Man Who Forgot Nothing." *Christianity Today* 32:63 (September 1988).

Partridge, Jeffrey F. "The Politics of Ethnic Authorship: Li-Young Lee, Emerson, and Whitman at the Banquet Table." *Studies in the Literary Imagination* 37, issue no. 1:103-126 (spring 2004).

Roderick, David. "*Book of My Nights:* Li-Young Lee." *Prairie Schooner* 77, no. 3:171–173 (fall 2003). (Review.)

Slowik, Mary. "Beyond Lot's Wife: The Immigration Poems of Marilyn Chin, Garrett Hongo, Li-Young Lee, and David Mura." *MELUS* 25, no. 3–4:221–242 (fall-winter 2000).

Smock, Frederick. "So Close to the Bone." *American Book Review* 10, no. 1:7, 14 (March-April 1988).

Tabios, Eileen. "Li-Young Lee's Universe-Mind—A Search for the Soul." In her *Black Lightning: Poetry in Progress.* Philadelphia: Temple University Press, 1998. Pp. 110–132.

Yao, Steven G. "The Precision of Persimmons: Hybridity, Grafting, and the Case of Li-Young Lee." *LIT: Literature Interpretation Theory* 12, no. 1:1–22 (April 2001).

Xiaojing, Zhou. "Inheritance and Invention in Li-Young Lee's Poetry." *MELUS* 21, no. 1:113–132 (spring 1996).

Xu, Wenying. "Li-Young Lee." *Asian American Poets: A Bio-Bibliographical Critical Sourcebook.* Edited by Guiyou Huang. Westport, Conn.: Greenwood Press, 2002. Pp. 205–211.

INTERVIEWS

"A Conversation with Li-Young Lee." *Indiana Review* 21, no. 2:101–108 (1999).

Bilyak, Dianne. "Interview with Li-Young Lee." *Massachusetts Review* 44, issue 4:600-612 (winter 2003).

Jordan, Marie. "An Interview with Li-Young Lee." *Writers' Chronicle* 34, no. 6:35–40 (May/summer 2002).

Lee, James K. "Li-Young Lee." *Words Matter: Conversations with Asian American Writers.* Edited by King K. Cheung. Honolulu: University of Hawaii Press, 2000. Pp. 270–280.

Marshall, Tod. "To Witness the Invisible." *Kenyon Review* 22, no. 1:129–147 (winter 2000). Reprinted in Tod Marshall, *Range of the Possible: Conversations with Contemporary Poets.* Spokane: Eastern Washington University Press, 2002.

Moyers, Bill. *The Power of the Word.* Program 4: *Voices of Memory.* Videotape. Moyers Collection, 1994. (Interviews and readings featuring Gerald Stern and Li-Young Lee, first aired on PBS in 1989.) Transcribed interview with Lee included in Moyers, *The Language of Life: A Festival of Poets.* New York: Doubleday, 1995. Pp. 257–269.

Pence, Amy. "Poems from God." *Poets & Writers* 29, no. 6:22–27 (November-December 2001).

Silverblatt, Michael. *Li-Young Lee,* vol. 2. Videotape. Lannan Foundation, 2001. (Reading with Interview).

Waniek, Marilyn Nelson. "A Multitude of Dreams." *Kenyon Review* 13, no. 4:214–226 (fall 1991).

Wong, Shawn. *Li-Young Lee,* vol. 1. Videotape. Lannan Foundation, 1995.

—BERT ALMON

Susanna Rowson

1762–1824

SUSANNA HASWELL ROWSON reinvented herself many times throughout her life, as an actor, playwright, lyricist, poet, writer, and educator. However, in all her pursuits, the desire to teach young women remained constant. It is evident in the professional manner in which she conducted herself in the theater; the independent women she created in her poems, plays, and fiction; and the progressive education she offered at her academy for women, the first of its kind in Boston.

During her lifetime, Rowson's many accomplishments made her a celebrated figure in the Northeast. Although several early biographies were written after her death, it was not until the 1960s that scholars began to recognize the significance of her work in the history of culture, literature, and women's education in the early American Republic. The simple, direct writing style of her novels is now seriously analyzed, revealing an early feminist ideology. Much has changed in how Rowson, like other women writers, is perceived by scholars. What has not changed is the source of Rowson's fame: she is still best known for her most successful novel, *Charlotte Temple* (1794), America's first best seller with more than two hundred editions. It continues to intrigue literary scholars, bibliographers, bibliophiles, and historians of American publishing.

CHILDHOOD AND YOUTH

Susanna Haswell was born in the vibrant seaport of Portsmouth, England, on February 5(?), 1762, the only child of William and Susanna Musgrave Haswell. When Susanna's mother died less than two weeks later, Haswell hired a nurse for his daughter. William Haswell, who served in the royal navy, shipped out to Massachusetts in 1763 and left his daughter in England with relatives. During his tour in the American colonies, Haswell bought a home and settled in Hull, Massachusetts, a town lying at the entrance to Boston Harbor. In 1765, he married Rachel Woodward, the daughter of a successful merchant. Two years later, he returned to England and brought his now five-year-old daughter with her nurse to America. During the journey, the threesome faced storms and possible starvation, which left a deep impression on Susanna; she described disastrous sea voyages repeatedly in her later fiction.

Once settled in America, the Haswell family grew; Robert was born in 1768 and William Jr. sometime later. Information on Susanna's relationship with them and her stepmother is scant. She wrote nothing about her brothers, but scholars suggest similarities between the stepmother in the 1792 novel *Rebecca*, Mrs. Littleton, and Rowson's own stepmother. Of Mrs. Littleton, Rowson writes: "her sentiments were therefore narrow and illiberal, and she possessed that kind of worldly knowledge, which rendered her suspicious of the integrity of every human being." (1794 ed., 9)

The Haswells lived in an old house, performed their own chores, and owned only one cow, but they possessed a small library that gave Susanna access to Homer, Edmund Spenser, John Dryden, and William Shakespeare. James Otis

(1725–1783), an influential politician, writer, and family friend, became her de facto tutor by frequently spending time with Susanna in conversation, a relationship she would proudly recall later in life. Otis was the brother of the first American female playwright and historian, Mercy Otis Warren (1728–1814). A self-educated woman, Rowson was, throughout her life, alternately self-conscious about her lack of formal education and self-confident in her ability to instruct women.

When the Revolutionary War broke out in 1775, the Haswells felt divided in their loyalties. Hull was populated almost entirely by American patriots, and the town had been boycotting British goods since 1770. William Haswell was married to an American, had two sons born in America, and owned property, but was still an officer in the royal navy. As the fighting drew closer to Hull during the first year of the war, it became increasingly difficult for Haswell to remain neutral. In 1775 the patriots denied his request to return to England and the family was imprisoned in a house in Hingham, Massachusetts. In December 1777, they were moved to a small house in Abington, where Rachel Haswell and Susanna's brothers grew ill. Throughout the winter of 1777–1778, the family lived on Indian bread and potatoes and the goodwill of friends. In May 1778, Haswell was moved to Nova Scotia in a prisoner's exchange; from there, the family sailed to England. Susanna never lost her respect for Americans, but she was deeply affected by the war and it infused her imagination. Later, she would become one of the first writers to draw on her experiences of the American Revolution in fiction.

Few details of Susanna's life in London are known. She attended the theater with her father, and when she began writing plays as an adult, Susanna found inspiration in the works of women playwrights such as Harriett Lee (1757–1851). A third brother, John Montresor, was born, and her father and stepmother became ill. At the age of sixteen Susanna began supporting her family. Scholars surmise that she, like the protagonist of *Rebecca,* worked as a governess. Susanna possessed the necessary requirements—she could sing, sew, was well-read, and intelligent.

MARRIED LIFE IN THE THEATER

In 1786, after her father finally secured a pension from the royal navy, Susanna Haswell married William Rowson (1766–1843), a hardware merchant who worked periodically in the London theater as an actor and musician. Scholars speculate that she married him more for social respectability than financial support. William drank heavily and was often unemployed, forcing Susanna Rowson to assume the position of breadwinner in the marriage. The couple had no children of their own, but Rowson raised her husband's illegitimate son.

Through William's connections in the theater, Rowson began performing, most likely as a strolling player for an acting company outside London. (She appeared only once in London, in 1792, as Charlotte in Hannah Cowley's *Who's the Dupe.)* The Rowsons probably earned a little more than laborers, although the work was more enjoyable. Possessing only average talent, Susanna Rowson nevertheless performed more often than her husband and won substantial roles because she learned her lines and consistently attended rehearsals. Rowson believed acting was a respectable profession and took it seriously—although many people inside and outside of the theater did not. With every performance she was vulnerable to insults from the audience. The reputation of theater folk had improved during the mid-1700s, but a married woman could assume only a limited measure of respectability.

VICTORIA: ROWSON'S FIRST NOVEL

In the late eighteenth century, writers frequently modeled their plots on Samuel Richardson's *Clarissa* (1747–1748), in which the female protagonist is seduced, abandoned, and then dies as punishment for her immoral behavior. Although provocative, these seduction novels were tolerated as their proclaimed intent was to warn young, single women away from disreputable men. When Rowson decided to augment her income from the theater, she chose to follow this successful formula and write a seduction novel titled *Victoria* (1786). She followed precedents set by other British writers before her, such as Hannah Moore (1745–1833) and Maria Edgeworth (1767–1849), by writing novels for women that revolved largely around the domestic sphere and promoted eighteenth-century ideals of womanhood, including purity, submission, and a strict morality.

The main plot of *Victoria,* written in epistolary form, follows the life of Victoria Baldwin. Her father dies, leaving her vulnerable to Harry Finchly, a baronet. Finchly seduces Victoria, lures her into a fake marriage, and abandons her once she is pregnant. Victoria loses her sanity upon the birth of her child and eventually dies. Like all seduction novel heroines, she illustrates that sex outside marriage is unacceptable under any circumstances and must be punished. *Victoria* also contains five additional subplots involving various other women and their life choices. The correspondence of many characters creates multiple points of view, and it is a tribute to Rowson's literary talent that the novel remains cohesive and intelligible.

Needing support for her first literary effort, Rowson published *Victoria* through subscription, a practice almost obsolete in England by the 1780s. Georgiana Cavendish, duchess of Devonshire (1757–1806), served as Rowson's patron, and her influence secured 270 subscribers for the novel, printed by J. P. Cooke in two volumes. *Victoria* sold well and at least ten American booksellers carried the book between 1789 and 1816. The book received two routine reviews in London publications, describing it as simply another women's novel promoting female purity and filial piety or parental obedience. This was not unusual; male critics possessed no literary expectations regarding women's novels. Women writers needed only to instruct their readers on womanly virtues, such as submission and purity.

Rowson's novel did not alarm the male-dominated literary establishment, but modern scholars identify early feminist themes in *Victoria* that the author continued to explore in her fiction. For example, her views on filial piety may seem uncompromising, as Victoria is punished for her behavior. But Rowson advocated forgiveness and support for unmarried mothers. Victoria's mother, sister, and friends come to her aid during her time of need. Rowson also questions obedience to husbands and men's freedom when Victoria says: "The world will never pardon us; while men may plunge in every idle vice and yet be received in all companies, and too often caressed by the brave and worthy. Can you tell me why this is, Bell? Are crimes less so when committed by men than by women?"

Rowson presents a realistic view of the world in *Victoria* that she will build upon in her later fiction. The scholar Dorothy Weil considers her a precursor to the realism of writers such as Jane Austen (1775–1817). Rowson's female characters possess foibles, and she avoids idealizing women, thus creating a range of female characters including villains such as Lady Maskwell, who lies and steals to satisfy her ambitions. Rowson never romanticizes love. In fact, the character of Bell Hartley views marriage as more of a necessary evil than a union of souls. And despite her abhorrence of class distinctions, Rowson makes it clear that Finchly would never consider marrying a woman of Victoria's lower social rank.

THE INQUISITOR

In her second novel, *The Inquisitor* (1788), Rowson raises social, moral, religious, and artistic issues while satirizing sentimental literature. Eighteenth-century English novels of this genre illustrate the value of sensibility, or a strong reliance on emotions as a means of discovering truth while stressing the importance of true virtue exemplified by honor and strict morals. The works of Laurence Sterne (1713–1768), Samuel Richardson (1689–1761), and Richard Fielding (1707–1754) were particularly influential and inspired many other writers, male and female. *The Inquisitor* is based on Sterne's *A Sentimental Journey through France and Italy* (1768), in which Parson Yorick, a gallant man possessing great sensibility, travels on the journey of the title.

A loosely structured series of short stories or scenes, *The Inquisitor* is narrated by a man wearing a ring that allows him to become invisible. He fulfills his role as a sentimental hero by using this power to help the poor and others in need. In the story of Annie, Rowson exaggerates the negative effects of sentimental literature on impressionable young women in order to promote the use of reason over emotion, a theme also developed in the works of Fanny Burney (1752–1840), a popular British author. Annie's suggestibility to the ideas about romance portrayed in the numerous sentimental novels she reads leaves her vulnerable to the dishonorable Mr. Winlove, who seduces her with Jean-Jacques Rousseau's *La Nouvelle Héloïse* (1761) and the works of Charles Churchill (1731–1764).

In this didactic novel, as in much of her other work, Rowson encourages women to support one another in times of need and to obey their parents. She promotes financial responsibility, virtue, and quality education for women, while admonishing excessive pride and idleness. A Protestant suspicious of Catholicism, she believed religion was exemplified in good works, not attendance at rituals or tearful sympathy. Rowson also awards no deference to class or rank in her fiction; she remained true to basic democratic ideals throughout her life, applying them to religion as well.

Rowson addresses artistic integrity in *The Inquisitor* through the character of a woman writer who refuses to plagiarize stories from magazines at the suggestion of a bookseller. Later in the novel she defends all women of letters through the words of an old gentlemen: "I never heard a woman, who was fond of her pen complain of the tediousness of time; nor, did I ever know such a woman extravagantly fond of dress, public amusements, or expensive gaiety; yet, I have seen many women of genius prove themselves excellent mothers, wives, and daughters."

Reviews of *The Inquisitor* were brief and offered scant remarks on Rowson's literary style. The *Critical Review* maintained that the ring with magic powers was contrived, while the *Monthly Review* praised Rowson's compassion and recommended the book for young readers.

A TRIP TO PARNASSUS

Along with *The Inquisitor,* Rowson published two books of verse in 1788: *Poems on Various Subjects,* of which no known copy exists, and *A Trip to Parnassus; or, The Judgment of Apollo on Dramatic Authors and Performers.* This thirty-page poem in couplets and anapestic quatrameter illustrates Rowson's views on drama with levity.

Rowson, as narrator, imagines her contemporaries in the theater as they seek the god Apollo's approval. He sits on his throne and either praises or rejects thirty-four playwrights and actors, most of whom were associated with Covent Garden. *Parnassus* begins with dramatists, the best known of whom is Richard Sheridan (1751–1816). Through Apollo, Rowson reveals her high moral standards and expresses her disapproval of vanity. For example, Apollo condemns Hannah Cowley (1743–1809), the creator of many successful plays that Rowson found morally suspect: "When your sex take the pen, it is shocking to find, / From their writing loose thoughts have a place in their mind." As the actors approach Apollo, we find many are rejected for their lack of naturalness. Others, such as Charles Macklin, a well-known actor who introduced realism into his characters, are highly praised by the god. The poem ends with Apollo rejecting Rowson herself. "He seem'd much offended, and gave me a look," she writes. Rowson then awakens, and the reader learns it has all been a dream.

Relatively new to the London theater world, Rowson wisely published *Parnassus* anonymously with John Abraham, a small London publisher. Rowson demonstrates a talent for rhyme in *Parnassus,* and the *Monthly Review* complimented her style. The *Critical Review,* however, disagreed with her opinions. Unfortunately, no evidence exists of the reactions of Rowson's contemporaries in the theater.

MARY; OR, THE TEST OF HONOUR

The following year, 1789, Rowson published *Mary; or, The Test of Honour,* also anonymously. She had agreed to take material, most likely from the publisher John Abraham, and rework it into a novel. Rowson condemned this practice in *The Inquisitor* but felt compelled by financial need to accept the job. However, she never acknowledged authorship of *The Test of Honour,* going so far as to feign being a new author in the preface.

Abraham operated a circulating library, and *The Test of Honour* was written for lower- and middle-class women paying for the privilege of borrowing books they could not afford to buy. The novel is written to appeal to their desire for adventure with the main plot focusing on Mary Newton, a strong and effective protagonist.

Mary, an orphan, travels by ship to Jamaica to claim an inheritance from her uncle. Along the way she survives a storm at sea, desertion on a remote island, Spanish pirates, and Algerian kidnappers. After she recovers her inheritance from a dishonest cousin, the man she has loved for years, Frederick Stephens, is released by the Algerians and they marry. Subplots concern an adulterous woman named Emily, who dies, and a courageous woman named Semira, who orchestrates an escape from the Algerian kidnappers.

In *The Test of Honour,* Rowson formulates her first critique of women's schools, which she believed should offer a more practical education. This became a prominent theme in her writing, culminating in a pioneering role in American women's education in the next century. In a description of Mary's boarding school, Rowson writes:

> … every method was taken to counteract and undermine the excellent precepts and solid virtues her mother had so ardently laboured to inculcate. She learnt to jabber bad french, and sing worse Italian; the more essential branches of needlework were neglected, that she might learn embroidery, clothwork, and fifty other things, equally useless.

The Test of Honour is not Rowson's best work—the writing is flamboyant and trite, the various plots improbable, and the structure confusing. Rowson was probably not writing up to her abilities because she agreed to use material provided by Abraham. Neither the *Critical Review* nor the *Monthly Review* seriously considered the novel.

MENTORIA

In 1791 Rowson published *Mentoria; or, The Young Lady's Friend,* a book that reflects her developing interest in educating women. This collection of ten letters, three short stories, and one essay is similar to eighteenth-century female courtesy books. According to the scholar Sarah Emily Newton, Rowson and other women writers, such as Hannah Foster, attempted to avoid criticism of their fiction by creating a "literary hybrid" which illustrated examples of proper female conduct through narrative.

The book opens with the poem "The Young Lady's Friend: Verses, Addressed to a Young Lady, on Her Leaving School." Following is a short biography of Mentoria, a pseudonym adopted by the fictional letter-writer of the book, Helena Askam. Askam, governess to four girls who have recently moved to London, writes to her former students about their behavior and offers advice, often illustrating it with a short fictional narrative. These letters discuss issues often found in Rowson's fiction, such as filial piety, contentment with one's social status, and supporting women friends in times of need, while minimizing romantic notions about marriage. In her last letter, Askam encourages the fictional Gertrude Winworth to refrain from teaching her newborn daughter that marriage is her only destiny. She writes: "Teach them the difference between right and wrong, and convince their reason, by pointing out the real way to promote their own happiness, and merit the regard and esteem of their friends." (1794 ed.)

The short stories in *Mentoria* reinforce the themes promoted in the letters. "Lydia and Marian" and "Urganda and Fatima" explore the same theme—the dangers of social ambition. "The Incendiary" condemns the behavior of those who gossip. In this story, Rowson's realism is coarse: " Cursed dissembler, said the enraged Albert, and he spurned her from him with his foot. She shrieked and fell, her head struck the bed-post, and the blood gushed in a torrent from her forehead." (1794 ed.)

Mentoria is so heavily didactic as to make it dull reading compared to Rowson's other novels. It was published by William Lane at Minerva Press, a highly successful publisher with a large network of circulating libraries. No known reviews of *Mentoria* exist, although a second edition was printed in Dublin, and subsequent editions appeared in Philadelphia and Boston, indicating the book was considered profitable among those in the publishing trade.

CHARLOTTE: A TALE OF TRUTH

Charlotte: A Tale of Truth (London, 1791) would become the United States' first best seller, but in England where it was first published, it was simply another seduction novel. The fifteen-year-old Charlotte attends boarding school in Chichester, when Montraville, a handsome military officer, asks her to elope with him to America. Charlotte's French teacher, Mademoiselle La Rue, advises her to go, as La Rue herself wishes to journey to America with Montraville's friend, another officer, named Belcour. Once the four arrive in New York, Montraville falls in love with Julia Franklin, a wealthy woman.

Belcour abandons La Rue and begins to seduce Charlotte by telling her that Montraville has engaged himself to another woman. Meanwhile, he lies to Montraville, telling him that Charlotte has betrayed him. Once Charlotte is pregnant, Belcour abandons her.

When Charlotte asks for help from La Rue, now married to a rich older man, her former teacher refuses, demonstrating (as Rowson's novels so often do) the way that women are capable of cruelty to other women. Fortunately, some of La Rue's servants take Charlotte in just before she gives birth to a daughter and loses her sanity.

Meanwhile, Charlotte's father arrives from England to find his daughter. Just before Charlotte dies, he forgives her and promises to care for his grandchild. The evil characters are punished: Belcour dies in a duel with Montraville; La Rue dies poor and alone; and Montraville suffers the rest of his life with bouts of guilt and depression.

Charlotte is written in a direct, conversational style, and the plot progresses at a steady pace, distinguishing it from Rowson's earlier works of fiction. The shortest of her novels, it is largely written in the third person, although it also includes engaging addresses to the reader in first person, such as:

Let not the reader imagine Belcour's designs were honourable. Alas! When once a woman has forgot the respect due to herself, by yielding to the solicitations of illicit love, they lose all their consequence, even in the eyes of the man whose art has betrayed them, and for whose sake they have sacrificed every valuable consideration. (1797 ed.)

Parental obedience is just one of many lessons Rowson hoped to impart to readers, including purity, aid for women in trouble, and disdain for class distinctions. Quality education for women is stressed, as Charlotte's reasoning ability has been stunted at her boarding school and her lack of sophistication leads her to trust the villainous Mademoiselle La Rue and the charming but unworthy Montraville. Nevertheless, Rowson holds Charlotte responsible for her behavior: "no woman can be run away with contrary to her own inclination," she writes. (1797 ed.)

Charlotte's romantic inclinations are not unlike those of her father, who disobeyed his own father and sacrificed great wealth to marry the woman he loved. Rowson holds the Temples' loving marriage up in stark contrast to the other sordid relationships in the novel, but does not waiver in her stance against overly romantic notions concerning marriage. In fact, the death of his daughter can be interpreted as punishment for Mr. Temple's own romanticism and neglect of his parental responsibilities toward his daughter, who clearly needed his guidance.

Mr. Temple and Montraville move beyond the stereotype often presented in seduction novels. A father is usually a resentful victim, his reputation having been damaged by his daughter's immoral behavior. But Mr. Temple cares only for his daughter and readily agrees to care for his newborn granddaughter. He is a complex male character, as is Montraville, who victimizes Charlotte but is victimized in turn by Belcour.

The *Critical Review* praised the novel's plot and descriptions, but the reviewer found Charlotte to be innocent and undeserving of her harsh punishment. The novel is now considered Rowson's best work of fiction, but a second printing of the book did not appear in England until 1819, well after *Charlotte* achieved unrivaled success in the United States.

REBECCA

Rebecca, or, The Fille de Chambre, published in 1792, is considered Rowson's best work of fiction after *Charlotte*. Rebecca Littleton, age sixteen, is the daughter of a retired army lieutenant. Her father dies soon after the death of her patron, Lady Mary Worthy, and Rebecca is left to fend for herself. She begins work as a governess for Lord and Lady Ossiter but is forced to leave when Lord Ossiter attempts to seduce her. After several adventures, including a journey to America during the Revolution, Rebecca marries the man she loves, Lady Worthy's son, George.

Rowson admitted in the preface to the 1814 edition that the novel is largely autobiographical. Many of Rebecca's experiences mirror those of Rowson, including a storm encountered on her voyage to America, Rebecca's role as a governess, and various Revolutionary War experiences, such as the torching of the Boston lighthouse. Historians find Rowson's descriptions of the Revolution valuable, and literary scholars consider the descriptions some of her best fiction writing. In describing a wounded soldier, Rowson writes:

He had fainted, a mattress was laid on the ground, and as they all united in endeavouring to remove him upon it, the motion increased the anguish of his wounds, and recalled his languid senses.

"Oh, Spare me! do not kill me!" said he looking round with a terrified aspect. (1794 ed.)

At its best, *Rebecca*'s plot advances rapidly, holding the reader's interest. The writing is clear and occasionally humorous. At its worst, the plot appears contrived, as when Rebecca's dying nurse reveals that George, switched at birth, is not Lady Worthy's true son. This leaves Rebecca free to marry George Worthy despite her earlier promise to Lady Worthy that she would not.

In *Rebecca,* Rowson once again explores the themes of filial obedience, social ambition, and virtue unrelated to wealth or social rank. Unlike Charlotte, Rebecca serves as a good example to other young women. She expands the definition of filial obedience to include other authority figures, such as Lady Worthy. In addition, Rebecca is not wealthy and possesses no social ambitions. She is, however, rich in virtue, reinforcing Rowson's contention that good moral character is unrelated to social or financial standing.

Although the novel proved popular in the United States years later, its reception in London is a mystery. No known reviews of *Rebecca,* Rowson's last novel published in England, exist. In fact, no copies of the 1792 first edition, published by William Lane, have been found.

RETURN TO AMERICA

While honing her writing skills, Rowson continued working in the theater. In 1793 she and William and William's sister, Charlotte, journeyed to Edinburgh to join the company of the Theatre Royal in Shakespeare Square, managed by the actor Harriet Bennett Pye Esten. The company was not successful, and soon the Rowsons accepted a position in the United States with the New Theater of Philadelphia, managed by Thomas Wignell.

The Rowsons and about fifty others arrived in Philadelphia in the fall of 1793 only to be greeted by a yellow fever epidemic. Quickly changing plans, the company instead made its debut in Annapolis, Maryland, with *Who's the Dupe,* in which Rowson appeared. In January 1794, the company returned to Philadelphia, where Rowson and her husband lived and worked for two years. Rowson accomplished much during her first few years in the United States, developing into a popular supporting actor, lyricist, fiction writer, and playwright.

SLAVES IN ALGIERS AND OTHER PLAYS

Few plays written by Americans were performed on stage in postrevolutionary America, so it is noteworthy that Rowson wrote at least six plays beginning in 1794 and all were performed in American theaters. Although she is considered only an average playwright, Rowson's first American play generated a tremendous amount of controversy and subsequent publicity. *Slaves in Algiers; or, A Struggle for Freedom* (1794) explored the connections among liberty, slavery, and women's rights through a dramatization of recent attacks by Barbary pirates on American ships. Hoping to collect ransom, pirates from the Barbary States captured ships, goods, crews, and passengers. When ransom was not paid, those captured were held prisoner. By the late 1700s, over one hundred American sailors were enslaved in Algiers.

Rowson shamelessly revised her novel, *Mary; or, The Test of Honour,* in the creation of *Slaves in Algiers,* turning the Greek heroine into a young American woman and substituting the United States for England as the symbol of liberty and democracy. But, like Judith Sargent Murray (1751–1820), Rowson deviates from the sentimental plot formula by creating proactive female characters who orchestrate their own escape, reject patriarchal authority, and do not marry.

The heroine of the play, Olivia, is an American who has been captured and sold to the dey of Algiers. Her father, Constant, and her fiancé, Henry, have also been captured. Rebecca, another American captive, converts Fetnah, the daughter of her Jewish captor, to Christianity. Fetnah, who develops a love of liberty and freedom, helps Rebecca and the other captives in a failed attempt to escape. Olivia agrees to marry the dey if he will set the others free, but before he can respond to her offer, a slave revolt forces him to free all the slaves. Olivia reunites with her fiancé, and Rebecca reunites with her long-lost daughter and husband, Olivia and Constant.

Slaves in Algiers proved exceedingly popular despite its weaknesses in plot, characterization, and language. The play's timely topic and vindication of American values contributed to its success. Rowson even dedicated the printed version of the play to "the citizens of the United-States of North-America." Performed in Philadelphia and Baltimore, it was published during the first year it was produced.

In *Curtain Calls: British and American Women and the Theater, 1660-1820,* Doreen Alvarez Saar considers *Slaves in Algiers* "an important feminist transcription of the ideas of the American revolution," for the audience comes to identify women's powerless social condition in the United States with slavery. It is Fetnah, forced to serve her master sexually, who gives voice to Rowson's abhorrence of the sexual dominance men hold over women: "woman was never formed to be the abject slave of man. Nature made us equal with them, and gave us the power to render ourselves superior." Fetnah also dreams of the freedom she will have once she travels to America, but in fact the enslaved American women have been speaking only of the freedoms men in the United States enjoy. With subtle irony, Rowson illustrates the double standard at work in America.

In 1795 William Cobbett (1763–1835), a British journalist and pamphleteer, published *A Kick for a Bite,* in which he criticized Rowson's writing style, her public life in the theater, and her feminism, particularly her claim that women were superior to men. Cobbett also disapproved of the play's overt patriotism and questioned the sincerity of Rowson's democratic ideals. The pamphlet was signed "Peter Porcupine," Cobbett's first use of this pseudonym under which he would later attack such political luminaries as Benjamin Franklin (1706–1790) and Thomas Paine (1737–1809).

In response to Cobbett, John Swanwick (1740–1798), a congressman, merchant, and banker from Pennsylvania, published a defense of Rowson entitled *A Rub from Snub* (1795). He discredited Cobbett as a critic and defended Rowson, but dismissed her feminist comments as "merely a sally of humor, intended to excite a smile, and not to enforce a conviction of woman's superiority." To his credit, he supported education for women and agreed with Rowson's portrayal of Americans as charitable, loyal, and philanthropic.

While the two men continued lambasting each other through pamphlets, Rowson remained dignified, confident that publicity would only increase the size of her audience. Her response to Cobbett was measured and appeared in the preface of her new novel, *Trials of the Human Heart,* published later that same year. Rowson maintains that Cobbett's accusations are "false and scandalous," but she refrains from defending her feminism, secure in the knowledge that her message had gotten through to the public.

No known copies of Rowson's other plays exist. With *The Female Patriot; or, Nature's Rights* (1794), the title indicates that Rowson may have continued the feminist theme she explored in *Slaves in Algiers.* Scholars can only hypothesize on her intentions, but Rowson may have based the play on a work by Philip Massinger (1583–1640) titled *The Bondman* (1624), which dramatizes a slave revolt with a female hero. *The Volunteers* (1795) explored the political and timely topic of the Whiskey Rebellion of 1794 in Pennsylvania, in which farmers objected to a federal excise tax. In this play, the militia honor American freedom, primarily through song; Rowson collaborated with Alexander Reinagle (1799–1877), with whom she had already worked on several pieces of music for other productions. The music and lyrics, which are all that remain of *The Volunteers,* consist of romantic and humorous songs with memorable melodies. The title of another play, "The American Tar; or, The Press Gang Defeated" (first performed in Philadelphia on June 17, 1796), implies a political theme; it was subtitled "A Ballet." Rowson collaborated with Raynor Taylor (1747–1825) on the music for this production. No known copy of the play exists, but it was probably never published.

REPRINTS IN THE UNITED STATES

Ambition and a need for money led Rowson to secure American publishers for several of her English novels beginning in 1793. Of the four novels that reappeared in U.S. editions—*The Inquisitor, Mentoria, Rebecca,* and *Charlotte*—*Rebecca* and *Charlotte* sold extremely well, but it is unknown how much Rowson received for these reprints.

H. & P. Rice and J. Rice & Co. of Philadelphia published the first American edition of *Rebecca* under its subtitle *The Fille de Chambre* in 1794. George Keating published another edition later that same year as well as two more editions in 1795. Subsequent editions were printed in Boston in 1814, 1831, and 1832, and the book was available through booksellers' catalogs for another forty years.

The Fille de Chambre was more popular in the United States than England. America had only recently gained independence from England, its mother country. In her essay "Mothers and Daughters in the Fiction of the New Republic," Cathy Davidson clarifies how this coming-of-age novel, one of many featuring young female protagonists struggling on their own against "evil" mother figures, resonated with the citizens of a young and struggling nation. She further asserts that sentimental novels of the early republic, in the way they chronicle the process by which daughters become mothers, parallel the story of America, the former British colony, becoming a nation. The reading public of the new United States also identified with Rebecca's free spirit and her harsh experiences during the Revolutionary War.

Rowson sold *Charlotte* to the prominent publisher and patriot Mathew Carey (1760–1839), who printed two editions in 1794 and a third in 1797. This third edition was published with a new title that most subsequent American editions used: *Charlotte Temple.* The novel became the first U.S. bestseller, with 161 editions over the next 140 years.

Charlotte Temple is generally considered an American novel in part because it is set in the United States and the author became a citizen and spent the remainder of her long life there. Its importance in American literary history is undisputed, and the reasons for *Charlotte Temple's* exceptional popularity in the United States are numerous: its villains are atypical in their complexity, but still punished fairly; its direct, conversational style is strikingly different from other American novels of the time; virtues of the middle class, such as thriftiness, are valued; and the novel denigrates class consciousness. In "Mothers and Daughters," Davidson maintains that sentimental novels with seduction narratives were plentiful and popular because they reflected central truths of women's lives in the early republic: the most certain means to a secure life was marriage, and virtue was essential to securing a husband. Donna Bontatibus asserts that these novels used seduction as a euphemism for rape, and they illustrate the social and political inequality experienced by women of the early republic.

Charlotte Temple's popularity was further advanced by the subtitle of the novel ("A Tale of Truth") and Rowson's assertion in the preface that the story was relayed to her by an acquaintance of Charlotte's. Readers set out to find the people on whom the characters were modeled. By the early nineteenth century, considerable evidence existed that Montraville was modeled on Lieutenant John Montresor (1736–1788?), Susanna Rowson's first cousin (for whom her youngest brother was named). However, there is little to support the popular contention that Charlotte was drawn from the life of Charlotte Stanley (d. 1775), the daughter of the eleventh earl of Derby. Nevertheless, the intrigue generated by these conjectures ultimately propelled Charlotte to fame. For example, a New York edition in 1840 contained an illustration of Charlotte's alleged gravestone in Trinity Churchyard in New York. Before long, the churchyard was the preferred destination of Charlotte Temple fans. A sequel to this literary phenomenon did not appear until 1828, after Rowson's death.

FIRST AMERICAN NOVEL

In 1795 Rowson produced a novel, *Trials of the Human Heart,* to be sold by subscription; it was published in Philadelphia and presented in four volumes. As in England, publishing by subscription was almost obsolete. But Rowson felt unsure of her ability to sell her fiction in the United States, so she secured Anne Bingham (1764–1801) as her patron. An influential Philadelphia socialite, Bingham enlisted members of important Philadelphia families as subscribers, including Martha Washington (1732–1802).

The novel, written in the epistolary form, presents the letters of Meriel Howard to her friend Celia, whom she has left behind in a French convent. Meriel has traveled to England to reunite with her parents, who are in fact her aunt and uncle. Her "father" attempts to rape her and cheats her out of an inheritance. Meriel, who must now care for herself and her "mother," endures numerous difficulties and traumas over the following sixteen years. For example, she is seduced by a married man, lives in poverty, marries for money, loses her children, and survives a shipwreck. Not surprisingly, Meriel grows to mistrust all men and vows "to despise the whole sex; they may wear a semblance of virtue, but the reality of it is foreign to their hearts." Reason and love triumph, however, and Meriel remains resilient and hopeful. In the end, she marries the man she loves, Frederic Rainsforth.

Trials of the Human Heart contains several autobiographical elements: the heroine longs to be a writer, survives a frightening storm at sea, and attends the play *The Tragedy of Jane Shore* (1714), which Rowson's theater company performed in 1795. It explores several of Rowson's favorite themes: filial piety, the virtues of the middle class, purity, the importance of reason over romance, and disdain for class distinctions. As always, Rowson also encourages women to support one another in times of need.

This novel, the first Rowson wrote in the United States, may be her weakest. Although Meriel is one of Rowson's most complex characters—she possesses as many faults as virtues—the novel's credibility and appeal are undermined by the novel's excessive length, stilted one-dimensional characters, and a melodramatic plot. No reviews exist for *Trials of the Human Heart,* and it was never reprinted.

BACK TO NEW ENGLAND

In the fall of 1796 the New Theater's financial troubles forced the Rowsons and several of their colleagues to travel to Boston to join the Federal Street Theater. Boston was an attractive destination for Rowson—she could be closer to her two half-brothers, Robert and Bill Haswell. In addition, she had learned from Robert that she held an excellent reputation in Boston as an author of fiction.

Rowson performed frequently at the Federal Street Theater and in April 1797 her comedy *Americans in England; or, Lessons for Daughters,* was performed. No known copy survives, only a list of characters, although the basic premise of the play can be inferred from its title. According to a review in the *Massachusetts Mercury,* it was well received.

Ever ambitious, Rowson also found time to compose lyrics with immigrant musicians from the theater. Her first musical collaboration had been with Alexander Reinagle in Philadelphia, with whom she composed "America, Commerce, and Freedom"(1804), which accompanied a patriotic ballet pantomime:

> The under full sail we laugh at the gale,
>   And the landmen look pale never heed 'em;
> But toss off the glass, to a favorite lass,
>   To America, Commerce and Freedom.

In Boston, Rowson collaborated with musicians who would contribute significantly to theater music in the early American republic. Most, like Reinagle, were English and European immigrants, such as James Hewitt and Gottlieb Graupner. With them, Rowson produced numerous popular songs for the theater—songs of love and patriotism—that were often sold as sheet music. While her most popular songs were sea chanties, Rowson was capable of writing romantic lyrics. But her typical love song was humorously brazen, such as "I Never Will Be Married, I'd Rather Be Excus'd" or "He Is Not Worth the Trouble."

REUBEN AND RACHEL

The end of Rowson's first season with the Federal Street Theater marked the end of the theater itself. It closed due primarily to competition from another theater, the Haymarket. During her short time there, Rowson wrote her next novel, *Reuben and Rachel; or, Tales of Old Times* (1798). This book is a departure from the domestic novels and seduction narratives Rowson had previously written—it is expansive, and attempts to explore the development of democracy in six countries over three hundred years.

The story begins in the fifteenth century with Christopher Columbus and the Spanish explorers. It follows the descendents of Columbus into sixteenth-century England and then seventeenth-century America. The story ends in the nineteenth century when Columbus' descendents, the twins Reuben and Rachel, become American citizens. The narrative relates important historical incidents, including biographies of esteemed women, and follows Reuben and Rachel as they overcome numerous adversities, such as poverty, slander, and shipwrecks. Both marry for love at the end of the novel and settle in Pennsylvania.

The overarching theme tracing the growth of democracy provides unity to *Reuben and Rachel* and allows Rowson to advance the narrative with extensive leaps in time. But Rowson explores other familiar themes in this novel: parental obedience, disdain for wealth and privilege, and the support of women in need. She successfully engages the reader with strong characters and illuminating descriptions. Rachel, like many previous Rowson heroines, is confident and independent, and she differs from the heroines of most American novels of the early republic in her ability to succeed without a mother's guidance. The novel is unique in its attempt at a realistic portrayal of Native Americans as complex human beings, depicting them as victims as well as aggressors: "Two or three unprincipled and licentious Europeans having made incursions amongst them, plundering their little settlements, burning their wigwams, and practising other enormities, as must certainly awaken a spirit of revenge in the bosom of persons better regulated than those of untutored savages."

The historical focus of *Reuben and Rachel* indicates Rowson was moving in a pedagogical direction. For years, she had been promoting through her fiction the theory that women must learn to reason in order to be successful in life. *Reuben and Rachel* is the first indication that Rowson desired to literally teach women how to develop their intellects. Entertaining and educational, it foreshadows Rowson's later textbooks. In the preface to the book Rowson clarifies her intentions:

> When I first started the idea of writing "*Tales of Old Times,*" it was with a fervent wish to awaken in the minds of my young readers, a curiosity that might lead them to the attentive perusal of history in general, but more especially the history of their native country.

Reuben and Rachel was not published until 1798, a year after Rowson opened her first school for girls. No reviews have been found, but a second edition was printed in 1799.

EDUCATING WOMEN

Rowson had attempted for years to educate young women through her fiction, so perhaps it is unsurprising that when she relinquished her financially unstable life in the theater, she opened a private school for girls. Mrs. Rowson's Young Ladies' Academy on Federal Street, the first ladies' academy in Boston, opened in November 1797, but unlike most schools for women, its central premise was not simply to educate future mothers. Rowson believed in discipline, and her school's curriculum reflected the central idea Rowson had put forth in her fiction: women must learn practical skills and rely on their reason, not their emotions, in making decisions.

Rowson's academy offered academic subjects, such as reading, writing, arithmetic, English grammar, history, geography, and composition, combined with practical subjects, such as financial and household management, hygiene, ethics, and deportment. Rowson also assumed the responsibility of overseeing her students' ethical and religious education. As she had in her novels, Rowson attempted to entertain in order to teach, and she brought her theatrical experience to her teaching, introducing music, drama, and dance to the curriculum.

Rowson made a dignified headmistress—elegant, creative, and affectionate—and her reputation as a respectable writer attracted elite Massachusetts families who wished to educate their daughters in Boston. Still, Rowson made a concerted effort to gain entry into Boston society and enhance her reputation by writing patriotic verses for special occasions, such as the ode she wrote to celebrate George Washington's birthday in 1798. By its first anniversary, the academy had more than one hundred students enrolled. The bibliographer Robert Vail claims that it was "one of the most famous girls' schools in America."

In 1800, Rowson moved her school to Medford, a rural northwestern suburb of Boston. Daughters of many of the wealthiest New England families attended Rowson's academy, leading her to add French, drawing, painting, and needlework to the curriculum for an additional fee. Success depended on Rowson's good reputation, and in 1802 her husband accepted a job in the Customs Service, after becoming a naturalized American citizen.

In 1803 the Rowsons moved the academy to Newton, another Boston suburb, and Rowson assumed the responsibility of raising her brother William's illegitimate son William Jr. Mary Cordis Haswell, Rowson's sister-in-law, began sharing the responsibilities of headmistress and then came, with her two daughters, to live with the Rowsons after Susanna Rowson's brother Robert died at sea in 1801. With Mary Haswell's help, familial obligations did not prevent Rowson from continuing to write.

AN EXEMPLARY WIFE, EDUCATOR, AND WRITER

Beginning in 1802, Rowson began contributing to the *Boston Weekly* magazine, published by the printing company Gilbert and Dean. Early biographers maintain that Rowson edited the magazine, pointing to the style and content of the periodical as well as contemporary sources. More recent biographers do not agree. Patricia Parker cites examples within the *Boston Weekly* that refer to the publishers as editors and suggests the unlikelihood of Rowson accepting another job when her academy was financially successful and demanding much of her time.

The *Boston Weekly* left most articles unsigned, but Rowson appears to have consistently written its "Gossip" column, which usually focused on topics such as the education of women, obedience to parents, female friendships, and other topics often explored by Rowson in her fiction. Some columns may have been written by others, such as one on church music which objects "to hearing a jumble of songs, dancing tunes, and sacred music performed within a few seconds of each other," a view Rowson would be unlikely to espouse, and another column (on June 25, 1803) recommending Rowson's novels.

In addition to the "Gossip" column, Rowson published a serial novel titled *Sincerity* from June 1803 to June 1804, published in book form as *Sarah; or, The Exemplary Wife* in 1813. No known reviews exist of *Sarah,* but many copies of the book in excellent condition have been found, which suggests that the book did not sell well.

Most sentimental novels of the early 1800s end with marriage, but *Sarah* begins with the marriage of George and Sarah Darnley. Sarah has married George at the insistence of others, despite her doubts, and George proves to be a poor husband—unfaithful, violent, and unloving. Sarah makes a noble effort to be a good wife, only to have George announce that he wishes to live without her. The position she takes as a lady's companion and governess leads to a string of personal tragedies for Sarah. Her sense of moral duty compels her to reunite with George and raise his illegitimate child, causing Sarah more financial and emotional problems. Late in life Sarah befriends Mr. Hayley, a country curate, and believes she may have married a man like him had she not married George so hastily. Sarah dies at an early age, resigned to her fate and believing she has retained her dignity despite an unhappy marriage.

The majority of the letters in this epistolary novel are from Sarah to her friend Anne and from Anne to her friend Eleanor, with several letters from other characters. All together, they offer numerous points of view, which gives this rather simple story a measure of complexity. Having originally been a serial novel, *Sarah* moves at a slower pace than Rowson's previous novels. *Sarah* also differs from Rowson's novels in its somber tone and sad ending. But it is similar to other novels of the time in its didacticism, offering advice to married and unmarried women alike. Rowson advises unmarried women to choose their future husbands with care and married women to remain dutiful to their husbands. As Sarah writes:

> … I married him; he was affluent then. If I bound myself by a sacred oath at that time, contrary to my own better judgment, to share his fortunes, be they better or worse, I will not now, in opposition to my sense of duty, forsake him in the hour of humiliation.

Rowson claimed in the preface to *Sarah* that the plot was drawn from real life, but that the characters no longer existed. Her nineteenth-century biographer, Elias Nason, maintains that the novel is based on Rowson's own experiences and that the quotation on the title page of the novel refers to Rowson's own marriage (an assessment with which her twentieth-century biographers would agree): "Do not marry a fool; he is continually doing absurd and disagreeable things, for no other reason but to shew he dares do them."

In 1804, Rowson published her last collection of poetry, titled *Miscellaneous Poems,* by subscription. The book listed 245 subscribers, including many elite New England families. The *Monthly Anthology* reviewed the book but did not praise the poems, only the intentions of the author. Indeed, Rowson is merely an average poet. But she holds the reader's interest with varied subjects, rhyme schemes, lengths, and forms, including odes and ballads. Some poems are actually song lyrics. The best of the collection are patriotic, such as "The Standard of Liberty." These poems are conservative in tone, most likely written with the aim of securing a respectable reputation among the parents of her students. Rowson seemed comfortable adapting her political views as necessary to enhance her reputation in the community. "Women as They Are," in which she makes a strong case for the development of women's intellect, is balanced by such poems as "Rights of Woman," in which Rowson asks: "Know you not that woman's proper sphere / Is the domestic walk?"

Rowson contributed less frequently to the *Boston Weekly* after the publishers sold it in 1805, and she stopped contributing completely when the publication changed hands again in 1806, preferring to submit her work to the *Monthly Anthology; or, Magazine of Polite Literature.* Scholars have not been able to identify the articles she wrote for this magazine, as all were unsigned. The only other known material Rowson published in periodicals are poems she submitted years later to the *New England Galaxy.* Most of those later poems were religious, such as "The Mighty Lord" (1818) and "The

Wedding Supper" (1818). A lukewarm review exists as proof of one last play written by Rowson in 1810 or 1811 titled "Hearts of Oak," most likely an adaptation of John Till Allingham's comedy of the same name first produced in London in 1803. No published version exists, only a review claiming it deserved "merit."

EDUCATIONAL WRITINGS: FROM GEOGRAPHY TO HISTORY

During her first years of teaching, Rowson discovered that the materials she desired were not available. Her textbooks are a teacher's solution to a genuine educational need. Today, these textbooks not only reveal information about Rowson's academy and her pedagogical methods, but her level of knowledge and personal biases.

Although geography texts existed, Rowson did not find them satisfactory, so in 1805 she published *An Abridgment of Universal Geography: Together with Sketches of History.* The textbook, written for adolescents, is 256 pages long and includes additional pages of geographical and historical exercises. She published another geography text for younger students in 1818 titled *Youth's First Steps in Geography,* which presented lessons in a question-and-answer format.

Well organized and written with clarity, Rowson's *Universal Geography* begins with Europe, explores each region and country around the world, and then discusses the United States, including each territory and state. Rowson freely borrowed information from geography texts previously written by Jedidiah Morse (1761–1826) and others, an acceptable practice in the early eighteenth century. She provides information concerning the location, boundaries, topology, resources, climate, industry, government, religion, and inhabitants of each country. In addition, Rowson includes information on navigation, map and globe reading, and definitions of terms

It was acceptable in the early nineteenth century for textbooks to reflect their authors' values, and Rowson's are clearly distinguishable in her geography text. In general, Rowson reveals a strong preference for Western, Protestant, democratic countries, namely Scotland, England, and the United States. Her disapproval of slavery is made clear in the section on Africa:

On Guinea, or the western coast, the English exchange their linen and woollen manufactures for slaves. Not only the English, but other European nations, together with Americans, join in the horrid traffic, and grow rich by the purchase and sale of their fellow creatures. Let LIBERTY blush, and CHRISTIANITY hide her dishonoured head.

Rowson's *Universal Geography* is unique among similar texts in its focus on the treatment of women in undemocratic, non-Christian countries, such as Egypt: "The women in this country are not admitted to the society of the men, not even at table, but remain standing or seated in a corner of the room while the husband dines."

After teaching for several years, Rowson discovered that her students' spellers taught them how to spell but did not instruct them on the meaning of words. Since dictionaries intended for adults proved too difficult for her students, Rowson desired a textbook that would do both. In 1807 her *A Spelling Dictionary: Divided into Short Lessons for the Easier Committing to Memory by Children and Young Persons* was published by John West. It was popular enough to warrant a second edition in 1815 in Portland, Maine.

This textbook provides over four hundred lessons, each focusing on twenty to twenty-five words. Each word is spelled syllabically, identified by its part of speech, defined, and given a synonym. For example, "wrench" is identified as a verb, and defined as "to pull by force, to wrest." Rowson chose words from many aspects of life, such as the law, classical literature, and natural science. At the end of her dictionary, she provides "A Concise Account of the Heathen Deities, and Other Fabulous Persons; with the Heroes and Heroines of Antiquity." Rowson wanted to move beyond rote learning with her students. She wrote in the preface: "Children study with more cheerfulness, when the lesson is short and determined, and if they are early habituated to connect ideas with words as they advance in life this pleasing association continues. Their minds become informed, the studies and readings are pleasures, for they afford some degree of amusement."

In 1807, Rowson moved the academy back to Boston on Washington Street, which offered several advantages. The students benefited from their exposure to live theater and music as well as the expertise of their new music teacher, Gottlieb Graupner. He and his wife, Catherine Hillyer, were longtime friends. Rowson's growing interest in religion prompted her to join charitable groups, such as the Boston Fatherless' and Widows' Society. In Boston, William became more productive. He played the trumpet for the Boston Philharmonic Society organized by Graupner, helped start the Handel and Haydn Society, and played with the Park Street Choir.

The academy thrived and in 1809 Rowson bought a house on Hollis Street and opened a second school, which she oversaw, leaving Mary Haswell to run the Washington Street school. Rowson also adopted two daughters at this time: Fanny Mills, the daughter of the actor John Mills, who had recently died, and Susan Johnston, the daughter of William's sister, Charlotte, also deceased.

Since 1802 Rowson had been organizing annual exhibitions during which her students recited essays, poems, dialogues, and biographical sketches she wrote for an audience of parents and friends. At a time when women rarely spoke in public, and apologized if they did, Rowson's female students were taking the podium without apology. By 1811, the event was popular enough for Rowson to charge a fifty-cent admission to locals and publish *A Present for Young Ladies,* which collected presentations from the exhibition.

The poems collected in *A Present for Young Ladies* illustrate themes Rowson had explored for years in her fiction, such as devotion to family, religion, and virtue. Given her theatrical background, it is not surprising that she wrote dialogues for her students to perform. They were didactic, but humorous—dramatizing Rowson's values, including the need for a quality education and the danger of sentimental novels—and occasionally political; one dialogue paints Napoleon as a tyrant, particularly in his treatment of his wife. But it was her "Sketches of Female Biography" that proved to be the most popular.

Rowson's concept of history contrasts sharply with the traditional approach with its emphasis on war and the pursuit of power. She was essentially a humanist who sought to include all aspects of human endeavor in her stories of the past. The women in her sketches were not necessarily famous, and they were chosen as much for their values as for their achievements. Lucretia Cornaro of Venice (1646–1684), a mathematician and philosopher, was the first woman to earn a doctoral degree at the university in Rome and the "perfect mistress over her own passions, a victory more praiseworthy and more difficult to achieve." Catherine Clive (1711–1785), an actor from England, was "as distinguished by her virtues as her extraordinary dramatic powers."

Rowson grew ill, and in 1822 Fanny Mills and Susan Johnston took over the responsibilities of running the Hollis Street school. By this time, Rowson had lost many loved ones: her father, her three brothers, and her adopted son, who drowned sometime after 1811. Biographers claim that she worried about the extensive debts her husband had incurred and felt embarrassed by his alcoholism and irresponsible behavior.

Ever industrious, Rowson hid her unhappiness from others as she assisted in the teaching of composition and continued to write. She completed and published her last two textbooks in 1822, *Exercises in History, Chronology, and Biography, in Question and Answer* and *Biblical Dialogues between a Father and His Family.*

Few history books existed at this time, and fewer still covered world history. *Exercises in History* chronicles world history from the creation to the beginning of the American republic with thirteen exercises in a question and answer format. Rowson combines secular and biblical sources, as the Bible was considered a factual text, and covers the histories of most countries, omitting Africa and parts of Asia due to a lack of sources. Rowson not only discusses politics, but literature, art, architecture, and inventions as well, and her biographies include many women, such as Queen Anne of England and Margaret of Denmark.

Scholars identify a growing interest in religion by Rowson as she aged, culminating in *Biblical Dialogues,* which retells the primary stories of the Old and New Testaments as well as selected stories from ancient and medieval church history. The Bible stories are framed by a narrative in which a fictonal Mr. Alworth tells the stories of the Bible to his children (three sons and two daughters) and the family discusses them. During these conversations, Mr. Alworth offers logical explanations for biblical events and explores the metaphorical implications of the Bible stories with the children. The family members and biblical characters are fully developed and realistic, resulting in a more entertaining book for young readers. Naturally, a respect for women permeates the text, evident in Rowson's focus on women of the Bible (such as Queen Esther) and her careful characterization of the Alworth sisters, who are encouraged to ask questions and offer opinions. Themes commonly identified in Rowson's fiction surface in this textbook: virtue, humility, filial obedience, and the benefits of reason over emotion—in this case, concerning matters of religion.

ONE LAST NOVEL

Sometime during the years after she retired from teaching, Rowson wrote a sequel to *Charlotte Temple* titled *Charlotte's Daughter; or, The Three Orphans* (commonly known as *Lucy Temple,* the title from the 1842 edition). The manuscript was discovered after her death and published by Richardson and Lord in 1828 with an endearing memoir by Samuel Lorenzo Knapp.

The novel set in Hampshire, England, focuses on three orphans, Mary Lumly, Aura Melville, and Lucy Blakely, Charlotte Temple's daughter. All three young women are eighteen years of age and share the same guardian, the Reverend Matthews. Mary exemplifies the poor values she learned from her mother and elopes with a disreputable man who abandons her and steals her inheritance. Aura personifies the ideal, marrying a man of great wealth who admires her good character. Lucy and her fiancé, John Franklin, pay for the sins of their parents. After learning that they share the same father, Montraville, both young people decide to live a life of celibacy. John travels to India and Lucy opens a school for girls.

Lucy Temple is written in the same direct, conversational style as *Charlotte Temple* and the plot progresses steadily. Its characters are not fully developed, but they are interesting nonetheless. For example, Mary, although easily seduced and robbed of her inheritance, develops into a strong, self-reliant woman. Some scholars maintain that the sequel excels *Charlotte Temple* in its realism and graphic descriptions, which drew on Rowson's own nostalgia for her homeland:

It was on one of those mornings when the visitants of Brighton sally forth to ransack libraries, torment shopkeepers, and lounge upon the Stiene, when Edward Ainslie taking Lucy under one arm and Lady Mary under the other, having taken a walk upon the downs, strolled into one of the public Libraries, where raffles, scandal and flirtation were going forward amongst an heterogeneous crowd assembled there. (1991 ed.)

Lucy Temple's sensationalism revolves around the subject of incest, which is present in several late-eighteenth-century English novels. Concurrent with this sensational use of incest are Rowson's numerous references to religion. Though she had always espoused a Christian morality, Rowson demonstrated a strong Protestant bias in her earlier work that is tempered in her last novel.

Independent women are featured in Rowson's last novel as they were in her first. Lucy Temple chooses her future for herself and selects a career Rowson knew to be fulfilling. Julia Franklin, John Franklin's mother, becomes a prominent landowner when her husband dies. And Rowson's own independent spirit comes forth as she breaks with literary tradition and allows Mary Lumly to live a happy life despite her seduction and pregnancy.

Lucy Temple's reviews lacked serious literary critique. John Greenleaf Whittier admired the book's moral beauty in his review in the *Essex Gazette* of Haverhill, Massachusetts. The *American Ladies' Magazine* recommended *Lucy Temple* for young women, but the reviewer also noted that the novel seemed underdeveloped and attributed this fault to a lack of ambition among women writers. *Lucy Temple* was popular, nevertheless, perhaps due to its connection to *Charlotte Temple* or Susanna Rowson herself.

When Rowson died on March 2, 1824, obituaries ran in the *Columbian Centinel* and the *Boston Evening Gazette,* which also reprinted the memoir by Samuel Lorenzo Knapp. This is the first known account of Rowson's life, and many more followed. Serious analysis of her life and work will continue, for as feminist scholarship grows, so does interest in Susanna Rowson.

Selected Bibliography

WORKS OF SUSANNA HASWELL ROWSON

NOVELS

Victoria. London: J. P. Cooke, 1786.

The Inquisitor; or, Invisible Rambler. 3 vols. London: G. G. J. & J. Robinson, 1788. Philadelphia: William Gibbons, 1793.

Mary; or, The Test of Honour. 2 vols. London: John Abraham, 1789.

Mentoria; or, The Young Lady's Friend. 2 vols. London: William Lane, 1791. Philadelphia: Samuel Harrison Smith, 1794.

Charlotte: A Tale of Truth. 2 vols London: William Lane, 1791. Philadelphia: Mathew Carey, 1794. Republished as *Charlotte Temple: A Tale of Truth.* Philadelphia: Mathew Carey, 1797. Modern edition. New York: Oxford University Press, 1986. (There are numerous reprints of this novel; the 1986 reprint includes an introduction by Cathy N. Davidson.)

Rebecca; or, The Fille de Chambre. London: William Lane, 1792. Republished as *The Fille de Chambre.* Philadelphia: H. & P. Rice and J. Rice & Co., 1794. Baltimore: George Keating, 1794, 1795.

Trials of the Human Heart. 4 vols. Philadelphia: Wrigley & Berriman, 1795.

Reuben and Rachel; or, Tales of Old Times. Boston: Manning & Loring, 1798.

Sarah; or, The Exemplary Wife. Boston: Charles Williams, 1813.

Charlotte's Daughter; or, The Three Orphans. Boston: Richardson & Lord, 1828. New York: Penguin Books, 1991. (There are numerous reprints of this novel; this 1991 reprint includes an introduction by Ann Douglas together with a reprint of *Charlotte Temple.*)

POETRY

Poems on Various Subjects. London: G. G. J. & J. Robinson, 1788.

A Trip to Parnassus; or, The Judgment of Apollo on Dramatic Authors and Performers. A Poem. London: John Abraham, 1788.

Miscellaneous Poems. Boston: Gilbert and Dean, 1804.

PUBLISHED DRAMATIC WORKS

Slaves in Algiers; or, A Struggle for Freedom. Philadelphia: Wrigley & Berriman, 1794.

The Female Patriot; or, Nature's Rights. Philadelphia: n.p., 1794.

The Volunteers. With Alexander Reinagle. Philadelphia: Self-published, 1795.

Americans in England; or, Lessons for Daughters. Boston: n.p., 1796.

EDUCATIONAL WRITINGS

An Abridgment of Universal Geography: Together with Sketches of History. Boston: John West, 1805.

A Spelling Dictionary: Divided into Short Lessons, for the Easier Committing to Memory by Children and Young Persons. Boston: John West, 1807.

A Present for Young Ladies: Containing Poems, Dialogues, Addresses, &c. as Recited by the Pupils of Mrs. Rowson's Academy. Boston: John West, 1811.

Youth's First Steps in Geography. Boston: Wells & Lilly, 1818.

Exercises in History, Chronology, and Biography, in Question and Answer. Boston: Richardson & Lord, 1822.

Biblical Dialogues between a Father and His Family. 2 vols. Boston: Richardson & Lord, 1822.

BIBLIOGRAPHIES

Piacento, Edward J. "Susanna Haswell Rowson: A Bibliography of First Editions of Primary Works and of Secondary Sources." *Bulletin of Bibliography* 43:13–16, (no. 1, 1986).

Vail, Robert W. G. *Susanna Haswell Rowson, the Author of "Charlotte Temple": A Bibliographical*

Study. Worcester, Mass.: American Antiquarian Society, 1933.

White, Devon. "Contemporary Criticism of Five Early American Sentimental Novels, 1970–1994: An Annotated Bibliography." *Bulletin of Bibliography* 52:293–305 (December, 1995).

CRITICAL AND BIOGRAPHICAL STUDIES

Bontatibus, Donna R. *The Seduction Novel of the Early Nation: A Call for Socio-Political Reform.* East Lansing: Michigan State University Press, 1999.

Brandt, Ellen B. *Susanna Haswell Rowson: America's First Best-Selling Novelist.* Chicago: Serba Press, 1975.

Davidson, Cathy N. "The Life and Times of Charlotte Temple: The Biography of a Book." In *Reading in America: Literature and Social History.* Edited by Cathy N. Davidson. Baltimore: Johns Hopkins University Press, 1989. Pp. 157–179.

Davidson, Cathy N. "Mothers and Daughters in the Fiction of the New Republic." In *The Lost Tradition: Mothers and Daughters in Literature.* Edited by Cathy N. Davidson and E. M. Broner. New York: Frederick Ungar, 1980. Pp. 115–127.

Knapp, Samuel Lorenzo. "A Memoir of the Author." Preface to *Charlotte's Daughter: or, The Three Orphans,* by Susanna Rowson. Boston: Richardson & Lord, 1828. Pp. 3–20.

Kornfeld, Eve. "Women in Post-Revolutionary American Culture: Susanna Haswell Rowson's American Career." *Journal of American Culture* 22:56–62 (winter, 1983).

Nason, Elias. *A Memoir of Mrs. Susanna Rowson, with Elegant and Illustrative Extracts from Her Writings in Prose and Poetry.* Albany, N.Y.: Munsell, 1870.

Newton, Sarah Emily. "Wise and Foolish Virgins: 'Usable Fiction' and the Early American Conduct Tradition." *Early American Literature* 25: 139–167 (no. 2, 1990).

Parker, Patricia L. *Susanna Rowson.* Boston: Twayne, 1986.

Saar, Doreen Alvarez. "Susanna Rowson: Feminist and Democrat." In *Curtain Calls: British and American Women and the Theater, 1660–1820.* Edited by Mary A. Schofield and Cecilia Macheski. Athens: Ohio University Press, 1991. Pp. 231–246.

Weil, Dorothy L. *In Defense of Women: Susanna Rowson (1762–1824).* University Park: Pennsylvania State University Press, 1976.

Rowson's papers are located in the Barrett Collection, University of Virginia.

—DENISE LARRABEE

Gjertrud Schnackenberg

1953–

PERHAPS MORE THAN any other contemporary American poet, Gjertrud Schnackenberg defies easy classification. Despite the attempts of varied camps to claim her for their own, she has slipped free from any description imposed on her from critics. She is a successful woman poet who has never written explicitly on feminist issues. She is at times beloved of New Formalist poetry critics, yet she writes as often in free verse as not. Her move away from the stern formalism of her first books has occasioned a number of impassioned responses, largely from those who think she should return to her original style. She has written intimate autobiographical elegies as well as poems of broad historical sweep. Her use of language has moved from the quietly picturesque to the extravagantly ambitious. She has been described as a poet of private familial moments as well as of icy emotional distance. This immense variety constitutes one of her great strengths: her ability to write in numerous styles and yet retain the praise of most literary critics and readers. It is also the font of much critical division.

Born on August 27, 1953, in Tacoma, Washington, Gjertrud Cecilia Schnackenberg is considered one of America's most accomplished poets, writing in a style inherited from H.D., Elizabeth Bishop, James Merrill, and Robert Lowell. Her father, Walter Charles Schnackenberg, a Lutheran of Norwegian descent, was a professor of medieval and Russian history at Pacific Lutheran University. Father and daughter were close and spent much time together, both in outdoor activities such as fishing and in more domestic ones like reading. He appears to have been a chief source of inspiration, particularly in her early poetry, as a principal subject and in more oblique ways, as for example when she writes about Charles Darwin (1809–1882), the father of modern biology. Her mother, Doris Storm Schnackenberg, does not seem to have exerted as much pull on her daughter's imagination and does not appear to be the subject of any published poems.

Gjertrud Schnackenberg attended Mount Holyoke College, where she first began to write poetry. Her father's death in 1973 came to define her early poetry and became a central theme of her first collection, *Portraits and Elegies,* published in 1982. While an undergraduate, she won the Kathryn Irene Glascock Poetry Prize twice, in 1973 and 1974. After graduating summa cum laude in 1975, she received a Radcliffe College fellowship for 1979–1980, an Ingram Merrill Foundation fellowship, and won a Pushcart Prize in 1979. The famous classicist Robert Fitzgerald selected Schnackenberg for the Lavan Younger Poets Award from the Academy of American Poets in 1983. She received a Rome fellowship from the American Academy and Institute of Arts and Letters in 1983 and lived in Italy for a year, a residency that was extended for two more years when she won an Amy Lowell Traveling Fellowship in 1984. She was a National Endowment for the Arts fellow in 1986 and a Guggenheim fellow in 1987. That year, on October 5, she married the Harvard philosophy professor Robert Nozick, who died at the age of sixty-three in 2002. She also received a grant from the National Endowment for the Arts and a Guggenheim Fellowship in 1988.

LITERARY CONTEXTS

The *New Princeton Encyclopedia of Poetry and Poetics* cites Schnackenberg among a group of heirs to the elegant formalism of James Merrill, including Alfred Corn, Marilyn Hacker, and Brad Leithauser. She has also been identified as a member of the late 1980s culturally conservative group known collectively as the New Formalists, who view formal technique in poetry as a "recovery of the liberating potential of limits." These poets were thought to constitute a "resistance to the more autobiographical and vatic modes of the 1960s." This is certainly true of Schnackenberg, but it should be emphasized that she has always maintained a genuine independence in matters of style, and this independence is clearly reflected in her growth as a poet. Over the course of her career she has never composed poetry in the prevailing style of any given period. Aside from her occasional use of recognized poetic forms, Schnackenberg actually shares little with the New Formalist camp, certainly nothing of their self-publicizing tendencies.

After twenty-five years of publishing poetry, Schnackenberg has yet to settle on a single governing style. Nonetheless readers and critics have claimed that she is recognizable in all of her various attires. Hers is a style of formality that does not require emotional aloofness, and a distinctive elegance persists despite her unpredictability, along with a refusal to appropriate the colloquialisms or vernacular of American speech. Use of everyday speech is a trend in American poetry that began with Walt Whitman, extended through Robert Frost, William Carlos Williams, and became the domain of John Ashbery and James Tate in the late twentieth century. Schnackenberg exists on a separate plane, one inhabited by Wallace Stevens and T. S. Eliot, what Robert McPhillips characterizes in his book *The New Formalism: A Critical Introduction* (2003) as the "high style." Similarly, while Schnackenberg's poems might be compared in form alone to those of such poets as Edna St. Vincent Millay, she shares nothing of Millay's public posturing or her poetic quaintness.

Schnackenberg's poetry might be described as stately. Historically speaking, poetry in English before modernism was written in an elevated style to set it apart from the language of commerce and ordinary conversation. Occasionally this led to extremes, and poetry became burdened by ornamentation. Since at least the beginning of the nineteenth century, when William Wordsworth and Samuel Taylor Coleridge published several editions of their *Lyrical Ballads,* there has been a compensatory trend toward simplification of poetic language, casting off unnecessary complications and cluttered, impractical diction. In the twentieth century, a century of extremes in all directions, this also led to overcompensation. While Robert Frost sought to express familiar speech patterns, he did so explicitly in the framework of iambic pentameter. In the 1960s poetry in America exploded in many directions at once, and the enduring result of the rebellion against tradition and form in all things was a relaxed form of poetic expression, usually combined with an anguished outpouring of emotion or public rage. Against the backdrop of this prosaic frenzy in American poetry Schnackenberg stands out as a stately artisan of biographical subjects and a gifted visionary who owes far more to the English poets Robert Browning and Gerard Manley Hopkins than to the nativist American Walt Whitman.

Within the first decade of Schnackenberg's career, the New Formalists claimed her, but she was already writing largely free verse by the time the movement began to gain notice. Schnackenberg has never been a standard-bearer for the New Formalists, and no evidence indicates that she ever recognized herself as a constituent of the group, much less an ambassador or apologist. Her poems rest uneasily in such company for several reasons. Even though she wrote in form and engaged her subjects with narrative rhetorical arrangements, she continued the old formalist or New Critical 1950s postwar tradition of highly allusive, classically inflected poetry, based on the models of the seventeenth-century metaphysical poets John Donne, George Herbert, Henry Vaughan, and others, whose poems were held up as ideals of graceful compression and delicate wit by T. S. Eliot. Most of the New Formalists eschewed their sophistication in favor of clear, accessible, even folksy poems that could be read and easily understood outside an academic setting. Unlike the poetry of the New Formalists Dana Gioia and Timothy Steele, Schnackenberg's close contemporaries in terms of age, one finds in her work traces of Eliot, Anthony Hecht, and Richard Wilbur. Comparisons are more often made with poets from the established canon of European literature than with her contemporaries. In a review of Schnackenberg's *The Lamplit Answer* (1985) the critic Phoebe Pettingell identifies the poet's models as "Dante, W. B. Yeats, T. S. Eliot, and the early (Catholic) Robert Lowell."

Critics and readers greeted Schnackenberg's first two books with enthusiasm, some of which continued unabated for her third and fourth as well. Writing in the culturally conservative *New Criterion*, William Logan explains that Schnackenberg had "published slowly, rarely in the current mode (she was writing formal verse before the bandwagons were drawn up to the bandbox, though her recent poetry has been in stately free verse)." In a review in *Poetry* magazine, Christian Wiman compares Schnackenberg to Robert Lowell and Elizabeth Bishop and observes that her "particular gift is for a kind of clear density, for making many different strands of experience part of a single, deceptively simple weave." A younger critic, Adam Kirsch, thinks highly of her "delightful strangeness." Rosanna Warren believes that Schnackenberg's

poetry "has set extremely high standards for contemporary poetry." And the South African Nobel laureate Nadine Gordimer wrote that the poems "move me in a way that I don't really think I have experienced since I first read Rilke at sixteen or seventeen."

Schnackenberg is sometimes most noticed as a result of her absence from anthologies or critical treatments. In 1986, Liz Rosenberg chastised Alicia Ostriker for excluding Schnackenberg from her book *Stealing the Language: The Emergence of Women's Poetry in America*. Rosenberg protests that the book makes "no mention of the new formalist movement in women's poetry represented by poets like Amy Clampitt, Mary Jo Salter and Gjertrud Schnackenberg, ... whose work may not fit Mrs. Ostriker's particular taxonomy." Although Robert McPhillips devotes an entire chapter to Schnackenberg in *The New Formalism,* she is conspicuously left out of the anthology *Rebel Angels: 25 Poets of the New Formalism* (1996), edited by Mark Jarman and David Mason. This is not as unusual as one might think. She has on occasion requested that her poems not appear in explicitly New Formalist anthologies. She has also had some trouble shaking off the surfeit of laurels placed on her brow. Six years after the publication of her first book and a decade after her first accolades, she was still being depicted as a "brilliant newcomer" by Christina Robb, when she appeared, perhaps reluctantly, in *The Direction of Poetry: An Anthology of Rhymed and Metered Verse Written in the English Language since 1975* (1988), edited by Robert Richman. Great things were expected from her, and for the most part great things were delivered, although she has published books slowly. By her own account she works up to seven years on a single collection of poetry. This intense devotion to her craft places her among poets like Philip Larkin and Elizabeth Bishop, who produced on average one book per decade during their careers.

The slow appearance of books notwithstanding, Schnackenberg's poems have enjoyed wide publication, having appeared in such venues as the *Atlantic Monthly, Harper's,* the *New Yorker,* the *Kenyon Review,* the *Paris Review, Ploughshares, Poetry,* the *Yale Review,* and the *Carolina Quarterly.* The larger pattern that becomes apparent in her books is movement away from childhood, away from America, away from formal poems, toward more complex ones that require a wealth of supporting notes. After her shift from formal constructions in her poems, some, such as Cynthia Haven, insisted that "meter reined in her excesses and ordered her pandemonium of literary, historical and religious allusions. Plus, she had an extraordinary dexterity and inventiveness in form. It's missed." But in the *New Republic* the poet Glyn Maxwell provides a more moderate assessment:

The changes that Schnackenberg has wrought upon the shapes of her verse over the years attest to an essential struggle with the nature of form itself, of art and artifice, resulting in a sort of flowering through anxiety. Each book, from the confident young display of *Portraits and Elegies* to the tremulous, fractured repetitions of *The Throne of Labdacus,* seems to indicate a changed attitude to the art itself, a genuine pause for thought in the silence between volumes. This is rare, for most contemporary poets take as few breaths between books as they do between lines. But Schnackenberg's aesthetic remains constant: after twenty-five years of published work, she is still gazing from darkness into lamplight and giving voice to those whom she imagines are warmed by it.

In her use of classical imagery and myth she can be compared to the contemporary poets Louise Glück and Anne Carson, though the three share almost nothing else in common. Schnackenberg is a unique presence in American poetry, and Glyn Maxwell feels that she "has rarely seemed to be in dialogue with any contemporary, and perhaps for this reason she is one of the few American poets whose voice one might recognize in a line." Yet Robert McPhillips, in *The New Formalism,* has written that "unmoored from traditional meter and form … and lacking narrative tension," Schnackenberg seems "even farther from the 'source of poetry.'" Although her metrics have loosened—and rhymes have become rare and somewhat eerily distant from one another when they do appear—Schnackenberg has never abandoned form altogether, as one will find in the acts of pure expression written by champions of a liberating free verse such as Diane Wakoski. Even in her later books Schnackenberg holds strictly to fixed stanzaic forms, usually couplets or tercets.

Her move away from strict form follows a pattern often observed in American poetry, one mourned by some and applauded by others. Robert Lowell began writing in an elaborate and highly formal style in *Lord Weary's Castle* (1946). This later gave way to autobiographical free-form expression in his landmark book *Life Studies* (1959), which in turn influenced Anne Sexton and Sylvia Plath, both of whom studied with him. This was seen as a path of emancipation, and it is one notably followed by Adrienne Rich as well. Rich began her career writing cautious poems such as "Aunt Jennifer's Tigers" in the 1950s. She described this reliance on form as a way to handle her emotions with "asbestos gloves." By the 1970s, with the publication of *Diving into the Wreck* (1973), she had adopted the formerly neglected first person pronoun and began writing in free verse on autobiographical feminist issues. The unusual thing about Schnackenberg's adoption of this career pattern is the time frame in which she did it. It was certainly odd for a young poet to write in tight formal stanzas in the mid-1970s, and by the time she had thrown off the mantle of formalism it was the late 1980s, when the New Formalists were at their peak and the so-called "culture wars" flared the hottest.

PORTRAITS AND ELEGIES

Praise came early for Schnackenberg. In winning the prestigious Glascock Poetry Prize at Mount Holyoke, she early joined the likes of former winners Sylvia Plath, Robert Lowell, and James Merrill. In his September 2, 1979, review in the *New York Times* of *The Pushcart Prize, IV* anthology, John Romano singled out Schnackenberg's poem "Laughing with One Eye" (which would later be retitled "Walking Home") as "extraordinary," "pictorial and dramatic and accessible in a way that we have all but ceased to expect from contemporary poetry." The poems written between her college years and 1982 appeared in her first collection, the chapbook *Portraits and Elegies,* published in 1982 by David R. Godine. These earlier, more traditional poems remain her most frequently discussed and perhaps most widely read. Nearly two decades later, in 2000, Mary Jo Salter made use of the poem "Elizabeth, 1905" from the book's closing sequence, "19 Hadley Street," as a centerpiece of her baccalaureate address at Schnackenberg's alma mater, describing Schnackenberg as "one of America's most distinguished poets."

A mere forty-eight pages, *Portraits and Elegies,* being a first collection, initially received little critical notice. However, David St. John, writing at the time in the *Antioch Review,* felt that it was "a special pleasure and relief to find a young poet writing in traditional forms who also has in her grasp both powerful subject matter and the intelligence to command her technique." He pronounced it an "exceptional first book of poems." This sentiment would be echoed by a number of critics who would have the opportunity to mention *Portraits and Elegies* in reviews of Schnackenberg's subsequent books. When it was reprinted in the collection *Supernatural Love: Poems 1976–1992* (2000), it became apparent that *Portraits and Elegies* remained for some her most popular and most remembered book. Looking back over her four books, Christian Wiman wrote in *Poetry* magazine that it was her "best book," and "a substantial and rare accomplishment." The poems are calm, prim but casual in their way, reminiscences, portraits of family and historical figures, both real and imagined. Glyn Maxwell wrote in the *New Republic,* "It has the successes and the failures of early work—the freshness and the impact, along with the overgrown lines." The poems are defined by delicate displacements that arise from remembered images or sounds, much like the madeleine dipped in tea that inspires such washes of remembered past in Proust. In one sense Schnackenberg can be thought of as a miniaturist with a vast scope, as when a lost marble becomes an entire planet in one poem. She uses details to shift dimensions.

The book is divided into three sequences, "Laughing with One Eye," the single long poem "Darwin in 1881," and "19 Hadley Street." The first was written in 1977, when she was twenty-four, and most of the poems are memories of her father, to whom the sequence is dedicated. "Laughing with One Eye" is prefaced by an epigraph from Yeats's poem "Vacillation," from *The Winding Stair and Other Poems* (1933). The lines are taken from the third part of that poem, where Yeats warns that by the age of forty—"from the fortieth winter"—one should take stock of one's accomplishments and discard the dross, that which is "not suited for such men as come / Proud, open-eyed and laughing to the tomb." For her father, as for anyone, this is praise of the highest order, if indeed she views her father as a man so wise that he had somehow learned to accept his own death, or at least that he had accomplished so much that his death could not be thought of as cutting his life unreasonably short. She describes her father as a gentle, sometimes clumsy man, and her adoration seems unalloyed by dark memories. In this regard the poems can be considered memorials, personal by way of content but public in their cool formal exterior.

The first poem, "Nightfishing," is a perfect example of this style. Set in iambic pentameter with a regular rhyme scheme of *abab, cdcd,* and so forth, it is a beautiful meditation on the death of her father. In the first and third stanzas, the speaker of the poem sits in a kitchen observing a planter's clock (a clock with dials that indicate the phases of the moon; often these dials would depict a man's face in the moon):

> The kitchen's old-fashioned planter's clock
>   portrays
> A smiling moon as it dips down below
> Two hemispheres, stars numberless as days,
> And peas, tomatoes, onions, as they grow.

The longer central stanza allows the speaker to relate a memory of fishing with her father at night. She recalls looking at him and seeing how,

> Just as a fish lurks deep in water weeds,
> A thought of death will lurk deep down, will
>   show
> One eye, then quietly disappear in you.

Then back in the present she continues: "I'm in the kitchen. You are three days dead," and time is "Pushing me, oarless, from the shore of you." The subject matter is not unusual, nor is the theme itself. Her exceptional treatment is what compels admiration. Schnackenberg's intense metaphorical observation is rare in poetry of any age, and it is not difficult to understand the early accolades that her work accrued. In fact her pictorial sense is at its most solid and effective in these early poems:

> *Steinway* in German script above the keys,
> Letters like dragons curling stiff gold tails,
> Gold letters, ivory keys, the black wood cracked
> By years of sunlight, into dragon scales.

This is the beginning of the second poem in the book, "Intermezzo." By definition an intermezzo is a musical interlude of lighter, more fragile texture than the pieces that precede or follow it, or sometimes a brief lyrical entr'acte. For Schnackenberg the musical form becomes a symbol of the sort of quiet reverie that overtakes us at times when we are least distracted. Her setting is reminiscent of D. H. Lawrence's famous poem "Piano," in that both contain rhapsodic returns to early memory triggered by the sound of music, yet here it is the pianist himself who is drawn back into his own memories even within the larger memory of the speaker. The poem ends with a brilliant transposition of proportion, when "The marble long-lost under the piano" becomes

> … a planet secretive, cloud-wrapped and blue,
> Silent and gorgeous by your foot, making
> A god lost in reflection, a god of you.

The middle third of the book comprises what may well be her best-known poem, "Darwin in 1881," which she chose to reprint in her second collection, *The Lamplit Answer,* published a mere three years later. The poem has garnered much commentary in academic settings, largely because it lends itself so well to classroom analysis, blending as it does scientific, historical, and literary themes. As with many of her later poems on figures such as the poets Dante Alighieri (1265–1321) and Osip Mandelstam (1891–1938), a substantial amount of biographical information is needed to appreciate the poem fully. However, unlike later treatments, "Darwin in 1881" is not accompanied by notes to provide such information. The reader finds an elderly Darwin, who died in 1882,

> Sleepless as Prospero in his bedroom
> In Milan, with all his miracles
> Reduced to sailors' tales.

She succeeds in intermingling different phases of her subject's life in a tangle of memory that aims to become, in some respects, a memento mori. Darwin considers the fossils and other remains that have made his grand work possible—the "beetle jaws and beaks of gulls / And bivalve hinges"—as his life is drawing to its conclusion, "Done with fixed laws, / Done with experiments."

The poetic parallel with Shakespeare's magical exile, the Duke of Milan, works in contrary motion to Darwin's experience. As Prospero is restored to his former status Darwin is deposed in a sense. Both are finished with magnificent travels, exotic locales, momentous discoveries, but Darwin's were integral to his life's work rather than a disruption of it. The use of literary allusion, which prevails in Schnackenberg's later books, is in evidence—"Silence creeps by in memory as it crept / By him on water," just as in *The Tempest* Ferdinand recalls how the spirit Ariel's "music crept by me upon the waters." Schnackenberg mixes motion and time, comparing memories to islands that disappear over horizons, though one knows they remain real on maps and globes. Her thematic inclinations are perhaps best expressed in this poem, though they will be deployed with a grandiloquent baroque delicacy in her later poems.

Although the most direct comparisons are between the lives of Prospero and Darwin, who both undertook great sea voyages, some have observed that the descriptions might also be a subtle reference to her father. As Prospero relinquished his magical powers to live a quiet life in Italy, Darwin gave up his epoch-making scientific research in later life and retired to his country home, Down House, in Kent, England, intent on penning his memoirs. The choice of subjects in this poem is ambitious and even more surprising given that Schnackenberg wrote the poem while still in her twenties. Darwin's role as a father is more important in this poem than is his role as the famous and controversial naturalist. This domestication makes him seem vulnerable, venerable, and yet endearing, three qualities that Schnackenberg attached to her own father in the first sequence of *Portraits and Elegies*. Darwin was the father of seven children who survived into adulthood, and he was close to them, sometimes recruiting them as research assistants. Likewise, Prospero is depicted as the devoted and protective father of his daughter in *The Tempest*. "Darwin in 1881" is written in quatrains of *abba* rhyme, combining identical with slant rhymes. The rhyme scheme sometimes continues across stanzas of varying length, as one finds embedded in the sentence spanning lines 55 through 61:

> He wrote, Let your indulgence set me free,
> To the Academy, and took a nap
> Beneath a London Daily tent, [a]
> Then puttered on his hothouse walk [b]
>
> Watching his orchids beautifully stalk [b]
> Their unreturning paths, where each descendant [a]
> Is the last—

This metrically irregular lineation and stanza construction, sustained throughout by a uniform rhyme scheme, may be a stylistic representation of Darwin's discovery of patterns among vastly diverse bodies of evidence. Erika Taibl, in *Poetry For Students* has written that:

> Schnackenberg plays with form in the poem in a way that calls to mind the balance of the in-between times of history. Ultimately, she reveals a return to traditional poetic form that is engaged in a modern context. In the meeting of tradition and modernity, a hybrid form is created. The hybrid is a new self for the contemporary poet, a marriage of past and present, a joining that is carefully illustrated through the character of Darwin as he reinvents himself in the context of history and his own theories.

She goes on to say that "to employ tools of both the free verse and formalist schools" could serve as a way "to emphasize the dynamics of language struggle and evolution."

The final section, "19 Hadley Street," was written in 1976 in the years immediately following Schnackenberg's graduation from Mount

Holyoke. The poems are set in the house where she lived near the college. She traces a receding history of the house through snapshot portraits of imagined former inhabitants, from "Dusting," which is set in the present, through "Elizabeth, 1905" to "Ebenezer Marsh, 1725." In their formal confidence and pictorial framing these poems can be compared to character sketches written as much as a century earlier by Edwin Arlington Robinson, Edgar Lee Masters, and Robert Frost. The house is depicted as a sanctuary from a threatening world. In 1858,

> ... while Cousin Jed debates
>   With Pa, slavery and war
> . . . .
> ... Aunt Jerusha celebrates
>   By drinking sherry
>   And blushes red to see
> Bachelor Moody, hat in hand, opening the gates.

In 1843, when it is the end of the world to those under the spell of the millennial revivalism of that era, the girls sit inside, each sewing her "Ascension Gown" for the rapture, and closing the

> hem up with a gathering thread
> So sinners left on earth could not
> Look up her dress as she arose.

The dark peril of witchcraft in 1740 leads to "The Meeting in the Kitchen," and as early as 1725 the house's

> ... windows were the biggest in the town,
> Your walls were papered, pillows filled with
>   down
> On great four-posters under family portraits,
> The shelves laden with tamarinds, sweetmeats.

Schnackenberg's style is least referential in *Portraits and Elegies,* which is to say that any historical information needed to appreciate the poems should already be in place for most readers. The book does not directly refer to other books. Aside from basic biographical elements from Darwin's life and a rudimentary comprehension of Shakespeare's *The Tempest* for the center of the book, the reader needs to know little more than what a Steinway piano or a planter's clock looks like. Consequently *Portraits and Elegies* is the only one of her books collected in *Supernatural Love* that does not require a single entry in the extensive notes section. Over time Schnackenberg would begin to demand more and more of her readers in the way of outside knowledge, but in these first poems she has not yet donned such high modernist garb. It is also here that she is closest to the New Formalist ideal, with poems composed in neatly rhymed tetrameters and pentameters, though it should be remembered that she was composing these poems at a time when the only notable poets writing in form were either those who had continued to do so since the Second World War, like Anthony Hecht and Richard Wilbur, or were born outside America, like Seamus Heaney, Derek Walcott, and Joseph Brodsky.

THE LAMPLIT ANSWER

The Lamplit Answer (1985), which followed *Portraits and Elegies* by three years, marked Schnackenberg's first publication by a major house—Farrar Straus and Giroux in New York—which also reissued her first book the following year. Both books subsequently appeared in England, published by Century Hutchinson. *The Lamplit Answer* met with commendations equal to those of her first book. John Hollander in the *Yale Review* calls her "a poet of more than promise, just as she is more than skilled," while Geoffrey Stokes wrote in the *Village Voice Literary Supplement* that same year that she is "a major poetic voice—at this point, the most gifted American of her generation." In the *New Leader,* Phoebe Pettingell compares Schnackenberg to Amy Clampitt, suggesting that each possesses a "religious, metaphysical mind." In his *New Criterion* review William Logan also associates the two poets, writing that "*Portraits and Elegies* ... was an astonishing debut (with Amy Clampitt's *The Kingfisher*, the most remarkable of the decade)."

Although regularly praised for her formal accomplishments, others felt that they served equally as detriments. J. D. McClatchy, writing in the *New York Times*, decided that the "lulling regularity of the iambic rhythm hold[s] both the poet and her reader back from a more rigorous probing." Although he considers her to be a "formidable versifier" he points out that "her technique lacks variety." Despite these reservations he concludes that the book "shines throughout with a luminous craft and a wise reflective sense of culture and its claims on human feeling." It is true that despite the regular chorus of supporters who claim her as a great formalist in the long tradition of English literature, her metrical range is generally narrow, confined almost entirely to iambic pentameter and tetrameter, with the rare poem in trimeter, such as "The Heavenly Feast." Luckily for her readers she avoids such poetry workshop staples as the villanelle and the sestina, although some have identified a ghostly terza rima at work in her later poem "A Gilded Lapse of Time," which is addressed partially to Dante, who composed his *Divine Comedy* in that interlocking pattern *aba, bcb, cdc,* and so forth. For the most part avoiding rhyming couplets, Schnackenberg's schemes tend toward *abab* and *abba* patterns, though one will also find more complex, irregular patterns, such as the *abc abd bef bcd* of "Imaginary Prisons," which mimics the bizarre curling thorn bushes that overtake Sleeping Beauty's castle.

With *The Lamplit Answer*, Schnackenberg's progress toward her contested reputation begins. The collection, dedicated to her three sisters, is more bookish, so to speak, as indicated by its title. A "lamplit answer" is one found in a book under a lamp, such as her father seeks in the final poem of the collection, "Supernatural Love." She displays interest in more distant historical subjects, among them Frédéric Chopin (1810–1849), for which she relied on Adam Zamoyski's biography and the virtuoso's own letters and journals. Schnackenberg was already beginning to show her tendency to unmoor herself from previous classifications. Writing in the *Nation*, Rosetta Cohen admires the poet's first book, in which she proves "capable of working small miracles with cadence and rhyme." She explains that in the second book the author "seems to have made an attempt to move beyond the limits of subject and style on which her reputation is based." Cohen outlines what she considers a "Jamesian preoccupation ... with the nuances of small gestures and quiet moments." Similarly Daniel Mendelsohn observes in the *New York Review of Books*, "Schnackenberg has a vivid historical imagination, but it's the imagination of a historical novelist, rather than a historian." Certainly Schnackenberg's focus on historical figures in given settings lends itself to comparison with prose fiction, though this type of poetry would soon give way to her more visionary and passionate poems.

The book is divided into four sections. The first of these sections contains the lush, ironic poem "Kremlin of Smoke." A poem in eight sections, it depicts Chopin living in exile among the splendor of the Faubourg Saint-Germain, where the "tea steam hangs / Phantom chrysanthemums on long, evaporating stems / In the air of the winter apartment." The star of any salon or drawing room, Chopin is imprisoned by opulence and indulgence, "the cream cakes, the pale-skinned meringues, / And the candied violets," as the "pipes and cigars of bespectacled / Millionaire guests fling a kremlin of smoke overhead, / Dome upon dome." The twenty-year-old piano prodigy learns that his childhood city, Warsaw, has fallen to the Russians. He reminisces about times spent with his mother and his childhood piano teacher, who provides a comic litany of things a pianist must know, including "to ignore every so-called Italian composer" as well as "the conventions surrounding one's need / For a bath, since a rubdown with vodka will do." The poem alternates between the childhood memories and 1831, when he writes in his journal, "I too am an outcome withering from my cause." The artist is powerless to act, and he becomes a flower snapped off from its roots.

It might be suggested that Schnackenberg lacks a sense of humor, but her generally concentrated style sporadically permits such moments to surface. One such can be found in the rather brutal humor of "Two Tales of Clumsy," which J. D. McClatchy feels to be "ponderous":

> Disguised as Doctor of Philosophy
> In academic haberdashery
> By dint of hood and black capacious gown,
> No-No wipes off the blackboard up and down,
> His black sleeve floating outward with each
>   lunge,
> The black streaks glisten from his dampened
>   sponge.

Schnackenberg has had ample opportunity to meet and spar with such characters, but the mode of light verse does not suit her well. It resembles satirical personae mastered by T. S. Eliot, but his poems of this kind, like those about the impotent modern man "Sweeney," are not among his most admired. This type of satire has a long and fertile tradition, dating back in the modern era to Erasmus and Voltaire, and reaching its most accomplished states in English literature with John Dryden, Alexander Pope, and Jonathan Swift. It is not an area into which one can tread lightly. Nonetheless, the first part of the "Clumsy" poem has been anthologized in the ubiquitous *Norton Anthology of Modern Poetry,* which guarantees that Schnackenberg

will be measured at least in some part as a comic poet.

Along with "Darwin in 1881," the next section contains the long poem "Imaginary Prisons." It is a variation on the Sleeping Beauty myth, rooted partly in the haunting eighteenth-century copper etchings of Giovanni Battista Piranesi. As an example of *ekphrasis* it works well, and it presages Schnackenberg's use of works of Renaissance art in her following collection, *A Gilded Lapse of Time* (1992). The reader finds the castle of Sleeping Beauty, enveloped by thorn bushes that continue to grow around it even as the inhabitants of the castle remain frozen along with those suitors unwise enough to have attempted to pass through the spiny fortress. A single syntactical unit is allowed to spiral through as many as seven tercets at a time, what Daniel Mendelsohn describes as "sustained, onward-pushing periods that seem to climb tirelessly from tercet to tercet like Beauty's roses climbing the palace's abandoned arbors." The characters continue to dream in their stationary postures, outside of time, where "It isn't history if it isn't written":

> The kitchen boy distracted by a quarrel
> Is dreaming that he opens up a box
> Of banished knives blinding even at twilight
>
> And this way makes his adversary cower,
> But ducks in fact before the furnace-stoker
> Around whose lifted shovel embers sparkle
>
> And hang like bumblebees around a flower.

The grammar snakes away from conclusions and twines around the stanzas as if they were trellises. There is no sense of movement in the poem, except as a camera panning around a landscape, telling different stories that were stopped at a point in time. Until Sleeping Beauty is awakened, they will remain,

> But we have learned that here and now is where
> All time stops in a face we've held as dear
> As she is held who's overcome with roses.

The third part of *The Lamplit Answer* contains the strange poem "Love Letter," written in the style of Lord Byron's comic epic *Don Juan.* Just as critical consensus has aligned against Schnackenberg's attempts to write in comic styles, so it disapproves her fanciful love poems. Richard Eder in the *Los Angeles Times Book Review* described "Love Letter" as a "rueful and whimsical" poem that gives the "effect of a winged horse pulling a bakery cart." Writing in the *Washington Post,* Jane Cooper concluded that *The Lamplit Answer* in general is "uneven, full of experiments in the grand style (Lowell seems a presence behind the opening poems, the Byron of Don Juan behind her vigorous, self-mocking love poems)." "Love Letter" was, tellingly, left out of her selected poems perhaps for several reasons. The critics were anything but supportive, but it also is unusual in its playful sexuality: "I don't love you because you make me come / And come and come innumerable times." If any single line would be virtually unidentifiable as hers, this would be it—largely because such a line would be perfectly at home in most books of poetry written at that time, even within the New Formalist school. This playfulness does succeed to a degree in the poem "Sonata," which is self-referential and whimsical in a way found rarely in this poet's work. It begins as a poem "to inveigh against your absence," and so could be thought of as a love poem, but it seems more concerned with analyzing the demands of its own form. Combining sections of both sonata and concerto forms, she sighs that

> … true Sonatas close
> With what pedantic musicologists,
> Waving their Ph.D.s beneath my nose,
> Persist in calling Recapitulation.

She goes on to state, "Theme One: My life lacks what, in lacking you?" but soon leads the poem into a litany of pre-Socratic philosophers in order to symbolize "what-is-life-without-you-here":

> Like *nous* detached from Anaxagoras,
> Like cosmic fire glimmering without

> A Heraclitus there to find it out,
> Like square roots waiting for Pythagoras,
> Like One-ness riven from Parmenides,
> Like Nothing without Gorgias to detect it,
> Like paradox sans Zeno to perfect it,
> Like plural worlds lacking Empedocles.

As a love poem it is not entirely astray from that long, important tradition, even if it exists here in a simultaneously cerebral and light-hearted way.

The final section contains the poem "The Heavenly Feast," a memorial to Simone Weil. Schnackenberg deliberately trims the lines to an iambic trimeter in quatrains, to articulate the emaciation of the poem's subject, who died of tuberculosis in a sanatorium in England, during the Second World War, when she refused to eat more than the rations given to her countrymen in Nazi-occupied France:

> So four years into the war,
> And cut off from the ones
> Whose circumstance you felt
> And suffering as yours,
>
> You carved yourself a path
> Through ever-narrowing doors
> Of hunger and of thirst,
> And entered them day by day,
>
> Refusing all at first
> But that ration of food
> Your people could obtain
> Behind the lines in France.

The tone is also remarkably spare and prosaic for Schnackenberg, and this adds to the sense of ascetic duty felt by Weil in the sanatorium. Possibly owing to its historical consideration of sacrifice and suffering, the poem was later set for soprano and orchestra by the composer Robert Beaser and was performed in 1999 at Carnegie Hall in New York, although the composition failed to earn the approval of music critics.

The last poem in the book, "Supernatural Love," provides this collection with its title,

The Lamplit Answer, as well as the title for the volume of selected poems published in 2000, *Supernatural Love.* It is composed in tercets of *aaa, bbb, ccc* rhyme. In the poem a father looks at the etymology of the word "carnation," which his young daughter, knitting nearby, intuitively believes means "Christ's flower."

> My father at the dictionary-stand
> Touches the page to fully understand
> The lamplit answer, tilting in his hand
>
> His slowly scanning magnifying lens,
> A blurry, glistening circle he suspends
> Above the word "Carnation."

He concludes that it derives from

> … "A pink variety of Clove,
>
> *Carnatio,* the Latin, meaning flesh."
> As if the bud's essential oils brush
> Christ's fragrance through the room.

He then turns to the next lamplit answer and sees that the entry for "clove" is "a spice, dried from a flower bud" which in turn is from the "French, for *clou,* meaning a nail." At this discovery the daughter strikes her "finger to the bone" with the sewing needle. She lifts her hand in "startled agony" and calls "Daddy daddy," which echoes Jesus' cry on the cross of "Abba, Abba." The conclusion is driven by an emotional conviction and elegance that is rarely achieved elsewhere:

> My father's hand touches the injury
>
> As lightly as he touched the page before,
> Where incarnation bloomed from roots that bore
> The flowers I called Christ's when I was four.

Glyn Maxwell wrote of *The Lamplit Answer* in the *New Republic* that "the lines are slightly plainer than before" as Schnackenberg sails "outwards into uncharted waters." This would prove prophetic. In the years to come she would leave the intimacy and domestic modesty of her first two books behind entirely.

A GILDED LAPSE OF TIME

In many regards *A Gilded Lapse of Time* remains Schnackenberg's most problematic and contested book. Having virtually exhausted the well of available honors, and even receiving an honorary doctorate from her alma mater, Schnackenberg produced a book that continues to divide opinion in a singular fashion. It is ambitious, as allusive as any poetry since Ezra Pound's *Cantos* more than two decades earlier, as thematically elusive as anything that had gone before. Some saw in it a great achievement, a weighing of history and art against spiritual crisis, along the lines of Eliot's *The Four Quartets* (1943), to which it appears to owe a considerable debt both formally and philosophically. Others found it daunting and indulgent, reminiscent of the worst excesses of the high modernism of a half-century before, unable to move without the clank of footnotes, reaching so far that it overextended itself and finally collapsed in a heap of broken images.

A more baroque and less personal air had come to dominate her style, and her earlier adherence to form was partially discarded, or, as Adam Kirsch put it in the *New York Times,* she "sacrific[ed] pressure for speed," though he notes that her "verse is … anchored in the pentameter even when it veers into irregularity." Apart from the selected poems, *A Gilded Lapse of Time* is the longest of Schnackenberg's books, and in many ways it is the most striving. Its subjects are varied, its allusions countless. In his review of the book in the *New York Times Book Review,* William Logan proclaims her "the most talented American poet under the age of 40," a verdict to which he adheres, despite his diminished interest in her following book, *The Throne of Labdacus* (2000). He declares *Gilded Lapse* her "darkest and yet most radiant book," containing sequences "so enraptured, so lost in annunciations and resurrections, that they might be called visions." He writes that the poems "have a leisurely grandeur; they are written in a melodic free verse, unfolding phrase by phrase into long, barely sustainable sentences." Daniel McGuiness in the *Antioch Review* says that "these are poems of terrific intelligence, terrific belief, terrific technique, terrific learning." The British poet Ruth Fainlight, writing in the *Times Literary Supplement,* remarks that "the opulent language and the range of reference of these meditations" place her "among the best poets writing."

Such praise was not universal. While acknowledging that "it is more difficult and more ambitious than what went before," Glyn Maxwell lamented that "she relinquishes rhyme at the outer gate. The forms in which she has attained such facility, the pentameters and the tetrameters, are beaten out into a miscellaneous, often awkward jumble of lengths." Daniel Mendelsohn, who is not at all dismissive of the book, still notices its "sprawling tripartite" structure, "exhaustingly spun-out sentences," its "vatic obscurities," "thematic grandiosity and verbal bloat," its "mandarin … allusions and "sheer excess." Schnackenberg is bookish in the most positive sense of the term, and her arthistorical sense is remarkably accomplished. She is, for the most part, quite earnest, even if so tied to celestial language that her sincerity is difficult to detect except in the fully furnished rococo chambers she inhabits. The very "surface" of her work, as Wallace Stevens might suggest, completes the notion of her sincerity. Her surface *is* in some respects her sincerity. Rosanna Warren defines the "gilded lapse" from the book's title as "pulsations, the gilded lapses or rifts in time through which revelation gleams and in which history seems—fleetingly—absolved." Richard Eder explains it as "the silence, and the break between what preceded it and what follows," much like Emily Dickinson's "Stillness in the Air— / Between the Heaves of Storm—".

Daniel Mendelsohn identifies *A Gilded Lapse of Time* as a "religious epic." What is most odd about the book is its fixation on Catholic iconography and voluble spiritual longing, a choice all the more peculiar given Schnackenberg's protestant Lutheran upbringing and the consequent soberness of her early poems. Much of this has to do with circumstance. Dante's Catholicism is authoritative (some have deemed the *Divine Comedy* a third Testament), and the setting, Ravenna, is entirely Catholic with classical Roman underpinnings. Schnackenberg seems preoccupied with erecting a scaffold of scholarship to sustain her spiritual quest, which might be removed later to reveal the sculpture it enabled to be chiseled. The notes for this book, which occupy thirteen pages, feel at times unnecessary if not unwanted, and it becomes impossible to follow them all while reading the poems themselves. This trend of a poet's providing notes, initiated by Eliot in *The Waste Land* (1922), would appear to have reached its fullest extent here. Schnackenberg has to some degree written a dissertation on her own poems before they were even published.

The book is arranged in three sections, "A Gilded Lapse of Time," "Crux of Radiance," and a long elegy for the Russian poet Osip Mandelstam, "A Monument in Utopia." The initial sequence is in twenty parts, addressed at times directly to Dante, and was originally published in the *New Yorker* on June 15, 1992. The poet tours the mausoleum of Galla Placidia and the tomb of Dante at Ravenna, and, as Rosanna Warren puts it in her review in the *New Republic,* "manages to compress within its frame not only a private, learned and passionate reading of *The Divine Comedy,* but an equally personal courtship of God, mediated through the Bible and St. Augustine, and through contemplation of the ruined brilliance of Byzantine Ravenna." The first stanza works well without prior knowledge of the source of a superstition—hearing one's name from a disembodied source as a prophecy of impending death—which happens in this case to be taken from Nikolai

Gogol's short story "Old-World Landowners" (1835), a source rather far afield from the gilded Renaissance artifacts that charge the poems.

A romantic crisis of one sort or another sets off a sense of spiritual longing:

When love was driven back upon itself,
When a lapse, where my life should have been,
Opened like a breach in the wall, and I stood
At a standstill before the gate built with mud,
I thought my name was spoken, and I couldn't
  reply—
Even knowing that when you hear your name
It's a soul on the other side who is grieving
For you, though you're never told why.

Other passages, such as the closing one, require more explanation:

… a heavy honeycomb, and your words
Were a stream of bees floating toward me in
  sunlight.
When I opened your book I thought you spoke,

Or else it was Gabriel lifting to my lips
A tablespoon of golden, boiling smoke
So wounding to my mouth I turned my back

On the source of poetry, and then I woke.

Schnackenberg has in mind a peculiar nexus of reference here: Saul's forbidding the starving Israelites to eat the honey from a comb they find in the wilderness, and Jonathan's proceeding unawares to dip his staff and taste (1 Samuel 14:24–29); and the use of the same image in classical antiquity, when bees were thought "to embody the souls of the dead." Honey imparted the gift of poetry to any who tasted of it. Once the reader learns this, an already substantial poem gains greater depth. A formerly surreal step becomes precipitous, and the reader might experience vertigo, which is both exhilarating and terrifying. Yet the poems remain reassuringly anchored in the here and now, as when "a tour guide beckoned me in, / And lifted her flashlight beam to the low vault." We are reminded that between the visionary moments there is time for life to continue as it always has. She finally comes around at the end from the fugue, which was inspired as much by poetic crisis as a spiritual one. Note in the closing sequence that rhyme, not always in attendance, reappears to tie together important motifs, as with "spoke," "smoke," and "woke." Rosanna Warren describes this as "subjecting the lyric to the abrasion of history," something Warren believes Schnackenberg has done right from the start. She goes on to say that "in the magnitude and the intricacy of its design, *A Gilded Lapse of Time* may be compared to the art of tapestry. Whether woven or stitched, tapestry suggests a work whose complexity and tensile strength subordinate many disparate elements to one masterful order." Phoebe Pettingell compares it to another artistic métier when she writes in the *New Leader,* "The startling images that light these pages often suggest the bizarre pictures medieval illuminators drew in the margins of their texts."

The trend toward the inclusion of classical and renaissance motifs is amplified in the middle portion of the book, "Crux of Radiance." William Logan says of the sequence: "The poet seems beyond the consolation of religion, but not the consolation of the art religion has inspired. The biblical imagery, classical allusions and philosophy from which the poems are composed might be airless bookishness to another poet, but Ms. Schnackenberg can spin straw into gold." The title alone imparts the expressive and ambitious nature of the poems, which are derived from quattrocento paintings such as Piero della Francesca's mural in fresco and tempera *Resurrection* (1463), which is the basis of the poem "Soldier Asleep at the Tomb":

In Palestine,
Where you are counting stars
To stay awake,
There is a legend that
The world was built
From nothing. There is a plaster crack

Ascending through the air
Above your head,
And you have laid aside
Your headgear
Covered with wolf skin,
But don't sink back,
Don't let your head
Tilt back, don't look up toward
The heaven's starry gulf and close your eyes,
Because you must not fall
Asleep. You must not sleep—

The image seems to open right into the historical and theological moment, but it remains an artifact, subject to the despoilment of the ages. Warren believes it "tests the redemptive promise of the crucifixion against the brutal evidence of history." Like everything else, it is less permanent than it appears. Schnackenberg's evocation of an *ex nihilo* concept of the Creation is strangely set alongside her gentle chiding of the soldier. It is tender, as if there were no distance between the resurrection of Christ and the patient observation, in the twentieth century, of a five-centuries-old mural. Warren also writes,

As she weaves her historical data with the scene of Christ and the angels and her metamorphic images (silk worm eggs, waterfalls, bright rivers, gold wires, gold thread, scarlet threads, rivers of blood), she presses toward the central scandal of aesthetics. Must art rise from pain? Does art exploit pain, or collude with torture, by representing pain?

The final section is the most unified, though Warren remarks that the "drive toward unity" leads the "poet astray." "A Monument in Utopia" traces the life, exile, and death of Osip Mandelstam, who perished in a work camp in Stalin's Soviet Union. The poem addresses him directly and resembles an ode:

You! You, with your hair-raising tales
Your coat without buttons, your raging fits,
Your history of poverty, your torn cigarettes!
You, with your heart still set
On impossible things.

In her use of syntactic parallelism and exclamatory description, Schnackenberg briefly and oddly resembles the Allen Ginsberg of *Howl* and *Kaddish*. It is also in part a loving tribute to Mandelstam:

You will be free to wander
In the metropolitan library,
Free to stare,
Without arousing suspicion,
At the statue voted by the senate
To honor poetry.

A Gilded Lapse of Time is a formidable challenge for most readers, and there is almost nothing in American poetry of the past two decades to which it can satisfactorily be compared. Despite a wide range of critical responses, most agree that the book represents a considerable achievement even if not, with William Logan, that it is "as brilliant and disturbing as any book in recent American poetry."

THE THRONE OF LABDACUS

With the simultaneous publication in 2000 of Schnackenberg's fourth book, *The Throne of Labdacus,* and a volume of poems selected from her first three books, *Supernatural Love: Poems 1976–1992,* critics were again divided, and some used the latter as a stick to strike at the former. Her earlier identifiable formalism had become supplanted by what Glyn Maxwell describes as "a flinty austerity of foreshortened rhymeless couplets, stalling and reiterating." The book struck him as an "antipodes of bleakness and intractability," utterly removed from her earlier poems.

The Throne of Labdacus, appearing fully eight years later, is a turn away from the scorching ecstasy of *A Gilded Lapse of Time.* It becomes clear that each of her four books stands as a work unto itself and rests uneasily on the shelf with its mates. *The Throne of Labdacus,* which won the Los Angeles Times Book Prize for poetry, met with three basic responses: most critics found it to be either the apogee or perigee of her career, while a more patient third group viewed it as one stage in a long progression and felt that future books would make the entire arc of her work more clear.

That champion of New Formalism, Robert McPhillips writes somewhat predictably in *The New Formalism* that *The Throne of Labdacus* is a "rather anemic exercise in philosophical-literary speculation that ultimately falls short as a cogent and illuminating critical enterprise on Sophocles as it does as a work of poetry," while Carol Moldaw says in the *Antioch Review,* felt that the book is Schnackenberg's "most austere, and arguably most beautiful, work to date." Adam Kirsch in the *New York Times* calls it "a very rare achievement in contemporary poetry—a philosophical idea treated, not glibly, obscurely or melodramatically, but with due seriousness and real intelligence" and feels that the poet is "reaching towards a more comprehensive work of art, attempting to balance language and idea, grandeur and precision." Christina Davis, in the *Boston Review,* decides that it is "her most exceptional and integrated [work] to date."

While Cynthia Haven, writing in the *San Francisco Chronicle Sunday Review,* insists that the book seems "spun out through redundant abstraction and needless gloss," Glyn Maxwell describes it as displaying the "sense of how a god, existing outside of time, would experience chronology" and says that this explains the "repetitions and its uncanny sense of being motionless." The most severe, if not the most eloquent, denunciation of the book comes from a frustrated Christian Wiman, who describes it harshly as a "numb book-length poem focused on the nameless slave who saved Oedipus" and adds, "I don't know if I would have even figured this out without the book jacket information." Yet across the Atlantic, Ruth Fainlight continued

to champion Schnackenberg in the *Times Literary Supplement,* saying that all "the strengths of the earlier books have been absorbed into its loosely structured blank couplets."

The ten parts of *The Throne of Labdacus* concern the myth of Oedipus. As Adam Kirsch has pointed out, it "is not a retelling of the Oedipus legend but a meditation on it, and assumes a fair familiarity with the original." Despite its length it cannot be considered epic, as it contains none of the vigorous, expansive ambition, the heroic (or antiheroic) energies a reader might expect from a long American poem after William Carlos Williams's *Paterson* (1946–1958), Charles Olson's *Maximus* (1953–1974), Allen Ginsberg's *The Fall of America* (1973), James Merrill's *Changing Light at Sandover* (1982), or Derek Walcott's *Omeros* (1990). The book's closest relative might be H.D.'s late-career classical reinvention *Helen in Egypt* (1961). At root *The Throne of Labdacus* may be thought of as a telling of the Oedipus myth, and while Schnackenberg may be conscious of the historical distance a reader must span, she is not clumsily self-conscious of this fact. It is systematic, hushed; it progresses along a single taut circuit, refusing to yield resolution or finale. Unlike the aforementioned twentieth-century predecessors, Schnackenberg's poem remains in one place, not attempting to comprehend swathes of culture, history, or private memory. Its strategy lies elsewhere.

The opening lines of the poem describe in miniature the entirety of the story:

The first warning passing through Thebes—
As small a sound

As a houseful alighting from Persia
And stamping its foot on a mound

Where the palace once was;
As small as a moth chewing thread

In the tyrant's robe;
As small as the cresting of red

In the rim of an injured eye; as small
As the sound of a human conceived—

In these opening lines one finds Oedipus conceived, blinded, and deposed. Schnackenberg's achievements as a miniaturist work well here, as details come to stand for larger episodes. The book handles such freighted issues as free will and fate. Does the god Apollo, "tuning the strings," determine the fate of Oedipus or simply pass down a judgment that has always existed? Does the shepherd who rescues the abandoned infant Oedipus despite his awareness of the oracle's prophecy do so of his own volition? He confesses, in a truly human moment, that

> *at the sight of the infant's gaze*
> *I was riveted, chosen, beguiled.*
> *I knew what the oracle said.*
> *And I rescued the child.*

At the book's conclusion, however, Apollo touches a string "and replies: / *I rescued the child.*" The fate declared, but not determined, by the oracle at Delphi cannot be altered, even by those who must live through the tragedy.

Schnackenberg anticipates some familiarity with the Oedipus myth and with Sophocles's *Oedipus Tyrannus* in particular. Similarly Sophocles himself, our primary source of information on the myth, relied on his audience's familiarity with the story in order to convey his drama through tight sequences of dialogue, according to the unities of time, place, and action described by Aristotle in his *Poetics*. Our post-Freudian position in history notwithstanding, the myth is not as important to our culture as it was to that of Sophocles. Like the modernists, Schnackenberg expects her audience to have enough grasp of artistic and historical matters to comprehend the icy topography of the classical Greek moral landscape. Unlike an inhabitant of ancient Thebes, we are dislodged from the cultural circumstances that informed Sophocles' drama. We are free to grapple on difficult moral ground or simply to discard Oedipus as a barbaric, amoral projection of human suffering:

> For some, the tragedy unfolds without a moral—
> No how or why; no spelling out of fate
>
> Or sacrifice or punishment; merely the god's
> Swift brushing-by, scented with laurel.
>
> And for others it is only an ancient folktale
> About a guiltless crime:
>
> Not a judgment, not a warning,
> Not an example, not a command—
>
> Merely a tale in which neither the gods
> Nor the human ones can claim that they meant
>
> To harm or to save, to kill or to stay their hands.

The poet's principal concern is not the morality or even the tragic inevitability of the myth, but rather time itself. Though certain narrative methods are in place, Schnackenberg's story does not advance along a plot line. The plot is entirely knotted together and outside of time. Such an enormous subject may be easily loosed from an author's hands. Schnackenberg holds it in place by rethinking the act of storytelling. She submerges dramatic arcs and curves into a broth of eternal reflection. Modern versions of the Oedipus myth have worn a variety of dress, such as Igor Stravinsky's eerie two-act oratorio in Latin, interspersed with a chorus in English, so it is not as though Schnackenberg is without precedent. In fact it would be a challenge, without resorting to Shakespeare or the Bible, to find a more heavily trodden subject.

The poem can be understood as a procession of prophetic assertion, weightless narrative, and depth provided by image alone. Voices interpolate the narration. Some are adopted from other texts (duly cited in the end notes); some are Schnackenberg's creation, such as the speech of the shepherd, which comprises the whole of the fourth section:

> *From the shroud came*
> *The gaze an infant bestows,*
>
> *In untouchable, wavering, radiant waves;*
> *Like a god's gaze, found in solitude.*
>
> *An infant maimed and left for dead. I stood*

In the shrinking snows. I knew the oracle.

I knew what the god had said.
I covered eyes with my hands.

But there are things we do
Not for the sake of the gods

But for other men. I lowered hands again
And looked: an infant left for dead.

There was no arguing backward,
No looking ahead.

This sternly figured disquisition forms the thematic axis of the poem. In addition to enlarging on the myth itself, Schnackenberg capably invents scenes that are possible, if never before imagined, such as Laius sleepless with guilt after placing the crippled infant Oedipus on a hillside to die. It is impossible to know if Sophocles himself ever considered such a thing.

Schnackenberg, a poet hailed as practitioner of a high and formal style, has chosen to write a long poem that defies classification, in variable metrics, with frequent pursuit of philosophical assertion in a manner that might be thought to echo portions of Eliot's *Four Quartets*. She presents a visionary account that is relayed through constant variation of poetic technique, a tactic hardly befitting a leading member of a formalist school. She succeeds outside of all bounds. *The Throne of Labdacus* thrives despite its refusal to adhere to narrative streams, but it can do so only by casting its shadow against an existing bas-relief. Readers need to be familiar with Sophocles and the Oedipus myth (Freud and his students notwithstanding) before reading the poem. For readers who lack some of the subtleties Schnackenberg had in mind, she supplies suitable guidance—the five pages of notes at *Labdacus*'s conclusion.

William Logan describers the book as occurring "in slow motion," written "in the margins of the myth." *The Throne of Labdacus* embodies the poet's "depths without her passion. It has been conceived in a museum and executed in a library." This grim assessment is balanced by others' such as Daniel Mendelsohn's, which compares Schnackenberg's couplets to "the strings of some awesome archaic instrument." And Robert McPhillips hopes "that this phenomenally talented poet will find her way back to the source of her lyric strength in her future work," but Adam Kirsch was confident that, although *The Throne of Labdacus* had not yet found a "perfect balance, it is only because even more satisfying and impressive poems will surely follow it."

Selected Bibliography

WORKS OF GJERTRUD SCHNACKENBERG

POETRY

Portraits and Elegies. Boston: Godine, 1982. New York: Farrar, Straus and Giroux, 1986. London: Hutchinson, 1986.

The Lamplit Answer. New York: Farrar, Straus and Giroux, 1985. London: Hutchinson, 1986.

A Gilded Lapse of Time. New York: Farrar, Straus and Giroux, 1992. London: Harvill, 1995.

Supernatural Love: Poems, 1976–1992. New York: Farrar, Straus and Giroux, 2000. (Published only in paperback.) English edition, *Supernatural Love: Collected Poems, 1976–2000.* Tarset, UK: Bloodaxe, 2001. (British edition is retitled and includes *The Throne of Labdacus.*)

The Throne of Labdacus. New York: Farrar, Straus and Giroux 2000.

ESSAYS

"Prefaces: Five Poets on Poems by T. S. Eliot. Gjertrud Schnackenberg: 'Marina.'" *Yale Review* 78, no. 2:210–215 (winter 1989).

"The Epistle of Paul the Apostle to the Colossians." In *Incarnation: Contemporary Writers on the New Testament.* Edited by Alfred Corn. New York: Viking, 1990. Pp. 189–211.

ANTHOLOGIES

Academy of American Poets, *Fifty Years of American Poetry: Anniversary Volume for the Academy of*

American Poets. New York: Abrams, 1984.

Ellmann, Richard, and Robert O'Clair, eds. *Norton Anthology of Modern Poetry.* 2d edition. New York: Norton, 1988.

Fainlight, Ruth. *Times Literary Supplement,* February 8, 2002.

Ferguson, Margaret, Mary Jo Salter, and Jon Stallworthy, eds. *Norton Anthology of Poetry,* 4th ed. New York: Norton, 1996.

Glück, Louise, ed. *The Best American Poetry, 1993.* New York: Scribners, 1993.

McClatchy, J. D., ed. *The Vintage Book of Contemporary American Poetry.* 2d ed. New York: Vintage, 2003

Richman, Robert, ed. *The Direction of Poetry: An Anthology of Rhymed and Metered Verse Written in the English Language since 1975.* Boston: Houghton Mifflin, 1988.

Strand, Mark, and Eavan Boland, eds. *The Making of a Poem: A Norton Anthology of Poetic Forms.* New York: Norton, 2000.

REVIEWS AND CRITICAL STUDIES

Cohen, Rosetta. "Magnifying Lens." *Nation* 241, no. 19:621–623 (December 7, 1985). (Review of *The Lamplit Answer.*)

Cooper, Jane. "Words of Distance and Intimacy." *Washington Post Book World,* August 25, 1985, p. 4. (Review of *The Lamplit Answer.*)

Davis, Christina. Review of *Supernatural Love* and *The Throne of Labdacus. Boston Review* 26, nos. 3–4:46–47 (summer 2001).

Eder, Richard. Review of *The Lamplit Answer. Los Angeles Times Book Review,* July 28, 1985, p. 3.

———. "Of Painters and Poets." *Los Angeles Times Book Review,* December 27, 1992, p. 3. (Review of *A Gilded Lapse of Time.*)

Griffiths, Paul. "A Program of Protest and Tribute." *New York Times,* November 2, 1999, p. E4.

Haven, Cynthia. Review of *The Throne of Labdacus* and *Supernatural Love. San Francisco Chronicle Sunday Review,* November 5, 2000.

Hilbert, Ernest. "Oedipus Redivivus." *Contemporary Poetry Review* (December 2003). (Review of *The Throne of Labdacus.*)

Hollander, John. "Poetry in Review." *Yale Review* 74, no. 4:vi–xv (summer 1985). (Review of *The Lamplit Answer.*)

Kirsch, Adam. "All Eyes on the Snow Globe." *New York Times,* October 29, 2000. (Review of *Supernatural Love* and *The Throne of Labdacus.*)

Logan, William. "Angels, Voyeurs, and Cooks." *New York Times Book Review,* November 15, 1992, pp. 15–16. (Review of *A Gilded Lapse of Time.*)

———. "The Habits of Their Habitats (Amy Clampitt and Gjertrud Schnackenberg)." In his *Reputations of the Tongue: On Poets and Poetry.* Gainesville: University Press of Florida, 1999. Pp. 70–89.

———. "Author! Author!" *New Criterion* 19, no. 4:65 (December 2000). (Review of *The Throne of Labdacus.*)

Maxwell, Glyn. "Things Done on Earth." *New Republic,* November 12, 2001, p. 53. (Review of *Supernatural Love* and *The Throne of Labdacus.*)

McClatchy, J. D. "Three Senses of Self." *New York Times,* May 26, 1985. (Review of *The Lamplit Answer.*)

McGuiness, Daniel. Review of *A Gilded Lapse of Time. Antioch Review* 51, no. 4:656–657 (fall 1993).

McPhillips, Robert. "Gjertrud Schnackenberg." In *Dictionary of Literary Biography,* Vol. 120, *American Poets since World War II.* Third Series. Edited by R. S. Gwynn. Detroit: Gale, 1992. Pp. 276–280.

McPhillips, Robert. *The New Formalism: A Critical Introduction.* Charlotte, N.C.: Volcanic Ash Books, 2003.

Mendelsohn, Daniel. "Breaking Out." *New York Review of Books* 48, no. 5:38–40 (March 29, 2001). (Review of *The Throne of Labdacus* and *Supernatural Love.*)

Moldaw, Carol. Review of *The Throne of Labdacus. Antioch Review* 59, no. 3:638–639 (summer 2001).

Pettingell, Phoebe. Review of *The Lamplit Answer. New Leader* 68:15 (September 23, 1985).

———. Review of *A Gilded Lapse of Time. New Leader* 75, no. 15:15–16 (November 30, 1992).

———. "Painful Mysteries." *New Leader* 83, no. 4:38 (September 2000). (Review of *The Throne of Labdacus.*)

Preminger, Alex, and T.V.F. Brogan, eds. *The New Princeton Encyclopedia of Poetry and Poetics.* Princeton: Princeton University Press, 1993. P. 1383.

Romano, John. "Large Work in Little Magazines." *New York Times,* September 2, 1979. (Review of *The Pushcart Prize, IV: Best of the Small Presses.*)

Rosenberg, Liz. "The Power of Victims." *New York Times,* July 20, 1986. (Review of *Stealing the Language: The Emergence of Women's Poetry in America* by Alicia Suskin Ostriker.)

St. John, David. "Raised Voices in the Choir: A Review of 1982 Poetry Selections." *Antioch Review* 41, no. 2:231–244 (spring 1983). (Review of *Portraits and Elegies.*)

Stokes, Geoffrey. Review of *The Lamplit Answer. Village Voice Literary Supplement,* May 7, 1985.

Warren, Rosanna. Review of *A Gilded Lapse of Time. New Republic* 209, no. 11:37–42 (September 13, 1993).

Wiman, Christian. "Short Reviews." *Poetry* 179, no. 2:91–95 (November 2001). (Review of *Supernatural Love.*)

—*ERNEST HILBERT*

Elizabeth Stoddard

1823–1902

ELIZABETH STODDARD'S LITERARY reputation remains a puzzle. An accomplished and versatile writer, from the 1850s through the 1890s Stoddard published poetry, prose sketches, three novels, nearly fifty short stories, and a children's book. In addition, she was a respected and popular journalist, writing for more than three years as the "lady correspondent" for *The Daily Alta California,* a San Francisco newspaper. For many years Stoddard and her husband, the poet Richard Henry Stoddard, circulated widely in New York City's literary and cultural circles, meeting many of the most prominent literati of their day. The couple's own more intimate circle was comprised of other, if less important, literary figures, including most centrally Bayard Taylor, Edmund Clarence Stedman, and George Boker. Reprinted twice in her lifetime, Stoddard's novels were widely and typically quite favorably reviewed in the most important periodicals of the day, and she was flattered by praise from such towering literary figures as Nathaniel Hawthorne and William Dean Howells. Nineteenth-century readers encountered her stories and sketches in a variety of prominent venues, including the *Atlantic Monthly, Putnam's,* and the *Literary World.* Despite such a promising record of accomplishment and connection, however, Stoddard never achieved the recognition she craved and deserved. Her long fiction never sold well, and throughout her career she was plagued by the knowledge that she was, as the critic Richard Foster has put it, "writing for audiences not yet born."

Given her work's insistently experimental stylistic qualities and its commitment to exploring such explosive issues as female sexual desire, religious hypocrisy, and the destructive effects of patriarchal power structures, Stoddard's struggle to find a wide audience in her own lifetime does not come as a particular surprise. What is more surprising, given those very same qualities and tendencies, is her difficulty in finding such an audience today. The literary historian James Matlack was the first to try to establish Stoddard's critical reputation among contemporary readers and critics, writing an extraordinarily detailed, meticulously researched dissertation, "The Literary Career of Elizabeth Barstow Stoddard," in 1967. The critic Richard Foster followed Matlack's lead, publishing editions of all three of Stoddard's novels in 1971 and an article on her work in 1972. But both Matlack's and Foster's efforts seemed to fall largely on deaf critical ears: only a handful of critics really wanted to talk about Stoddard and her work.

It was not until 1984 that Elizabeth Stoddard's reputation showed signs of faring better. In that year Lawrence Buell and Sandra Zagarell published their crucial collection *The Morgesons and Other Writings, Published and Unpublished.* In an effort to establish Stoddard as a writer of impressive range and of contemporary interest, this collection made available for the first time not only her 1862 novel but also selections from her short fiction, journalism, letters, and an 1866 journal. For a time Stoddard seemed poised on the verge of critical visibility: Buell and Zagarell forwarded the work they had begun in their collection with individual treatments of Stoddard's fiction in monographs and articles. Other critics, such as Susan K. Harris and David Reynolds, followed Buell and

Zagarell's lead and offered studies of Stoddard and her work (particularly *The Morgesons*) in articles and book-length studies. Stoddard's story "Lemorne *versus* Huell" appeared first in Sandra Gilbert and Susan Gubar's *Norton Anthology of Literature by Women* (1985), then in the *Norton Anthology of American Literature* (1989), and finally in the *Heath Anthology of American Literature* (1990). When Penguin published *The Morgesons* as part of their Penguin Classics series in 1997, Stoddard's reputation appeared to be at last secure.

But despite such critical efforts and publishing ventures, Stoddard still remains largely absent from contemporary critical consciousness. Her work garners only cursory (and typically reductive) treatment in such "comprehensive" studies of American literary history as the *Columbia Literary History of the United States* (1988) and the *Columbia History of the American Novel* (1991). While the articles published on Stoddard since the appearance of *The Morgesons and Other Writings* in 1984 are in the main very good, there are comparatively few of them. Perhaps most ominously, "Lemorne *versus* Huell" was dropped from the subsequent (1994, 2002) editions of the *Norton Anthology of American Literature*—a fact that seems to indicate that those critics seeking to bring Stoddard to the attention of a larger audience have reached some sort of impasse. Though made in 1984, Sandra Zagarell's assertion in "The Repossession of a Heritage," that "Stoddard's place in American literature has remained negligible primarily because readers have never known how to place her" still seems to hold. Those efforts by critics to determine "how to place" Stoddard and her work, and to argue for her centrality to American literary history, have gone largely unheeded, a fact that Robert McClure Smith and Ellen Weinauer, following Zagarell, attribute in part to "Stoddard's disturbing of neat boundaries" and her "writing's fraying of established generic categories."

If in both the nineteenth and the late-twentieth centuries Stoddard's work proved to be, in essence, too difficult to "place," signs point to a more promising turn of mind in the early twenty-first century. In 2003 alone, Stoddard studies bloomed. Smith and Weinauer's collection of essays *American Culture, Canons, and the Case of Elizabeth Stoddard* is joined by the first two critical monographs to treat Stoddard and her work: Regula Giovani's "*I Believe I Shall Die an Impenetrable Secret*": *The Writings of Elizabeth Barstow Stoddard* and Lynn Mahoney's *Elizabeth Stoddard and the Boundaries of Bourgeois Culture.* Perhaps most importantly, at least in terms of making Stoddard more visible to contemporary audiences, 2003 also witnessed the publication of a collection of Stoddard's short fiction, *Stories: Elizabeth Stoddard,* which introduces students, scholars, and general readers to sixteen of Stoddard's stories, more than a dozen of which had been previously available only through original archival research. These publications, along with the relatively small but qualitatively strong body of critical material that precedes them, suggest that criticism is becoming more responsive to Stoddard's "disturbing of neat boundaries," both generic and cultural. More and more, scholarship has begun to devote itself to understanding Stoddard's (often implicit) engagement in the cultural debates of her moment—racism and the Civil War, property rights legislation, women's health, separate-spheres ideology and domestic space—along with her effort to challenge, throughout her career and in a range of vocalities, the premises of dominant literary categories, genres, and forms. As these issues move to the forefront of Stoddard scholarship, it becomes increasingly apparent that if we omit Elizabeth Stoddard from the literary historical record, we miss an opportunity to complicate our understanding of nineteenth-century literary history and of women writers' participation in that history.

BIOGRAPHY

Elizabeth Drew Barstow was born on May 6, 1823, in Mattapoisett, Massachusetts, a coastal town at the base of Cape Cod, where she would spend the majority of her first three decades. She was the second of nine children, only five of whom survived beyond infancy, born to Wilson Barstow, a prosperous shipbuilder, and Betsey Drew, the daughter of a tailor. Although the Barstows often lived in affluence and played a leading role in Mattapoisett society and politics, the Barstow business, precariously reliant on the perils of seafaring and whaling, failed several times between 1843 and 1856, and the family was frequently embarrassed by financial setbacks and entanglements. But despite occasional vicissitudes, Stoddard was largely privileged in her youth by her family's financial status. In particular she received the boarding school education that her family's economic prominence might seem to warrant. Among the schools she attended was Wheaton Female Seminary in Norton, Massachusetts, where she was enrolled in 1837 and again in the winter of 1840–1841. But Wheaton's rigid educational philosophy, and perhaps even more its aggressive evangelicalism, were unappealing to Elizabeth Barstow, whose unsystematic intellectual curiosity, lifelong aversion to religious dogmatism, and defiance of conventional expectations with regard to female piety seem to have emerged quite early on.

Given her early religious skepticism it is ironic that the young Stoddard benefited more from the informal education she received in the library of Mattapoisett's Congregational minister, Thomas Robbins (fictionalized as Dr. Snell in *The Morgesons*), than she did from her formal schooling. Known as having one of the most extensive personal libraries in antebellum New England, Robbins was an antiquarian and a literary eclectic: despite his conservatism (he edited Cotton Mather's *Magnalia Christi Americana* and authored a sympathetic history of New England's founding religious fathers), he collected the "classic" works of eighteenth-century English writers, from Joseph Addison and Richard Steele to Henry Fielding and Oliver Goldsmith. A girl retrospectively described by Richard Henry Stoddard in his *Recollections* as having "a passion for reading, but a great disinclination for study," Stoddard embarked, at Robbins' invitation, on an unsystematic but extensive project of self-education. Her early reading habits extended into adulthood, and in the 1850s she turned her attention to contemporary European and American authors including George Sand, Elizabeth Barrett Browning, the Brontës, Alfred, Lord Tennyson, Charles Dickens, Nathaniel Hawthorne, Walt Whitman, Ralph Waldo Emerson, Henry David Thoreau, and Edgar Allan Poe. Stoddard's unusual opportunities with regard to a literary education extended to other spheres of intellectual and artistic culture. She traveled, often with her father, to such places as Boston and Salem, Massachusetts, the Berkshires, Washington, D.C., Maine, and perhaps most importantly, New York City, where she would meet her eventual husband and spend the majority of her adult life.

In summing up Stoddard's childhood and young adolescence, James Matlack notes that what emerges from the historical record is the "image of an active, somewhat rebellious girl in a seaside village." Stoddard's husband takes note of her "somewhat rebellious" nature, describing her in his *Recollections* as "one of those irrepressible girls who are sometimes born in staid Puritan families, to puzzle their parents, and to be misunderstood. Her spirits were high, and her disposition wilful [*sic*]." Like many of her most prevalent themes and plot devices (social class membership, financial reverses and their effects, the influence of the sea on human life and community), Stoddard's concern throughout her long and short fiction with "willful" female characters—women who challenge conventional expectations regarding female behavior and decorum—appears to have deeply autobiographical roots. In the 1865 novel *Two Men,* Stoddard's central female protagonist declares that "I am not like other girls, and I shall not try to be." Such a determined refusal to resist the script of conventional womanhood was one that Stoddard manifested throughout her life and her writing career. While this resistance often took forms that readers today cannot help but admire—a fictional commitment to sexually passionate female characters, an incisive investigation into the costs of separate-spheres ideology for women's development, an outspoken devotion to art as an acceptable vocation for women and to her own artistry—it often shaded over into an almost venemous outspokenness. Dubbed "the Pythoness" by some of those who knew her best, with her sometimes self-promoting candor Stoddard would alienate many in the years to come.

Whatever its privileges, comforts, and moments of defiance, Stoddard's youth came to an abrupt and traumatic end in the late 1840s, with the deaths, just twelve weeks apart, of her only sister, Jane (October 1848) and of her mother, Betsey (January 1849). In the years that immediately followed the deaths of Jane and Betsey Barstow, Stoddard seems to have quite consciously broadened her world, a spirit of restlessness motivating her to travel away from Mattapoisett, often to more cosmopolitan settings. On one such trip to New York City in 1851 she was introduced to the poet Richard Henry Stoddard, who was two years her junior. Just over a year later, in December of 1852, the two were married, in a ceremony they kept secret for two months.

For Elizabeth and Richard Henry Stoddard, the path from meeting to marriage was not a smooth one. While Richard fretted about how to establish himself as a poet and provide for a wife, Elizabeth seemed concerned with, among other things, the compromises that marriage involved for a nineteenth-century woman. In a letter to her friend Margaret Sweat written two weeks after her marriage, she addresses both her attraction to Richard Stoddard ("You must think how rare is an intellectual marriage between two wonderfully sensuous persons!") and her concerns about marriage as an institution, announcing her hope that "you will have no children. I have signified my intention to that effect—and [we] will walk the world together two *single* married women." Whatever her reluctance and its sources, Stoddard seems by the summer of 1853 to have settled quite fully and happily into both the intellectual and the sensual dimensions of her marriage. With striking frankness, for example, she writes Sweat in June about the "paradisal" nights she shares with her husband: "last night a great yellow moon shone down on our beds, our eyes, our bodies. Yes we have Eden, only better cooking than Adam had...." Despite its rather rocky and uncertain beginnings, the marriage between Elizabeth Barstow and Richard Henry Stoddard would last, weathering many personal tragedies and setbacks, until Elizabeth Stoddard's death in 1902.

Although Richard Henry Stoddard sought to support the couple through the work of his pen, he found it impossible to do so. Under the auspices of Nathaniel Hawthorne, whom he had met in July 1852, Richard Stoddard secured a job in the New York Custom House, where he worked from 1853 until 1870. The income was welcome but never sufficient to support the couple in the style they sought. Financial difficulties would plague them throughout their married lives and would leave them both, by all accounts, frustrated and embittered. Embittering too were the devastating personal tragedies the couple experienced. Their first child, Wilson, was born in June 1855; a second—unnamed—son was born, deformed, in the late spring of 1859, dying just a few weeks afterward. Two years later Wilson, six years old, died after a short illness, leaving both Elizabeth and Richard Stoddard devastated. A third son, Edwin Lorimer ("Lorry"), was born in December 1863. Lorry lived to maturity, and the Stoddards watched him succeed as both an actor and a writer for the stage. But they outlived this son too: he died in 1901 of tuberculosis, his death further darkening the last year of Elizabeth Stoddard's life. The Stoddards struggled with their own health as well; many of Elizabeth Stoddard's letters take note of the crippling effects of her bouts with illness and suggest an almost chronic invalidism.

It would appear that the couple's mutual intellectual and literary commitments solidified their bond and helped them weather the manifest difficulties of their married lives. Critics tend to agree that Richard Henry Stoddard's devotion to an outmoded high romanticism, coupled with his arguably limited poetic gifts, may at times have inhibited Stoddard, who looked to her husband as an established literary authority early on. (Characteristically, she would come to mock what she perceived as the literary pretensions of her husband and his romantic compatriots in her newspaper column, her fiction, and in direct comments and remarks.) Yet critics also recognize Richard Henry Stoddard for his tireless encouragement of Elizabeth Stoddard's literary career, both early and late. She was galvanized in her early literary efforts not only by her husband—she published her first piece, the impressionistic reverie "Phases," in October 1852, just two months before her marriage—but also by the world they inhabited together. The couple's home became a kind of intellectual gathering place where members of their circle met to discuss matters literary and cultural, and the Stoddards themselves attended the salons of Anne Lynch and Alice and Phoebe Cary along with such illustrious nineteenth-century figures as William Cullen Bryant, Emerson, Horace Greeley, Henry Ward Beecher, Edwin Booth,

Helen Hunt Jackson, George Ripley, and Julia Ward Howe.

It was against this enlivening cultural backdrop that Elizabeth Stoddard launched her own literary career. Having begun with apparent intentions to cultivate herself as a poet, she moved quickly to focus on prose. Between 1854 and 1858 she wrote a biweekly column for a San Francisco newspaper, the *Daily Alta California.* Her work for the *Alta* functioned largely as a kind of literary apprenticeship, the column providing a testing ground for her evolving, manifestly unique voice and style. Shortly after her engagement with the *Alta* came to a close, Stoddard began publishing short fiction, beginning with "Our Christmas Party," published in *Harper's New Monthly Magazine* in 1859. Not long after, Stoddard placed her long story, "My Own Story," in the *Atlantic Monthly,* one of the most respected journals of her age. Thus would Stoddard embark on the most productive decade-and-a-half of her career: between 1860 and 1875 she published three novels—*The Morgesons* (1862), *Two Men* (1865), and *Temple House* (1867)—some thirty-five short stories, including the widely anthologized "Lemorne versus Huell" (1863), and a strange and fascinating children's book, *Lolly Dinks' Doings* (1874).

Stoddard managed to sustain this productivity despite her awareness that her work was not finding a ready audience. "Indications are that it will be misunderstood," she wrote with prescience to her friend Edmund Clarence Stedman shortly after publication of *The Morgesons.* Five years later, after her predictions were borne out by poor sales of her second and third novels, Stoddard seems to have given up on her hopes of winning an audience for her long fiction. Beginning in 1868 she devoted herself exclusively to poetry and short prose works, and after *Lolly Dinks' Doings,* her literary production all but ceased for more than a decade. In the late 1880s, however, Stoddard received new inspiration from an unexpected flurry of interest in her works. Her longtime friend Edmund Stedman persuaded a New York publishing firm to bring out new editions of all three of her novels, the realist qualities of which seemed more suited to late-nineteenth-century audiences. Though the books did not sell well, the surge of interest led to an uptick in Stoddard's literary output, and she published fourteen short pieces (stories, sketches, reviews) between 1889 and 1891 alone. She was publicly praised by such well-respected literary authorities as William Dean Howells and Julian Hawthorne, the latter of whom called *The Morgesons* "one of the best novels ever written by a woman, and superior to all but a very few produced before or since by any American author." In 1893 her novels were included as part of an exhibit recognizing women writers at the World's Columbian Exposition in Chicago, and in 1895 she brought out *Poems,* a collection published by Houghton, Mifflin. In 1897, when Richard Henry Stoddard was honored for his service to American letters by the New York Authors' Club, Stoddard herself received many tributes. Once more the literary world seemed ready fully to acknowledge Elizabeth Stoddard, and in 1901 her novels were issued for a third time, again through the agency of Stedman and with a new preface by Stoddard herself. But Elizabeth Stoddard was destined never to find a wide audience, even with those readers schooled in the sort of realism to which her fiction often tends. Once again sales figures for her work were discouragingly low. Largely unrecognized by the public whose acclaim she sought, Stoddard died of double pneumonia on August 1, 1902. Her husband died just one year later.

"OUR LADY CORRESPONDENT": STODDARD AND THE *DAILY ALTA CALIFORNIA*

Little is known about how the virtually unpublished Stoddard landed a position as the New York correspondent for the only daily paper in the West. In "Literary Folk As They Came and Went with Ourselves," a memoir published in the *Saturday Evening Post* in 1900, Stoddard wrote simply that she "made an engagement" to write "New York letters," noting that "This engagement proved useful to me in two ways; teaching me to write prose and the earning of money. Every month I received a check for twenty-four dollars, which possessed many imaginative possibilities which were never realized. At any rate, I was the first female wage-earner that I had known, and it gave me a curious sense of independence." In this remark, made nearly fifty years after her engagement with the *Alta* came to an end, Stoddard touches on several issues central to the column itself throughout its more than three-year run: her interest in learning to "write prose"—to find and define her literary voice; the pull, for her, between domestic demands (the prosaic uses of her "twenty-four dollars") and "imaginative possibilities"; and the "independence" she feels as a result of her wage-earning. Witty, incisive, outspoken, and wide-ranging, Stoddard's columns from the beginning bear witness to one woman writer's effort to find a place for herself in an evolving American literary field, to negotiate the complex and competing demands of domesticity and artistry, and to preserve her "independence" in a culture that prized white female passivity and submissiveness.

Stoddard's first *Alta* column, published on October 8, 1854, establishes the tone and subject matter that she would largely maintain over the next several years; it also speaks to the complexity of her effort to find and claim her own literary authority—an effort that is clearly complicated by her gender. In this first letter Stoddard employs the mode of direct address that would characterize virtually all of her work for the *Alta,* declaring to her readers her intention to "send you letters containing facts and opinions." Offering a humble disclaimer that "most of those" facts and opinions "shall emanate from worthier minds than mine," Stoddard expresses her "hope" that readers would "thin[k] there may be 'solid chunks of wisdom' therein." But her conventionally feminine posture of humility is belied in that same column by commentary she offers on the recently published *Walden*—commentary that "emanates" from no mind other than her own. *Walden,* she notes, is "the latest effervescence of that peculiar school, at the head of which stands Ralph Waldo Emerson." Refusing to bow unquestioningly at the foot of the transcendental altar, Stoddard asserts that Thoreau's "ideas of beauty are positive, but limited. The world of art is beyond his wisdom." Yet she also declares that "The Book is full of talent, curious and interesting. I recommend it as a study to all fops, male and female."

In its carefully articulated judgment on a recent literary "event"—the publication of *Walden*—this first column reveals a great deal about Stoddard's agenda as a "lady correspondent": quite accurately, she perceived herself as a mediator between San Francisco, a rapidly growing city that was becoming the cultural center of the West, and the much more deeply established and culturally sophisticated East. Just as she draws attention in this first column to the recent appearance of *Walden,* later columns would offer her western readers information and opinions about the most current literary happenings. In various of Stoddard's columns one finds praise for the work of George Sand, a woman "who has dared to live her own way" (October 22, 1854); criticism for the "exceeding narrow[ness]" of Susan Warner's *The Wide, Wide World* (January 8, 1855); recognition of Edgar Allan Poe as a "man of great original and peculiar genius" (March 19, 1855); comparisons between Robert Browning and Alfred Lord Tennyson (the former "has more genius than Tennyson, but a great deal less art," she declares on January 20, 1856); and ambivalence regarding the "thoughtful, talented, licentious" Walt Whitman (November 9, 1856). While virtually all of her *Alta* columns

involve reviews of new books and accounts of literary events and personalities, Stoddard did not limit herself to comments on literature and writers. Indeed, she seems committed to informing her readers about all facets of life in the East, cultural and political: her columns are filled with references to such "happenings" as passage of the Maine law outlawing alcohol (Stoddard declares that the law is "unconstitutional" and predicts that it will be ineffectual [May 19, 1855]), women's rights conventions, the New York Crystal Palace Exhibition, the sinking of a ship, the repercussions of the economic Panic of 1855. Less often, and typically more obliquely, she discusses her own domestic situation (housekeeping arrangements, her family's "want" of money) and takes her readers with her on walks through New York City or on her summer journeys to her native coastal town. Reading the columns one is struck by their range and liveliness; one is also struck by the complexity of Stoddard's effort to establish her own literary authority in a culture that valued women for their piety, domesticity, and submissiveness.

This effort is apparent from her very first column, in which Stoddard disclaims the opinions she intends to offer in her column (they "emanate from worthier minds than mine") even as she passes her own confident judgment on *Walden* and the transcendental "school." Stoddard is aware of the anomaly of her seemingly "unfeminine" strong-mindedness, for which, she indicates, she can find no suitable models among her fellow women writers: "This being my first essay to establish myself in the columns of your paper," she notes, "I debate in my mind how to appear most effectively, whether to present myself as a genuine original, or adopt some great example in style; such as the pugilism of Fanny Fern, the pathetics of Minnie Myrtle, or the abandon of Cassie Cauliflower" (October 8, 1854). Rejecting both what she sees as the edgy activism of Fern and the base emotionalism of "flowery" female sentimentalism, Stoddard seems interested in using her California letters to carve out an alternative literary space. Other columns offer further evidence of her frustration with the available models of female authorship. "Why will writers, especially female writers, make their heroines so indifferent to good eating, so careless about taking cold, and so impervious to all creature comforts?" she asks in a column from August 1856: "The absence of these treats compose their good women, with an external preachment about self-denial, moral self-denial. Is goodness, then, incompatible with the enjoyment of the senses? In reading such books I am reminded of what I have thought my mission was: a crusade against Duty" (August 3, 1856). Not surprisingly, in Stoddard's own short stories and especially in her novels, one finds "heroines" manifestly concerned with "good eating" and other "creature comforts"—Cassandra Morgeson, the first-person narrator of Stoddard's first novel, comes to mind—indicating Stoddard's quite radical commitment to a model of "goodness" that is not predicated on female "self-denial" and that allows women to pursue their sensual desires.

Yet even while Stoddard offers criticism of the conventionalism, sentimentalism, and unrealistic high-mindedness of her fellow female authors (and indicates her own alternative literary project), she is mindful of the ways in which those qualities are valued and perpetuated by a culture that is largely not of women's own making. In her second *Alta* column she excoriates critics for their low expectations of women writers—expectations that perpetuate the very qualities she finds most distasteful in the work those writers produce. "No criticism assails" women writers, she notes on October 22, 1854; "Men are polite to the woman, and contemptuous to the intellect. They do not allow woman to enter their intellectual arena to do battle with them. Hence the intolerable van-

ity of our female writers." The divergence of which Stoddard takes note here—between the female writer's "womanhood" and her "intellect"—is one that she would treat over and over again in her columns, letters, poetry, and fiction. For Stoddard, cultural definitions of and the duties attendant upon "womanhood" (marriage, domesticity, maternity) existed in radical contradiction to the demands of the "intellect"—the demands of art. At times Stoddard would treat this contradiction with an appealingly self-deprecating humor. Describing her family's move from a boarding house to an apartment, Stoddard draws a domestic set-piece for her readers' enjoyment: "My little boy sits in a bamboo chair at the family board, and divides his mashed potato between his mouth and the floor with generous impartiality. In a few words you have the tout-ensemble of the family. It is a romantic picture, and it is a bore." Noting her "sympathy" with Mrs. Jellyby, a popular character from Dickens' *Bleak House,* Stoddard remarks that "Her eyes were fixed on Africa, and her letter envelopes dropped in the gravy; mine are fixed on California, and I forget to buy anything to eat, so famine comes into the house" (June 21, 1857). Although Stoddard is clearly having fun with the stereotype of the literary bluestocking—the woman whose commitment to a life of the intellect prevents her from properly performing her domestic duties—she is also marking the very real pull between her role as a "woman" and her role as a "writer." Thus, in a more serious column (November 18, 1855) offering praise for the work of the French painter Rosa Bonheur, admirable for being both a "remarkable woman and a remarkable artist," Stoddard offers a paean to all women artists who create in the face of deeply challenging cultural and material odds:

I like to chronicle the success of a woman. If there be any so valiant as to trench on the domain appropriated by men to themselves, I hasten to do them honor. And I say—O courageous woman!

What you have done for song, or art, under the disadvantage of crying, teething babies, the contemptuous silence of your husband, the incredulity of all your male acquaintances, shows that a parity of circumstances would bring about a parity of intelligence, between you and our good lords and patrons.

Here Stoddard lays down a kind of gauntlet, as much for herself as for her readers. Beginning with her columns for the *Alta,* she would spend the rest of her life trying to negotiate the seemingly competing demands of literary artistry and culturally defined "womanhood" ("I am never going to do any more housework if I can help it, I am an AUTHOR," she wrote her husband in 1861) and to earn for herself the sort of recognition usually reserved for men. The authorial voice that she cultivates through her years with the *Daily Alta California* is one that at once recognizes the cultural constraints under which (literary) women operate and insists, as she flatly declares in a March 1856 column, that "Intellect has no sex."

Despite—or perhaps even because of—her willingness to speak her mind and compel her readers to examine their own stereotypes and assumptions about (among other matters) literary women, Stoddard's column appears to have been quite popular. Her work for the column survived four changes in the *Daily Alta*'s ownership and several more turnovers in editorial staffing. While for the first year or so her columns usually appeared adjacent to the editorials and on the second page of the newspaper, beginning in 1856 they appeared almost invariably on the first page of the paper's Sunday edition. A year after she began writing for the *Alta,* the paper retooled her byline: originally offered under the heading "Letter from a Lady Correspondent," in October of 1855 her column was retitled, becoming "From Our Lady Correspondent." The change suggests that the editors had an interest in claiming an exclusive relationship with Stoddard (she is "our … correspondent") and thus that her column was

one of the paper's selling points. In this context the abruptness of Stoddard's departure from the paper is somewhat surprising: unaccompanied by any sort of formal announcement or journalistic leave-taking, Stoddard's final column appeared on the back page of the paper on February 28, 1858. Indeed, just as the circumstances surrounding Stoddard's initial employment with the paper remain hazy, so too are those surrounding her column's end. One possibility, of course, is that her literary ambitions had grown and that she believed she had learned enough about "writing prose" to bring her relationship with the paper to an end. Regardless of the reasons for her departure, Stoddard had clearly made good use of her career as a "lady correspondent," establishing her distinctive literary voice and paving the way for the "crusade against Duty" to which she would largely devote the rest of her long literary career.

EMERGENCE OF A FICTION WRITER

During her tenure with the *Alta,* Stoddard had also begun publishing poetry, placing a few pieces in *The Knickerbocker* in 1854 and another poem, "The House by the Sea," in the popular *Home Journal* in 1855. The poetry gained her the notice of the literary tastemaker Rufus Griswold, who remarked favorably on Stoddard in his 1855 anthology *Poets and Poetry of America.* Thanking him for his "kind notice" of her work, Stoddard took the opportunity to remark on the emergence of women writers on the antebellum literary scene: "The Literary Female is abroad," she wrote, "and the souls of the literary men are tried. I am afraid to think of writing a book, and only intend to keep up a guerilla [sic] kind of warfare by sending out odds and ends." Encouraged perhaps by the acclaim she had received from Griswold, Stoddard did continue to send out poetic "odds and ends," publishing more poems in 1857 and 1858, two of them in highly influential journals

("A Woman's Dream" was published in *Harper's New Monthly Magazine* in 1857 and "Mercedes" appeared in the even more prestigious *Atlantic Monthly,* edited by James Russell Lowell, in 1858). But increasingly, Stoddard seemed interested in conducting her "guerilla kind of warfare" on a new front: that of prose fiction. And by 1861 she had clearly gotten over her fears about "writing a book": in November of that year she signed a contract for publication of *The Morgesons,* which would appear in 1862. Sandra Zagarell has suggested that Stoddard turned to prose in part because it offered a realm where she could chart her own literary course: having written poetry largely under her husband's tutelage, Stoddard may well have sought some freedom from Richard Henry Stoddard's influence and authority. The fact that she signed her *Daily Alta* columns with the initials of her maiden name—"E.D.B."—suggests that, from the beginning, prose constituted a realm of comparative independence and autonomy for the blossoming writer. Whatever the reasons behind the shift, while Stoddard would continue to publish poetry throughout her career, beginning in the 1860s it was primarily in the realm of prose, and in particular prose fiction, that she undertook her literary "crusade."

In the preface to the 1901 edition of *The Morgesons,* Stoddard describes the origins of her first published work of fiction, "Our Christmas Party," which appeared in *Harper's New Monthly Magazine* in January 1859. She situates her authorship as the product of the "idle hours" she spent alone while her husband was filling his post at the New York Custom House. One day, she writes,

> I sat by a little desk, where my portfolio lay open. A pen was near, which I took up, and it began to write, wildly, like "Planchette" upon her board, or like a kitten clutching a ball of yarn fearfully. But doing it again—I could not say why—my mind began upon a festival in my childhood, which my mother arranged for several poor old people at Thanksgiving. I finished the sketch in private.... It pleased the editor of *Harper's Magazine,* who accepted it, and sent me a check which would look wondrous small now.

Stoddard's description of her sketch's origins is in certain respects disingenuous. Most strikingly, she denies her own agency with regard to "Our Christmas Party" by figuring her writing as unintended ("I could not say why") and instinctively, even supernaturally, automatic. As she tells it, it was not she herself but rather the pen that "began to write," and it writes "wildly," with a kind of occult energy (the "planchette" was a "spirit writing" instrument used by mediums in the nineteenth century).

Like so much of what Stoddard says with regard to her own authorship, this description must certainly be read in gendered terms: echoing Harriet Beecher Stowe, who insisted that God had written the phenomenally popular *Uncle Tom's Cabin,* Stoddard disclaims both her status as conscious creator and her thoughtful "crafting" of a literary career. But while she seems bent on carving out a safe space for the woman writer (one is reminded of her description to Rufus Griswold of the mere "odds and ends" she intended to write), she also reveals in this preface something quite genuine about her struggle to find her fictional voice. Having insisted upon the almost occult ease with which she wrote this early story and other "similar sketches" that followed on its heels, she goes on to discuss her very real struggle to produce something more substantial. When she "announced" her "intention of writing a 'long story,'" she "was told by him of the customs [Richard Henry Stoddard] that he thought I 'lacked the constructive faculty.'" As she tells it, she was undaunted by this discouragement: "I labored daily, when alone, for weeks; how many sheets of foolscap I covered, and dashed to earth, was never told." The result of this daily "labor"—labor that exists in marked contrast to the (as she describes it) unwilled and automatic writing of "Our Christmas Party"—was "My Own Story," Stoddard's first long work of fiction.

The publication history that surrounds "My Own Story"—a first-person narrative of romantic entanglements and passion among a group of men and women brought together during a summer in a seacoast village—suggests a labor involving more than Stoddard's private effort to construct a longer tale. In November 1859 Richard Henry Stoddard submitted the story to the literary giant James Russell Lowell for the *Atlantic Monthly.* Lowell agreed to publish the piece, but only after Stoddard made it more "respectable" by muting its explicit eroticism. Stoddard complied with Lowell's suggestions, and "My Own Story" was published in May 1860. But in the aftermath of the story's publication, Stoddard indicated in a letter to Lowell that she was struggling with, even questioning, his fictional mandates. "Your warning strikes me seriously," she explained to Lowell:

> —Am I indeed all wrong, and are you all right about the "going near the edge" business? Must I create from whose, or what standard? ... Do I disturb your artistic sense by my want of refinement? I must own that I am coarse by nature. At times I have an overwhelming perception of the back side of truth. I see the rough laths behind the fine mortar—the body within its purple and fine linen—the mood of the man and the woman in the dark of the light of his or her mind when alone.

It is important to note that while Stoddard defers on one level to Lowell's authority, she does not do so unquestioningly. Indeed, not only do her questions juxtapose her own fictional standards with those established by male monitors such as Lowell; through those questions she also admits the possibility that her standards are the right ones. Even in the earliest stages of her fictional career, then, Stoddard is willing to acknowledge, albeit in a qualified way, the validity of her own vision of what "stories" can, indeed must, do. While she would always remain aware of established literary authority and decorum, from this point on Stoddard's literary "crusade" would take the form of offering what she saw as the unvarnished truth of men's and women's lives—showing the "rough laths behind the fine mortar." At the end of her revealing letter to Lowell, a letter written from Mattapoisett, Stoddard tells him that she is "about to commence a story here in sight of the hoary sea, which I hope will not have the faults you have spoken of." In all likelihood the "story" to which she refers is the manuscript of what would eventually become *The Morgesons*—viewed by most contemporary critics as Stoddard's finest work of fiction. And contrary to her expressed "hope" (but consistent with her commitment to her own vision of fictional truth), that "story" would indeed have some of the "faults" that so troubled the "respectable" Lowell: candor, sexual explicitness, and a manifestly unconventional treatment of female agency and desire.

THE MORGESONS

The Morgesons indicates its unconventionality from its very first line: "'That child,' said my aunt Mercy, looking at me with indigo-colored eyes, 'is possessed.'" The "child" in question is ten-year-old Cassandra Morgeson, who explains that "When my aunt said this I was climbing a chest of drawers, by its knobs, in order to reach the book-shelves above it." The book that the intrepid Cassandra is trying to "capture" in her climb to the top of the chest is the *Northern Regions,* an 1827 narrative of polar exploration that is juxtaposed in this scene to the *Saint's Everlasting Rest,* a devotional classic by Richard Baxter in which, Cassandra makes clear, she has no interest. As Cassandra goes on noisily to drop her shoes on the floor, announce to her mother that she "hate[s] good stories," and "defiantly" plug her ears against her aunt's ministrations, it becomes clear why Aunt Mercy would describe her as "possessed." It also becomes clear that this story will be, in large part, about the extent to which Cassandra can preserve her (transgressive) independence in a world that would subject her to the codes of genteel femininity enacted and articulated in this first scene by her aunt and mother. With this central issue in mind the novel goes on to chart Cassandra's growth from youth to adulthood, tracking her evolving sense of self through a series of journeys away from her native town of Surrey and into ever-widening social and emotional spheres.

On each of those journeys, Cassandra learns something about the codes of femininity to which she is supposed to adhere as well as about the alternative standards that govern her. She is sent first to Barmouth to live for a year in the repressive home of her maternal grandfather, a "Puritan, without gentleness or tenderness"; in Barmouth she is tormented by her schoolmates, suffers chilblains, and becomes the (resistant) object of conversion efforts. Despite her determination to be a "thorough reprobate" and the hardships to which she is subjected, Cassandra grows and thrives: "I assumed a womanly shape," she writes; "I had lost the meagerness of childhood and began to feel a new and delightful affluence. What an appetite I had, too!" On Cassandra's second journey, the question of appetite becomes more pressing and manifestly more sexual. She goes to live for a year with her married cousin Charles Morgeson, a brooding, Byronic figure (Stoddard's fiction is populated by many such darkly attractive men) with whom she falls in love. More disturbed, interestingly, by Charles' obsession with mastery (his effort to gain Cassandra's affections goes hand in hand with his efforts to break an unruly horse) than by his status as a married man, Stoddard stages a riding accident that kills Charles and leaves Cassandra's face forever scarred. Those scars become, simultaneously, the mark of her transgression and of her growth into a kind of self-understanding and sexual maturity: "You crawled out of a small hole, my child," the doctor tells Cassandra in the aftermath of the accident, suggesting that she has been on some level reborn.

Cassandra's third journey takes her to the town of Belem (a fictional Salem), where she meets Desmond Somers, the man who will eventually become her husband. Unlike many of the other men (and women) in the novel, Desmond is compelled by Cassandra's strength and by the sexual agency manifested by her scars; nor does he seek to contain and control her. "I am yours," he writes her in a letter, "as I have been, since the night I asked you 'How came those scars?' Did you guess that I read your story?" Desmond too is scarred, in particular by family tendencies toward alcoholism, cruelty, and dissipation; his willingness to conquer his alcoholism (he goes off for two years to make his own living and to get sober) so that he can come to Cassandra as an equal partner suggests Stoddard's interest in models of male/female partnership that are based not on dominance but rather on parity, emotional maturity, and mutual acceptance.

While *The Morgesons* is notoriously difficult to place with regard to genre (it has been variously identified as gothic, domestic, anti-domestic, anti-sentimental, realist, romantic, and proto-modernist), critics generally agree that the novel borrows from, among other forms, the conventions of the bildungsroman, the novel of initiation. Like the bildungsroman, which typically charts a male protagonist's movement from youth to adulthood, often by tracing his journeys through ever-widening social milieux and environments, *The Morgesons* depicts Cassandra's maturation through a series of emotional, psychological, and sexual "expeditions." But *The Morgesons* takes pains to show the ways in which, by contrast to men, women's development is constrained within narrowly prescribed limits: Cassandra's journeys, as Sandra Zagarell notes in "Repossession," are never self-initiated; they are rather "always by invitation or family decree, and they always confine her within other people's homes." This is, in short, no novel of the open road: Cassandra returns to her childhood home in Surrey between each of the three significant journeys the novel depicts, and much of her narrative is devoted to careful, even minute depictions of interior spaces and domestic arrangements. From very early on it is clear that the freedom and autonomy offered to male "initiates" are simply not available to Cassandra. By at once deploying the forms of the bildingsroman and recognizing the form's fundamental inability to describe women's actual lives, Stoddard thus draws attention to the circumscribed limits within which women live—and to the need to expand those limits so that women can achieve full self-development. Most explicitly, she explores the meanings of her culture's most cherished and oft-discussed aspect of female "Duty": domesticity.

One of Cassandra's most significant trials in the novel is one she faces upon her return from Belem, when she finds her mother dead and determines to take on the responsibilities of running the Morgeson household. Having decided that she must "give up" herself to the family's domestic needs, Cassandra notes that "A wall had risen up suddenly before me, which divided me from my dreams; I was inside it, on a prosaic domain I must henceforth be confined to." But while it is clear that Cassandra's domestic "imprisonment" involves at least a partial renunciation of the very selfhood that the novel works so hard to valorize and affirm, Stoddard refuses to reduce the narrative of domesticity to one of simple incarceration. Thus when Cassandra eventually inherits the family residence and is "left alone" in the house, she explains, "I regained an absolute self-possession." Nor does that self-possession ap-

pear to be compromised when Desmond returns and the couple marries. But even as *The Morgesons* seems to hold out the possibility of a redefined and less imprisoning domesticity, the novel's utterly grim final scene undermines that possibility once again. Cassandra writes the "last words" of her narrative from a bedroom that opens onto the sea, an emblem of sexuality and female possibility throughout the novel that she describes in this scene as "relentless," "monotone," pitiless and uncompassionate. Next to Cassandra is her sister Veronica, a chronically sick, childlike woman whose husband, Desmond's brother Ben, has died as a result of complications from his own alcoholism; and Veronica's year-old baby, who "smiles continually, but never cries, never moves, except when it is moved." In a final line that questions the very spiritual premises on which bourgeois culture is based, Cassandra describes Desmond's despairing response to Ben's death: "'God is the Ruler,' he said at last. 'Otherwise let this mad world crush us now.'" Coupling images of perverse and shattered domesticity with this deeply qualified expression of religious belief, the end of *The Morgesons* contests many of the key values and tenets of nineteenth-century bourgeois culture.

Ultimately Stoddard's first novel leaves its readers with more questions than answers. Refusing the narrative coherence to which her contemporary audience was largely accustomed, Stoddard's novel, as Sandra Zagarell has pointed out, offers an ending but not a conclusion. Such a refusal, Zagarell suggests in "Strenuous Artistry," indicates a more radical refusal to endorse a coherent vision of selfhood: in the end, "We must come to terms with Cassandra, not as a unitary character who unfolds and develops in keeping with a discernible pattern," Zagarell writes, "but as a multifarious, sometimes contradictory self-in-process." Thus Stoddard mobilizes the bildungsroman not only to indicate the narrow straits within which women are allowed to "develop" but also to ask even more fundamental, and unsettling, questions about the very nature of the self. It is perhaps no wonder that the novel was "misunderstood." Reviews were generally very favorable, with critics singling out for special praise Stoddard's insistently detailed and realistic depiction of the New England world in which *The Morgesons* is set and her intense artistic vision. (Stoddard was understandably pleased by the private commendation she received in a letter from Nathaniel Hawthorne, who asserted that the first part of *The Morgesons* was "as genuine and lifelike as anything that pen and ink can do." But critics also seemed uncertain about how to describe or make sense of Stoddard's unconventional style (elliptical dialogue, comparative lack of narrative exposition, abrupt shifts in scene and focus), and some believed the book to be immoral and unwholesome. Perhaps because of her experience with her *Alta* readers, Stoddard seems to have been hopeful about her ability to gain a popular audience even while questioning the very conventions, beliefs, and sense of "Duty" which that same audience would likely hold dear. Her hopes were not borne out: the novel's sales were slim, and she was bothered by the censure that some critics heaped on her and her characters. But Stoddard persisted in her literary efforts, moving despite some discouragement into the most productive phase of her literary career.

STORIES OF RACE AND RECONSTRUCTION: *TWO MEN* AND *TEMPLE HOUSE*

In an 1887 letter to her friend Edmund Stedman, Stoddard reminded him that "*The Morgesons* was published ten days before Bull Run. It was selling but from that day stopped." As Lawrence Buell and Sandra Zagarell point out, here Stoddard makes plain her belief that "the news of the Union's disastrous defeat" had "crippled her sales." Stoddard's remark also

draws important attention to the Civil War context of her early fictional career—a context that is notable in part for its near absence, in any explicit sense, from either *The Morgesons* or from her corpus more generally. With the exception of a few sketches and short stories ("What Fort Sumter Did for Me" and "Gone to War" from 1861, "Tuberoses" and "Sally's Choice" from 1863, for example), Stoddard seems to have eschewed the war either as substantive setting or backdrop for her fictional plots. Largely or entirely absent from Stoddard's work are the staples of war-era fiction: wounded soldiers, mourning mothers, letters to or from the battlefront, fugitive slaves, or impassioned speeches about the causes of union or abolition. This omission is particularly striking given the fact that Stoddard's most beloved brother, Wilson, served as a captain in the Union Army and that another brother, Zaccheus, died on active duty for the army in North Carolina in October 1862. But while the war and its aftermath do not appear as explicit content, in several of the works that follow *The Morgesons*, including her second and third novels, Stoddard investigates a variety of issues raised by the Civil War and Reconstruction eras: the destructive effects of economic systems (like slavery) that commodify individuals; the prevalence of and the harm wreaked by northern racism; and most substantially, the new meanings of citizenship and nation in the aftermath of Emancipation and in the years of early Reconstruction. While Stoddard would continue to explore in her fiction the complex dimensions of women's subjectivity and female agency, in much of her war-era work she broadens her scope, moving from an almost relentlessly interiorized exploration of the boundaries of the self (enhanced in works like *The Morgesons* by the first-person point of view) to an exploration of the boundaries of the nation and the meanings of national identity.

Often viewed as one of Stoddard's finest short stories, "Lemorne v*ersus* Huell" (1863) can effectively be read as a bridge between those texts that offer an interiorized examination of female selfhood and those that engage, typically symbolically and allegorically, more identifiably "national" issues. In "Lemorne," Stoddard returns to many of the issues and narrative devices that galvanized *The Morgesons* and such stories as "My Own Story" and the 1862 "Eros and Anteros" (*New York Leader*): all of these texts have first-person female narrators, explore the struggles for power that undergird relationships between men and women, and depict the explosive force of (often transgressive) sexual desire. As in *The Morgesons* and "Eros and Anteros" in particular, Margaret, the first-person narrator of "Lemorne *versus* Huell," is in love with a man who, she comes to learn, is a domineering "scoundrel." The impoverished Margaret is, unbeknownst to herself, "sold" to her lawyer-lover, Uxbridge, by her aunt, who persuades Uxbridge to throw a case in her favor by promising to enrich Margaret if she wins. As Margaret tells her story, she turns repeatedly to the language of ownership and enslavement. Most strikingly, when Uxbridge comes upon Margaret—a self-described "slave" to her imperious aunt—sitting "*free* and *alone*" and looking upon the sea, she tells him that "I am a runaway." Making reference to a federal law passed in 1850 that required people, whether in free or slave states, to remand fugitive slaves to the custody of federal authorities, Margaret asks him, "What do you think of the Fugitive Slave Bill?" Uxbridge's reply—"I approve of returning property to its owners," he insists—is telling. He views Margaret as property, owned not by herself (or, yet, by him) but rather by her aunt. Her value having increased as a result of a favorable end to "Lemorne *versus* Huell," Margaret is, in the end, simply transferred from one owner to another: "I was not allowed to *give* myself—I was *taken*," she notes.

"Lemorne *versus* Huell" is not a story about slavery per se. Nor does Stoddard want readers to equate the genteel poverty in which Margaret exists to the experience of slavery in the American South. But by insisting on the violation of selfhood to which Margaret is subjected by both her aunt and her lover, a man whose "white nervous fingers" look like they would "pinch like steel," Stoddard makes the grounds of an antislavery position clear. "Every person's individuality was sacred to me," Margaret explains, "from the fact, perhaps, that my own individuality had never been respected by any person with whom I had had any relation." For Margaret, as for Stoddard, the violation of individuality that is at work in slavery's recasting of people as property involves an intolerable kind of social death. "Lemorne *versus* Huell" is an anti–love story precisely because Margaret is viewed not as a "sacred" individual but rather as an object of exchange. It is no wonder that the novel ends with Margaret's (literal and figurative) awakening to the incontrovertible fact that "*My husband is a scoundrel.*"

Like slavery, race is absent in "Lemorne *versus* Huell" except as metaphor: the story is shot through with images of whiteness and blackness, that which is pale and that which is dark. But in Stoddard's 1865 novel *Two Men*, race plays a much more explicit and substantial role. As she is in virtually all of her published narratives, Stoddard is concerned in *Two Men* with the extent to which social forces work to subject and constrain the individual. But new to this novel, at the heart of which is a love affair between a white man and an African American woman, is an effort to situate race and racial "otherness" in the constellation of those forces. Turning from the first person to a third-person point of view and from a female to male protagonists, in *Two Men* Stoddard tells the story of Jason Auster and his son, Parke. Jason is a would-be reformer who, rather inexplicably, sacrifices his progressive beliefs when he marries the cold and tyrannical town heiress, Sarah Parke. Several years into the novel's action, Sarah's long-lost cousin and co-inheritor, Osmond Luce, appears, bringing his enigmatic young daughter, Philippa, to live with Sarah and Jason. Philippa becomes Jason's ward and surrogate daughter. She eventually falls in love with Parke, but he neither is aware of nor reciprocates her love. A privileged, beautiful, and aimless young man, Parke meets Charlotte Lang, a fair-skinned African American woman whose mother is reputed to have been the mistress of a white man. Parke seduces Charlotte, who becomes pregnant. He vows to marry her, but before he can do so his mother dies, followed shortly after by Charlotte and her infant. Parke determines to leave with his uncle for South America, and Jason and Philippa are left alone. Jason is freed by Sarah's death and Parke's departure to reveal his enduring love for Philippa. She eventually returns his love, and the novel implies that they will marry.

Like most of Stoddard's fiction, *Two Men* works unconventional variations on the conventionally "feminine" themes of love, romance, and marriage. Lisa Radinovsky, one of the few critics to have written on *Two Men,* notes in "(Un)Natural Attractions" that "Stoddard rejected traditional marriage plots in favor of unions that unsettled families and crossed social barriers between races and classes," offering "unusually realistic representations of interracial and incestuous relationships, daring to assert the naturalness of transgressive desire." As her characters make anomalous, socially deviant choices—Parke announcing his intention, in the face of virulent racism, to marry Charlotte and, later, to bury her and her child in his family's burial ground; Jason falling in love with and proposing to the woman who had long been his ward and surrogate daughter—Stoddard explores once again, and here from the perspective of male characters, whether one can

maintain one's integrity and autonomy against the swift tide of social convention. But Stoddard also uses the story of her "two men" and the family of which they are a part to explore, as Jennifer Putzi has suggested, issues of membership and belonging that had moved to the center of the American political stage. Written in the final years of the war and published just two months after the Confederate Army surrendered to Union forces at Appomattox, *Two Men* asks questions that were assuming increasing urgency as the Civil War moved to a close: Whose "country" is this, and who can claim membership in it? Who can claim to be a citizen within the borders of the nation, a member of the national family, and who cannot? At one point a hateful Sarah describes Philippa (associated, like Charlotte Lang, with the South and with a kind of exotic mystery) as a foreigner: she is not, Sarah insists, "in her own country." Parke reassures Philippa that "my country is your country," and by novel's end Philippa seems to have found her place. But with respect to Charlotte Lang, explicitly marked by racial otherness, the novel is far less sure. While the novel's depiction of an interracial love affair (and its critique of the virulent racism to which Charlotte and her family are subjected in the North) seems to hold out the hope that the national family emergent in the postwar years will be one predicated on racial diversity, Charlotte's death suggests that there is still no "country" for her, even in Stoddard's fictional world.

Stoddard's third novel, *Temple House* (1867), is similarly equivocal on the matter of race. Written in the aftermath of and amidst heated cultural debates about new laws governing the content of freedom and the meaning of citizenship—the Thirteenth Amendment (1865), the Civil Rights Act (1866), the Fourteenth Amendment (passed by Congress in June of 1866)— *Temple House* explores, as Ellen Weinauer has argued, "the role that freedom might play in constituting a national 'family,'" along with the "terms on which one might claim kinship in the national 'household.'" Once again focusing on a male protagonist and using the third-person point of view, *Temple House* tells the story of the eccentric Argus Gates, a retired ship captain, and the house he inherits from a female relative. While the widowed Argus has long lived alone at Temple House, by the time of the novel's action he has been joined there by his self-possessed sister-in-law, Roxalana, and her "wild[ ]" and willful daughter, Temple. In the novel's course a number of other individuals come within the house's precincts, including Sebastian, a "Spaniard" whom Argus has saved from a shipwreck; Virginia Brande, the emotionally hungry daughter of the domineering and oppressive town financier; and Chloe, an outspoken and unruly servant who is the daughter of a "Gay Head Indian" and an African American man.

As do Stoddard's earlier novels, but with a looser narrative structure, *Temple House* offers a highly unconventional rendering of family relationships and transgressive love: one of the most powerful relationships in the novel is the homoerotic one between Sebastian and Argus, and the marriage between Argus and Virginia that the novel in the end portends involves yet another union between an older man and a woman who could well be his daughter. Above all, however, the novel's main interest is in the extent to which Temple House can function as a repository of freedom for the divergent group of people who come to visit and inhabit it. As Lisa Radinovsky writes in "Gender Norms," the house that gives the novel its title becomes a place where "people who do not conform to white, middle-class Christian standards can congregate." Stoddard uses Temple House (the place) to pose questions about freedom and national "belonging"/citizenship—and works to provide answers to those questions by imagining within its precincts a (national) family that is constituted on principles of difference, nonconformity, and acceptance. But the novel is in the end unable to find an equal place in that family for the one figure whose "otherness" is figured in insistently racial terms: the African American/Native American servant, Chloe. Although the novel seeks repeatedly to valorize Chloe's transgressive speech and behavior—she stands up most notably to Virginia's father, Cyrus, a man whose domineering behavior has driven his wife mad and violated the psychic integrity of his daughter—she never escapes the servant status to which her racial identity apparently consigns her. While Chloe's fate is different from that of Charlotte Lang, whose transgressions across lines of race and class leave her dead, Chloe's movements, like Charlotte's, are circumscribed within very narrow limits: she is transferred back and forth between the Brande household and Temple House, given as a "loan or gift," then reclaimed. Thus, however unruly, Chloe in the end remains abject, her rebellion contained by her seemingly inescapable role as family "servant." In this novel, whose investigation of kinship, diversity, and (re)union situates it at the heart of postwar debates about the meanings of nation and national membership, Stoddard fails to find a seat at the family table for those who are marked by racial "otherness."

So too, in certain respects, does Stoddard fail to find a seat for herself at the literary table with her second and third novels. Reviews of *Two Men* were quite strong—William Dean Howells called it "one of the most original books written by an American woman"—but readers continued to find Stoddard's elliptical style and her characters' unconventionality off-putting. Interestingly, perhaps because of the ways in which Stoddard eschews the most radical dimensions of the interracial relationship she depicts in the novel (the marriage between a white man and a black woman is averted by Charlotte's death), critics seemed by and large untroubled by her treatment of the miscegenation theme. But the book did not sell, and just two months after it appeared its publishers went bankrupt. "*Two Men,*" Stoddard would later write to Edmund Stedman, "met with a violent death." The "death" of *Temple House* was less "violent," perhaps, but more resounding for Stoddard, who viewed it even late in her career as her best work. The novel was reviewed much less extensively and also less positively than either *The Morgesons* or *Two Men.* Stoddard's insistent violations of readerly expectations with regard to plotting and narrative explanation had become apparently insurmountable stumbling blocks for nineteenth-century readers. As a reviewer for *The Nation* wrote, "We pay [Stoddard] the compliment of always thinking she was saying something worth hearing, and of trying to comprehend what it was, yet sometimes we understand her ... simply not at all." No doubt frustrated by such a lack of understanding, Stoddard would never write another novel, and she would be forever plagued by an awareness that her distinctive brand of literary "genius" would likely never find its audience.

LATE CAREER

In some respects it seems strange to refer to the period after 1867 as Stoddard's "late" career: at this point she had been writing fiction for less than ten years, and she would go on to write and to publish for thirty years more. Indeed, in the years between the publication of *Temple House* and that of *Lolly Dinks' Doings* in 1874, Stoddard would appear more often in contemporary periodicals than she ever had before. But the term is nonetheless apt, for although she would continue to publish short pieces and poetry throughout most of the rest of her life, she had already written the bulk of her best work. Driven in part by financial exigencies and in part by the lack of recognition that so troubled her, Stoddard seemed more and more willing to try to cater to the tastes of her popular audiences, writing short and relatively unambitious regional sketches or tales offering melodramatic renderings of by now familiar Stoddardian plots. Some of the stories from the period after *Temple House* are admittedly interesting for their continued interrogation of such matters as the complex positive and negative pulls on women of culturally mandated domesticity ("Lucy Tavish's Journey," 1867), patriarchal imprisonment of women ("A Dead-Lock and Its Key," 1871), and homoerotic relationships between men ("Out of the Deeps," 1872). But in general Stoddard's work after *Temple House* manifests a falling off. Nor was Stoddard's 1874 foray into children's literature, *Lolly Dinks' Doings*—a manifestly bizarre collection of tales, some of which had been previously published in a journal edited by Richard Stoddard—destined to turn the tide. Apparently emerging from stories that Elizabeth Stoddard (identified in the text as the "alias" of "Mrs. Dinks") told her son Lorry (called Lolly Dinks as a child), *Lolly Dinks' Doings* is notable for an amalgamation of tones and styles (it is at once macabre and affectionate, gently humorous and incisively satirical, conventional and unpredictable), abrupt narrative shifts, and complex pacing. The book received some notice, most of which was positive, and Stoddard, with characteristic immodesty, described it in an 1880 letter to her friend and fellow writer Julia Dorr as the "cleverest child's book written here." But whatever she and her critics felt about the book itself, *Lolly Dinks' Doings* marked the beginning of a virtual silence for Elizabeth Stoddard. For nearly fifteen years she published almost nothing, and though her ambitions flickered again with the republication of her works in the late 1880s, she seemed aware, as James Matlack writes, that "her last real chance to achieve a significant reputation had come and gone."

In one of the most notable and complex of her "late" stories, "Collected by a Valetudinarian," Stoddard visits the issue of literary reputation with an elegiac treatment of a dead writer, a "woman of genius" named Alicia Raymond, whose works remain largely unpublished and who has been "forgotten" by all but a few family members. In the story, Stoddard's first-person narrator is asked by a friend to read Alicia Raymond's diary and give her opinion as to "whether any of her manuscript should be published." The fact that Alicia's diary is a fictionalized version of Stoddard's own 1866 journal makes it clear that "Collected" functions as a veiled interrogation of Stoddard's own literary career, the fate of her own "genius." In Alicia, Stoddard depicts a woman writer who eludes the literary marketplace and remains satisfied with being a "solitary" genius—"I am alone with my own power," Alicia writes, echoing a similar claim from Stoddard's own journal; "What I decide to be, that I am for myself." Aware of Alicia's self-satisfaction as a "solitary" genius, the narrator of the story argues against publication of her work: it is "enough," she asserts, that the family "cherishes Alicia's memory tenderly." But Stoddard's career makes it plain that she could never be fully satisfied with being "alone with her own power." Indeed, by representing her own diary as Alicia's, she figures herself as a dead woman writer; as early as 1870, then, Stoddard had in essence written a funeral oration for her own career. More than thirty years later, her own grave would bear witness to the fact that, like Alicia Raymond, she too would have to be satisfied with being tenderly "cherished": the inscription in part reads, "Novelist, Poet, / strong original thinker and / steadfast loving friend / will long be remembered."

CONCLUSION

Critics have often remarked on the similarities between Elizabeth Stoddard and Emily Dickinson: both grew up in privileged, eccentric, and close-knit New England families; both were educated at female seminaries where they resisted evangelical conversion efforts; both were iconoclastic writers devoted to formal and thematic experimentation—both were writers, in essence, before their times. But Stoddard also can be usefully compared to Herman Melville. Both Stoddard and Melville had roots in New England but lived a good portion of their lives in New York City; both were emotionally (and materially) connected to the sea—indeed, in one of the more intriguing coincidences in American literary history, the Barstow shipbuilding firm in Mattapoisett built the *Acushnet,* the whaler on which Melville shipped in 1841; years later, Stoddard's husband helped Melville land a job in the New York Custom House. The connections go beyond the biographical, though. Like Melville, Stoddard was committed to speaking the "truth" about human life, however transgressive that truth might be, but was frustrated with and even embittered by the public's seeming unwillingness (or inability) to accept or embrace that truth. At the turn into the twentieth century, William Dean Howells wrote appreciatively of Elizabeth Stoddard and her work: "In a time when most of us had to write like Tennyson, or Longfellow, or Browning," he declared in *Literary Friends and Acquaintance,* "she never would write like any one but herself." That remark could of course apply as well to Melville, whose literary iconoclasm is well known. But unlike Melville, whose once-forgotten work was revived in the early twentieth century and seems unlikely ever again to be overlooked, Elizabeth Stoddard has experienced no full-scale revival. As it did in her own day, today her critical reputation continues to flicker and sputter. The flurry of new interest in Stoddard—interest that extends to heretofore neglected aspects of her career, including her poetry and her chronically unread second and third novels—involves an effort to fan the flames of that reputation. One can hope that the effort succeeds. In the meantime, the puzzle of Stoddard's critical fate warrants reflection and scrutiny. In the end, the divergence of that fate from Melville's much more promising one suggests that, even today, we are less tolerant of experimentation, and more insistent on neat categorization, for female than we are for male fictionists. In the *Daily Alta*, Stoddard had expressed her view that "Intellect has no sex." The critical inability to find a place for Stoddard—for Stoddard's generic, stylistic, and thematic challenges—on the map of American literary history suggests that, like those of Stoddard's contemporaries, our notions of literary "intellect" are still, on some level, gendered ones.

Selected Bibliography

WORKS OF ELIZABETH STODDARD

NOVELS

The Morgesons. New York: Carleton, 1862. Rev. ed., New York: Cassell, 1888–1889; reprints, Philadelphia: Coates, 1901, and New York: Johnson, 1971. Also republished in *The Morgesons and Other Writings, Published and Unpublished.* Edited by Lawrence Buell and Sandra Zagarell. Philadelphia: University of Pennsylvania Press, 1984. Pp. 5–262. (All quotations come from this edition.)

Two Men. New York: Bunce & Huntington, 1865. Rev. ed., New York: Cassell, 1888–1889; reprints, Philadelphia: Coates, 1901, and New York: Johnson, 1971.

Temple House. New York: Carleton, 1867. Rev. ed., New York: Cassell, 1888–1889; reprints, Philadelphia: Coates, 1901, and New York: Johnson, 1971.

SHORT STORIES

"Our Christmas Party." *Harper's New Monthly Magazine,* January 1859, pp. 202–205.

"My Own Story." *Atlantic Monthly,* May 1860, pp. 526–547.

"What Fort Sumter Did for Me." *Vanity Fair,* May 1861, pp. 241–242.

"Gone to the War." *Vanity Fair,* December 1861, pp. 275–276.

"Eros and Anteros." *New York Leader.* February 1862, p. 2.

"Tuberoses." *Harper's New Monthly Magazine,* January 1863, pp. 191–197.

"Lemorne *versus* Huell." *Harper's New Monthly Magazine,* March 1863, pp. 537–543. Also republished in *The Morgesons and Other Writings, Published and Unpublished.* Edited by Lawrence Buell and Sandra Zagarell. Philadelphia: University of Pennsylvania Press, 1984. Pp. 267–283. (All quotations come from this edition.)

"Sally's Choice." *Harper's Weekly,* May 1863, p. 342.

"Lucy Tavish's Journey." *Harper's New Monthly Magazine,* October 1867, pp. 656–663.

"Collected by a Valetudinarian." *Harper's New Monthly Magazine,* December 1870, pp. 96–105. Also republished in *The Morgesons and Other Writings, Published and Unpublished.* Edited by Lawrence Buell and Sandra Zagarell. Philadelphia: University of Pennsylvania Press, 1984. Pp. 285–308. (All quotations come from this edition.)

"A Dead-Lock and Its Key." *Harper's Weekly,* November 1871, pp. 1042–1043.

"Out of the Deeps." *Aldine,* May 1872, pp. 94–95.

OTHER WORKS

"From a Lady Correspondent." *Daily Alta California,* October 8, 1854–February 28, 1858.

Remember: A Keepsake. With Richard Henry Stoddard, coeditor. New York: George A. Leavitt, 1869. Reissued by Belford, Clarke in 1886 as *Readings and Recitations from Modern Authors.* *(Edited collection.)*

Lolly Dinks' Doings. Boston: William F. Gill, 1874. (Children's book.)

Poems. Boston and New York: Houghton, Mifflin, 1895.

"Literary Folk As They Came and Went with Ourselves." *Saturday Evening Post,* June 30, 1900, p. 1223.

Preface to the 1901 edition of *The Morgesons*. In *The Morgesons and Other Writings, Published and Unpublished*. Edited by Lawrence Buell and Sandra Zagarell. Philadelphia: University of Pennsylvania Press, 1984. Pp. 259–262.

JOURNALS, CORRESPONDENCE, AND MANUSCRIPTS

The largest collection of manuscripts related to Elizabeth Stoddard is in the Edmund Clarence Stedman Collection at Columbia University. Among the most crucial holdings in the Stedman Collection is Elizabeth Stoddard's only extant journal (1866). The New York Public Library also holds an extensive Stoddard collection, including numerous letters received by both Elizabeth and Richard Henry Stoddard along with a number of manuscripts (primarily poems) and personal documents (invitations, publishers' agreements, letters of appointment). Colby College, Middlebury College, the Boston Public Library, the American Antiquarian Society, and the Pennsylvania State University Library also have important Stoddard holdings. The Taylor Collections at Cornell and Harvard offer extensive holdings with regard to the Stoddard circle. James Matlack offers the most detailed list of manuscript sources related to Stoddard in "The Literary Career of Elizabeth Barstow Stoddard."

COLLECTIONS

The Morgesons and Other Writings, Published and Unpublished. Edited by Lawrence Buell and Sandra Zagarell. Philadelphia: University of Pennsylvania Press, 1984. (This collection remains the most useful introduction to Stoddard's work. In addition to Stoddard's most widely known novel, Buell and Zagarell include two of Stoddard's short stories, "Lemorne *versus* Huell" and "Collected by a Valetudinarian," selections from her *Daily Alta California* column, letters by Stoddard to Edmund Clarence Stedman and Elizabeth Akers Allen, and Stoddard's 1866 journal. Buell and Zagarell offer an extremely thorough and incisive critical/biographical introduction to Stoddard and the challenges her work poses to contemporary readers, along with very useful framing material throughout the collection.)

Stories: Elizabeth Stoddard. Edited by Susanne Opfermann and Yvonne Roth. Boston: Northeastern University Press, 2003. (The first collection of Stoddard's stories ever to appear, this book gives readers access to much work that has heretofore been available only in archives. The sixteen stories allow readers to trace Stoddard's fictional evolution from her beginnings in 1859 through her later career and represent her range and versatility as a writer of short fiction.)

BIBLIOGRAPHIES

Buell, Lawrence, and Sandra Zagarell, eds. *The Morgesons and Other Writings, Published and Unpublished*. Philadelphia: University of Pennsylvania Press, 1984. (Includes "A Guide to Writings by and about Elizabeth Stoddard" that lists both primary and secondary sources. Unique to this volume and thus of particular use is the section on "Early Reminiscences and Assessments," which lists memoirs that make mention of Stoddard and her husband, along with early criticism and reviews of Stoddard's work.)

Giovani, Regula. *"I Believe I Shall Die an Impenetrable Secret": The Writings of Elizabeth Barstow Stoddard*. Bern, Switzerland, and New York: Peter Lang, 2003. (Includes comprehensive appendices listing Stoddard's "Letters" to the *Daily Alta California* that helpfully indicate both the dates of the letters and their placement in the newspaper, her short prose, organized both by date of publication and by periodical, and her poems, organized by date of publication and by periodical.)

Matlack, James Hendrickson. "The Literary Career of Elizabeth Barstow Stoddard." Ph.D. Dissertation, Yale University, 1968. Ann Arbor: UMI, 1968. (Matlack provides a comprehensive "Publication Check-List" for all of Stoddard's works, with her short prose pieces listed by date of publication, along with a "Bibliography of Primary Sources" that indicates archival holdings of letters and personal papers by or related to the Stoddards and their "circle.")

CRITICAL AND BIOGRAPHICAL STUDIES

Alaimo, Stacy. "Elizabeth Stoddard's *The Morgesons*: A Feminist Dialogue of *Bildung* and Descent." *Legacy* 8:29–37 (1991).

Baumgartner, Barbara. "Intimate Reflections: Body, Voice, and Identity in Stoddard's *The Morgesons.*" *ESQ* 47:186–211 (2001).

Belasco, Susan. "Elizabeth Barstow Stoddard, the *Daily Alta California,* and the Tradition of American Humor." *American Periodicals* 10:1–26 (2000).

Buell, Lawrence. "Provincial Gothic: Hawthorne, Stoddard, and Others." In his *New England Literary Culture: From Revolution through Renaissance.* Cambridge, U.K., and New York: Cambridge University Press, 1986. Pp. 351–370.

Foster, Richard. "The Fiction of Elizabeth Stoddard: An American Discovery." In *History and Fiction: American Prose in the Nineteenth Century.* Edited by Alfred Weber and Hartmut Grandel. Göttingen, Germany: Vandenhoek and Ruprecht, 1972. Pp. 161–193.

Giovani, Regula. *"I Believe I Shall Die an Impenetrable Secret": The Writings of Elizabeth Barstow Stoddard.* Bern, Switzerland, and New York: Peter Lang, 2003.

Harris, Susan K. *Nineteenth-Century American Women's Novels: Interpretive Strategies.* Cambridge, U.K., and New York: Cambridge University Press, 1990.

———. "Stoddard's *The Morgesons:* A Contextual Evaluation." *ESQ* 31:11–22 (1985).

Howells, William Dean. *Literary Friends and Acquaintance.* Edited by David F. Hiatt and Edwin H. Cady. Bloomington, Ind., and London: Indiana University Press, 1968.

Matlack, James Hendrickson. "Hawthorne and Elizabeth Barstow Stoddard." *New England Quarterly* 50:278–302 (1977).

Mahoney, Lynn. *Elizabeth Stoddard and the Boundaries of Bourgeois Culture.* New York: Routledge, 2003.

———. "The Literary Career of Elizabeth Barstow Stoddard." Ph.D. dissertation, Yale University, 1967. Ann Arbor, Mich: UMI, 1968. (Matlack's 600-plus page dissertation remains the most important source on Stoddard, offering detailed biographical information, extensive quotations from letters to, from, and about Stoddard and her husband, summary and critical analysis of virtually all of her significant work, and reference to numerous reviews of and commentary upon Stoddard's work throughout her lifetime.)

Putzi, Jennifer. "The 'American Sphinx' and the Riddle of National Identity in Elizabeth Stoddard's *Two Men.*" In *American Culture, Canons, and the Case of Elizabeth Stoddard.* Edited by Robert McClure Smith and Ellen Weinauer. Tuscaloosa and London: University of Alabama Press, 2003. Pp. 184–201.

Radinovsky, Lisa. "Gender Norms and Genre Forms: Elizabeth Stoddard's Challenges to Convention." Ph.D. dissertation. Duke University, 1999. Ann Arbor, Mich.: UMI, 1999.

———. "(Un)Natural Attractions? Incest and Miscegenation in *Two Men.*" In *American Culture, Canons, and the Case of Elizabeth Stoddard.* Edited by Robert McClure Smith and Ellen Weinauer. Tuscaloosa and London: University of Alabama Press, 2003. Pp. 202–231.

Smith, Robert McClure. " 'A Peculiar Case': Masochistic Subjectivity and *The Morgesons.*" *Arizona Quarterly* 28:1–32 (2002).

Smith, Robert McClure, and Ellen Weinauer, eds. *American Culture, Canons, and the Case of Elizabeth Stoddard.* Tuscaloosa and London: University of Alabama Press, 2003. (This collection of essays treats a range of Stoddard's work, from her poetry, journalism, and short fiction to all three of her novels, locating that work in the context of nineteenth-century cultural trends and issues, including slavery, race, female illness, domesticity, nationalism, and the Civil War and Reconstruction. In addition to essays by Putzi, Radinovsky, and others, the volume includes Smith and Weinauer's introduction, Smith's " 'Among a Crowd, I Find Myself Alone': American Culture, Canons, and the Case of Elizabeth Stoddard," and Weinauer's "Reconstructing Temple House.")

Stoddard, Richard Henry. *Recollections, Personal and Literary.* Edited by Ripley Hitchcock. New York: A. S. Barnes, 1903.

Weir, Sybil. *"The Morgesons:* A Neglected Feminist *Bildungsroman.*" *New England Quarterly* 49:427–439 (1976).

———. "Our Lady Correspondent: The Achievement of Elizabeth Drew Stoddard." *San Jose Studies* 10:73–91 (1984).

Zagarell, Sandra. "Profile: Elizabeth Drew Barstow Stoddard (1823–1902)." *Legacy* 8, no. 1:39–49 (1991).

———. "The Repossession of a Heritage: Elizabeth Stoddard's *The Morgesons.*" *Studies in American Fiction* 13:45–56 (1985).

———." 'Strenuous Artistry': Elizabeth Stoddard's *The Morgesons.*" In *The Cambridge Companion to Nineteenth-Century American Women's Writing.* Edited by Dale M. Bauer and Philip Gould. Cambridge and New York: Cambridge University Press, 2001. Pp. 284–307.

—*ELLEN M. WEINAUER*

Louis Untermeyer

1885–1977

*T*HE POET, ANTHOLOGIST, novelist, satirist, and editor Louis Untermeyer published some one hundred books (not counting juvenile titles) and, by the end of his life, had become a prime example of "a minor poet with a major career." Over the course of six decades, from the 1910s to the 1960s, he reigned as "gatekeeper," responsible in large part for making the careers of such poets as Robert Frost and Edna St Vincent Millay. To know and gain Untermeyer's approval was, in effect, to be knighted and welcomed into a kingdom whose borders he had already defined. Untermeyer consolidated his version of the kingdom of poetry in 1919 when he published the first of his wildly successful anthologies of modern American poetry, as well as a book of essays on the subject. Both works would go into multiple editions and become central to the curricula of high schools and colleges throughout the United States. His anthology *Modern American Poetry* in particular became the standard against which all others would measure themselves.

Despite that power, by the time of his death in 1977, his vision of American poetry, not to mention his anthologies of it, had fallen into disfavor, out of print, forgotten. As a result, at the dawn of the twenty-first century, his role in establishing the contours of American poetry had been largely forgotten, as was his own poetry. Yet in his day his poetry was as highly regarded as was that of those whose reputations he was the first to make: Robert Frost, Edna St. Vincent Millay, Vachel Lindsey, Carl Sandburg, Amy Lowell, and Edgar Lee Masters to name just a few.

EARLY YEARS

Born October 1, 1885, to a wealthy Jewish family in New York City, Louis Untermeyer grew up in a privileged late-nineteenth-century urban environment complete with cooks, butlers, and German-speaking maids. He enjoyed all the apparatus of high society, from urbane living to piano lessons and the like. His grandfather, Meyer Untermeyer, had emigrated from Bavaria, settling initially in Maine. Later, his children, including Louis's father, Emanuel, founded a jewelry company, Untermeyer and Keller. By the time of Louis's birth, the firm had become quite successful as a manufacturer of rings. Louis, together with a brother, Martin, and a sister, Pauline, grew up on Lexington Avenue near 91st Street in a house devoted to culture particularly through the influence of his mother, Julia Michael. Her family, the Michaels, also German Jewish, had come to the United States from Alsace, a French element that perhaps explains why they settled in New Orleans. Taking her youthful exposure to the French Creole world of art and music from her youth to her new life in New York City, Untermeyer's mother made sure to educate her children in the arts.

As it happened, even as a child Louis had an unusual aptitude for music as well as an uncanny ability to turn a rhyme. In his memoir *From Another World* (1939), Untermeyer recalls that, in his grammar school years, he learned German from the family cook, fell deeply in love (at the age of fourteen), discovered the power of the German Jewish poet Heinrich Heine, and decided, despite his own first attempts at poetry, to be "America's leading composer and the world's greatest pianist." Cultivated and nurtured in the arts, and a free spirit by nature, Untermeyer inevitably strafed against the structured environment of the early-twentieth-century schoolroom. Although he accelerated quickly through high school and was ready, at age sixteen, to take his entrance exams for Columbia University, he in fact dropped out, never graduating from high school or attending college. (Toward the end of his life, in 1965, however, he was finally awarded his high school diploma from what had once been P.S. 6 in New York City and is now Dewitt Clinton High School.)

Between 1902 and 1904, in what should have been his senior year of high school and first years of college, Untermeyer became a member of the family business, devoting himself, in his off hours, to music and poetry. By the time he was nineteen, he became a traveling salesmen for the jewelry firm and had begun to cultivate a reputation as something of a rake, a lady's man with a "girl in every port." Soon, however, he met the woman, Jean Starr, with whom he would have perhaps one of the most tempestuous relationships known to American letters. Starr, who came from Zanesville, Ohio, was boarding at the prep school that Untermeyer's sister attended in New York City. According to Untermeyer, Starr had come with his sister to the family home, where Louis had impressed her with his piano playing. It was not long before they became secretly engaged. In 1907 they married, and in 1908, their only child, Richard, was born. By then, according to Untermeyer, he had composed over four hundred poems. But, as he himself later admitted, these early years were essentially spent as a lazy bon vivant: "I escaped responsibilities by letting my parents assume them; enjoying a bifurcated existence, I was serious neither about business nor art."

With so many poems, and enough friends working in the various New York City media, however, Untermeyer began to publish. Also at this time, one of the nation's most widely read columnists, Franklin P. Adams, began to feature Untermeyer's poetry in his nationally distributed column, "Always in Good Humor." Untermeyer achieved a national reputation through Adams's column, and he soon became a book reviewer for what was then the nation's most prominent book review magazine: the *Chicago Evening Post's* literary supplement, which gave him two columns: "Pierian Handsprings" and "—and Other Poets."

Meanwhile, in New York, his poet friends—Joyce Kilmer, James Oppenheim, and several others—had established a literary magazine, *Moods,* to which Untermeyer contributed a column on music, "Chords and Dischords." The magazine itself, like the early poetry of the young men who created it, was designed to return poetry to its earthier roots in lust and what would today be called machismo. The song of the male libido proved worthy of ultimately of a small anthology published in 1910 as *The Younger Choir.* Despite his association with these poets and their songs of youthful passion, Untermeyer used his acerbic satirical wit to lampoon the effort behind *Moods:* his first book, in 1911, was a small bound pamphlet of twenty-four pages titled *The Younger Quire.* Published in an edition of one hundred copies and opening with an introduction by "Daffy-downdilly" (Untermeyer's pseudonym), it offered parodies of the style and theme of each of the poets associated with *Moods,* including Untermeyer himself. In that self-parody, Untermeyer pens one stanza that perhaps best captures the spirited exuberance of this group as a whole:

Oh, the whole world seemed to love us,
And we knew that high above us
All the gods were jealous of us,
In the young June days,
And our songs were full of pity

For the lovers in the city,
Who had never heard a ditty,
Wild and witty as our ways.

Untermeyer's first genuine book of poetry followed this satire in the same year. *First Love: A Lyric Sequence* (1911) was published by a vanity press with financing from his father and dedicated to Jean Starr. In seventy-two poems and an "envoy," it fictionalizes the stormy courtship and romance of Untermeyer and Starr in a sequence of poems with stanzas such as:

A new religion stirs me now
With sacred fervor, and I vow
To be its votary, and share
With song and sunshine everywhere.

Looking back years later at this first volume, Untermeyer himself could not help but cringe recalling that it was little more than "a long drawn out sigh of self-dramatization." The poetry's celebration of love and eros, however, was very much in keeping with Untermeyer's New York life. By 1911, he was thoroughly drawn into the world of Greenwich Village modernist avant-garde radicalism, where the songs of lust and love danced in counterpoint to leftist politics and youthful rage against materialism. Through his friendship with the Dutch anarchist Piet Vlag, who managed the cooperative restaurant of the Rand School in New York, Untermeyer met a crowd of politicized writers and artists who had ideological stands behind their lusty jabs against American Victorian codes of sexual, political, and social repression: the poet journalist John Reed, the socialist and publisher William English Walling, the painters John Sloane, Stuart Davis, and George Bellows. The group, centered around the writer Max Eastman, had, with Floyd Dell, in 1911 established its own magazine, the *Masses,* a monthly that published poetry, fiction, and reproductions of artwork, as well as reviews, essays, and the like. Soon, Untermeyer became one of the magazine's editors.

By 1913, the twenty-seven-year-old Untermeyer had established a national reputation primarily as a poetry reviewer. But his own poems were respected enough to gain him acceptance to the Poetry Society of America, located in New York City. The society's president, Monroe Wheeler, and its secretary, Jessie Rittenhouse, were both poets of high reputation. Untermeyer, a new member of the society, quickly became its principle advocate for what he termed "the new spirit" of freedom then sweeping American poetry in both theme and form.

Such was his reputation that when the poet Sara Teasdale learned that Untermeyer would review her first collection of poetry, she "seized the occasion to write the poet directly herself praising his work and asking for an autograph," according to her biographer William Drake. Later, when Teasdale came to New York, Untermeyer invited her for a visit. Evidently his reputation preceded him, for, afraid to be alone with him, she wrote to Rittenhouse to see if he was "a nice fellow." She soon developed a crush on him—in part because, as Drake explains, she found in the Untermeyer home "something of the youthful sophistication, the wit, and the freer atmosphere she looked for in New York."

Untermeyer was never, despite later criticism to the contrary, an unthinking supporter of poets who flattered him. When Teasdale published her next book, *Rivers to the Sea* (1915), Untermeyer, who had praised it privately to her, blasted it in a review. Similarly, when the poet Amy Lowell published her first collection of poems in 1912, Untermeyer condemned it in print. She later told him that his was the "only review to make her cry." When soon thereafter she changed her style and began to adopt precisely the sort of poetics Untermeyer himself had begun to advocate, by contrast, he praised her to the skies and became an ardent champion. (When, in 1955, *The Complete Poetical Works of Amy Lowell* were published they came with an introduction by Louis Untermeyer. For all that, however, he ultimately concluded that the controversial Lowell "lacked genuine and lasting talent, attempting to substitute motion and commotion for outright inspiration.")

Not only was Untermeyer making reputations in America by 1913, but he was also entering the world of English letters by writing reviews in England for Harold Monro's quarterly magazine, *Poetry and Drama,* among others. In that magazine, he came across the work of Robert Frost. Untermeyer assumed that Frost was another English poet and was surprised to learn that Frost was in fact an American living in England. Eventually, Untermeyer would do more than any one else to advance the career and reputation of Robert Frost.

POET, PARODIST, ADVOCATE: 1914–1917

Between 1911 and 1914, (marriage and fatherhood notwithstanding), Untermeyer cultivated a reputation as a lively, free-spirited Romeo and also as a serious advocate of a new poetry of passion, musicality, and lyricism. Appropriately enough, his first major book, *Challenge* (1914), comprising three sections, revealed the divided aspects of Untermeyer's personality. In the first two sections, "Summons" and "Interludes," thirty-eight poems explore the inner life of passion and the material expressions of beauty and life. The final section, "Protests," asserts the more political and social commitments he derived from his association with the *Masses* crowd.

In the book's first poem, "Summons," Untermeyer asserts that "Love, and the faces of a world of children, / Swept like a conquering army through my blood—." In "The Great Carousel," he says:

Death can never take from me
   My warm, insatiate energy;

He shall not dare touch one part
   Of the gay challenge of my heart.

In this same poem, he asserts his youthful power: "Death cannot quench my love of life." In "God's Youth," he extends this idea to God himself. There, he imagines the deity as a lusty young man:

To feel Himself branch out, let go, dare all,
Give utterance to His vaguely-formed desires,
And loose a flood of fancies, wild and frank.

In the second section, "Interludes," dedicated to his wife, Untermeyer depicts the "challenge" death makes to life. In one of that section's poems, "Invocation," he says that "Beauty's a challenge as fierce and as stirring as conflict." The entire section contains frankly sexual poems dedicated to carnal passion ("A Birthday") as well as poems that locate beauty in unexpected places: Broadway, Fifth Avenue, even the cabs ("In a Cab," "Summer Night— Broadway," "Fifth Avenue—Spring Afternoon"). In the book's final section, dedicated to his friend James Oppenheim, Untermeyer expresses his social, political ideas and feelings. Here one finds the book's title poem, "Challenge," which concludes:

And while Life's lusty banner flies,
   I shall assail, with raging mirth,
The scornful and untroubled skies,
   The cold complacency of earth.

In this section such poems as "Caliban in the Coal Mines," "Strikers," "In the Subway," and "Any City" describe prostitutes, outcasts, and failures of contemporary American life pointing, all the while, a sharp finger at policy and social convention.

In the *Boston Evening Transcript,* the reviewer William Stanley Braithwaite, an African American poet whose annual anthologies collecting *The Best Magazine Verse* were among the most important gatekeepers of the day, praised the book as prophetic. Writing in the *Yale Review,* Edward Bliss Reed, another major tastemaker of the era, said that the volume exhibited two extremes—one an intense commitment to artistry and the other an equal fervor for prophecy—that made Untermeyer representative of a poetic renaissance, a new movement in which "the modern poet is not merely an artist, a singer, but a prophet and preacher of righteousness."

By contrast, the poet Eunice Tietjens, writing in the *Little Review* (a bastion of the new poetic turn to a more innovative use of aesthetic form and an opponent of the prophetic, preacherly wing of the movement) had little praise to offer: "The book is a revolt," she wrote, "but a careful perusal of its pages fails to reveal against what it revolts." Among the more notable objections beyond its lack of innovative form was its insistent machismo: "Unfortunately, virility ... has a way of oozing out of [Untermeyer's poems], leaving them empty of everything save a painful determination to be manly at all costs."

This split among reviewers set the stage for all subsequent reaction to Untermeyer's work. Among the most avant-garde modernists his work would never be appealing because it was too concerned with theme rather than craft. As Tietjens also said, "it is unfortunate that Mr. Untermeyer, who writes so much and so readably on the subject of poetry, should put out so pretentious and undeveloped a volume as this." By contrast, those already in the poetry establishment, like Braithwaite, Reed, and others, would see in his themes, and even his forms, a fresh voice, a new energy. (A group of students at Columbia University who shared the positive sentiments of Braithwaite and Reed in fact founded a student poetry magazine that called itself *Challenge,* and they considered Untermeyer their mentor.)

After the publication of *Challenge,* Untermeyer continued to build his literary reputation, aligning himself increasingly with Amy Lowell, who was then in the full force of her advocacy of imagism in American poetry and engaged in a public dispute with Ezra Pound for "control" over the publicity of the new free-verse poetry movement. But rather than continue to publish more poem in the new spirit, he turned instead to his own critical flair for humor and parody. His next book, a collection of poetic parodies dedicated to Franklin P. Adams, "—*and Other Poets*" (1916), returned to the sort of effort he had done six years earlier in *The Younger Quire.* Only now instead of mocking an obscure anthology he was poking fun at an entire movement and at his friends who had now achieved international prominence: Sara Teasdale, Amy Lowell, Vachel Lindsay, Edgar Lee Masters. The parody of Robert Frost's "Death of the Hired Man," for example, is here called "Death of the Tired Man," while his parody of Ezra Pound is called, "Ezra Pound: Putting on a Greek Headress, Provencal Slippers, and an Imagiste Air Recites." The actual title is given in the Greek alphabet. The first stanza is: "Come, my songs, let us sing about something— / It is time we were getting ourselves talked about." Untermeyer also parodies a wide range of British and Irish poets, including William Butler Yeats and Rudyard Kipling.

In the staid *Nation,* an unamused O. W. Firkins gave the book a thumbs down. His review mattered since, as the poet Conrad Aiken claimed, he was one of only two reviewers (the other was H. L. Mencken) who "stand clear of ax-grinding and nepotism, who analyse sharply, who delight to use words as poniards." Similarly, the *Springfield Republican,* a paper that had lauded *Challenge,* found little to praise in the parodies. By contrast, the *New York Times,* found "real rollicking fun" in the parodies, as did the *Dial* (which had not yet been transformed into the high modernist journal it would later become), whose reviewer Raymond Aldon enjoyed the lampooning "of such current phenomena as imagism, free verse, and polyphonic prose." Among the radical crowd, Untermeyer's poet friend Clement Wood went even further, claiming in the Socialist *New York Call* that the book "does not parody individual poems, but the whole spirit of the singer." This sentiment was also echoed in the *Yale Review,* where Edward Bliss Reed said the poems were in fact a "subtle criticism" of contemporary poetry.

By contrast with such praise, the *Little Review* published an attack. Untermeyer, said the reviewer, is "really parodying his colleague Walt Mason's prose-printed jingles which are syndicated throughout newspaperdom." The reviewer concludes: "No matter what may have been your attitude toward the poets parodied these things leave your feeling unchanged—except that he makes more definite your attitude towards him." (Much later, in the 1930s, Untermeyer used his memoir to respond to such criticism, reflecting that in his view, "Parody is not a kind of cheap burlesque, an exhibition of buffoonery, but one of the lesser arts, a light-hearted exposure, a combination of compliment and criticism.")

The split in the kingdom of American poetry that had been growing ever since the feud between Pound and Amy Lowell by 1916 had reached a crisis point. By then, Untermeyer was understood to be on one side while poets like T. S. Eliot and Ezra Pound were on the other. Describing the situation in his own book of essays on the poetry scene, *Skepticisms* (1919), Conrad Aiken wrote that "the competition among poets in this country just now is, as a matter of fact, severe to the point of deadliness." Much of that competitive situation had been created by Untermeyer, Aiken argued. In "The Ivory Tower: Louis Untermeyer as Critic," Aiken defines Untermeyer as part of a "red-blooded Americanism" school of poetry that had the effect of erasing and devaluing the work of vital poets including T. S. Eliot, John Gould Fletcher, Wallace Stevens, and the imagists. Aiken identified Untermeyer's "chief tenets" as

"Americanism, lustihood, glorification of reality (facing the world of fact), democracy (a word which few of his pages lack) and, of course, the postponed, though not to be omitted, inevitable beauty." Furthermore, according to Aiken, Untermeyer's premise that art is a "community expression" had reduced any aesthetic discussion, eliminated any consideration of craft, from one's evaluation of poetry. Says Aiken, Untermeyer's view had the effect of saying: "away, therefore, with the pernicious doctrine of 'art for art's sake'; and down with the ivory tower. Art has a human function to perform. It has no right to cloister itself, to preoccupy itself with beauty." Aiken disagreed with Untermeyer's every tenet, as did his good friend from college days, T. S. Eliot. "To put it curtly," says Aiken about Untermeyer, "he likes poetry with a message—poetry which is politically, from his viewpoint, on the right side. Surely he must perceive the shortsightedness of and essential viciousness of this."

Untermeyer, however, was in fact convinced that a broad and socially informed idea of craft was the only means of evaluating American poetry—indeed, of evaluating any of the arts—and to this end in 1916 he had cofounded a short-lived but historically important magazine, the *Seven Arts,* whose sole purpose was to champion in all the arts what the poet John Gould Fletcher had disparagingly called "the Whitmanian, cosmic, social brotherhood spirit." Such important literary and cultural critics as Randolph Bourne, Waldo Frank, and Van Wyck Brooks all participated. James Oppenheim edited the magazine while Waldo Frank and Van Wyck Brooks did the majority of editorial labors. In these issues were published such famous essays as Van Wyck Brooks's "Young America," the antiwar essays of Randolph Bourne, the art criticism of Leo Stein, and reproductions of original work by Marsden Hartley. Here, too, were the first stories of Sherwood Anderson and a printing of one of the rare plays of Robert Frost. Untermeyer contributed both on and off the page. In the first issue he published a review of new trends in modern dance as well as his own new poems.

In April 1917, he had written a general essay for *Seven Arts* on the current poetry scene in which he drew the lines that so bothered Aiken. In "Growth and Decay in Recent Verse," he wrote, "Two years ago the name of Ezra Pound was the last word in radical literary circles; today his least agile disciples have surpassed him in his contortions and *chinoiseries,* or have turned to Amy Lowell as their imagistic leader." Not only did he demote Pound, but he also stated, as fact, that Amy Lowell was now the principle advocate of the new poetry. Following that statement he offered a role call of the only significant American poets, naming Robert Frost, Edwin Arlington Robinson, Amy Lowell, Arturo Giovanitti, James Oppenheim, Carl Sandburg, Vachel Lindsey, and calling their work "the sign of a healthy expansion; of something which is intensely casual and intensely spiritual."

In 1917, Untermeyer published a collection of translations from the German Jewish poet Heinrich Heine, a volume that was intended to serve as a justification for his favored kind of poetry, a precedent for poetry he meant to champion. It was yet another way to distance himself from the overly obscure aestheticism of the Pound and Eliot wing of the new poetry movement. Through Heine, Untermeyer could champion hard hitting emotional realism, the use of traditional rhyme pattern, and metrical verse. Pound reacted to the translations by claiming that Heine was not an antidote or alternative to his own imagism but was rather its inspiration: in a letter to *Poetry* magazine editor Harriet Monroe, he protested, "If Untermeyer had read my original imagist outlines he'd see that Heine is one of the very people on whom one wish to focus attention."

THE CULTURAL VANGUARD, IN A COUNTRY AT WAR

The United States's entry into World War I in 1917 created a politicized environment for the arts that had serious consequences for Untermeyer as both a poet and an editor. In the pages of *Seven Arts,* John Reed rebelliously condemned the United States war effort, so angering the magazine's patron that she pulled her money out of the venture and the young magazine collapsed. At the socialist journal the *Masses,* dissent against U.S. involvement in the war precipitated a legal crisis forcing that magazine out of publication as well: the August 1917 issue of the *Masses* was determined to be seditious by the U.S. Post Office, which suspended the magazine's second-class mailing privilege, and soon thereafter the editors themselves were indicted under the charge of violating the Espionage Act. In his short poem "Portrait of a Supreme Court Judge," Untermeyer made his views of the proceedings plain:

> How well this figure represents the Law—
> This pose of neuter justice, sterile cant;
> This Roman emperor with the iron jaw
> Wrapped in the black silk of a maiden aunt.

Perhaps this politicization explains why, as the *Masses* trial was occurring and as the *Seven Arts* was closing its doors, Untermeyer, despite being a member of management in his family's jewelry business, chose in 1917 to convince his own workers to unionize. In the same year, his father died, leaving a legacy that enabled him to reduce his daily working hours. Amid the personal loss and the professional turmoil of 1917, Untermeyer brought to publication his third collection, titled *These Times.*

One poem in the volume, "Portrait of a Jewelry Drummer," offers a veiled self-portrait of his years working as a traveling salesman for the family's jewelry firm and expresses his cynicism concerning such work:

Adventure hangs about him, like a friend;
Romance he buys and sells on six months' time.
In his small wallet lust and heedless crime
Come to a safe and profitable end.

Elsewhere in the volume, one finds poems of strong masculine erotic themes ("Swimmers," "The Wave," "Victories"), cynical portraits akin to the work of Edwin Arlington Robinson (a section of poems, "Thirteen Portraits'), leftist social critiques reminiscent of Sandburg (in a section of poems titled "Battle-Cries"), Frostian portraits of regular folk, epic poems one would expect from Pound, and free-verse polyphony of the sort Amy Lowell wrote, as well as his own unique blend of music: a rhyming meter dedicated to the pursuit of beauty, eros, and love.

Divided into seven sections with an introductory poem, "These Times," and an epilogue, "Reveille," this is also Untermeyer's longest book so far. Published just before the *Masses* trials had come to an end, and before *Seven Arts* stopped publishing, the book expresses Untermeyer's sense that he and his friends are on the cultural vanguard and must defend themselves. The title poem begins: "This is my hour, the sum of tireless ages." Its first stanza concludes: "I come: a challenge hurled at creeds and cages." Expressing the general attitude of the book his poem "Immortal" declares: "I shall not be content to loaf and lie / Inactive in that strait and slothful bed." The book concludes in a mythic mode with two long poems: "Eve Speaks" and "Moses on Sinai." These poems, which constitute a final section titled "Two Rebels," ground Untermeyer's own newfound poetry of wisdom and love in a Biblical, Hebraic precedent.

Given Untermeyer's presence in the literary world, the collection predictably was widely reviewed and much publicized, and it went into several printings. For all of its success in sales, however, reviews were decidedly mixed. The most insightful readers understood that, in this book, Untermeyer was not only expressing his own philosophy but that of a whole generation associated with the *Masses* and *Seven Arts*. In the *New Republic* the reviewer asserted that "one is grateful to Mr. Untermeyer because he takes beauty into account, because he feels it, strives for it, and often, as he deserves, wins it for his own."

Edward Bliss Reed, writing for the *Yale Review,* summarized precisely what made Untermeyer so popular a poet but at the same time expressed his ambivalence:

Mr. Untermeyer has included too much in *These Times.* The best of his volume has his well-known qualities—a trenchant expression, an intolerance of social injustice, and an exhilaration in the force and beauty of nature, the strength and beauty of human affection. But there are poems here which are journalistic; that is, they interest us for the moment and we never return to them. At times it would seem that free verse has harmed his ear.

Amy Lowell offered an eight-page essay in *Poetry* in which she attempted to locate Untermeyer as a poet of the new school, a group she refers to as the "poets of revolt." She then argues that "the poets of revolt" fall into three phases: "vague unrest," "conscious revolution," and "accomplished evolution." She places Untermeyer in the second group. Fearing that may be faint praise, Lowell adds that in Untermeyer one does not find the attack on the Puritan spirit and conventions of a Sandburg but rather one finds instead a "religious fire." According to Lowell, Untermeyer's Jewishness accounts for the prophetic, emotional, and spiritual caliber of his work: "Much of his work," she says, "reminds one of the ritualistic dances of the Old Testament" and it is "just this religious fire which makes *These Times* such an important contribution to the poetry of today." In effect, Lowell had blessed Untermeyer and, in her own way, passed the baton of gatekeeper to the new poetry to him.

FROM GATEKEEPER TO KINGMAKER: 1919

In 1919, Untermeyer published three books that established his reign over the kingdom of poetry once and for all. Although one of the volumes was another collection of parodies, *Including Horace* (1919), it was his anthology *Modern American Verse* (1919), and his book of criticism *The New Era in American Poetry* (1919) that established his reign.

The New Era demonstrates that it was substantial critical work to account for the wide range of experiment then dominating American poetry: carved out of nearly a decade of reviews, the book was designed as an argument in favor of "the new spirit." Rather than organize his discussion chronologically, Untermeyer built it in terms of quality, discussing the best poets first: Robert Frost, James Oppenheim, Vachel Lindsay, Carl Sandburg, Edwin Arlington Robinson, Amy Lowell, Edgar Lee Masters, Arturo Giovannitti, Ezra Pound, John Hall Wheelock, Charles Erskine Scott Wood. Following those chapters, he then included chapters on poets as representative of larger movements: "Sara Teasdale and the Lyricists," "H.D. and the Imagists." The more avant-garde poets were discussed in a chapter devoted to Alfred Kreymborg's magazine and anthology, *Others*. Notable in all of the chapters was his inclusiveness. Indeed, the book's concluding chapter was titled, "The Melting Pot." Altogether, this book of essays made eclecticism itself a defining feature of American poetry.

Drawing on the influence of his friends, Van Wyck Brooks, H. L. Mencken, and Randolph Bourne, Untermeyer argued that only in the first decades of the twentieth century had American poetry become, in fact, "American." He argued that the Puritan spirit of repression had been poetry's single most enduring handicap. He then defines the spirit of the new poetry as "human, racy and vigorous" in theme. He finds its use of words refreshing, its diction modern, and its new musical possibilities, both in free verse and

meter, intriguing. He claims that both in form and theme the new poetry creates for the reader a sense of "actuality," "heartiness and lustihood" that the old poetry had been too shy, too tempered, too moral to attempt. Said Untermeyer, such poetry was American insofar as it was the very definition of the highest American ideal, "democracy." "This democracy is twofold: a democracy of the spirit and a democracy of speech." With regard to history, Untermeyer would look no further back than Walt Whitman, who, according to him, is the precursor of every new poet of the age. Quoting his friend Van Wyck Brooks, Untermeyer says: "Every strong personal impulse, every cooperating and unifying impulse, everything that enriches the social background, everything that impels and clarifies the modern world owes something to Whitman."

In a book that gave prominence to Italian immigrant Catholics, Yiddish-speaking immigrant Jews, women, men, high born and low, the volume's final chapter "The Melting Pot" emphasizes again the importance of every kind of variety: "What a medley of clans and nationalities! America is truly a melting pot in a poetic as well as an ethnic sense.... Our poetry, leading our literature, has become polyglot and universal and, like art and science, is fast becoming first national and then international." He concludes, then, that "poetry in these days is something more than a graceful literary escape from life. It is a spirited encounter with it."

Reviews of the book were published in virtually every American city, and sales of the book were brisk. What the reviews make plain is that among the literati Untermeyer's partisan views had ruffled more than a few feathers. In the *Boston Evening Transcript,* for example, William Stanley Braithwaite approved of four of Untermeyer's top six poets—Frost, Lindsay, Sandburg, Robinson, Lowell, and Masters—but disagreed with the inclusion of two decidedly ethnic, radical, free-verse poets: the Jewish James Oppenheim and the Italian Catholic Arturo Giovannitti. In a similarly mixed review, the *Nation* called the book "indispensable for its general facts and outlines as Amy Lowell's is for its doctrine." The staid *Springfield Republican,*, however, sniffed merely that "as a survey his book has some interest."

The most annoyed reviewers were those experimental poets who had been demoted as minor. Although he had chapters on H.D. and Pound, Untermeyer had relegated other poets working in similar aesthetic terrain—such as John Gould Fletcher, Conrad Aiken, Wallace Stevens, and T. S. Eliot—to less than chapter-length status. Of them all, Conrad Aiken did the most to confront Untermeyer publicly. That year, he published two reviews as well as his own book of essays in order to correct Untermeyer's bias. As it happened, however, Aiken's Skepticisms did not outcompete *The New Era:* only Untermeyer's book was taken up by the nation's colleges and high schools, and it became the textbook primer on the new American poetry. Writing in the *New Republic,* Aiken praised Untermeyer's essays as "the only comprehensive survey we have had," but expressed his worry that readers might interpret Untermeyer's opinions as objective fact. He laments that "a writer should be guided by principles so specious and biases so obvious." In the more literary *Yale Review,* meanwhile, Aiken argued that Untermeyer had overrated the free-verse democratic, working-class, and immigrant tales of Oppenheim, Sandburg, Giovannitti, and Alter Brody. This, he argued, was because of "a strong bias toward poetry which is consciously 'democratic'". As a result, said Aiken, "poetry which exists only to be true, or beautiful, or strange, leaves [Untermeyer] a little unsatisfied" because it seems to be an art without purpose.

Of all the responses, however, a review by Alice Corbin Henderson in the magazine *Poetry* was the most telling for what it implied. In it, she sounded a triumphant note of acclamation.

Together with Harriet Monroe, Henderson had, through the vehicle of *Poetry* magazine, been at the forefront of the new movement. Indeed, all of the poets Untermeyer championed had at one time or another been published in *Poetry*. In her omnibus review of three critical books, she chose the occasion of the review to declare: "The New Movement in poetry is more than a name or a hope. It has definitely arrived." To say this was to admit that Untermeyer's notice was, itself, a mark of one's arrival. Nonetheless, she could not help but distance herself from many of his tenets about the art of poetry. She disagreed, for example, that art was a community affair. "Art and poetry are individualistic," she maintained. She also denied Untermeyer's premise that the new poetry originated in Whitman. "The link which he seeks to tie Robert Frost, among others, to Whitman is pretty slight," she wrote. Her real objection to Untermeyer's position, however, was based on aesthetic principles:

> At one time his standard *is* poetic; at the next one finds it social or topical or something else. Topical it very often is to an irritating degree. Mr. Untermeyer is always talking as if the poet's 'job' were to express something outside himself: the streets, or the countryside, or the social ferment, rather than the man himself, to whom these things are accidents of experience."

Meant as criticism, attacks like this did not have any immediate effect on Untermeyer's ability to define American poetry. Only until the views held by Henderson, Aiken, and Eliot gained ascendancy in the American academy under the name New Criticism would Untermeyer's reign come to an end. By 1919, however much they might have disapproved, those poets who claimed to be more interested in art than in the "spirit" of an age, or in democracy, had to content themselves with the fact that Louis Untermeyer had captured the intellectual and literary public's attention: his was the definition that would stick. Henderson herself all but publicly lamented this fact when, in her review, she revealed just how weak the critical argument in Untermeyer's chapter on Lowell's poetry was: "I don't know how Miss Lowell does it, but she obviously paralyzes the critical faculty—or nerve!"

Reflecting back on this era of divisiveness from the perspective of 1939, Untermeyer wrote in *From another World* that in the intervening years he had "grown to admire Eliot's combination of flat statement and rich rhetoric, of power and triviality." When Eliot's early poems first appeared, Untermeyer said, he had condemned them

> not from a poetic but from a personal standpoint. I was a confirmed yea-sayer, full of the social fervor of *The Masses* and the liberalism of *The Seven Arts.* I believed in the possibility of man's salvation, only through art and education. Eliot seemed to me a voice crying all too effectively in a literary cactus-land. A fairly young and outraged disciple of affirmation, I flew at Eliot as at an apostle of everything that was negative and disillusioned. Looking back now, I think the uncritical praise provoked me more than the poetry: the group sometimes known as 'the younger ineffectuals' triumphantly hailed the poems as a gospel of defeat.

Despite this more generous assessment, one immediate result of his 1919 book of essays was a further consolidation of his own power to define the new poetic movement. *The New Era in American Poetry,* like his previous two books, had been published by Holt. That year, however, his editor Alfred Harcourt left Holt to start, with a partner, his own publishing company. As part of their new list, Harcourt understood, as only a publisher could, that there was money to be made in anthologies. In the final months of 1919, then, Untermeyer released a companion anthology to his book of essays and so launched what would be a publishing "chestnut": one of the central textbooks used in new editions year after year for decades in American classrooms. The book, *Modern American Poetry,* was at first

rejected by educators, but within two years it had become the standard textbook, indeed the standard anthology, on the subject—requiring, in 1921, a second revised edition.

In the preface to *Modern American Poetry,* Untermeyer traced the originality of American verse to Whitman, claiming "the influence of Whitman can scarcely be overestimated." He argued that not only in form but in theme Whitman was the great precursor: "our great poetic emancipator." Altogether, the anthology was even more eclectic, catholic, and various than was his book of essays: it represents not only men and women, Protestants, Catholics, Muslims (Kahlil Gibran), and Jews, but also the full geographical sweep of the United States. In this book one finds poets from the Far West, Southwest, Mid-West, and South who are given far more prominence than had been the case in any other American poetry anthology. Most remarkably, the anthology begins with the work of Emily Dickinson whom Untermeyer claims offered "one of the most original contributions to recent poetry." In 1919, Dickinson's work was still only available in a bowdlerized edition and would not gain serious academic attention until the 1950s. Particularly useful in this anthology were the headnotes offering biographical and critical appreciations of each of the poets—including his wife, Jean Starr Untermeyer, who had, in 1918, just published her own first book of poems, *Growing Pains.* As with Untermeyer's book of essays, so, too, did this anthology spark the expected debate among the old guard and the avant-garde.

What the book also did was enhance his own reputation as a poet. Both *Challenge* (1914) and *These Times* (1917) were still in print, the first already into a third printing. In keeping with the critical inspiration that had overcome him, however, his next creative book, a collection of parodies titled *Including Horace*—and dedicated to H. L. Mencken, for whose magazine *Smart Set* Untermeyer had been writing—was a kind of mock history and mock anthology. It begins with a straightforward translation of Horace's "Integer Vitae." There then follow twenty-four other "translations" as they might have been written by poets as various as his beloved Heine to the Englishmen Robert Bridges and A. C. Swinburne to Americans like Edgar Allen Poe, Walt Whitman, James Whitcom Riley, and Robert Frost.

Given the split in the world of poetry, one of the most intriguing translations is the one said to be by "Conrad Aiken and T. S. Eliot," which begins in a mockery of Eliot's "The Love Song of J. Alfred Prufrock"

> It is late, says Fenris, and the evening trembles
> Like jelly placed upon an old man's table.
> It is late, he says, and I am scarcely able
> To keep my collar up, attend the latest play,
> Mumble stale gossip; cough and turn away;
> Grope in confusion down an endless hall.
> The evening drags.... and why should I dis-
> semble?
> I am tired, I tell you, tired of it all ...

Even more humorous is the translation said to be by Irving Berlin:

> Mister Horace, won't you come and sit with me;
> > Play a tune that's made an awful hit with me.
> > > Go up and get your fiddle;
> > Rosin up your bow;
> > > > Here's a little riddle
> > > That I'd like to know.
> So—
> > Tell me why your music makes me fee so
> good;
> > Cheers up everybody in the neighborhood.

Following that section are more than sixty similarly humorous, lighthearted translations of various odes of Horace. If nothing else, the publication of this book in conjunction with the two critical works made it impossible to label Untermeyer a stuffy, overly serious advocate of anything. This, indeed, became precisely a new means of attacking him. Writing in the *New Republic,* Alvin Johnson—reading with a classicist's eye—disapproved of Untermeyer's "conception of Horace as a rioting adventurer and occasional poet." But he admitted, "Louis Untermeyer is not to be held to strict personal responsibility for thus distorting and cheapening the quality of Horace. He is merely following the established American convention." Again, his Americanness was used as a mark against him. In fact, however, reviewers had, for the most part, only praise to offer. As the reviewer said in the *Springfield Republican,* echoing the overwhelming critical reaction to the book, it "will tickle not only everyone who as a freshman clambered over the tough spot in the Latin odes, but all who enjoy clear and facile versification."

THE EARLY 1920s

By the end of 1920, Untermeyer had published three more books, including a new book of poetry that, to those who knew Louis and his wife, would reveal just how fractured their marriage had become. Writing in his memoir *Bygones* (1965), Untermeyer admits to being anything but faithful throughout his marriage. But what took him by surprise was the fact that in the course of his infidelities he happened to fall in love, with a woman who lived in Baltimore. The affair itself would be recorded in his fourth book of poetry, *The New Adam* (1920). Although that book was dedicated to his wife, it contained such poems as "Equals," "Almost," and "Hair Dressing" that were, by his own account, written for a lover whom he calls Sylvia. In fact, the whole book is dedicated to the single theme of love and even begins with a prose preface, "A Note on the Poetry of Love," in which he argues that no poets in English have really been as honest about love as those who wrote in the Middle Ages. Happily, he says, "In the last few years we have been witnessing a return to the upright vigor, the wide and healthy curiosity of our outspoken ancestors." The

poetry of love, he says, "is written with a directness that tells of a living and intimate relation.
It is addressed to a woman rather than Woman,
to one who is not only mistress but friend, the
fellow-mortal, the divine average." As if to
prove his own thesis, "Hair-Dressing," about
his illicit affair in Baltimore, concludes:

> My pretty, proper darling,
> With not one hair amiss,
> Who turns, like some calm duty,
> One powdered cheek to kiss,
>
> Are you the same wild creature
> I held last night, and found
> Sleeping on my shoulder
> With all her hair unbound?

Meanwhile, his poem "A Marriage" proved to
be far more honest than those who did not know
him might have imagined. It begins:

> I tell you it is over and I mean it.
> You have been tugging at my joy too long.
> The coming of the end—you must have seen it—
> Finds us still struggling, stubborn but not strong.

The instability of the Untermeyer marriage had
become infamous within their circle of friends.
According to Sara Teasdale, who had become
close friends with Jean, she "flirted outrageously
with other men to even the score with Louis, in
order, she said, to make him love her the more."

Publishing a new collection of poems so
closely on the heels of his own rise to the top
of the critical pyramid was itself a bold act.
Older critics such as William Stanley Braithwaite made their impatience known, seeing in
the book "nothing about love or woman" that
was new and little that had not been done better
"by any number of poets in the past two
centuries." Mark Van Doren, whose criticism
would help pave the way for the New Criticism, had the most scathing comment: "Mr. Untermeyer, glib of phrase and smug of meter,
merely writes poetry of another sort. He is
casual, as he promised, and flippant, and frank,

dutifully vulgar; but seldom is his effect other
than that of an agile pen tracing a facile passion."

For all this complaint, however, there was far
more praise. Most illuminatingly, it came often
from poets whose career Untermeyer had
already nurtured, such as Babette Deutsche,
whose first book of poetry Untermeyer had
praised. Certainly appreciative, Deutsche penned
two reviews of *The New Adam,* one for the *New
York Evening Post* and one for the *Dial.* When,
in 1921, Untermeyer revised his increasingly
popular anthology, he found room to include
her poems and a short biographical note about
her in it.

Despite the praise of his poetry, however, it
was clear that Untermeyer was making his mark
more as an anthologist than as a poet. As a
result, his publisher convinced him to do a
similar anthology for British poetry. Published
in 1920 to the same sort of divided but equally
vociferous reviews as the American anthology,
Modern British Poetry also became a standard
textbook within just a few years.

Meanwhile, sensing just how much power he
had to make or break a poetic career, a number
of his friends joined with Untermeyer on
another anthology project: *A Miscellany of
American Poetry* (1920). This would be an annual volume that would print previously unpublished work from the leaders of the new poetry
movement. The first volume (also published in
1920) included work by Louis Untermeyer, Jean
Starr Untermeyer, Robert Frost, Carl Sandburg,
Amy Lowell, Conrad Aiken, John Gould
Fletcher, and T. S. Eliot, among others. A new
miscellany was published almost every year
between 1920 and 1927.

In 1922, the great year of "high modernism,"
T. S. Eliot's *The Waste Land and Other Poems*
and James Joyce's novel *Ulysses* presented a
double-barreled assault on Untermeyer's conception of American poetry. In fact, however,
he met this threat with his usual wit. In a review

titled "Disillusion and Dogma" that appeared in the *Freeman* in January 1923, he labeled "The Waste Land" a "pompous parade of erudition"; he derided its "twitching disillusion" and its "mingling of willful obscurity and weak vaudeville." His attack was based on matters of craft—he felt the poem had no "integrated design"—and on matters of principle: he objected to its "desiccated sensations," its overwhelming pessimism.

Meanwhile, that same year he produced another book of parodies, *Heavens* (1922), and two more anthologies: the one-volume *Modern American and British Poetry* and *American Poetry, 1922: A Miscellany. Heavens* was, according to Braithwaite, "a volume without its like in contemporary American literature." In it, a character is offered a choice of 976 different heavens out of which five are described. These five are actually parodies of such writers as G. K. Chesterton, Sinclair Lewis, and H. G. Wells. In a parody of each writer's style, Untermeyer has each author describe his version of heaven. In addition to these parodies, he also offers fantasy previews of many other heavens, all invented with the objective of mocking the contemporary poetry scene in a variety of comic send-ups.

Even before Untermeyer's assault on Eliot's *The Waste Land,* Eliot had, himself, made his own negative assessment of Untermeyer public. Writing in his regular "London Letter" for the *Dial* in April 1922, Eliot took up the problem of Untermeyer's *Modern American Poetry.* In a single paragraph, he dismissed its view of contemporary poetry: "I am told that Mr. Sandburg is now the great American representative poet. Some of his smaller verse is charming; but appears to be rather an echo of Mr. Pound, who has done it better." He then went further into Untermeyer's list of great modern American poets:

The same is true of Mr. Lindsay, whose verse has no moral significance; and that of Mr. Masters, whose verse has not enough; and Miss Lowell appears to have nothing that she has not borrowed from Mr. Pound or from Mr. Fletcher. Mr. Frost ... it is regretfully said, is uninteresting, and what is uninteresting is unreadable, and what is unreadable is not read. There, that is done.

In 1923, Louis Untermeyer officially resigned from the family firm. By the time he left, he had become a vice president and manager of a factory in Newark, New Jersey. He had also been a principle designer for a line of rings. After quitting, and in quick succession, he published four more books in 1923, including revised versions of earlier anthologies.

A new edition of *Modern American and British Poetry* was designed entirely for the school market, complete with "suggestions for study" written by a high school teacher from the South Philadelphia High School for Girls. A new collection titled *This Singing World: An Anthology of Modern Poetry for Young People* set its sights on the juvenile market. And *The New Era in American Poetry* appeared as a completely rewritten and revised edition, published this time as *American Poetry since 1900.* In this new version, Untermeyer sealed his commitment to the Whitmanian spirit even as he made Robert Frost the one true poet of the age. For the book's frontispiece, he chose a photograph of a plaster cast of Robert Frost's head. In this book of essays, only nine poets get individual chapters: Robert Frost, Edwin Arlington Robinson, Carl Sandburg, Vachel Lindsay, Edgar Lee Masters, Amy Lowell, Ezra Pound, Conrad Aiken, and Alfred Kreymborg. And while he did include such modernist poets as Aiken, Pound, and Kreymborg, he also relegated such poets as John Gould Fletcher, William Carlos Williams, Wallace Stevens, Marianne Moore, and even Eliot himself to the minor status of members of various groups. Following his nine chapters on individual poets, for example, he then offered chapters on "Lyricists," "Rhapsodists," "Traditionalists," "Imagists," "Impressionists," "Expressionists," and "Cerebralists."

It was in those chapters that one found Williams, Fletcher, and Stevens. The smallest group, the "Cerebralists," had only two poets: Eliot and Marianne Moore. Perhaps acknowledging the opinions of his earlier critics, in this book Untermeyer also demoted a number of poets to whom he had earlier given entire chapters: Brody, Oppenheim, Giovannitti.

The most striking aspects of the book, however, were its section "Native Rhythms," which included chapters on Native American and African American poetry, and the abundance of women, many of whom owed their initial reputation to Untermeyer's reviews of their early books: Sara Teasdale, Elinor Wylie, Edna St. Vincent Millay, Lola Ridge, and, of course, his wife, Jean Starr Untermeyer. Supplanting his earlier book of essays, *American Poetry since 1900,* like his anthology, became a standard textbook (the essays by 1927 went into a fifth printing while the anthology that year entered its twelfth printing).

In addition to the new anthologies, in 1923 Untermeyer also published *Roast Leviathan* (1923), a collection of his own poems organized on the theme of Judaism and Jewishness. Given the spiritual, often nearly pagan, lust for life in his earlier books of poetry (not to mention the poets he chose to champion), this turn to specifically Jewish themes struck some as a new departure. In fact, however, Untermeyer had always been a champion of otherwise neglected Jewish American poets such as Brody and Oppenheim. Throughout his career, moreover, he had grown accustomed to his own sensibility being described as "Jewish." In *Roast Leviathan,* then, Untermeyer simply highlighted and brought to the surface what had always been present in his work. In the book's first poem, "Lost Jerusalem," he makes Judaism a source for his combined interest in freedom of the mind and body, passion and liberty:

A race that burns, an ever fiery sword,
To rescue tolerance and set freedom free.

This is our mission, let us never cast
Away our boldness which hath great reward ...

And in "Monolog from a Mattress," he offers a dramatic monologue of Heinrich Heine meditating on his own Jewishness as if to echo Untermeyer's own newfound sense of his religious heritage. Ultimately, then, the book grounds Untermeyer's eroticism, love, and social justice poems in Judaism and his Jewish heritage.

Overall the reviews of *Roast Leviathan* were among the best that any of Untermeyer's books of poetry ever received. Even former enemies like Fletcher and Van Doren offered tempered praise. In part because of Untermeyer's growing reputation as a critic of English poetry, the book was also widely reviewed there.

DIVORCE, TURMOIL, AND PAIN: 1923–1928

Like so many other writers in the 1920s, Untermeyer in 1923 joined the general exodus of artists and intellectuals who chose to leave the United States for the more romantic fields of Europe. By 1924, he had settled in Vienna, Austria. His son had been enrolled in an elite boarding school in Switzerland and, as Untermeyer says in his memoirs, he embarked on a life of cultural Jewishness, meeting such well-known literary figures as the playwright and novelist Arthur Schnitzler and such musical figures as the composer Max Reinhardt. His wife, Jean, meanwhile, began to revive her own singing career—but the life of culture, art, and the Vienna of legend did little to prevent the dissolution of Untermeyer's marriage. By December 1924, he and Jean Starr had separated. He began to work on the libretto of an opera with Reinhardt, and he met the journalist Dorothy Thompson, who was then foreign correspondent for the *Philadelphia Ledger.* Through Thompson, Untermeyer soon became a part of a bohemian circle of Viennese intellectuals and artists.

Meanwhile, after eight printings, it was time, he felt, to bring out another edition of his anthology *Modern British Poetry*. To gather material, Untermeyer went to England, where he met numerous poets—many of whom realized he was the man to know if they wanted a piece of the American market. Of them all, Untermeyer struck up a genuine friendship with the great poet of World War I, Siegfried Sassoon. Also, while in London, Untermeyer met John Gould Fletcher, who, in a fit of pique, said: "I should have remembered what everyone says, that you have no standards and wouldn't know a good poem from a bad one unless you knew who wrote it—and then you'd be wrong." Clearly this attack stung Untermeyer enough to want to record it, for it speaks to a certain buzz that had begun to circulate as Untermeyer's influence grew.

That buzz became public when, in 1925, another notable and influential critic, Edmund Wilson, wrote in the *New Republic* that Untermeyer was no longer a critic but rather "an expert politician bent on maintaining his power." Said Wilson, in an echo of Eliot:

> as the anthologies and the reviews tack back and forth before the wind, we reflect at last, not without regret, that Mr. Untermeyer has ceased to be interesting. For my part, I prefer to believe that Louis Untermeyer has become no longer even an active political figure, but rather a political machine.

Such negative views dampened neither his personal influence nor the influence of his anthologies, which continued to mushroom. The central tale of Untermeyer's life during these years, however, was a series of personal ruptures and disasters. First, he fell intensely in love with a young poet, Virginia Moore, and asked his wife for a divorce. She refused. The only way to get a divorce in those years was to establish residency in a foreign country and get a divorce there. Untermeyer and Moore therefore went to Mexico. The trip was a disaster, and Moore got dysentery. Nonetheless, the divorce was granted and, in 1926 Untermeyer and Moore were married.

In the meanwhile Jean's and Louis's son, Richard, had enrolled as a freshman at Yale. Sara Teasdale, who had become a friend of both Jean's and Louis's, was literally made sick by the saga of their marriage; her biographer writes that Teasdale attempted to alleviate Jean's suicidal depression by inviting Jean and Richard to stay with her, and that she was "keenly sensitive to the suffering of ... Dick ... whose emotional life had already been warped, she felt, by the instability of his parents."

On January 26, 1927, the publisher Alfred Harcourt, through a variety of circumstances, was given the awful task of telling Untermeyer that his son, Richard, age nineteen, had died—an apparent suicide in his Yale College dormitory room. In the memoir *Bygones,* Untermeyer described his subsequent actions: "Looking back, I cannot believe that any man could have been so irresponsible, so unrealistic. The only excuse I can give is that I was out of my mind." Soon after his son's death, he and Virginia traveled to Italy, Switzerland, England. Virginia was pregnant. In London, she gave birth to a boy, John.

Meanwhile, Jean Starr had also traveled to Europe. By the end of 1927, Untermeyer had left his second wife and once more taken up residence in Germany with his first wife. With his new baby in London under the care of a nanny, and his second wife now living at her parent's home in Saint Louis, Untermeyer returned to the United States to get divorced once more. According to Untermeyer, since "cruelty" would be the only sufficient grounds for a legal divorce in Missouri, he had to stage a violent act with Virginia Moore's mother and father acting as witnesses. With her father egging him on, Untermeyer reports in *Bygones,* the following surreal encounter ensued: "'Then strike her now,' he said to me. I walked across the room and patted her cheek. 'Harder,' said Mr. Moore. I made a kind of fist and tapped her brow. 'Did you see that?' he called to his wife." With the violence duly witnessed, the divorce was granted. To complete his reconciliation with Jean, they remarried under the authority of an Orthodox rabbi.

It was 1928, and Untermeyer, now married for the second time to the same woman and living once more in New York City, published two creative books: a collection of poetry, *Burning Bush,* and a novel, *Moses.* In *Burning Bush* (1928), dedicated "for all that is Richard," the first section, "Unreasoning Heart," contains some of his most powerful and disturbing poetry. In the bleak "Long Feud," he follows the metaphor of grass growing wild on a well-kept lawn:

Man's the aggressor, for he has
Weapons to humble and harass

The impudent spears that charge upon
His sacred privacy of lawn.

The poem concludes in weary bitterness:

His are the triumphs till the day
There's no more grass to cut away,
And, weary of labor, weary of play,

Having exhausted every whim,
He stretches out each conquering limb.
And then the small grass covers him.

The poem "Unreasoning Heart" includes these poignant lines:

And, a broken life can be made whole
By looking at the slant of the one long hill,
In this eternity of peace, the heart
Forgetting all forgets that it can hurt.

Meanwhile, the title poem, "Burning Bush," serves as a kind of apologia for the turmoil that was Untermeyer's romantic life. The poem takes the biblical episode of a bush that burned but was not consumed as a metaphor for the combination of the carnal and the spiritual. In the second of the poem's two stanzas Untermeyer writes:

The martyrdom of fire is not enough
For bodies eager to be doomed;
Burning in one long agony of love,
Burning but not consumed.

Almost without exception the collection was widely praised. In the most representative review, O. W. Firkins admitted: "I am not yet ready to call him a great artist, but I have reached even now the stage where I should be angry with anybody who made a point of denying him that title."

By contrast, *Moses,* Untermeyer's first and only novel, was universally panned. In this novel, Moses is split between earthly passion and desire, on the one hand, and a prophetic urge to do justice, on the other. Although he must overcome his more base instincts, he fails both to repress his carnal self and to activate fully his own ethical sensibility. Clearly a mask for the turmoil in Untermeyer's own life, Moses, as a character, struck virtually every reviewer as an unbelievable anachronism. The reviewer for the *New York Evening Post,* E. B. Barrett, summarized what was, in fact, a general consensus: "Mr. Untermeyer has made of Moses a pitiful hero, a lustful prophet, half mystic, half hypocrite, whom we dislike and condemn."

The stock market crash and the onset of the Great Depression did not mark the ruin of Untermeyer's financial livelihood. His textbook sales continued to improve as his anthologies of modern English and American poetry continued to go into multiple printings. Rather than rest on these laurels, however, he continued to produce new poetry anthologies, including *Yesterday and Today: A Comparative Anthology of Poetry* in 1926, an overview of Walt Whitman's poetry in 1926, overviews of Conrad Aiken's and Emily Dickinson's poetry in 1927, and also the last of the *American Miscellany* series, published in 1927.

THE 1930s

Throughout the 1930s, Untermeyer reaped the rewards that his status as gatekeeper had earned. Among them were not only a significant income from lectures around the country but also invitations to be poet in residence at a number of American colleges and universities: the University of Michigan (1939–1940), Knox College (1939), Kansas City University (1939). In 1937, he had been invited to give the prestigious Henry Ward Beecher Lectures at Amherst College. When those lectures were published as *Play in Poetry* (1938), they marked his first substantial critical work since the 1923 essay collection on American poetry.

At the outset of the decade, his creative work also flourished. He published two new collections of poems, *Food and Drink* (1932) and *First Words before Spring* (1933). He also published short stories, *The Donkey of God* (1932); a children's novel, *Chip* (1933) about the life of a chipmunk; and a travel book based on his years in Austria and Germany, *Blue Rhine, Black Forest* (1930). The stories proved to be particularly eventful. Because they concerned a misbegotten idea of raising donkeys imported from Italy, and because most of the book took place in Italy, it won a prestigious prize for best book on Italy by a non-Italian, sponsored by the government of Benito Mussolini. The result of the prize was a face-to-face meeting with the fascist dictator. Adolf Hitler had just been elected chancellor of Germany and Untermeyer, referring to that fact, said to Mussolini: "I am not a politician. I am not always a poet. But I am undeniably a Jew. As a self-appointed spokesman for my people, let me say that the Jews of America appreciate your sense of fair dealing and sympathy with Jews in Italy—especially in these times." Writing about that event later, in

1939, Untermeyer could not help but feel a bit sick: "But Mussolini has betrayed every dream for which he spoke. Age, thou art shamed."

If his creative work was flowing, so, too, at the outset of this decade, was his production of new anthologies: *A Critical Anthology* (1930), which brought together revised editions of his Modern American Poetry and Modern British Poetry; *American Poetry from the Beginning to Whitman* (1931); and *The Book of Living Verse: English and American Poetry from the Thirteenth Century to the Present Day* (1932)

His relationship with Jean Starr continued to be stormy; attempting a solution, they moved to a farm they named Stony Water, located in the Airondack Mountains of upstate New York. They also adopted two boys, Joseph and Lauren. Untermeyer later wrote that although the household servants (a hired man and a nanny) largely raised the boys, the addition of children and a substantial farm in the country did, for a while, purchase a bit of bliss. But only for a short while. On a trip to Toledo, Ohio, as part of a cross-country lecture tour, Untermeyer met a lawyer, Esther Antin, and once more fell in love. Once more, he asked Jean for a divorce. Once more, she refused. Untermeyer, through a series of subterfuges, attained yet another divorce through the Mexican authorities and in 1933 married Esther Antin, his third wife.

Jean left Stony Water to settle in New York City, while Untermeyer divided his time between the farm and Toledo. Eventually, Esther gave up her law practice, and the couple settled permanently at Stony Water.

By the end of the 1930s, Untermeyer had once again begun having clandestine affairs. In 1939, the fifty-three-year-old Untermeyer published his first memoir, *From Another World* (1939). It was a remarkable book mostly for what it did not say. After tracing his early life, it offered virtually no biographical detail at all. Instead readers were given a series of delightful anecdotes and stories about the many writers, artists, and intellectuals he had known and whose careers he had often fostered. It is very much the book of a public figure whose reputation is based on his circle of influence more than on his own particular circumstances.

THE 1940s

World War II brought Untermeyer once more to New York City, where he worked in the Office of War Information as senior editor of publications. Eventually, Untermeyer's creative talents were employed by the theater and dance division of the War Information Office, where he wrote broadcast propaganda scripts on the triumphs and virtues of American culture. But his real talent, as gatekeeper, was tapped in 1944 when he went to work for the nonprofit corporation Armed Services Editions, whose only client, the armed services of the United States, demanded a regular stream of books to be sent to the soldiers fighting in battle theaters across the globe. Even in war, in other words, Untermeyer had the power to make or break reputations. It was up to him to choose up to forty titles a month: he selected which poets and writers the federal government would distribute.

Meanwhile, with an eye on the future, Untermeyer in 1943 once more entered the world of business. Signing on as the cultural editor for Decca Records, where he was responsible for their spoken word and recorded drama division, he entered a job that he held until 1956.

Meanwhile, Untermeyer's editorial judgement and literary prestige had also won for him a place on the advisory committee of the Pulitzer Prize in Poetry. From the 1940s to the 1960s he was one of the few people to select the annual winner of perhaps the most important national prize offered to poets in any given year.

By the late 1940s, New York had become the center of two new media empires: network radio and the new medium of television. Untermeyer found himself a regular celebrity on both. In 1947, he had his own radio show, *Let's Balance the Books,* and, in 1949 Untermeyer was invited to be part of the regular panel of the CBS game show, *What's My Line?* For the first time in his career, Untermeyer was a genuine celebrity.

By the mid-1940s, however, Untermeyer and Esther Antin had separated, with Untermeyer taking an apartment in Brooklyn. He soon fell in love again, this time with the fiction editor of *Seventeen* magazine, Bryna Ivens. In 1948, he asked Esther for a divorce. She refused. For the third time, Untermeyer found himself compelled to resort to the Mexican "solution." He and Bryna went to Mexico to establish residency. Untermeyer achieved his divorce and, in July, married for the fifth time, to his fourth wife. In the fall of 1948, the new couple bought a home in Connecticut, but Untermeyer's troubles were only just beginning.

THE 1950s

Unlike Jean Starr, Esther did not concede to the Mexican solution. Instead, she sued Louis for bigamy. The ensuing legal wrangle lasted from 1948 to 1951. The conclusion was as complex as Untermeyer's various marriages, but in the end the judge decided that Untermeyer had only ever had one wife, Jean Starr: none of the Mexican marriages and divorces was valid. By this time, Jean (herself now an established poet with a life of her own) was as ready to legally part from Untermeyer as he had been willing on numerous occasions to part from her. The two went to Reno, Nevada, where they were legally and officially divorced. As a result, Untermeyer, in November 1951, married Byrna Ivens again, this time in a legally recognized ceremony.

Even as he was unsnarling his personal marital situation, larger events were having a debilitating effect on his public life. The influence of Senator Joseph McCarthy was at its peak in the entertainment industry, and throughout 1949 and 1950 a smear campaign against the liberal politics and supposed "Communism" of Untermeyer flooded the offices of CBS and its advertising sponsor of *What's My Line? Life* magazine even did a spread on Untermeyer that attempted to taint him with the brush of treason. CBS, conceding to the criticism, required Untermeyer to be examined by its board to see if, in fact, he was too leftist. Astounded and disgusted, Untermeyer quit the show. Even after McCarthy was censured by the Senate in 1954, the national political climate continued to support widespread anticommunist sentiment; when he went to southern California on a lecture tour in 1956, the seventy-year-old Untermeyer found that his lectures were the occasion of boycotts and that demonstrations were planned against him. Untermeyer says in the memoir *Bygones* that his book of biographical sketches, *Makers of the Modern World* (1955), was, in the context of that repressive political era, a defense of liberalism worldwide, told through the life tales of ninety-two famously liberal men and women.

For all these headaches, however, the 1950s—and especially the late 1950s—were years of triumph for Untermeyer. His reputation was at its height. His greatly expanded textbooks *Modern American Poetry* and *Modern British Poetry* had become the standard texts in high schools and colleges nationwide. He was very much a public literary figure. And in his marriage he was, at last, a happy man. He and his new wife traveled extensively in Europe between 1954 and 1960. Eventually, Bryna became a notable editor of children's books, and together with her, Untermeyer published close to a dozen children's books between 1948 and 1968.

THE 1960s

By the time Untermeyer was in his mid-seventies, he had achieved a new level of prominence. With the election of John F. Kennedy, Untermeyer's famous liberalism became a major asset. In 1961, he was appointed consultant in poetry to the Library of Congress, a position today known as poet laureate, a post he held until 1963. As part of his duties, he was instrumental in establishing an official White House–sponsored National Festival of Poetry, and he regularly appeared on television. Asked by the State Department to represent American literature in the cold war effort to promote American culture, in 1961 he went to India and in 1962 he went to Japan.

Altogether, Untermeyer's 1960s were a decade of triumph both nationally and internationally. And for the first time in nearly thirty years, he returned to his own poetry, which had by then fallen out of print. *Long Feud: Selected Poems* appeared in 1962. In 1965 he published his first book of new poems in over thirty years, *Labyrinth of Love,* as well as a self-revealing, highly personal autobiography, *Bygones.*

CONCLUSION

Louis Untermeyer died at his house in Newtown, Connecticut, on December 18, 1977. In a mock obituary published much earlier, the poet e. e. cummings had amusingly written:

> mr u will not be missed
> who as an anthologist
> sold the many on the few
> not excluding mr u

In the *New York Times* obituary marking his death, however, Untermeyer was more seriously described, as "a minor poet and a major anthologizer." That assessment still holds true. But if today his poetry is still neglected, his idea of poetry, and the operating principle behind his influential *Modern American Poetry,* has never been more powerful. His inclusive vision has now become the reigning orthodoxy of the twenty-first century. In his own day, Untermeyer never accepted the strict divisions between free verse and metrical verse that, until the 1990s, governed the understanding of American poetry. For him, poetry was defined as a kind of force, an event, and it could arrive as easily in the original cadence of free verse as in fixed forms. Describing his joy in the poetry of his friend James Oppenheim, he said: "the sense was unorthodox, the phrasing was fresh, the spirit rather than the form was free." And describing his own poetry, he wrote: "My natural impulse was toward a pronounced pattern; in poetry as in music, I delighted in expressions free in spirit but fixed in form. My ear craved all the sensual properties of traditional verse, the alternating caress and clang of rhythm, the little bells of rhyme." He felt no compulsion to choose sides in what would, throughout the post–World War II period, be an ever-expanding list of dichotomies: men versus women, city versus nature, fixed form versus free verse, ethnic poetry versus some sort of neutral standard, national versus regional. Untermeyer's anthologies, like his criticism and poetry, were eclectic, welcoming, broad in interest, generous in principle.

In American literary study, something of a revolution occurred in the early 1990s after the critic Paul Lauter published *The Heath Anthology of American Literature* (1990). Suddenly, ethnic, regional, and women writers as well as a whole neglected stylistic spectrum returned to the American textbook. In fact, however, all that had happened was a return to the principles of Louis Untermeyer.

Reflecting on his own talent as anthologist, Untermeyer admitted in *Bygones,* "I was born a collector; I had the mind of a magpie." In the earlier memoir, *From Another World,* he had attempted to explain how he made his selections, how he came to include and exclude the poems and poets he ultimately chose: after several pages of reflection, however, he had admitted, "Time is, of course, the final anthologist." A glance at any current anthology of American literature reveals that, when it came to vision and understanding, the open-hearted, democratic, Whitmanian idea of American literature that governed Untermeyer's choices was, if anything, far ahead of its time.

Selected Bibliography

WORKS OF LOUIS UNTERMEYER

POETRY AND PARODIES

The Younger Quire. New York: Moods, 1911. (Parodies.)

First Love: A Lyric Sequence. Boston: Sherman, French, 1911.

Challenge. New York: Century, 1914.

"—and Other Poets." New York: Holt, 1916. (Parodies.)

These Times. New York: Holt, 1917.

Including Horace. New York: Harcourt, Brace and Howe, 1919. (Parodies.)

The New Adam. New York: Harcourt, Brace and Howe, 1920.

Heavens. New York: Harcourt, 1922. (Parodies.)

Roast Leviathan. New York: Harcourt, Brace, 1923.

Collected Parodies. New York: Harcourt, Brace, 1926.

Poems. With Richard Untermeyer. Privately printed, 1927.

Burning Bush. New York: Harcourt, Brace, 1928.

Adirondack Cycle. New York, Random House, 1929. (Pamphlet.)

Food and Drink. New York: Harcourt, Brace, 1932.

First Words before Spring. New York: Knopf, 1933.

Selected Poems and Parodies of Louis Untermeyer. New York: Harcourt, Brace, 1935.

Long Feud: Selected Poems. New York: Harcourt, Brace, and World, 1962.

Labyrinth of Love. New York: Simon and Schuster, 1965.

PROSE

The New Era in American Poetry. New York: Holt, 1919. (Essays.)

American Poetry since 1900. New York: Holt, 1923. (Essays.)

The Forms of Poetry: A Pocket Dictionary of Verse. New York: Harcourt, Brace, 1926.

Moses. New York: Harcourt, Brace, 1928. (Novel.)

Blue Rhine, Black Forest, a Hand- and Day-Book. New York: Harcourt, Brace, 1930. (Travel journal.)

The Donkey of God. New York: Harcourt, Brace, 1932. (Short stories.)

Poetry: Its Appreciation and Enjoyment. With Carter Davidson. New York: Harcourt, Brace, 1934.

Doorways to Poetry. Edited with others. New York, Harcourt, Brace, 1938. (Textbook.)

Play in Poetry. New York, Harcourt, Brace, 1938. (Henry Ward Beecher Lectures.)

From Another World: The Autobiography of Louis Untermeyer. New York: Harcourt, Brace, 1939.

A Century of Candymaking, 1847–1947. N.p.: Privately printed, 1947.

Makers of the Modern World. New York: Simon and Schuster, 1955. (Biography.)

Lives of the Poets: The Story of One Thousand Years of English and American Poetry. New York: Simon and Schuster, 1959.

Edwin Arlington Robinson: A Reappraisal, Washington D.C.: U.S. Government Printing Office, 1963.

Lives of the Poets 1963. New York: Simon and Schuster, 1963.

Robert Frost: A Backward Look. Washington D.C.: U.S. Government Printing Office, 1964.

Bygones: The Recollections of Louis Untermeyer. New York: Harcourt, Brace & World, 1965. (Autobiography.)

The Paths of Poetry: Twenty-Five Poets and Their Poems, New York: Delacorte, 1966.

The Pursuit of Poetry: A Guide to Its Understanding and Appreciation with an Explanation of Its Forms and a Dictionary of Poetic Terms, New York: Simon and Schuster, 1969.

Said I to Myself, Said I: Reflections and Reappraisals, Digressions and Diversions. N.p.: Privately printed, 1978.

BOOKS EDITED

Modern American Poetry. (Revised edition) New York: Harcourt, Brace, & Howe, 1921.

A Miscellany of American Poetry. New York: Granger, 1920.

Modern British Poetry. New York: Harcourt, Brace, & Howe, 1920.

Modern American and British Poetry. Harcourt, Brace, 1922.

American Poetry, 1922: A Miscellany, New York: Granger, 1922.

American Poetry, 1925: A Miscellany. New York: Granger, 1925.

Walt Whitman. New York: Simon and Schuster, 1926.

Yesterday and Today: A Comparative Anthology. New York: Harcourt, Brace, 1926. Rev. ed. *Yesterday and Today: A Collection of Verse (Mostly Modern) Designed for the Average Person of Nine to Nineteen and Possibly Higher.* New York: Harcourt, Brace, 1927.

American Poetry, 1927: A Miscellany. New York: Granger, 1927.

Emily Dickinson. New York: Simon and Schuster, 1927.

Conrad Aiken. New York: Simon and Schuster, 1927.

A Critical Anthology: Modern American Poetry, Modern British Poetry. New York: Harcourt, Brace, 1930. (Revised editions *of Modern American Poetry and Modern British Poetry.*)

American Poetry from the Beginning to Whitman. New York: Harcourt, Brace, 1931.

The Book of Living Verse: English and American Poetry from the Thirteenth Century to the Present Day. New York: Harcourt, Brace, 1932. 2nd ed., rev. *The Book of Living Verse: Limited to the Chief Poets.* New York: Harcourt, Brace, 1939.

The New Treasury of Verse. London: Odhams, 1934.

A Treasury of Great Poems: English and American, New York: Simon and Schuster, 1942. Rev. ed. *A Concise Treasury of Great Poems, English and American, from the Foundations of the English Spirit to the Outstanding Poetry of Our Own Time.* Garden City, N.Y.: Permabooks, 1953. Rev. ed., enlarged. *A Treasury of Great Poems, English and American, with Lives of the Poets and Historical Settings Selected and Integrated by Louis Untermeyer.* 2 vols. New York: Simon and Schuster, 1964.

The Poems of Edgar Allan Poe. New York: Heritage, 1943.

The Poems of Henry Wadsworth Longfellow. New York: Heritage, 1943.

Robert Frost: Come In, and Other Poems. New York: Holt, 1943. Rev. ed., enlarged. *The Road Not Taken: An Introduction to Robert Frost.* New York: Holt, 1951.

Great Poems from Chaucer to Whitman. New York: Editions for the Armed Services, 1944.

The Poems of Ralph Waldo Emerson. New York: Heritage, 1945.

The Pocket Book of Story Poems. New York: Pocket Books, 1945. Rev. ed., enlarged. *Story Poems: An Anthology of Narrative Verse.* New York: Washington Square Press, 1957.

The Poems of John Greenleaf Whittier. New York: Heritage, 1945.

Love Poems of Elizabeth Barrett Browning and Robert Browning. New Brunswick, N.J.: Rutgers University Press, 1946.

A Treasury of Laughter. New York: Simon and Schuster, 1946.

The Book of Noble Thoughts. New York: American Artists Group, 1946.

The Poems of William Cullen Bryant. New York: Heritage, 1947.

The Pocket Treasury. New York: Pocket Books, 1947. (Prose selections.)

The Rubáiyát of Omar Khayyam. Translated by Edward FitzGerald. New York: Random House, 1947.

Anthology of the New England Poets from Colonial Times to the Present Day, New York: Random House, 1948.

The Love Poems of Robert Herrick and John Donne. New Brunswick, N.J.: Rutgers University Press, 1948.

The Pocket Book of American Poems from the Colonial Period to the Present Day. New York: Pocket Books, 1948.

The Inner Sanctum Edition of the Poetry and Prose of Walt Whitman. New York: Simon and Schuster, 1949.

The Best Humor of 1949–50. With R. E. Shikes. New York: Holt, 1951.

The Best Humor of 1951–52. With R. E. Shikes. New York: Holt, 1952.

The Poems of Emily Dickinson. New York: Heritage, 1952.

The Magic Circle: Stories and People in Poetry. New York: Harcourt Brace, 1952.

Early American Poets. New York: Library Publishers, 1952.

The Book of Wit and Humor. Concord, N.H.: Mercury Books, 1953. (Prose selections.)

A Treasury of Ribaldry. Garden City, N.Y.: Hanover House, 1956.

The Britannica Library of Great American Writing. 2 vols. Chicago: Britannica Press, 1960. (Prose selections.)

Collins Albatross Book of Verse. London: Collins, 1960.

Lots of Limericks: Light, Lusty and Lasting. Garden City, N.Y.: Doubleday, 1961.

An Uninhibited Treasury of Erotic Poetry. New York: Dial, 1963.

The Pan Book of Limericks. London: Pan, 1963.

Love Sonnets. New York: Odyssey, 1964.

Love Lyrics. New York: Odyssey, 1965.

A Time for Peace: Verses from the Bible. New York: World, 1969.

Men and Women: The Poetry of Love. New York: American Heritage Press, 1970.

Treasury of Great Humor: Including Wit, Whimsy, and Satire from the Remote Past to the Present. New York: McGraw-Hill, 1972.

Fifty Modern American and British Poets, 1920–1970. New York: McKay, 1973.

TRANSLATIONS

Poems of Heinrich Heine. New York: Holt, 1917. Rev. ed. New York: Harcourt, Brace, 1923.

The Fat of the Cat, and Other Stories, by Gottfried Keller. New York: Harcourt, Brace, 1925.

The Poetry and Prose of Heinrich Heine. New York: Citadel, 1948. (Poetry translated by Untermeyer.)

Cyrano de Bergerac, by Edmond Rostand. New York: Limited Editions Club, 1954.

Poems, by Heinrich Heine. New York: Limited Editions Club, 1957.

Heinrich Heine: Paradox and Poet. 2 vols. New York: Harcourt, Brace, 1937.

CHILDREN'S LITERATURE

Chip: My Life and Times, as Overheard by Louis Untermeyer. New York: Harcourt, Brace, 1933. (Fiction.)

The Last Pirate: Tales from the Gilbert and Sullivan Operas, New York: Harcourt, Brace, 1934.

Songs to Sing to Children. With Albert Ernest Wier. New York: Harcourt, Brace, 1935.

The Wonderful Adventures of Paul Bunyan. New York: Heritage, 1945.

French Fairy Tales. New York: Didier, 1945. (Retelling of tales by Charles Perrault.)

All the French Fairy Tales. New York: Didier, 1945. (Retelling of tales by Charles Perrault.)

More French Fairy Tales. New York: Didier, 1946. (Retelling of tales by Charles Perrault.)

For You with Love: A Poem. New York: Golden Press, 1961.

The Kitten Who Barked. New York: Golden Press, 1962. (Fiction.)

One and One and One. New York: Crowell-Collier, 1962. (Poetry.)

This Is Your Day: A Poem. New York: Golden Press, 1964.

The Second Christmas. Kansas City, Mo.: Hallmark Cards, 1964.

The World's Great Stories: Fifty-Five Legends That Live Forever. New York: Evans, 1964. Published as *The Firebringer, and Other Great Stories: Fifty-Five Legends That Live Forever.* New York: Evans, 1968.

Thanks: A Poem. New York: Odyssey, 1965.

Merry Christmas. New York: Golden Press, 1967.

Lift up Your Heart. New York: Golden Press, 1968.

Your Lucky Stars. New York: Golden Press, 1968. (Poems.)

Thinking of You. New York: Golden Press, 1968. (Poems.)

A Friend Indeed. New York: Golden Press, 1968. (Poems.)

You: A Poem. New York: Golden Press, 1969.

Plants of the Bible. New York: Golden Press, 1970.

Cat o' Nine Tales. New York: American Heritage, 1971. (Fiction.)

BOOKS EDITED FOR CHILDREN

This Singing World: An Anthology of Modern Poetry for Young People. Vol. 1. New York: Harcourt, Brace, 1923. Vol. 2, *Junior Edition.* New York: Harcourt, Brace, 1926. Vol. 3, *For Younger Children.* New York: Harcourt, Brace, 1926.

New Songs for New Voices. New York: Harcourt, Brace, 1928. (Poems.)

Rainbow in the Sky. New York: Harcourt, Brace, 1935. (Poems.)

Stars to Steer By. New York: Harcourt, Brace, 1941. (Poems.)

The Golden Treasury of Poetry. New York: Golden Press, 1959.

Fairy Tales: The Complete Household Tales of Jakob and Wilhelm Grimm. With Bryna Untermeyer. New York: Limited Editions Club, 1962.

Legendary Animals. With Bryna Untermeyer. New York: Golden Press, 1963.

Aesop's Fables. New York: Golden Press, 1965.

The Golden Treasury of Children's Literature. With Bryna Untermeyer. New York: Golden Press, 1966.

Songs of Joy from the Book of Psalms. New York: World, 1967.

Words of Wisdom. With Bryna Untermeyer. New York: Golden Press, 1968. (Quotations.)

Tales and Legends. With Bryna Untermeyer. New York: Golden Press, 1968.

Adventure Stories. With Bryna Untermeyer. New York: Golden Press, 1968.

Animal Stories. With Bryna Untermeyer. New York: Golden Press, 1968.

Favorite Classics. With Bryna Untermeyer. New York: Golden Press, 1968.

Tales from the Ballet. New York: Golden Press, 1968.

The Golden Book of Fun and Nonsense. New York: Golden Press, 1970.

Roses: Selections. New York: Golden Press, 1970.

The Golden Book of Poems for the Very Young, New York: Golden Press, 1971.

The Golden Treasury of Animal Stories and Poems. New York: Golden Press, 1971.

Stories and Poems for the Very Young. With Bryna Untermeyer. New York: Golden Press, 1973.

A Galaxy of Verse. With Bryna Untermeyer. New York: Evans, 1978.

SELECTED UNCOLLECTED ESSAYS

Review of modern dance. *Seven Arts,* November 1916, , pp. 79–81.

"Growth and Decay in Recent Verse." *Seven Arts,* April 1917, pp. 668–671.

"Disillusion and Dogma." *Freeman,* January 1923.

Introduction to *The Complete Poetical Works of Amy Lowell.* Boston: Houghton, Mifflin, 1955.

CRITICAL AND BIOGRAPHICAL STUDIES

Aiken, Conrad. *Selected Letters of Conrad Aiken.* Edited by Joseph Killorin. New Haven, Conn.: Yale University Press, 1978.

———. *Skepticisms.* New York: Knopf, 1919.

de Chasca, Edmund S. *John Gould Fletcher and Imagism.* Columbia: University of Missouri Press, 1978.

Drake, William. *Sara Teasdale: Woman and Poet.* San Francisco: Harper & Row, 1980.

Eliot, T. S. "London Letter." *Dial,* April 1922, 510–513.

Heymann, C. David. *American Aristocracy: The Lives and Times of James Russell, Amy, and Robert Lowell.* New York: Dodd, Mead, 1980.

"Louis Untermeyer." In *World Authors 1900–1950.* Edited by Martin Semour-Smith and Andrew C. Kimmens. New York: H. W. Wilson, 1996.

"Louis Untermeyer." In *Current Biography.* New York: H. W. Wilson, 1967.

Mencken, H. L. "The New Poetry Movement." *Prejudices: First Series.* New York: Knopf, 1919.

Pound, Ezra. *EP to LU: Nine Letters Written to Louis Untermeyer by Ezra Pound.* Edited by J. A. Robbins. Bloomington: Indiana University Press, 1963.

———. *The Letters of Ezra Pound, 1907–1941.* Edited by D. D. Paige. New York: Harcourt, Brace, 1950. (See letter to Harriet Monroe, January 21, 1916.)

Gregory, Horace, and Marya Zaturenska. *A History of American Poetry: 1900-1940.* New York: Harcourt, Brace, 1946.

Sandburg, Carl. *The Letters of Carl Sandburg.* Edited by Herbert Mitgang. New York: Harcourt, Brace & World, 1968.

The Letters of Robert Frost to Louis Untermeyer. New York: Holt, Rinehart & Winston, 1963.

Torrey, E. Fuller. *The Roots of Treason: Ezra Pound and the Secret of St Elizabeths.* New York: McGraw-Hill, 1984.

Wilson, Edmund. *New Republic.* 1925.

BOOK REVIEWS

"And Lesser Things." *Little Review* 3:33–34 (1916). (Review of "*–and Other Poets.*")

Aiken, Conrad. Review of *The New Era in American Poetry. New Republic* 19:58 (May 10, 1919).

———. Review of *The New Era in American Poetry. Yale Review* 9:413–416 (January 1920).

Aldon, Raymond. "Recent Poetry." *Dial* 61: 64 (July 15, 1916). (Review of "*–and Other Poets.*")

Barrett, E. B. Review of *Moses. New York Evening Post,* October 12, 1928, p. 11.

Braithwaite, William Stanley. Review of *Challenge. Boston Evening Transcript,* September 26, 1914, p. 6.

———. Review of *Heavens. Boston Evening Transcript,* April 5, 1922, p. 7.

———. Review of *The New Adam. Boston Evening Transcript,* December 31, 1920, p. 4.

Doren, Mark Van. Review of *The New Adam. Nation* 112:86 (January 19, 1921).

Firkins, O. W. Review of *Burning Bush. Saturday Review of Literature* 5:84 (September 1, 1928).

Henderson, Alice Corbin. "On 'The Movement.' " *Poetry* 14:159-167 (1919). (Review of *The New Era in American Poetry.*)

Johnson, Alvin. "Horace Reprocessed." *New Republic,* December 17, 1919, pp. 83–84. (Review of *Including Horace.*)

Lowell, Amy. "A Poet of the Present." *Poetry* 11:157–164 (1917). (Review of *These Times.*)

———. Review of *The New Adam. New York Times,* October 10, 1920, p. 8.

Nation 108:793 (May 17, 1919). (Review of *The New Era in American Poetry.*)

New Republic 13: 899 (December 15, 1917). (Review of *These Times.)*

New York Times, March 26, 1916. (Review of *"–and Other Poets.")*

Reed, Edward Bliss. Review of *Challenge. Yale Review* 4:178–186 (1914).

Reed, Edward Bliss. Yale Review (New Series) 6: 419. (January 1917).

———. Review of *These Times. Yale Review* 6:862 (July 1917).

Springfield Republican, April 6, 1919, p. 17. (Review of *The New Era in American Poetry.)*

———, January 2, 1920, p. 6. (Review of *Including Horace.)*

Tietjens, Eunice. "The Revolt of the Once Born." *Little Review* 1: 51–53 (1914). (Review of *Challenge.)*

Wood, Clement. Review of *"–and Other Poets." New York Call,* May 21, 1916, p. 15.

MANUSCRIPTS AND PAPERS

A collection of the papers of Louis Untermeyer are held at Lilly Library. Indiana University, Bloomington, Indiana.

—*JONATHAN N. BARRON*

Wendy Wasserstein

1950–

WENDY WASSERSTEIN WAS born on October 18, 1950, in Brooklyn, New York. Her father, Morris W. Wasserstein, owned a textile factory and is noted for inventing velveteen and wired ribbon. The family became wealthy. Wasserstein's mother, Lola Schleifer Wasserstein, danced throughout her life after emigrating from Poland with her family to escape extermination by the Nazis. Besides Wendy, the Wassersteins had three older children. The oldest, Sandra Meyer, died of cancer in 1996, at the age of sixty, after breaking through several major barriers for women. Wendy proudly reports in her essay "Don't Tell Mother," included in *Shiksa Goddess; or, How I Spent My Forties* (2001), "Sandra was the first female product-group manager at General Foods, in 1969; the first female president of a division of American Express, in 1980; the first female to run corporate affairs as a senior officer at Citicorp, in 1989." Another daughter, Georgette Levis, owns and operates an inn in Vermont with her psychiatrist husband. Wasserstein's brother, Bruce, became an enormously successful entrepreneur and author. Bruce could not attend the opening of Wendy's Pulitzer Prize–winning play, *The Heidi Chronicles* (1988), because he was finalizing the $25 billion merger of R. J. Reynolds and Nabisco; posters of Wendy's plays regale his office walls. He told Phoebe Hoban for her article "The Family Wasserstein" in *New York* magazine in 1993 that the siblings have always been a "very reinforcing family" because "it works better that way." Wendy Wasserstein has known since childhood that growing up with her family gave her rich material, and she has put it to good use.

The theater made its mark on her at birth. She was named after the character in J. M. Barrie's play *Peter Pan*. Other circumstances nudged her toward writing plays. Slightly dyslectic, she was less interested in the written word than talk, so she has always had a strong memory for conversations. Her grandfather, Shimon Schleifer, had been a school principal and an amateur playwright in Poland, and her parents and siblings loved the theater, so from a young age, Wendy accompanied them to plays, musicals, variety shows, and movies.

While her family lived in Brooklyn, Wendy attended primary school at the Yeshiva of Flatbush and, later, the Brooklyn Ethical Culture School where she especially enjoyed dancing to colors called out by a teacher, a history Wasserstein discovered she shares with the legendary Betty Comden. When she was twelve, the family moved to Manhattan, and Wendy established the habit of taking dance lessons on Saturday mornings from June Taylor, who had been the choreographer for the popular *Jackie Gleason Show* in the 1950s. After dance class, Wasserstein typically attended a matinee with her parents. Those afternoons in the theater gave her the idea that one could make a living doing something one loved. All the hours she sat immersed in Broadway musicals and shows at Radio City Music Hall may help explain why Wasserstein always includes songs in her plays and sometimes dancing.

Her sister Sandra showed her that one could have interesting experiences by not following orders. Wasserstein often tells of the day her sister was supposed to pick her up and take her out for a grilled cheese sandwich, followed by the Rockettes and a Doris Day movie. Instead Sandra bought them a decidedly nonkosher meal of spareribs and shrimp and then took her sister to a film called *Expresso Bongo* (1959) featuring topless women wearing kilts. Wasserstein says this adventure gave her a glimpse of the variety of options available to women brave enough to seize them.

Since Wendy needed a new school once the family moved to Manhattan, her mother donned uncharacteristically conservative clothing and took her daughter to the exclusive Dalton School for an entrance interview. At first Wendy tried to please the interviewer, but when it dawned on her that she could easily gain admittance if she were willing to lie about herself, she lost interest in attending Dalton. She asserted her integrity by losing herself in another character: after slipping a piece of gum into her mouth, she said in a heavy Brooklyn accent that she wanted to go to public school with all her friends. She was turned down. This episode offers an early example of Wasserstein's ability to achieve authenticity by speaking through the voices of other people.

Over and over she says that she loves writing plays because doing it well requires honest speech. When asked how she teaches playwriting, Wasserstein answers that she tries to coax her students to trust their own voices. In "New York Theater: Isn't It Romantic," another essay included in *Shiksa Goddess,* she explains that despite the attractions of writing for film and television, playwrights always return to the theater because of "the theater's endurance as the great art form of the individual voice." And the voice of the play seems wiser than that of the mortal who penned it. Wasserstein's preface to the published *Sisters Rosensweig* (1993) tells of her seeing a moving performance of the play and concluding that the "author must be very mature"—a person who believes in family, tradition, challenge, possibilities, and well-made plays and therefore "could not possibly be me."

The author achieves this wisdom by losing herself in the variety of perspectives assumed by the characters, just as Wasserstein's beloved Anton Chekhov does. "He has the overall vision of a changing society, and the individual insight into each character," she says in "Theater Problems? Call Dr. Chekhov." "He doesn't reprimand his characters, he just puts them out on the stage as honestly and with as much craft as possible."

She describes writing a play as an exploration of character, and she loves listening to different voices. None of these characters are herself or even the other people from her life who sometimes inspire them, but every one of them reflects some part of herself. Before the birth of her daughter, Lucy Jane, on September 12, 1999, Wasserstein arranged her life so she could often sit alone with these people in small rooms that reminded her of life in a college dorm, and she even took "writing holidays" to hotels near college or university campuses to finish projects. Perhaps to coax herself to let go of the characters in a play, Wasserstein usually gets the idea for the next play as she's finishing whichever one she's working on at the time. But she does not immediately begin the next project; she must make space for that event—and all those new people.

Many years passed between Wendy Wasserstein's performance at the Dalton School's entrance interview and her realization that she could spend the rest of her life losing herself in the voices of others. After being turned down by the Dalton School, Wasserstein attended another private school, the Calhoun School, where the only playwriting she did was scripts for fashion shows that she produced solely because it got her exempted from physical education class. She did not begin writing seriously until her undergraduate years at Mount Holyoke College, a place whose influence saturates Wasserstein's first widely known play, *Uncommon Women and Others* (1978).

Mount Holyoke College is the oldest institution of higher learning for women in the United States. The grave of its founder, Mary Lyon, sits in the center of campus, reminding the students daily that they attend a school established in 1837 by someone who not only believed women had capabilities that deserved cultivating, but who also thought that these women should put their educations to socially responsible use. Wasserstein makes the links between *Uncommon Women* and her experience at Mount Holyoke very clear: the characters, all Mount Holyoke graduates, get together for a reunion in 1978, seven years after graduation; Wasserstein graduated from Mount Holyoke in 1971. At Mount Holyoke, the characters lived in North Stimson Hall where they had a housemother named Mrs. Plumm; her freshman year, Wasserstein's housemother was Camilla Peach, and in her senior year she lived in North Mandelle Hall. Framing the play's action is a male voice-over that uses the comments of former Mount Holyoke administrators to speak of the accomplished women who have graduated from the college.

Wasserstein thinks women's schools are invaluable because they help women respect themselves and their minds. She attributes her willingness to trust her own voice to the women's schools she attended and the women's movement. Wasserstein says that she took women's history when it was first offered at Mount Holyoke and claims the course changed the way she saw the world. But coming of age during the late-twentieth-century wave of feminism presented problems as well as new possibilities.

Mount Holyoke itself reflected the ambivalence this transition precipitated by providing women with fine educations that encouraged them to take their minds seriously while retaining rituals of gracious living, such as sit-down meals with linen napkins. Since Wasserstein and her Mount Holyoke friends had grown up with the notion that all women should aspire to get married and have children, they had no real need to have traditional values reinforced. As a history major Wasserstein realized that no matter how clearly contemporary Mount Holyoke women understood the importance and value of shaping their own lives, their past training held them in a tight grip, stunting liberation into ambivalence.

While at Mount Holyoke, Wendy Wasserstein also personally experienced the psychic power that the illusion of male superiority continued to hold over women. She was one of twenty-three Mount Holyoke women who spent a year at the all-male Amherst College; it took a while before she and her roommate found the courage to stop eating peanut butter and jelly sandwiches in their dorm suite and join their male classmates in the dining hall. And she noticed that in classes the women did not speak nearly as freely or as confidently as the men.

Wasserstein didn't begin writing seriously until a friend persuaded her to take Leonard Berkman's writing course at Smith College in nearby Northampton, Massachusetts, so that they could explore the town's shops. When David Savran interviews her for *The Playwright's Voice: American Dramatists on Memory, Writing, and the Politics of Culture* (1999), Wasserstein explains that Berkman "was the first person who made me feel confident with my own voice." Although Wasserstein characterizes herself as a poor student at Mount Holyoke, in fact her grades rose substantially as the years passed, suggesting that she learned a great deal there.

After graduation in 1971 with a bachelor's degree in history, she was one of the first students in the creative writing program at the City University of New York, which she describes glowingly, in a report held in the Mount Holyoke library archives, as a new but serious program where distinguished writers teach small classes. Wasserstein studied with the novelist

Joseph Heller and the playwright Israel Horovitz. She received her master's degree in 1973, and soon thereafter Playwrights Horizons produced the play that was her thesis, *Any Woman Can't,* beginning Wasserstein's long association with that group. She subsequently applied to Columbia Business School and the Yale School of Drama; when accepted at both, she followed her heart to Yale where she received her master of fine arts degree in 1976. Her first widely known play, *Uncommon Women and Others* (1978), grew from a one-act play she wrote at Yale.

UNCOMMON WOMEN AND OTHERS

In *Uncommon Women,* while the male voice-over speaks confidently of the futures these Mount Holyoke students will enjoy, the women of whom he seems so sure converse with each other about their confusion. The play suggests that since every woman can suddenly have it all, every woman will fail because achieving this ideal is a practical impossibility, something asserted by a woman who eventually assumes control of the play's voice-overs. At the beginning of the last scene of the play she announces, "Women still encounter overwhelming obstacles to achievement and recognition despite gradual abolition of legal and political disabilities." *Uncommon Women* shows these difficulties through a series of vignettes that present the same women interacting at college and at their seventh-year reunion.

Two of the major characters, Kate Quin and Samantha Stewart, successfully realize the goals they established in college. Kate Quin has achieved distinction as a lawyer and Samantha Stewart has devoted herself to her husband. But both worry about what they have failed to achieve. Kate's attaché case "alternately makes her feel like a successful grown-up, or handcuffed," because she has no free time and she wonders if she'll ever have a child. Samantha married Robert Cabe with the intention of supporting his greatness. The day after she met him in college she said, "I want to be his audience, and have my picture, behind him, in my long tartan kilt, in the *New York Times* Arts and Leisure section." Now she feels that she has accomplished little, even as she awaits the birth of her first child. The doubts expressed by Kate and Samantha seem to validate Rita Altabel's analysis late in the play of the two bad options available to women as all of them are about to graduate from college:

> God knows there is no security in marriage. You give up your anatomy, economic self-support, spontaneous creativity, and a helluva lot of energy trying to convert a male half-person into a whole person who will eventually stop draining you, so you can do your own work. And the alternative— hopping onto the corporate or professional ladder is just as self-destructive. If you spend your life proving yourself, then you just become a man.

Unlike Kate and Samantha, when Holly Kaplan and Muffet Di Nicola try to imagine what they want after graduation, they collapse into confusion. Holly, a character whose father, like Wendy Wasserstein's, invented velveteen, claims to hate sex and then announces that she would happily turn her life over to a man. She certifies the truth of the latter claim by making a desperate phone call to a doctor in Minneapolis whom she briefly encountered nearly a year earlier in Harvard's Fogg Museum; he has forgotten their meeting. Muffet claims she wants to live independently, then worries where she'll meet men once she graduates, then abandons Leilah after they plan to go out together because her boyfriend, "Pink Pants," calls. After graduation Holly collects three master's degrees while Muffet drifts into an insurance job that she enjoys. Ironically perhaps, as a result of their inability to choose clear goals and pursue them Muffet and Holly seem happier with their relatively amorphous lives than the focused and successful Kate and Samantha.

The irrepressible Rita has also failed in her plan to train her boyfriend to help nourish her writing career the way Leonard Woolf helped his wife Virginia, but she has no doubt that she will one day write and that all these Mount Holyoke graduates will one day be "amazing." While she's in college she thinks this will occur at the age of twenty-five; she then immediately moves back the deadline to thirty—just to be safe. As the play closes she keeps moving the big moment back: "When we're forty we can be pretty amazing. You too, Muffy and Samantha. When we're ... *forty-five,* we can be pretty fucking amazing." So the curtain comes down on five women still trapped in ambivalence, who also have the comfort of knowing that they will console one another as they encounter more disappointments.

Wasserstein has said that she got the inspiration for this ending from Chekhov's play *The Three Sisters* (1901), and the resolution of her characters' conflicts is as elusive as getting to Moscow is for Chekhov's. But despite their problems, in the final stage direction these women *"exit with their arms around each other,"* signaling that they will always have one another. Indeed Wasserstein suggests that writing the play helped her reestablish contact with her friends. And in "Female Laughter and Comic Possibilities: *Uncommon Women and Others,*" included in Claudia Barnett's *Wendy Wasserstein: A Casebook* (1999), Miriam M. Chirico argues that the play's humor makes it feel optimistic: "As spectators we have a secure emotional realization that the uncommon women before us will continue to strive and grow because of their laughter and wit."

This play did well, opening at the Phoenix Theatre in New York City on November 21, 1977, and appearing on the PBS *Great Performances* series the following year. This success suggested to Wasserstein that she could make a life out of writing plays. When *Uncommon Women* was revived in 1994, many critics thought the play showed its age, but in 1988, Wendy Wasserstein's good feelings about the work persisted. She told Esther Cohen in "Uncommon Woman: An Interview with Wendy Wasserstein": "I have a real love ... for 'Uncommon Women.' I really ... find it very dear. I think because whoever wrote it really cared a lot. There's a lot of raw emotion there."

When Wasserstein sat down to write the play, she cared passionately about the lack of roles for female actresses. She first noticed this when watching Broadway shows as a child; by the time she attended the Yale drama school, she had the conscious aim of writing a play for an all female cast. In the late 1970s Wasserstein cherished her new writing career for a reason that would make Mount Holyoke's founder, Mary Lyon, proud: she believed that by doing something she loves, she could help improve society's understanding of women. Writing in "Comic Textures and Female Communities 1937 and 1977: Clare Boothe and Wendy Wasserstein" (1990), Susan L. Carlson agrees that with this play Wasserstein not only "shows how a comedy full of women no longer needs to be a bitter dead end," she "creates a comic world where women can work within a female community to challenge social roles." The wit and humor that pervade the play persist through Wasserstein's subsequent work.

ISN'T IT ROMANTIC

In an interview on October 9, 1991, Wasserstein says to Leslie Jacobson, "My plays tend to be semiautobiographical or come out of something that's irking me, and it's got to irk me long enough for me to commit to spend all that time alone writing and turn it into a play." When she wrote *Isn't It Romantic* (1984), apparently her mother irked her. The description of the play's protagonist, Janie Blumberg, recalls characterizations of her creator: "Her appearance is a little kooky, a little sweet, a little unconfident— all of which some might call creative, or even witty." Anyone who has read Wasserstein's stories about her mother has no trouble identifying her as the inspiration for Janie's tap-dancing mother, Tasha Blumberg: both Mrs. Wasserstein and Mrs. Blumberg urge their daughters to dress nicely when they take out the trash because they could meet someone promising at the garbage receptacle; both urge their daughters to nourish their self-esteem by chanting "I am" to themselves; both rely on takeout to meet their families' nutritional needs; and both desperately want their daughters to get married. Lola Wasserstein has commented that, unlike Tasha Blumberg, she wears black leotards, not tie-dyed ones. In *Isn't It Romantic,* Wasserstein emphasizes that family pressures often add another layer to the conflict in women's roles she traced to social norms in *Uncommon Women.*

Janie's parents frequently invade her apartment to get an update on her romantic status, sometimes bringing along a Russian cabdriver whom they consider a promising marital prospect. Janie would happily fulfill her parents' expectations; she would like to marry but takes exception to the idea of settling down with a Russian cabdriver who can't speak English. Instead she becomes involved with a kind, idealistic Jewish doctor, Marty Sterling, telling him on their first date that even though she doesn't appreciate his sexist judgment of female doctors, "I want you to like me very much."

Janie's best friend, Harriet Cornwall, has a mother who barely pays attention to her because doing so would take time and focus from her role as a successful executive. Harriet, well on her way to being as successful an executive as her mother, urges Janie to trust herself more and stop fearing solitude, citing the cautionary example of Cynthia Peterson, a mutual friend who leaves accounts of her frantic, unsuccessful search for a man on Janie's answering machine. Harriet tells Janie, "What women like Cynthia

Peterson don't understand is, no matter how lonely you get or how many birth announcements you receive, the trick is not to get frightened. There's nothing wrong with being alone." Harriet establishes her indifference to enduring romantic ties by having an affair with a cruel married man.

As Janie comes to find Marty, like her parents, overbearing, his habit of calling her "Monkey" becomes extremely annoying, especially after he discourages her from taking her writing seriously, telling her, "You want to interview at 'Sesame Street,' fine. They do nice work. But don't let it take over your life. And don't let it take over our life. That's a real trap." Then, without consulting Janie, Marty rents an apartment for the two of them and arranges for a truck to come pick up her belongings. An hour before the movers appear, Janie tells Marty she can't live with him just yet; Marty walks away from her, declaring that she doesn't love him enough.

Harriet's affair also fails to satisfy her, in large part because she fears turning into a woman as passionless as her mother, someone who considers having a hot dog and a hot fudge sundae during the same afternoon deliriously irresponsible. So about the same time Janie tells Marty that she's not ready for the movers, Harriet flees into marriage with Joe Stine, a man she barely knows. Janie not only feels abandoned by Harriet, she finds it hard to believe that her friend has ever talked honestly with her since Harriet has consistently warned Janie against relying on marriage to redeem her life but then does it herself. Although the play definitely shows the conflicts that women who want it all will probably encounter as a result of social circumstances, the women in the play also rebel against their parents' advice and their parents' lives.

In *Isn't It Romantic* the confusion in women's roles as social norms change becomes all the more intense because the messages women get from those nearest and dearest to them have at least as much impact as those sent by the media and society at large. As Janie explains, she even gets profoundly conflicting messages from her own mother. Tasha, who urges her daughter to settle for any man, participates in a rich marriage of equals; she wants her daughter to give up her passions, as she has consistently refused to do; she expects her daughter to become a conventional housewife even though she herself cooks nothing. Janie decides to attend to what her mother does rather than what she says and as the play closes, she picks up a hat and umbrella and dances alone to "Isn't it Romantic" as Cynthia Peterson's latest pathetic phone message plays out in the background. Janie has learned that marriage to a kind doctor won't save her life; that no matter how confident friends may seem, they have at least as many conflicts as she does; and that even her apparently adult mother has no notion of the disjunction between her advice and her behavior. This leaves Janie finally and utterly on her own—a place she embraces. As the play ends, *"a spot picks up Janie dancing beautifully, alone."*

Like Janie's, Wasserstein's conflicts with women's roles originated in her family, not at Mount Holyoke or when the women's movement began in the 1960s. In "How I Spent My Forties" in *Shiksa Goddess* Wasserstein explains that both she and her sister Sandra chose to ignore their mother's advice about getting dressed up to take out the garbage, focusing instead on her message that "'God helps those who help themselves.' ... All things being equal, we both preferred not to hang around the garbage in formal attire. We'd rather help ourselves." Although Wasserstein sees *Isn't It Romantic* as a political play, she confesses to Phoebe Hoban in "The Family Wasserstein" that "it's the ultimate revenge to be enormously successful in a very public way while working out your family baggage."

THE HEIDI CHRONICLES

Wasserstein's next play, *The Heidi Chronicles* (1988) was her greatest success of all, winning the Pulitzer Prize, the first Tony Award ever given to a woman playwright, the New York Drama Critics' Circle Award for best play, and several others. It presents the story of Heidi Holland, an art historian, using a series of vignettes to delineate the path that led her to the front of an art history class at Columbia University where she lectures as the play opens. Bringing attention to previously ignored female artists has become the center of Heidi's professional life, just as her creator has spent her theatrical career describing the conflicts that consume the lives of contemporary women.

After this brief introductory scene which takes place in 1989, the action shifts to Heidi at a high school dance in 1965, where Susan, the first of three other characters who will serve as foils to Heidi, urges Heidi to leave, freeing Susan to pursue a boy who can do the twist and smoke at the same time. Susan consistently follows fashion. The next time she appears, in 1970, she studies law in Ann Arbor while participating in an antimale women's consciousness group. When going back to the land becomes popular, Susan moves to Montana. And when the greedy 1980s arrive, Susan joins a television production company and pursues money. In 1984 at her last meeting with Heidi, she confesses that "I've been so many people, I don't know who I am. And I don't care." Then she asks Heidi to serve as consultant for a show about three single women in their thirties who "don't want to make the same mistakes we did." When Heidi asks what these mistakes are, Denise, Susan's assistant, explains that "a lot of women your age are very unhappy. Unfulfilled, frightened of growing old alone." This development is seen as a mistake, Susan explains, because "blaming everything on being a woman is just passé." Heidi turns down the offer, protesting that she doesn't think the women of her generation made "such big mistakes." While Susan has flitted from one trend to another, Heidi has spent her life facing and trying to resolve the social obstacles that prevent women in general and her in particular from living fully, and she does not believe women deserve the blame for them.

When Susan abandons her at the dance, Heidi meets her second foil, Peter Patrone, who remains her lifelong friend, just as Christopher Durang has been an important friend to Heidi's creator ever since he approached Wendy Wasserstein at Yale, speaking the same line that Peter addresses to Heidi: "You look so bored you must be very bright." Even though Peter is gay, when Heidi tries to leave town to begin a new life, he reprimands her for trying to leave him and the rest of her past behind. He reminds her that men also have problems: because of AIDS, he spends much of his time attending the funerals of friends who have died too young. Heidi, who took offense when Peter first confessed his homosexuality to her, vows to stay and remain part of his family, discussing with him the men who attract him.

The love of Heidi's life is Scoop Rosenbaum, her third foil, an arrogant journalist she meets while campaigning for Eugene McCarthy in 1968. He approaches her aggressively and treats her contemptuously; although she tries to fight back, when he invites her to sleep with him, she follows him out the door. When she attends the consciousness raising group with Susan in 1970, she confesses that Scoop treats her badly but irresistibly attracts her. When Scoop marries Lisa in 1977, Heidi attends the wedding and tells Scoop that she plans to go to England and write a book. He retorts, "Heidella, if you haven't won this particular round, it doesn't mean you have to drop completely out of the match," explaining that he didn't marry her because he couldn't dominate her. He knew that she would have insisted on her own life, and he needed a wife focused on him. Then he predicts that she will never be happy because, unlike him, she refuses to settle: "But if you aim for ten in all things and get six, you're going to be very disappointed. And, unfortunately, that's why you 'quality time' girls are going to be one generation of disappointed women. Interesting, exemplary, even sexy, but basically unhappy. The ones who open doors usually are." That Scoop's wife is a promising illustrator of children's books does not deter him from expecting her submissiveness and devotion to him; but all the same by 1980, although still married, he escorts a young woman wearing a leather miniskirt and fishnet stockings.

At the end of the book, while the new single mother Heidi holds the child she just adopted, Scoop arrives to announce that he has given up editing his glamorous magazine, *Boomer,* in order to live in a way that will do credit to his children. He tells Heidi that when he heard she had adopted a baby, "I thought, 'Fuck you. If you had the courage to make the move and go for your ten, then what am I waiting for?'" Heidi immediately takes offense: "Wait a minute! Why is my baby my ten, and your work your ten?" But Heidi adds that even if traditional gender roles have distorted and continue to distort their relationship, it seems reasonable to hope that things will change so that if her daughter and his son ever meet, they will not have the same problems that Scoop and Heidi did: "He'll never tell her it's either/or, baby. And she'll never think she's worthless unless he lets her have it all. And maybe, just maybe, things will be a little better."

And so *The Heidi Chronicles* repeats and extends the central theme from earlier Wasserstein plays: contemporary women have enormous difficulty developing both successful professional lives and personal lives. Her plays also become increasingly pessimistic about the comfort women can offer each other. In *Uncommon Women* most of the women remain loyal to one another, but the relatively minor relationship between Kate and Leilah apparently ends because of jealousy. In both *Isn't It Romantic* and *The Heidi Chronicles,* the female friend whom the major character trusts the most disappoints her.

But *The Heidi Chronicles* also points out that gender roles have harmed men. Indeed the play suggests that all members of the baby boom generation have huge hopes that reality frustrates. Peter suffers because of AIDS; Scoop realizes the shallowness of the success he achieves with his magazine. In this play everyone fails, but everyone also learns from struggling with obstacles; and their friendships, no matter how untraditional, make it all endurable—along with the hope that one can help prepare the way for the next generation to enjoy fuller lives, Heidi as a mother, Scoop as a father, and Peter as a pediatrician.

Ironically Wendy Wasserstein's most prize-winning and acclaimed play has also received sharp criticism from those who believe that it betrays feminism. Jill Dolan writes in *Presence and Desire: Essays on Gender, Sexuality, Performance* (1993),

> *The Heidi Chronicles* is an example of misdirected rage, in which white feminist anger is suppressed by the realist text and erupts inappropriately to trash the history of the movement.... The movement becomes a historical backdrop against which the same domestic stories traditionally recounted by American realism play out.

Some critics even suggest that Wasserstein had Heidi embrace conventional values for commercial reasons, but when asked if making money was her primary goal when writing *The Heidi Chronicles,* Wasserstein responds that she wrote it in a cold London room subsidized by a $4,000 grant.

In *Speaking on Stage: Interviews with Contemporary American Playwrights* (1996), when Jan Balakian asks Wasserstein about feminist criticism of Heidi's decision to embrace the traditional women's role and adopt a baby, Wasserstein responds, "She's a woman who wants a baby. I think it takes enormous courage to do what she does." Almost a decade later Wasserstein would find out for herself what single motherhood requires: at the age of forty-eight, she gave birth to Lucy Jane. And like Heidi, Wasserstein considers her family to be the friends she has accumulated over the years. In fact she felt it important to include a sympathetic homosexual character in *The Heidi Chronicles* as a testimony to her friendship with a gay man stricken with AIDS.

BACHELOR GIRLS

Bachelor Girls, which was published in 1990, collects essays Wasserstein wrote for periodicals between 1984 and 1990. Since she found writing in her own voice threatening, Wasserstein decided she had better do it, and the volume offers a clear look at the values motivating Wasserstein. One of these is love. In "My Mother Then and Now," an essay mostly making fun of her colorful mother, Wasserstein admits that she admires her mother's passionate pride in her children and grandchildren so much that she wonders if she'll "ever be able to love as totally and selflessly as she does." Wasserstein also cherishes being herself. In "The Good, the Plaid, and the Ugly" she says, "I've discovered that I'm happiest when the burden of creating an image is completely off me." She feels fortunate to live in a society, unlike that she visited in Romania, where she not only can write the truth but wins accolade for doing so. Speaking of the barrage of awards she won in 1989 for *The Heidi Chronicles,* she says, "Nothing is quite as gratifying as recognition for work one is truly proud of." And so, Wasserstein concludes, she is "a very lucky girl."

Wasserstein says she came up with the title *Bachelor Girls* because as a child watching television, the role of the bachelor father in the series with that name seemed vastly superior to that of a spinster. So as an unmarried woman she prefers to characterize herself as a "bachelor girl." And with her title she generously attempts to redeem other single women from negative stereotypes. In "The Sleeping Beauty Syndrome: The New Agony of Single Men," she even imagines a world where single men struggle to find mates while the women attend to their own lives.

Not surprisingly, many of the essays in this collection lament those social norms that make it difficult for women simultaneously to achieve authenticity and love, but Wasserstein softens her attacks, as usual, with humor, telling in "The Razor's Edge" of holding down a woman who lived in her college dorm while she waxed her legs, and presenting in "To Live and Diet" a comical review of her own attempts to lose weight. In "The New Capitalist Tool" she talks about those women who supposedly succeed in a world that encourages them to focus on their appearance, not their minds and hearts—those attractive second wives who marry rich older men. Wasserstein doubts that they lead happy lives. For one thing, they must worry constantly about some even younger third wife. She concludes, "We haven't come such a long way, baby, if the ultimate privilege for women is in being a first-class support system."

She jokingly deals with the reality of abusive male partners in "The World's Worst Boyfriends" which concludes with a list of creepy men through the ages, from Aethelred the Unready (968?–1016) to the polygamist Brigham Young, "said to have had twenty-seven wives," and the diet doctor Herman Tarnower. She even goes for laughs in her essay about her disastrous weekend in Paris with a boyfriend, "Jean Harlow's Wedding Night," but exposes her desolation as the essay draws to a close.

Wasserstein somehow manages to end this essay on an upbeat, but when she turns to commenting on other women's trials, she sometimes rests in sadness or anger, as in "The Messiah" where she talks of women blaming themselves for their problems and concludes: "The self-recrimination for not being a certain kind of woman, a certain kind of mother, a certain kind of complete person is a quiet but constant undertow, a persistent dull ache. I wish all my friends could accept how fine and admirable they really are." After telling in "Tokyo Story" about Japanese women, who are considered unmarriageable after the age of twenty-six, crying their way through a performance of *Isn't It Romantic,* the play where Janie Blumberg joyfully accepts her solitude, Wasserstein remarks, "Perhaps I had to travel this far to understand why I write."

The essays also include accounts of good relationships Wasserstein enjoys with men, including her brother Bruce, her friend and a frequent director of her plays André Bishop, and Peter, a friend struggling with AIDS. Her discussion of Geraldine Ferraro and the women who have followed into politics and about her kind, socially aware young male relative suggest that Wasserstein expects the stereotypes now obstructing healthy relationships between men and women will eventually fall away. It seems safe to assume that she hopes her work will help speed this evolution.

THE SISTERS ROSENSWEIG

Wasserstein admits to basing the central characters in her next play, *The Sisters Rosensweig* (1993), on herself and her two sisters. Wasserstein's sister Sandra, the anglophile, inspired Sara Goode; her sister Georgette shares some characteristics with the character Gorgeous Teitelbaum, including her nickname and passion for dressing well; and Pfeni Rosensweig, the wandering journalist, has some of the qualities of Wasserstein herself, including a talent for recalling conversations. But Wasserstein contends that the characters so successfully came to life as she worked on the play that she hated to finish because then she would no longer hear their voices.

She proposed a number of challenges for herself. She first conceived of the play while finishing *The Heidi Chronicles* in London and decided to write something that would explore what happens to Americans in London. She wanted to produce a play that would not only provide jobs for middle-aged actresses needing a showplace for their talents, but one that would also have an attractive man fall madly and instantly in love with a middle-aged woman, and she wanted the play to end with a happy relationship between a man and a woman. Furthermore she hoped to achieve all these goals while fulfilling the classical unities of time, place, and action. In addition she sought to strike a balance between happiness and sorrow, a technique she associates with her idol, Anton Chekhov, although in the preface to the play she acknowledges that George S. Kaufman, Moss Hart, and Noel Coward also influenced *The Sisters Rosensweig*. Some of these goals nudge Wasserstein to move beyond the central theme of her earlier plays: the difficulties that prevent men and women from establishing good relationships with each other.

Although the three women in this play are middle-aged, their lives still need work, for each nourishes an illusion that prevents her from living fully. During the weekend when the action takes place, they help each other face reality and move on to the next stage of their lives. Thus each sister takes a step away from self-deceit toward fuller integrity as the play progresses.

Gorgeous is a suburban housewife married to a supposedly successful lawyer. Appearances matter a great deal to her, so she pretends that her superficially flawless life qualifies her to dispense advice on a radio show. Her passion for fake designer clothes hints at the falsity of her façade. By the end of the play she admits to her sisters, Pfeni and Sara, that her husband has lost his law partnership and spends his evenings hanging out in bars in a trench coat looking for material he can write about in their basement from early morning until noon. After yearning for genuine designer apparel, when she receives an authentic Chanel suit and accessories, Gorgeous manifests her newfound honesty and maturity by selling them in order to collect money for her daughter's tuition.

Pfeni is a journalist who travels too often to settle down and do serious work; her niece Tess, Sara's daughter, reports her mother's opinion that Pfeni travels out of a fear of commitment. Pfeni also deludes herself into thinking she has a solid relationship with a bisexual man named Geoffrey Duncan. Gorgeous bluntly tells her to face facts: "And don't tell me you have Geoffrey. I know you can't judge a book by its cover, but sweetsie, you're at the wrong library altogether." Finally Geoffrey persuades Pfeni that her sisters are right; he confesses to missing men and urges Pfeni to devote herself to serious work:

> People like you and me have to work even harder to create the best art, the best theatre, the best bloody book about gender and class in Tajikistan that we possibly can. And the rest, the children, the country kitchen, the domestic bliss, we leave to others who will have different regrets. Pfeni, you and I can't idle time.

At the end of the play Pfeni takes off for Tajikistan to write her book. Although her relationship with Geoffrey impeded her, he gets no blame for this; she willfully deceived herself, and he coaxed her toward reality. And indeed if he misled her, it was because of his own confusion: "Pfeni, the only time I have a real sense of who I am and where I'm going is when I'm in a darkened theatre and we're making it all up."

Sara, the anglophile who has disowned her history as a Jewish girl from Brooklyn, meets and falls in love with Mervyn Kant, an American manufacturer of fake fur who has recently traveled to Eastern Europe with the American Jewish Confederacy. After they spend an evening together, Sara sends him away; but at the urging of her sisters she invites him back and admits that she cares for him. But this does not mean Sara has desperately settled for any man; before she commits to him, Kant assures her that even though his first wife stayed home, it now seems to him unfair that she didn't have a chance to pursue her interest in art until shortly before her death. He has no interest in keeping another woman from living fully.

In acknowledging her attachment to Mervyn Kant, Sara owns not only her sexuality, but also her Jewish background. This dissolves the alienation that has developed between her and her daughter, Tess. Angry at her mother's pretense, Tess became involved with a rebellious young man who promised to take her off to join the Lithuanian resistance. When her mother protests, "Don't you think it's just slightly irregular for a nice Jewish girl from Connecticut to find her calling in the Lithuanian resistance?" Tess replies, "But I'm not a nice Jewish girl from Connecticut. I'm an expatriate American who's lived in London for five years and the daughter of an atheist." When her mother embraces her past by accepting Mervyn Kant, Tess abandons her boyfriend and Lithuania and begins asking her mother about her background for a school project. Things go smoothly at first: her mother admits she comes from Brooklyn. When Tess asks when her mother first sang, Sara replies, "I made my debut at La Scala." Tess objects, and Sara returns to the truth: "I first sang at the Hanukah Festival at East Midwood Jewish Center. I played a candle." As the play ends, reconciled, Tess and Sara sing "Shine on Harvest Moon" together.

Wasserstein's insistence that she has constructed a play that uses some details of her family life rather than one about her family seems persuasive, but her account of the last time she saw her sister Sandra alive, long after the play was produced, suggests that *The Sisters Rosensweig* does accurately depict the Wasserstein sisters' support for one another. After Geoffrey leaves Pfeni in the play, Sara cheers her by saying, "Pfeni, you're a beautiful and brilliant woman. Next time just don't agree to marry the man you're sitting next to at *Giselle*." According to Wasserstein's account in "How I Spent My Forties," the last thing Sandra said to Wendy before falling into a four-day terminal coma was similar: "You should go look at yourself in the mirror. You're very pretty."

Wasserstein's deep affection for her sisters may help explain why she managed to write a play that many believe successfully evokes a rich layering of joy and sadness. Nonetheless some critics believe she fails to achieve the balance she reached for. Gaylord Brewer writes in "Wendy Wasserstein's Three Sisters: Squandered Privilege," included in Claudia Barnett's *Casebook,* "The several serious and topical concerns of the play ... are routinely dismissed and demolished by the characters (and therefore finally by the play) with an *a priori* habit of glibness, dismissal, and general wisecracking for the sake of a laugh."

AN AMERICAN DAUGHTER

Wasserstein once again produces a unified piece taking place over a weekend in *An American Daughter* (1998); this time she decides to stretch herself even more by attempting to write a work drenched in politics. In the preface to the published play Wasserstein says, "My intention with *An American Daughter* was not to overhaul but to widen the range of my work: to create a fractured fairy tale depicting both a social and a political dilemma for contemporary professional women." Wasserstein took her inspiration from "Nannygate," the fates of Zoe Baird and Judge

Kimba Wood when nominated for attorney general during the first administration of President Bill Clinton: both women had to remove their names from nomination because of outrage over their child care arrangements.

In Wasserstein's play Lyssa Dent Hughes, a successful doctor, has been nominated for surgeon general and looks forward to fulfilling her liberal agenda which includes a determination to improve women's health care options. When Timber Tucker interviews her for a television show after her nomination, her husband, Walter Abrahmson, lets it drop that she once missed jury duty. Lyssa's father, Senator Alan Hughes, adroitly changes the subject, but Morrow McCarthy, a gay conservative friend also present, pulls the conversation back to Lyssa's lapse: "My best friend, Dr. Lyssa Dent Hughes, Surgeon General nominee, a woman of impeccable commitment, at the forefront of women's health issues, pro-choice, pro-gay, has never served on a jury." Everyone else begins to defend her, but her "best friend" Morrow, has a response: "Not everyone can believe that their innate goodness, their superior agenda, simply gives them the right to ignore the invitation." To add to her media problems, Lyssa calls her mother "the kind of ordinary Indiana housewife who took pride in her icebox cakes and cheese pimento canapés," and the public relations frenzy begins.

Insulted housewives constitute Lyssa's most adamant attackers; her husband, a sociologist of American culture explains why: "You're pretty, you have two great kids, you're successful, you're admired, you're thin, and you have a great soul. Face it, Lizard, in the heartland that means you're one prissy privileged ungrateful-to-her mother, conniving bitch." Lyssa's father hires her a spin artist and she attempts to play the game, donning a headband and pastel clothing for a follow-up talk with Timber, but she abandons her role in the middle of the interview and speaks the truth, saying that the women of

America should be concerned about the way their health issues are ignored, not about her private life. She offers a decidedly tactless explanation of why people condemn her: "A woman from good schools and a good family? That kind of woman should be perfect! And if she manages to be perfect, then there is something distorted and condescending about her. That kind of hard-working woman deserves to be hung out to dry."

Lyssa withdraws her name from nomination, but after her father presents her with a letter written by their ancestor Ulysses S. Grant urging his daughter "to rise and continue," she vows to do the same, and as the play ends she climbs the stairs to take on the people her sons report are attacking her in Internet chat rooms. Although Lyssa's father plays the role of a smooth politician throughout the play, he apparently shares her integrity; her treatment has so sickened him that he decides he'd prefer life on an Indiana farm to another term in the Senate.

Lyssa's best friend, Judith Kaufman, an African American Jewish doctor named in honor of Wasserstein's cousin "the late Barry Kaufman, who taught African-American studies in the New York City public school system," shares a dilemma with her creator: she tries without success to have a child. About the same time Lyssa withdraws her name from nomination, Judith decides to stop trying to give birth. After leading astonishingly successful lives both women come face to face with limits beyond their control.

The play's other characters constitute an unappealing, hypocritical, manipulative lot. Timber Tucker, devoted to exposing Lyssa's so-called moral lapses, admits to her off camera that he enjoys picking up the kind of woman who "gets you a beer and turns into a sandwich." Lyssa's husband Walter may well have mentioned her failure to appear for jury duty because his own career has lagged since his big book appeared five years earlier. A former graduate student, Quincy Quince, not only makes a successful pass at him, she builds her reputation by pointing out the failings of the women in the prior generation. After television shows display Lyssa's comments, they bring on Quincy Quince to explain what they mean.

Wasserstein acknowledges in her preface that this play had a relatively short run, in part, she suggests, because critics thought it was about "too many things." And indeed critics have complained that the play covers so much so quickly that some characters do not develop beyond stereotypes. Wasserstein counters that she received plenty of letters from women praising the play and notes that "Linda Winer, the drama critic at *Newsday,* and one of the few female critics, wrote that it was my best play." Some men have agreed. Christopher Bigsby argues in *Contemporary American Playwrights* (1999) that with this play

> Wendy Wasserstein … seems to have accomplished that transition from comedy with a redeeming streak of seriousness to seriousness with a redeeming streak of comedy…. The wise-cracking author of *Uncommon Women and Others,* for whom character, plot and construction were secondary, now chooses to move character to the centre of her attention and create a classically structured plot

In any case Wasserstein has no intention of letting negative judgments of *An American Daughter* persuade her to create smaller work:

> I do have a theory about writing for the theater. If you aim for a six and get a six, you'll do fine. If you aim for a ten and get a six, or even an eight, you won't do well at all. But I believe the purpose of writing plays, or practicing any art form, is to try for a ten every time.

SHIKSA GODDESS

Wasserstein's next book, *Shiksa Goddess; or, How I Spent My Forties* (2001), collects thirty-five essays, most of which she published in such periodicals as *Harper's Bazaar, The New Yorker, Allure, Vogue,* and the *New York Times* during the 1990s. In the preface she refuses to apologize for the wide range of the essays, many of which are humorous, arguing that comedy "embraces the widest human conditions." Touching on real estate, Bette Midler, the Wassersteins' first Manhattan Thanksgiving, the theater, and her family (of course), the women's issues that more or less dominated *Bachelor Girls* play a smaller role in this volume, which also has some things to say about the arts and writing.

Wasserstein provides an especially impassioned essay with "The State of the Arts." She says that the arts gave her life a purpose. Her involvement in the arts also taught her the joy of community and the importance of discipline. She goes on to argue that arts education, far from being a frill, plays a fundamental role. In "A Place They'd Never Seen: The Theater," Wasserstein draws upon one of her own contributions to arts education—taking eight students from the DeWitt Clinton High School in the Bronx to plays for a year, including a performance of *An American Daughter.* Wasserstein is pleased when the students report that this experience changed their attitudes toward plays.

In addition to including more public service essays in this collection, Wasserstein concludes it with two intensely personal and moving pieces: "How I Spent My Forties," about her sister Sandra and her death from cancer, as well as about Wasserstein's attempt to become pregnant, and "Days of Awe: The Birth of Lucy Jane," about the difficult birth of Wasserstein's premature daughter. Women's issues surface in these accounts, but they come wrapped in an intimate and loving perspective. And so in *Shiksa Goddess,* Wendy Wasserstein takes her readers on a journey at once more expansive and more intimate than that provided by *Bachelor Girls.*

During the late 1990s, Wasserstein undertook a variety of new writing projects, including a children's book, *Pamela's First Musical* (1996), and an opera libretto, "The Festival of Regrets," built around the *tashlich,* a Rosh Hashanah (Jewish new year) ritual of repentance in which Jews throw pieces of bread, symbolizing their sins, on flowing water. The Orthodox Jewish composer Deborah Drattel set Wasserstein's words to music, and the one-act opera was one of three included in *Central Park* (1999), composed for the New York City Opera.

OLD MONEY

Given Wasserstein's generally expansive direction, it is not surprising that when she wrote her next play, *Old Money* (2002), she made it even larger and more inclusive than *An American Daughter.* If the critics who complained that she took on too much in *An American Daughter* had any impact on Wasserstein, they simply strengthened her determination to prove them wrong. *Old Money* presents two wealthy families who occupy a Manhattan mansion a century apart. Some things distinguish them: Tobias Vivian Pfeiffer, the man who becomes wealthy on the cusp of the twentieth century, deals in things, while his twenty-first century counterpart, Jeffrey Bernstein, gets rich by manipulating numbers. When they become wealthy, both men have artistic ambitions, but by the twenty-first century defining what constitutes art has become murky, especially since the arts and celebrity have become intertwined. So while Tobias Pfeiffer interests himself in a Botticelli painting, Jeffrey Bernstein has a statue by Saulina Webb, the woman responsible for *The Tampon Totem Pole* whose work has been collected by Jane Fonda.

But the similarities between these two generations are also striking. Both newly rich men aspire to the arts, have social-climbing women vying for their romantic attentions, and fraternize with eccentric women artists. The sons of both are drawn to attractive young women and show little interest in devoting their lives to collecting money, much to the anguish and disappointment of their fathers. To underline the similarities between these two groups of people separated by a century, the same actors play roles in both eras, and at one point parts of both family groups appear on stage at the same time. Music and dancing often take place during the shifts between different times and sets of characters. Having the same actors play roles in different generations and song and dance mark the ends of acts lifts the play above realism in a way that invites the audience to see it as a work about human patterns rather than as the kind of timely social commentary that characterizes Wasserstein's earlier plays. Once again Wasserstein produces a work that seems to call upon new dimensions of her imagination.

Her magazine contributions and some essays included in *Shiksa Goddess* hint at the growing sense of class awareness that appears full-blown in *Old Money.* Wasserstein explains in her preface to the printed play that the idea for it first came to her when she attended a party of wealthy people and heard them debate the financial worth of a successful producer not in attendance. She clearly sees herself as outside of the discussion, much like the eccentric women artists in her play:

> The guests were certified members of the Hollywood and Wall Street A-lists, or at least they considered themselves that way. They seemed thrilled to be in each other's company.... I was not a regular member of this group. Instead of private planes, I still relish a taxi. But I was a college friend of one of the businessmen, and just like the pomegranates it's a nice touch to sprinkle the table with artists.

Setting the play in a beautiful house also gives Wasserstein a chance to exploit her interest in architecture, nurtured in part by auditing Vincent Scully's history of architecture class when she studied at Yale.

Wasserstein links the use of song and dance for the entrances and exits in this play to the fact that her sister Sandra had died just before she began writing it. Because Sandra had introduced her to the ballet, attending ballet performances became consoling to Wasserstein after her sister's death. She explains, "Mostly, I wanted to lose myself in the patterned and silent beauty." So, she introduced the beauty of bodies in motion that so fascinated her into *Old Money* and even aspired to make its overall pattern like that of a dance: "In creating the structure of my play, doubling eight characters in the past and the present, I hoped to find the rhythm of a dance." About a year after her sister's death, she became pregnant with Lucy Jane, and as a result "the pattern of life never seemed quite so vivid to me, nor did the theatrical impact of exits and entrances."

Wasserstein explains that she wrote the play at the American Academy in Rome, which meant not only that she worked in a beautiful place, but that she had people with whom to discuss architecture. All this helps explain why this play seems more consciously artful and less topical than her others. Wasserstein concludes her preface by saying that she thinks all her plays reveal "how a group of people live at a certain time" and that any true American playwright inevitably must deal with money, but she adds that "more than anything, writing and rehearsing this play reminded me of the challenge and pleasure of writing for the theater." So even though most of the characters in *Old Money* care about art only as a way of certifying class, their creator takes it very seriously.

Nor surprisingly some critics complained that Wasserstein once again took on too much in *Old Money,* while others praised the play. One thing seems certain: no matter what the final judgment of this work, Wasserstein will continue to write plays that reveal and probably also create new dimensions of herself. Although Wasserstein has used much biographical material in her plays, she always presents it in a way that speaks to concerns larger than her personal joys and pains, and in doing so she undoubtedly experiences the same kind of broadening awareness her audiences do. Once having achieved an insight, Wasserstein seems determined to move on to another. If seeing things in a new way requires that she extend her technical repertoire, so much the better. As Wasserstein explains to Claudia Barnett, "In some ways you don't even know who you are or what you're thinking unless you're writing, and that helps. More than anything."

Selected Bibliography

WORKS OF WENDY WASSERSTEIN

PLAYS

Uncommon Women and Others. New York: Dramatists Play Service, 1978.

Isn't It Romantic. Garden City, N.Y.: Nelson Doubleday, 1984.

The Heidi Chronicles. Garden City, N.Y.: Fireside Theatre, 1988.

The Heidi Chronicles and Other Plays. San Diego: Harcourt Brace Jovanovich, 1990. (Includes *Uncommon Women and Others, Isn't It Romantic,* and *The Heidi Chronicles.*)

The Sisters Rosensweig. New York: Harcourt Brace, 1993.

An American Daughter. New York: Harcourt Brace, 1998.

Seven One-Act Plays. New York: Dramatists Play Service, 2000. (Includes "Bette and Me," "Waiting for Philip Glass," "Tender Offer," "Workout,"

"Medea," "Boy Meets Girl," and "The Man in a Case.")

Old Money. New York: Harcourt, 2002.

OTHER WORKS

Bachelor Girls. New York: Knopf, 1990. (Essays.)

Pamela's First Musical. New York: Hyperion Books for Children, 1996. (A children's book about going to see a Broadway musical.)

Shiksa Goddess; or, How I Spent My Forties. New York: Knopf, 2001. (Essays.)

PRODUCTIONS FOR FILM AND TELEVISION

Uncommon Women and Others. Adapted for *Great Performances* from Wasserstein's play by the same title. Public Broadcasting Service (PBS), 1978.

The Sorrows of Gin. Adapted for *Great Performances* from the short story with the same title by John Cheever. Public Broadcasting Service (PBS), 1979.

Sketches for *The Comedy Zone,* CBS Broadcasting, 1984-85.

"Drive," She Said. Public Broadcasting Service (PBS), 1987.

The Object of My Affection. Screenplay by Wasserstein, adapted from a novel by Stephen McCauley. Directed by Nicholas Hytner. Twentieth Century Fox, 1998. (A motion picture.)

PRODUCTIONS FOR STAGE

Any Woman Can't. Playwrights Horizons, New York, 1973.

Happy Birthday, Montpelier Pizz-zazz. New Haven, Conn., 1974.

When Dinah Shore Ruled the Earth. With Christopher Durang. Yale Cabaret, New Haven, Conn., 1975.

Uncommon Women and Others. Produced as a one-act play. New Haven, Conn., 1975. Revised and produced as a full-length play. Phoenix Theatre at Marymount Manhattan Theatre, New York, 1977.

Isn't It Romantic. Phoenix Theatre at Marymount Manhattan Theatre, New York, 1981. Revised version produced by Playwrights Horizons, New York, 1983.

Tender Offer. Ensemble Studio Theatre, New York, 1983. (One act.)

Miami. Music by Jack Feldman. Song lyrics by Bruce Sussman and Jack Feldman. Playwrights Horizons, New York, 1986. (Musical.)

The Man in a Case. Adapted from the short story with the same title by Anton Chekhov. Lucille Lortel Theatre, New York, 1986. (One act.)

The Heidi Chronicles. Seattle Repertory Theatre, Seattle, 1988. Playwrights Horizons, New York, 1988. Plymouth Theatre, New York, 1989.

The Sisters Rosensweig. Mitzi E. Newhouse Theater at Lincoln Center Theater, New York, 1992.

An American Daughter. Mitzi E. Newhouse Theater at Lincoln Center Theater, New York, 1997.

Waiting for Philip Glass. Guthrie Theater Lab, Minneapolis, 1998. Joseph Papp Public Theater, New York, 1998. (Part of a one-act play production titled *Love's Fire.* Six other playwrights contributed. All seven plays were inspired by Shakespearean sonnets.)

The Festival of Regrets. Libretto by Wasserstein. Music by Deborah Drattel. Glimmerglass Opera, Cooperstown, New York, 1999. (One of three one-act operas presented together in a production titled *Central Park.*)

Old Money. Mitzi E. Newhouse Theater at Lincoln Center Theater, New York, 2000.

Third and *Welcome to My Rash.* Theater J, Washington, D.C., 2004. (Companion one-act plays.)

PAPERS

Wendy Wasserstein has donated her papers to the library at Mount Holyoke College.

CRITICAL AND BIOGRAPHICAL STUDIES

Alter, Iska. "Wendy Wasserstein." In *Jewish American Women Writers: A Bio-Bibliographical and Critical Sourcebook.* Edited by Ann R. Shapiro. Westport, Conn.: Greenwood Press, 1994. Pp. 448–457. (Bibliography of Wasserstein's work and of criticism about it.)

Balakian, Jan. "*The Heidi Chronicles:* The Big Chill of Feminism." *South Atlantic Review* 60, no. 2:93–101 (May 1995).

Barnett, Claudia, ed. *Wendy Wasserstein: A Casebook.* New York: Garland, 1999. (Includes interviews and a bibliography as well as critical essays.)

Becker, Becky K. "Women Who Choose: The Theme of Mothering in Selected Dramas." *American Drama* 6, no. 2:43–57 (spring 1997).

Bigsby, Christopher. "Wendy Wasserstein." In his *Contemporary American Playwrights*. Cambridge, UK: Cambridge University Press, 1999. Pp. 330–368.

Carlson, Susan L. "Comic Textures and Female Communities 1937 and 1977: Clare Boothe and Wendy Wasserstein." In *Modern American Drama: The Female Canon*. Edited by June Schlueter. Rutherford, N.J.: Fairleigh Dickinson University Press, 1990. Pp. 207–217.

Ciociola, Gail. *Wendy Wasserstein: Dramatizing Women, Their Choices, and Their Boundaries*. Jefferson, N.C.: McFarland, 1998. (Includes bibliography.)

Czekay, Angelika. "'Not Having It All': Wendy Wasserstein's Uncommon Women." In *The Playwright's Muse*. Edited by Joan Herrington. New York: Routledge, 2002. Pp. 17–44. (The book also includes Czekay's interview of Wasserstein, pp. 45–51.)

Dolan, Jill. *"The Heidi Chronicles:* Choking on the Rage of Postfeminism." In her *Presence and Desire: Essays on Gender, Sexuality, Performance*. Ann Arbor: University of Michigan Press, 1993. Pp. 50–55.

Hoban, Phoebe. "The Family Wasserstein." *New York* 26, no. 1:32–37 (January 4, 1993).

Keyssar, Helene. "Drama and the Dialogic Imagination: *The Heidi Chronicles* and *Fefu and Her Friends*." *Modern Drama* 34, no. 1:88–106 (March 1991).

Mandl, Bette. "Feminism, Postfeminism, and *The Heidi Chronicles*." *Studies in the Humanities* 17, no. 2:120–128 (December 1990).

Rose, Phyllis Jane. "An Open Letter to Dr. Holland: Dear Heidi." *American Theatre* 6, no. 7:26–29, 114–116 (October 1989).

Whitfield, Stephen. "Wendy Wasserstein and the Crisis of Jewish Identity." In *Daughters of Valor: Contemporary Jewish American Women Writers*. Edited by Jay L. Halio and Ben Siegel. Newark: University of Delaware Press, 1997. Pp. 226–246.

INTERVIEWS

Balakian, Jan. "Two Interviews with Wendy Wasserstein," *Journal of American Drama and Theatre* 9, no. 2:58–84 (spring 1997).

———. "Wendy Wasserstein." In *Speaking on Stage: Interviews with Contemporary American Playwrights*. Edited by Philip C. Kolin and Colby H. Kullman. Tuscaloosa: University of Alabama Press, 1996. Pp. 379–391. Betsko, Kathleen, and Rachel Koenig. "Wendy Wasserstein." In their *Interviews with Contemporary Women Playwrights*. New York: Beech Tree Books/William Morrow, 1987. Pp. 418–431. Biggs, Melissa E. "Different Textures to Different Lives: Wendy Wasserstein." In her *In the Vernacular: Interviews at Yale with Sculptors of Culture*. Jefferson, N.C.: McFarland, 1991. Pp. 178–189. Cohen, Esther. "Uncommon Woman: An Interview with Wendy Wasserstein." *Women's Studies* 15, no. 1:257–270 (October 1988). Franklin, Nancy. "The Time of Her Life," *New Yorker,* April 14, 1997, pp. 62–68, 70–71.

Isenberg, Barbara. "Writing 'Bout Her Generation: Playwright Wendy Wasserstein Taps into the Witty, Ironic, Self-Absorbed, Confused Essence of Her Contemporaries." *Los Angeles Times,* October 7, 1990, Calendar section, p. 48.

Jacobson, Leslie. "Wendy Wasserstein." in *The Playwright's Art: Conversations with Contemporary American Dramatists*. Edited by Jackson R. Bryer. New Brunswick, N.J.: Rutgers University Press, 1995. Pp. 257–276.

Savran, David. "Wendy Wasserstein." In his *The Playwright's Voice: American Dramatists on Memory, Writing, and the Politics of Culture*. New York: Theatre Communications Group, 1999. Pp. 289–310.

Winer, Laurie. "The Art of Theater XIII: Wendy Wasserstein." *Paris Review* 39, no. 142:165–188 (spring 1997).

—NANCY L. BUNGE

C. D. Wright

1949–

WITH THE PUBLICATION of C. D. Wright's long poem *Deepstep Come Shining* in 1998 it became clear that a good American poet had become an extraordinary one, and the appearance of *Steal Away: Selected and New Poems* in 2002 (a Griffin Prize nominee) consolidated her position. Another major collection published in 2003, *One Big Self: Prisoners of Louisiana* (with photographs by the distinguished photographer Deborah Luster), made it clear that she has grown into a major poet. She has made a long journey from the Arkansas Ozarks to Rhode Island, where she has been State Poet Laureate and teaches in the outstanding creative writing program at Brown University. In 2004, she received a John D. and Catherine T. MacArthur Foundation Grant for $500,000 (a so-called "genius grant") which she plans to use for further collaborations with Deborah Luster.

She has playfully said in "The Wages of Poetry," an essay published in the *Associated Writing Programs Chronicle,* that she "was born in a warren of no great distinction in the vicinity of the middle hillbilly class." She even describes herself on questionnaires as "White, Anglo-Saxon, Protestant," a self-identification that has nothing to do with racism, which she has consistently deplored. The people of the Ozarks are the epitome of the hillbilly image, something that Wright sought to correct by curating a multimedia show called *The Lost Roads Project: A Walk-In Book of Arkansas,* which toured the state for two years between 1994 and 1996.

Carolyn Doris Wright (who goes by "CD" to avoid confusion with another poet, named Carolyne Wright) was born on January 6, 1949, to Ernie E. Wright, a probate and chancery judge, and Alyce E. Wright, his court reporter. The family moved from Mountain Home to nearby Harrison when she was in the first grade. The WPA guide to Arkansas, published in 1941, described Harrison as "the metropolis of the northern part of the state." It had a population of 4,238 at the time. From her parents and their courtroom vocations she seems to have picked up her interest in human drama and accurate reporting. She is particularly acute at rendering colloquial speech, especially the rich idiom of the Ozarks. In an essay called "Provisional Remarks on Being / A Poet / of Arkansas" (1994), she suggests that her background is "relevant to every word I lay down," and she praises hill people and African Americans for "keeping the language distinct."

She has written about her childhood and youth in an evocative memoir published in the *Contemporary Authors Autobiography Series* (1996). The essay is highly episodic rather than continuous, with typographical marks separating events. The work follows her life in chronological order but is elliptical in style, emphasizing images, anecdotes, and influential figures rather than linear order. Wright begins with her birth and emphasizes her mother's insistence on continuing with a dinner in spite of contractions. It also stresses her mother's beauty, physical strength, and independence: she learned to fly against her husband's wishes. The mother is clearly presented as a role model, the first of a series in the essay. Her mother's professionalism as a court reporter encouraged "certain writerly traits" in the daughter.

Along with memories of childhood play and pets, she describes experiences—"sparks" she calls them—that also encouraged "writerly traits." Reading created sparks, and she says that she "read her childhood away." The only poetry collection in her parents' house was *Forty Beloved Verses,* edited by the host of a radio program of the 1930s, "Major Bowles' Original Amateur Hour." When she was given a copy of Seymour Krim's 1960 anthology *The Beats,* "that was a spark," she says. Wright learned from the sexual frankness and shock tactics of the Beats. Another spark was struck when a history teacher put "Buffalo Bill's Defunct" on the board and signed it simply "ee." Wright herself almost always uses her initials with capitals but without periods. The poetry of e. e. cummings often stimulates young writers by its freedom and audacious attitudes—and no doubt through its bursts of sentimentality. By the time she entered college she had read only four women writers: Louisa May Alcott, Jane Austen, and Charlotte and Emily Brontë. The charged emotional atmosphere of Wright's early poems suggests the Brontës much more than Jane Austen. She observes that on graduating from college she had only doubled the number of women writers familiar to her. All of the new ones were fellow southerners: "Flannery O'Connor, Katherine Anne Porter, Eudora Welty, Carson McCullers." The gothic imagery and redneck characters of O'Connor and McCullers seem likely influences on her early work, though its major source is the late poet Frank Stanford, who entered her life later.

The autobiographical essay mixes revelation with reticence. She provides a long list of the "wealth of crimes" that impel her writing. The "crimes" begin with minor items, like screaming "I hate you" at her mother, and ascend to major events: "If I had not loved a married poet only to have love end in the bottomless tragedy of his suicide, I would not write." Her conclusion about these "crimes" and her writing is worth quoting at length, as it defines her stance in relation to the confessional tendency in American poetry:

> Not that when I do write, I feel compelled to confess. I feel compelled to selectively confess when I sense that the literal truth is relevant. As a writer, I am not interested in my self as a burning matrix of material. I am interested in my self as sociology, someone whose early stimuli were necessarily fixed but whose responses vary. I feel much more at liberty to examine my self than the self of a bail bondsman or of the woman who sold Dutch Masters cigars out of the back of her stationwagon in my hometown, either of whom would offer far more opportunities for dramatic involvement. And in which case I would write fiction. As a social organism who needs to write in order to begin to understand, I will serve.

At times Wright manages to be both bold and reticent. For the daughter of a judge and a court reporter, she can be vague about times, places, and people: she mentions an abortion in New York in her autobiographical essay but give no further details.

In spite of her disclaimer about not writing fiction, one of the most effective elements in her poetry is the use of narrative, which is expectable in a southern writer attuned to storytelling in writers like O'Connor and Welty. Her work contains frank autobiography but it also contains pure invention about imagined characters. Real life offered her lots of models. Her autobiographical essay brings in a variety of local characters, like a dog poisoner, a guitarist named Snake Maynard, and an antivivisectionist who also managed to be a racist, Dee Dee Smith. At times her work suggests the anecdotes and character sketches familiar to readers of William Faulkner.

The most powerful personality in the autobiographical essay is "Mrs. Vittitow," born Margaret Kaelin. Vittitow almost carries off the essay, receiving more than two full pages, more than anyone else, and the pages are the concluding ones. The essay, then, begins with Wright's mother as a fundamental role model and ends with another model, a woman who served as a mentoring rather than mothering figure. Mrs. Vittitow, she told Robert N. Casper and Nadia Colburn in a 2002 interview in *Jubilat,* was a "ferocious autodidact" Wright met in 1967. In her essay Wright declares that Mrs. Vittitow (given the "Mrs." out of respect, not condescension) is her chief mentor: "If I were among writers customarily asked if anyone were interested in what kind of mud I am made or whose thunder I stole, I would point to her." In the introduction to *Further Adventures with You* in 1986, Wright described herself as "largely Ms. Vittitow educated but I cannot stop to explain." The intellectual passions conveyed outside of classes during the years of university education do not appear on registrars' transcripts. She admires Vittitow not only for her deep knowledge of writers like James Joyce and Gerard Manley Hopkins but for her passionate engagement with the civil rights movement. Vittitow lost her family over her antiracist views and was escorted over a bridge linking Arkansas to Tennessee by the Arkansas police. She wound up in Memphis, living in a residential hotel, where Wright met her while attending Memphis State University.

EARLY POETRY

Wright received a B.A. degree in French from Memphis State in 1971. After trying law school briefly and working in New York for an art auction house, she entered the University of Arkansas in Fayetteville for graduate work in creative writing in 1973. She received an M.F.A. in 1976 for a thesis entitled *Alla Breve Loving,* which became her first book under the same title, published by Mill Mountain Press in Seattle in the same year. Her supervisor was the poet Miller Williams. She has paid tribute to him in "Preliminary Remarks on the Poetry in the First Person," an article in a testimonial volume edited by Michael Burns, *Miller Williams and the Poetry of the Particular* (1991). Her committee included another poet, James Whitehead, whose second collection, *Local Men* (1979), displays the same interest in picturesque southern characters as Wright's early poems, though the older writer relies on laconic understatement while Wright aims for dramatic, even shocking effects.

Her great debt as an artist in the 1970s was not to established writers like Williams and Whitehead but to a remarkable poet whose premature death by suicide has permanently marked her work. Writers often get their sense of vocation, craft, and aesthetic excitement from their peers, especially in an age of creative writing programs. Frank Stanford (1948–1978) was the great influence. As she told the *Jubilat* interviewers: "The poet whose work I fell deepest into was Frank Stanford's. His poems were very potent, romantic, mysterious." He founded Lost Roads Publishers to create a publishing outlet in Arkansas. As Eric Loberer says in an essay published in *Rain Taxi Review of Books* (1998), "in 1976, Frank Stanford took out a loan, and—aided and abetted by fellow poet C. D. Wright—bought an 1850 multilith printer, an old carbon arc burner, and a camera, thus beginning Lost Roads Publishers." He managed to publish twelve titles before his death less than two years later. Wright became a coworker with him and has kept the press active right into the 2000s, collaborating on the work with Forrest Gander.

Frank Stanford was married to the painter Ginny (Crouch) Stanford, and a quarrel with his wife over his affair with Wright led to his suicide on June 3, 1978. Wright has written brilliantly about Stanford in an elegiac essay, "Frank Stanford of the Mulberry Family: An Arkansas Epilogue," published in the Tributes issue of *Conjunctions* in 1997. The essay reads like a poem rather than an exposition. It is built on repeated, almost choral references to the botanical properties of the bois d'arc tree, which grows abundantly in the Ozarks and is also known as the Osage orange. The tree and its fruit (the horse apple) are linked symbolically with the love affair of Stanford and Wright, and italicized horticultural passages are interspersed through the text, which is written in brief paragraphs. The distinctive odor of the Osage orange is strongly associated with the odor of Stanford, and a passage about the aromas left on the body of the narrator after their lovemaking is followed by a suggestive quotation: *Sap like that of rest of tree, milky and sticky.* A reference to the heartwood of the tree is followed by a description of Stanford's death: he shot himself three times in the heart with a target pistol. Not as abundant as the bois d'arc references are invocations of a mockingbird, a songbird common in the South, as a symbol of poetic creativity. The mockingbird "tells it differently every year" and "has a million licks."

The essay is an extraordinary mixture of grief and remembered sensuality. It ends with the suicide of Stanford and his funeral. The poet was left with an unresolved emotional conflict, a situation terminated by a traumatic loss. Trauma must, according to Freudian theory, be compulsively revisited in the mind. As Wright says, using a tree metaphor, "The memory of it is very hard. It goes down. There. Geotropic. It would take a long time to fell. It is not poetry. It is a scratched, repetitive record of loving. Unloving. Losing. Leaving." The "it" in these words has no antecedent, but Wright implies that trauma is a kind of tree growing into Hades, something different from the bois d'arc she identifies with love. She also acknowledges that the compulsive reiteration of trauma is not art in itself but a kind of scratched record. Her relationship to confessional poetry is a subtle one. She has made art out of this loss in various ways, while recognizing that simply speaking pain again and again is counter to art. One difference between her traumas and those of poets like Sylvia Plath, Anne Sexton, and Robert Lowell is that the trauma occurred during adulthood. Wright's husband, Forrest Gander, has also (rather unusually) dealt with Wright's trauma in his own poems. The brief "June the Third" in *Lynchburg* refers to it as an occasion of grief, and in one of his later collections, *Deeds of Utmost Kindness,* he includes "Librettos for Eros," a set of poems dedicated to Stanford. Biographers dealing with Wright and Stanford will find the poems interesting to interpret: they abound in imagery from Stanford's poems and no doubt reflect Wright's understanding of the relationship. The sequence ends with a "Repeating Dream," in which a woman dreams that a dead man has driven from the cemetery to her house and "sits grotesquely / Still in the parked car."

EARLY POEMS

Wright's first collection, *Alla Breve Loving,* was based on her M.F.A. thesis of the same title. It appeared in 1976 from Mill Mountain Press in Seattle, which also published seven collections of poetry by Stanford. "Alla Breve Loving" is one of the few early poems to survive the rigorous winnowing carried out for Wright's selected poems, *Steal Away* (2002). The musical term "alla breve" refers to a dramatic increase in the tempo of a selection. The poem describes a love triangle between a woman, an ex-lover referred to as the saxophonist, and a second man, who goes to bed with the woman but thinks of someone else. The implication of the title is that these people are living at a quickened tempo. For the saxophone player, who figuratively retreats into the bell of his instrument, the pace may be dangerous: he and the instrument are compared to an "ancient terrapin / at the approach of the wheel."

Wright's three early books may be grouped together. In *Alla Breve Loving, Room Rented by* a Single Woman (1977), and *Terrorism (1979),* the influence of Stanford is clear in the short lines, the narrative drive, the graphic and often violent imagery. Both poets use bits of story from the bottomless well of southern American anecdotes, and they often mimic southern colloquial speech. Her poetic line is usually short and grammatically self-contained in these poems, and the syntax is rarely complex even when a sentence is spread over a number of lines. The brief title poem of *Terrorism* manages to be southern gothicism and black humor at the same time:

> A man in a green dress
> is not answering the telephone.
> When the doorbell rings
> he goes in the closet,
> looks at his reflection
> in his wife's shoes.
> When he comes out he sees
> the parakeet hanging from the lightstring.

She rarely gives names to her characters: poem after poem describes people identified only as a woman, or a man, or a girl; sometimes she resorts to pronouns, talking about a he, or a she, or they.

One character who is named in the early poems seems a version of the author. "Lucia" is the daughter of a judge, and she and her friend Mona (someone not refined enough for the judge, who doesn't want them to associate) get into mild trouble exploring their boring southern town. A number of poems deal with domestic abuse, like women being beaten or a child kicked to death. Several male protagonists are under sentence of death for murder. "Soldier of Fortune," a poem in *Room Rented by a Single Woman,* takes the form of a letter to "Mama" from a mercenary on death row. It fails for two reasons: the poet is not able to create a convincing foreign reality, and the mercenary's bravado is bathetic. The most powerful poem about capital punishment is "The Night before the Sentence Is Carried Out" in *Terrorism,* which focuses not on the condemned man but on a woman riding a bus "with a sack of black apples in her lap." Her connection to the condemned man is left mysterious, like her actions in the poem, which include throwing a half-opened knife into a lake.

One of Wright's hallmarks as a writer is the use of mysterious anecdotes. In summing up her work in a *Boston Review* article (1997), Stephen Burt speaks of her "narrativity," by which he means that she does not tell entire stories; rather, she hints at narratives. The American poet and critic Yvor Winters once suggested that modern experimental poetry employed a device he called "reference to a non-existent plot," citing T. S. Eliot's early poem "Gerontion" as an example. Adam Kirsch speaks of her "elliptical narratives" in his article "Discourtesies" (2002). The strategy is a legitimate one when used skillfully, and in her masterpiece, *Deepstep Come Shining,* Wright is very skillful indeed. When the method hints at too little or relies too heavily on melodrama, it can fail.

From 1976 to 1978 Wright worked for the Arkansas Arts and Humanities Office. In 1979 she moved to San Francisco. As Nadia Herman Colburn says in "About C. D. Wright," a profile published in *Ploughshares* (2002), the poet "had two major encounters in her first week: an earthquake and language poetry." The effects of her readings and dialogues with language poetry, a literary movement that foregrounds language rather than content, would eventually have a deep affect on her work. After a year as director of writing workshops at the Intersection Center for the Arts, she got a job as office manager for the Poetry Center at San Francisco State University, where she worked from 1980 to 1982. She also taught at the university. Wright has described this period in a brilliant essay, "The Adamantine Practice of Poetry" (1989), which manages to be a detailed portrait of her life in the period, a sketch of personal relationships (she met her future husband, Forrest Gander, at the center), and a discussion of her artistic development.

The most interesting part of the essay is her consideration of the art of poetry. Wright came to San Francisco as a promising young poet preoccupied with her own pain and loss, particularly the trauma of Stanford's suicide. She says: "My poems were filled with personal pain. I tried to make them beautiful and interesting. That is I tried to be artful about my limited but particular experience with pain." Eventually she changed her goals, and "instead of aiming to give beautiful expression to pain, I discharged my wrath less the beauty. Then humor against the wrath. Finally form begin to matter, and so to materialize." She sees form not as an end in itself but as "an ambulance, to carry the wounded towards some place where we might hope to recover from whatever afflicted us." She expresses the hope that it is not blasphemous "when I say I look to poetry for supernatural help."

The influence of language poetry is not apparent in her next two volumes, but a new commitment to form and precision is. In "The Adamantine Practice of Poetry," Wright uses the alchemical image of the lodestone, the adamantine and transforming substance, to evoke the nature of poetry. Like the lodestone, the poem can be "Brilliant. Impenetrable." She says that poetry is "what is brought about by some of the most lustrous, least attractive wordsmiths. What cannot be fashioned into prose. Let that go as a very hard and a very cold definition." Like William Butler Yeats, who imagined writing "a poem maybe as cold / And passionate as the dawn," Wright has sought to remake herself as a stylist, and she has succeeded, though not all at once.

Her next book, *Translations of the Gospel Back into Tongues* (1982), was her first to be issued by a mainstream publisher, the State University of New York Press. The year before,

she had received a National Endowment for the Arts fellowship that enabled her and Forrest Gander to live for awhile in Dolores Hidalgo, Mexico. Later they stayed in the Ozarks at a place called Hog Jaw near Lead Hill. *Translations of the Gospel Back into Tongues* is not a radical break. Six of the poems were reprinted from *Terrorism,* and the atmosphere is still, as Stephen Burt says, out of the "Southern Gothic prop closet." He also observes that she relies on "generically portentous nouns—moons, rivers, dead roses, 'others,' 'someone,' 'dusk, Sarah, harvest.'" It can be added that she still tends to talk about anonymous persons called "she" or "he," "a man" or "a woman." But the stories told are more subtle. Burt detects a new influence, W. S. Merwin. In "The Adamantine Practice of Poetry," Wright writes admiringly of a motto from Merwin that used to hang in the graduate writing building at Brown: "Practice practice put your faith in that." Certainly Merwin's oblique and apocalyptic narratives of the 1970s have influenced some of the poems in the opening section, "True Accounts from the Imaginary War." The Vietnam War is not mentioned by name, but many of the details, like women fleeing burning townships, suggest that conflict. One of the best poems, "Fields," dedicated to the Vietnam War poet Bruce Weigl, evokes "nineteen and seventy" by opening with a woman "Blowing dust off a record by The Doors." The scene is a party, and one man there remembers a moment in the war when the sergeant yelled "Haul ass," and men scrambled for a riverbank.

In the preface to her next book, *Further Adventures with You,* Wright says that *Translations of the Gospel Back into Tongues* was "a lamentation for the late Frank Stanford, and a tribute to the great American experience of jazz." Only one poem appears to deal directly with Stanford: "Who Sit Watch in Daylight" imagines a visit from a ghost. But many of the poems are influenced by Stanford's ability to create a mysterious atmosphere with inexplicable details. The jazz poems are a new turn in Wright's work. One of the best ones is "The Secret Life of Musical Instruments," an account of life on a band tour. It is dedicated to the Fayetteville, Arkansas, jazz pianist Claudia Burson.

FURTHER ADVENTURES WITH YOU

In 1983 the year after *Translations,* Wright was hired by the creative writing program at Brown University. She has said with self-deprecating humor that her reaction was to assume that something had gone awry in the selection committee. She served as director of the program from 1989 to 1992 and 1998 to 2001 and is now the Israel J. Kapstein Professor of English. She received the Witter Bynner Prize for Poetry from the Academy of American Arts and Letters in 1986. Her next book, *Further Adventures with You,* appeared in that same year. It has a remarkable preface, "hills," in which she discusses her Ozark origins and her literary aspirations. She observes that her first writing was "strictly dialect," with southern atmosphere, but she is now able to recognize "the pitch of that speech" from outside and no longer finds it sufficient, though she does not renounce its use when appropriate. Her persistent interest in the Ozarks is indicated by the cover of the book, which foregrounds a dog on a farm. As Jenny Goodman has noted in *Dictionary of Literary Biography (1992),* the dog has only three legs; Wright is perhaps sending up the southern grotesque tradition. She defines her themes in "hills": "My poems are about desire, conflict, the dearth of justice for all. About persons of small means. They are succinct but otherwise orthodox novels" in a page or less. The preface also makes it clear that she has become aware of literary theory through her years in San Francisco: there is more to say about that when discussing the later poetry.

The book shows some new stylistic dimensions. Her earlier poems were almost always written in brief lines, but some of the new poems reach for the amplitude of longer lines. More important as a development is her interest in the prose poem: there are seven of them. Like many contemporary prose poems, they are saturated in realistic detail and tend to make startling, even surreal leaps in the narrative. An important example is "Treatment," which presents the rape of a schoolgirl by a bus driver in the format of a deeply disturbing sketch for a film. The text is written from an objective camera-eye view that is occasionally replaced by scenes from the point of view of the bus driver. It ends with a scene in a church in which the jazz musician Pharoah Sanders appears as an angel with a choir in a church (perhaps at the girl's funeral). The bus driver comes down the aisle transformed into a snake. A prose poem about the loss of Frank Stanford, "Scratch Music," has powerful, bleak images of the suicide: "you blew your heart out like the porchlight," and "You picked up a gun in winter as if it were a hat and you were leaving a restaurant: full, weary, and thankful to be spending the evening with no one."

Not all of the collection is dark. Humor was not a mark of Wright's early work, but "Handfasting" shows a gift for grimly amusing poetry, dealing as it does with the speaker's wish to die along with her husband like an old couple who froze going out to get the mail: the wish is to "freeze our flabby asses off together." The volume is marked by several love poems that make a strong contrast with the lament for Frank Stanford. A perfect lyric poise in "The Complete Birth of the Cool" expresses a moment of quiet satisfaction while sitting on a cement step. The affirmative conclusion—earned by the preceding images—is "Awe provides for us." In "The Adamantine Practice of Poetry," Wright speaks of poetry as offering supernatural help, and a poem like "The Complete Birth of the Cool" demonstrates what she means.

Several poems make good on the claim in the preface that she writes about "persons of small means": lives of poverty glimpsed in a rented house are juxtaposed several times with Ludwig Wittgenstein's famous philosophical dictum: "the world is all that is the case." And part of the case is poverty. In 1984, two years before *Further Adventures with You,* Wright published an essay on her political views in *Five Fingers Review,* a San Francisco magazine. The title "Arguments with the Gestapo Continued: Literary Resistance" alludes to Thomas Merton's *My Argument with the Gestapo: A Macaronic Journal.* Merton's book, written in 1940 but published only in 1969, was deeply cynical about both sides in the war; it repudiated ideology and deluded patriotism. Wright expresses a similar disillusionment, expressing scorn for Ronald Reagan's administration. She does not believe that writing can be neutral, but her article also rejects sectarianism as she sees it in the work of Ron Silliman. What her political consciousness seems to come down to is sympathy with the poor and opposition to injustice rather than commitment to a particular cause or ideology. One important revelation in the essay is that by the time of its writing she had become interested in the ideas of San Francisco language poets like Silliman and Carla Harryman. Since 1976, many of the poets grouped in this category (some resisting the label) have seen experimental writing as a means of critiquing the ideology of capitalist society.

Her 1987 sequel, "Arguments with the Gestapo Continued: II," is based on a rather rambling talk given at the Intersection Center for the Arts in San Francisco where she had worked in 1979. Wright reveals a considerable knowledge of literary theory, including the work of Michel Foucault. She talks less about national politics than about the politics of the universities, which is perhaps natural as she had become involved in a major creative writing program. She suggests that poetry cannot be neutral: "Regardless of specific subject poem by poem, human experience is partly, not wholly political. How can language, unless it avoids experience, avoid the political weather wherein it launches itself." This point of view seems bland and helps explain why, in his review of *Deepstep Come Shining* in *Poetry* (2000), an astute critic like F. D. Reeve could speak of "the absence of political engagement in Wright's work." If revealing tragic inequities in American society (the tradition of James Agee, a writer Wright admires) is political, Wright's *One Big Self: Prisoners of Louisiana* would prove Reeve wrong. It cries out against the attempts to solve social problems by putting a sizable portion of the population in prison. In "Politics and the Personal Lyric in the Poetry of Joy Harjo and C. D. Wright" (1994), Jenny Goodman has suggested that raising the awareness of readers and influencing their attitudes is a valid engagement with politics.

In 1987, the year after *Further Adventures with You,* Wright received a Guggenheim Fellowship, and the same year she was named Poet Laureate of Boone, her home county. The awards have accumulated since: a second National Endowment for the Arts fellowship in 1988, a GE Foundation award in the same year, a Whiting Writers' Award in 1989, a Rhode Island Governor's Award for the Arts in 1990, and in 1992, both the Poetry Center Book Award from San Francisco State University and a Lila Wallace–Readers' Digest Foundation Fellowship in 1992. In 1994 she was named to a five-year term as State Poet of Rhode Island.

In spite of all the awards, Wright has not become a complacent literary figure. Her essays on poetry are combative and witty. The best of them is "69 Hidebound Opinions, Propositions, and Several Asides from a Manila Folder concerning the Stuff of Poetry," an often revised collection of aphorisms, jibes, statements on poetics, and polemics. The sixty-nine entries cover schools of poetry in a fiercely independent way. Statement 4, for example, says, "My purpose is neither to hack away at the canon nor to contrive a trend." She addresses matters of technique but affirms her belief that poetry is a spiritual practice. The essay is probably the best introduction to Wright's attitudes toward poetry and her poetic practice.

STRING LIGHT

Stephen Burt has said of *String Light,* published in 1991, that it is her "first whole book no one else could have written." As Burt suggests, the opening poem, "Lake Return," implies that the poet will find her images in the local and in the "undersides of things." The poem speaks of things found in a southern lake: "water weeds," "nipples," "shoehorns," "leftovers from the singed pot." The lake also has purer light in its lower reaches, and she uses an intimate metaphor to convey this: "clitoral light." In the sequence entitled "Ozark Odes," she begins with the same poem and then ends with a short one, also called "Lake Return": "Why I come here; needs of a bottom, something to refer to; where all things visible and invisible commence to swarm."

A geniality pervades this volume, displayed in the poems of marital love and the celebrations of a child. Wright's son, Brecht Wright Gander, was born in 1986. The first poem about childbirth, however, is a poem about the birth of Frank Stanford: "King's Daughters, Home for Unwed Mothers, 1948." The poem speculates about the child's unknown background in a style imitating Stanford's huge narrative poem *The Battlefield Where the Moon Says I Love You.* It concludes that the unknown parents will never know what became of "this boychild": "That he will do things they never dreamed."

This apparent exorcism frees the writer to talk about pregnancy and child rearing. The next

poem, "Narrativity Scenes," a title making an obvious pun on "nativity," for the poem is set on Christmas Eve, talks about the moment when "two people" will become "more." In droll way, the narrative imagines a comfortable domestic life, in which "I'll milk while you paint" and "You'll paint while I milk." Even more amusing is the following poem, "More Blues and the Abstract Truth," which describes a series of calls to "grandmother" for advice about tender nipples, bleeding, and household chores during pregnancy. The responses are always irrelevancies about blue rugs and gardening. The final irrelevancy from the grandmother is perhaps implied good advice by example for an overanxious mother-to-be: "Even. If. The. Sky. Is. Falling. / My. Peace. Rose. Is. In. Bloom."

In "Our Dust," the speaker speaks as an ancestor, perhaps to her child, perhaps to more distant descendents. She describes herself through the objects and places she has known and written about: "I was the poet / of shadow work and towns with quarter-inch phone books, of failed / roadside zoos." In the last poem in *String Light,* she defines her poetic even further through objects. Additional poems on the progeny theme include some candid shots of the baby doing things like peeing on the paper plate that a guest has put down. There is perhaps a little too much raw transcription of daily life in this collection. "Living," for example, reads like a journal entry.

The range of the volume is wide. She includes two poems about living in Fayetteville, "The Night I Met Little Floyd" and "The Next Time I Crossed the Line into Oklahoma." They are not prose poems but a hybrid form: the texts are not justified but they are not in lines either, as the separations between utterances are made by dashes, creating a rapid, telegraphic utterance suitable for the chaotic events described. In "The Night I Met Little Floyd," the speaker narrates a terrifying account of a friend's abortion, a car breakdown, a ride with another friend who wanted to stop in Oklahoma to buy marijuana from two albino boyfriends: we appear to be in redneck territory. But the speaker returns home to a duplex (shared with Sonnyman, an obvious refraction of Frank Stanford) where she finds Little Floyd sitting and reading a book of poetry. Little Floyd has appeared in *Translations of the Gospel Back into Tongues,* where the narrator describes him in "Bent Tones" as "changing his shirt for the umpteenth time," an action required by anyone who wants to stay crisp and neat in the southern summer. Wright deliberately undercuts the assumptions of anyone who assumes that "a big full-bearded hillbilly" (as she describes Little Floyd in "The Next Time I Crossed into Oklahoma) must be an unlettered savage. The poem about crossing into Oklahoma, a less interesting effort, describes a wild drive to "buy a lid of homegrown." For all the frenetic driving, nothing very interesting occurs.

In an essay published by *Antioch Review* in 1989, "The New American Ode," Wright suggested that American poetry was ready for a revival of this traditional form, which tends to exalt and celebrate its subject. A good example in *String Light* is "Our Dust," with its serious treatment of imagined descendants, and "Mount Venus," which celebrates women often overlooked in poetry: elderly women with three-pronged canes and single women "who work to support our cars." "Old Man with a Dog" is a clever turn on William Wordsworth's "Resolution and Independence." The Romantic poet describes the consolation achieved during a period of depression through an interview with an immensely old and feeble man who made his living gathering leeches. The speaker in Wordsworth's poem asks the man, "How is it that you live, and what is it you do?" In Wright's poem the old man climbs a hill to the old age home to comb his wife's hair. Wright gives the man his dignity by letting him speak for himself, in terms borrowed from Words-

sworth: "What will I do? / How will I live?" In "Ozark Odes" she evokes people and places of the Ozarks, sometimes with an exalted tone, at other times with a comic slant. The ode-making drive becomes steadily more important in her work.

The poem in *String Light* that clearly foreshadows Wright's development is "Remarks on Color." In it, form is used in a radical way: the poem is written in numbered lines, the kind of radical use of format found in the language poets she has found useful. Some lines connect with a previous or following line, some do not. Some deal with skin color, others with "strip-ed melons" or a "white car." Like the language poets, she follows procedures suggested by the philosopher Ludwig Wittgenstein in his Philosophical Investigations: we should not assume that words like "game" and color names like "red" or "white" always have the same meaning. Wittgenstein says "Don't think but look!" to see if they are the same. Wittgenstein suggests that we often assume identity where there is only what he calls a family resemblance. Wright demonstrates such a confusion in line 10 when she talks about Lopez's white car and in line 39 quotes someone saying, "just don't compare me to any white musicians." White as a car color is value-neutral, white as a racial term definitely is not. It is sly to use what appears to be an anti-white saying in a poem about colors. Presumably she is quoting a black jazz musician. Certainly line 40 ("the symphony they got seventy guys all playing one note") is an unacknowledged quotation from Miles Davis, who was affirming the superiority of the black musical tradition over what he considered the inflexibility of the classical (white) orchestral tradition.

JUST WHISTLE

Wright's next book, *Just Whistle: A Valentine* (1993), radically dislocates meaning. It manages to be confessional and reticent at the same time. The title comes, of course, from the famous line in the film *To Have and Have Not* (1944) spoken by "Slim" (Lauren Bacall) to Harry Morgan (Humphrey Bogart): "If you need me, just whistle." Slim follows that line with "You know how to whistle, don't you? Just put your lips together and blow." This suggestive line is spoken early in a film in which the evolving love relationship of the protagonists is marked by emotional ambivalence and mistrust, and ambivalence marks what Wright, in a 2001 interview with Kent Johnson has called a "long twisted erotic poem." The collection is a departure for Wright in its intertextual quality: other texts are interwoven with it in a way that goes beyond mere allusions. Other works intertwined with *Just Whistle* include two of Gerard Manley Hopkins' "Terrible Sonnets" ("Carrion Comfort" and "No worst, there is none") and Ted Hughes's sequence *Crow*.

In her interview with Robert N. Casper and Nadia Colburn, Wright says that the book came out of "obsessing with form." She had been interested in the complete commitment to form in the language poets she knew in San Francisco. They were steeped in French theory and Russian formalism, she notes. Stephen Burt has demonstrated that *Just Whistle* represents the kind of writing of the female body advocated by the French feminist Hèléne Cixous. The poem also employs the kind of "defamiliarization" advocated by the Russian formalists of the 1920s: the reader often puzzles over images that seem to imply parts of the body and sexual actions without quite—as the cliché goes—calling a spade a spade. In her poem, testicles are called plums, the sexual organs of the male are a scuttling armadillo, and the vagina seems at times to be a crow, or so Adam Kirsch believes. In the *Jubilat* interview Wright says that for the first time "I wrote from a place that didn't have anything to do with geography and the vocabulary attached to that geography." But she has a new geography in the poems, the contours and cavities of human bodies, and a new vocabulary, terms derived from anatomy, like "glans" and "crura," both denoting parts of the penis and clitoris. The vocabulary is richly scientific, as she tells Casper and Colburn: "I wrote out of a calculated vocabulary, and a psychic pain I had to give shape to or else I was going to make a big mess." Along with a medical vocabulary she uses ordinary objects as symbols of sexuality in the tradition of Gertrude Stein's *Tender Buttons:* pennies represent semen and a bowl the vulva.

The plot of the poem is left obscure, but much is implied. The emotional action begins in an intimate moment: the third-person protagonist is asked by her partner not to wear her panties to bed. And later she is asked to "go check on the dogs." The hostility aroused by these requests drives the poem. Naturally, there is a background for the hostility. The speaker is at an emotional impasse, a sexual dryness rather than the spiritual dryness of the "Terrible Sonnets" that she mingles with her own words. The details are intimate indeed: the panties are marked with a thin issue of piss, and the speaker's concern with trying acidophilus as a cure suggests that the cause is a yeast infection.

Images of crows literally fly through the poems, and one poem is a parody of Ted Hughes's "Examination at the Womb Door." The poem by Hughes is a series of questions posed to Crow, who is a supernatural being, a symbol of survival. Wright's poem "A Brief and Blameless Outline of the Ontogeny of Crow" is written in split lines in a call-and-response pattern. In Wright's version the last line is not as it is in Hughes, "Pass, Crow," but a pair of statements: "Whistle it said Asshole it thought it said."

"Just whistle" implies an invitation, an acceptance of desire, while "asshole" is a rejection. Ambivalence and miscommunication seem to be at the root of the narrator's erotic turmoil.

Wright has a deep admiration for the feminist movement and has said she would not have survived without it. Her book is in part a rehearsal of grievances: various exploiting men, known epithets like "the first inseminator," "the second inseminator," "the grunt," and "the liar" are scorned. One man is disliked for not being present at "the termination," presumably an abortion. But poets, Robert Frost said once, are best when they have a grievance, not a grief, and the litany of wrongs leads to an outpouring of grief for one of these men, "the liar," whose identity suggests Frank Stanford. Hughes wrote the devastating poems in *Crow* out of despair over the suicides of a wife and lover: it is not surprising that he is one of the sources of Wright's poem. At one point she says that "we do not heal but harden," but the powerful description of a male suicide lying on a bed is probably her most direct poetic confrontation so far of the trauma of Stanford's death.

The resolution of the sexual ambivalence comes about by means that the poet does not make clear, but some kind of intense reconciliation and renewal takes place, perhaps simply because grief and grievance have been purged. The original small-press edition of the work has its mystery heightened by the *mordançage* prints of Deborah Luster. Luster, a prize-winning photographer, became a frequent collaborator with Wright in the 1990s. *Mordançage* is a method of etching away the surfaces of prints with a corrosive substance. The result is a ghostly image resembling a negative. The human bodies illustrating *Just Whistle* are eerily erotic but not explicit nudes. Luster says of the images, "I am interested in this penetration zone, this edge of line and relief. Along these edges the bodies are gnawed and wounded: parts of arms, leg, hair are eroded and fall away into the surrounding space." The illustrations are as effective in conveying the wounds and erosions of Wright's poems as Leonard Baskin's pared-down and grim illustrations of gods and carrion

in Hughes's *Crow.* Although the text of *Just Whistle* is available in Wright's selected poems, *Steal Away,* the scarce original edition is worth seeking out for the illustrations and the leisurely layout of the poems over many more pages.

With the assistance of Luster, Wright assembled an exhibition on the writers of their native state, *The Lost Roads Project: A Walk-In Book of Arkansas.* A book based on the exhibition was published under the same name in 1994. After touring the state for two years the exhibition is now in the Berg Collection at the New York Public Library. Wright was in a way writing an updated version of the WPA volume *Arkansas: A Guide to the State,* a work she admires. The original guide gave little attention to literature. Wright has included the eccentric regionalists as well as nationally known writers like James Whitehead and Maya Angelou. She also created a separate *Reader's Map of Arkansas* to show where in the state writers live or have lived.

TREMBLE

Her next collection, *Tremble* (1996), is not as difficult as *Just Whistle,* but it continues the preoccupation with form: some poems are centered on the page, one is written in columns of three words each, others use spaces for punctuation, turning the text into a series of short phrases in the manner of some of James Dickey's late poems. In the *Jubilat* interview she states that the book was an attempt to see if she could be a lyric poet, by which she means that she wanted to perfect the lyric line. The opening poem, "Floating Trees," shows great delicacy in effects like parallelism and enjambment. The book continues to grapple with the Stanford trauma, though with some optimism: "And It Came to Pass," a poem written for the June 3 anniversary of his suicide, suggests that the poet wants to strike other notes, if only with a glass and spoon. And "Song of the Gourd" declares that in gardening "I felt less responsible for one man's death one woman's long term isolation." The mood is often tender, a celebration of love: "The Shepherd of Resumed Desire" playfully evokes sexuality through euphemisms without the bitterness of the *Just Whistle* poems in which things are not named because they are hard to confront. A new note comes in the "Girl Friend Poems," which commemorate friendship between women.

DEEPSTEP COME SHINING

Wright's next book, *Deepstep Come Shining,* is a single long poem based on a road trip through the South with Deborah Luster. The project, which was formulated by Luster, was to talk to blind people about their dreams. They widened their project to talk to "outsider artists." The trip took them through North and South Carolina and northern Georgia. They ended up at Paradise Gardens in Summerville, Georgia, a center for the folk art of Reverend Howard Finster. Finster, who died in 2001 at eighty-four, had a vision while smearing paint on a bicycle: a face appeared on one of his fingertips. Simultaneously a voice told him to create sacred art. He attempted to evade this vocation but eventually became one of the best-known folk artists in the United States. Wright admires the eccentric artists: she has edited the poems of besmilr brigham, a poet who spent much of her life in Horatio, Arkansas, in a three-room house with a husband and many cats.

The poem proceeds by a dreamlike logic. It belongs to the tradition of American long poems united by a consciousness assembling memories of people and places, along with scraps of literature and history: Ezra Pound's *Cantos,* William Carlos Williams' *Paterson,* and Charles Olson's *Maximus Poems* are analogues. In his review in *Poetry,* F. D. Reeve shrewdly compares Wright's work with Muriel Rukeyser's American road journey poem, "The Book of the Dead," published in 1938 in *U.S. 1.*

The bits of vivid American speech are as important as the citation of Hugues de Montalembert's book about his blinding: *Eclipse, a Nightmare.* A postscript to *Deepstep Come Shining* entitled "Stimulants, Poultices, Goads" lists many sources, literary and personal, including Flannery O'Connor, the Book of Common Prayer, Bob Dylan, the Lumière brothers (who invented movies, and whose surname means "light"), Aunt Mildred, and many others. The most important written sources are *King Lear,* in which Gloucester learns to see metaphorically after he has lost his real eyes, and Matthew 5:29, which preaches a hard text: "If thy right eye offend thee, pluck it out." The poem assumes a hard world but records a search for illumination. Along with written texts, the poem cites exchanges between the speaker and the other person in the car, and vivid phrases overheard on the journey become motifs.

The title of the book comes from a tiny town in Georgia, Deepstep, founded in 1828 by several families, including the Veals, which explains Wright's references to the Veals of Deepstep. Wright may have been impressed by the sign at the city limits, which commemorates the community for producing several Methodist ministers, including a Veal. The quest for vision in the poem does not take an orthodox route, but the evocative word "Deepstep" suggests profundity. Sometimes the poet uses it as a verb and tells the reader to "deepstep," while at other times the word is used as a noun, suggesting a being or process, as in the phrase "Deepstep come shining." The associated plea "lead me along your light bearing paths" is a kind of prayer. One of the texts cited is Bob Dylan's song "I Shall Be Released," in which the imprisoned narrator (whether in literal or symbolic prison is not clear) says "I see my light come shining / From the West unto the East." Near the end of the book a promise of light comes in the ironic form of a mock sermon by a radio evangelist, whose audience is told it needs an elevator to "the auditorium of light," a rather vulgarized version of Dante's journey into the heart of light. Illumination is ambiguous, not always positive: Wright records a scene in which a swan is hit by a lightning bolt and explodes. She cites cases of people whose iridectomies cause them to see in a kind of hyperreal and disturbing way.

The work is often very funny as well as portentous. A rather dubious healer appears, "the boneman," who supposedly can cure the blind. His methods are grotesque, but perhaps no odder than the use of spittle and clay by Jesus in the Bible. Counterpoised to the boneman is a sinister figure, the snakeman. Rome, Georgia, comes in for some satirical comment. It is a far cry from Rome, Italy. Some of the humor is disturbing, as in a story drawn from Oscar Wilde about a family cat eating an eye removed by Wilde's father, a Dublin surgeon. A sign is glimpsed with the words "God is Louise" rather than "God is Love," an error that perhaps indicates just how far astray human beings have gone. Can "Louise," whoever she is, fill in for the deity? "If Louise is god, can her evanescence be fixed?" Wright goes on to present Louise as an avatar of the very worldly woman in Bob Dylan's song "Just Like a Woman," who cannot be blessed until she sees "she's just like all the rest," which would establish her humility.

For once Frank Stanford does not seem to be a presence in the text, though he is acknowledged in the list of sources. The recurring references to a woman whose mother played a white piano and was murdered by gunshots fired through a pillow are obscure unless a reader knows that Deborah Luster's mother was murdered in this manner. The book ends with a reference to the loss of the mother. But it is permeated with images of light as well as blindness. An exhibition of Deborah Luster's photographs was mounted at the Light Factory in Charlotte, North Carolina, in 1999 with the title:

"Come Shining: The Spiritual South." Some of the photos were published under that title with an introduction by Wright.

STEAL AWAY

Wright and Deborah Luster were winners of a major prize in documentary photography in 2000, the Tenth Dorothea Lange–Paul Taylor Prize, an award of $10,000 given by the Center for Documentary Studies at Duke University and named for Dorothea Lange, a celebrated photographer, and her husband, Paul S. Taylor, whose *American Exodus* was a class study of uprooted farmers and workers moving west during the Depression. Wright and Luster received the prize for what was then a work-in-progress on Louisiana prisoners, *One Big Self,* published in 2003. The publication of *Steal Away: Selected and New Poems* in 2002 made it clear what a fine body of work the poet had produced since 1976, and it was generally reviewed very favorably. She was extremely hard on her early poems in making selections. The arrangement of work from her books is chronological, with interludes of *"retablos"*—and "Girl Friends." The *retablos* are based on images by Deborah Luster and are accompanied by translations into Spanish by Gabriel Bernal Granados. A *retablo* is a Mexican folk art form, usually paintings of sacred scenes on wood. Luster's *retablos* are mysterious images, like the picture on the cover of *Deepstep Come Shining,* which depicts an old woman with hummingbirds hanging around her neck. Wright's poems manage to survive on their own without the pictures by Luster. She does not seek to write meticulous descriptions of individual photographs.

The major effort at assessing Wright's career on the basis of *Steal Away* was a long review by Adam Kirsch in the *New Republic.* His rather condescending commentary is based on his own eccentric division of modern poetry into categories of "courteous" and "discourteous." "Courteous" work is easily understood, "discourteous" work is difficult. His complaint about Wright is that her poetry appears difficult but has "a fundamentally unchallenging criticism of life." Some of his comments on her poetic practice are perceptive, as when he suggests that "deliberate withholding of the story, this placing of the reader at a disadvantage, has become the main strategy of Wright's poetry," and he also comments on her similar use of "elliptical narrative." Her work, he says, is mostly about marriage—or "couples," and her attitudes are tinged with 1960s radicalism. These are not sufficient themes for a true criticism of life, in Kirsch's view. He would prefer accessible ("courteous") form and difficult subject matter to discourteous form and easy subject matter. His essay is not as probing as Stephen Burt's survey in 1997, a warm appreciation that still manages to point out some defects in Wright's work.

ONE BIG SELF: PRISONERS OF LOUISIANA

Deborah Luster's loss of her mother led her to a surprising effort at understanding crime, a series of powerful photographs of prisoners in the overpopulated Louisiana prison system. Wright accompanied her on some of her visits to three prisons, and the result is *One Big Self: Prisoners of Louisiana,* a lavishly produced collection of poems and photographs. The very title affirms human community. It comes from a quotation by Terrence Malick, a film director whose work probes criminal behavior and includes *Badlands* (1973), the story of two killers on a mindless rampage. The quotation, which is used as an epigraph to the book, says: "Maybe all men got one big soul where everybody's a part of—all faces of the same man: one big self." The sating is found in Malick's film, "The Thin Red Line," but its real source is Steinbeck's novel about oppressed humanity, *The Grapes of Wrath.* Luster and Wright may not have known this fact. The pictures present the prisoners as individuals marked by their histories but full of intense emotions. In her introductory essay, Deborah Luster says that "Louisiana incarcerates more of its population than any other state in the union." And she points out that the United States imprisons more of its population than any other Western country in what she ironically calls "the free world."

It is not unusual for writers to visit prisons. Naturally moral questions arise when the lives of prisoners are the subject. In an essay that Wright prepared in 2001 for *Crossroads,* the journal of the Poetry Society of America, she notes that she and Luster could be seen as intrusive, with "our naïveté, our guilt, our whiteness, our visitor's passes." Wright did not attempt to interview prisoners: this is a subjective study, the creators note, not a sociological treatise. Mostly Wright sat on a bench and let prisoners talk to her. She notes that the writing in the book "is hectored by questions that collect around the forms of harm and the quality of mercy." Wright's poems are marked by a sympathy that is mostly unstrained, but she is aware that the crimes committed by some of the prisoners were heinous in the extreme.

Much of the text contains poems built from scattered single lines containing quoted speech or sharp perceptions of life in the prisons. For example, a prisoner is quoted as saying, "The last time you was here I had a headful of bees," creating a striking metaphor. The poet notices a sign on a weight machine that says PUSH TO FAILURE, an accidental piece of irony in a prison where many have done just that. This drifting series of lines is similar in method to *Deepstep Come Shining,* and both works perhaps owe a debt to a celebrated American prison writer, Ezra Pound, whose *Pisan Cantos* record his imprisonment in the "death cells" of a detention center at the end of World War II. As in Pound's work, Wright's poems seem a mixture of contingent observation and striking motifs. One motif is the prosecution of former Louisiana

Governor Edwin Edwards on racketeering charges: she notes that he was able to hire a celebrity lawyer and that he would not wind up doing hard labor in the prison farm at Angola. Wright's text was finished before Edwards went to a federal prison in Texas. He announced that he would be writing his memoirs in jail. His destiny is different from that of the underprivileged who fill the Louisiana state prisons. Another recurring element is based on a sign in a prison library, an announcement that "DUE TO THEFT" true crime and black studies books "are housed in closed shelving / Limit 3 books per person / 0 exceptions so don't ask." The ironies of the sign are clear (theft in prison, the popularity of books about crime among criminals), and the bureaucratic regulations of prison life are conveyed by "0 exceptions so don't ask," a phrase that Wright repeatedly uses in other contexts.

Another motif is the board game "Mansion of Happiness." The game was invented in 1843 by a clergyman's daughter and is a prototype in format of Monopoly. But unlike Monopoly, the older game stresses moral rather than financial success, and the object is to land on squares like Justice and advance to the Mansion of Happiness. The moral world of the game is simple, without shades of ambiguity, as in the statement quoted right after the mention of the PUSH TO FAILURE sign: "Whoever becomes a DRUNKARD must be taken to the Whipping Post," a grimmer fate than the Monopoly card that says "Go Directly To Jail, Do Not Pass Go."

In Monroe, Louisiana, near the East Carroll Parish Prison Farm, a criminal in jail might have used the services of a bail bondsman, like Mr. Ditty Bop. Wright gets considerable humor by quoting a radio ad for Ditty Bop. The ad was written and delivered by Sister Pearlee Toliver, the "Jewel of the Dial." Toliver was an African American broadcaster who wrote hilarious ads for clients and read them on her gospel music show. Sister Pearlee gets special mention in the source list for *One Big Self,* a list entitled "Why not check it out and lock it down," a play on the sentence that ended every one of Sister Pearlee's ads: "Why not check it out and lock it in?" "Lock it down" alludes to the lockdown, a security measure when prisoners are returned to their cells or placed in an isolation block. The Jewel of the Dial, who died in 2002, was famous enough to get an obituary in the *New York Times.* Some of her ads were for Mother Helen, a psychic that some of the prisoners at East Carroll rely on. Wright also gets humor from southern evangelism, as when she cites the claim on an evangelical radio program that God "has a wrong-answer button and we are all waiting for it to go off," a contemporary and simplified version of the penalties in the Mansion of Happiness game. Her satire is more universal when she decries Monroe's Pecanland Mall, which has been built by razing pecan groves, a kind of erosion of the environment not limited to the South.

The most powerful poems come in the form of imaginary letters. The addressees include the Afflicted Reader, the Affluent Reader, A Prisoner, and, more disturbing than almost anything in the book, a letter to a condemned man addressed: "Dear Unbidden, Unbred." In a passage of Swiftian irony, the doomed man is described as worthless, as one whose execution will be greeted by the "schadenfreudes" (the German term for those who delight in the pains of others) with "howls of execration." Those howls of execration are a phrase from Albert Camus' *The Stranger,* a work in which a man faces execution more for his apparent heartlessness in going to a comic film after his mother's funeral than for his ambiguous shooting of a man on a beach. The quality of poetic mercy is not strained in the book: it does not reek of schadenfreude. The great saying by Walt Whitman comes to mind: "The poet judges not as a judge judges but as the sun falling around a helpless thing." In her autobiographical essay

Wright suggested that her poems were driven by "crimes," and the crimes ranged from minor discourtesies to more profound guilt: in effect, her poems present a contemporary version of original sin, the assumption that human nature is defective.

Photographer and poet were both haunted by tragedies in their own lives: in one passage, Wright mentions the murder of her friend's mother and the suicide of her own lover "with his partner's target pistol." Such awareness inoculates against schadenfreude. Luster's photos of the prisoners show them as they wished to be photographed, in chef's hats, in Mardi Gras or Halloween costumes, bare-chested and flexing their muscles, turning their faces to conceal or reveal scars. The pictures are definitely not condemnations. One prison saying repeated in the book is that "NO ONE NO BODY IS BAD FOREVER." The final words of Wright's text are a tribute to Luster and to the prisoners who were so eager to see their portraits. The master copies of the pictures were printed on metal; the prisoners could see but not take away those versions because the metal could be turned into weapons. "And so. I took out her tintypes / And drew the prisoners around me." What Wright called her "mutinous text" in her *Crossroads* article has counted some of the costs of violence in America, costs for perpetrators as well as victims. The book is a rare document of a poet and a photographer's vision of the so-called underbelly of America. Wright has traveled a great distance from the gothic imagery of her early poetry. The prisons of Louisiana manifest horrors in American life, and Wright is artist enough to convey the pathos and terror of what the last words of the book call "a cultural landscape of violent activity." Her *Deepstep Come Shining,* which does not rely on another artist's work for its effect, is more aesthetically effective in its autonomy, but *One Big Self* as a whole is an outstanding commentary on America, the product of a photogra-pher and a poet at the height of their powers. We can expect more collaborations between these two artists, as Wright has said that she intends to finance further work with the aid of the $500,000 MacArthur Foundation Grant she received in 2004.

In 2005, Wright published *Cooling Time: An American Poetry Vigil.* The title phrase comes from a legal practice in Texas which, as she says, was defined in a novel by William Humphrey, The Ordways: if an injured or insulted person kills the perpetrator before having time to cool down and reflect, a murder charge cannot be laid. Wright has found an interesting metaphor to tell us that these assembled reflections on poetry are sober—if sometimes extreme—reflections, not simply products of the heat of the moment. But the very term "cooling time" is a reminder that her reactions have often been hot-blooded at the start. The book contains extracts drawn from her writings on poetry over the years. It is a distillation of her critical writings and polemics rather than a collection of them in their original form. The dedication of the volume to her husband and son is revealing: "for Forrest and for Brecht / who live with this contrarian." She is willing to be the nay-sayer, but where American poetry is concerned, she is also ready to keep a vigil, a mark of passionate commitment.

Selected Bibliography

WORKS OF C. D. WRIGHT

POETRY

Alla Breve Loving. Seattle: Mill Mountain Press, 1976. (Chapbook.)

Room Rented by a Single Woman. Barrington, R.I.: Lost Roads Publishing, 1977.

Terrorism. Barrington, R.I.: Lost Roads Publishing, 1979.

Translations of the Gospel Back into Tongues. Albany: State University of New York Press, 1982.

Further Adventures with You. Pittsburgh: Carnegie-Mellon University Press, 1986.

String Light. Athens: University of Georgia Press, 1991.

Just Whistle: A Valentine. Photographs by Deborah Luster. Berkeley, Calif.: Kelsey Street Press, 1993.

Tremble. Hopewell, N. J.: Ecco Press, 1996.

Deepstep Come Shining. Port Townsend, Wash.: Copper Canyon Press, 1998.

Come Shining: The Spiritual South—Photographs by Deborah Luster. Edited with Bruce Lineker, introductory essay by C. D. Wright. Charlotte, N.C.: Light Factory, 1999.

"Retablos: Poems and Photographs." With Deborah Luster. *Conjunctions* 32:109–125 (spring 1999).

The Tenth Dorothea Lange–Paul Taylor Prize: Deborah Luster and C. D. Wright in Collaboration. Edited by Iris Tillman Hill. Durham, N.C.: Center for Documentary Studies at Duke University, 2001. (Contains poems by Wright.)

Steal Away: Selected and New Poems. Port Townsend, Wash.: Copper Canyon Press, 2002.

One Big Self: Prisoners of Louisiana. Photographs by Deborah Luster. Santa Fe, N.M.: Twin Palms, 2003.

OTHER WORKS

The Lost Roads Project: A Walk-in Book of Arkansas. Fayetteville: University of Arkansas Press, 1994.

The Reader's Map of Arkansas. Fayetteville: University of Arkansas Press, 1994.

A Reader's Map of Rhode Island. Barrington, R.I.: Lost Roads, 1999.

Cooling Time: An American Poetry Vigil. Port Townsend, Wash.: Copper Canyon Press, 2005.

UNCOLLECTED ESSAYS

"A Note on *The Battlefield Where the Moon Says I Love You.*" *Ironwood* 17:157–164 (spring 1981).

"Arguments with the Gestapo Continued: Literary Resistance." *Five Fingers Review* 1:30–34 (1984).

"Mission of the Surviving Gunner." *Field* 35: 19–20 (fall 1986).

"Argument with the Gestapo Continued: II." *Five Fingers Review* 5:79–89 (1987).

"The Adamantine Practice of Poetry." *Brick: A Journal of Reviews* 35:55–58 (spring 1989).

"The New American Ode." *Antioch Review* 47, no. 3:287–296 (summer 1989).

"And the Last Shall Be First." *Brick* 39:63–65 (summer 1990).

"The High Euclidean Songs of Evan S. Connell." *Brick* 40:24–25 (winter 1991).

"Infamous Liberties and Uncommon Restraints: Writing Past the Margins of Free Verse." *AWP Chronicle* 23:1–4 (May 1991).

"Preliminary Remarks on the Poetry in the First Person." In *Miller Williams and the Poetry of the Particular.* Edited by Michael Burns. Columbia, Mo., and London: University of Missouri Press, 1991. Pp. 62–65.

"Provisional Remarks on Being / A Poet / Of Arkansas." *Southern Review* 30, no. 4:808–811 (autumn 1994).

Untitled Contribution to a Symposium on "What I'd Be If I Were Not a Writer." *Brick* 50:10 (fall 1994).

"The Wages of Poetry." *AWP Chronicle* 29, no. 1:13–15 (September 1996).

"C. D. Wright." *Contemporary Authors Autobiography Series.* Vol. 22. Edited by Joyce Nakamura. Detroit: Gale, 1996. Pp. 307–317.

"C. D. Wright." Modern American Poetry website (http://www.english.uiuc.edu/maps/poets/sz/cdwright/cdwright.htm). Compiled and prepared by Edward Brunner and Cary Nelson as a supplement to Nelson's *Anthology of Modern American Poetry.* New York: Oxford University Press, 2000. (Includes her "69 Hidebound Opinions," "hills," and other prose and poetry.)

"A Taxable Matter." In *A Field Guide to Contemporary Poetry and Poetics.* Rev. ed. Edited by Stuart Friebert, David Walker, and David Young. Oberlin, Ohio: Oberlin University Press, 1997. Pp. 240–242.

"Frank Stanford of the Mulberry Family: An Arkansas Epilogue." *Conjunctions* 28:297–308 (fall 1997).

"69 Hidebound Opinions, Propositions, and Several Asides from a Manila Folder concerning the Stuff of Poetry." In *By Herself: Women Reclaim Poetry.*

Edited by Molly McQuade. St. Paul, Minnesota: Graywolf Press, 2000. Pp. 380–397.

"One Big Self: Prisoners of Louisiana." *Crossroads: PSA Journal* 56:14–17 (spring 2001).

"Collaborating with Deborah Luster." *Brick* 68:89–91 (fall 2001).

"Gertrude Stein." In *Poetry Speaks.* Edited by Elise Paschen and Rebekah Presson Mosby. Naperville, Ill.: Sourcebooks, 2001. Pp. 39–40.

"Introduction." *Ploughshares* 28, no. 4:7–8 (winter 2002–2003).

"In a Ring of Cows Is the Signal Given: Ruminations on Mothering and Writing." In *The Grand Permission: New Writings on Poetics and Motherhood.* Edited by Patricia Dienstfrey and Brenda Hillman. Middletown, Conn.: Wesleyan University Press, 2003. Pp. 195–200.

CRITICAL AND BIOGRAPHICAL STUDIES

Burt, Stephen. "'I Came to Talk You into Physical Splendor': On the Poetry of C. D. Wright." *Boston Review* 22, no. 6:31–33 (December–January 1997–1998)

Colburn, Najia Herman. "About C. D. Wright: A Profile." *Ploughshares* 28, no. 4:204–210 (winter 2002–2003).

Curtis, Mary Jo. "Giving Voice to Louisiana Prisoners." *George Street Journal* 25, no. 3:1 (September 15, 2000).

Gander, Forrest. *Deeds of Utmost Kindness.* Hanover, N.H.: Wesleyan University Press, 1996.

———. *Lynchburg.* Pittsburgh: University of Pittsburgh Press, 1993.

Goldensohn, Lorrie. Review of *A Translation of the Gospels Back into Tongues. Poetry,* April 1984, pp. 46–47.

Goodman, Jenny. "C. D. Wright." In *American Poets since World War II. Dictionary of Literary Biography.* Third Series. Edited by R. S. Gwynn. Detroit: Gale, 1992. Pp. 329–333.

———. "Politics and the Personal in the Poetry of Joy Harjo and C. D. Wright." *Melus* 19, no. 2:35–57 (summer 1994).

Keller, Lynn. "'Ink and Eyes and Veins and Phonemes': C. D. Wright's Eclectic Poetics." *Arizona Quarterly: A Journal of American Literature, Culture, and Theory* 59, no. 3:115-149 (autumn 2003).

Kirsch, Adam. "Discourtesies." *New Republic,* October 21, 2002, pp. 32–36.

Lorberer, Eric. "Lost Roads Press." *Rain Taxi Review of Books* 11:37–38 (fall 1998).

Longenbach, James. Review of *Steal Away: New and Selected Poems. Yale Review* 90, no. 4:171–185 (October 2002).

Mayes, Frances. Review of *Translations of the Gospel Back into Tongues. Ironwood,* spring 1984, pp. 174–178.

Muske, Carol. "Poetry in Review." *Yale Review* 87, no. 4: 160-161 (October 1999).

Neely, Mark. Review of *Steal Away: Selected and New Poems by C. D. Wright. Jacket* 22 (May 2003). Available online (jacketmagazine.com/22/neely-wright.html).

Reeve, F. D. Review of *Deepstep Come Shining. Poetry* 176, no. 4:236–239 (July 2000).

Shaw, Robert. Review of *Translations of the Gospel Back into Tongues. New York Times,* September 4, 1983, pp. 8, 11.

INTERVIEWS

Casper, Robert N., and Nadia Colburn. "Interview with C. D. Wright." *Jubilat* 5:117–132 (2002).

Holman, Bob. "Trace of a Tale: C. D. Wright, an Investigative Poem." *Poets & Writers* 30, no. 3:12–23 (May–June 2002).

Jensen, Charles, and Sarah Vap. "A Risk and Trust: An Interview with C. D. Wright." *Hayden's Ferry Review* 34:120-134 (spring-summer 2004).

Johnson, Kent. "Looking for 'One Untranslatable Song': An Interview with C. D. Wright." *Jacket* 15 (December 2001). Available online (http://jacketmagazine.com/15/cdwright-iv.html).

Prince, Ruth E. C. "The Dreams of the Blind: An Interview with C. D. Wright." *Radcliffe Quarterly* 85, no. 2:32 (fall 1999).

—BERT ALMON

Index

Arabic numbers printed in bold-face type refer to extended treatment of a subject.

A Complete Listing of Authors in
American Writers

Gunn Allen, Paula   Supp. IV
Gurney, A. R.   Supp. V
Haines, John   Supp. XII
Hammett, Dashiell   Supp. IV
Hansberry, Lorraine   Supp. IV
Hardwick, Elizabeth   Supp. III
Harjo, Joy   Supp. XII
Harrison, Jim   Supp. VIII
Harte, Bret   Supp. II
Hass, Robert   Supp. VI
Hawthorne, Nathaniel   Vol. II
Hawthorne, Nathaniel   Retro. Supp. I
Hay, Sara Henderson   Supp. XIV
Hayden, Robert   Supp. II
Hearon, Shelby   Supp. VIII
Hecht, Anthony   Supp. X
Heller, Joseph   Supp. IV
Hellman, Lillian   Supp. I
Hemingway, Ernest   Vol. II
Hemingway, Ernest   Retro. Supp. I
Henry, O.   Supp. II
Hijuelos, Oscar   Supp. VIII
Hoffman, Alice   Supp. X
Hogan, Linda   Supp. IV
Holmes, Oliver Wendell   Supp. I
Howe, Irving   Supp. VI
Howe, Susan   Supp. IV
Howells, William Dean   Vol. II
Hughes, Langston   Supp. I
Hughes, Langston   Retro. Supp. I
Hugo, Richard   Supp. VI
Humphrey, William   Supp. IX
Huncke, Herbert   Supp. XIV
Hurston, Zora Neale   Supp. VI
Irving, John   Supp. VI
Irving, Washington   Vol. II
Isherwood, Christopher   Supp. XIV
Jackson, Shirley   Supp. IX
James, Henry   Vol. II
James, Henry   Retro. Supp. I
James, William   Vol. II
Jarrell, Randall   Vol. II
Jeffers, Robinson   Supp. II
Jewett, Sarah Orne   Vol. II

Jewett, Sarah Orne   Retro. Supp. II
Johnson, Charles   Supp. VI
Jones, James   Supp. XI
Jong, Erica   Supp. V
Justice, Donald   Supp. VII
Karr, Mary   Supp. XI
Kazin, Alfred   Supp. VIII
Kees, Weldon   Supp. XV
Kennedy, William   Supp. VII
Kennedy, X. J.   Supp. XV
Kenyon, Jane   Supp. VII
Kerouac, Jack   Supp. III
Kincaid, Jamaica   Supp. VII
King, Stephen   Supp. V
Kingsolver, Barbara   Supp. VII
Kingston, Maxine Hong   Supp. V
Kinnell, Galway   Supp. III
Knowles, John   Supp. XII
Koch, Kenneth   Supp. XV
Komunyakaa, Yusef   Supp. XIII
Kosinski, Jerzy   Supp. VII
Kumin, Maxine   Supp. IV
Kunitz, Stanley   Supp. III
Kushner, Tony   Supp. IX
LaBastille, Anne   Supp. X
Lacy, Ed   Supp. XV
Lanier, Sidney   Supp. I
Larcom, Lucy   Supp. XIII
Lardner, Ring   Vol. II
Lee, Harper   Supp. VIII
Lee, Li-Young   Supp. XV
Leopold, Aldo   Supp. XIV
Levertov, Denise   Supp. III
Levine, Philip   Supp. V
Levis, Larry   Supp. XI
Lewis, Sinclair   Vol. II
Lindsay, Vachel   Supp. I
Locke, Alain   Supp. XIV
London, Jack   Vol. II
Longfellow, Henry Wadsworth   Vol. II
Longfellow, Henry Wadsworth   Retro. Supp. II
Lowell, Amy   Vol. II
Lowell, James Russell   Supp. I
Lowell, Robert   Vol. II

Powers, Richard   Supp. IX
Price, Reynolds   Supp. VI
Proulx, Annie   Supp. VII
Purdy, James   Supp. VII
Pynchon, Thomas   Supp. II
Rand, Ayn   Supp. IV
Ransom, John Crowe   Vol. III
Rawlings, Marjorie Kinnan   Supp. X
Reed, Ishmael   Supp. X
Reznikoff, Charles   Supp. XIV
Rice, Anne   Supp. VII
Rich, Adrienne   Supp. I
Rich, Adrienne   Retro. Supp. II
Ríos, Alberto Álvaro   Supp. IV
Robbins, Tom   Supp. X
Robinson, Edwin Arlington   Vol. III
Rodriguez, Richard   Supp. XIV
Roethke, Theodore   Vol. III
Roth, Henry   Supp. IX
Roth, Philip   Supp. III
Roth, Philip   Retro. Supp. II
Rowson, Susanna   Supp. XV
Rukeyser, Muriel   Supp. VI
Russo, Richard   Supp. XII
Salinas, Luis Omar   Supp. XIII
Salinger, J. D.   Vol. III
Salter, James   Supp. IX
Sandburg, Carl   Vol. III
Santayana, George   Vol. III
Sarton, May   Supp. VIII
Schnackenberg, Gjertrud   Supp. XV
Schwartz, Delmore   Supp. II
Sexton, Anne   Supp. II
Shanley, John Patrick   Supp. XIV
Shapiro, Karl   Supp. II
Shepard, Sam   Supp. III
Shields, Carol   Supp. VII
Silko, Leslie Marmon   Supp. IV
Simic, Charles   Supp. VIII
Simon, Neil   Supp. IV
Simpson, Louis   Supp. IX
Sinclair, Upton   Supp. V
Singer, Isaac Bashevis   Vol. IV
Singer, Isaac Bashevis   Retro. Supp. II

Smiley, Jane   Supp. VI
Smith, Logan Pearsall   Supp. XIV
Smith, William Jay   Supp. XIII
Snodgrass, W. D.   Supp. VI
Snyder, Gary   Supp. VIII
Sontag, Susan   Supp. III
Southern, Terry   Supp. XI
Stafford, William   Supp. XI
Stegner, Wallace   Supp. IV
Stein, Gertrude   Vol. IV
Steinbeck, John   Vol. IV
Stern, Gerald   Supp. IX
Stevens, Wallace   Vol. IV
Stevens, Wallace   Retro. Supp. I
Stoddard, Elizabeth   Supp. XV
Stone, Robert   Supp. V
Stowe, Harriet Beecher   Supp. I
Strand, Mark   Supp. IV
Styron, William   Vol. IV
Swenson, May   Supp. IV
Tan, Amy   Supp. X
Tate, Allen   Vol. IV
Taylor, Edward   Vol. IV
Taylor, Peter   Supp. V
Theroux, Paul   Supp. VIII
Thoreau, Henry David   Vol. IV
Thurber, James   Supp. I
Toomer, Jean   Supp. IX
Trilling, Lionel   Supp. III
Twain, Mark   Vol. IV
Tyler, Anne   Supp. IV
Untermeyer, Louis   Supp. XV
Updike, John   Vol. IV
Updike, John   Retro. Supp. I
Van Vechten, Carl   Supp. II
Veblen, Thorstein   Supp. I
Vidal, Gore   Supp. IV
Vonnegut, Kurt   Supp. II
Wagoner, David   Supp. IX
Walker, Alice   Supp. III
Wallace, David Foster   Supp. X
Warren, Robert Penn   Vol. IV
Wasserstein, Wendy   Supp. XV
Welty, Eudora   Vol. IV

ISBN 0-684-31306-5

9 780684 313061